CW00726390

Leaves of the Twin Divine Trees

Leaves of the Twin Divine Trees

An In-depth Study
of the Lives of Women Closely Related to
the Báb and Bahá'u'lláh

by

Baharieh Rouhani Ma'ani

GR
George Ronald
Oxford

George Ronald, *Publisher*
Oxford
www.grbooks.com

© Baharieh Rouhani Ma'ani 2008
All Rights Reserved

Reprinted 2009

A catalogue record for this book is available from the British Library

ISBN 978–0–85398–533–4

Printed in Great Britain by the MPG Books Group,
Bodmin and King's Lynn

Cover design: Steiner Graphics

Contents

Dedicated to the imperishable memory of

Amatu'l-Bahá Rúḥíyyih Khánum,

'Bahá'í world's last remaining link with the family of 'Abdu'l-Bahá'[1]

Rúḥíyyih Khánum was born in August 1910 to William Sutherland Maxwell, appointed by Shoghi Effendi a Hand of the Cause of God, and May Maxwell, designated by him a disciple of 'Abdu'l-Bahá. She was named Mary at birth. In 1937 she married Shoghi Effendi, the grandson of 'Abdu'l-Bahá and head of the worldwide Bahá'í community from 1921 to 1957. After her marriage she became known as Amatu'l-Bahá Rúḥíyyih Khánum. When her father passed away in March 1952, Rúḥíyyih Khánum was appointed by Shoghi Effendi a Hand of the Cause of God. She served as liaison between Shoghi Effendi and the International Bahá'í Council and was his English secretary.

After Shoghi Effendi passed away in November 1957, Rúḥíyyih Khánum devoted her full attention to the promotion of the Cause of Bahá'u'lláh. She travelled extensively, met with heads of state, delivered talks to large gatherings of people, and met with seekers and believers alike. She wrote many books and articles. She passed away in Haifa in January 2000.

The reason a detailed account of her life 'so noble in its provenance, so crucial to the preservation of the Faith's integrity, and so rich in its dedicated, uninterrupted and selfless service'[2] is not included in this book is the immensity of the task. A comprehensive account of her life and services a volume will not suffice. A book entitled *The Maxwells of Montreal* is in the works and covers her life until March 1952 when her father passed away and she was appointed Hand of the Cause of God. It is expected to be published by George Ronald in the near future. The services Rúḥíyyih Khánum rendered to the Cause of Bahá'u'lláh since 1952 are well documented. Good sources are volumes of the *Bahá'í World* and back issues of the Bahá'í International News Service.

Introduction

Women are generally absent from the pages of the early history of the Bábí–Bahá'í Faith and there are reasons for it. Their absence is better understood by older believers from Iran and other Middle Eastern countries, for they are familiar with the dynamics at work. These believers rarely saw a woman's name and particulars appear in a history book and this seemed acceptable. They were raised in the cradle of gender inequality and witnessed biases against women all their lives. Almost all women were victims of prejudices that pushed them into oblivion. The older believers were well familiar with the social and religious background giving rise to the marginalization of women in history. They knew that the causes had deep roots and could not be eliminated without education and concerted effort. Some had more important things to do, such as struggling to stay alive and saving their souls. Others did not know any better. To them things looked all right as they were. However, it became increasingly difficult for them to convince the younger generation – the beneficiaries of the principle of gender equality brought by Bahá'u'lláh – not to challenge the *status quo*. The slow pace of progress acceptable to older Bahá'ís is insufficient for those who crave tangible and meaningful change.

One area where change is desperately needed is in the way women are treated in history. Lack of information about most of the early women believers, including the women closely related to the Central Figures of the Faith, raises questions about who they were, how they lived their lives, what contribution they made to the progress of the Faith and so on. Bridging the gap between the exercise of unlimited patience towards the unequal treatment of women in history advocated by older believers and the eagerness of the younger generation to ensure that they are not deprived of an important part of their heritage requires conscientious and systematic effort. A significant part of that effort lies in delving into and studying the lives of the early women believers who played an important role, through suffering and working behind the scenes, in shaping historical events. The effort also includes an analysis and assessment of the factors that prompted historians to discuss historical events without disclosing in full the names and particulars of female participants.

The early Bábí and Bahá'í historians and chroniclers followed a pattern prevalent at the time the Báb and Bahá'u'lláh revealed their missions in the 19th century. By then the plight of women had reached the lowest conceivable level. Muḥammad had introduced certain improvements in the status of women, which benefited the early Muslim believers. With the passage of time and biased interpretations of scripture, improvements gave way to the imposition of strict but arbitrary restrictions on women. Consequently, the status of women towards the end of the Muhammadan dispensation became worse than it had been when Muḥammad revealed His mission.[3] Women were gradually divested of their human rights on the grounds that they were intrinsically inferior to men. Women's inferiority was taught and accepted as an indisputable fact. Referring to the plight of Iranian women, a well-known Iranian poetess, Parvin I'tiṣámí, says: 'Women lived and died in the gloomy corners of misery. What were they in those days if not prisoners?'[4]

Written history, especially in Middle Eastern countries of the 19th century, dealt almost exclusively with men's concerns and events associated with them. Men were major participants in what they termed historical events. They formulated rules for evaluating what constituted important roles and measured contributions made by individuals to historical events by standards arbitrarily set. The system was based on convention with deep roots many centuries old. It was designed by men and operated by them with no room for the work performed by women. Women were generally invisible and had no voice.

According to *One Common Faith,*

> . . . moral justification was unquestionably supplied by people's understanding of the intent of the scriptures themselves. With few exceptions, these texts address themselves to men, assigning to women a supportive and subordinate role in the life of both religion and society.[5]

Those who did anything 'worthwhile' were hardly noticed because they worked silently and often behind the scenes. Women had been raised to be unconcerned about their place in history and men saw no reason to acknowledge what women did. The more invisible women became, the more brilliant the work of the men appeared. Women constituted the bulk of the blessed 'nameless and traceless' on earth. The plight of women reached its nadir in the mid-19th century with the advent of the Báb and Bahá'u'lláh.

Emboldened by the teachings of the Báb, a heroic soul known as Ṭáhirih Qurratu'l-'Ayn, unable to bear the injustices meted out to womankind, raised her voice in protest, challenged the *status quo* and set out to pull down barriers constructed between women and the heights they could scale. She knew intuitively that 'clinging to primitive norms in the present day would defeat the very purpose of religion's patient cultivation of moral sense'.[6] She refused to honour restrictions imposed on women and fulfilled her preordained measure by focusing on the development of her talents and demanding her God-given rights. She achieved historical notoriety by showing utter disregard for tradition. By going against the norm, she forced historians to go against convention, to find out as much information about her as they could and to publish without hesitation. Only when she rose above the restrictions and limitations imposed on her did her name become public knowledge and were the particulars of her life disclosed.

Another woman in the early history of the Faith about whose activities and sacrifices we have much information is Zaynab, the 14 year old in Zanján who also defied convention and entered the arena of activity reserved for men.

Thus women have been historically noteworthy when they have shown boldness, courage, audacity, fearlessness, keen intuition and, above all, an indomitable spirit. The way in which Ṭáhirih and Zaynab have been portrayed in the literature has, however, unfortunately been interpreted by many to imply that there were no other women in the early stages of the history of the Bábí–Bahá'í Faith whose struggles in the field of service merited historical mention. The women who worked assiduously and quietly for the promotion of the Faith in the first few decades of its history – and there were countless of them – were either ignored or relegated to a passing reference. The women of the twin Holy Families were no exception, especially those who remained faithful to the Covenant. In fact, they suffered more stringent limitations than women in general. Although they shared with acquiescence the sufferings of the Manifestation of God to whom they were closely related and served Him and His Cause with devotion and sacrificial deeds, unlike their male counterparts they had no identity of their own. No one in the outer circle knew them or was aware of the value of the work they performed. They lived in traditional societies and tradition expected them to be obscure. Their close relationship to the Manifestation of God required them to be even more obscure. It was considered disrespectful to Him, people thought, to probe into the lives of His female relatives, to find out who they were, how they lived their lives, what aspirations they had, how they responded to the new Revelation, how they served the newly revealed Cause, how lifelong persecution affected them and so forth. As a result, basic and crucial information about them has been lost to posterity.

The early historians, when compelled to acknowledge a woman's involvement in a historical event, instead of mentioning her name and particulars, stated the name of a man closely related to her and specified the nature of her relationship to him. This kind of quasi-identification, while keeping the identity of the women undisclosed, provided historians with a way to mention a woman without explaining who she was. When a woman was introduced as the wife of a certain man, it did very little to identify her, for men in Iran and other Middle Eastern countries in those days had more than one wife. Introducing a woman as the sister or daughter of a man was likewise ambiguous, for almost invariably he would have more than one sister or daughter. The only relationship that was not open to speculation was that of a child to his or her mother and that was almost never used, although a good precedent for it existed in religious history: Christ is known as Jesus, son of Mary.

Readers will find instances of these ways of identifying women in the accounts of the lives of the women who are the subject of this book.

The unavailability of adequate documented information about the early women believers in general and the women of the twin Holy Families in particular became the driving force for undertaking an in-depth study of their lives. The genesis of the quest goes back over two and a half decades. The scope of the research, the scarcity of accurate information and lack of time prolonged the process of bringing the project to fruition. To present a factual account of the lives of the women covered in this book required bringing together material from sources published in English and Persian. Shedding light on those aspects of the lives of these women that remained dark and ambiguous also required looking beyond published sources. Permission was sought and most gratefully received from the Universal House of Justice to study the unpublished writings revealed in their honour. This inestimable privilege has vastly enriched the accounts given, for in the writings of the Central Figures of the Faith are enshrined gems of invaluable information about these women which is unavailable elsewhere. The information gleaned from the sacred writings has filled crucial gaps. Another source of hitherto unavailable information has been the unpublished memoirs of the early believers, pilgrim and resident Bahá'ís alike. For this, too, I am indebted to the Supreme Body for its permission and to the Archives Office at the Bahá'í World Centre for its cooperation.

A word about the title of the book. Arabic is a gender-specific language. All things, animate and inanimate, as well as concepts, abstract and otherwise, are either feminine or masculine. Some such words are used symbolically in scripture and take on meanings other than those originally assigned to them. For example, '*sadrih*' meaning 'tree', is feminine and is used in reference to the Manifestation of God. The last paragraph of the Tablet of Visitation reads:

> Bless Thou, O Lord my God, the Divine Lote-Tree and its leaves, and its boughs, and its branches, and its stems, and its offshoots as long as Thy

most excellent titles will endure and Thy most august attributes will last.[7]

In this passage the original term translated as 'Divine Lote-Tree' is 'Sadratu'l-Muntahá'. The feminine pronoun referring to 'Sadratu'l-Muntahá' is *há* meaning 'her', which has been translated as 'its' in English.

The parts of the tree are also frequently used in the writings and these too have taken on symbolic meanings. Among these are *awráq* (leaves), plural of *waraqih* (leaf); *athmár* (fruits), plural of *thamarih* (fruit); *aghṣán* (branches), plural of *ghuṣn*; and *afnán* (boughs), plural of *fanan* (bough). While *waraqih* and *thamarih* are feminine, *ghuṣn* and *fanan* are masculine. Bahá'u'lláh has used *ghuṣn* and *aghṣán* for His direct male descendants, especially those eligible for succession. *Ghuṣn-i-A'ẓam* (the Most Great Branch) is used in reference to 'Abdu'l-Bahá, Bahá'u'lláh's eldest son and successor. In the Kitáb-i-Aqdas Bahá'u'lláh has referred to 'Abdu'l-Bahá as He 'Who hath branched from this mighty Stock'.[8] 'Abdu'l-Bahá used the term in a similar manner, referring to Shoghi Effendi, whom He appointed as the Guardian of the Cause of God and the interpreter of the writings, as *Ghuṣn-i-Mumtáz* (the Distinguished Branch).

The terms 'branch' and 'branches' are used in both the generic and specific senses in the Old and New Testaments. Examples of the generic use of the terms are provided in John 15:1–6.[9] The term 'branch' has been also used in the Old Testament to refer specifically to the future Manifestation of God (Isaiah 11:1[10]) and to 'Abdu'l-Bahá (Zechariah 6:12–13[11]).

The terms 'leaf' and 'leaves' have likewise been used in both generic and specific senses. Bahá'u'lláh used *'waraqih'* (leaf) and *'awráq'* (leaves) to refer specifically to the women among His kindred, also to the women related to the Báb. He refers to his eldest daughter Bahá'íyyih Khánum as the Greatest Holy Leaf, 'a leaf that hath sprung from this preexistent Root'.[12] For the male relatives of the Báb, He used *afnán*. The term '*afnán*' is also used as a family name by both male and female relatives of the Báb. Almost all Afnáns trace their relationship to the Báb through His wife and His mother.[13]

The terms *waraqih* and *awráq* are also used to address the women believers individually and collectively. In a Tablet that begins with the words 'O My handmaiden, O My leaf!' Bahá'u'lláh explains the reason why He addresses the recipient as 'leaf':

> We have designated thee 'a leaf' that thou mayest, like unto leaves, be stirred by the gentle wind of the Will of God – exalted be His glory – even as the leaves of the trees are stirred by onrushing winds. Yield thou thanks unto thy Lord by virtue of this brilliant utterance.[14]

In the *Lawḥ-i-Sulṭán* (Tablet to Náṣiri'd-Dín Sháh), Bahá'u'lláh says:

> This is but a leaf which the winds of the will of thy Lord, the Almighty, the All-Praised, have stirred. Can it be still when the tempestuous winds are blowing? Nay, by Him Who is the Lord of all Names and Attributes! They move it as they list. The evanescent is as nothing before Him Who is the Ever-Abiding.[15]

There are equivalents in Persian for the parts of the tree that have been used in the writings symbolically. Unlike Arabic, Persian is a non-gender-specific language and the pronouns are unisex. When the terms meaning 'tree', 'leaf', 'fruit', 'branch' and 'twig' are used in Persian, they refer to male and female alike. The word for 'tree' in Persian is *'darakht'* or '*dár*'; for 'branch', '*shákhih*' or '*shakhsár*'; for 'leaf', '*barg*'; and for 'fruit', '*bar*' or '*bár*'. In some instances these terms are used in the writings of the Báb and Bahá'u'lláh to refer to the believers in general; in other instances they are used to refer to the members of the human race. Thus when Bahá'u'lláh says, 'O well-beloved ones! The tabernacle of unity hath been raised; regard ye not one another as strangers. Ye are the fruits of one tree, and the leaves of one branch'[16] He is addressing humanity as a whole. A similar statement is made by the Báb:

> We have created you from one tree and have caused you to be as the leaves and fruit of the same tree, that haply ye may become a source of comfort to one another.[17]

But when He says, 'Send down Thy blessings, O my God, upon the Tree of the Bayán, upon its root and its branch, its boughs, its leaves, its fruits and upon whatsoever it beareth or sheltereth',[18] He is speaking of His Revelation, those related to Him and those who come under the shade of the tree of His Cause.

What is intended by 'Leaves' in the title of this book is the specific application of the word in the writings of Bahá'u'lláh, that is, His close female relatives and the close female relatives of the Báb. The 'Twin Divine Trees' is a reference to the twin Manifestations of God for this Day, the Báb and Bahá'u'lláh.

Acknowledgements

The challenge of writing about women in the early history of the Bábí–Bahá'í Faith, especially those shrouded in obscurity, is a lack of authentic and documented information. To unravel the unknown, the writings of the Central Figures of the Bahá'í Faith revealed in their honour have proved invaluable, for they contain important information unavailable elsewhere. Such writings shed light not only on the lives of the women concerned but also on the general history of the Faith.

For the preparation of this book, access to unpublished writings and historical manuscripts was crucial. I am deeply indebted to the Universal House of Justice, the Supreme Body of the Bahá'í Faith, for granting me unfettered access to these sources and also for allowing me to include the provisional English translation of a large number of these Tablets in the book.

Encouragement from family and close friends, especially when the task seemed daunting, sustained me throughout the project. I am most grateful for the encouraging words of those who urged me forward and helped me to carry on until the project was complete. Two names from among many stand out: Dr Peter Khan and my daughter Sovaida Ma'ani Ewing.

For the publication of the book, I have been fortunate to work with the editorial board of George Ronald, Publisher, especially Dr Wendi Momen who has edited the book. My loving appreciation goes to them for their tireless efforts in providing the Bahá'í world with a noble and highly valuable service.

I

Prominent Women Closely Related to the Báb

1

Fáṭimih Bagum, the Mother of the Báb, Titled the Most Virtuous of All Women

Family Background

Fáṭimih Bagum's father was Mír Siyyid Muḥammad-Ḥusayn, from the lineage of Imám Ḥusayn, the grandson of the Prophet Muḥammad. Her mother's name cannot be traced. In sharp contrast to her father's forebears, whose names have been recorded over several generations, no information is available about her mother's ancestry. Traditionally, mothers, on the whole, did not matter, therefore their particulars were not recorded and their lineages, except in exceptional circumstances, were not traced. Early Bábí and Bahá'í historians, in line with time-honoured traditions, focused attention mainly on the father, his paternal ancestry and the male line in general.

Fáṭimih Bagum had three brothers: Jináb-i Ḥáj Mírzá Siyyid Muḥammad, later known as Khál-i Akbar (the Greater Uncle), who was, according to Muḥammad-'Alí Faizí, the eldest of the three brothers;[1] Jináb-i Ḥáj Mírzá Siyyid 'Alí, later known as Khál-i A'ẓam (the Most Great Uncle); Jináb-i Ḥáj Mírzá Siyyid Ḥasan 'Alí, later known as Khál-i Aṣghar (the Younger Uncle). The use of 'Mírzá' before their names indicates that their mother was a Siyyid.

Nabíl-i-A'ẓam, when writing of the Báb's lineage, made a brief reference to His mother:

> He [the Báb] was the descendant of a house renowned for its nobility, which traced its origin to Muḥammad Himself. Siyyid Muḥammad-Riḍá, as well as His mother, were descendants of the Prophet, and belonged to families of recognized standing.[2]

Birth and Early Life

The date and exact place of Fáṭimih Bagum's birth are unknown. Of her childhood and early life, including where she was raised, whether she received instruction in the art of reading and writing, and how she spent her time before marriage, nothing is known. What has come to hand pertains to the later stages of her life, especially after her husband died and she became a single parent to a son whose outstanding spiritual qualities everyone admired.

Marriage, Motherhood and Widowhood

Fáṭimih Bagum was probably in her early teens when she married Siyyid Muḥammad-Riḍá. The age of maturity, and therefore marriage, for girls, according to the Qur'án, is nine. The practice of marrying girls off at the age of 12 and 13 was common in 19th-century Iran. Based on this information, we can surmise that Fáṭimih Bagum probably married quite young. Exactly when her marriage to Jináb-i Áqá Siyyid Muḥammad-Riḍá took place is unknown. However, it is certain that a child who became world renowned was born to the couple in 1819. Had He been the first child and born about a year after His parents' marriage, one could conjecture the approximate date of their marriage to have been 1818. However, according to Furúgh Arbáb, Fáṭimih Bagum had given birth to other children who had died in infancy,[3] so it is difficult to determine when the marriage might have been.

The death of their infants caused the young couple much grief and sadness.[4] Fáṭimih Bagum and her husband prayed hard for the blessing of having children. Their prayers were answered when on the 1st of Muḥarram 1835 (20 October 1819) Fáṭimih Bagum gave birth to a son named Siyyid 'Alí-Muḥammad. He survived and became the joy of His parents' lives. The date of His birth, which caused His parents and relatives exceeding gladness, later became a day of celebration and jubilation for those who adhered to the latest world religion, the followers of the Greatest Name, whose advent the Báb had come to herald and to prepare the people.

The birth of Siyyid 'Alí-Muḥammad changed Fáṭimih Bagum's life in ways she never could imagine. Initially, it busied her with the responsibilities and functions of motherhood. She and her husband were happy and grateful for having been blessed with a wonderful child. A few years thus elapsed then calamity struck, casting sorrow and grief once again in the heart of Fáṭimih Bagum. Her husband, Siyyid Muḥammad-Riḍá, passed away a few years after their son was born. The written accounts of the early history of the Bábí–Bahá'í Faith vary concerning the exact age of the Báb at the time His father passed away but none provides any information about how he died or how Fáṭimih Bagum coped with the tremendous loss she sustained so early in her life. Regarding the Báb's age at the time of His father's death, H. M. Balyuzi writes:

> According to Mírzá Abu'l-Faḍl-i-Gulpáygání, Siyyid Muḥammad-Riḍá, the Báb's father, died when his only child was an infant, unweaned. Then the care of the child devolved upon a maternal uncle, Ḥájí Mírzá Siyyid 'Alí . . . But according to a manuscript history of the Bábí–Bahá'í Faith in Shíráz by Ḥájí Mírzá Ḥabíbu'lláh-i-Afnán, Siyyid Muḥammad-Riḍá passed away when his son was nine years old . . .[5]

Siyyid 'Alí-Muḥammad (the Báb) may well have been younger than nine and older than an infant when His father passed away, for elsewhere in Balyuzi's book we read:

> Siyyid 'Alí-Muḥammad had some six to seven years of schooling with Shaykh 'Ábid. In all probability He left the school at the Qahviy-i-Awlíyá' before He was thirteen.[6]

If the Báb left the school of Shaykh 'Ábid before he was 13 and he had six to seven years of schooling, then he must have been about six years old when he entered that school. This confirms a footnote in *The Dawn-Breakers*:

> According to Mírzá Abu'l-Faḍl (manuscript, p. 41), the Báb was six or seven years of age when He entered the school of Shaykh 'Ábid . . . The Báb remained five years at that school, where He was taught the rudiments of Persian.[7]

The question of the Báb's age when His father passed away is directly linked to His entering Shaykh 'Ábid's school, for it is generally believed that:

> In His early childhood He lost His father, Siyyid Muḥammad-Riḍá . . . He was reared by His maternal uncle, Ḥájí Mírzá Siyyid 'Alí . . . who placed Him, while still a child, under the care of a tutor named Shaykh 'Ábid.[8]

The Báb's age at the time His father passed away is important in connection with the account of Fáṭimih Bagum's life because it provides insights into her age when her husband died. Assuming that Fáṭimih Bagum married at the age of 13 or thereabouts, even if she had lost two or three children before the Báb was born, she would have been in her early twenties when she was widowed and became a single parent. If the Báb's father died when the Báb was an infant, she would have been even younger, in her mid to late teens (perhaps 15 or 16) – and younger still if indeed He was the first child.

Whether Siyyid 'Alí-Muḥammad was an infant, five, six or slightly older when His father passed away, it stands to reason that His mother continued to rear Him. Indeed, the absence of the father made the mother's role even more crucial in the upbringing of her son. However, since the society in which the Báb grew up had little regard for the role that women played in their children's care, and in accordance with Islamic jurisprudence, it was necessary in the absence of the father that a man, preferably a male relative, act as the legal guardian of the under-aged fatherless child. Thus the untimely death of Siyyid Muḥammad-Riḍá called for the appointment of a male relative to be the guardian of Fáṭimih Bagum's son. The person who undertook this responsibility was, as recorded by Nabíl, His maternal uncle Jináb-i Ḥájí Mírzá Siyyid 'Alí.[9]

The absence of any reference in the early Bábí–Bahá'í history books to the role played by the Báb's mother in His upbringing matches the practices common at the time which ignored or marginalized contributions made by women to major historical events, especially if those events revolved around the figure of a Messenger of God. On the whole, whatever work was carried out by women, widow or not, was considered their duty and merited no acknowledgement, let alone appreciation. Lack of consideration for the need to treat women with the same standard and respect used for men has created gaps in the early history of our Faith which present and future generations will find impossible to fill. As a result, we do not know, for example, what Fáṭimih Bagum went through to raise as a single parent a child who had lost His father at a very young age and depended solely upon His mother for parental love and support. That she 'endured patiently' for her son's sake and that she enjoyed a lofty station by virtue of her being the mother of 'the mighty Word of God' there is no doubt, for the Báb Himself testifies to it in chapter 28 of His first major work, the Qayyúm al-Asmá':

> O thou Mother of the Remembrance! May the peace and salutation of God rest upon thee. Indeed thou hast endured patiently in Him Who is the sublime Self of God. Recognize then the station of thy Son Who is none other than the mighty Word of God. He hath verily pledged Himself to be answerable for thee both in thy grave and on the Judgement Day, while thou hast, in the Preserved Tablet of God, been immortalized as the 'Mother of the Faithful' by the Pen of His Remembrance.[10]

The Báb was very close to His mother. He was her only child. The bond uniting the mother and the son was extraordinarily strong. His special regard and consideration for His mother are evident from the contents of the letters He wrote to her and to His wife during His trip to Mecca. In a letter to His wife sent from Búshihr, before leaving for pilgrimage to Mecca, He says:

> It was not possible to see the Lady of the Household, the Honourable mother at the time of departure. Convey to her My salutations, and beseech her prayers.[11]

Temporary Separation

When the Báb came of age He joined his maternal uncles in business and when nearly 16 moved to Búshihr.[12] A footnote in *The Dawn-Breakers*, quoting from Appendix 2 of the *Táríkh-i-Jadíd* (*New History*), puts His age at the time of moving to Búshihr at 17:

> He left Shíráz for Búshihr at the age of 17, and remained there for five years engaged in commercial pursuits.[13]

There is nothing to suggest that Fáṭimih Bagum moved with her son to Búshihr or that she visited Him during His long stay there. On the whole, women in those days did not travel, for travelling was done by mule and the roads in the interior of Iran, especially in the mountainous areas of the south, were, if they existed at all, very insecure. Hence it does not seem likely that she visited Him. However, to suggest that the mother and son did not meet during that long span of time is unreasonable, especially considering the strong ties between the Báb and His mother. What is highly plausible is that, during His sojourn in Búshihr, the Báb made trips to Shíráz to see His mother, grandmother and other relatives there.

The length of the Báb's stay in Búshihr has been stated by one source to be four years[14] and by another to be six.[15] After engaging in business for several years, the Báb left Búshihr for the holy cities of Najaf and Karbilá in the spring of 1841. His sojourn in Iraq lasted nearly seven months.[16] The Báb's mother was unhappy about her son living so far away from home. She wanted Him to return to Shíráz, marry and settle down. As travelling for women entailed untold hardship, she pleaded with her brother, Ḥájí Siyyid 'Alí, who had acted as her son's guardian, to go to Iraq and convince Him to return. Ḥájí Mírzá Siyyid 'Alí did as asked. In Iraq he found the Báb reluctant to leave. He enlisted the help of Siyyid Javád-i-Karbilá'í, an old family friend, as H. M. Balyuzi notes:

> According to Ḥájí Mírzá Ḥabíbu'lláh's[17] narrative, as the sojourn of the Báb in the holy cities lengthened into months, His mother, anxious to have her only son back in Shíráz, asked her brother, Ḥájí Mírzá Siyyid 'Alí, to go to 'Iráq and persuade Him to return. He could not deny his sister's request, but when he reached 'Iráq he found that his nephew, who

had once been his ward, was unwilling to leave the holy cities. Thereupon he appealed to Ḥájí Siyyid Javád-i-Karbilá'í for help, who was at first reluctant to lend his support, not wishing to lose the company of the young Shírází Siyyid whom he had over the course of years so tremendously admired. However, when he learned that His mother was greatly concerned, he consented to intervene. At last the Báb complied with their request and agreed to return.[18]

The Báb's Return to Shíráz and Subsequent Developments

Fáṭimih Bagum's happiness at having her beloved son back in Shíráz can be well imagined. He was now 23 years old and it was time for Him to get married, thought His mother. The Báb, however, had other plans. After visiting His mother, He wanted to return to the holy cities in Iraq. His mother had to act fast. She needed her brother's help to ensure success. Ḥájí Mírzá Siyyid 'Alí was happy to lend assistance. According to Balyuzi,

> After a few months in Shíráz He declared His intention of going once again to 'Iráq. His mother, alarmed and agitated by this decision, once more sought the aid of her brother. Their efforts resulted in the marriage of the Báb to Khadíjih-Bagum, daughter of Ḥájí Mírzá 'Alí, the paternal uncle of His mother. The marriage took place in August 1842.[19]

The Báb's marriage to Khadíjih Bagum fulfilled Fáṭimih Bagum's most cherished hope. She had devoted her life to raising a son with unique endowments. He was revered by everyone. In His childhood an erudite man, Shaykh 'Ábid, had refused to teach Him for he found Him in need of no teacher. That child was now a married man and, together with His wife, lived in the same house as His mother. No greater happiness and joy than that could be imagined for Fáṭimih Bagum.

The blessings and favours of God to Fáṭimih Bagum seemed complete when her daughter-in-law conceived and in 1843 gave birth to a son, who was named Aḥmad. There are different views about exactly how long Aḥmad lived. Ḥájí Mírzá Ḥabibu'lláh indicated that the child was stillborn.[20] Balyuzi states that Ahmad 'did not live long'.[21] Muḥammad-'Alí Faizi says that 'He died in early infancy'.[22] However long the child lived, his death made Fáṭimih Bagum and the immediate members of his family profoundly sad. Nabíl says that 'The Father did not lament His loss', offering him as a sacrifice to God.[23] However, Fáṭimih Bagum was devastated by her grandson's death and angry that his life could not be saved. Thus the happiness which for a while seemed complete was greatly diminished by this tragic event.

Fáṭimih Bagum's Life Undergoes Permanent Change

About a year after Aḥmad's death the Báb declared His mission to Mullá Ḥusayn on the eve of 23 May 1844. The declaration took place in the same house that Fáṭimih Bagum shared with her son and His wife. The house that has become known as the House of the Báb had several rooms on the lower and upper floors and a small courtyard. Fáṭimih Bagum occupied a room on the lower floor. The room was so positioned that entry into and exit from the house could be monitored from its vantage point. Because of this it would have been unlikely for her to be oblivious of what was going on in the upper part of the House where the Báb received visitors and discussed with them His mission. It is clear from the recorded recollections of Khadíjih Bagum that the Báb's mother was not directly informed of the significance of the events taking place on the glorious night of His declaration. But this does not mean that she did not suspect something extraordinary going on, either intuitively or through other sources. Leaving speculation aside, it is certain that with the declaration of the Báb, Fáṭimih Bagum's life underwent drastic change. At the least it marked the beginning of the end of the mother and son being together. The Báb's decision to embark on a pilgrimage to Mecca soon after the declaration of His mission, followed by the proclamation He made in Mecca and Medina, precipitated events that led to Fáṭimih Bagum's eventual separation from her son, as Nabíl notes:

> Entrusting His wife to His mother, and committing them both to the care and protection of His maternal uncle, He joined the company of the pilgrims of Fárs who were preparing to leave Shíráz for Mecca and Medina.[24]

The Báb left Shíráz for Mecca on the last day of September 1844, returning thereto in early July 1845. During His long and arduous voyage He kept in touch with His mother through correspondence, as evidenced by the contents of a letter He wrote to her from Mukhá:

> He is God, the Most High!
> In the name of God, the Most Merciful of the Merciful!
> This is a letter written from the port of Mukhá to the honourable mother, may God, the Most Exalted, keep her safe! She is most certainly eager to know about the well-being of her son. A letter was sent from Búshihr. I trust God, the Most High, that it hath been illumined with the honour of thy perusal. I explained in the letter sent from Búshihr the details up to Musqat. Surely, it hath been conveyed to thy noble presence.
>
> Praised be God, my health until this day that I arrived in Mukhá hath

been good and there hath been no change in my condition. With assistance from God, exalted be He, soon I shall reach the spot where prayers are answered. I will most certainly pray on thy behalf and on behalf of honourable grandmother. Through God's bounty, no ground for doubt exists and refusal cannot be imagined.

Mubárak[25] continues to find life in service. He does what he needs to do with the help of the accompanying religious students.

Convey greetings to everyone.

To the sister of Áqá Mírzá Siyyid Ḥasan,[26] surely the letter I sent from Musqat hath been received and she will also peruse this page.

Kiss the faces of *núr-i-chashmán* (those who solace the eye).[27]

The sister of Jináb-i Shaykh together with Áqá Siyyid Mírzá . . . have, praised be God, arrived.

Peace be upon thee, and God's mercy and His blessings.

Dated: The 10th day of the month of Dhí Qa'dih. Praised be God, the Lord of all the worlds.[28]

This letter was sent to Ḥájí Mírzá Siyyid Muḥammad, Fáṭimih Bagum's brother, who was then in Búshihr. He was to forward it to his sister in Shíráz. In those days it was considered improper to put a woman's name on an envelope. This practice continued in many parts of Iran until the mid-20th century. When Ḥájí Mírzá Siyyid Muḥammad opened the envelope and found a letter addressed to the Báb's wife, he forwarded it to Shíráz. He did not realize, however, that there was another letter inside for Fáṭimih Bagum, his sister. Later he sent that letter to Shíráz together with a letter of explanation addressed to his mother and sister, i.e. the Báb's grandmother and mother respectively. By then the Báb had returned to Búshihr from His pilgrimage. Below is the translation of a part of Ḥájí Mírzá Siyyid Muḥammad's letter:

In the name of the Best of All Protectors!
May this attain the illumined gaze of the honourable and exalted mother and sister, may God, exalted be He, keep both of them safe!

First of all, may your eyes and mine and everyone's be solaced! Praise and gratitude be to God! His Highness Jináb-i Ḥájí [the Báb] has arrived safely and in perfect health. I have had the honour of attaining His presence and am at His service. Prudence dictates that He stay here for some time then proceed [to Shíráz]. God willing, He will soon proceed in that direction. Be assured.

From Musqat He sent a detailed letter and wrote a separate one for my honourable sister. Although they were received after His arrival, when

I opened the letter I did not realize that it was addressed to my beloved sister. There was also a brief separate letter for the sister of Áqá Mírzá Abu'l-Qásim [Khadíjih Bagum, the wife of the Báb]. I forwarded that one. When I discovered that He had also written separately to my sister [Fáṭimih Bagum], I sent that one as well. You must have perused all of them and felt elated that in truth His Self, the source of munificence, is the light of the eye of this world and the next. He is our pride. Praised be God, praised be God!

It is hoped that you have certainty in His Cause and that you have not allowed doubt to enter your heart because of people's idle talk. Let not any tale cause you fear or produce vain imagining. The Creator of the universe is His Protector and Helper.

I have nothing further to say. I am myself very eager to be of service and beseech prayers. Peace be upon you, and mercy of God and His blessings. The loved ones all wish you peace and say may your eyes be illumined! The mother of the ones who are the solace of the eye [i.e. the children][29] sends her regards and says to my sister: 'I wish I were there.' Say to the mother of Áqá Mírzá Abu'l-Qásim [Khadíjih Bagum's mother, the mother-in-law of the Báb], 'Praised be God, I have nothing to be ashamed of. You have a son-in-law who is peerless in the world. The inhabitants of the globe should all obey Him . . .'[30]

This is a significant letter, for its contents demonstrate that the Báb's uncle was aware, at that early stage, of the Báb's advent and tried at the outset to allay the apprehension caused by the repercussions of the Báb's declaration in Shíráz and proclamation in Mecca, preparing His mother and grandmother in a timely manner to handle with prudence the rumours that were bound to reach their ears. It also reveals how potent were the effects of those rumours and idle talk.

The letter shows as well the keen insight of the wife of the Báb's uncle. The message that she asked her husband to convey to Khadíjih Bagum's mother regarding her son-in-law testifies to this. The simple and straightforward message shows also how the women of the family related to one another and tried to calm the situation at times of crisis.

The Báb's family was closely knit. The women, although voiceless in public, exerted influence from behind the scenes. The mother and grandmother of the Báb in particular enjoyed special standing and respect within the family circle and in the larger community. The members of the family, often blood related, provided support at times of need. In keeping with traditional practice, when warranted, women expressed their views and, as deemed appropriate, took action in unobtrusive ways.

Exactly how long the Báb stayed in Búshihr before proceeding to Shíráz is not clear. What we know is that Quddús did not accompany Him back to Shíráz. To avoid arrest, the Báb told him to travel back to Shíráz alone and gave him instructions regarding the things that needed to be done in that city before the Báb's arrival. The Báb then set out for Shíráz, fully anticipating what was to befall Him on the way.

In the meantime, news of the Báb's claim and His proclamation that He was the promised Qá'im spread and reached the inhabitants of His native city. To pacify the 'ulamá who vehemently demanded action against the Báb, the governor of Fárs, Ḥusayn Khán, dispatched soldiers to Búshihr with specific orders to arrest and escort Him in chains back to Shíráz. The Báb met them en route to Shíráz, introduced Himself to them and asked them to fulfil their mission. Upon His return to His native city, the Báb became the object of the wrath of Ḥusayn Khán, whose animosity towards Him was fuelled by the religious leaders of Shíráz. The Báb was interrogated and treated with disdain, and at the instigation of a Ḥájí 'Abdu'l-Ḥusayn, a brother of the wife of Ḥájí Mírzá Siyyid Muḥammad, the Báb's Greater Uncle, three of the divines of Shíráz 'passed the verdict of death on the Báb'.[31] Ḥusayn Khán confirmed the sentence. Had the Imám-Jum'ih of Shíráz, Shaykh Abú-Turáb, signed the verdict, the Báb would have been executed then.

News of the Báb's arrest, maltreatment and the conspiracy to put Him to death alarmed His mother, who initiated certain actions to frustrate the evil intentions of His enemies. Together with two other women, Fáṭimih Bagum appealed to the Imám-Jum'ih to stay the hand of the oppressor and let not any harm befall her beloved son. According to Balyuzi,

> By now Zahrá Bagum [the sister of the wife of the Báb], the mother of the Báb, and the wife of Ḥájí 'Abu'l-Ḥasan[32] had together persuaded the Imám-Jum'ih to find a way out of the impasse.[33]

One might wonder how it was that women who were generally invisible were at the same time apparently so 'powerful' and persuasive that they were able to influence such an important individual as the Imám-Jum'ih. It should be remembered that the systems of government and judiciary in Iran in mid-19th century were different from such systems today, especially in the West. The Imám-Jum'ih enjoyed unique powers, his judgement carried special weight and his approval was needed to execute religious edicts, such as the death sentence. One can surmise from the fact that the Imám-Jum'ih of Shíráz officiated at the marriage of the Báb and Khadíjih Bagum that he was a close friend of the family, knew the Báb personally and was well known to the Báb's mother and the other two women who succeeded in persuading him to intervene in favour of the Báb. At the same time, when the women acted in unity to achieve a common purpose and when they were not hindered and opposed by men, they could be very persuasive.

The women's timely intervention helped. The Imám-Jum'ih refused to sign the edict issued by the 'ulamá. Instead, he arranged for the Báb to declare from the pulpit of the Vakil Mosque that He was neither the representative of the promised Qá'im, nor the intermediary between Him and the faithful.[34] After the Imám-Jum'ih's announcement, the Báb was released to the care of His uncle, Ḥájí Mírzá Siyyid 'Alí, 'with the condition that at whatever time the governor should deem it advisable, Ḥájí Mírzá Siyyid 'Alí would at once deliver the Báb into his hands'.[35] Nabíl says:

> Ḥájí Mírzá Siyyid 'Alí, his heart filled with gratitude to God, conducted the Báb to His home and committed Him to the loving care of His revered mother . . . In the quiet of His own home, the Báb led for a time a life of undisturbed retirement. No one except His wife, His mother, and His uncles had any intercourse with Him.[36]

That God-given opportunity enabled His mother and wife to spend some precious time with Him. Together they celebrated Naw-Rúz 1846. Knowing that that reunion with the immediate members of His family would be the last one in this transient world, the Báb made it particularly memorable. It was during this time that He transferred all of His earthly possessions to His mother and wife:

> The second Naw-Rúz after the declaration of the Báb's Mission, which fell on the twenty-first day of the month of Rabí'u'l-Avval, in the year 1262 AH [1846 AD], found the Báb still in Shíráz enjoying, under circumstances of comparative tranquillity and ease, the blessings of undisturbed association with His family and kindred. Quietly and unceremoniously, He celebrated the festival of Naw-Rúz in His own home, and, in accordance with His invariable custom, bountifully conferred upon both His mother and His wife the marks of His affection and favour. By the wisdom of His counsels and the tenderness of His love, he cheered their hearts and dispelled their apprehensions. He bequeathed to them all His possessions and transferred to their names the title to His property. In a document which He Himself wrote and signed, He directed that His house and its furniture, as well as the rest of His estate, should be regarded as the exclusive property of His mother and His wife; and that upon the death of the former, her share of the property should revert to His wife.[37]

Then arrived the fateful night when 'Abdu'l-Ḥamíd Khán, the Chief Constable of Shíráz, at the expressed order of the governor, Ḥusayn Khán, instructed his men to break into the house of Ḥájí Mírzá Siyyid 'Alí, where the Báb was meeting with one of His followers, Siyyid Káẓim-i Zanjání.[38] The Báb and Siyyid Káẓim were arrested and taken away. After this incident the Báb must have been allowed to return temporarily to His house, before He was arrested again for, recollecting that episode, Khadíjih Bagum says:

> It was summer-time in the month of Ramaḍán. We slept on the roof, and my mother-in-law slept in the courtyard. *Farrashes* of the Governor made their way to our home from a neighbour's roof. That Blessed Being rose up and told me to go downstairs. The intruders took away every book and every piece of writing that they found in the upper chamber. To Him they said, 'You have to come with us to the house of 'Abdu'l-Ḥamíd Khán (the Dárúghih).' ... God knows what His mother and I suffered that night. We were thankful that His grandmother, an elderly lady, was not there.[39]

The following account by H. M. Balyuzi is based on a letter written by Ḥájí Mírzá Abu'l-Qásim, Khadíjih Bagum's brother, to Ḥájí Mírzá Siyyid Muḥammad, the Báb's uncle:

> Not long after that night when the privacy of His home had been stealthily invaded, the authorities arrested the Báb and detained Him, under lock and key, in the house of the Dárúghih. And it was rumoured in the city that he would be put to death in the same house.[40]

The arrest and detainment of the Báb that night set in motion a chain of events. Cholera broke out in the city and claimed many lives. Fear and consternation seized the inhabitants of Shíráz. When the news of the epidemic reached the governor, he fled Shíráz, to save his life. 'Abdu'l-Ḥamíd Khán's sons contracted the disease, prompting him to implore the Báb to intercede on their behalf. When He did so and his sons recovered, he decided to release the Báb, as sign of his gratitude. He pleaded with the governor who had colluded with Ḥájí Mírzá Áqásí, the then Prime Minister of Iran, to put the Báb to death in secret,[41] to let Him go free. Ḥusayn Khán complied with the request but stipulated that the Báb had to leave Shíráz.[42]

The Báb's Exile from Shíráz

According to Nabíl, before leaving Shíráz the Báb sent a message to his uncle, Ḥájí Mírzá Siyyid 'Alí, asking him to come to see Him in the home of

'Abdu'l-Ḥamíd Khán. During that farewell meeting,

> He informed His uncle of His intended departure from Shíráz, entrusted both His mother and His wife to his care, and charged him to convey to each the expression of His affection and the assurance of God's unfailing assistance. 'Wherever they may be', He told His uncle, as He bade him farewell, 'God's all-encompassing love and protection will surround them.'[43]

In her recollections, Khadíjih Bagum gives a slightly different version of the circumstances surrounding the Báb's departure for Iṣfahán:

> One day, to our indescribable joy, He came home and stayed two or three days. Only Ḥájí Mírzá Siyyid 'Alí and two others of the believers knew of His release. But these were the last days of my life with Him. A few days before the arrival of the month of Ramaḍán, He announced that His sojourn in Shíráz was no longer advisable and that He would leave the city that very night. We, who had known how much He had suffered in Shíráz, were happy and contented that He could now reach a place of safety. In the afternoon He called on Ḥájí Mírzá Siyyid 'Alí and Ḥájí Mírzá Zaynu'l-'Ábidín and his wife, who was my sister, to bid them farewell, returned home about sunset, and two hours later, all alone, left the house. His clothes and the necessities for the journey had been sent out of the city earlier. Accompanied by one of the believers He took the road to Iṣfahán.[44]

The hour of separation from His mother and wife had arrived, a separation with no reunion in sight. Ironically, Fáṭimih Bagum had for unknown reasons remained unaffected by her son's claim and was seemingly unaware of the significance and implications of what was happening. Her beloved son was leaving His native city, never to return to it again in His lifetime. She was agitated that people's religious feelings had been stirred and wished her son would disavow Himself of the declaration He had made. The poignancy of the situation was profound. The Báb was careful not to upset His mother and she was eager to rescue Him from that which was destined to happen.

The Báb left Shíráz for Iṣfahán in the last days of September 1846.[45] Little is known about how His mother coped with the pangs of separation and what she did after her beloved son left Shíráz. After the Báb's departure for Iṣfahán it was some time before the news of His safety reached His mother through the intermediary of her younger brother, Ḥájí Mírzá Ḥasan-'Alí, who lived in Yazd.

> Ḥájí Mírzá Ḥasan-'Alí, a younger brother of Ḥájí Mírzá Siyyid 'Alí, lived in Yazd. Once every few months he would send a messenger to Shíráz with a letter for his sister, the mother of the Báb, to console and comfort her, and give her whatever news he had of the Báb. At times there was a letter from the Báb Himself, addressed to His wife, mother and grandmother.[46]

As stated earlier, the Báb, before departing Shíráz, had entrusted His mother and wife to the care of His maternal uncle, Ḥájí Mírzá Siyyid 'Alí. While in Shíráz, this uncle had fulfilled his responsibility. Then came a time when he had to leave for Yazd. In his absence, his son, Ḥájí Mírzá Javád, and Ḥájí Mírzá Muḥammad-'Alí, the son of Ḥájí Mírzá Siyyid Muḥammad, another nephew of Fáṭimih Bagum, looked after her affairs and ensured her well-being and comfort. This is confirmed by Khadíjih Bagum:

> Then Ḥájí Mírzá Siyyid 'Alí left for Yazd. Of the young members of the family, Ḥájí Mírzá Javád and Ḥájí Mírzá Muḥammad-'Alí came to see us oftentimes and provided us with our means of livelihood. They were exceedingly kind. Whenever they met my mother-in-law, they invariably kissed her hand and spoke such words as would bring her peace of mind.[47]

Several months elapsed, then the news of the Báb's exile to the mountain fortresses of Ádharbáyján reached Shíráz and caused His mother and wife great distress. Had the women been able and allowed to travel and move about freely, the Báb's mother would have no doubt gone there herself to see what had befallen her beloved son. Unfortunately, the restrictions imposed upon women made such travel untenable. Therefore, she did the only thing she could under the circumstances. She 'appealed to her brother, Ḥájí Mírzá Siyyid 'Alí, to do something'.[48] Ḥájí Mírzá Siyyid 'Alí decided to visit the Báb in Ádharbáyján, where He was imprisoned.

Ḥájí Mírzá Siyyid 'Alí's Visit to the Báb and Martyrdom

Nabíl writes of Ḥájí Mírzá Siyyid 'Alí and what befell him after he visited the Báb in Ádharbáyján:

> It was he who surrounded Him, while under his care, with unfailing solicitude, who served Him with such devotion, and who acted as intermediary between Him and the hosts of His followers who flocked to Shíráz to see him . . . Towards the middle of the year 1265 AH [1848–9 AD] . . . Ḥájí Mírzá Siyyid 'Alí left Shíráz and visited the Báb in the castle of Chihríq.

> From thence he went to Ṭihrán and, though having no special occupation, remained in that city until the outbreak of the sedition which brought about eventually his martyrdom.[49]

Ḥájí Mírzá Siyyid 'Alí was the only member of the Báb's family who visited Him after He left Shíráz. Unfortunately, he never came back to share his observations with Fáṭimih Bagum, at whose request he had undertaken the trip, nor did he have a chance to convey to her in person what the Báb had said. The reason he did not return to Shíráz immediately after he visited the Báb in Ádharbáyján was probably his notoriety, which put his life in grave danger. As a leading merchant of Shíráz who had accepted his nephew's claim to be the promised Qá'im, he was an attractive and easy target for persecution by the city's religious leaders and the governor. Thus, after visiting the Báb in Chihríq he proceeded to Ṭihrán, and as he had settled his accounts and closed his books before leaving for Ádharbáyján, he remained in Ṭihrán for several months.

While in Ṭihrán he sent a letter to his brother, Ḥájí Mírzá Siyyid Muḥammad. In that letter, a part of which is quoted by H. M. Balyuzi in *The Báb*, he tried to convince his brother of the truth of their nephew's claim and expressed the desire for 'all the members of his family to see his letter'.[50] It is not certain whether Ḥájí Mírzá Siyyid Muḥammad shared the contents of his brother's letter with all the members of his family, as requested. If he did, there is no record of their reaction.

Ḥájí Mírzá Siyyid 'Alí was still in Ṭihrán when hostilities against the Bábís broke out. He was arrested for espousing the cause of His nephew. The only condition set for his release was recanting his belief in Him, which he refused to do. His refusal caused the Amír Niẓám, the Grand Vazír, to issue orders that 'he be taken out and beheaded'.[51] Six other Bábís were put to death during the same episode and became known as the Seven Martyrs of Ṭihrán.

In the meantime, Fáṭimih Bagum eagerly awaited the return of her brother, who she thought would come with fresh news from her son. A considerable time passed. He did not return, nor did any communication arrive from him. 'How strange!' Fáṭimih Bagum must have thought.

The Martyrdom of the Báb

Nearly four years intervened between the Báb's departure from Shíráz in late September 1846 and His martyrdom in Tabríz on 9 July 1850. During this time He had been taken from place to place and had spent about three years in the mountain fortresses of Máh-Kú and Chihríq in the province of Ádharbáyján.

There must have been communication between the Báb, His mother and other immediate members of His family during His imprisonment, although nothing has come to hand. As a result, we do not know the extent to which His mother was aware of what was happening to Him, how she coped with the prolonged separation from her beloved son or what were her hopes and fears during those dreadful years. History is silent on these and similar questions.

The Báb, after spending nearly two years in Chihríq, was brought to Tabríz, the capital of the province of Ádharbáyján. There He was interrogated in front of the Crown Prince, the Amír Niẓam and the leading 'ulamá of the city. His emphatic assertion in response to explicit questions regarding His station confirmed His claim to be the promised Qá'im and earned Him the condemnation of the 'ulamá present. They used that occasion and the interrogation as valid grounds for demanding His execution. Unlike the Imám-Jum'ih of Shíráz who was favourably inclined towards the Bab, the Imám-Jum'ih of Tabríz was happy to add his signature to the death sentence prepared by religious leaders in that city. The Báb was condemned to death in a province very far from home and very different from Fárs and in a city where the Báb had no loved ones to make appeals on His behalf. Within months of the date of the interrogation, the Báb was recalled to Tabríz and, together with a companion titled Anís, executed before public gaze.

Disclosure of the News of the Martyrdom of the Báb

We know from Khadíjih Bagum's memoirs that the news of the martyrdom of the Báb and His uncle, Ḥájí Mírzá Siyyid 'Alí, was 'concealed from the women of the family'.[52] This was very much in keeping with the way women were traditionally treated. They were generally perceived as fragile beings incapable of handling trauma. As they showed emotion when faced with devastating events, such as the tragic death of a loved one, men interpreted it as a sign of weakness. The conventional sign of strength was being in control of one's feelings to the extent of showing no emotions. Men were in charge and dictated to women how they were to behave. The only time women could legitimately pour their hearts out, let off steam and scream – in other words be emotional and not be blamed – was when they mourned the death of a loved one or broke down because a tragic event proved utterly devastating. Men felt vulnerable when dealing with women in such situations. Postponing the disclosure of bad news for as long as it could be delayed was a tactic used in the hope that the passage of time would lessen the poignancy of the tragic event and mitigate its ravaging effect.

There was yet another element of men's general lack of understanding of the way women behaved: they did not understand women's intuitiveness, a female characteristic confirmed by 'Abdu'l-Bahá[53] and supported by recent studies. Women often know intuitively when something is wrong, especially when it has to do with their loved ones. They also feel it when information is deliberately withheld from them. Keeping them in the dark incapacitates them, prevents them from being pro-active and demanding that action be taken in a timely and appropriate manner. It is not possible to initiate action when information and evidence are withheld. Thus, in the past, women constantly lived in a state of fear and anxiety that something important was being concealed from them. The practice of keeping women uninformed and usually at a safe distance from the reality of 'traumatic' experience neither spared them, nor men, from the discomfort of having to deal with the unpleasant realities of life. It only delayed the process, at times with devastating effects.

Regarding the news of the Báb and His uncle's martyrdom being kept from the women of the family, Khadíjih Bagum says, 'whenever we mentioned rumours that had come to our ears, the men would hotly deny them – all lies they would say'.[54] As a result of keeping the news a secret, neither the mother nor the wife of the Báb, or the wife of Ḥájí Mírzá Siyyid 'Alí, knew for sure the fate of their loved ones for over a year. Everything came to the fore when another member of the family, the young Ḥájí Mírzá Javád, the son of Ḥájí Mírzá Siyyid 'Alí, passed away at the age of 18. He had gone with his father-in-law, Ḥájí Mírzá Abu'l-Qásim, the brother of Khadíjih Bagum, on pilgrimage to the holy cities in Iraq. He passed away on the way back to Iran. Upon his return, Ḥájí Mírzá Abu'l-Qásim had no choice but to disclose the heartbreaking news to the deceased's mother, his wife and other members of the family. The tremendous effect of this shocking news on the family, especially on the women concerned, can well be imagined. It was at this juncture that the news of the martyrdom of the Báb and His uncle, Ḥájí Mírzá Siyyid 'Alí, was also disclosed.[55]

Keeping secret the news of the martyrdom of two prominent members of a closely-knit family and disclosing it simultaneously with the news of the tragic death of a third appears most unusual, if not incomprehensible, today. Yet it was normal in those days. That is how it was done and the devastation it caused was incredible. The women were the ones who suffered the most. Fáṭimih Bagum was the worst affected. She had lost her beloved son and her dearly-loved brother as well as her nephew. The castle of false hopes she had built for so long suddenly came crashing down and the weight of anguish it caused was more than she could bear. The tears of blood she shed in separation from her beloved son were unceasing. She was also the one at whom fingers of blame were pointed. Her son was perceived as the cause of the problems the family was facing, and Ḥájí Mírzá Siyyid 'Alí, her brother, had, on her behalf, undertaken a trip to Á<u>dh</u>arbáyján to visit the Báb, a trip that culminated in his tragic death in Ṭihrán.

Fáṭimih Bagum's Departure from <u>Sh</u>íráz and Iran

The enormous weight of her loss, coupled with the enemies' hostile attitude, as well as the reproof shown by some relatives, reached unendurable proportions, prompting Fáṭimih Bagum to seek a way out. Secluding herself and devoting the rest of her life to meditation and communion with God appealed to her. She first thought of moving to Ma<u>sh</u>had, the capital of the province of <u>Kh</u>urásán, where the shrine of Imám Riḍá is situated, but she changed her mind and chose Najaf and Karbilá, the twin holy cities in Iraq, as an alternative place of residence. She packed her belongings and moved as far away as she could. Balyuzi writes of this decision:

> The mother of the Báb was inconsolable. The spiteful attitude and the lashing, wounding tongues of some members of the family, who were still bitterly hostile, intensified her agonies, until she could not bear any longer the injuries inflicted upon her and decided to take herself away from <u>Sh</u>íráz. At first she wished to go to Ma<u>sh</u>had . . . and have her mother with her. But she changed her mind, leased the house of the Báb to Mírzá Muḥammad-Ḥusayn-i-Bazzáz, and, accompanied by Bíbí Gawhar – a sister of Ḥájí Mírzá 'Abdu'lláh <u>Kh</u>án-i-Bályúz – and Ḥájí Mubárak, the faithful black servant of the Báb, went to Karbilá and resided there for the rest of her life. Later, Mírzá 'Abdu'l-Majíd and his wife, both believers, went to live in the same holy city. The wife of Mírzá 'Abdu'l-Majíd served the mother of the Báb with exemplary devotion.
>
> <u>Kh</u>adíjih Bagum, recalling those days of desolation and distress, would say: 'Her departure from <u>Sh</u>íráz added greatly to my burden of sorrow and deepened the sadness of my heart. I had no longer by my side a comforter whose love and sympathy and care had sustained me over the years.'[56]

Moving to Iraq deprived Fáṭimih Bagum of the blessing of living with her beloved daughter-in-law, <u>Kh</u>adíjih Bagum, and other relatives who sympathized with her plight but provided her with a priceless opportunity. Providentially she was placed in a country that served as Bahá'u'lláh's place of exile for ten years. While Bahá'u'lláh was in Ba<u>gh</u>dád, Fáṭimih Bagum lived in Najaf. The close proximity of Bahá'u'lláh's place of exile to the place of her residence in Iraq made contact between her and the believers possible. Another advantage she enjoyed in Iraq was the comfortable distance that existed between her and her hostile relatives and general public.

This further facilitated her realization of the glory of her beloved son when it was presented to her.

Life in Iraq and Recognition of the Báb's Station

The exact date of Fáṭimih Bagum's arrival in Iraq and the details of her life in that country are unclear. She seems to have left Shíráz sometime in 1854. Her arrival in Iraq may have coincided with Bahá'u'lláh's withdrawal to the mountains of Kurdistán. All accounts point to her taking residence in the twin holy cities of Karbilá and Najaf. Being despondent and grief-stricken after the martyrdom of her son and her brother and the tragic death of her young nephew, she seems to have lived a life of seclusion, spending a lot of time in prayer and meditation.

Some time after Bahá'u'lláh's return to Baghdád from Sulaymáníyyih, Fáṭimih Bagum received a visit from two Bahá'ís with whom she was acquainted from her earlier days in Shíráz: Ḥáj Siyyid Javád-i-Karbilá'í and a woman believer identified as the wife of Ḥáj 'Abdu'l-Majíd-i-Shírází. They were sent by Bahá'u'lláh for the specific purpose of laying bare before her eyes the truth of the claim of her martyred son. Nabíl notes the significance of that meeting:

> The mother of the Báb failed at first to recognize the significance of the Mission proclaimed by her Son. She remained for a time unaware of the magnitude of the forces latent in His Revelation. As she approached the end of her life, however, she was able to perceive the inestimable quality of that Treasure which she had conceived and given to the world. It was Bahá'u'lláh who eventually enabled her to discover the value of that hidden Treasure which had lain for so many years concealed from her eyes. She was living in 'Iraq, where she hoped to spend the remaining days of her life, when Bahá'u'lláh instructed two of His devoted followers, Ḥájí Siyyid Javád-i Karbilá'í and the wife of Ḥájí 'Abdu'l-Majíd-i-Shírázi, both of whom were already intimately acquainted with her, to instruct her in the principles of the Faith. She acknowledged the truth of the Cause and remained, until the closing years of the thirteenth century AH[57] when she departed this life, fully aware of the bountiful gifts which the Almighty had chosen to confer upon her.[58]

We also read in *The Dawn-Breakers* that the Báb's wife, Khadíjih Bagum, who had 'perceived at the earliest dawn of His Revelation the glory and uniqueness of His Mission', had been directed by Him 'not to divulge this secret to His mother'.[59] No reason has been given for this directive. Was it because His mother was unready to deal with so magnificent a development at a time when she was surrounded by relatives generally unsympathetic to her son's claim, some even hostile to Him? Were there other considerations? The only member of the family, other than Khadíjih Bagum, who had recognized the station of the Báb was Ḥájí Mírzá Siyyid 'Alí, Fáṭimih Bagum's brother. But he was martyred in Ṭihrán shortly after he had visited the Báb in Ádharbáyján and had no opportunity to relate to his sister the greatness of the station of her son. On the other hand, he, too, may have been admonished by the Báb not to divulge His station to His mother. The withholding of information from Fáṭimih Bagum may have been for her own protection, as well as for the protection of Khadíjih Bagum. Well aware of their precarious situation, the Báb may have desired to protect them from unforeseen and dangerous consequences.

When Fáṭimih Bagum removed herself from the circle of her friends and relatives and lived in a place far away from her native city, the time was propitious for her to learn of the truth of her son's claim. Bahá'u'lláh in His consummate wisdom chose the time to initiate her into the secret of her son's mission. For the purpose, He chose a man, Siyyid Javád-i Karbilá'í, who was intimately associated with the Báb and His family in Shíráz before the declaration of His mission and a woman with whom she was well acquainted, the wife of Ḥájí 'Abdu'l-Majíd-i Shírází.

Fáṭimih Bagum, according to a Tablet from Bahá'u'lláh, did not immediately embrace the Cause of the Báb. The stumbling block was her objection to an odious act by Mírzá Yaḥyá Azal. Fáṭimih Bagum could not understand how someone like Mírzá Yaḥyá who had pledged allegiance to her beloved son and claimed to be His successor could, after His martyrdom, dishonour His wife by marrying her,[60] then offering her to his closest associate and staunch supporter, Siyyid Muḥammad-i Iṣfahání. Bahá'u'lláh lamented this repugnant behaviour of Mírzá Yaḥyá in His writings and revealed the following in a Tablet signed by Khádimu'lláh:

> . . . the dawning place of the Sun of Existence, the mother of the Primal Point, may the life of all except Him be His sacrifice, was in Najaf. As she hesitated in her acknowledgement of the Cause of the Báb, in accordance with His [Bahá'u'lláh's] instructions, some people were dispatched to explain to her the details of His Revelation. After the matter was explained and discussed in her presence, she said, 'How could the people convinced of His claim to be the Qá'im, those who have given their allegiance to Him, dishonour His wife?'[61] This remark occasioned much embarrassment. By the One who caused the pebbles to speak as a sign of His power [Prophet Muḥammad], the Ancient Beauty was for some time overtaken by sadness . . .[62]

When Ḥabíbu'lláh Afnán and his father were in the presence of Bahá'u'lláh 'one late afternoon in the Garden of Riḍván', they heard Him speak about Mírzá Yaḥyá's abhorrent behaviour and witnessed how sad He became. H. M. Balyuzi has recorded Ḥabíbu'lláh Afnán's recollection of what Bahá'u'lláh said that day:

> Bahá'u'lláh spoke to them on that day about Mírzá Yaḥyá and his crew, during the Baghdád period; how Mírzá Yaḥyá took as his wife the sister of Mullá Rajab-'Alí, the second wife of the Báb, and then gave her to Siyyid Muḥammad-i-Iṣfahání, despite the injunction of the Báb. This shameful deed, Bahá'u'lláh said, had prevented the mother of the Báb from giving her allegiance to the Faith. Ḥájí Mírzá Ḥabíbu'lláh states that traces of sorrow appeared on the face of Bahá'u'lláh, as He spoke of those days in Baghdád. His father, 'Aqá Mírzá Áqá, was greatly affected, but Bahá'u'lláh said, 'Do not grieve. Praise be to God, the mother of that Blessed Being came to believe, at the end.'[63]

Another significant event in the life of Fáṭimih Bagum during her stay in Iraq was the visit of her two brothers Ḥájí Mírzá Siyyid Muḥammad and Ḥájí Mírzá Siyyid Ḥasan-'Alí in 1862. The two brothers were not yet convinced of the truth of the claim of their nephew. Ḥájí Mírzá Siyyid Muḥammad, who was eager to attain Bahá'u'lláh's presence and investigate the truth of the new religion, convinced his brother to join him on the trip to Iraq, ostensibly for the purpose of seeing their sister and visiting the holy shrines in Karbilá and Najaf. According to the memoirs of Ḥabíbu'lláh Afnán,[64] the two brothers did first visit the holy shrines in Iraq but afterwards Ḥájí Mírzá Siyyid Ḥasan-'Alí returned to Shíráz while Ḥájí Mírzá Siyyid Muḥammad proceeded to Baghdád where he attained Bahá'u'lláh's presence.[65] It was in response to his questions regarding the prophecies of the past that the Kitáb-i-Íqán was revealed.

The Passing of Fáṭimih Bagum and Her Resting-Place

Fáṭimih Bagum spent the rest of her life in Iraq. There are no indications or evidence that she ever returned to her home town to visit her family and friends. The exact date of her passing is not certain. Some sources have suggested that it was close to the end of the 13th century AH, *circa* 1882. If so, she lived to be about 80 years old and died during the year her daughter-in-law, Khadíjih Bagum, passed away.

No information is available about the last days of her life or the cause of her death. She was buried in either Najaf or Karbilá. The exact place of her interment will be made public at an appropriate time in the future and her remains will be transferred to the Bahá'í cemetery of Baghdád, in fulfilment of Shoghi Effendi's wishes, which he set as a goal of the Ten Year Plan (1953–63).

Fáṭimih Bagum's Station and Her Place in History

Bahá'u'lláh bestowed on the mother of the Báb the title of Khayru'n-Nisá' – 'Most Virtuous of All Women' – and forbade its use for others, for this reason: Mírzá Yaḥyá Azal, Bahá'u'lláh's half brother and the breaker of the Báb's Covenant, had several wives, some of questionable repute, whom he called Khayru'n-Nisá'. This was a transgression that could not be tolerated and caused disquiet among the believers. The details have been set out in the Kitáb-i-Badí':[66]

> His [Mírzá Yaḥyá's] shamelessness hath reached such a state that he hath titled his wives Khayru'n-Nisá' ('best of women'). He took possession of the wife of the Báb and then gave her away. Woe betide them for the torment of the Most Great Day!
>
> In this regard these wondrous and sweet verses have been revealed by God, the Exalted, the Most Glorious.
>
> This is that which hath been now sent down from the Highest Realm of Glory: O people! Know ye that We have singled out for special favour the mother of the Primal Point, who hath been mentioned before the Throne as the most virtuous of all handmaids. The use of this title for aught beside her hath been forbidden. Thus hath it been revealed by the Pen of the Most High in the Tablet of decree which is preserved in the inviolable treasury of thy Lord. She is indeed the Khayru'n-Nisá'. After her, it will be applied to the wife of the Point, who hath not set foot beyond the fortress of chastity and hath not been touched by the betrayers' hand. Thus hath the command been decreed. As to the handmaid who hath breached the trust and left the sanctuary of the Point, she hath verily severed her relationship with God, Who hath ordained all things in a perspicuous Tablet . . .
>
> In this day the Khayru'n-Nisá' is the mother of the Primal Point. The use of this title for the other handmaids of God hath been strictly forbidden. However, it hath been permitted that after her this title be used for the wife of the Point, who is residing in Fárs, who hath not transgressed the divine fortress of God's protection and who hath had due regard for God's sanctity, the one whose garment of purity hath not been touched by the hand of the betrayers. By My life, the True One, she is the immaculate

> maiden, the consort of the Most High, the most chaste. Render her service, O My friends, with utmost sincerity, for she is the remnant of God amongst you, if ye are of those who truly understand. We beseech God to enable her to stand firm in her duty and to protect her from the touch of the violators, whom the winds of passion and carnal desire move as they please. They, verily, are in manifest error. May she remain steadfast in this Cause. He is verily supreme over all things . . . It is incumbent upon all to show respect to the consort of God. It is most desired to have consideration for her under all conditions . . .[67]

Fáṭimih Bagum's greatest and most lasting glory is that she bore and raised the martyred Herald of Bahá'u'lláh's Revelation and that she recognized the station of her son and of the one whose advent He heralded.

2

Khadíjih Bagum, the Wife of the Báb

Family Background

Khadíjih Bagum's parents were Ḥájí Mírzá Siyyid 'Alí and Ḥájíyih Bíbí. They resided in Shíráz. The family was related to the family of the Báb through Mírzá Siyyid 'Alí, who was a paternal uncle of the mother of the Báb. The family bond became stronger when several marriages took place between members of the two families.

Ḥájíyih Bíbí, originally from Jahrúm, was first married to Áqá Muḥammad Taqí, a Shírází merchant, and had two children from that marriage: Ḥájíyih Bíbí Ján Ján and Muḥammad Mihdí, whose *nom de guerre* was Ḥijáb and became known as Ḥájí Ḥijáb. Ḥájíyih Bíbí Ján Ján married Jináb-i Ḥáj Siyyid 'Alí, the Báb's uncle, entitled Khál-i-A'ẓam (the Most Great Uncle). Unlike her husband, who recognized the station of the Báb and became a martyr in His path, Ḥájíyih Bíbí Ján Ján does not seem to have fully understood the significance of the Báb's Revelation. She is believed to have remained unconvinced to the end of her life of the validity of His claim. Her brother, Ḥájí Ḥijáb, likewise wondered to the end of his life about the Báb's claim and the truth of His Cause.

Ḥájí Mírzá Siyyid 'Alí and Ḥájíyih Bíbí had, in addition to Khadíjih Bagum, three other children: Zahrá Bagum, Siyyid Ḥasan and Mírzá Abu'l-Qásim. Zahrá Bagum is also known as 'Ukht-i-Ḥaram' (Sister of the Honourable Wife). After Khadíjih Bagum, she is the most prominent female member of the Afnán family and a chapter in this book is devoted to her life.

Siyyid Ḥasan, known as Afnán-i-Kabír (the Great Afnán) has been immortalized by 'Abdu'l-Bahá in *Memorials of the Faithful*. His son, Siyyid 'Alí, became the first Afnán to marry a member of Bahá'u'lláh's family. When Munírih Khánum visited Shíráz on her way to the Holy Land to marry 'Abdu'l-Bahá, Khadíjih Bagum asked her to present to Bahá'u'lláh on her behalf three requests. One of the requests was for her nephew, Siyyid 'Alí, to marry one of Bahá'u'lláh's daughters. The request was honoured with a favourable response. Later, with 'Abdu'l-Bahá's intercession, Furúghíyyih Khánum, Bahá'u'lláh's youngest daughter, married Siyyid 'Alí. Siyyid Ḥasan spent the last years of his life in the Holy Land. He passed away shortly after Bahá'u'lláh's ascension and is buried in 'Akká.

Mírzá Abu'l-Qásim, known as Saqqákhánih'í,[1] lived and worked as a merchant in Shíráz. He suffered tremendously at the hands of local authorities in Shíráz after the Báb's return from His pilgrimage to Mecca. His daughter, Maryam Sulṭán Bagum, married Mírzá Áqá, Khadíjih Bagum's favourite nephew. Of Khadíjih Bagum's two brothers, Ḥáj Mírzá Abu'l-Qásim was the closest to her.

Birth and Early Life

Khadíjih Bagum was born in 1238 AH (1822 AD). Her full name is recorded on her marriage certificate as Khadíjih-Sulṭán Bagum.

Little is known of Khadíjih Bagum's early life. A part of what is presented here is based on deductions made from historical events recorded about the life of the Báb. The rest is based on her own recollections as related by Munírih Khánum, the wife of 'Abdu'l-Bahá, in her autobiography, and also by Khadíjih Bagum's niece, Maryam Sulṭán Bagum, daughter of Mírzá Abu'l-Qásim, who 'recalled all that she had heard from her saintly aunt', and recorded by 'her grandson, Abu'l-Qásim Afnán'.[2]

There is no consensus about how old the Báb was when His father passed away. According to one source, He was an unweaned infant, some believe that He was five, yet others maintain that He was eight years old. After His father's death, He and His mother went to live with His uncle, Ḥájí Mírzá Siyyid 'Alí, who acted as His legal guardian.[3] Ḥájí Mírzá Siyyid 'Alí, as stated earlier, was married to Khadíjih Bagum's sister, Ḥájíyih Bíbí Ján Ján. As the dwellings of Ḥájí Mírzá Siyyid 'Alí, the Báb's uncle, and that of Mírzá 'Alí, Khadíjih Bagum's father, were adjacent to each other, the children of the two families played together. Thus the Báb and Khadíjih Bagum, who was three years His junior, were childhood playmates. This fact is confirmed in *Khadíjih Bagum: The Wife of the Báb*.[4] No information is available on whether Khadíjih Bagum received any schooling as a child. The general practice of the time and place was not favourable towards women receiving even an elementary education.[5]

Khadíjih Bagum seems to have had a happy childhood. When she was about 12 years old, Siyyid 'Alí-Muḥammad, who had reached the age of maturity, joined Ḥájí Mírzá Siyyid Muḥammad, His uncle, in business and moved to Búshihr. How often He visited His mother and other members of the family in Shíráz during His several years' stay in that town is not known. The nature of the dreams that Khadíjih Bagum had during the years of separation from her young cousin indicates the spiritual bond that existed between them:

> . . . when Siyyid 'Alí-Muḥammad had gone to Búshihr (Bushire), Khadíjih Bagum had a vivid dream in which she saw her young Cousin in a verdant plain, with flowers in profusion, facing towards the Qiblih (Mecca) in an attitude of prayer. He wore a *labbádih* (an outer coat) on which Qur'ánic verses were embroidered with threads of gold. His face was radiant . . . At this time Siyyid 'Alí-Muḥammad could not have been more than sixteen years old.[6]

Marriage

Siyyid 'Alí-Muḥammad spent nearly seven years in Búshihr engaging in business. He then proceeded to Karbilá in Iraq. When He prolonged His sojourn in the 'Atabát (Shí'í holy places in Iraq), His mother, eager for Him to marry and settle down in Shíráz, entreated Him to return. She also persuaded her brother, Ḥájí Mírzá Siyyid 'Alí, the legal guardian of the Báb, to go to Karbilá and plead with Him to return. Ḥájí Mírzá Siyyid 'Alí complied with his sister's wish but was unable to achieve the purpose of the trip. Finally, he enlisted the help of Ḥájí Siyyid Káẓim-i Rashtí, who asked the Báb to return to Shíráz for the sake of His mother and her good pleasure.[7] The Báb agreed. After nine months in the 'Atabát, He returned to Shíráz in 1258 AH (1842 AD).[8] Seizing the opportunity, His mother began preparations for His marriage to a woman of His choice.

After the Báb's return from Iraq, Khadíjih Bagum had a dream which indicated to her that she had been chosen to be His consort. In her dream she saw Fáṭimih Zahrá, the daughter of the Prophet Muḥammad, visiting her house to discuss a marriage proposal. As she and her sisters entered the room to greet and welcome her, she rose up and kissed Khadíjih Bagum on the forehead. This loving gesture signalled to her that she had been chosen for the honour. She woke up feeling elated. However, modesty prevented her from sharing the dream with the members of her family.[9]

In the afternoon of that day the mother of Siyyid 'Alí-Muḥammad paid a visit to Khadíjih Bagum's mother. Being closely related, these women had visited one another many times before but this visit was different: it was made with a very specific purpose in mind. This honoured visitor had come, according to the custom of the time, to ask for the hand of Khadíjih Bagum in marriage with Siyyid 'Alí-Muḥammad. Had the Báb's father been alive, he would have also been involved in the protocol preceding the union of the two families through the marriage of their children. The focus of that significant visit was Khadíjih Bagum. When she and her two sisters entered the room, the mother of the Báb rose up, kissed Khadíjih Bagum on the forehead and took her in her loving embrace. After she left, Khadíjih Bagum's older sister told her that Fáṭimih Bagum had come to ask for her hand in marriage with her son. Since Khadíjih Bagum's older sister, Ḥájíyih Bíbí Ján Ján, was married to Fáṭimih Bagum's brother who acted as the Báb's guardian, she no doubt knew the purpose of the visit beforehand and had intimated it to her mother and other sister. When Khadíjih Bagum heard her sister's remark about the forthcoming marriage proposal, she responded that she felt very honoured and related the dream that she had had the night before.[10]

In those days in Iran it was usually the groom's family that initiated negotiations regarding a proposed marriage. After the groom expressed the desire to marry a specified young woman whom he knew from childhood, or whose name had been suggested to him for consideration, the parents of the parties involved and elders of the family would get busy negotiating and obtaining necessary agreements. If successful, they would move on to making arrangements for the realization of the proposed union. In the case of Siyyid 'Alí-Muḥammad and Khadíjih Bagum, the union was probably contemplated long before it was formally proposed and agreed upon. It was not uncommon in 19th-century Iran for children born to two families well known to one another to be named for each other and to marry when they came of age. Siyyid 'Alí-Muḥammad and Khadíjih Bagum were closely related. Their families lived in close proximity to each other. They were childhood friends and playmates and they were close in age. Khadíjih Bagum did not marry until the age of 20, in an era when girls were eligible for marriage, according to Qur'ánic laws, at the age of nine. Had the marriage not been contemplated beforehand, more time would have been needed for the families to reach agreement regarding the proposed marriage. Khadíjih Bagum herself has explained how smooth and fast the process of reaching agreement was. She says that several days later marriage negotiations took place and gifts were sent to formalize the engagement.[11]

When Fáṭimih Khánum, later known as Munírih Khánum, stopped in Shíráz on her way to the Holy Land to marry 'Abdu'l-Bahá in 1872, Khadíjih Bagum related the account and added,

> The Báb and his uncle set out for Bushihr [sic] at this time to engage in some commerce . . .
>
> I cannot remember now how long the Báb's trip lasted. While he was in Bushihr I dreamt that it was our wedding night and that I was sitting in His presence. He was wearing a green cloak around which there was writing. Within those writings, verses from the Qur'án were inscribed. One of the verses was the *Áyatu'l-núr* [the Verse of Light; Qur'án 24:35], and light emanated from His person. The intensity of my happiness at seeing Him in this state woke me up. After this dream, I felt assured that He was

> a great personage and a great love for Him filled my heart. Yet I could not confide these thoughts to anyone. He returned from Bushihr after some time, and His uncle arranged the wedding ceremony. So, the marriage took place [in 1842]. And still I found myself completely detached from material things and my heart attracted only by Him. I could see by His behaviour, His words, His tranquillity, and dignity that He was a great person. But I never imagined that He was the Promised Qá'im . . .[12]

The Báb Himself has spoken in the Qayyúm al-Asmá' of His betrothal:

> In truth I have become betrothed before the throne of God with Sara, that is to say, the dearly beloved, because 'dearly beloved' is derived from Dearly Beloved (the Dearly Beloved is Muhammad which signifies that Sara was a Siyyid). In truth I have taken the angels of heaven and those who dwell in Paradise as witnesses of our betrothal.[13]

In his chronicle Nabíl makes only a brief statement about the Báb's marriage with Khadíjih Bagum: 'Some years later the Báb was united in wedlock with the sister of Mírzá Siyyid Ḥasan and Mírzá Abu'l-Qásim.'[14]

Traditionally, the marriage ceremony was held in the house of the bride's parents and the reception in the house of the parents of the bridegroom. In the case of the Báb and Khadíjih Bagum, the ceremony was held in the house of her parents, the reception in the house of the uncle of the Báb and his wife.

> Shaykh Abú Turáb, the Imám-Jum'ih of Shíráz, presided over the ceremony and read the usual oration. As it was customary for a relative of the bridegroom to respond, His uncle, Ḥájí Mírzá Siyyid 'Ali, accepted the suit.[15]

Khadíjih Bagum was well aware of and grateful for the bounties that God had bestowed upon her. When relating the story to the members of her family, she would say, 'No words can ever convey my wonderful feeling of good fortune.'[16] She would also say, 'His kindness towards me and His care for me were indescribable. He and His mother alike showered me with kindness and consideration.'[17]

From the time of the wedding until the Báb embarked on His pilgrimage to Mecca at the end of September 1844, except for the birth and death of Aḥmad, life was relatively tranquil for the couple. However, the Báb's declaration in Shíráz on the night of 22 May 1844 followed by His proclamation in Mecca that He was the promised Qá'im set in motion a chain of hostile reactions turning His life and that of Khadíjih Bagum into a whirlwind of unprecedented events that culminated in His permanent departure from Shíráz. But before all that happened, Khadíjih Bagum had a terrifying dream, which she related to her husband. His interpretation served as an early warning that the span of their union on the earthly plane was short.

> . . . not long after her marriage, she dreamt one night that a fearsome lion was standing in the courtyard of their house, and she herself had her arms round the neck of the lion. The beast dragged her twice round the whole perimeter of the courtyard, and once round half of it. She woke up, alarmed and trembling with fright, and related her dream to her Husband. His comment was: 'You awoke too soon. Your dream portends that our life together will not last more than two-and-a-half years.' Khadíjih Bagum was greatly distressed, but her Husband's affection and His words of comfort consoled her and prepared her to accept every adversity in the path of God.[18]

The Birth and Death of the Child of the Báb and Khadíjih Bagum

The fruit of the Báb's marriage with Khadíjih Bagum was a son, named Aḥmad. He was born in 1843 and did not have long to live. The exact circumstances of his death are not known. He is believed to have died shortly after birth. The difficulties associated with his birth almost claimed Khadíjih Bagum's life:

> And when the time came, her accouchement was exceedingly difficult and fraught with danger. Her mother-in-law reported to Siyyid 'Alí-Muḥammad that His wife was on the point of death. There was a mirror beside Him, on which He wrote a prayer, and instructed His mother to hold the mirror in front of His wife. That done, the child was safely delivered; but its life was short.[19]

Nabíl has recorded the birth and death of Aḥmad:

> The child which resulted from this union, [the Báb] named Aḥmad. He died in the year 1259 AH [1843 AD], the year preceding the declaration of the Faith by the Báb. The Father did not lament His loss. He consecrated His death by words such as these: 'O God, my God! Would that a thousand Ishmaels were given Me, this Abraham of Thine, that I might have offered them, each and all, as a loving sacrifice unto Thee. O my Beloved, my heart's Desire! The sacrifice of this Aḥmad whom Thy servant 'Alí-Muḥammad hath offered up on the altar of Thy love can never suffice to

quench the flame of longing in His heart. Not until He immolates His own heart at Thy feet, not until His whole body falls a victim to the cruellest tyranny in Thy path, not until His breast is made a target for countless darts for Thy sake, will the tumult of His soul be stilled. O my God, my only Desire! Grant that the sacrifice of My son, My only son, may be acceptable unto Thee. Grant that it be a prelude to the sacrifice of My own, My entire self, in the path of Thy good pleasure.[20]

Aḥmad's death caused immense grief to the members of the family. Siyyid 'Alí-Muḥammad's grief can be discerned from the references that He made to Aḥmad's death in His writings. In the Súratu'l-'Abd, a chapter of the Qayyúmu'l-Asmá', He says:

All praise be to God Who bestowed upon the Solace of the Eyes,[21] in His youth, Aḥmad. We did verily raise him up unto God . . . O Solace of the Eyes! Be patient in what thy God hath ordained for thee. Verily He doeth whatsoever He willeth. He is the All-Wise in the exercise of His justice. He is thy Lord, the Ancient of Days, and praised be He in whatever He ordereth.[22]

Well aware of the depth of sorrow surging in the heart of Khadíjih Bagum, in another chapter of the same book,[23] the Báb speaks tenderly of His marriage with her, bids her to be patient in what God had decreed and assures her of the glory ordained for Aḥmad in the worlds of God:

O concourse of Light! Hear My call from the point of Fire in this ocean of snow-white water on this crimson earth. Verily, I am God, besides Whom there is no other God. On the exalted throne a beloved noble woman, bearing the same name [Khadíjih] as the beloved of the First Friend [the Prophet Muḥammad], was wedded to this Great Remembrance;[24] and verily I caused the angels of Heaven and the denizens of Paradise, on the day of the Covenant, to bear witness, in truth, to God's Remembrance.

O well-beloved! Value highly the grace of the Great Remembrance, for it cometh from God, the Loved One. Thou shalt not be a woman, like other women, if thou obeyest God in the Cause of Truth, the greatest Truth. Know thou the great bounty conferred upon thee by the Ancient of Days, and take pride in being the consort of the Well-Beloved, Who is loved by God, the Greatest. Sufficient unto thee is this glory which cometh unto thee from God, the All-Wise, the All-Praised. Be patient in all that God hath ordained concerning the Báb and His Family. Verily, thy son, Aḥmad, is with Fáṭimih,[25] the Sublime, in the sanctified Paradise.[26]

Aḥmad's body was buried under a cypress tree in the large courtyard of the tomb of Bíbí Dukhtarán. No other details are available about the burial and those who attended. The tomb of Bíbí Dukhtarán is in the centre of the courtyard surrounded by graves on all sides.[27] About the end of 1333 AH (late 1954–early 1955 AD) the Department of Education in Shíráz decided to build a school in the precincts of the tomb. When the excavation to lay the foundation of the school began, the Local Spiritual Assembly of Shíráz wrote to Shoghi Effendi and sought permission to transfer the remains of Aḥmad to Gulistán-i-Jávid (Bahá'í cemetery). In response, Shoghi Effendi's secretary sent the following cable on his behalf:

> GUARDIAN APPROVES TRANSFER REMAINS PRIMAL POINT'S SON GULISTAN JAVID. ENSURE BEFITTING BURIAL.[28]

Muḥammad-'Alí Faizi says that the remains were exhumed at a depth of two metres and placed in a bag made of silk. The bag was then placed in a casket made of cement and kept safe for three months in a room in the western section of the Ḥaẓíratu'l-Quds awaiting a suitable time for its interment in the Gulistán-i-Jávid. On 1 Urdíbihisht 1334 (first day of Riḍván 1955), coinciding with the anniversary of the martyrdom of the Báb according to the lunar calendar, the remains were transported to the Bahá'í cemetery and, after the recitation of the sacred writings, buried in a designated spot in the presence of the members of the Assembly and a large number of friends.[29] When the completion of the project was reported to Shoghi Effendi, he sent the following cable dated 24 April 1955:

> SHÍRÁZ ASSEMBLY CARE KHADEM TEHRAN OVERJOYED HISTORIC ACHIEVEMENT CONGRATULATE VALIANT FRIENDS LOVING REMEMBRANCE SHRINES SUPPLICATING BOUNTIFUL BLESSINGS SHOGHI.[30]

Khadíjih Bagum's Recognition of the Station of the Báb

About a year after Aḥmad's birth and death, on the night of 22 May 1844, Siyyid 'Alí-Muḥammad declared to Mullá Ḥusayn in the upper chamber of His house in Shíráz that He was the promised Qá'im. Khadíjih Bagum's response to the Báb's claim is recorded in *The Dawn-Breakers*:

> The wife of the Báb . . . perceived at the earliest dawn of His Revelation the glory and uniqueness of His Mission and felt from the very beginning the intensity of its force.[31]

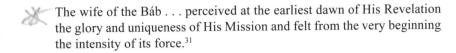

Through her close association with the Báb and her observation of every aspect of His life, Khadíjih Bagum, long before His declaration to Mullá Ḥusayn, had discovered her husband's extraordinary spiritual endowments. However, she was unaware of the claim He was to make and the nature of His mission until she experienced something unique which confirmed her belief in Him. Furúgh Arbáb in *Akhtaran-i Tábán* has given an account of what Khadíjih Bagum experienced on the night the Báb declared His mission to Mullá Ḥusayn. The source of her account is the historical manuscript of Ḥájí Mírzá Ḥabíbu'lláh Afnán, a great nephew of Khadíjih Bagum. Here is the English translation of the pertinent parts of that account:

> The sun was setting . . . when the Countenance of the Peerless Beloved illumined His home with the light of His effulgent Face. According to the usual custom, tea was served in the chamber of His mother and the dinner table was set. That night His blessed Person was not hungry but accompanied others and had a little food, then He went to bed.
>
> Around midnight His wife noticed His absence. She became worried and searched the courtyard of the House and the room of His mother, but did not find Him anywhere. As she was not yet aware of His inner heart's secret, her anxiety heightened with the passing of every second. She involuntarily climbed up the staircase [leading to the second floor] and, lo and behold, she saw the upper chamber of the House immersed in light. What was the source of all this light, and where had the lamps come from, she asked herself. But this was not tangible light; it was divine light, and she did not see it with her outward eyes but with her inner sight. She proceeded towards the guest room. There she saw that world-illuminating Sun and light-shedding Moon standing in the middle of the room with His hands raised heavenward. While her eyes were fixed upon the dazzling light emanating from His Being, a feeling of awe and fright came over her. She wanted to return but was unable to move. Her awe grew to such intensity that she felt stupefied. At this point His Blessed Person relieved her of her bewilderment. By uttering the words 'go back' He gave her new life and revived her faculties. She returned to bed but could not sleep. She communed with the Almighty saying 'O my God, what power and grandeur! What greatness and glory! What is the wisdom in your revealing to me that effulgent Sun? Is He my Siyyid 'Alí-Muḥammad? Will I henceforth be able to live with that luminous Sun? Nay, nay, the rays of this Resplendent Sun will consume me, and will reduce me to ashes. I possess not the power to withstand it.'
>
> Her thoughts were all night revolving around this episode until she heard the voice of the mu'adhdhin from the adjacent mosque. At that time

the Immaculate Being descended the steps. His esteemed wife, who had beheld the majesty and greatness of her glorious husband, was trembling as she thought of meeting Him face to face, and tried to conceal herself. When the breakfast table was spread and she went, according to the usual practice, to the room of His mother, she was still trembling, and would not lift her head. The Exalted Being poured tea and offered it to her. He enquired, 'What is the matter with you?' She replied, 'What was the condition I saw you in?' The Tongue of Grandeur uttered such words that caused her anxiety to vanish, and confirmed her in what she had seen. He spoke words such as these: 'Know thou that the Almighty God is manifested in Me. I am the One whose advent the people of Islam have expected for over a thousand years. God has created Me for a great Cause, and you witnessed the divine revelation. Although I had not wished that you see Me in that state, yet God had so willed that there may not be any place in your heart for doubt and hesitation.'[32]

A similar account with slight variations is found in H.M. Balyuzi's *Khadíjih Bagum*.[33]

Just as Khadíjih, the wife of the Prophet Muḥammad, witnessed the first emanations of the Spirit of Truth manifesting in her exalted husband and became the first to perceive the divinity of the mission with which He had been entrusted, so it was nearly 13 centuries later when a descendant of hers, also named Khadíjih, became the first to recognize the Sun of Reality shining through the person of Siyyid 'Alí-Muḥammad, a lineal descendant of Prophet Muḥammad and His wife Khadíjih. Khadíjih Bagum was the recipient of this tremendous bounty without preparation and expectation, for despite her awareness that her husband was above other men in stature and spiritual endowments, she never imagined that her intimate and loving companion would be the promised Qá'im. The discovery was no doubt an overwhelming and awe-inspiring experience.

Bahá'u'lláh's words in the Tablet revealed in Khadíjih Bagum's honour after her death confirm that 'before the creation of the world of being', she had 'found the fragrance of the garment of the Merciful'.[34]

Khadíjih Bagum's Response to the Declaration of the Báb

Nabíl has recorded in detail the account of the Báb's declaration of His mission to Mullá Ḥusayn on the night of 22 May 1844. What we are concerned with here is how deeply Khadíjih Bagum was aware of its significance and what her feelings and responses were. For that we have her own words, as spoken to Munírih Khánum:

> What an extraordinary night that was! The Báb said to me: 'Tonight we will entertain a dear guest.' His whole being was ablaze. I was most eager to hear what He had to say, but He turned to me and told me: 'It is better if you go and sleep.' I did not wish to disobey Him, but I remained awake all night and could hear His blessed voice until the morning, conversing with the Bábu'l-Báb, chanting verses, and presenting proofs and arguments.
>
> Every day, from then on, the Báb entertained an unknown guest and they would converse in the same way.[35]

With the declaration of the Báb began a period of intense activity followed by severe persecution of Him and His followers. Seekers desiring to discuss their perplexities with the one who claimed Qá'imíyyat would be received as guests in His house. They would stay for long hours for spiritual enlightenment and would return for further meetings with Him until they were confirmed in their belief. Khadíjih Bagum was the gracious hostess to those who thronged the house.

The Báb's Pilgrimage to Mecca

Four months elapsed. Eighteen believers on their own found and recognized the Báb and became known as the Letters of the Living. Others from the ranks of the 'ulamá and the common people declared their belief in Him and began to spread the new faith. Then came the time for the Báb to go on pilgrimage to Mecca, to proclaim His mission in the stronghold of Islam. The trip to Mecca in September/October 1844 marks the first time after their marriage that Khadíjih Bagum was separated from the Bab. Nabíl relates:

> Entrusting His wife to His mother, and committing them both to the care of and protection of His maternal uncle, He joined the company of the pilgrims of Fárs who were preparing to leave Shíráz for Mecca and Medina. Quddús was His only companion, and the Ethiopian servant His personal attendant. He first proceeded to Búshihr . . .[36]

In a letter written by the Báb to Khadíjih Bagum two days after His arrival in Búshihr, where He stayed for two weeks before leaving for Jiddah, He speaks of the effect of His separation from her:

> God is my witness that since the time of our separation, such griefs encircled me as are beyond description. But since destiny is so all-powerful, it is due to a fitting purpose that this [separation] occurred in this way. May God, in the name of Five Holy Souls,[37] provide the means of my return

> as may be best. It is two days since I entered Búshihr. The weather is intensely hot, but God will protect [me]. At any rate, it appears that in the very month the ship will sail. Gracious God shall protect us.[38]

In Mecca the Báb proclaimed His mission. The repercussions of that proclamation were more far-reaching in Shíráz and its surrounding areas in Fárs, where the Báb was known, than in Mecca, the Arabian peninsula or other parts of Iran. The agitation caused by His fellow pilgrims after their return to Shíráz prompted the governor, Ḥusayn Khán, to take preemptive measures to forestall His influence before His return. As a result, the Báb reentered the city escorted by soldiers sent by the governor to Búshihr to apprehend Him. Upon arrival in Shíráz, the Báb appeared before the governor and answered questions in the presence of the Imám-Jum'ih which led to His declaration from the pulpit of the Vakíl Mosque that He was not claiming to represent the promised Qá'im. Was Khadíjih Bagum immediately informed of what was happening to her husband? If so, how did she react and what did she do in response? Answers to such questions remain unknown. The strong likelihood is that she and the Báb's mother, as well as other female members of the family were, at least initially, shielded from knowing the true nature of events taking shape around them and affecting their lives.

The Báb's Return to Shíráz and Subsequent Developments

After the Báb returned to Shíráz from His pilgrimage to Mecca, events of an unprecedented nature unfolded rapidly. The severe persecutions that He and His followers suffered as a result of His claim created consternation in the hearts and bewildered members of His family. Except for Khadíjih Bagum and Siyyid 'Alí, the Báb's uncle and guardian, others wished in vain that the Báb would desist from making statements they considered provocative and dangerous. However, the Báb's declaration in Shíráz followed by His proclamation in Mecca had set in motion a process of significant consequences that could not be reversed, culminating in orders that He leave His native city, never to return to it again. Khadíjih Bagum has spoken about an episode which brought about the Báb's departure from Shíráz and sealed the decree of separation between Him and her, a separation that was not followed by a reunion on this earthly plain:

> One night [23 September 1846] we were asleep. Suddenly, the chief of police, the accursed 'Abdu'l-Ḥamíd Khán, entered with his men through the roof of the house and seized the Báb, who was clad only in a thin robe. They took Him away without any explanation. I never saw Him again.

> I cannot describe the terrible trials, ordeals, and difficulties that occurred after this. I did not see even one of His friends or followers after his arrest. The doors were shut on all sides, and communications were cut off completely.[39]

Aware of what the future held in store for Him and of the suffering and ordeals that Khadíjih Bagum was to sustain, the Báb spent as much time as He could with His family before He was separated from them for good[40] and, concerned with their well-being, ensured that in His absence their needs were met.[41]

Khadíjih Bagum was the first member of the Afnán family to recognize the station of the Báb. Áqá Siyyid ‘Alí, entitled Khál-i-A‘ẓam, who acted as the Báb's guardian, was the second. According to A.M. Faizi, Áqá Siyyid ‘Alí was confirmed in his belief after he received from the Báb a special epistle, entitled Sha‘á'ir-i-Sab‘ih. This epistle was sent to Áqá Siyyid ‘Alí from Búshihr after the Báb's pilgrimage to Mecca and Quddús delivered it to him in Shíráz.[42] Nabíl says:

> The Báb's maternal uncle, as a result of the endeavours exerted by Quddús, was the first, after the Letters of the Living, to embrace the Cause in Shíráz. As the full significance of the new-born Faith had remained as yet undivulged, he was unaware of the full extent of its implications and glory. His conversation with Quddús, however, removed the veil from his eyes.[43]

When the Báb was in Chihríq this loving uncle undertook a historic pilgrimage to the abode of His beloved nephew. After that visit he was arrested in Ṭihrán and put to death for his belief. Thus he became the first martyr among the members of the Báb's family and bore testimony with his blood to the truth of the mission of his glorious nephew.

The Martyrdom of Jináb-i Ḥájí Mírzá Siyyid ‘Alí, the Báb's Uncle

It is unclear how and when the news of the martyrdom of Áqá Siyyid ‘Alí reached Shíráz. As discussed in the chapter on Fáṭimih Bagum, it took more than a year for the tragic news to be disclosed to his wife and the female members of the family. Khadíjih Bagum, who was eagerly expecting firsthand news from and about her beloved husband, kept hoping that her brother-in-law, Ḥájí Mírzá Siyyid ‘Alí, would soon return, bringing with him credible information about the Báb's plight. Ḥájí Mírzá Siyyid ‘Alí was the only member of the family who shared with Khadíjih Bagum knowledge of the truth of the Báb's claim. He was not only a loving uncle and guardian to the Báb but also Khadíjih Bagum's brother-in-law. His wife, Ḥájíyih Bíbí Ján Ján was, as mentioned above, Khadíjih Bagum's half sister. Ḥájíyih Bíbí Ján Ján could not understand why Siyyid 'Alí-Muḥammad had to persist in His claim and endanger His life and the lives of many. To acquaint her with the truth of the Báb's mission, nearly three decades later Khadíjih Bagum arranged for her to meet Munírih Khánum, when she was in Shíráz on her way to the Holy Land in 1872.

One of the outstanding characteristics of Khadíjih Bagum was her great capacity for knowing things that others could not bear to hear. It was for the reason of this unique capacity that the Báb shared with her information regarding events that were to transpire and their significance. He also advised her lovingly of the best way to deal with her woes and tribulations. According to Nabíl:

> To her the Báb confided the secret of His future sufferings, and unfolded to her eyes the significance of the events that were to transpire in His Day. He bade her not to divulge this secret to His mother and counselled her to be patient and resigned to the will of God. He entrusted her with a special prayer, revealed and written by Himself, the reading of which, He assured her, would remove her difficulties and lighten the burden of her woes. 'In the hour of your perplexity,' He directed her, 'recite this prayer ere you go to sleep. I Myself will appear to you and will banish your anxiety.' Faithful to His advice, every time she turned to Him in prayer, the light of His unfailing guidance illumined her path and resolved her problems.[44]

The Báb's admonition 'not to divulge this secret to His mother' made Khadíjih Bagum circumspect in spreading the Báb's message among the members of her family, for any teaching activity on her part would have made His mother aware of the secret that He did not wish to be divulged to her. The Báb gave no reason for not wanting His mother to know 'the secret'. She may have been unwilling to hear anything contrary to the popular belief and resistant to the idea of her son going against the traditional way of thinking. It may have been that the Báb wished to spare her from the agonies and tribulations that awaited the adherents of His Cause. It could also be that her own mother was not favourably inclined towards the claim of the Báb and would have made the life of Fáṭimih Bagum, with whom she had to live amicably, unbearable. Or a combination of these and other factors may have been at work, inscrutable to all but the Báb Himself. Whatever the reason or reasons, we know that she did everything in her power to rescue her beloved son from the clutches of His enemies in Shíráz and in the end died confirmed in the belief that He was indeed the promised Qá'im.

The Martyrdom of the Báb and Its Aftermath

After a sojourn of just over five months in Iṣfahán, the Báb had been taken to the province of Ádharbáyján where He spent the rest of His life as an exile and prisoner in the mountain fortresses of Máh-Kú and Chihríq before He was executed in Tabríz by a firing squad on 9 July 1850.

As explained in chapter 1, the news of the martyrdom of the Báb was not immediately conveyed to His mother and His wife. History is silent about when and how the news reached them and how they reacted to it. More than a year later Mírzá Javád, who had accompanied his father-in-law, Mírzá Abu'l-Qásim, on pilgrimage to Mecca, died in Jiddah and was buried there. Mírzá Abu'l-Qásim returned to Shíráz alone and disclosed what had happened to Mírzá Javád. It was then that the news of the martyrdom of the Báb and His uncle was also made known.[45]

Considering that Khadíjih Bagum's relatives had mixed feelings about the Bab's claim, one can well imagine the difficult and awkward situation she was in. Devastated and grief-stricken, Khadíjih Bagum mourned the loss of her beloved husband and the object of her adoration. It had been over four years since she had last seen Him. Now she knew that they would not be reunited on the earthly plane.

The news of the horrific fate awaiting the adherents of the nascent faith could not have escaped Khadíjih Bagum's attention. Although the armed conflicts between government forces and Bábís in Mázandarán and Zanján were far away from Shíráz, Nayríz was very close. The news of the heroism of the Bábí defenders there could not be kept a secret, for the survivors had been brought to and paraded in Shíráz, where Khadíjih Bagum lived. When the Bábí women captives were released in Shíráz after the first Nayríz episode in 1850, Khadíjih Bagum wished to see them but doing so was unwise. 'Two of the captives came to our house in the guise of beggars', she says, 'but no one dared speak to them.'[46]

When the second Nayríz upheaval took place some two years later and the women captives were again taken to Shíráz, Khadíjih Bagum received them lovingly and gave each a fine linen scarf. A pregnant woman captive who had given birth to a baby girl on the way from Nayríz to Shíráz brought her baby to Khadíjih Bagum. She named her Humáyún, which means 'lucky'.[47] Of these women captives, Khadíjih Bagum says:

> When the captives of Nayríz and Zanján were brought to Shíráz, they could not approach us nor could we approach them. But after a while the daughters of Ḥujjat and some ladies from Nayríz visited us in the house of Ḥájí Mírzá Siyyid 'Alí. Thereafter we were able to visit one another.[48]

The Effect of Fáṭimih Bagum's Departure from Shíráz

When the news of the martyrdom of the Báb and His uncle as well as the untimely death of Mírzá Javád was disclosed, the devastation felt by Fáṭimih Bagum, the Báb's mother, coupled with the hostile attitude of those who pointed a blaming finger at her son as the cause of the adversities the family had suffered, became unbearable. She decided to leave Shíráz. She arranged her affairs and moved to Karbilá, a Shí'í stronghold in Iraq where she devoted the rest of her life to prayer and meditation. Her departure added tremendous grief to the already sorrow-laden heart of Khadíjih Bagum, who was very close to her mother-in-law. Fáṭimih Bagum's move to another country put a great distance between the two women dearly loved by the Báb. After Fáṭimih Bagum left, Khadíjih Bagum felt lonelier than ever before.

Khadíjih Bagum's Teaching Activities

The mystery of suffering in its plenitude manifested itself in the life of Khadíjih Bagum, who seemed intrinsically endowed with a superhuman capacity to endure patiently in the path of her beloved. She sustained for many years the crushing weight of afflictions visiting her in rapid succession. She bore the tremendous burden of her woes and tribulations in solitude and silence. She did not breathe a word for a long time about all that surged forcefully within her heart and soul. And now she was separated from the Báb's mother whom she loved, admired and whose support she enjoyed.

Painful as separation from Fáṭimih Bagum was for Khadíjih Bagum in those dire circumstances, it was a blessing in disguise. Faithful to the Báb's admonition, Khadíjih Bagum had not divulged the secret of the Báb's mission to His mother or to any other member of His family. Now that Fáṭimih Bagum was no longer in Shíráz, Khadíjih Bagum felt the urge to share what she knew with a receptive soul, a reliable person, who could shoulder the responsibility of ensuring that the Cause of the Báb would shine brilliantly in the hearts of the members of His family. The person she chose for the purpose was her 13 year old nephew. In him she found the pure soul she could trust. He was known as Áqá Mírzá Áqá, the only child of Zahrá Bagum and Áqá Mírzá Zaynu'l-'Abidín. Khadíjih Bagum gradually familiarized him with the truth of the mission of the Báb, planted in him the seed of the new faith and generated in him the love of the glorious kinsman for whose sake so many worthy souls had sacrificed their lives. The ready soil of Áqá Mírzá Áqá's heart absorbed the spiritual sustenance that his loving aunt so graciously and generously shared with him. Áqá Mírzá Áqá in turn taught the Faith to his parents, who well understood the significance of what Khadíjih Bagum was going through.

Ḥabíbu'lláh Afnán, the son of Áqá Mírzá Áqá, describes the success of Khadíjih Bagum's efforts to teach her nephew after she received a Tablet from Bahá'u'lláh:

> At that time no one among the family of the Afnán had embraced the Faith, and therefore the wife of the Báb had no close friend in whom she could confide. For this reason, she entered into conversations about the Faith with . . . Jináb-i-Afnán, Áqá Mírzá Áqá, who was her nephew (her sister's son), and was then thirteen years of age.
>
> . . . Because of the purity of her heart, Áqá Mírzá Áqá was deeply attracted to the Cause of God, recognized its truth and was filled with such enthusiasm that he was unable to withhold himself from teaching it, and proceeded to do so with courage and steadfastness. First he succeeded in teaching his own father ... and then his own mother, the sister of the Báb's wife.[49]

It is to Áqá Mírzá Áqá and his son Ḥabíbu'lláh Afnán that we owe the bulk of the information we have available about the life of Khadíjih Bagum. Ḥabíbu'lláh Afnán recorded episodes in her life and left to posterity a manuscript which has been widely quoted by all who have attempted to write about her. Ḥabíbu'lláh Afnán married Maryam Sulṭán, his cousin and a niece of Khadíjih Bagum. Her recollections form the basis of the monograph about Khadíjih Bagum's life written by H. M. Balyuzi.

Among Khadíjih Bagum's siblings the closest to her was her sister Zahrá Bagum. When Zahrá Bagum's son embraced the Faith of God and guided his parents to the path of truth, it opened a new page in the book of Khadíjih Bagum's life. She now had loving members of her family in whom she could confide and with whom she could discuss the truths she had known but concealed for so long. Khadíjih Bagum was also eager to teach the Faith to her other sister, Ḥájíyih Bíbí Ján Ján, the widow of the Báb's martyred uncle. Ḥájíyih Bíbí Ján Ján had questions that puzzled her. As stated earlier, when Munírih Khánum was in Shíráz in 1872, Khadíjih Bagum arranged for her to meet her sceptical sister. Munírih Khánum records in her autobiography:

> I found her to be a holy and pure woman, pious and prayerful, but she was

> not fully convinced about the truth of this Cause. She remarked: 'What a commotion our Mírzá 'Alí-Muḥammad has caused in the world! So many important people have perished, and so much blood has been shed!'[50]

Munírih Khánum goes on to describe a dialogue between her and Ḥájíyih Bíbí Ján Ján about the mission of the Báb, then states: 'I heard after we left Shiraz, the lady accepted the Faith.'[51] However, according to M.A. Faizi: 'After the martyrdom of Jináb-i Khál, she lived in a state of bewilderment regarding the blessed Cause, and remained in that state to the end of her life.'[52]

Khadíjih Bagum's Recognition of the Station of Bahá'u'lláh

Adib Taherzadeh, author of *The Revelation of Bahá'u'lláh*, states: 'Khadíjih Bagum recognized the station of Bahá'u'lláh from the early days in Baghdád and remained one of His most devoted followers.'[53] Taherzadeh's statement is based on an entry in the narrative of Ḥabíbu'lláh Afnán:

> The Blessed Beauty after His arrival in Baghdád sent many Tablets, with His own signature, 152 (which signifies Bahá), to various parts of Persia. These were taken to their intended destinations by some trustworthy individuals. Among these was a Tablet revealed in honour of the Exalted Leaf, the wife of the Báb.[54]

Exactly when, how and under what circumstances Khadíjih Bagum learned of Bahá'u'lláh's Revelation and accepted that He was the person for whom her beloved husband had offered Himself as a ransom, has fortunately been described by Khadíjih Bagum herself. That description shows that she recognized His station early in His ministry.

> Years passed, and Mírzá Áqá grew up. He was greatly attached to me. The Blessed Beauty [Bahá'u'lláh] was in Baghdád. Mírzá Áqá wrote to Him on my behalf and I was honoured with a reply. Then came a day when Mullá Muḥammad-i-Zarandí, Nabíl-i-A'ẓam, travelled to Shíráz with a mandate from the Blessed Beauty to announce His Mission to the People of the Bayán in this city. In the house of Mírzá Áqá he told the believers gathered there that the Promised One of the Bayán had come, and they, one and all, pledged their loyalty. One day I asked him to come. I was behind a curtain, and as soon as I heard him say that the Blessed Beauty was 'He Whom God shall manifest', promised in the *Bayán*, I experienced the same feeling as I had that night, standing at the threshold of the upper

> chamber of our home, and became certain that what God had promised for the 'Year Nine' had come to pass. I immediately put my forehead on the ground in adoration and thanksgiving. Then, I could only whisper: 'Offer at His sacred threshold my most humble devotion.' I did not hesitate for a moment and my submission was instantaneous and total.[55]

Khadíjih Bagum's recognition of Bahá'u'lláh's station reassured her that the Báb's sufferings and His martyrdom were for a lofty purpose and reinforced her hope in an immeasurably glorious future.

Seeking Advice about Joining Fáṭimih Bagum

It is evident from the contents of Tablets Khadíjih Bagum received from Bahá'u'lláh that she sought and received Bahá'u'lláh's approval for major decisions she had to make in her life. In one Tablet Bahá'u'lláh replies to her question as to whether she should respond affirmatively to an invitation from the Báb's mother to join her in Iraq:

> Thou hast mentioned that the mother of Ḥaḍrat-i A'lá (His Highness the Exalted One), may the spirits of all except Him be His sacrifice, wisheth for thee to direct thy steps towards that land. This is most desirable. Shouldst thou decide to go, no harm would befall thee.[56]

The trip did not take place for reasons unknown. However, travelling alone from Shíráz to Iraq would have been unthinkable for a woman of her stature at that time in the Middle East and she would have had to wait until a reliable person could be found to accompany her. Further, her health was a major concern. Also, the means were not immediately in place for her to undertake the trip. There could have been a number of reasons for her not embarking on the journey.

After encouraging Khadíjih Bagum to join the mother of the Báb, Bahá'u'lláh exhorted her not to let tribulations make her despondent, for, He said:

> . . . calamities have always been and will continue to be the lot of God's chosen ones. Therefore, blessed is the one who is satisfied with and thankful for all that hath visited him. For nothing from God touches a person except what is best for him of all that hath been created between the heavens and the earth. Since people are unaware of this mystery and its secrets, they are saddened when calamity strikes. God willing, thou wilt be always seated upon the seat of assurance and nourished with the fruits

of understanding. Verily, He is the best of all providers and protectors.
May the Spirit and Glory be upon thee and upon those who are with thee, and upon every believing servant. Praised be God, the Lord of all worlds.[57]

In the text of the Tablet, Bahá'u'lláh reveals a prayer for Khadíjih Bagum to recite. In it mention is made of a malady afflicting her:

> O my God! I beseech Thee by Thy Beauty Whom Thou hast revealed and made manifest in truth, He Whom Thou hast sent to all the inhabitants of the world. Among the Highest Concourse Thou hast called Him the Most Great Announcement, and among the people of the world Thou named Him 'Alí. I beseech Thee moreover by His next appearance in the vesture of Abhá, to deprive me not of the fragrances of the glory of Thy mercy and suffer me not to be far from the shore of the bounty of Thy nearness and beneficence. Thou verily rulest over all things.
>
> O my God! Give me to drink from the Kawthar of Thy favour and from the outpourings of Thy bounty and bestowal, that I may be purified from all that is abhorrent to me and freed from this malady which hath afflicted me. Thou art verily to Thy servants the Most Forgiving and the Most Merciful. O my God! Rend asunder the veils that have intervened between me and Thee. Heal me then with the Kawthar of healing proffered from the fingers of Thy mercy that hath overtaken all things and encompassed all the dwellers of the world. O my God, disappoint me not of the wonders of Thy bounty and grace. Nourish me then from the everlasting chalices that Thou dost possess, and make me firm in Thy Cause. Thou art verily Powerful over all things.[58]

Khadíjih Bagum's Petitions to Bahá'u'lláh

Khadíjih Bagum's closeness to Bahá'u'lláh and His family, as well as the trust and respect that she enjoyed, prompted her brother, Siyyid Ḥasan, to request her to ask Bahá'u'lláh for the hand of one of His daughters in marriage with his son, Siyyid 'Alí. Knowing Khadíjih Bagum's lifelong desire to attain Bahá'u'lláh's presence, Siyyid Ḥasan promised that if the request were granted, he and his son would take Khadíjih Bagum with them to the Holy Land to attain her heart's desire, a hope which had kept her alive. She submitted the request through a special person who visited Shíráz together with her brother on their way to the Holy Land. In her autobiography Munírih Khánum explains the nature of the request:

> Just before we left, the wife of the Báb said, 'I wish for two things from the Ancient Beauty: first, that one of the Blessed Leaves be united to the family of the Primal Point [the Afnán family], so that these two blessed Trees might also be united outwardly; second, I would like permission to visit Him.' When I later attained the presence of Bahá'u'lláh and conveyed these two requests, He granted them immediately.[59]

H. M. Balyuzi provides more detail:

> Munírih Khánum carried to the presence of Bahá'u'lláh three requests from Khadíjih Bagum. She longed for the house of her Husband to be repaired so that she might live there. She asked for the hand of Furúghíyyih Khánum, a daughter of Bahá'u'lláh, on behalf of her nephew, Ḥájí Siyyid 'Alí. And she begged for permission to travel to 'Akká and have the bounty of attaining the presence of her Lord, in Whose path her Husband had gladly offered His life. Bahá'u'lláh granted all her requests.[60]

Both accounts confirm that Khadíjih Bagum's requests were adorned with Bahá'u'lláh's acceptance.

Concerning the House of the Báb

The House of the Báb in Shíráz is the focal centre of pilgrimage in Iran. It has been so designated by Bahá'u'lláh in the Kitáb-i-Aqdas.[61] The House was originally purchased by the Báb's father, Jináb-i-Áqá Siyyid Riḍá.[62] The date of the purchase is unknown. The Báb's early years were spent in that House. When the Báb's father passed away, He and His mother transferred their residence to the house of the Báb's uncle, Jináb-i-Ḥáj Mírzá Siyyid 'Alí, known as Khál-i-A'ẓam. It seems that the Báb and His mother stayed in the house of Khál-i-A'ẓam until He left for Búshihr. It is unclear who occupied the House during the years the Báb was in Búshihr. When He returned to Shíráz several years later and married Khadíjih Bagum, He, His wife and His mother settled in the House where He had lived as a child.

It was in the upper chamber of this House that the Báb declared His mission to Mullá Ḥusayn on the night of 22 May 1844. When He returned from His pilgrimage to Mecca, He, His wife and His mother continued to live in the same House until the night when 'Abdu'l-Ḥamíd Khán, the Chief Constable, and his men entered the House through the roof and arrested the Báb, resulting in His confinement in the house of His uncle and subsequent departure for Iṣfahán and Ádharbáyján. According to Nabíl, before the Báb left Shíráz for Iṣfahán, He bequeathed His possessions to His wife and mother and transferred the title to His property to them.[63]

After the Báb's departure from Shíráz, His mother and His wife continued to live in the House together with Mubárak and Fiḍḍih, their faithful servants. When the news of the Báb's execution in Tabríz on 9 July 1850 finally reached His mother, she was so grief-stricken and disconsolate that, as previously noted, she decided to leave Shíráz. She made arrangements to reside in the vicinity of the Shí'í holy places in Iraq and after some time left for Karbilá together with Mubárak and a female relative, Bíbí Gawhar, a great-aunt of H. M. Balyuzi.

Before Fáṭimih Bagum left Shíráz, it was clear that Khadíjih Bagum could not live in the sacred House alone. Therefore, she relates,

> I went to live with my sister, the widow of Ḥájí Mírzá Siyyid 'Alí. She herself had lost both her husband and her only son within the space of one year. As great as was my sorrow, hers was even greater and I had to comfort her. The loyal, faithful Fiḍḍih was with me.[64]

To provide for the protection of the sacred House, before Fáṭimih Bagum left Shíráz a contract was drawn up between her and a Mírzá Ḥasan, son of Mírzá Asadu'lláh, who received it in trust. He was not a believer but was known to the family. The contract stipulated that the man was to repair the House, which had been damaged by earthquake, at his own expense in order to make it habitable. It also specified that he had to vacate the House when the owner wanted it back and that he had no claim to it.

Fáṭimih Bagum left Shíráz for the holy cities of Iraq in about 1854. She spent the rest of her life there and there is no indication or evidence that she ever returned to Iran for a visit. Mírzá Ḥasan did not vacate the House and over time used it as his own property. After him, another person who was not a believer lived in the House. In the meantime, further earthquakes and lack of repair caused more damage to it.

Eventually the House fell into a state of disrepair; something had to be done. Áqá Mírzá Áqá took the initiative. He consulted with Jináb-i Ḥáj Siyyid Muḥammad who authorized him to do what was necessary to evacuate the usurper. Áqá Mírzá Áqá met with the occupier and offered to mortgage another house for him to live in. The tenant agreed to move out. After necessary repairs were carried out, a believer by the name of 'Abdur-Razzáq lived there for about three years. After him, two other believers, Ḥájí Abu'l-Ḥasan-i-Bazzáz and Mullá Áqá Buzurg-i Zarqání, lived there one after the other. In the meantime, further earthquakes caused considerable damage to the House.

In 1872 when Munírih Khánum was in Shíráz on her way to the Holy

Land, one of the petitions Khadíjih Bagum asked her to present on her behalf to Bahá'u'lláh was that she be allowed to make certain changes to the House of the Báb and live there herself. Permission was granted, changes were made and Khadíjih Bagum transferred her residence there.

Khadíjih Bagum's initiative shows that she was keenly aware of the significance of the House where her beloved husband had lived, where He had declared His mission to Mullá Ḥusayn and where He had received souls earnestly seeking Him. After Fáṭimih Bagum passed away, Khadíjih Bagum was the Báb's sole heir and as such she had the right to occupy the House and treat it as her own. However, as a devoted follower of Bahá'u'lláh fully cognizant of His station as the centre of authority, she sought His permission to introduce changes in the House and to live there. Bahá'u'lláh granted her request and later, in a Tablet addressed to '*awlíyá*' (those in authority) in Shíráz, written in His hand and bearing His seal, confirmed that Khadíjih Bagum had the '*tawlíyat*' (custodianship) of the House of the Báb, and that after Khadíjih Bagum, her sister, Zahrá Bagum, who had been Khadíjih Bagum's mainstay after the Báb's martyrdom, was granted the custodianship of the sacred House. In the same Tablet Bahá'u'lláh confirms that after Zahrá Bagum her offspring would have the honour.[65]

Under the supervision of Áqá Mírzá Áqá the work on the House of the Báb was completed and Khadíjih Bagum moved there. She was in effect the first custodian of the House of God, the focal point of pilgrimage in Iran.[66] With Khadíjih Bagum living in the House, the friends were able to visit her and at the same time visit the House itself. The number of people visiting the House increased and attracted the attention of the opponents of the Faith. The matter was reported to the governor, Prince Farhád Mírzá, uncle of Náṣiri'd-Dín Sháh, who decided to have the House demolished. Two devoted believers, who worked for the Prince, heard the report and were able to prevent that course of action. They immediately conveyed the information to Jináb-i-Afnán with the recommendation that it was best for Khadíjih Bagum not to live in the House for a while and to wait for the rumours to die down and the situation to become calm.[67] Áqá Mírzá Áqá reported the situation to Bahá'u'lláh. In a Tablet revealed in his honour on 19 Ṣafar 1295, Bahá'u'lláh stated:

> If in these days the stay in the True House of Ḥaram-i-Athar (the Purest Wife), upon her be all glory and loftiness, is the cause of people's uproar, their jealousy and enmity, it is not permissible by reason of the wisdom that God hath revealed in the Book, until the right time arrives. It is absolutely necessary to have regard for the considerations of wisdom. If in these days, for reasons of wisdom and discretion, it is not possible for

Ḥaram (the Wife) and the Afnáns to live in the House, its door must be closed and it is not permissible for anyone to live there . . .[68]

When Khadíjih Bagum returned to the House she exercised great caution and wisdom. For example, she did not use the entrance of the House but instead used the entrance of the newly acquired house next door. The visitors did likewise. The purpose was to deflect the attention of the populace away from the House.

Khadíjih Bagum lived happily in the House of her beloved husband, exhilarated by the continuous outpourings of grace and favour coming from Bahá'u'lláh, for the remainder of her earthly life. It was in that House, the House that the Báb had bequeathed to her, that she passed away.

The Marriage between Bahá'u'lláh's Daughter and Khadíjih Bagum's Nephew; Permission for Khadíjih Bagum to Attain Bahá'u'lláh's Presence

The realization of Khadíjih Bagum's third request to Bahá'u'lláh hinged on His approval of the second. Khadíjih Bagum had requested that the families of Bahá'u'lláh and the Báb be united through the marriage of His daughter with her nephew. She had also sought permission to attain Bahá'u'lláh's presence. The two requests were linked, for her brother and nephew had promised to take her to the Holy Land if Bahá'u'lláh approved the marriage. The thought of attaining the presence of the Blessed Beauty so enraptured her that she lived for the day when she could gaze upon that heavenly countenance, her supreme consoler, and forget her lifelong suffering. These requests Bahá'u'lláh granted as well but, alas, Ḥájí Siyyid 'Alí and his father failed to fulfil their promise. Together with Ḥájí Siyyid 'Alí's mother and sister, they travelled from Yazd to the Holy Land via 'Ishqábád, without taking Khadíjih Bagum with them. The news of their betrayal caused Khadíjih Bagum immense sorrow. Her hopes, upon which she had built the foundation of the last years of her life, were shattered. This deprivation, the last and most drastic in a chain of suffering she had heroically endured, broke her tender heart. Nothing could console her. She bewailed her plight and shed tears of anguish. This blow tore her delicate being apart. She became ill and never recovered. She had completely lost hope of ever being able to see Bahá'u'lláh on this earthly plane. H.M. Balyuzi relates:

> Khadíjih Bagum was heart-broken. Her health deteriorated and despite the attentions of several physicians, within two months of the receipt of that distressing intelligence, she passed away in the house of her glorious

> Husband, three hours before sunset on Monday, 2 Dhi'l-Qa'dih 1299 AH (15 September 1882). And strangely, the faithful servitor, Fiḍḍih, died two hours after the death of her mistress, in the same house.[69]

Exactly how long it took from the time the marriage request was granted to the time it actually took place is unclear. A decade intervenes between the date of Munírih Khánum's visit to Shíráz and the date of Khadíjih Bagum's passing. Therefore there must have been a lapse of several years between the granting of the request and the actual date of the marriage.

In her autobiography, Munírih Khánum makes a brief reference to Khadíjih Bagum's passing and what caused it. The reason for her circumspection may be close family relationships, for this brother of Khadíjih Bagum in time became the father-in-law of 'Abdu'l-Bahá and Munirih Khánum's daughter, Ṭúbá Khánum:

> [Bahá'u'lláh] commanded her brother (that is, the father of Mírzá Muḥsin) to set out from Yazd and travel to Shíráz in order to transport the wife of the Báb [to the Holy Land] as if she were going on pilgrimage to Mecca.
>
> But because of various difficulties, when the gentleman set out from Ashkhabad ('Ishqábád) he wrote to his sister, the wife of the Báb, saying, 'I have left. God willing, the means for your journey will somehow be provided.' When she received this message, she was so grief-stricken that she fell ill. Two days later she passed away from this world of pain.[70]

The Passing of Khadíjih Bagum

Khadíjih Bagum survived the Báb by 32 years. During those long years of separation and anguish she endured tribulations far beyond what ordinary human beings can sustain but never flinched in her deep devotion to her best beloved. In the midst of her woes and sufferings she took it upon herself to console other suffering souls who had sustained misfortunes and ordeals for their faith. When she heard of the plight of the women survivors of the second upheaval of Nayríz, for example, she immediately extended to them consolation and help. These were the women captives who had been brought to Shíráz riding on the bare backs of camels and mules, carrying their children and infants with them. They had been paraded half naked and to the sound of loud music before the public gaze. After untold miseries and sufferings these women had been set free but were stranded in the city. In spite of the dangers involved, Khadíjih Bagum summoned them to her presence, received them lovingly, consoled their grieving hearts and extended to them loving sympathy. The sincerity of feelings and the depth of concern with which Khadíjih

Bagum received and treated these helpless and grief-stricken women touched their hearts deeply and lightened the burden of their suffering.

When Khadíjih Bagum passed away, her favourite nephew, Áqá Mírzá Áqá, was living abroad. In a letter that Jináb-i Mírzá Abu'l-Qásim, Khadíjih Bagum's brother and the father-in-law of Áqá Mírzá 'Áqá, sent to him in Bombay on 28 Dhi-Hajjih 1299 AH (1882 AD), he describes the circumstances leading to her death:

> In my previous letter, I wrote about the condition of her honour, the sister, and her illness. At that time I expressed regret that her illness is no longer treatable. It was a most difficult situation. Jináb-i Áqá Mírzá Aḥmad was her physician. Jináb-i Áqá Mírzá Ḥasan likewise paid her visits. Occasionally, I also brought Jináb-i Áqáy-i Ḥakímbáshí to her bedside. Jináb-i Áqá Mírzá Aḥmad said that medically all that could have been done was done, but it was all in God's hand. The predestined decree was something different. Nothing can change the preordained time. On Monday evening, the 2nd, just over three hours after sunset,[71] God's mercy took over and she said yea to His call. I am unable to describe what we and the servants have gone through. I hope that the loving Lord will grant all of us patience and endurance. It has been most difficult . . . I know that once you hear of it, you, too, will have a hard and difficult time. But there is no escape. Whatever the Lord of existence decrees, that shall be.
>
> Nowadays, there is no discussion or information regarding a will, neither is there any mention as to what the survivors would do after her . . .
>
> Memorial services were held on Monday and Tuesday at the grave side. On Thursday, before noon, a group of notables, including His Excellency, Mushíru'l-Mulk and His Honour Áqáy-i Imám-i Jum'ih, ordered that the service end. In obedience to his instruction, the service ended and we have been staying at home. The friends who did not come to the memorial service troubled themselves and came. We are now returning their visits.[72]

The news of Khadíjih Bagum's passing caused Bahá'u'lláh immense sorrow. He was well aware of the flimsy excuses that had been used to deprive her of attaining His presence. In a Tablet dated 4 Rabí'u'l-Avval 1301 AH (1883–4 AD) and signed by Khádimu'lláh, Bahá'u'lláh states:

> The Afnáns arrived in Beirut. After some time they received permission to come in small groups. Finally, they entered the shelter of grace and the canopy of grandeur. After the visit they returned in small groups.
>
> Regarding that which had been promised, it was mentioned here that

> the intention was this: After arriving in Beirut, Áqá Siyyid 'Alí was to go to Shíráz, make arrangements for the Exalted Leaf's travel, then direct their steps towards Him. For it was thought that if in those days, prior to the trip, he had gone to Shíráz, the enemies and stirrers of mischief would have created a situation and prevented all [from making the trip]. It so happened that although the trip was a well-kept secret, the stirrers of mischief were hard at work but God freed us, protected us and saved us through His bounty, and He is the All-Bountiful, the Most Beneficent. Yea! Such excuses were heard from some of them. The true knowledge is with our Lord, the All-Knowing, the All-Informed.
>
> Would that the good pleasure of Her Highness the Exalted Leaf had been obtained! This would have been most loved and desired by the True One. However, what happened hath happened. God is aware and testifieth that her deprivation from coming on pilgrimage is consuming the heart, and all the leaves of the Tabernacle of virtue, decency and grandeur are sorrowful and grieved.
>
> One day this exalted statement was heard from the Tongue of the Possessor of Names. He said: 'O Servant in Attendance! The effect of that which hath come to pass will become manifest in the world.' And today another Word was uttered by the Blessed Tongue: 'Write to My Afnán that the Exalted Leaf asked for something, We responded positively and made a promise. The people involved are still hopeful and waiting, although they have not to date mentioned anything.' And He said: 'Write this explanation to the Afnán, upon him be My Glory, and he had been informed previously. We have not liked it in the past and do not like it now to leave unfulfilled what We have promised the Exalted Leaf. If God wills it, He will adorn His promise with fulfilment although all affairs are today contingent on the requirements of wisdom. It must be seen what Divine wisdom will require and what command will be issued forth and manifested from the Source. People know not what is with God, but He knoweth what the servants possess, and He is the All-Knowing, the All-Wise.'[73]

The contents of a Tablet revealed in honour of Áqá Mírzá Áqá and signed by Khádimu'lláh, dated 11 Rabí'ul-Úlá 1298 AH (*circa* 1880–1 AD), indicate that after it became clear that Siyyid 'Alí was not going to fulfil his promise, efforts were made to enable Khadíjih Bagum to travel to the Holy Land with someone other than a family member:

> Thou hast written regarding your consultation with Ḥaḍrat-i Muballigh (His Highness, the Teacher of the Cause) concerning the Exalted Leaf,

> Ḥaḍrat-i-Ḥaram (Her Highness, the Consort [of the Báb]), upon her be Bahá'u'lláhu'l-Abhá. This is most desired. It would be most certainly better if she would travel with him.[74]

Another Tablet revealed in honour of Ḥájí Mírzá Muḥammad-Taqí Afnán and signed by Khádimu'lláh, dated 6 Dhi'l-Ḥajjih 1307, indicates that those efforts did not yield the hoped-for result:

> Concerning the Leaf of the Blessed Tree, the Consort, upon her be Bahá'u'lláhu'l-Abhá, sometime ago Jináb-i Ḥájí Mullá Ḥusayn-i-Lárí, upon him be God's Glory, sought permission to come on pilgrimage. After permission was granted, he came and attained His presence. Bahá'u'lláh consulted him regarding the Leaf of the Tree, the Consort, upon her be Bahá'u'lláhu'l-Abhá. He said that this year Ḥajj (pilgrimage to Mecca) fell in the month of Tamúz [June–July], and in view of certain considerations that he mentioned, her journey was halted . . .[75]

Siyyid 'Alí Afnán never admitted his failure or apologized for what he had done to Khadíjih Bagum. He did not appear serious about fulfilling his promise to her either during his stay in Iran or after he left for the Holy Land. His pretentious behaviour could be discerned from vague and controversial statements he made to exonerate himself. He gave the impression that he intended to do the honourable thing and fulfil his promise but self-interest and self-preservation caused him to fail miserably. In his letter of 19 Ramaḍán 1299 AH (circa 1882 AD), in response to a letter from Khadíjih Bagum, who had obviously written to him saying that he had broken a solemn promise he had made to her, he says:

> . . . Your letter indicative of the steadfastness and good health of that esteemed and blessed being was the cause of rendering to God praise and gratitude. God willing, you will be always under divine care and protection. The unkind statements in your letter have made me completely disappointed in myself. I wonder what has happened! I have not failed to render service to the degree possible. However, I have not completely given up hope. God willing, the Lord will arrange affairs in a happy manner. At the time of my travel to Simnán, I did not quite know father's intention; whether he was going to Mashhad or continuing further. When he was leaving Yazd, he wrote that he was going to Mashhad and said you, too, would travel thereto. In Mashhad it became clear that he intended to proceed to those directions [Holy Land]. I was preoccupied with my own thoughts when your letter arrived. It made me sad and

despondent. God willing, the Lord will let affairs happen as they should. It is not possible for me to return from here, otherwise I would have attained your presence. That is how things have happened and there is no problem. I stand firm and am faithful to the promise I have given. Rest assured. Even now, if you agree and consider it prudent, I have asked my uncle, Áqá Mírzá Buzurg, to make arrangements for your travel. Áqá Siyyid Áqá, my cousin, and Jináb-i Mírzá 'Abdu'l-Ḥamíd are also travelling to render service. There is no point in going to Mecca. From Búshihr go directly to Alexandria and stay there for several days. I will come from the other side and attain your presence. I will send Áqá Siyyid Áqá back to Bombay from Alexandria. And if you do not like it this way, I will myself attain your presence and arrange for your travel . . .[76]

The disheartening letter from her nephew, the man who had betrayed her, broke Khadíjih Bagum's heart. She wept and bemoaned her plight. The depression she suffered worsened day by day until she winged her way to her most beloved. Her illness lasted five and a half months.[77]

Khadíjih Bagum passed away on the afternoon of 15 September 1882. Her body was buried later that 'same night . . . within the Shrine of Sháh-i-Chiragh, in the section known as Ṣadru'l-Ḥifáẓ'.[78] Sháh-i-Chirágh is a shrine built in Shíráz over the tomb of Mír Siyyid Aḥmad, believed to be the son of Imám Músá Káẓim. According to H. M. Balyuzi, Khadíjih Bagum's faithful maid Fiḍḍih, who died two hours after the death of Khadíjih Bagum in the same house, 'was buried within that Shrine in a chamber facing the Ṣadru'l-Ḥifáẓ (to the north of the tomb of Mír Siyyid Aḥmad), which was called Masjid-i-Zanánih (Women's Mosque)'.[79]

After Khadíjih Bagum passed away, Áqá Mírzá Áqá sent to the Holy Land a sum of money belonging to her. He must have also mentioned something about the balance of the money and her clothes. A Tablet signed by Khádimu'lláh, dated 26 Jamádíy'l-Úlá 1303 (*circa* 1885 AD) states:

> Thou hast written about the sum belonging to Ḥaḍrat-i-Varaqiy-i-'Ulyá (Her Highness, the Exalted Leaf) . . . Whatever was sent, hath been received. The balance must be sent to the exalted handmaid, thy mother. According to His instructions, the decision regarding her [Khadíjih Bagum's] clothing has likewise been left to that handmaiden.[80] He said: 'If they could preserve some of it in a box, it would be loved and acceptable before the Lord.'[81]

And in response to a question from Áqá Mírzá Áqá about Khadíjih Bagum's belongings, Bahá'u'lláh states:

> These laws relate to the Kitáb-i-Aqdas, and in this matter thou hast been empowered to decide. Do that which thou deemest advisable. Send thou one of her belongings, which tell and remind one of her, to the Holy Presence, that it may be a remembrance of her before the Lord, her Creator.[82]

Describing the effect of Khadíjih Bagum's ascension, the Tablet goes on: 'This sorrow, like unto the life-vein, coursed throughout the body and in every artery produced its effect.'[83]

Khadíjih Bagum's Station and Her Place in History

In the Kitáb-i-Badí' Bahá'u'lláh refers to Khadíjih Bagum as 'the immaculate virgin', 'the consort of the Most High', 'the most chaste', 'the consort of the Point', 'the consort of God', 'the remnant of God'. He enjoins His followers to serve her with absolute sincerity and show her respect and consideration. In the same book, after praising the virtues of the mother of the Báb, Fáṭimih Bagum, and His wife, Khadíjih Bagum, Bahá'u'lláh confers upon them the designation *Khayru'n-Nisá'* (the Most Virtuous among All Women), and forbids the use of the name for others:

> In this day the Khayru'n-Nisá' is the mother of the Primal Point. The use of this title for the other handmaids of God hath been strictly forbidden. However, it hath been permitted that after her this title be used for the wife of the Point, who is residing in Fárs, who hath not transgressed the divine fortress of God's protection and who hath had due regard for God's sanctity, the one whose garment of purity hath not been touched by the hand of the betrayers. By My life, the True One, she is the immaculate maiden, the consort of the Most High, the most chaste. Render her service, O My friends, with utmost sincerity, for she is the remnant of God amongst you, if ye are of those who truly understand. We beseech God to enable her to stand firm in her duty and to protect her from the touch of the violators, whom the winds of passion and carnal desire move as they please. They, verily, are in manifest error. May she remain steadfast in this Cause. He is verily supreme over all things . . . It is incumbent upon all to show respect to the consort of God. It is most desired to have consideration for her under all conditions . . .[84]

In another Tablet, Bahá'u'lláh directs Khadíjih Bagum to render praise to God that she had been the throne upon which the Merciful was established in the temple of His name 'Alí. He says that she became the throne of God without any of the believers knowing it, that she associated with God, her Lord, that she entered the sea of union from time immemorial, that she was united with the Self of God, that she was overtaken by the splendours of the dawn of union with Him, and that this was a station not attained by any other. He says moreover that she attained the Day of Judgement and entered the highest paradise in His presence, that she was honoured with meeting God before the creation of the heavens and earth. Bahá'u'lláh explains that her eyes met the eye of the one through whose glance all created things sacrificed their spirits, that she heard God's melodies with her ear, that she was a dweller of the highest Paradise. He calls Khadíjih Bagum Mir'átu'lláh (Mirror of God), Varaqatu'l-Baqá (Leaf of Eternity), Arḍu'l-Vafá (Land of Fidelity), Madíntu'l-A'lá fí rafraf-i qurb-i aminá (the Most Exalted City in the highest retreats of nearness to the Most Trusted). He says that she was the first throne that appeared in the world, the first land upon which rained the water of yearning springing from the river of crystal clear water, that she was the first Rose Garden in which the Nightingale of Holiness sang verses encompassing all created beings, that she was the first station upon which shone the Ancient Sun at a time when she was unaware of it. In the same Tablet, Bahá'u'lláh reaffirms that Khadíjih Bagum was the most virtuous among all women provided that she remained steadfast in her love for God.[85]

And in yet another Tablet Bahá'u'lláh pays glowing tribute to Khadíjih Bagum, to her steadfastness in the Covenant of God and to her unswerving devotion to Him:

> . . . thy letter hath been presented before the Throne, and the glance of thy Lord, the Most High, the Most Great, hath been turned thereto. Well is it with thee for having remained faithful to the Covenant of God and His Testament and for having turned thy back to the traitors. We have perceived from thee the fragrance of unswerving devotion. Take pride among the people of the world in that to which God hath testified. Let nothing sadden thee. By My life, He is with thee at all times. It behoveth everyone to venerate thee, glorify thee and through thee pay heed to the truth of God and His Cause. Thus hath the command been sent down from the Almighty, the All-Powerful. Render thanks to God and praise Him with joy and radiance for that which He had revealed for thee from the Pen of Revelation in this perspicuous Tablet.[86]

Khadíjih Bagum is the only female member of the Báb's family honoured with the station of a martyr. Bahá'u'lláh singled her out for this very special privilege, as stated in a Tablet, dated 14 Ṣafar 1300 AH (*circa* 1883 AD), signed by Khádimu'lláh:

In that city she was visibly a sign from the Exalted Lord and the Sovereign of Existence, exalted be His mention and glorified His praise. In her transfer from one place to the next there is a sadness that behoveth blood to flow from my eyes and the eyes of those who are clinging to the Blessed, Exalted, Manifest and Living Tree . . .

Yet another favour for the Blessed Leaf, revealed by God, our Lord and the Lord of all who are in the heavens and earth: 'O servant in attendance! The heart of Thamariy-i 'Ulyá (the Most Exalted Fruit) was verily consumed in the fire of separation. For that reason, before God she is regarded as a martyr. The reward of this deed is the statement revealed by the Pen of the Most High in the Visitation Prayer that on the night and day [of her ascension], whoever passed away would be adorned with the vesture of forgiveness, except those who have openly denied the Divine Truth, His Manifestation and His verses. She hath been singled out for this favour.'[87]

The visitation prayers revealed by Bahá'u'lláh in honour of Khadíjih Bagum attest to the depth of His sorrow and grief and testify to her exalted station. The translation of one of the Tablets reads:

He is the comforter of the sorrowful!

O Pen! Verily Thou hast been visited by a great calamity, an immense affliction, which hath caused the inhabitants of the highest Heaven and most lofty Paradise to lament. Through this affliction sorrow hath ascended until it seized the hem of the robe of the Merciful. Blessed be the man who arose to render her service in her lifetime and visited her grave after she winged her flight and ascended to the world beyond. Blessed likewise be the handmaiden who betook herself to her shrine and through her drew nigh unto God.

The glory shining from the horizon of My luminous Brow, and the splendour of the light manifested from the heaven of My Name, the Most Glorious, be upon thee, O thou the fruit of the divine Lote-Tree, the blessed and luminous leaf, the consort of the One through Whose revelation the kingdom of immortality and the realm of creation were wreathed in smiles! I testify that thou art in truth the first leaf who attained the cup of a sure union and the last fruit who offered up her soul because of her separation from Him. Thou art the one whose inner being was consumed, whose heart melted, and whose limbs were set aflame by reason of thy remoteness from the presence of the One Whom God hath made to be the Dawning-place of His Signs, the Dayspring of His Proofs, the Manifestation of His Names, the Source of His laws, and the Seat of His Throne.

O My leaf and the fragrance of the paradise of My good pleasure! Thou art with the Supreme Companion, and this Wronged One maketh mention of thee in the prison of 'Akká. Thou art she who, before the creation of the world of being, discovered the fragrance of the garment of the All-Merciful. Thou wert honoured with meeting Him, attained union with Him, and drank the wine of nearness from the hand of His bestowal. I testify that in thee two signs have been conjoined: The sign of union revived thee in the beginning and the sign of separation encompassed thy death in the end. How many a night did thy sighs ascend because of thy love for God and thy tears flow at the mention of His Name, the Most Glorious! He hath verily been with thee, witnessing thy burning, thy fervour, thine eagerness, thy yearning, and hearing the lamentation of thy heart and the wailing of thine inner being.

O thou who art the fruit of My tree! Through thine affliction the ocean of sorrows hath surged and the breezes of forgiveness have wafted. I bear witness that on the night thou didst ascend to the Abhá Horizon and to the throne of the Most High, and on the following day, in honour of thee and as a bounty unto thee, God verily forgave the trespasses of every servant and handmaiden who ascended, save those who openly denied God's truth and that which He hath revealed. Thus hath God singled thee out, O My leaf, for this most great bounty and this everlasting and preeminent station. Well is it with thee, with those who visit thee, with those who dwell in thy vicinity, with those who circle round thee, and with those who have besought and will continue to beseech God through thee.

Thou art she through whose afflictions the Maid of Heaven lamented and the leaves of the Tree of Revelation grieved. Thou art she who upon hearing the call from the tongue of the Possessor of the kingdom of names turned thy face unto Him and wert so attracted that the reins of composure were well-nigh seized from thy hand. O My leaf! O thou who art soaring in the atmosphere of My love, hast turned thy face unto Mine, and art occupied with my praise! Verily, We have revealed for thee a remembrance which neither the affairs of the centuries nor the passing of the ages can obliterate. We have through My Supreme Pen immortalized thy mention in the Crimson Book, which is known to none except God, the Source of all created things, and We have made mention of thee in this Tablet in such wise that those who enjoy near access to God will remember thee and the believers in the divine unity will direct their steps towards thine earthly remains. Blessed art thou, and well is it with thee and with whosoever standeth before thy resting-place reciting that which the Lord of Bounty hath now revealed.[88]

Khadíjih Bagum's Resting-Place

One of the prominent believers in Shíráz, named Faḍlu'lláh, beseeched Bahá'u'lláh to honour him and four other believers in Shíráz with the custodianship of the resting-place of Khadíjih Bagum and the Báb's uncle, who also passed away in Shíráz and was buried in Sháh-i-Chirágh. In a Tablet revealed on 19 Muḥarram 1301 (*circa* 1884 AD) and signed by Khádimu'lláh, Áqá Mírzá Áqá was informed of the permission granted to Jináb-i-Faḍl, who had attained Bahá'u'lláh's presence in the prison, and certain other people whose names are mentioned in the Tablet, regarding the custodianship. The Tablet quotes the text of what had been revealed by Bahá'u'lláh in this regard:

> He is the Wise Commander!
>
> O Faḍla'lláh! We have verily made thee and four other known believers, mentioned in Our presence, the custodians of the shrine of the Exalted Leaf and the shrines of those related to us in that land. We have placed the custodianship in thy hands as a glory for thee and thy children for so long as this world and the kingdom may endure. Render thanks to God for this everlasting bounty (*dawlat*) and eternal favour (*'ináyat*). He verily doeth what He pleaseth and commandeth what He wisheth. He is the Omnipotent Protector, the Self-Subsisting. Arise with resolution and steadfastness to render the service entrusted to you by God, the Possessor of all that hath been and all that will be.[89]

After Khadíjih Bagum's death, Áqá Mírzá Áqá wrote to the Holy Land asking Bahá'u'lláh for words to be engraved on her tombstone. The request was favoured with acceptance. Later Bahá'u'lláh instructed Mírzá Muḥammad-'Alí, whom He sent to Bombay in 1890–1 to publish the Kitáb-i-Aqdas and some other Tablets, to write the following verse for Khadíjih Bagum's tombstone: 'He is the Eternal! Verily, the exalted leaf hath heard the call of the divine Lote-Tree and hath taken her flight unto it. 1299.'[90] The verse was engraved on marble and kept in the home of Ḥáj Mírzá Muḥammad-'Alí Afnán, the maternal cousin of the Báb. About two decades later it was transported to Shíráz by Áqá Mírzá 'Abdu'l-Vahháb Afnán. Owing to unfavourable circumstances, the tombstone could not be erected.[91]

In a Tablet revealed in honour of the distinguished Afnáns in Shíráz, 'Abdu'l-Bahá says:

> Concerning the holy, fragrant, and luminous resting-place of the illustrious wife – My soul yearneth to inhale the holy savour of its dust – it must

> be cared for with the utmost respect until the time cometh when it shall be exalted. The Afnán of the blessed Tree must, on behalf of this Servant, circumambulate that focal point round which the holy ones circle in adoration and must visit the perfumed and sacred resting-place of the wife of the Glorious One.[92]

One of the goals of Shoghi Effendi's Ten Year Plan for Iran was the transfer of Khadíjih Bagum's remains to the Bahá'í cemetery in Shíráz but unfavourable circumstances prevented the transfer from taking place.

3

Zahrá Bagum, the Sister of the Wife of the Báb

Family Background

Zahrá Bagum was born to Ḥájíyih Bíbí and Áqá Mírzá 'Alí, residents of Shíráz. She had two sisters and three brothers. One sister, Ḥájíyih Bíbí Ján Ján, and one brother, Muḥammad Mihdí, known as Ḥájí Ḥijáb, were from a different father. Her full sister and brothers were Khadíjih Bagum, the wife of the Báb; Siyyid Ḥasan, entitled Afnán-i-Kabír; Ḥájí Mírzá Siyyid Abu'l-Qásim, known as Saqqákhánih'í.[1]

Birth and Early Life

No information is available regarding Zahrá Bagum's date of birth. She seems to have been older than Khadíjih Bagum. Since her parents lived in Shíráz, it is assumed that she was born and raised in that city. Of her early life we know nothing.

Marriage and Subsequent Developments

Zahrá Bagum married Áqá Mírzá Zaynu'l-'Ábidín, son of Ḥáj Mírzá Siyyid Muḥammad, uncle of the Báb's father. Exactly when that marriage took place is unknown. However, we do know that their marriage preceded the marriage of the Báb and Khadíjih Bagum, which took place in 1842.

Zahrá Bagum and her husband had one son, named Siyyid Muḥammad. He later became known as Mírzá Áqá, whom Bahá'u'lláh entitled Núru'd-Dín. Of the children born to Khadíjih Bagum and her sisters, Mírzá Áqá is the only one who survived, married and had children of his own.[2] Zahrá Bagum and her son played a very important role in the life of Khadíjih Bagum after the Báb was martyred. Indeed, the first person in whom Khadíjih Bagum confided the truth of the Báb's mission was Mírzá Áqá. At the age of 13 he embraced the Cause of the Báb. As a result of that transformation, the loving bond between him and his maternal aunt was strengthened and continued to the end of Khadíjih Bagum's life and beyond. Mírzá Áqá rendered outstanding services to the Cause of Bahá'u'lláh, the most significant of which was the restoration of the House of the Báb to its original design during 'Abdu'l-Bahá's ministry.

Having been confirmed in the truth of the mission of the Báb, Mírzá Áqá became the cause of the enlightenment of the hearts of his mother and father. He then widened the scope of his teaching activities and engaged Jináb-i-Siyyid Muḥammad, the Báb's greater uncle, in discussions about the truth of his nephew's divine mission. However, to be absolutely convinced, Jináb-i-Siyyid Muḥammad needed further proof and evidence. Acting upon a suggestion from Mírzá Áqá, he proceeded to Baghdád. The purpose of the trip was to meet Bahá'u'lláh and personally investigate the truth of the nascent Faith. While there, he was encouraged to submit the questions that he had regarding the prophecies that needed to be fulfilled at the time of the Promised One's appearance. It was in response to those questions that the Kitáb-i-Íqán (the Book of Certitude) was revealed in 1862.

The recognition of the station of the Báb and Bahá'u'lláh by Mírzá Áqá, Zahrá Bagum and other members of the family opened before Khadíjih Bagum, the mother teacher of the Afnán family, a new and glorious horizon. It made it possible for her to open her heart to them, sharing with them her own experiences of perceiving at an early stage the glory of the Báb's station. Those recollections her nieces and nephews living in Shíráz, especially the son and grandchildren of Zahrá Bagum, remembered fondly and later recorded and preserved for posterity.

The Custodianship of the House of the Báb

Zahrá Bagum was a devoted believer. She was also a most loving sister and staunch supporter of Khadíjih Bagum. The services that she rendered to her bereaved sister received high praise and commendation from Bahá'u'lláh, who bestowed upon her, according to a Tablet revealed in His own hand and adorned with His seal, the custodianship of the blessed House of the Báb, after Khadíjih Bagum passed away. He also ordained that the custodianship of the blessed House would remain in Zahrá Bagum's lineage, thus perpetuating her memory through ages and centuries.[3]

The custodianship of the sacred House, wherein the promised Qá'im had lived and declared His mission, a place ordained in the Kitáb-i-Aqdas as one of the two focal centres of pilgrimage in the Bahá'í world, is an inestimable honour and privilege. In the past such exalted positions were reserved for men of high rank and stature. Even today it is extraordinary for such honour to be bestowed upon a woman; how much more revolutionary it must have been in mid-19th century, when women throughout the world and especially in the

Middle East were deprived of far less significant rights and honours. When Khadíjih Bagum passed away and the custodianship of the House, including the right to reside there, was conferred upon Zahrá Bagum, the believers, influenced by the traditions of their backgrounds, learned a valuable lesson in the application of the principle of gender equality. The honour to look after the House of God was great, the mission glorious and the responsibilities it entailed tremendous. Zahrá Bagum was the designated custodian of the holy House to the end of her life. Unfortunately no record has been left of how she carried out the duties associated with the task assigned to her. On the whole, little is known about her life from beginning to end.

After Zahrá Bagum passed away her son, Mírzá Áqá, called Núru'd-Dín by Bahá'u'lláh, became, as ordained by Him, the designated custodian of the House of the Báb. Mírzá Áqá had one daughter, Ḥájíyih Ṭúbá Khánum, and five sons: Mírzá Aḥmad-'Alí, known as Áqá Siyyid Áqá; Mírzá Jalál; Ḥáj Mírzá Zaynu'l-'Ábidín, known as Ḥáj Mírzá Buzurg; Ḥáj Mírzá Ḥabíbu'lláh; and Ḥáj Mírzá Ḍíyá.[4] Those who assumed custodianship of the House of the Báb after their father passed away were Mírzá Buzurg and Mírzá Ḥabíbu'lláh Afnán. After Mírzá Ḥabíbu'lláh Afnán, two of his sons, Abu'l-Qásim Afnán and Abu'l-Ḥasan Afnán, served as custodians. Future custodians will be appointed by the Universal House of Justice from the lineage of Zahrá Bagum and that is her greatest legacy in this contingent world.

The Passing of Zahrá Bagum

Zahrá Bagum outlived Khadíjih Bagum by eight years. The two sisters were extremely close. Life after Khadíjih Bagum must have been most difficult for Zahrá Bagum, especially since her only son and his family moved to Egypt. She passed away in Shíráz in 1890 and was buried next to Khadíjih Bagum in the Shrine of Sháh-i-Chirágh.

Bahá'u'lláh's Writings Revealed in Honour of Zahrá Bagum

Zahrá Bagum was addressed by Bahá'u'lláh as Ukht-i-Ḥaram (Sister of the Honourable Wife). Ḥaram (honourable wife) is a reference to Khadíjih Bagum, the Báb's wife. While Khadíjih Bagum was alive, Zahrá Bagum was addressed as Ukht-i-Ḥaram but after Khadíjih Bagum passed away, Zahrá Bagum was addressed as Umm-i-Afnán (the mother of the Afnán), a reference to her only son, Áqá Mírzá 'Aqá. Zahrá Bagum was the recipient of several Tablets of Bahá'u'lláh and she was also mentioned in Tablets dealing with the custodianship of the House of the Báb.

Two of the Tablets revealed in her honour have been published in *Khánidán-i-Afnán* by the late Muḥammad-'Alí Faizi. Neither has been translated into English. In one Tablet, Bahá'u'lláh expresses the hope that through God's favour she would cling to the divine *sidrih* (tree) in every one of His worlds. He then assures her of God's bounty and advises her to be thankful for having attained the greatest of all honours, that of fixing her gaze upon the Most Great Countenance. He expresses the hope that she will always remember God with joy and radiance, turning her back on all else. He adds that the world is a place of changes and vicissitudes and is therefore worthless in the sight of God. What is constant and eternal exists with God, He says. At the end He beseeches God to enable all to do that which is loved and praiseworthy, and to ordain for them what is concealed behind hidden veils.

The second Tablet is addressed to Umm-i-Afnán. In this Tablet Bahá'u'lláh speaks of Zahrá Bagum having sustained that which had saddened the hearts of the denizens of the cities of justice and fairness. He admonishes her to be patient, for these difficulties had happened in the path of God. He assures her that she and the Exalted Leaf, Khadíjih Bagum, were always remembered by Him. He then speaks of what God has ordained for the Afnáns, with which nothing in the world can compare, and emphasizes the fleeting nature of the world. He says that what the Pen of the Most High had revealed for the Afnáns were for them to remember God and to teach His Cause to the highest degree possible. He praises the station of the teacher, stating that nothing in the world compares with a word revealed in the Tablets. Bahá'u'lláh again stresses His love for them, conveys His condolences for what had happened to them and beseeches God to protect them, assist them and enable them to show patience and submission. He then says that the Afnán (Siyyid 'Alí[5]) was present, resting under the shadow of God's mercy and the tabernacle of His majesty. He advises her to render thanks to God for this conspicuous bounty and to be happy for having been honoured with this exalted Tablet which was revealed for her. Speaking of the Afnán again, Bahá'u'lláh says that the Provider of means had made it possible for His Afnán to join the Sidrih. He then beseeches God to confirm her in such a way that the doubts of the ignorant and the insinuations of the deniers would not become barriers. He admonishes her to always fix her gaze upon the Highest Horizon and cling to His cord. He then remembers the wife of the Afnán (Maryam Sulṭán Bagum[6]) and assures her of God's favour. He again advises Zahrá Bagum not to be sad, for soon, He says, will appear that which will cause the visible and hidden existence to smile. Ending the Tablet, Bahá'u'lláh says that that Household, including the women and children, are related to God. He gives praise to God and beseeches Him to draw them nigh unto Him, to protect them from the evil deeds of the enemy.[7]

4

Fáṭimih Khánum, the Second Wife of the Báb

The Báb's second marriage took place during His sojourn in Iṣfahán. After He left Shíráz in the summer of 1846 and before His exile to Ádharbayján, the Báb spent nearly six months in Iṣfahán. The exact date of His marriage to Fáṭimih Khánum is unknown. Of the approximately six months that He spent in Iṣfahán, 40 days were spent in the Imám-Jum'ih's residence[1] and about four months in the 'Imárat-i-Khurshíd, the private residence of the governor, Manúchihr Khán, the Mu'tamidu'd-Dawlih.[2] The second marriage of the Báb is believed to have taken place while He lived in the private residence of the Mu'tamidu'd-Dawlih.

Family Background, Birth and Early Life

Fáṭimih Khánum's father was Mullá Ḥasan, the preacher, one of the early Bábís of Iṣfahán. There are many unknowns about her. They include the name of her mother, the exact date of her birth, her age when she got married, her education if any, and other particulars. On the whole, almost nothing is known about her early life, which is not unusual for a woman of that era. She was presumably born and raised in Iṣfahán where her father preached.

Edward G. Browne in his book *Materials for the Study of the Bábí Religion* says that she died in 1916 at the age of 84.[3] If the statement is accurate, we can work backwards and come up with the approximate date of her birth – about 1832 – and her age at the time of marriage – about 14.

Marriage

It has been reported that when the governor of Iṣfahán, the Mu'tamidu'd-Dawlih, rescued the Báb from the schemes of the 'ulamá of the city designed to execute Him, and arranged for Him to reside in his private residence known as 'Imárat-i-Khurshíd, he was eager to keep the Báb's whereabouts a secret. To ensure that his own employees would not learn the secret, he suggested to the Báb that a reliable Bábí woman be hired to carry out the work that needed to be done in His quarters. The Báb agreed. Fáṭimih Khánum had the needed qualifications and was chosen for the honour.[4]

According to the Shí'í Muslim practice, the only way a man could employ a maid for service in his residence was to enter into a marriage contract with her. To comply with this religious requirement, the Báb married Fáṭimih Khánum. Abu'l-Qásim Afnán, the author of *'Ahd-i-A'lá: Zandigáníy-i Haḍrat-i Báb*, relates a statement which he heard from Siyyid Muḥammad-'Alí Jamálzádih, who heard it from Ḥáj Mírzá Yaḥyá Dawlatábádí, who attributed it to Fáṭimih Khánum, who is reported to have said:

> After they married me to His Holiness the Báb, I went to the Mu'tamid's residence and entered a room where I found the Master (the Báb) seated, engaged in writing. I said *Salám* and stood there. With the movement of His hand He invited me to sit down. I sat down. He continued writing for several hours while I sat there. When I was overcome with sleep, I got up and went to another room. My meeting with the Báb consisted of that and nothing else.[5]

Whatever the circumstances of that marriage contract, she was regarded as the Báb's second wife and occupied a position of honour in the Bábí community. The position, however, entailed certain responsibilities and protocol that she and the members of the community were expected to uphold and respect. In Islam and the Bábí Faith the wife of the Manifestation of God is regarded as the mother of the believers and it is thus forbidden for any other man to marry her. As we will see later, Fáṭimih Khánum and her family, after the martyrdom of the Báb, failed to honour this requirement and caused an uproar among the believers.

After the Báb's Departure from Iṣfahán

After the Báb had stayed in the 'Imárat-i Khurshíd for about four months, the Mu'tamidu'd-Dawlih died. His nephew and successor reported the Báb's whereabouts to Muḥammad Sháh and was instructed to send Him with escort to Ṭihrán. That journey took the Báb to the mountains of Ádharbayján where He was imprisoned for nearly three years before He was taken to Tabríz and executed on 9 July 1850.

After the Báb's departure from Iṣfahán, Fáṭimih Khánum remained in that city and lived with her family. Nothing is known of her life during the years she lived in Iṣfahán after the departure of the Báb. She must have been well respected among the believers for the position she had acquired by virtue of her marriage to the Báb.

After the Martyrdom of the Báb

When the Báb was martyred in 1850, Fáṭimih Khánum lost all hope for an earthly reunion with Him. If the date of Fáṭimih Khánum's birth was indeed about 1832, at the time the Báb was martyred she would have been about 18 years old. Her family, although proud of her position among the believers, were concerned about her future, so they arranged for her to go to Baghdád together with her mother and brother, Mullá 'Alí-Muḥammad. They left Iṣfahán, ostensibly to escape persecution, and arrived in Baghdád during Bahá'u'lláh's sojourn in the mountains of Sulaymániyyih. Soon after their arrival in Baghdád, Fáṭimih Khánum married Mírzá Yaḥyá Azal,[6] who considered himself the Báb's nominee and successor. The circumstances leading to this marriage are obscure and the real reason prompting Mírzá Yaḥyá to enter into this marriage is unclear.

In a Tablet revealed in honour of one of His aunts who was a staunch supporter of Mírzá Yaḥya, 'Abdu'l-Bahá enumerates Mírzá Yaḥya's misdeeds, including his marriage with Fáṭimih Khánum. To refute 'Abdu'l-Bahá's statement, Ismá'íl-i Ṣabbágh-i Sidihi, a well-known Azalí, wrote a fictitious letter which he claimed to have been written on behalf of Fáṭimih Khánum and sealed it with her seal. In that letter it is claimed that the Imám-Jum'ih, after the martyrdom of the Báb, tried in vain to marry her. Then Fáṭimih Khánum received a letter from Mírzá Yaḥyá's sister saying that if she wanted to be protected from the harm coming from the people, she should go and see 'Ḥaḍrat-i Thamarih' (Mírzá Yaḥyá) in the company of Ḥáj Siyyid Muḥammad. The letter said that Fáṭimih Khánum, her mother and other members of the family who could no longer live in Iṣfahán went to Káẓimayn. While in Káẓimayn, according to the letter, Jináb-i Mírzá Músá (Áqáy-i-Kalím) arrived from Baghdád and together with Ḥáj Siyyid Muḥammad went to see Mírzá Yaḥyá. At that time Fáṭimih Khánum's brother, Jináb-i Qahír (Mullá Rajab-'Alí), lived in Najaf. Áqá 'Alí-Muḥammad, Fáṭimih Khánum's other brother, informed the brother in Najaf that they had come from Iṣfahán to Káẓimayn and had brought his wife and children along. The brother in Najaf responded that he was going to Karbilá and said that they should also go there. Therefore, they all set out for Karbilá. The forged letter continues:

> To follow his instruction and avoid doing anything contrary to it, and in order to seek his permission to leave, I [Fáṭimih Khánum], too, went to see 'Haḍrat-i Thamarih' in the company of my brother and Ḥáj Siyyid Muḥammad. 'Ḥaḍrat-i Thamarih' showed me the will and testament of the Primal Point in which He addressed me by the title He had bestowed upon me in Iṣfahán and which no one else knew, instructing me to obey

> Ḥaḍrat-i Thamarih's commands. The purpose of my coming to see you, I said, is to obey whatever you order, for I do not want to do anything contrary to God's command. Ḥaḍrat-i Thamarih wedded me and gave me into the care of Ḥáj Siyyid Muḥammad. Together with Ḥáj Siyyid Muḥammad and my brother we went to Karbilá.[7]

Ismá'íl-i Ṣabbágh is reported to have given the above letter to Dr Sa'íd Khán-i Kurdistání to send to Professor Browne in England.[8] Sa'íd Khán, according to Abu'l-Qásim Afnán, wrote in the margin of the book which deals with the letter:

> This lady was my patient in Ṭihrán for many years. I asked her many questions about important historical matters. She herself told me that she obeyed Azal and married him. A month later, Azal's wives raised hell. 'They forced him to separate from me and he offered me to Siyyid Muḥammad' (Sa'íd Ṭabíb-i-Kurdistání 10-4-22 [10 April 1922].)[9]

The reason the marriage of Mírzá Yaḥyá with Fáṭimih Khánum was short lived was apparently his wives' refusal to coexist with her, probably because she enjoyed an advantage over them: she had been married to the Báb. As such and regardless of the duration of that marriage, she was entitled to special respect and consideration. This anomaly must have been difficult to deal with. The wives reportedly voiced strident objections to the new addition to Mírzá Yaḥyá's harem, forcing him to give her up after one month. The details and actual reasons for Mírzá Yaḥyá's humiliating and unscrupulous behaviour towards Fáṭimih Khánum are unclear. What is known is that he committed a dishonourable act by marrying her in utter disregard of the clear prohibitions in Islam and the Bábí Faith against marrying the wife of the Manifestation of God.[10] And when things became difficult, he committed another heinous act by offering her in marriage to his henchman, Siyyid Muḥammad-i Iṣfahání.

Fáṭimih Khánum's brothers have been implicated in arranging the marriages she contracted with Mírzá Yaḥyá and Siyyid Muḥammad. Traditionally, women lacked economic and financial independence. They were raised to be completely dependent on men, be they their fathers, brothers, husbands or sons. Lack of education turned them into helpless beings. When a young woman became a widow, the family faced a dilemma, especially if she had no independent means of livelihood. In such a case she would normally go back and live with her parents if her father was still alive and had the means to look after her. In the absence of the father, her brothers were expected to provide 'protection'. Although some brothers fulfilled this duty with varying degrees of grace, generally they tried to find a way out of the responsibility.

Remarriage was one option they often pursued. The woman, being in a bind, very often reluctantly agreed to the arrangements. In the case of Fáṭimih Khánum, it seems that her brothers compromised her honour by looking for an easy way out of their responsibility for her, while at the same time trying to advance their own lot in life. The arrangements that they made for her trip to Baghdád at a time when the community was going through a period of confusion and uncertainty, and the unfortunate developments that ensued, caused much controversy and displeasure among the believers and brought devastating consequences. One of her brothers and Siyyid Muḥammad-i-Iṣfahání, the man she married after Mírzá Yaḥyá Azal, later lived in 'Akká, spied on Bahá'u'lláh and His followers, teamed up with the adversary, made false reports to those in authority and made life for the believers unbearable. Finally, the two of them and another one of their accomplices were murdered in 'Akká for their heinous deeds.

Had Fáṭimih Khánum and her brothers observed patience and pursued a wiser course of action, had they resisted temptation to capitalize on her plight and seek to advance their lot in life, had they not followed the path of perdition led by Mírzá Yaḥyá Azal, arrangements would have been made for her to live honourably and the humiliating treatment she was subjected to would have been avoided. Many were the needy in the early days of the Faith, for whom Bahá'u'lláh made arrangements to be helped: how much more He would have done to help a woman in Fáṭimih Khánum's position had she and her family adopted the course of action that was proper and praiseworthy.

Bahá'u'lláh has referred with great sorrow to Mírzá Yaḥyá's despicable behaviour of marrying Fáṭimih Khánum after the Báb's martyrdom and subsequently offering her to his henchman Siyyid Muḥammad. He condemned the repugnant act in several of His Tablets. He says in the Kitáb-i-Badí' that to gratify his carnal desires, Mírzá Yaḥyá did not spare the wife of God's Manifestation, that he violated the honour of the wife of the Báb and that he rent asunder the 'most great veil'.[11]

In the Epistle to the Son of the Wolf, He says:

> Reflect a while upon the dishonour inflicted upon the Primal Point. Consider what hath happened. When this Wronged One, after a retirement of two years during which He wandered through the deserts and mountains, returned to Baghdád, as a result of the intervention of a few, who for a long time had sought Him in the wilderness, a certain Mírzá Muḥammad-'Alí of Rasht came to see Him, and related, before a large gathering of people, that which had been done, affecting the honour of the Báb, which had truly overwhelmed all lands with sorrow. Great God! How could they have countenanced this most grievous betrayal? Briefly,

We beseech God to aid the perpetrator of this deed to repent, and return unto Him. He, verily, is the Helper, the All-Wise.[12]

'Abdu'l-Bahá too refers to Mírzá Yaḥyá's dishonourable act in one of His Tablets:

> After the Supreme Martyrdom, he [Mírzá Yaḥyá] married the wife of His Highness [the Báb], the mother of the believers, who according to the explicit text of the Bayán was forbidden to all. And when he found her unappealing, as if that humiliation were not enough, he offered that honourable woman, i.e. the sister of Mullá Rajab-'Alí, the wife of His Highness [the Báb], to Siyyid Muḥammad-i-Iṣfahání . . .[13]

Fáṭimih Khánum is believed to have remained married to Siyyid Muḥammad-i Iṣfahání until he was murdered in 'Akká in 1872. There is, however, no evidence that she actually lived in 'Akká herself.

Fáṭimih Khánum's Passing and a Brief Review of Her Life

According to the statement by Edward G. Browne, mentioned above, Fáṭimih Khánum died in December 1916 at the age of 84. She probably died in Ṭihrán and was buried there. It was in Ṭihrán that her physician, Dr Sa'íd Khán, became acquainted with her.

When the Báb was martyred, Fáṭimih Khánum was about 18 years old. She was living with her family in Iṣfahán and probably had no control over her future. Had she been a strong woman of independent means, she would have been able to withstand the pressure put upon her and would not have allowed her brothers to determine her destiny. Instead of submitting to Mírzá Yaḥyá's lustful appetites, she would have refused to enter into a marriage contract with him and later with Siyyid Muḥammad, who smeared her honour and ruined her reputation. Had she done that, she would have had the respect of the members of the community and arrangements would have been made for her to live honourably to the end of her life. Since that was not the case, one wonders whether she herself, with some encouragement from her brothers, did not consider it an honour to be married to a man who claimed to be the Báb's nominee and successor. Whatever her reasons for remarrying, the fact remains that she lost the honour that could have been hers had she remained faithful to the Báb and lived up to the requirements of the position she had gained in the community. As it was, Fáṭimih Khánum's notoriety in Bábí–Bahá'í history is due to the unusual circumstances of the marriages she contracted after the Báb was martyred.

II

Prominent Women Closely Related to Bahá'u'lláh

5

Khadíjih Khánum, the Mother of Bahá'u'lláh

Scanty as is our information about Fáṭimih Bagum, the mother of the Báb, there is no comparison between what we know about her life and that of Khadíjih Khánum, Bahá'u'lláh's mother. Almost every aspect of Khadíjih Khánum's life is wrapped in obscurity. Reasons for this disparity regarding historical information about the mother of the Báb and the mother of Bahá'u'lláh will be discussed later in this account.

Family Background

Khadíjih Khánum's family, according to Malik-Khusrawví, author of *Iqlím-i Núr*, belonged to the Namadsáb tribe. Members of this tribe occupied areas in close proximity to Tákur in the district of Núr in Mázandarán where Bahá'u'lláh's father and paternal ancestors came from. The literal meaning of *namadsáb* is 'pulverized in felt'. The reason for the appellation is said to be this: In times past this tribe had rebelled against the government. The head of the tribe was arrested and pulverized in felt until he died, thus his offspring became known as Namadsáb.[1]

It is not known who Khadíjih Khánum's parents were or whether she had any siblings.

Birth and Early Life

No information is available about Khadíjih Khánum's childhood or early life. All aspects of her life before she married Mírzá Buzurg, Bahá'u'lláh's father, remain unexplored. The date and place of her birth are also unknown. Since her parents belonged to a tribe that resided in Fíyúl and Avyá (or Ívá), about three kilometres from Tákúr, she was probably born in one of those villages, unless they had settled elsewhere before her birth.

Following the traditional pattern, Khadíjih Khánum probably married very young. The name of her first husband, his background and occupation are unknown. He died sometime after the birth of their third child. The couple and their children were probably residing in Ṭihrán when the husband died. After his death, Khadíjih Khánum married Mírzá Buzurg. Exactly how long after the death of her first husband she remarried is not known.

That Khadíjih Khánum was a widow with three children when she married Mírzá Buzurg has been acknowledged by several sources. The children from the first marriage were Sakínih Khánum, Mírzá Muḥammad-'Alí and Sughrá Khánum. We also know that Sakínih Khánum married Mírzá Buzurg's younger brother, Mírzá Muḥammad, about the same time her mother married Mírzá Buzurg.[2]

Marriage to Mírzá Buzurg

The only aspect of Khadíjih Khánum's life briefly discussed in the early history of the Bahá'í Faith is her marriage to Mírzá Buzurg. H. M. Balyuzi, author of *Bahá'u'lláh: The King of Glory,* writes:

> Mírzá Buzurg's second wife was Khadíjih Khánum, who had been married once before and was widowed . . . Mírzá Buzurg took Khadíjih Khánum as his wife and wedded her daughter, Sakínih Khánum, to his younger brother, Mírzá Muḥammad. Khadíjih Khánum was the mother of Bahá'u'lláh (Mírzá Ḥusayn-'Alí). The first-born of that marriage was a daughter, Sárih Khánum: she is generally known as 'Ukht', Arabic for sister, because Bahá'u'lláh has thus referred to her. The next was a son, Mírzá Mihdí, who died in his father's lifetime; and Mírzá Ḥusayn-'Alí (Bahá'u'lláh) was the third-born. The fourth was another son, Mírzá Músá, entitled Áqáy-i-Kalím in later years, and the fifth was another daughter, Nisá' Khánum, who was married eventually to Mírzá Majíd-i-Áhí, a secretary of the Russian Legation.[3]

That Mírzá Buzurg, 'a favoured minister of the Crown',[4] would marry a widow with three children signifies something extraordinary about her: She was either very wealthy, enjoyed an alluring social standing in the community, was exceedingly beautiful or was a close relative who needed the protection of a male member of the family after her husband's death. These were generally the considerations prompting men of stature in 19th-century Iran to marry a widow with children. Since there is no indication that Mírzá Buzurg and Khadíjih Khánum were closely related, it is assumed that one or more of the other considerations were at work. The fact that at the time Mírzá Buzurg married Khadíjih Khánum he arranged for his younger brother to marry her eldest daughter is another indication that something about Khadíjih Khánum's personality and background made her particularly attractive and appealing to would-be marriage partners.

Khadíjih Khánum as the Mother of the Supreme Manifestation of God

The reason we know about Khadíjih Khánum's marriage to Mírzá Buzurg is that through this union Mírzá Ḥusayn-'Alí, entitled Bahá'u'lláh, the Inaugurator of the Bahá'í dispensation and cycle, was conceived and born. The irrefutable fact that this information conveys is that Khadíjih Khánum was the one who bore and reared the Supreme Manifestation of God for the age in which the human race is destined to come of age, achieve unity and live in peace. This is sufficient reason and a fair expectation for humanity to want to have much more information about her than the bits and pieces available thus far. The significance of her station has been implicitly acknowledged in *The Dawn-Breakers* when reference is made to Bahá'u'lláh's birth:

> One of the most mighty signs that shall signalize the advent of the promised Hour is this: 'A woman shall give birth to One who shall be her Lord.'[5]

Immediately after the above sentence, the focus of the statement shifts to Bahá'u'lláh's father:

> In those days, there was born a Child in an ancient and noble family of Núr, whose father was Mírzá 'Abbás, better known as Mírzá Buzurg, a favoured minister of the Crown. That Child was Bahá'u'lláh. At the hour of dawn, on the second day of Muḥarram, in the year 1233 AH [12 November 1817 AD), the world unaware of its significance, witnessed the birth of Him who was destined to confer upon it such incalculable blessings.[6]

Although the name of Bahá'u'lláh's father, his position and home district are all stated in the above passage, no mention is made of the name and particulars of His mother. The woman who carried from the time of conception to birth the precious gem embodying the temple and soul of Bahá'u'lláh, who nurtured Him with the substance of her life and raised Him in the bosom of her love, was generally unknown. Traditional norms required that women remain obscure. Historians on the whole did not overstep the bounds of 'propriety' that tradition imposed. The result has been the loss to humanity of valuable historical information regarding the identity, personality and life of a remarkable woman, a most crucial figure in the history of the new cycle inaugurated by Bahá'u'lláh, her son.

The exact date of Khadíjih Khánum's marriage to Mírzá Buzurg is unknown but based on Bahá'u'lláh's birth date (1817) and the fact that he was the third of the children born to Mírzá Buzurg and Khadíjih Khánum, it may be surmised that it probably took place between 1810 and 1812. This assumption is based on the premise that the siblings were born about two to three years apart, as was the norm in those days.

The absence of reliable information makes it difficult to know whether Khadíjih Khánum lived in Núr or Ṭihrán before she married Mírzá Buzurg. What is certain is that she was living in Ṭihrán when Bahá'u'lláh was born on 12 November 1817. We also know, based on 'Abdu'l-Bahá's utterances, that Khadíjih Khánum was living in the part of the capital known as Maḥalliy-i Darváziy-i Shimírán, when Bahá'u'lláh was born.[7] 'Abdu'l-Bahá further indicates that Bahá'u'lláh often spent the summers in Tákúr, Mázandarán.[8] It stands to reason that His mother did likewise.

As previously stated, the number of children born to Mírzá Buzurg and Khadíjih Khánum was five. What we know of Khadíjih Khánum's married life with Mírzá Buzurg, other than the number of children they jointly had, is confined to the few stories 'Abdu'l-Bahá has recounted regarding the early years of Bahá'u'lláh's life. These stories He must have heard from Khadíjih Khánum herself.

Concerning Bahá'u'lláh's infancy, 'Abdu'l-Bahá says that the mother of the Blessed Beauty was attached to Him to such a degree that she could not for a moment separate from Him. He also says that Bahá'u'lláh's demeanour astonished His mother. He quotes her saying that in infancy Bahá'u'lláh never cried, nor did He evince the qualities characteristic of other suckling babies, such as screaming, crying, weeping, impatience and restlessness.[9]

And regarding His father's childhood, 'Abdu'l-Bahá says that one day when Bahá'u'lláh was seven years old He went strolling. His mother, admiring the gracefulness of the blessed body, remarked that He was slightly short in size. His father responded that she was ignoring the capacity and aptitude He had, how intelligent and smart He was. He said that Bahá'u'lláh was like a flame of fire, that at that tender age He was more mature than those who had reached adulthood. He said that it mattered not that He was not tall.[10]

This story about Bahá'u'lláh's childhood goes back to about 1824. After that nothing is known of Khadíjih Khánum's life until 1835 when Mírzá Buzurg loses his belongings, including the complex of houses in Ṭihrán occupied by him and his family. After that, according to H.M. Balyuzi, Mírzá Buzurg moved to the house 'close to the entrance of Masjid-i-Sháh' which Kulthúm Khánum, his third wife, had inherited from her father, while

> . . . Mírzá Ḥusayn-'Alí (Bahá'u'lláh) rented the house 'near the Gate' of Shimrán, and took His mother, His wife, His other step-mothers and

the rest of His brothers and sisters to live with Him. This rented house remained His residence for the remaining years He spent in Írán. It was near the Madrisiy-i-Mírzá Ṣáliḥ, the theological college where Mullá Ḥusayn-i-Bushrú'í would stay when bearing the message of the Báb to Ṭihrán.[11]

The Marriage of Bahá'u'lláh and Ásíyih Khánum

The above passage is significant, for it confirms that Khadíjih Khánum was alive when Bahá'u'lláh married Ásíyih Khánum in 1835. It also confirms that she lived in Ṭihrán in the same house where Bahá'u'lláh and Ásíyih Khánum resided. It is puzzling, though, that no mention is made of her in connection with her son's marriage. The following is an account of that marriage by H. M. Balyuzi:

> When Bahá'u'lláh was nearly fifteen years old, His elder sister Sárih Khánum and Mírzá Maḥmúd, the son of Mírzá Isma'íl-i-Vazír of Yálrúd, were married. This Mírzá Maḥmúd, who never espoused the new Faith, had a younger sister, Ásíyih Khánum: winsome, vivacious and exceedingly beautiful. As soon as she came of age, and Bahá'u'lláh was nearly eighteen, Sárih Khánum requested her father, Mírzá Buzurg, to ask the hand of this sister-in-law for her Brother, Mírzá Ḥusayn-'Alí. Their marriage took place in Jamádiyu'l-Ukhrá (Jamádíyu'th-Thání) AH 1251 (about October 1835). Ásíyih Khánum was the mother of 'Abdu'l-Bahá.[12]

Those familiar with Persian culture know that mothers have traditionally played an important role in the decision-making process involving the marriage of their children. Therefore, it seems strange that Khadíjih Khánum would have been completely sidelined in matters regarding her son's marriage. It is even stranger that her own daughter, Sárih Khánum, who approached her father to arrange for the marriage of Bahá'u'lláh to Ásíyih Khánum, would have bypassed her mother, or that Bahá'u'lláh would have kept His mother in the dark and married without her blessings and consent. A more plausible scenario would be for Sárih Khánum to discuss the desirability of that marriage with her mother first and having obtained her agreement, then to approach her father 'to ask the hand of [her] sister-in-law for her Brother'. H. M. Balyuzi had to rely on accounts obtained from earlier sources about Bahá'u'lláh's marriage to Ásíyih Khánum. Since Khadíjih Khánum's name and the role she played in the process have been completely overlooked, it is suspected that the general bias against women, so deeply rooted in the culture and tradition of the time, has caused the oversight.

Khadíjih Khánum's Life from 1835 to the Time She Passed Away

Penetrating the thick clouds obscuring Khadíjih Khánum's life from 1835 to the end of her life is a most difficult task, for the torches of information necessary to shed light on the path of search for the events associated with her life are non-existent. In the absence of authentic information, the best that can be done at this stage of our history is to ask questions, to use what is known to draw conclusions, even to employ conjecture. Below are some facts that may prove helpful in our quest to know more about Khadíjih Khánum's life.

We know that some nine years intervened between Bahá'u'lláh's marriage to Ásíyih Khánum and the date of the Báb's declaration. By the time the Báb declared His mission, Mírzá Buzurg had passed away but Khadíjih Khánum was most probably still living with Bahá'u'lláh and His family in the house close to the Gate of Shimírán where her grandson, 'Abdu'l-Bahá, was born on 23 May 1844, the night of the Báb's declaration. 'Abdu'l-Bahá was about five months old and the family was living in the same house when Bahá'u'lláh in October 1844 received the Báb's message, carried to Ṭihrán by Mullá Ḥusayn-i Bushrú'í and conveyed to Him by Mullá Muḥammad-i Núrí through Mírzá Músá, the younger son of Khadíjih Khánum and Mírzá Buzurg. When Bahá'u'lláh unfolded the scroll sent to Him by the Báb and began to read aloud some of the passages, His mother could not have been far. She may have actually heard His voice when He turned to Mírzá Músá and said:

> Músá, what have you to say? Verily I say, whoso believes in the Qur'án and recognizes its Divine origin, and yet hesitates, though it be for a moment, to admit that these soul-stirring words are endowed with the same regenerating power, has most assuredly erred in his judgement and has strayed far from the path of justice.[13]

Then Bahá'u'lláh went to the district of Núr to promote the Bábí Faith. As a result of His teaching activities 'a considerable number among' the 'ecclesiastical dignitaries, State officials, traders, and peasants'[14] became Bábís, among them were many members of Bahá'u'lláh's family. According to *The Dawn-Breakers*,

> . . . the very stones and trees of that district seemed to have been quickened by the waves of spiritual power which emanated from His person. All things seemed to be endowed with a new and more abundant life, all things seemed to be proclaiming aloud: 'Behold, the Beauty of God has been made manifest! Arise, for He has come in all His glory.'[15]

Bahá'u'lláh's conspicuous success aroused the opposition and hostility of His uncle 'Azíz, alarmed the fanatical element in the area and opened wide the gate of persecution. The question is: How at times such as these could Bahá'u'lláh's mother remain unaffected by events in the centre of which was her own beloved son? How could she be oblivious of things that happened openly in her own home district and caused so much turmoil?

And there are other questions: What did Khadíjih Khánum do, after Bahá'u'lláh's return to Ṭihrán from His nine months' sojourn in Karbilá, when He was arrested, humiliated and thrown into the Síyáh-Chál for four months? Where was she when Bahá'u'lláh's house in Ṭihrán was plundered, forcing Ásíyih Khánum to rent two rooms in an obscure corner of Ṭihrán and move there with her three children? Did she see Bahá'u'lláh when He was released from prison and during the month He was recuperating in the house of Mírzá Riḍá Qulí and Maryam, His half brother and sister-in-law, in Ṭihrán? Was she there to say goodbye to her beloved son and His family, as well as to her other son, Mírzá Músá, when they left Ṭihrán for Baghdád? How did she cope with the pangs of separation till the end of her earthly life? No trace can be found of her on the pages of history books during those terrible times. The period of Khadíjih Khánum's life that is most obscure is the time between Bahá'u'lláh's active involvement with the Bábí Faith and her death. Is it because she did not embrace the Bábí Faith or she was prevented from doing so by some elements in her family who held sway over her? Not knowing anything about her side of the family, how and where she lived after Bahá'u'lláh's departure from Iran or anything about her life in general makes it difficult even to conjecture.

Nothing exists to indicate whether Khadíjih Khánum was dead or alive by the time Bahá'u'lláh left Ṭihrán and Iran, never to return. If she was alive, we do not know her reaction to the Báb's advent, to Bahá'u'lláh's full commitment to the promotion of the Bábí Cause; to the sufferings He endured as a Bábí leader in Ṭihrán; to His imprisonment, release, exile from His native land; and finally to the claim that He was the Promise of all ages. Although Khadíjih Khánum's children were devoted to Bahá'u'lláh, her own stand is unclear. The absence of any information about the date of her death makes it impossible to know whether she was alive when Bahá'u'lláh's Cause became known in Iran and abroad. It is interesting to note that there is a reference to Ásíyih Khánum's great aunt, whose name we do not know, and her husband Mírzá Yúsif[16] regarding the assistance they rendered when Bahá'u'lláh was in the Síyáh-Chál.[17] They were apparently Russian subjects. The protection they enjoyed as foreign nationals enabled them to extend a helping hand without fearing persecution or prosecution. There is also a reference to Ásíyih Khánum's mother in *Robe of Light* regarding the day that Bahá'u'lláh and His family left Ṭihrán for Baghdád:

> None of the relatives dared to come to say farewell on that fateful day, save only lady Ásíyih's mother who was to care for her little grandchild Mihdí.[18]

Was Khadíjih Khánum among the relatives in Ṭihrán who stayed away? If Ásíyih Khánum's mother was there, why couldn't she be? Did the hostile members of her family surround and restrain her so severely that she could not see Bahá'u'lláh and His family at the time of their departure from Iran? If so, what were the lamentations of her heart? And was she at all involved with the raising of her grandson, Mírzá Mihdí, during the several years he lived in Iran after Bahá'u'lláh and Ásíyih Khánum left their native land? The answers to these questions may never be known.

The complete silence observed by historians regarding Bahá'u'lláh's mother makes one wonder whether she had passed away before Bahá'u'lláh was arrested in Ṭihrán, imprisoned in the Síyáh-Chál and exiled to Baghdád. Such a conjecture would have been plausible were it not for a passing reference in one of Bahá'u'lláh's Tablets revealed in Adrianople (Edirne) suggesting that she was alive at that time and that her woes and tribulations had caused her endless distress:

> Would that I had perished ere My mother had delivered Me, and that she had not heard of what I have had to endure at the hands of those who worship names, yet kill Him Who hath revealed them, Who hath created them, hath brought them into being and sent them forth.[19]

The Passing of Khadíjih Khánum and Her Place in History

It is not clear exactly when Khadíjih Khánum passed away and where she has been buried. Here again I turn to conjecture and propose the following.

In a Tablet revealed in honour of one of His sisters, most probably Sárih Khánum, Bahá'u'lláh says:

> Shouldst thou desire to know My situation, 20 years have passed since I have seen the light of day. I swear by the Sun of the Celestial Beauty that during this time I have not partaken even a glass of water in comfort and have been denied even a moment's rest owing to the venom of the ungodly. Like unto one constantly tormented in the mouth of a dragon, I have ever been confined in the prison of envy and afflicted by the claws of enmity. The tale of this Youth increaseth sorrow, His remembrance a book does not suffice and its end the pen of creation is unable to describe.
>
> O My Sister! By God, I have so blotted out from memory the remem-

brance of everything that I know not what hath been written down. Sorrow hath so surrounded Me that I have forgotten Mine own Self, how much more the writing of letters. O that My Mother had never given birth to Me!

May thou be always under the protection of God and abide in the shade of His mercy. Convey My sincere wishes to honourable mother.[20]

In the first line of the Tablet Bahá'u'lláh says that 20 years have passed since He had seen the light of day. If the beginning of the 20 years is calculated from the time He was imprisoned in the Síyáh-Chál, i.e. the latter part of 1852, we would obtain 1872. By then Bahá'u'lláh was incarcerated in the walled city of 'Akká. Before closing the Tablet Bahá'u'lláh conveys His 'sincere wishes to honourable mother'. If that reference is to His own mother, then she would still have been alive in 1872 and would have heard of her son's final place of exile. She would have also heard about the martyrdom of the Purest Branch in 1870. She may have even been alive when 'Abdu'l-Bahá got married in 1873.

When Khadíjih Khánum passed away, Bahá'u'lláh revealed a visitation prayer in her honour. It is signed "Abdu'lláh Ḥusayn-'Alí' and is the only writing of Bahá'u'lláh that the present author has seen that is signed in this manner. The style of writing, the composition and mode of expression is the same as His other writings. Had His mother passed away while He was in Iran, He would have eulogized her in person. The reason He signed it 'Abdu'lláh Ḥusayn-'Alí is probably because it was being sent to Iran and was going to be read by His relatives antagonistic to His claim. The prayer bears no date and there is no indication as to where it was revealed. Here is a translation:

The most honoured, esteemed and respected mother. He is God!

Praised be Thou O Lord, My God! This is My mother who hath acknowledged Thy oneness, confessed Thy unity, attained the honour of meeting Thy Manifestations in Thy days, reached the station of recognition and entered the tabernacle of Heaven, for she loved Thyself and Thy Servant and held fast to the cord of Thy love through the sanctified Temples of Thy Sovereignty.

I beseech Thee, therefore, O My God, to grant her the honour of beholding Thy Beauty, and vouchsafe unto her the gift of Thy Presence. Give her to drink then from the ocean of Thy mercy and the chalice of Thy forgiveness. Make her to dwell, O My God, in the precincts of Thy mercy in the Heaven of eternity. Grant her to hear Thy holy melodies that she may cast the veil from her head in her eagerness to meet Thee and speed through the domains of Thy nearness and union. Thou art verily powerful over all that Thou desirest, and Thou art verily the Mighty, the Most Luminous.

The Servant of God Ḥusayn-'Alí.[21]

Whatever Khadíjih Khánum's lot in life may have been, however grievous the sufferings she endured, and regardless of whether or not she openly confessed her allegiance to the nascent Faith, she was the mother of Bahá'u'lláh, the inaugurator of the cycle of fulfilment, the redeemer of humankind, the author of a new world order, the Prince of Peace. Her legacy, like that of the mother of the Báb, is that she bore, raised and gave to the world the Manifestation of God whose advent all past religions, including the Báb's, had promised.

The Treatment in History of the Mothers of the Twin Manifestations of God

Insufficient information makes a comprehensive comparison between the lives of these two prominent women in the history of the Bábí and Bahá'í Faiths impossible. However, the available material, scanty as it is, highlights factors causing differences in the way they have been treated by history. These differences may hold the key to our understanding of the eclipse dimming forever our vista of Khadíjih Khánum's life and personality.

Fáṭimih Bagum was married once and had only one son. Her son was very young when her husband died and she became a single parent. The absence of the father and the fact that the Báb had no siblings caused a closer tie between the mother and her son and made room for Fáṭimih Bagum to be deeply involved with events associated with His life. When the Báb's father passed away, the focus of attention was shifted to His mother and her brother who served as His legal guardian, shedding light, negligible as it has been made to appear, on the role she played in His upbringing and some later developments in His life. A similar situation eighteen hundred years earlier had helped the mother of Jesus Christ to move into the limelight. Had it not been for the circumstances of Christ's birth, His mother would not have been accorded the fame and recognition she received years later.

When the Báb went on pilgrimage to Mecca, and undoubtedly during the time He was in Búshihr and Karbilá, He kept in touch with His mother through correspondence. The letters that have survived are a wonderful source of information regarding the loving bond that existed between the mother and son. Unfortunately, none of Bahá'u'lláh's letters to His mother have come to light. This has deprived the world of gaining a deeper insight into her life.

After the martyrdom of the Báb and His guardian-uncle, Fáṭimih Bagum enjoyed the blessing of having a faithful and understanding daughter-in-law who treated her with deference and, in her recollections, spoke of her lovingly and with respect. As for Khadíjih Khánum, we know nothing about how, where and with whom she lived after the departure of Bahá'u'lláh and His family, which included Mírzá Músá, from Iran. With their departure, she was deprived of most of the members of her family who could have provided solace and enlightenment regarding Bahá'u'lláh's Revelation.

Fáṭimih Bagum had the opportunity to leave her native land and remove herself from the hostile elements surrounding her. She spent the last years of her life in Iraq, which made it possible for Bahá'u'lláh to send trusted believers to familiarize her with the Báb's claim and station. Khadíjih Khánum, probably deprived of independent means of livelihood, continued to live with the members of her family in the familiar surroundings of Núr and Ṭihrán, where her movements and activities were tightly controlled. Of the children born to her and Mírzá Buzurg who remained in Iran, the one utterly devoted to Bahá'u'lláh was Sárih Khánum. She, too, was surrounded by hostile elements and severely persecuted, as Bahá'u'lláh attests in a Tablet revealed in her honour.[22]

Nisá' Khánum who married Mírzá Majíd-i Áhí, died young. Of Bahá'u-'lláh's half brothers and sisters, the one faithful to Bahá'u'lláh, Mírzá Muḥammad-Qúlí, accompanied Him on His exiles. Others were either hostile to Bahá'u'lláh or, to protect themselves and their interests, kept a comfortable distance from Him. So Khadíjih Khánum lived among relatives who were either hostile to Bahá'u'lláh or chose to be indifferent, yet she had to survive their onslaught by keeping her feelings to herself and not breathing a word to deniers and betrayers of her son. Moreover, there are no indications or evidence that anyone ever attempted to convince her of the glory of her son's mission and station, a bounty vouchsafed to Fáṭimih Bagum by Bahá'u'lláh.

The circumstances of Bahá'u'lláh's arrest, imprisonment in the Síyáh-Chál and subsequent departure from Iran were very different from those attending the departure of the Báb from Shíráz. The persecution in Shíráz before the Báb's departure for Iṣfahán was confined to His person and a few of His followers. It was just two years after the declaration of His advent. The flow of information was slow. It was basically by the word of mouth and people were generally unaware of the significance of His mission. Consequently, His family and friends were not so frightened as to completely avoid contact with Him. However, Bahá'u'lláh's departure from Iran had been occasioned by an attempt by two Bábís on the life of the Sháh, causing an uproar against the Bábís in general and the martyrdom of many prominent believers, among them Ṭáhirih. As a result, people in general and members of Bahá'u'lláh's family in particular kept their distance from Him and those who confessed the Bábí Faith to ensure their own safety. The fact that K͟hadíjih K͟hánum was not present when Bahá'u'lláh and His family left Iran may be attributed to one of the following factors: perhaps she was not in Ṭihrán at that time, or she was too afraid to see her beloved son off, or she was prevented from doing so by the hostile members of her family, upon whom she depended for survival, or she was too ill to leave her home.

Illiteracy was the lot of the generality of women at that time and there is no evidence to indicate that K͟hadíjih K͟hánum was literate.[23] She did not have loving and understanding brothers, as did Fáṭimih Bagum, who had her interests at heart and helped her to communicate privately with her son away from the eyes of intruders. Had she been able to write, she would have undoubtedly written about the woes and tribulations that she sustained in separation from Him and recounted the afflictions that she endured by virtue of her being the mother of so glorious and enviable a son. Such correspondence would have provided historians with some source material on which to base their treatment of her.

6

Ásíyih Khánum, the Most Exalted Leaf, Titled Navváb, the Wife of Bahá'u'lláh

Family Background

Ásíyih Khánum's father was Mírzá Ismá'íl Vazír-i-Yálrúdí.[1] He was known as Navváb, a title of honour meaning 'deputy', 'noble'. Her mother's name has not been mentioned in any of the available historical sources. In 19th-century Iran it was not customary for people to trace their lineage through their mother's line. As a result, little attention was paid to information about who the mother was and what her particulars were.

Ásíyih Khánum had a brother, Mírzá Maḥmúd, who married Sárih Khánum, Bahá'u'lláh's older sister, in 1832. This marriage strengthened the bond of relationship between the family of Mírzá Buzurg and Khadíjih Khánum, Bahá'u'lláh's parents, and that of Mírzá Ismá'íl and his wife, Ásíyih Khánum's parents. The marriage of Sárih Khánum and Mírzá Maḥmúd was the precursor of a far more significant marriage that took place three years later, that of Bahá'u'lláh and Ásíyih Khánum.

Birth, Childhood and Early Life

The date of Ásíyih Khánum's birth is unknown. Her tombstone bears only the date of her death. Birth certificates did not exist in Iran when Ásíyih Khánum was born. The registration of births and deaths is a relatively recent phenomenon. It was introduced in Iran in the late 1920s/early 1930s. Before this time families kept the record of the birth of their children, especially the firstborn son, by noting the date inside the cover of the Qur'án or a book the family held dear. If the date of Ásíyih Khánum's birth was thus noted, the information was never looked up or inquired about, for none of the available history books record it. Ásíyih Khánum was probably born in Yálrúd, where she may have spent her childhood and early life.

Little is known of Ásíyih Khánum's early life. The fact that she was called Navvábih, the feminine form of Navváb, indicates that she was considered 'the secret essence of [her] sire', that from early childhood she evinced attributes of nobility and graciousness. Bahá'u'lláh later referred to her in His Tablets as Navváb and used the masculine pronoun when referring to her in the third person singular. This is the title by which she is known in the Bahá'í world.

'Abdu'l-Bahá has confirmed that His mother's name was Ásíyih. In a Tablet revealed in honour of a believer in the United States, He wrote:

> The name Aseyeh is accepted in the Threshold of Oneness, for the daughter of Pharaoh had this name, who, when (Moses) the Light of Guidance dawned, became confirmed by the Merciful One, left the court of Pharaoh with its grandeur and sovereignty and became perfumed with the fragrances of holiness. Then she assisted in the service of His Holiness (Moses) – upon him be peace! Also, Aseyeh was the name of my mother.[2]

In another Tablet He says:

> That blessed name which thou hast asked to remain with thee forever and become the cause of spiritual progress – that name is 'Aseyeh', which is the name of the mother of 'Abdu'l-Bahá. I give the blessed name to thee. Be therefore in the utmost joy and happiness, and be engaged in all gladness and attraction (or ecstasy) for thou hast become the object of such a favour.[3]

The generality of the population of Iran in the 19th century was illiterate. The illiteracy rate of women was much higher than that of men. Some women who were taught the art of reading could not write. The rationale was that writing enabled them to engage in clandestine correspondence, thus making control over their lives most difficult, if not impossible. Ásíyih Khánum was among the tiny minority who enjoyed the ability to read and write. It is assumed that in her childhood she had received instruction in the arts of reading and writing. A specimen of her handwriting is extant. Bahá'í pilgrims have the opportunity to view it when they visit the International Archives Building at the Bahá'í World Centre.[4]

Ásíyih Khánum's life as a girl of tender age growing up in her parents' home assumed significance when her brother married Bahá'u'lláh's sister. When Sárih Khánum moved from her parents' home to that of her husband, she got to know her young sister-in-law. Ásíyih Khánum at the time could not have been much older than nine or, at the most, ten years old. Sárih Khánum so liked the rare physical beauty and wonderful spiritual qualities of Ásíyih Khánum that she planned her marriage to her beloved brother Mírzá Ḥusayn-'Alí.

The custom of the time did not allow young men and women who were eligible for marriage to meet and plan their future together. It was generally the man's family, and particularly his mother or sister, who was responsible for choosing a suitable wife for him. If the choice was satisfactory, negotiations and arrangements would follow. The family of the woman had the right to approve or disapprove the proposition. Their approval, usually given after a lengthy process of negotiation, made it possible for the arrangements to proceed. As men and women married very young in those days, the families had to support them initially until they had an independent means of livelihood. This factor was taken into consideration when negotiations for marriage were in process. Although marriage arrangements and customs were not uniform everywhere in Iran, the following was more or less the norm.

The parents of the bride usually provided *jaház* or *jahízíyyih* (a form of dowry consisting, in accordance with the wealth of the family, of furnishings for a house (particularly soft furnishings such as drapery and linen), dinner and tea sets, utensils, silverware, all kinds of accessories, servants and maidservants, often slaves who lived more or less as members of the family. The parents of the groom provided the cost of the wedding, very elaborate in those days, and *mahr* or *mahríyyih* (dowry – a mutually agreed amount – usually considerable).[5] The dowry did not have to be paid in cash; it was often in the form of the transfer of a title deed or a promissory note. If the marriage ceremony and the reception were not combined, the ceremony usually took place in the bride's family house and the expenses defrayed by her parents. The wedding reception and the expenditures involved were the responsibility of the groom's parents.

Marriage

Almost all Bahá'í historical sources say that Ásíyih Khánum married Bahá'u'lláh as soon as she came of age but do not specify her age at marriage. H.M. Balyuzi says:

> When Bahá'u'lláh was nearly fifteen years old, His elder sister Sárih Khánum and Mírzá Maḥmúd, the son of Mírzá Ismá'íl-i-Vazír of Yálrúd, were married. This Mírzá Maḥmúd, who never espoused the new Faith, had a younger sister, Ásíyih Khánum: winsome, vivacious and exceedingly beautiful. As soon as she came of age, and Bahá'u'lláh was nearly eighteen, Sárih Khánum requested her father, Mírzá Buzurg, to ask the hand of this sister-in-law for her Brother, Mírzá Ḥusayn-'Alí. Their marriage took place in Jamádíyu'l-Ukhrá (Jamádíyu'th-Thání) AH 1251 (about October 1835).[6]

Since Bahá'u'lláh and Ásíyih <u>Kh</u>ánum married according to Islamic law and the age of maturity for girls in the Qur'án is nine, we do not know exactly how old she was when she got married. Although the coming of age has been assumed by at least one source to mean that she was 15,[7] her exact age at the time of her wedding is uncertain. She may have been any age between nine and 15. According to Bahá'íyyih <u>Kh</u>ánum, the Greatest Holy Leaf, her mother married her father 'when she was very young'.[8]

After the families of Mírzá Buzurg and Mírzá Ismá'íl became closely related through the marriage of Sárih <u>Kh</u>ánum and Mírzá Maḥmúd, and especially before Ásíyih <u>Kh</u>ánum came of age, there would have been opportunities for Bahá'u'lláh and Ásíyih <u>Kh</u>ánum to see one another in family gatherings and functions. Therefore the possibility that He would have intimated to Sárih <u>Kh</u>ánum His intention of marrying Ásíyih <u>Kh</u>ánum and authorizing her to approach their parents with a request to proceed with formalities and arrangements for their union cannot be ruled out. In a Tablet, Bahá'u'lláh makes a passing reference to having visited the grandmother of the Most Great Branch (the mother of Ásíyih <u>Kh</u>ánum) when she was married to Mírzá Ismá'íl (Ásíyih <u>Kh</u>ánum's father). The visit took place at a time when He had not yet come of age, which means that He was not yet 15, the age of maturity for boys in the Qur'án:

> One day during My childhood, I set out intending to visit the grandmother[9] of the Most Great Branch[10] at a time when she was the wife of Mírzá Ismá'íl-i-Vazír. Upon My arrival I saw a man seated and wearing a large turban. With him was another person. The faithful and holy Leaf was conversing from behind a curtain. One of the things he mentioned was this: We must know and understand whether Gabriel is higher than Qanbar-i-Amíru'l-Mu'minín.[11] This Wronged One, although I had outwardly not yet come of age, was utterly astonished at the level of the intelligence of those two ignorant ones. Yea! The aforementioned man considered such utterances to be the sign of learning and vainly imagined that he had attained the highest level of understanding, unaware that before God, he was reckoned among the worshippers of names . . .[12]

As an intermediary arranging the marriage of her brother to her husband's sister, Sárih <u>Kh</u>ánum would have first discussed the intended plan with her mother, <u>Kh</u>adíjih <u>Kh</u>ánum. After obtaining her agreement, she would have gone to her father with the request. When Mírzá Buzurg and <u>Kh</u>adíjih <u>Kh</u>ánum acceded to Sárih <u>Kh</u>ánum's request, in accordance with the customs of the time, they would have approached the parents of Ásíyih <u>Kh</u>ánum to seek their approval for the marriage, unless Sárih <u>Kh</u>ánum had already secured their agreement. In any case, acquiring consent for the marriage from the parties concerned does not seem to have been difficult. Already related to each other by the marriage of their older children, the families were well acquainted; they came from the same region of Núr; they were prominent, wealthy and renowned.

The preparations for the wedding were elaborate. The marriage certificate specifies the vast extent of the dowry which included two maidservants, one servant, a considerable sum of money and a large piece of property. The size of Ásíyih Khánum's *jaház* – the dowry provided by her parents – was such that, according to the spoken chronicle of her daughter Bahá'íyyih Khánum, 'forty mules were loaded with her possessions when she came to her husband's home. For six months before the marriage a jeweller worked at her home, preparing jewellery – even the buttons of her garments were of gold, set with precious stones.'[13]

The reason the bride's parents provided her, in accordance with their ability, with an elaborate *jaház* is because the Islamic law of inheritance affords the female offspring of the deceased father only half of what his male offspring inherit. To compensate for this inequity the female offspring are given at the time of their marriage as much as their parents can afford in the form of *jaház*.

The First Decade of Ásíyih Khánum's Married Life

What is known of Ásíyih Khánum as a young married woman is that she lived some times in Ṭihrán, at other times in Tákur. She undoubtedly visited Yálrúd as well and spent time with her family there. According to H.M. Balyuzi, 'Whenever He returned to His home in Tákur, Bahá'u'lláh would usually stop for a while in Yálrúd, and here He would visit the mujtahid,[14] who was distantly related to His family.'[15] Since the family of Bahá'u'lláh's faithful sister, Sárih Khánum, and Ásíyih Khánum's family had ancestral homes in Yálrúd, Ásíyih Khánum no doubt accompanied Bahá'u'lláh on many such journeys. And as the means of travel was by mule, whenever she undertook trips to Yálrúd and Tákur she probably stayed for a considerable time.

The course of Ásíyih Khánum's life during the first ten years of her marriage was, compared with the later years, smooth and rather uneventful. As a young woman of noble lineage married to a renowned nobleman, she was provided with the needs of a comfortable life. Her time must have been spent in association with the members of the family which, in those days, was much more closely knit together than it is now. She also engaged in charitable pursuits. According to Bahá'íyyih Khánum:

> . . . in the early years of their married life, they, my father and mother, took part as little as possible in State functions, social ceremonies, and the luxurious habits of ordinary highly-placed and wealthy families in the land of Persia; she, and her noble-hearted husband, counted these worldly pleasures meaningless, and preferred rather to occupy themselves in caring for the poor, and for all who were unhappy, or in trouble.
>
> From our doors nobody was ever turned away; the hospitable board was spread for all comers.
>
> Constantly the poor women came to my mother, to whom they poured out their various stories of woe, to be comforted and consoled by her loving helpfulness.
>
> Whilst the people called my father 'The Father of the Poor', they spoke of my mother as 'The Mother of Consolation', though, naturally, only the women and little children ever looked upon her face unveiled.[16]

During the first decade of her marriage, Ásíyih Khánum bore three children: Káẓim, Mihdí and 'Abbás. The first two died in infancy. Her later children seem to have been born about two years apart. If this pattern prevailed earlier, then it is likely she was extremely young, possibly below childbearing age, when she married in 1835. Otherwise her first child would most likely have been born about 1836, the second about 1838 and the third about 1840. As 'Abdu'l-Bahá was born in 1844, and if the two-year-apart pattern is realistic, it seems likely that her first child was born around 1840 and the second around 1842. Ásíyih Khánum's extreme youth may have been a reason for the death of her first two children, as her body may not have been sufficiently developed to bear healthy children.[17]

What affected Ásíyih Khánum's life more than anything during the period under discussion was the passing of Mírzá Buzurg, Bahá'u'lláh's father, in 1840. During the later years of his life Mírzá Buzurg's fortunes had suffered a setback and he had lost almost everything, including the complex of houses wherein lived all his family. This house, Bahá'u'lláh says 'was sold at auction, for a negligible sum' and was purchased by two Qájár princes who 'divided it between themselves'.[18] According to H.M. Balyuzi, Mírzá Buzurg then moved to the house that his third wife, Kulthúm Khánum, had inherited from her father.[19] Kulthúm Khánum and Mírzá Buzurg had three children, who presumably lived in the same house. Bahá'u'lláh rented the house

> 'near the Gate' of Shimrán, and took His mother, His wife, His other step-mothers and the rest of his brothers and sisters to live with Him. This rented house remained His residence for the remaining years He spent in Írán. It was near the Madrisiy-i-Mírzá Ṣáliḥ, the theological college

> where Mullá Ḥusayn-i-Bushrú'í would stay when bearing the message of the Báb to Ṭihrán. The children of Bahá'u'lláh – 'Abdu'l-Bahá (the Most Great Branch), Bahá'íyyih Khánum (the Greatest Holy Leaf) and Mírzá Mihdí (the Purest Branch) – were all born in this rented house; their mother was his first wife, Ásíyih Khánum.[20]

Mírzá Buzurg did not live long after he was divested of his worldly possessions. He passed away leaving a number of dependents, including several wives and children, some of them minors. They lived under Bahá'u'lláh's care. Considering the lifestyle of traditional Iranian families at the time, this change must have been readily accepted by Ásíyih Khánum. She quickly adapted to the new requirements of her life as the wife of a senior member of the family, who, after the passing of His father, had shouldered responsibility for his unprotected survivors. There is no mention of Bahá'u'lláh and Ásíyih Khánum having any living children by 1840 when Mírzá Buzurg passed away. Ásíyih Khánum, although young in age, shared, by virtue of her position, the responsibility of caring and providing for this large family and no doubt had the respect and appreciation of those under Bahá'u'lláh's care. Her gentle and loving disposition, her captivating demeanour and selfless attitude facilitated the creation of the atmosphere desirable in such circumstances.

The Báb's Advent and Subsequent Developments

The Báb declared His mission in Shíráz on the eve of 23 May 1844. On that same night Bahá'u'lláh and Ásíyih Khánum's third child was born. He was named 'Abbás after His grandfather. To the delight of His parents, this child survived; he would in the future adopt 'Abdu'l-Bahá (Servant of Bahá) as His title. Bahá'u'lláh referred to Him as the Most Great Branch. At the age of ten, long before Bahá'u'lláh declared His mission in Baghdád, 'Abdu'l-Bahá would recognize His father's station and consecrate His life to the service of His Cause. He would share all His father's exiles and represent Him at meetings with government officials and dignitaries. He would be named, in a document in the handwriting of Bahá'u'lláh, as His successor, the Centre of His Covenant and the authorized Interpreter of His writings. In the latter part of His life He would travel extensively in the countries of Europe and North America and promulgate the principles of His father's Faith.

Ásíyih Khánum's joy was complete as she saw her son grow and become stronger day by day. He was an infant when Mullá Ḥusayn, the Báb's envoy, arrived in Ṭihrán and stayed in the school of Mírzá Ṣáliḥ, known as Madrisiy-i-Páy-i-Minár, which was situated in close proximity to the house that Bahá'u'lláh had rented near the 'Gate of Shimrán'. It was in this *madrisih* that Mullá Ḥusayn met Mullá Muḥammad-i-Núrí, who led him to Bahá'u'lláh, the 'Hidden Secret' the Báb had sent him to Ṭihrán to find and to whom he was to deliver a message on His behalf. Upon receiving the message, Bahá'u'lláh accepted the Báb as the promised Qá'im of Islam and arose to promote His Cause.

As 'Abdu'l-Bahá grew older, Bahá'u'lláh's involvement with the Bábí Faith became more intense. Ásíyih Khánum not only had to cope with the demands of motherhood but also had to adjust to the rapid changes that were taking place around her.

Bahá'u'lláh's house became the focal centre of the activities of the followers of the nascent Faith in Ṭihrán and Ásíyih Khánum, the lady of the house, was their gracious and loving hostess. Her life underwent the same kind of drastic change that affected all those who accepted the Revelation of the Báb. The conditions of the time did not allow her to associate with her husband's guests, who were generally men, or participate in the meetings they held. But she could, from her private parlour, witness the movements of the guests and follow developments.[21] She was undoubtedly aware of the many events that were being shaped. Unfortunately, no details are available to indicate the degree of her knowledge, involvement and reaction, which would have provided a sure basis for a historical description and analysis. In the absence of such details, one has to rely upon scraps of evidence and draw conclusions.

During the time when Ásíyih Khánum was in Ṭihrán and observed the frequent comings and goings of the Bábís, she must have met and closely associated with prominent female believers such as Ṭáhirih and Varaqatu'l-Firdaws. These two women were Bahá'u'lláh's house guests for a while. Ṭáhirih lived in Bahá'u'lláh's house after she was rescued, at His behest, from imprisonment in Qazvín. No doubt she used the *andarún* of the house. The story describing Ṭáhirih addressing from behind a curtain her fellow-believers gathered in the *bírúní* of the house helps us to gain intriguing insights into some aspects of Ásíyih Khánum's life. 'Abdu'l-Bahá relates in *Memorials of the Faithful* the circumstances of a visit paid by Vaḥíd to Ṭáhirih, while the latter was staying in the home of Bahá'u'lláh in Ṭihrán:

> Ṭáhirih listened to him from behind the veil. I was then a child, and was sitting on her lap. With eloquence and fervour, Vaḥíd was discoursing on the signs and verses that bore witness to the advent of the new Manifestation. She suddenly interrupted him and, raising her voice, vehemently declared: 'O Yaḥyá! Let deeds, not words, testify to thy faith, if thou art a man of true learning . . .'[22]

As the story is about the early years of 'Abdu'l-Bahá's childhood, it must have occurred in His mother's residence. This is confirmed by the story related by 'Abdu'l-Bahá when He was in London. The story has been recorded by Lady Blomfield in her book *The Chosen Highway*:

> . . . He, being a little boy, was sitting on the knee of Qurratu'l-'Ayn, who was in the private parlour of His mother, Ásíyih Khánum, the door of this room being open, they could hear, from behind the curtain, the voice of Siyyid Yaḥyáy-i-Dárábí, who was talking and 'arguing with my Father'.
>
> Qurratu'l-'Ayn, that beautiful, fearless poetess, addressing the Siyyid with her musical, yet penetrating voice, said:
>
> 'O Siyyid this is not the time for arguments, for discussions, for idle repetitions of prophecies or traditions! It is the time for deeds! The day for words has passed!
>
> 'If you have courage, now is the appointed hour for manifesting it; if you are a man of deeds, show a proof of your manhood by proclaiming day and night:
>
> '"The Promised Herald has come!
>
> '"He has come, the Qá'im, the Imám, the Awaited One has come! He has Come!"'
>
> 'Abbás Effendi told us that He remembered this episode very distinctly; the expression of enthusiasm on her lovely, radiant face as she spoke those inspiring words from behind the curtain, which hung before the door, was wonderfully impressive.
>
> 'Abbás Effendi added:
>
> 'She used often, during her short visit, to take me on to her knee, caress me, and talk to me. I admired her most deeply.'[23]

Bíbí Kúchak, whom Bahá'u'lláh has entitled Varaqatu'l-Firdaws (Leaf of Paradise), had been a Shaykhí. She and her mother (sister and mother of Mullá Ḥusayn) attended the classes of Siyyid Káẓim-i-Rashtí in Karbilá. They recognized the station of the Báb through Ṭáhirih. Varaqatu'l-Firdaws later married Shaykh Abú Turáb-i-Ishtihárdí, whom Bahá'u'lláh appointed to 'watch over' Ṭáhirih 'and ensure her protection and safety' in Núr, after the incident in Níyálá.[24] It was probably because of his wife's intimacy with Ṭáhirih that he was chosen for this service. Ásíyih Khánum may have been in Núr when Bahá'u'lláh arrived there, accompanied by Ṭáhirih and her attendant.

Varaqatu'l-Firdaws became a prominent Bábí and renowned teacher of the Faith. Ishráq-i-Khávarí says she was with Ṭáhirih in Baghdád, Hamadán and other places; she was in Bahá'u'lláh's house in Ṭihrán; she attained

His presence several times; and was a close associate of Bahá'u'lláh's wife, Ásíyih Khánum. After the upheaval at Shaykh Ṭabarsí, she accompanied her mother to Bushrúyih, their native land, and became a target for intense persecution. She spent the last years of her life in 'Ishqábád serving the Faith. Bahá'u'lláh has revealed in her honour a visitation prayer for Mullá Ḥusayn and the martyrs of Shaykh Ṭabarsí.

Ásíyih Khánum's strong intuition, her utter devotion to Bahá'u'lláh, her observation of the leading role her husband played in guiding and inspiring the Bábís, coupled with her close association with the prominent Bábí figures who were aware of Bahá'u'lláh's exalted station, must have confirmed her in His glorious destiny. It is inconceivable that a person of Ásíyih Khánum's spiritual endowments would have remained untouched by the happenings that took place around her. The fact that she wholeheartedly fulfilled her responsibilities in connection with the new situation, despite the suffering and hardship they entailed, is a strong indication that she was aware of their significance.

An incident recorded by Nabíl-i-A'ẓam in His narrative indicates that Ásíyih Khánum was aware of the identity and needs of at least some of the people who frequented Bahá'u'lláh's house. The same record reveals the fact that Ásíyih Khánum was familiar with the preparation of home remedies:

> One day Mírzá Aḥmad conducted me [Nabíl] to the house of Bahá'u'lláh, whose wife, the Varaqatu'l-'Ulyá, the mother of the Most Great Branch, had already healed my eyes with an ointment which she herself had prepared and sent to me by this same Mírzá Aḥmad. The first one I met in that house was that same beloved Son of hers, who was then a child of six.[25]

After the Most Great Branch another son, named 'Alí-Muḥammad, was born. He lived to be about seven years old. He was 18 months younger than 'Abdu'l-Bahá, was probably born in late 1845 and died in early 1852, before Bahá'u'lláh's arrest and imprisonment in the Síyáh Chál.

The only daughter born to Bahá'u'lláh and Ásíyih Khánum was named Fáṭimih at birth. Later she became known as Bahá'íyyih Khánum, was honoured by Bahá'u'lláh with the title originally bestowed on her mother, which Shoghi Effendi has translated as 'the Greatest Holy Leaf', and has been designated as the most outstanding heroine of the Bahá'í dispensation. She was born in late 1846 or early 1847.

The last child born to Bahá'u'lláh and Ásíyih Khánum in Ṭihrán was Mírzá Mihdí, entitled the Purest Branch. He was born in 1849 in the midst of hectic Bábí activities.

For a period of 14 years, i.e. from the time of her marriage in 1835 until 1849, Ásíyih Khánum was Bahá'u'lláh's only life partner. During the last years of this period, her lifestyle underwent drastic change. She started off her married life with all the luxuries that people of her social standing enjoyed: position, wealth, comfort. She witnessed the adverse events and hardships which struck her father-in-law Mírzá Buzurg during the last years of his life. These developments affected her as deeply as they affected Bahá'u'lláh, as they shouldered responsibility for the members of the family and caring for their daily needs. Four years later, the Báb's declaration set in motion feverish activities by His followers to spread His Faith. Bahá'u'lláh was deeply involved in spearheading Bábí activities in Ṭihrán and the district of Núr. His house became the focal centre of the believers, who thronged to it seeking His advice and guidance. The Cause of the Báb completely changed the focus of Bahá'u'lláh's activities and deeply affected Ásíyih Khánum's life as well.

The imprisonment of the Báb in the mountains of Ádharbáyján and His isolation from the rank and file of His followers intensified Bahá'u'lláh's involvement with the affairs of the Bábí community. The conference at Badasht in 1848 and the episode at fort of Shaykh Ṭabarsí in 1849 saw Bahá'u'lláh in Khurásán to promote the Cause of the Báb and in Mázandarán to inspect the preparations at the Shaykh Ṭabarsí fort for its defence against the onslaught of its enemies. Added involvement meant increased visibility and persecution.

Bahá'u'lláh's second marriage took place in 1849 when events of far-reaching significance with regard to the Bábí Faith were in the making.[26] In May 1849 the upheaval at Shaykh Ṭabarsí came to an end. Bahá'u'lláh tried to join the defenders of the fort but was arrested, imprisoned and bastinadoed in Ámul. A few months later Ṭihrán witnessed the martyrdom of seven prominent Bábís, the agitation in Nayríz and Zanján reached its peak, and in July 1850 the Báb Himself was martyred. Following the Báb's martyrdom, Bahá'u'lláh left Iran, at the request of Mírzá Taqí Khán, the prime minister, for Iraq. His journey took about a year. He visited Kirmánsháh on the way, where Nabíl-i-A'ẓam and Mullá 'Abdu'l-Karím-i-Qazvíní, also known as Mírzá Aḥmad, attained His presence.

During His absence from the capital, Ásíyih Khánum and her children lived in Mázandarán, i.e. Tákur and Yálrúd, near her family, as mentioned by Nabíl:

> Ere Bahá'u'lláh's departure from Kirmánsháh, He summoned Mírzá Aḥmad and me to His presence and bade us depart for Ṭihrán . . . Mírzá Aḥmad was instructed to remain in Ṭihrán until His arrival, and was

entrusted with a box of sweetmeats and a letter addressed to Áqáy-i-Kalím, who was to forward the gift to Mázandarán, where the Most Great Branch and His mother were residing.[27]

During Bahá'u'lláh's sojourn in Iraq, Mírzá Taqí Khán was murdered and Áqá Khán-i-Núrí replaced him as the prime minister. Three months after Bahá'u'lláh's return from Karbilá, hardships reached their climax when three Bábí youth who held Náṣiri'd-Dín Sháh responsible for the Báb's martyrdom and the severe persecution of His followers made the attempt on his life. Their thoughtless act resulted in Bahá'u'lláh's arrest and imprisonment in the Síyáh Chál (Black Pit) of Ṭihrán in August 1852. When Bahá'u'lláh arrived in the capital in May 1852, His family may have been still in Mázandarán. Upon arrival, He was welcomed by Ja'far-Qulí Khán, the brother of the prime minister, Áqá Khán-i-Núrí, and was his honoured guest for one month. He remained there until His departure for Shimírán. From there He proceeded to Lavásán where He spent a month in Afchih. He was on His way to Ṭihrán when soldiers dispatched by the government took Him captive in Níyávarán. Bahá'íyyih Khánum, who was five years old when her father was arrested, related her recollections many years later:

> My father was away at his country house in the village of [Níyávarán], which was his property . . .
>
> Suddenly and hurriedly a servant came rushing in great distress to my mother.
>
> 'The master, the master, he is arrested – I have seen him! He has walked many miles! Oh, they have beaten him! They say he has suffered the torture of the bastinado! His feet are bleeding! He has no shoes on! His turban has gone! His clothes are torn! There are chains upon his neck!'
>
> My poor mother's face grew whiter and whiter.
>
> We children were terribly frightened and could only weep bitterly.
>
> Immediately everybody, all our relations, and friends, and servants fled from our house in terror, only one man-servant, Isfandíyár, remained, and one woman. Our palace, and the smaller houses belonging to it were very soon stripped of everything; furniture, treasures, all were stolen by the people.[28]

To protect Isfandíyár from the wrath of the enemies, and to forestall any unforeseen consequences that his arrest might have entailed for Bahá'u'lláh, Ásíyih Khánum sent him away to Mázandarán.[29]

Life conditions for the family during this time became very difficult and hazardous. Bahá'u'lláh was arrested and imprisoned. The house that He, Ásíyih Khánum, their children and other members of the family occupied near the Gate of Shimírán was plundered. Family members, friends and servants fled in terror. Ásíyih Khánum had suddenly become destitute. Her main concern was the safety of her husband and their children. She had to take charge and do the best she could under unbearable circumstances. She rented a small place in an obscure quarter of the city and moved there with her children. She then took action to find out about Bahá'u'lláh's condition. Describing those dreadful days, Bahá'íyyih Khánum says:

> My mother went daily to the house of her aunt for news of him and generally spent the entire day there, hoping that each hour would bring some tidings. These were long and weary days for my mother, young as she was and unaccustomed to sorrow.
>
> At first, on going to her aunt's, my mother would take me with her; but one day, returning unusually late, we found 'Abbas Effendi surrounded by a band of boys who had undertaken to personally molest him. He was standing in their midst as straight as an arrow – a little fellow, the youngest and smallest of the group – firmly but quietly *commanding* them not to lay their hands upon him, which, strange to say, they seemed unable to do. After that, my mother thought it unsafe to leave him at home, knowing his fearless disposition, and that when he went into the street, as he usually did to watch for her coming, eagerly expectant of news from his father for whom, even at that early age, he had a passionate attachment, he would be beset and tormented by the boys. So she took him with her, leaving me at home with my younger brother. I spent the long days in constant terror, cowering in the dark and afraid to unlock the door lest men should rush in and kill us.[30]

While living in the rented rooms, Ásíyih Khánum and her children were in want of the barest necessities of life. One day, despite the grave dangers facing her son, who was then about nine years old, Ásíyih Khánum was forced to send Him to seek help from His aunt, who lived in another part of the city. 'Abdu'l-Bahá has made mention in His talks in the West of an episode that occurred then:

> I was a Child about nine years old when we were surrounded by calamities and assaulted by the enemies. They had thrown so many stones into our house that it was full of stones. We had nobody except Mother, sister, and Áqá Mírzá Qulí.[31] To provide us with better protection, Mother took us from the Gate of Shimírán to the Sanglaj Location, where she found

> a house in an obscure lane and she looked after us there. She strictly forbade us to leave the house until one day our living circumstances became so difficult that Mother told Me to go to My aunt's (Bahá'u'lláh's sister) house and tell her to use all means at her disposal to find us a few 'qirán'.[32]
>
> My aunt's house was in the Takiyih of Ḥájí Rajab-'Alí, close to which lived Mírzá Ḥasan-i-Kaj Damágh. I went. The aunt tried very hard until she found five 'qirán', which she tied securely in the corner of a handkerchief, and gave to Me.
>
> On My return, in the Takiyih, the son of Mírzá Ḥasan-i-Kaj Damágh recognized Me and immediately proclaimed Me as a Bábí. The children ran after Me. The house of Ḥájí Mullá Ja'far-i-Istarábádí was near. When I reached there, I took shelter in the entrance area of the house. The son of Ḥájí Mullá Ja'far saw Me, but he neither prevented Me, nor did he disperse the children. I stayed there until it was dark. When I left that place, again the children pursued Me. They shouted and threw stones. When I reached the shop of Áqá Muḥammad-Ḥasan-i Ṣandúqdár, the children did not come any closer.
>
> In brief, when I reached home, I was so tired and fearful that I collapsed. Mother asked, 'What is the matter with you?' But I could not respond. I passed out suddenly. Mother took the handkerchief containing the money and put Me to sleep.[33]

And again in connection with the same subject He says:

> There was a time in Ṭihrán when we had every means of livelihood and comfort, but they were all pillaged in one day. Life became so difficult that one day Mother put a little flour in My hand and I ate it like that.[34]

In her chronicles Bahá'íyyih Khánum describes the prison into which her father was cast where 'no food was provided' and says how difficult it was for her mother 'to arrange to get any food or drink taken into that ghastly prison'.[35] She then explains how the butchers, shoemakers, blacksmiths and others were given the opportunity to carry out 'their pitiless inventions on the Bábís'. And as they were busy inflicting injuries upon the victim, 'a drum was loudly beaten' and the mob crowded to witness the scene.[36] She continues:

> These horrible sounds I well remember, as we three children clung to our mother, she not knowing whether the victim was her own adored husband. She could not find out whether he was still alive or not until late

at night, or very early in the morning, when she determined to venture out, in defiance of the danger to herself and to us, for neither women nor children were spared . . .

We listened eagerly to the accounts she gave to my uncle. This information came through the kindness of a sister of my grandfather, who was married to Mírzá Yúsif, a Russian subject, and a friend of the Russian Consul in Ṭihrán. This gentleman, my great-uncle by marriage, used to attend the courts to find out some particulars as to the victims chosen for execution day by day, and thus was able to relieve to some extent my mother's overwhelming anxiety as these appalling days passed over us.

It was Mírzá Yúsif who was able to help my mother about getting food taken to my father, and who brought us to the two little rooms near the prison, where we stayed in close hiding. He had to be very careful in thus defying the authorities, although the danger in this case was mitigated by the fact of his being under the protection of the Russian Consulate, as a Russian subject.[37]

Nobody at all, of all our friends and relations, dared to come to see my mother during these days of death, but the wife of Mírzá Yúsif, the aunt of my father.[38]

After giving an account of the circumstances which led to Bahá'u'lláh's release from the Síyáh Chál, Bahá'íyyih Khánum relates the joy of His homecoming and the preparations for their journey into exile:

And so he came to our two little rooms.

Oh, the joy of his presence!

Oh, the horror of that dungeon, where he had passed those four terrible months . . .

The glory had won so great a victory that the shame, and pain, and sorrow, and scorn were of comparatively no importance whatever!

Jamál-i-Mubárak [Bahá'u'lláh] had a marvellous divine experience whilst in that prison.

We saw a new radiance seeming to enfold him like a shining vesture, its significance we were to learn years later. At that time we were only aware of the wonder of it, without understanding, or even being told the details of the sacred event.

My mother did her best to nurse our beloved, that he might have some strength to set out upon that journey on which we were to start . . .

Now was a time of great difficulty.

How could she prepare?

The poor, dear lady sold almost all that remained of her marriage treasures, jewels, embroidered garments, and other belongings, for which she received about four hundred túmáns. With this money she was able to make some provision for the terrible journey.[39]

Departure from Iran and Journey to Baghdád

Bahá'u'lláh's release from the Síyáh Chál was contingent upon His departure from Iran. He accepted banishment to Iraq, which He had visited before. However, after four months' imprisonment in the dreadful dungeon, His health had deteriorated considerably and He needed to recuperate sufficiently to undertake the arduous trip. There were also preparations that needed to be made for the journey. They were given about a month to make necessary arrangements and for Bahá'u'lláh to recuperate. He spent part of this time in the house of His half brother and sister-in-law, Mírzá Riḍá-Qulí and Jináb-i-Maryam. Ásíyih Khánum and the children seem to have continued living in the rented rooms, for there is no mention of their being with Bahá'u'lláh during the time He spent in the house of Mírzá Riḍá-Qulí and Maryam. Also, the fact that Maryam provided nursing care for Him indicates that Ásíyih Khánum was not with Him at that time. She must have been busy making arrangements for the trip, so it was deemed advisable for Bahá'u'lláh to move to His brother's house to recuperate. Another reason may have been the inadequacy of the rented rooms for Bahá'u'lláh's quick recuperation, which prompted Him to agree to stay with His brother and His family.

Bahá'u'lláh, accompanied by several members of His family and a few others, set out from Ṭihrán on 12 January 1853. Among the members of His family were Ásíyih Khánum and two of the children: their eldest son, 'Abdu'l-Bahá, and their daughter, Bahá'íyyih Khánum, about nine and six respectively. Mírzá Mihdí, who was about three years old, was left in Ṭihrán. The separation from him was very hard for Ásíyih Khánum to bear but the long and arduous journey during the severe winter months would have endangered his life. It was therefore necessary for him to stay behind.

The journey lasted three months. Bahá'u'lláh, in a prayer which describes the intense sufferings He endured in the Síyáh Chál, makes reference to His banishment to Iraq soon after His release from imprisonment:

> . . . Thy decree was irrevocably fixed, and thy behest summoned this servant to depart out of Persia, accompanied by a number of frail-bodied men and children of tender age, at this time when the cold is so intense that one cannot even speak, and ice and snow so abundant that is impossible to move.[40]

The details of Ásíyih Khánum's journey from Ṭihrán to Baghdád during those winter months of 1853 are scanty. The exiles travelled by horse and mule, journeying through the mountain passes of western Iran and the areas bordering Iraq. The information available gives us some idea of the appalling conditions endured by the exiles. What we know of Ásíyih Khánum's ordeals during that journey we owe to Bahá'íyyih Khánum, whose spoken chronicle has been recorded by Lady Blomfield in *The Chosen Highway*:

> This journey was filled with indescribable difficulties. My mother had no experience, no servants, no provisions, and very little money left. My father was extremely ill, not having recovered from the ordeals of the torture and the prison. No one of all our friends and relations dared to come to our help, or even to say good-bye, but one old lady, the grandmother of Ásíyih Khánum.
>
> Our faithful servant, Isfandíyár, and the one negro woman who did not fear to remain with us, did their best. But we three children were very young, my brother eight, and I six years old. Mírzá Mihdí, the 'Purest Branch', was very delicate, and my mother allowed herself to be persuaded to leave the little fellow, only two years old, with her grandmother, though the parting with him was very sad . . .
>
> My poor mother! How she suffered on this journey, riding in a takht-i-raván,[41] born on a jolting mule! And this took place only six weeks[42] before her youngest son was born!
>
> Never did she utter one word of complaint. She was always thinking of some kindness for somebody, and sympathy she gave unsparingly to all in their difficulties . . .
>
> When we came to a city, my mother would take the clothes and wash them at the public baths; we also were able to have baths at those places. She would carry the cold, wet clothes away in her arms – drying them was an almost impossible task; her lovely hands, being unused to such coarse work, became very painful.[43]

Life in Exile: The Baghdád Period

Bahá'íyyih Khánum describes the little house which accommodated them after their arrival in Baghdád and the difficulties facing the exiles, especially her mother:

> When we first arrived there, we had a very little house,[44] consisting of my father's room, and another one which was my mother's, and in which were also my eldest brother, the baby, and myself.

> When Arab ladies came to see us, this was the only reception room. These ladies came because they had been taught by Ṭáhirih, Qurratu'l-'Ayn, during her visit to Baghdád . . .
>
> Ásíyih Khánum, my dear mother, was in delicate health, her strength was diminished by the hardships she had undergone, but she always worked beyond her force.
>
> Sometimes my father himself helped in the cooking, as that hard work was too much for the dainty, refined, gentle lady. The hardships she had endured saddened the heart of her divine husband, who was also her beloved Lord. He gave this help both before his sojourn in the wilderness of Sulaymáníyyih, and after his return.[45]

Ásíyih Khánum's agonizing ordeals in Baghdád reached their climax when Bahá'u'lláh, without prior notice, withdrew to the mountains of Sulaymáníyyih in Kurdistan.

> Our grief was intense when my father left us. He told none of us either where he was going or when he would return . . .
>
> So we, my mother, my brother 'Abbás and I, clung together in our sorrow and anxiety.[46]

The intrigues employed by Bahá'u'lláh's half brother Mírzá Yaḥyá, known as Ṣubḥ-i-Azal, increased in His absence. Mírzá Yaḥyá, who was not among the exiles when Bahá'u'lláh left Ṭihrán, had joined Him of his own free will; he went to Baghdád in disguise some two months later and further complicated the already difficult conditions of life for the family. He cherished in his heart the hope of leading the Bábí community but he had neither the courage and strength, nor the inner knowledge and wisdom, nor the substance required for such a position. However, Bahá'u'lláh, who had raised, nurtured and protected him after their father's death, provided him with every opportunity to recognize the truth. Bahá'u'lláh's retreat to the mountains of Sulaymáníyyih, so soon after His arrival in Baghdád, was yet another step intended to help Mírzá Yaḥyá realize the folly of his hopes and to assist the members of the community to fix their gaze upon Him whom God would make manifest. He left Baghdád on 10 April 1854, exactly one year after His arrival there. No one knew of His intended departure or destination. Ásíyih Khánum's agonizing concern for Bahá'u'lláh during His two years' absence was immense.

During the two years of Bahá'u'lláh's sojourn in Sulaymáníyyih, Mírzá Yaḥyá's unreasonable demands on the members of His family escalated. His intense fear of persecution had made him cynical and suspicious; in order to protect his own interests and ensure his safety, he did not wish the members of Bahá'u'lláh's family to associate with anybody. At the same time, he expected them to provide the means of comfort for him and his several wives. His expectations and behaviour, which betrayed his inner weakness of character and selfishness, made life unbearable for Bahá'u'lláh's family, with whom he lived. The precious child, 'Alí-Muḥammad,[47] that Ásíyih Khánum had carried during her arduous journey and had given birth to after her arrival in Baghdád, died during Bahá'u'lláh's absence. This tragic event broke the grieving heart of his sorely-tried mother. Mírzá Yaḥyá, who wished to remain undiscovered lest he become a target for retribution, did not allow the child a proper burial. The body was given to an anonymous person to bury. Bahá'íyyih Khánum says:

> During this time the darling baby brother, born after our arrival in Baghdád, became seriously ill. Our guest would not allow a doctor, or even any neighbour to come to our help.
>
> My mother was heart-broken when the little one died; even then we were not allowed to have anybody to prepare him for burial.
>
> The sweet body of our beautiful baby was given to a man, who took it away, and we never knew even where he was laid. I remember so clearly the sorrow of those days.[48]

The details of what Ásíyih Khánum went through during Bahá'u'lláh's retreat in Sulaymáníyyih have not been recorded. Shoghi Effendi, in his message in Persian of 25 December 1939, refers to the blame, dispraise and slander aimed at her by the people of envy during the two years that the Blessed Beauty spent in the mountains of Kurdistán. He also refers to the humiliation, cruelties and transgressions that she suffered at the hands of the stirrers of mischief. His review of Ásíyih Khánum's sufferings during that period reminds the reader of the prophecy of the Prophet Isaiah about her:

> For the Lord hath called thee as a woman forsaken and grieved in spirit, and a wife of youth, when thou wast refused, saith thy God. For a small moment have I forsaken thee; but with great mercies will I gather thee. In a little wrath I hid my face from thee for a moment; but with everlasting kindness will I have mercy on thee, saith the Lord thy Redeemer.[49]

A highly significant event occurred during the early years in Baghdád. Some sources have specified that 'Abdu'l-Bahá was at the time about ten years old, which indicates that Bahá'u'lláh had not yet left for the mountains of Kurdistán. If not before, it must have been immediately after His return to

Baghdád that 'Abdu'l-Bahá 'still in His childhood', recognized 'the full glory of His Father's as yet unrevealed station, a recognition which had impelled Him to throw Himself at His feet and to spontaneously implore the privilege of laying down His life for His sake'.[50] Whether the immensity of this highly charged spiritual experience and the feelings of ecstasy surging in the soul of 'Abdu'l-Bahá in His tender years were contained and escaped the attention of His mother is left to the imagination of the reader. If she was unaware of their significance, how could she bear the events taking place in Baghdád, which weighed so heavily on her sorrowful heart? Could her keen insight have remained untouched by the numerous evidences pointing to Bahá'u'lláh's extraordinary personality and station?

During Bahá'u'lláh's absence from Baghdád, His family moved to the house of Sulaymán-i-Ghannám 'known, at that time, as the house of Mírzá Músá, the Bábí, an extremely modest residence situated in the Karkh quarter, in the neighbourhood of the western bank of the river . . .' On this house Bahá'u'lláh later conferred 'the official designation of the Bayt-i-A'ẓam (the Most Great House)'.[51]

Bahá'u'lláh's return from Sulaymáníyyih on 19 March 1856 was by far the most happy event in years experienced by Ásíyih Khánum and the members of His family. Another happy occurrence was the reunion of Ásíyih Khánum with her son Mírzá Mihdí. He joined the exiles in Baghdád some time after Bahá'u'lláh's return from Sulaymáníyyih. Ishráq-i-Khávarí says the reunion took place about 1860. Mírzá Mihdí accompanied Fáṭimih Khánum, Bahá'u'lláh's second wife, on her return trip to Baghdád.[52] If the date is accurate, Mírzá Mihdí rejoined his family after seven years' separation. The means of communication in those days was by messenger post and messages took months to reach their destination. The delicate child that Ásíyih Khánum had left behind was rarely able to receive news of his beloved parents. And now after such a long time he could be again in the loving arms of his parents and the members of his family. It was truly a joyous occasion for all concerned. Mírzá Mihdí shared to the end of his life the anguish and hardships of a life in exile to which his beloved father and the rest of His family were subjected.

The authority and sovereignty of Bahá'u'lláh, upon His return from Sulaymáníyyih, became clearer day by day. His new residence became the focal centre of activity. Members of the Bábí community travelled from Persia to Baghdád to attain His presence and acquire from Him knowledge and wisdom. Seekers of enlightenment thronged His abode. Ásíyih Khánum's life was again filled with tremendous activity; she had to oversee the work in a house which had become the focus of attention for both believers and seekers.

The evidences of Bahá'u'lláh's might and sovereignty provoked the animosity of religious leaders, who brought pressure to bear on government authorities to take action to curb His influence. The Iranian government asked that He and His followers be returned to Iran. They were sorry to have let them leave their area of jurisdiction and to have lost authority over them. The Ottoman authorities could not entertain the request, for by then many of the Bábís had become citizens of the Ottoman Empire. Having failed in their attempt to bring Bahá'u'lláh and His followers back under their jurisdiction and to deal with them as they pleased, the Iranian authorities demanded that they be banished to areas farther away from Iran. The Persian religious leader in Iraq, Shaykh 'Abdu'l-Ḥusayn, spearheaded the campaign. His machinations caused the Ottoman authorities to issue a decree banishing Bahá'u'lláh from Baghdád.

Banishment to Constantinople (Istanbul) and Adrianople (Edirne)

When Bahá'u'lláh was officially informed of the decree of the government to leave Baghdád, He was given a month to proceed to Constantinople, the capital of the Ottoman Empire. On the morning of 22 April 1863 Bahá'u'lláh, accompanied by some members of His family and companions, left Baghdád and arrived in the Garden of Najíb Páshá, designated by Him the Garden of Riḍván, in the afternoon of same day.[53] Ásíyih Khánum and other members of the family stayed behind to make preparations for the journey. They were to follow Him shortly but were unable to do so owing to the flooding of the River Euphrates. Eight days later they joined Bahá'u'lláh in the garden. On the twelfth day, Bahá'u'lláh, His family and companions left the Garden of Riḍván on their way to Constantinople, where they remained for nearly four months. It was in this city that Sulṭán 'Abdu'l-'Azíz issued his 'infamous edict' banishing the exiles 'suddenly and without any justification whatsoever, in the depth of winter, and in the most humiliating circumstances, to Adrianople, situated on the extremities of his empire'.[54] According to Bahá'u'lláh's own testimony: 'They expelled Us from the city (Constantinople) with an abasement with which no abasement on earth can compare.' 'Neither My family, nor those who accompanied Me had the necessary raiment to protect them from the cold in that freezing weather.'[55]

The journey from Constantinople to Adrianople was long and arduous. It took place at the beginning of a very severe winter, lasted 12 days and entailed tremendous hardship. Upon arrival in Adrianople, Bahá'u'lláh, His family and companions stayed in a caravanserai called Khán-i-'Arab. After three nights He and His family moved to a house in the Murádíyyih quarter of the city. It took several months before a well-situated and spacious house in the centre of the city could be found. Called the House of Amru'lláh, it had an *andarún* and *bírúní*.

Although the family enjoyed ease in this house, the trickery employed by internal agitators such as Siyyid Muḥammad-i-Iṣfahání and Mírzá Aḥmad-i-Ká<u>sh</u>ání, supporters of Mírzá Yaḥyá Azal, assumed new proportions. Mírzá Yaḥyá's heedless attitude towards Bahá'u'lláh and the incessant intrigues he employed against Him became more extreme. His treachery was the cause of untold suffering to Bahá'u'lláh and His family. Recognizing his inability to gain the esteem and allegiance of the followers of the Báb, coupled with his intense passion for leadership, prompted him to plot to remove Bahá'u'lláh from the scene. His plan to induce Bahá'u'lláh's barber to assassinate Him in the bath exposed the extent of his malicious intentions but did not stop him from carrying out new schemes, such as poisoning the well from which water was drawn for use in Bahá'u'lláh's house, or inviting Bahá'u'lláh to his home and offering Him tea in a cup smeared with poison. Although his heinous act did not achieve the result he had hoped for, it made Bahá'u'lláh very ill. The illness lasted for a month and increased tremendously the anguish of Ásíyih <u>Kh</u>ánum and other members of the family for His safety and well-being. After Bahá'u'lláh recovered, the effect of the poison remained with Him to the end of His life.

Yet these treacherous acts, grave as they were, did not cause Bahá'u'lláh to sever ties with His half brother. What effected a complete separation was Mírzá Yaḥyá's response to the Lawḥ-i-Amr, in which Bahá'u'lláh made His claim and station conspicuously clear. A copy of the Tablet was delivered to Mírzá Yaḥyá. Facing the moment of truth, he had no choice but to make his position clear. His response was a counterclaim. The ensuing confusion severely tested members of the nascent community.

To provide the believers with the opportunity to decide who they wanted to follow, at this time (March 1866) 'Bahá'u'lláh withdrew with His family to the house of Riḍá Big . . . which was rented by His order, and refused, for two months, to associate with either friend or stranger, including His own companions'.[56] The wavering in heart were severely tested but the sincere longed for the time when Bahá'u'lláh would re-admit them to His presence, nourish their souls with spiritual sustenance and provide unfailing guidance. Mírzá Yaḥyá and his accomplices thenceforth committed their malicious acts against Bahá'u'lláh and His faithful believers openly and shamelessly.[57]

The separation of Bahá'u'lláh and Mírzá Yaḥyá came as a blissful relief to Ásíyih <u>Kh</u>ánum, who was extremely concerned about the safety of her husband in light of the internal enemy's ruthless designs to harm Him. Shoghi Effendi, in his message in Persian of 25 December 1939, refers to the events that transpired in the Land of Mystery (Adrianople). He says these events shook the believers and made the countenances of the beauteous Branch (Mírzá Mihdí) and the Most Exalted Leaf (Ásíyih Khánum) to glow with ever-increasing brightness in the midst of all calamities.[58]

Bahá'u'lláh and His family later moved back to the house of Amru'lláh for six months before moving to the house of 'Izzat Áqá, the last of their residences in Adrianople. Moving from residence to residence clearly had implications for Ásíyih Khánum. The responsibilities commensurate with her position as the lady of the house were great indeed. Except for the brief period of His withdrawal, Bahá'u'lláh received the friends regularly in the *bírúní*, responded to their needs for guidance and answered their questions. The proclamation of His divine mission further increased the activities of the community, which naturally impacted the work performed by Ásíyih Khánum.

'Akká, the Final Place of Exile

The trying years in Adrianople were five in all. Those who wanted Bahá'u'lláh as far away from Iran as possible and in a place where they hoped He would not survive the hardships continued to press for His banishment once again, this time to the most desolate city in the world. On 12 August 1868 Bahá'u'lláh, His family and companions left Adrianople, this far corner of the European continent, entitled by Him the 'remote prison' and the 'Land of Mystery', for the final place of exile, the penal colony of 'Akká. According to Shoghi Effendi,

> Suddenly, one morning, the house of Bahá'u'lláh was surrounded by soldiers, sentinels were posted at its gates. His followers were again summoned by the authorities, interrogated, and ordered to make ready for their departure. 'The loved ones of God and His kindred,' is Bahá'u'lláh's testimony in the Súriy-i-Ra'ís, 'were left on the first night without food . . . The people surrounded the house, and Muslims and Christians wept over us . . .'[59]

The journey was arduous, the future unknown and the final destination notorious for its inhospitable climate and disagreeable conditions. In the words of Shoghi Effendi:

> 'Akká . . . had sunk, under the Turks, to the level of a penal colony . . . It was girt about by a double system of ramparts; was inhabited by a people whom Bahá'u'lláh stigmatized as 'the generation of vipers'; was devoid of any source of water within its gates; was flea-infested, damp

> and honey-combed with gloomy, filthy and tortuous lanes. 'According to what they say,' the Supreme Pen has recorded in the Lawḥ-i-Sulṭán, 'it is the most desolate of the cities of the world, the most unsightly of them in appearance, the most detestable in climate, and the foulest in water. It is as though it were the metropolis of the owl.'[60]

The distance between Adrianople and Gallipoli was covered in five stages and took several days. After three days in Gallipoli the exiles left by an Austrian-Lloyd liner for Alexandria via Madellí and Smyrna (Izmír). In Alexandria they changed ship and set out by another Austrian-Lloyd for Haifa via Port-Sa'íd. The journey from Haifa to 'Akká was by sailing boat. Bahá'íyyih Khánum has described the vessel that carried the exiles to Haifa, and their arrival in 'Akká:

> There was no place in which we could lie down in that vessel. There were also some Tartar passengers in the boat. To be near them was very uncomfortable; they were dirty beyond description.
>
> Our lack of food had reduced us to a seriously weak state of health.
>
> At length we arrived at Haifa, where we had to be carried ashore in chairs. Here we remained for a few hours. Now we embarked again for the last bit of our sea journey. The heat . . . was overpowering. We were put into a sailing boat. There being no wind, and no shelter from the burning rays of the sun, we spent eight hours of positive misery, and at last we had reached 'Akká, the end of our journey.
>
> The landing at this place was achieved with much difficulty; the ladies of our party were carried ashore.
>
> All the townspeople had assembled to see the arrival of the prisoners. Having been told that we were infidels, criminals, and sowers of sedition, the attitude of the crowd was threatening. Their yelling of curses and execrations filled us with fresh misery. We were terrified of the unknown! We knew not what the fate of our party, the friends and ourselves would be.
>
> We were taken to the old fortress of 'Akká, where we were crowded together. There was no air; a small quantity of very bad coarse bread was provided; we were unable to get fresh water to drink; our sufferings were not diminished. Then an epidemic of typhoid broke out. Nearly all became ill.[61]

The exiles arrived in the prison-city of 'Akká on 31 August 1868. Exhausted by a long and arduous journey, the travellers were greeted by a hostile and contemptuous population. Some had gathered to see 'the God of the

Persians'. They had mocking glances and their language was derisory. The prisoners were accommodated in an army barracks which also served as a prison. The insanitary conditions and the inedible food made the prisoners ill. Ásíyih Khánum's accumulated sufferings through long years of exile were beginning to show their effect and had made her frail. The foul smell of their place of confinement was impossible to bear. Bahá'íyyih Khánum fainted before the eyes of her mother. 'Abdu'l-Bahá, who had acted as a shield for His father ever since the family had left Baghdád, had to tend the sick and look after their affairs. But He, too, fell ill and added to Ásíyih Khánum's anguish.

The Martyrdom of the Purest Branch

Living conditions in Bahá'u'lláh's last place of exile were woeful. He, His family and companions had been sent there to perish. They had been confined in a place where water and air were foul, food was scarce, people hostile. Some exiles succumbed to their miserable circumstances and were even denied a proper burial. Some Bahá'ís who undertook a long and arduous journey from Iran to 'Akká in the hope of attaining Bahá'u'lláh's presence were prevented from achieving their purpose and sent back. Nearly two years elapsed and no improvement was in sight. Ásíyih Khánum's greatest comfort and joy in those perilous days was her closeness to Bahá'u'lláh and her beloved children, who were all in their twenties. But that joy did not last long. She was destined to witness the tragic death of her beloved son, Mírzá Mihdí, the youngest of her surviving children, entitled by Bahá'u'lláh the Purest Branch. He was the one she had left in Iran at the time of Bahá'u'lláh's banishment to Iraq. He was the one with whom she had been joyfully reunited in Baghdád, after several years of agonizing separation. He was the one to whose meekness everyone testified. He was then 22 years old. He fell through an unguarded skylight in the roof of the barracks, the only place the prisoners were allowed to visit, and died less than 24 hours after his fall.

The martyrdom of the Purest Branch dealt Ásíyih Khánum the hardest blow. The account of his tragic death depicts its devastating effect on her but also reveals her unqualified acceptance of Bahá'u'lláh's decisive decree to offer him up for the quickening of mankind and its unification. The account, based on information provided in a booklet published in Persian on the occasion of the hundredth anniversary of the martyrdom of the Purest Branch, is as follows:

> Mírzá Mihdí was one of Bahá'u'lláh's amanuenses. On the afternoon of 21 June 1870 he presented himself to His exalted father and offered his

services. Bahá'u'lláh advised him to go back on the roof of the barracks – he often used the roof for prayer and meditation – and continue his prayers. Mírzá Mihdí returned to the roof. Immersed in prayers and unaware of the world around him, he paced the area of the roof chanting verses from one of Bahá'u'lláh's famous odes known as 'Qaṣídiy-i-'Izz-i-Varqá'íyyih'.[62]

> He was pacing the roof of the barracks in the twilight, one evening, wrapped in his customary devotions, when he fell through the unguarded skylight onto a wooden crate, standing on the floor beneath, which pierced his ribs . . .[63]

> The terrifying sound of the fall echoed in the surrounding area . . . It was as if the day of resurrection had been renewed. The loving, frail and weeping mother of the Purest Branch forced herself to the site where her beloved son was lying. As she beheld him soaked in blood, she gave an agonizing sigh and lost consciousness. The Purest Branch, despite his weakness and tormenting pain, took his mother in his arms.
>
> After a while, the relatives and those present removed the Purest Branch and placed him in a bed. The Most Great Branch 'Abdu'l-Bahá attained the presence of Bahá'u'lláh and, prostrating Himself before His Exalted Father, implored Him with tearful eyes to bestow healing [upon His brother]. The Blessed Beauty responded thus: 'O My Most Mighty Branch, leave him to his Lord', i.e. leave his affairs to God, so that He may do as He please. The Most Great Branch bowed His Head in submission and directed others to be resigned to the will of God.[64]

Nabíl says that at that time Ásíyih Khánum, the grief-stricken mother of the Purest Branch, attained the presence of Bahá'u'lláh, prostrated herself at the Threshold of His Grandeur, and said:

> 'My Lord, I entreat Thee to accept from me this ransom.' The Blessed Beauty conferred His bountiful favours upon her and advised her to be patient. Ásíyih Khánum responded: 'Whatever is Thy good-pleasure that indeed is my heart's desire and my best beloved . . .'[65]

Referring to the martyrdom of His son, Bahá'u'lláh says in a prayer: 'I have, O my Lord, offered up that which Thou hast given Me, that Thy servants may be quickened, and all that dwell on earth be united.'[66]

The body of the Purest Branch was washed in the barracks before the eyes of Bahá'u'lláh. The traditional restrictions on women probably compelled Ásíyih Khánum to remain on the upper floor of the barracks, where the family lived, and mourn the loss of her beloved son away from where his body was being washed. After the body was prepared for burial, according to Bahá'íyyih Khánum, 'It was carried out by our jailors, and we did not even know whither it was taken.'[67] The place of burial was the Nabí Ṣáliḥ cemetery in 'Akká.[68] What went on in the heart and mind of Ásíyih Khánum during those heart-wrenching hours is not recorded anywhere. All we know is that none of her numerous woes and sufferings compared in magnitude to the loss of her wonderful son in the prime of his life. After the martyrdom of the Purest Branch, Ásíyih Khánum's health deteriorated to the point that it caused concern. In relating an account of his tragic death, Bahá'íyyih Khánum says:

> The death of this youngest and favourite child – of a very gentle and sweet disposition – nearly broke his mother's heart. We feared for her reason. When the Blessed Perfection was told of the condition of his wife, he went to her and said: 'Your son has been taken by God that His people might be freed. His life was the ransom, and you should rejoice that you had a son so dear to give to the cause of God.' When our mother heard these words she seemed to rally, – knelt, and kissed the Blessed Perfection's hands, and thanked him for what he had said. After that she did not shed a tear.[69]

Life inside the Prison-City

Soon after the martyrdom of the Purest Branch the conditions of Bahá'u'lláh's confinement eased; the barracks were needed by the government for other purposes. Bahá'u'lláh and His family moved to several temporary dwellings before they settled in the House of 'Abbúd. During the seven years of Bahá'u'lláh's stay in this house several occurrences took place which had a direct bearing on Ásíyih Khánum's life.

Although Mírzá Yaḥyá did not accompany Bahá'u'lláh to 'Akká – from Adrianople he and his supporters were banished to Cyprus – his chief instigator, Siyyid Muḥammad-i-Iṣfahání, and four other Azalís were sent with Bahá'u'lláh to 'Akká. These five sympathizers of Azal did everything in their power to undermine Bahá'u'lláh in His final place of exile. They served as spies, reported the movement of Bahá'í pilgrims to authorities, spread distorted information, interpolated Bahá'u'lláh's writings and disseminated them among the populace inciting them against Bahá'u'lláh and His followers. Their misconduct caused confusion and immense suffering to Bahá'u'lláh, His family and followers. As the contents of the Fire Tablet revealed at that time shows, Bahá'u'lláh was highly distressed, withdrew from the community and refused to see anyone. His silence and isolation emboldened the stirrers of mischief; they used every means at their disposal to discredit Him and His companions. Seven of Bahá'u'lláh's ardent lovers, who could no longer bear to see Him suffer at the hands of these few evildoers, decided to exterminate the mischief-makers even at the cost of endangering their spiritual lives, for they knew that Bahá'u'lláh would be displeased with them. Thus on 22 January 1872 they killed three of the Azalís, an act that brought untold hardship to Bahá'u'lláh, His family and followers. Ásíyih Khánum witnessed with anxiety and deep concern the events that caused her beloved Husband so much grief and anguish. It was an hour after sunset when she saw an army officer arrive and take with him both Bahá'u'lláh and 'Abdu'l-Bahá. She spent long terrifying hours awaiting eagerly news of her loved ones. The interrogation lasted many hours. After 70 hours Bahá'u'lláh returned to the house but 'Abdu'l-Bahá was detained for several days.

During the stay of Bahá'u'lláh and His family in the House of 'Abbúd, 'Abdu'l-Bahá's marriage took place. This was undoubtedly one of the happiest events in Ásíyih Khánum's life. Her beloved and only son was 29 years old when His bride arrived from Iran. Bahá'u'lláh had arranged for Fáṭimih Khánum, upon whom He bestowed the name Munírih after her arrival in 'Akká, to come to the Holy Land. She arrived towards the end of the same year that the Azalís had been murdered. Five months later, in March 1873, the marriage of the Most Great Branch to Munírih Khánum took place. Ásíyih Khánum, assisted by her beloved daughter Bahá'íyyih Khánum, made all the arrangements for the wedding. She witnessed the blessings Bahá'u'lláh showered upon her new daughter-in-law on the afternoon of the wedding day, the seventh day of the month of fasting.

The simple wedding ceremony materialized the highest wish of Ásíyih Khánum's earthly life. She had lived to see with her own eyes that banishment and ordeals could not thwart God's purpose for mankind. 'Abdu'l-Bahá, destined to become the Centre of Bahá'u'lláh's Covenant, was happily married and, before long, His mother enjoyed the pleasure of having her grandchildren around her.

With the arrival of Munírih Khánum, members of her family, with Bahá'u'lláh's permission, began to settle in the Holy Land. Notable among them were Shamsu'ḍ-Ḍuḥá (Khurshíd Bagum),[70] her daughter, Fáṭimih Bagum,[71] and their children. They transferred their residence from Iṣfahán to the Holy Land at Bahá'u'lláh's behest. Their presence widened the circle of friends with whom Ásíyih Khánum associated closely.

Five years after 'Abdu'l-Bahá's marriage another significant event took place. At the invitation of Midḥat Páshá, the governor of Beirut, 'Abdu'l-

Bahá visited that city in 1878. It was 'Abdu'l-Bahá's first journey outside the confines of His place of exile and the first time Ásíyih Khánum was separated from her beloved Son for a considerable period of time. Although happy for the people who had the pleasure of seeing Him, the sadness that His absence caused was palpable. Bahá'u'lláh has made reference in one of His Tablets to the sorrow felt in 'Akká after 'Abdu'l-Bahá left for Beirut.

> Praise be to Him Who hath honoured the Land of Bá through the presence of Him round Whom all names revolve . . . Sorrow, thereby, enveloped this Prison-city, whilst another land rejoiceth . . . We beseech God – blessed and exalted be He – that He may honour us with meeting Him soon.[72]

In a letter that 'Abdu'l-Bahá wrote to Munírih Khánum during that trip, He speaks most affectionately of His beloved mother, whom He always referred to as 'Ḥaḍrat-i-Válidih' (Her Highness, the Mother). And Ásíyih Khánum addressed Him as 'Áqá Ján' (beloved Master).

> . . . Since My intention is to hasten home, the response to Her Highness, the Mother, as well as to Khánum,[73] will either be written in detail, or reported at length in person when I see them. My heart is not happy and content with such a brief response and I have not had the opportunity to write in detail. I hope from divine bounty that under His infinite loving care and favour all will be happy and protected.[74]

After nine years' confinement in 'Akká, 'Abdu'l-Bahá succeeded in renting a place situated several kilometres to the north of 'Akká. It was called the Mansion of Mazra'ih. He then pleaded with Bahá'u'lláh to change His residence to that area in the countryside, which was surrounded by trees and greenery. In late 1877 or early 1878 Bahá'u'lláh left the prison-city and took up residence in the Mansion of Mazra'ih. Two years later He transferred His residence to the Mansion of Bahjí, situated between Mazra'ih and 'Akká, which 'Abdu'l-Bahá acquired for His father after its owner fled owing to an epidemic in the area. After His departure from Iran, except for the two years that Bahá'u'lláh spent in Sulaymáníyyih, He and Ásíyih Khánum were never separated. However, when Bahá'u'lláh left the prison-city, Ásíyih Khánum and Bahá'íyyih Khánum remained with 'Abdu'l-Bahá and His family in 'Akká and continued to live in the House of 'Abbúd.

The primitive means of travel and restrictions imposed on women in those days made travelling for the female members of the Holy Family very difficult. It is unclear whether Ásíyih Khánum had the opportunity to visit Bahá'u'lláh at Mazra'ih and later at Bahjí. The accumulated effects of working beyond her endurance during the long years of banishment and imprisonment had affected her health and made her frail. However, Bahá'u'lláh visited her and other members of His family in 'Akká. At times He spent several days with them. During the last eight to nine years of Ásíyih Khánum's life when she lived a short distance from Bahá'u'lláh, in addition to visits, He was also in touch with her through written communications. Almost all His writings revealed in her honour belong to that period. In a Tablet, illuminated and displayed in the International Archives Building, He expresses the hope that she is well and advises her on health issues.

In another Tablet, the date of which is undetermined, Bahá'u'lláh testifies to the tribulations that had encompassed Ásíyih Khánum in the path of God. He exhorts her not to let such tribulations cause her sadness:

> In the Name of God!
>
> O Khánum, O Amatalláh! That is, O My handmaid, O thou the handmaid of God! It is hoped that in the path of His love thou art sanctified from all else save Him, fixing thy gaze upon the Holy Court in such wise that the tribulations encompassing thee in the path of God, the King, the Omnipotent Protector, the Self-Subsisting, will not cause thee sadness.[75]

During the final years of her life Ásíyih Khánum had high hopes of meeting the consort of the Herald of Bahá'u'lláh, the one who had sacrificed His life for her husband. The much anticipated meeting never took place for reasons discussed in the chapter on 'Khadíjih Bagum, the Wife of the Báb'. The untimely death of Khadíjih Bagum in 1882 made the Blessed Beauty very sad and deprived Ásíyih Khánum of meeting the person whose life in many ways resembled her own. Although Khadíjih Bagum and Ásíyih Khánum never met on this earthly plain, they were united through a strong invisible bond.

Ásíyih Khánum and Khadíjih Bagum were about the same age, suffered all their lives by virtue of being the consort of one of the Twin Manifestations of God for this day, were utterly devoted to the Báb and Bahá'u'lláh, wholeheartedly promoted the Cause of Truth, stood firm in the face of opposition and persecution, never wavered in their faith and remained faithful to the end.

The Passing of Ásíyih Khánum, Her Station and Place in History

The succession of heartrending events and protracted sufferings sapped Ásíyih Khánum's energy. During the last years of her life she suffered from poor health. The exact nature of her illness is not known. Based on advice

Bahá'u'lláh gave her in one of His Tablets displayed in the International Archives Building, she may have suffered some kind of stomach disorder which weakened her constitution. However, that does not seem to have been the cause of her death. According to the unpublished memoirs of Siyyid Asadu'lláh-i Qumí who lived in 'Akká and had a shoe-repair shop in the Súq-i-Abyaḍ,[76] "Abdu'l-Bahá's mother fell from a high elevation. Several days later she left this mortal world, joined the rays of the Sun of Truth, took her flight to the highest summit and with spiritual tongue said, "Verily we are God's, and verily to Him do we all return.""

When the end was near, Bahá'u'lláh visited her in the House of 'Abbúd. He was at her bedside when she breathed her last breath. The year was 1886. At her bedside were also her beloved children 'Abdu'l-Bahá and the Greatest Holy Leaf.

The funeral of Ásíyih Khánum, unlike that of her son which had occurred 16 years earlier, was held with the dignity that her position required. According to H. M. Balyuzi:

> Notables of 'Akká, as well as Muslim and Christian divines, came to follow the funeral cortège which was preceded by muezzins and reciters of the Qur'án. Schoolchildren joined the procession chanting verses and poems expressing their grief. Overwhelming was the sorrow of 'Abdu'l-Bahá . . . [77]

In his message of 21 December 1939 sent to the Bahá'ís of North America on the occasion of the transfer of the remains of Ásíyih Khánum and the Purest Branch to Mount Carmel, Shoghi Effendi included the translation of some of Bahá'u'lláh's Tablets revealed in her honour. The selected excerpts made known Ásíyih Khánum's exalted station, which had until then remained concealed, to the rank and file of the believers:

> The first Spirit through which all spirits were revealed, and the first Light by which all lights shone forth, rest upon thee, O Most Exalted Leaf,[78] thou who hast been mentioned in the Crimson Book! Thou art the one whom God created to arise and serve His own Self, and the Manifestation of His Cause, and the Day-Spring of His Revelation, and the Dawning-Place of His signs, and the Source of His commandments; and Who so aided thee that thou didst turn with thy whole being unto Him, at a time when His servants and handmaidens had turned away from His Face . . . Happy art thou, O My handmaiden, and My Leaf, and the one mentioned in My Book, and inscribed by My Pen of Glory in My Scrolls and Tablets . . . Rejoice thou, at this moment, in the most exalted Station and the All-

> highest Paradise, and the Abhá Horizon, inasmuch as He Who is the Lord of Names hath remembered thee. We bear witness that thou didst attain unto all good, and that God hath so exalted thee, that all honour and glory circled around thee.
>
> O Navváb! O Leaf that hath sprung from My Tree, and been My companion! My glory be upon thee, and My loving-kindness, and My mercy that hath surpassed all beings. We announce unto thee that which will gladden thine eye, and assure thy soul, and rejoice thine heart. Verily, thy Lord is the Compassionate, the All-Bountiful. God hath been and will be pleased with thee, and hath singled thee out for His own Self, and chosen thee from among His handmaidens to serve Him, and hath made thee the companion of His Person in the daytime and in the night-season.
>
> Hear thou Me once again, God is well-pleased with thee, as a token of His grace and a sign of His mercy. He hath made thee to be His companion in every one of His worlds, and hath nourished thee with His meeting and presence, so long as His Name, and His Remembrance, and His Kingdom, and His Empire shall endure. Happy is the handmaid that hath mentioned thee, and sought thy good-pleasure, and humbled herself before thee, and held fast unto the cord of thy love.

At the end of the passage Bahá'u'lláh sternly warns anyone attempting to deny her 'exalted station, and the things ordained' for her 'from God':

> Woe betide him that denieth thy exalted station, and the things ordained for thee from God, the Lord of all names, and him that hath turned away from thee, and rejected thy station before God, the Lord of the mighty throne.[79]

That it was necessary for such a warning to be voiced is of keen interest. The warning was specifically, it seems, in response to some in the family circle who had turned away from her and tried to deny her lofty station. But generally it concerns anyone who would try during the dispensation to marginalize her work, ignore the services she rendered and undermine her exalted station. This is not unfamiliar in religious history where women have often been marginalized and the worth of their achievements minimized, if not completely ignored. In his tributes Shoghi Effendi has issued a similar warning to those who might attempt to deny the exalted station of Bahá'íyyih Khánum, the Greatest Holy Leaf, and marginalize her contribution to major historical events.

In a visitation Tablet revealed after Ásíyih Khánum's death, Bahá'u'lláh refers to this as the second sorrowful event – the first being the passing of Khadíjih Bagum four years earlier – besetting the people of Bahá. He then testifies that Ásíyih Khánum attained His presence at daytime and in the night season, that she gazed upon His Countenance, circled round His throne, gave ear to His Call, resided in His House, clung to the Cord of His Covenant, held fast the Hem of the Garment of His Generosity and Bounty, until the fatal event, recorded in the Book, struck and weakened her. He then bears witness that she endured all the hardships and sufferings that He bore, until she offered up her soul in His path before His Countenance.

In the same Tablet, Bahá'u'lláh reassures Ásíyih Khánum of God's good-pleasure; bears witness that she drank the choice wine of recognition from the chalice of Utterance, that she endured patiently in the path of her Lord, that she believed firmly in God, in His Books, in His Prophets, and in all that has been sent down from the Heaven of His Will. He bids her rejoice in the highest Paradise for having been mentioned by the King of Names, and reaffirms that she attained unto all good, that God elevated her to a station round which circled every glory and high station. He addresses her as the Most Exalted Leaf, and confirms that the sorrow caused by her death changed the light of the day to the darkness of night, transformed joy to sadness, calmness to agitation, and that the whole world was overtaken by grief because of the bereavement of the One for whom the Qá'im had sacrificed Himself. He then confirms that she was with Him at all times, that she fled her home in the land of Ṭá and went with Him to Baghdád, from Baghdád to the Land of Mystery, from there to the Most Great Prison. He then addresses the people of Bahá thus:

> O faithful ones! Should ye visit the resting-place of the Most Exalted Leaf, who hath ascended unto the Glorious Companion, stand ye and say: 'Salutation and blessing and glory upon thee, O Holy Leaf that hath sprung from the Divine Lote-Tree! I bear witness that thou hast believed in God and in His signs, and answered His Call, and turned unto Him, and held fast unto His cord, and clung to the hem of His grace, and fled thy home in His path, and chosen to live as a stranger, out of love for His presence and in thy longing to serve Him. May God have mercy upon him that draweth nigh unto thee, and remembereth thee through the things which My Pen hath voiced in this, the most great station. We pray God that He may forgive us, and forgive them that have turned unto thee, and grant their desires, and bestow upon them, through His wondrous grace, whatever be their wish. He, verily, is the Bountiful, the Generous. Praise be to God, He Who is the Desire of all worlds; and the Beloved of all who recognize Him.[80]

In his messages, especially the one in Persian written at the time of the transfer of Ásíyih Khánum's remains in December 1939, Shoghi Effendi refers to Ásíyih Khánum as 'the most distinguished of all the people', 'the Shining Star of the Celestial Heaven', 'the Spiritual Mother of the people of Bahá', 'the Wronged Leaf' which hath sprung forth from 'the Tree of Faithfulness', the 'Precious and Exalted Treasure and the keepsake of the Abhá Beauty'[81] and that 'Brilliant Star of the Firmament of Faithfulness'.[82]

The dearth of documented information about this remarkable figure of our Faith is regrettable. However, the writings of Bahá'u'lláh and 'Abdu'l-Bahá, the utterances of 'Abdu'l-Bahá and the Greatest Holy Leaf, and the messages of Shoghi Effendi provide the needed spark to create in our hearts the fire of longing to draw nearer to our spiritual mother, who was sorely tried all her life for no other reason than the fact that she had been chosen to be the consort of the Supreme Manifestation of God. The prophecy of Isaiah in the 54th chapter of his book is an ancient testimony to Ásíyih Khánum's grandeur and uniqueness.

> Enlarge the place of thy tent, and let them stretch forth the curtains of thine habitations: spare not, lengthen thy cords, and strengthen thy stakes; For thou shalt break forth on the right hand and on the left; and thy seed shall inherit the Gentiles, and make the desolate cities to be inhabited. Fear not; for thou shalt not be ashamed: neither be thou confounded; for thou shalt not be put to shame . . . For thy Maker is thine husband; the Lord of hosts is his name; and thy Redeemer the Holy One of Israel; The God of the whole earth shall he be called . . .

He then assures her:

> For the mountains shall depart, and the hills be removed; but my kindness shalt not depart from thee, neither shall the covenant of my peace be removed, saith the Lord that hath mercy on thee.

Thereafter he imparts a most wonderful glad-tiding:

> O thou afflicted, tossed with tempest, and not comforted, behold, I will lay thy stones with fair colours, and lay thy foundations with sapphires. And I will make thy windows of agates, and thy gates of carbuncles, and all thy borders of pleasant stones. And all thy children shall be taught of the Lord; and great shall be the peace of thy children. In righteousness shalt thou be established . . . whosoever shall gather together against thee shall fall for thy sake.[83]

'Abdu'l-Bahá has made it clear in a Tablet revealed in honour of one of the believers in the West that this chapter is about His mother, Ásíyih Khánum:

> As to thy question concerning the 54th chapter of Isaiah: This chapter refers to the Most Exalted Leaf, the mother of 'Abdu'l-Bahá. As a proof to this it is said: 'For more are the children of the desolate, than the children of the married wife.' Reflect upon this statement, and then upon the following: 'And thy seed shall inherit the Gentiles, and make the desolate cities to be inhabited.' And truly the humiliation and reproach which she suffered in the path of God is a fact which no one can refute. For the calamities and afflictions mentioned in the whole chapter are such afflictions which she suffered in the path of God, all of which she endured with patience and thanked God therefore and praised Him, because He had enabled her to endure afflictions for the sake of Bahá. During all this time, the men and women (Covenant-breakers) persecuted her in an incomparable manner, while she was patient, God-fearing, calm, humble and contented through the favour of her Lord and by the bounty of her Creator.[84]

In another Tablet, speaking of His mother, 'Abdu'l-Bahá says:

> In the *andarún* [inner section of the house] the leaves were occupied with the remembrance of God and the discussion of subjects related to the Cause. Thus was their time engaged. 'Abdu'l-Bahá's mother was day and night engaged in prayer and meditation. She made mention of God and spoke on themes and proofs related to His existence. The difference between Bahá'í women and others is that in the East women are either attending to the affairs of the house or engaged in the pleasures of this world. But Bahá'í women do what they must to look after life's affairs and occupy the remainder of their time exploring the realities and meanings of things.[85]

Ásíyih Khánum's Distinguishing Characteristics

According to her daughter Bahá'íyyih Khánum, Ásíyih Khánum was

> . . . tall, slender, graceful, eyes of dark blue – a pearl, a flower amongst women.
>
> I have been told that even when very young, her wisdom and intelligence were remarkable. I always think of her in those earliest days of my memory as queenly in her dignity and loveliness, full of consideration for

> everybody, gentle, of a marvellous unselfishness, no action of hers ever failed to show the loving-kindness of her pure heart; her very presence seemed to make an atmosphere of love and happiness wherever she came, enfolding all comers in the fragrance of gentle courtesy.[86]

Her granddaughter Ṭúbá Khánum has described her and her room in the House of 'Abbúd:

> Her tiny room was simple and bare – the narrow, white bed, which was also the divan in the daytime; a very small table, on which was her prayer and other holy books, her 'qalam-dán' (pen case), and leaflets for writing; there was also her rosary, sometimes a flower in a pot, and lastly an old painted box holding her other frock and her other under-garment . . .
>
> My eyes will always see her in her blue dress, with a white 'niqáb' on her head, and little black slippers on her tiny feet. Her sweet, smiling face, and her wrapt expression, as she chanted prayers in her musical voice.[87]

Ásíyih Khánum's Resting-Place

In December 1939, after the lapse of 53 years from the date of her passing, the Guardian of the Cause of God Shoghi Effendi, Ásíyih Khánum's great-grandson, transferred her remains and those of her son the Purest Branch to the slopes of Mount Carmel, despite strong opposition from the Covenant-breakers.[88] He announced the joyous news in his message of 5 December 1939 to the American National Spiritual Assembly:

> BLESSED REMAINS PUREST BRANCH AND MASTER'S MOTHER SAFELY TRANSFERRED HALLOWED PRECINCTS SHRINES MOUNT CARMEL. LONG INFLICTED HUMILIATION WIPED AWAY. MACHINATIONS COVENANT-BREAKERS FRUSTRATE PLAN DEFEATED. CHERISHED WISH GREATEST HOLY LEAF FULFILLED. SISTER BROTHER MOTHER WIFE 'ABDU'L-BAHÁ REUNITED ONE SPOT DESIGNED CONSTITUTE FOCAL CENTRE BAHÁ'Í ADMINISTRATIVE INSTITUTIONS AT FAITH'S WORLD CENTRE. SHARE JOYFUL NEWS ENTIRE BODY AMERICAN BELIEVERS.[89]

And in his message of 21 December 1939 he referred to the 'capital institutional significance' of the transfer of the 'sacred remains':

> The transfer of the sacred remains of the brother and mother of our Lord and Master 'Abdu'l-Bahá to Mount Carmel and their final interment within the hallowed precincts of the Shrine of the Báb, and in the immediate neighbourhood of the resting-place of the Greatest Holy Leaf,

> constitute, apart from their historic associations and the tender sentiments they arouse, events of such capital institutional significance as only future happenings, steadily and mysteriously unfolding at the world centre of our Faith, can adequately demonstrate.[90]

Amatu'l-Bahá Rúḥíyyih Khánum, who was an eyewitness, has recorded the details of the transfer of the remains of Ásíyih Khánum and Mírzá Mihdí in *The Priceless Pearl* and has explained the reason for the transfer:

> It had long been the desire of the Greatest Holy Leaf to lie near her mother, who was buried in Akka, as was her brother, Mihdí. But when Bahíyyih Khánum passed away in 1932 she had been befittingly interred on Mt Carmel near the Shrine of the Báb. Shoghi Effendi conceived the idea of transferring the remains of her mother and brother, so unsuitably buried in Akka, to the vicinity of her resting-place and in 1939 he ordered in Italy twin marble monuments, similar in style to the one he had erected over her own grave. Fortunately these reached Haifa safely in spite of the war. Far from being a simple procedure, 'the consummation of this long, this profoundly cherished hope' proved to be extremely difficult . . . [From her diary] 'Whilst their tombs were still in process of excavation from the solid rock of the mountain, the Guardian had learned that the Covenant-breakers were protesting against the right of the Bahá'ís to remove the mother and brother of 'Abdu'l-Bahá to new graves, actually having the temerity to represent to the government their so-called claim as relatives of the deceased. As soon, however, as the civil authorities had the true state of facts made clear to them – that these same relatives had been the arch-enemies of the Master and His family, had left the true Cause of Bahá'u'lláh to follow their own devices, and had been denounced by 'Abdu'l-Bahá in His *Will and Testament* – they approved the plan of the Guardian and immediately issued the necessary papers for the exhumation of the bodies. Without risking further delay Shoghi Effendi, two days later, himself removed the Purest Branch and his mother to Mount Carmel.'
>
> After daybreak, accompanied by a few Bahá'ís, Shoghi Effendi went to Akka, opened one grave after the other, and brought the remains to Haifa . . . When the earth was removed from the coffin of the Master's mother he discovered the wood was still intact,[91] except for the bottom which had rotted away, and so he instructed them to gently remove the top. He told me the figure of 'Abdu'l-Bahá's mother, wound in her shroud, lay there so clearly outlined that one could almost discern her features, but it collapsed in dust and bones at the first touch. He descended into the grave and

> with his own hands helped to place the skeleton in the new coffin prepared for it; this was then closed, loaded on a waiting vehicle, and they all proceeded to the second Arab cemetery where the Purest Branch was buried and there opened his grave. As he had been buried two decades longer than his mother, and the interment had been hastily carried out in the days when Bahá'u'lláh was so strictly confined in the prison barracks of Akka, the coffin had entirely disintegrated and Shoghi Effendi again gathered up himself the few bones and dust that remained and again placed them himself in the second coffin that lay beside the grave to receive them.[92]

The coffins were then brought to Haifa by car. Shoghi Effendi and a few trusted servants of the Cause bore the coffins over their shoulders and carried them from the street up to a building adjacent to the resting-place of Bahá'íyyih Khánum. The coffins were deposited in a room in this building for three weeks.

> And now, again on the shoulder of the Guardian, they are borne forth to lie in state in the Holy Tomb of the Báb. Side by side, far greater than the great of this world, they lie by that sacred threshold, facing Bahjí, with candles burning at their heads and flowers before their feet . . . The following sunset we gather once again in that Holy Shrine . . . Slowly, held aloft on the hands of the faithful, led by Shoghi Effendi, who never relinquished his precious burden . . . Once they circumambulate the Shrines, the coffin of beloved Mihdí, supported by the Guardian, followed by that of the Master's mother, passes us slowly by. Around the Shrine, onward through the lighted garden, down the white path, out onto the moonlit road, that solemn procession passes. High, seeming to move of themselves, above the heads of those following, the coffins wend their way . . . They pass before us, outlined against the night sky . . . They approach, the face of the Guardian close to that priceless burden he bears. They pass on toward the waiting vaults. Now they lay the Purest Branch to rest. Shoghi Effendi himself enters the carpeted vault and gently eases the coffin to its preordained place. He himself strews it with flowers, his hands the last to caress it. The mother of the Master is then placed in the same manner by the Guardian in the neighbouring vault . . . Masons are called to seal the tombs . . . Flowers are heaped upon the vaults and the Guardian sprinkles a vial of attar of rose upon them . . . And now the voice of Shoghi Effendi is raised as he chants those Tablets revealed by Bahá'u'lláh and destined by Him to be read at their graves.[93]

When the entombment of the remains was successfully accomplished, Shoghi Effendi sent the following cable on 26 December 1939:

> Christmas eve beloved remains Purest Branch and Master's mother laid in state Báb's Holy Tomb. Christmas day entrusted Carmel's sacred soil. Ceremony presence representatives Near Eastern believers profoundly moving. Impelled associate America's momentous Seven Year enterprise imperishable memory these two holy souls who next twin founders Faith and Perfect Exemplar tower together with Greatest Holy Leaf above entire concourse faithful.[94]

In the messages he sent in English on 21 December 1939 and in Persian on 25 December of the same year, Shoghi Effendi referred to the monumental significance of the transfer of the remains of the Purest Branch and his mother Ásíyih Khánum. In his letter to American believers he wrote:

> The swiftness and suddenness with which so delicate and weighty an undertaking was conducted; the surmounting of various obstacles which the outbreak of war and its inevitable repercussions necessarily engendered; the success of the long-drawn out negotiations which the solution of certain preliminary problems imposed; the execution of the plan in the face of the continued instability and persistent dangers following the fierce riots that so long and so violently rocked the Holy Land, and despite the smouldering fire of animosity kindled in the breasts of ecclesiastics and Covenant-breakers alike – all combined to demonstrate, afresh and with compelling power, the invincible might of the Cause of Bahá'u'lláh.
>
> . . . Avenged, eternally safeguarded, befittingly glorified, they repose embosomed in the heart of Carmel, hidden beneath its sacred soil, interred in one single spot, lying beneath the shadow of the twin holy Tombs, and facing across the bay, on an eminence of unequalled loveliness and beauty, the silver-city of 'Akká, the Point of Adoration of the entire Bahá'í world, and the Door of Hope for all mankind. 'Haste thee, O Carmel!' thus proclaims the Pen of Bahá'u'lláh, 'for lo, the light of the countenance of God, the Ruler of the Kingdom of Names and Fashioner of the heavens, hath been lifted upon thee.' 'Rejoice, for God hath in this Day established upon thee His throne, hath made thee the dawning-place of His signs and the day-spring of the evidences of His Revelation.'[95]

And in Persian he said:

> O loved ones of God. These two precious and most exalted treasures, these two keepsakes of the sacred Beauty of Abhá, have now been joined to the third trust from Him, that is, to the daughter of Bahá and His remnant, the token of the Master's remembrance.

> Their resting-places are in one area, on an elevation close by the Spot round which do circle the Concourse on High, and facing the Qiblih of the people of Bahá – 'Akká, the resplendent city, and the sanctified, the luminous, the Most Holy Shrine.
>
> . . . For joy, the Hill of God is stirred at so high an honour, and for this most great bestowal the mountain of the Lord is in rapture and ecstasy.[96]

Shoghi Effendi then linked this remarkable event to the following excerpt in the Tablet of Carmel revealed by Bahá'u'lláh:

> These exalted words have been recorded in the Tablet of Carmel: '. . . Well is it with him that circleth around thee, that proclaimeth the revelation of thy glory, and recounteth that which the bounty of the Lord thy God hath showered upon thee . . .'[97]

In connection with the same theme he wrote:

> The conjunction of these three resting-places, under the shadow of the Báb's own Tomb, embosomed in the heart of Carmel, facing the snow-white city across the bay of 'Akká, the Qiblih of the Bahá'í world, set in a garden of exquisite beauty, reinforces, if we would correctly estimate its significance, the spiritual potencies of a spot, designated by Bahá'u'lláh Himself the seat of God's throne.[98]

Reviewing the achievements of the first Bahá'í century in his message of Naw-Rúz 101 BE addressed to the Bahá'ís of the East, Shoghi Effendi says that with the transfer of the remains of Ásíyih Khánum and the Purest Branch to the vicinity of the Shrine of the Báb and in close proximity of the resting-place of the Greatest Holy Leaf, the first step towards the establishment of the World Administrative Centre of the Bahá'í Faith according to what had been revealed by the Pen of the Most High in the Tablet of Carmel was implemented.[99] This statement makes the link between the transfer of the remains to Mount Carmel and the contents of the Tablet of Carmel, the charter for the development of the Bahá'í World Centre, very clear.

The Focal Point of the World Administrative Centre of the Future Bahá'í Commonwealth

Shoghi Effendi had an all-embracing and glorious vision. To translate his far-reaching vision to reality, he knew the milestones that had to be reached and the impetus needed to meet the challenge. He conveyed his vision and the means to achieve it through his illuminating and inspiring messages.

Soon after the remains of Ásíyih Khánum and her martyred son had been 're-interred under the shadow of the Báb's holy Shrine',[100] he wrote in his message of 30 December 1939 of the 'association of the First Mashriqu'l-Adhkár of the West with the hallowed memories of the Purest Branch and of 'Abdu'l-Bahá's mother' and of the inauguration of 'a new, and at long last the final phase of an enterprise which, thirty years ago, was providentially launched on the very day the remains of the Forerunner of our Faith were laid to rest by our beloved Master in the sepulchre specifically erected for that purpose on Mount Carmel'.[101] Returning to the theme of the transfer of the remains of the Purest Branch and his mother, he wrote:

> And now, while the Bahá'í world vibrates with emotion at the news of the transfer of the precious remains of both the Purest Branch and of 'Abdu'l-Bahá's mother to a spot which, watched over by the Twin Holy Shrines and in the close neighbourhood of the resting-place of the Greatest Holy Leaf, is to become the focus of the administrative institutions of the Faith at its world centre, the mere act of linking the destiny of so far-reaching an undertaking with so significant an event in the Formative Period of our Faith will assuredly set the seal of complete triumph upon, and enhance the spiritual potentialities of, a work so significantly started and so magnificently executed by the followers of Bahá'u'lláh in the North American continent.[102]

By choosing a specific spot on an elevation on Mount Carmel to serve as the ground for the permanent resting-places of 'Abdu'l-Bahá's sister, brother and mother, Shoghi Effendi was laying the foundation for the realization of a glorious vision several decades later. He was creating the axis of the Arc around which buildings housing the institutions of the world administrative centre of the future Bahá'í Commonwealth were to be constructed. Referring to the enterprise, he wrote:

> It marks, too, a further milestone in the road leading eventually to the establishment of that permanent world Administrative Centre of the future Bahá'í Commonwealth, destined never to be separated from, and to function in the proximity of, the Spiritual Centre of that Faith, in a land already revered and held sacred alike by the adherents of three of the world's outstanding religious systems.[103]

In his message to the Bahá'ís of the West he emphasized the theme:

> . . . the conjunction of the resting-place of the Greatest Holy Leaf with those of her brother and mother incalculably reinforces the spiritual potencies of that consecrated Spot which, under the wings of the Báb's over-shadowing Sepulchre, and in the vicinity of the future Mashriqu'l-Adhkár, which will be reared on its flank, is destined to evolve into the focal centre of those world-shaking, world-embracing, world-directing administrative institutions, ordained by Bahá'u'lláh and anticipated by 'Abdu'l-Bahá, and which are to function in consonance with the principles that govern the twin institutions of the Guardianship and the Universal House of Justice. Then, and then only, will this momentous prophecy which illuminates the concluding passage of the Tablet of Carmel be fulfilled: 'Ere long will God sail His Ark upon thee (Carmel), and will manifest the people of Bahá who have been mentioned in the Book of Names.'
>
> . . . the association of these three incomparably precious souls who, next to the three Central Figures of our Faith, tower in rank above the vast multitude of the heroes, letters, martyrs, hands, teachers and administrators of the Cause of Bahá'u'lláh, in such a potentially powerful spiritual and administrative Centre, is in itself an event which will release forces that are bound to hasten the emergence in a land which, geographically, spiritually and administratively, constitutes the heart of the entire planet, of some of the brightest gems of that World Order now shaping in the womb of this travailing age.[104]

Shoghi Effendi's master plan made it possible for the resting-places of the faithful and close relatives of the Founder of the Faith and of the Centre of His Covenant to be established in one spot on God's holy mountain. It is significant that three of the four buried in this area of the mountain are women, one of them being Ásíyih Khánum, the wife of the founder Himself, an honour unique in the annals of religion. The Monument Gardens are visited by 'such as . . . undertake . . . the meritorious and highly enviable pilgrimage' to the 'blessed shrines'.[105] To make it possible for those unable to come on pilgrimage who are 'aware of the greatness of their virtue and the pre-eminence of their lineage' who 'desire to commune with their spirits, and to strive to acquire an added insight into the glory of their position, and to follow in their footsteps', Shoghi Effendi provided to the believers the translation of 'testimonies written by Bahá'u'lláh and 'Abdu'l-Bahá' for 'their inspiration and guidance in their noble quest'.[106] This is indeed unique in the annals of religion.

7

Bahá'íyyih Khánum, the Most Outstanding Heroine of the Bahá'í Dispensation

Family Background

Bahá'íyyih Khánum was born to Mírzá Ḥusayn-'Alí, later known as Bahá'u'lláh, and Ásíyih Khánum, titled Navváb and the Most Exalted Leaf. Bahá'u'lláh and Navváb came from prominent families in the district of Núr in Mázandarán, Iran. Bahá'u'lláh's father, Mírzá 'Abbás-i-Núrí, entitled Mírzá Buzurg, was a celebrated calligrapher. Both he and Ásíyih Khánum's father, Mírzá Ismá'íl-i-Yálrúdí, held high-ranking positions in the government and were known as viziers. Almost nothing is known about Ásíyih Khánum's mother. For information about Bahá'u'lláh's mother, see the chapter on Khadíjih Khánum.

Four sons of Bahá'u'lláh and Ásíyih Khánum died in infancy and childhood. Two of them, Káẓim and Mihdí, were probably dead before Bahá'íyyih Khánum was born. Of the other two, one lived to be several years old. His name was 'Alí-Muḥammad. 'Abdu'l-Bahá speaks of him as a very clever, friendly and sociable child. The other, also named 'Alí-Muḥammad, died in Baghdád in 1854. He was then about one year old. Bahá'íyyih Khánum's surviving brothers were Mírzá 'Abbás and Mírzá Mihdí. Mírzá 'Abbás, later known as 'Abdu'l-Bahá, was about three years older than Bahá'íyyih Khánum; Mírzá Mihdí, entitled the Purest Branch, was about three years younger. He died at the age of 22 when he fell through an unguarded skylight in the roof of a section of the army barracks in 'Akká, where Bahá'u'lláh and His family were imprisoned for two years.

Birth, Childhood and Early Life

Shoghi Effendi gives 1846 as the year of Bahá'íyyih Khánum's birth. When exactly during that year she was born is uncertain but she was born in Ṭihrán. The name given her at birth was Fáṭimih. Later, Bahá'u'lláh bestowed upon her the feminine form of His appellation 'Bahá', meaning glory. Confirming this in a Tablet revealed in her honour, He says: 'She hath revealed herself in

My name and tasted of the sweet savours of My holy, My wondrous pleasure.'[1] The full text of that Tablet is inscribed in golden letters around the base of the circular dome of her monument. She sealed the letters that she wrote to Bahá'í institutions and individuals with a seal bearing the name Bahá'íyyih. The seal is on display in the International Archives Building. Bahá'u'lláh also bestowed upon her, after her mother passed away, the title of Greatest Holy Leaf. Bahá'íyyih Khánum is the name used predominantly throughout this account.

We have considerable information in English about Bahá'íyyih Khánum's early life which is owed to Madam Canavarro, who interviewed her in December 1902. The information she obtained through a translator was recorded and passed on to Myron Phelps for his book *Life and Teachings of Abbas Effendi,* published in 1903. Another source, widely quoted in this chapter and in the chapter on Ásíyih Khánum, is *The Chosen Highway* by Lady Blomfield, who spoke with Bahá'íyyih Khánum many years later through a translator, who was one of the younger daughters of 'Abdu'l-Bahá, and recorded her recollections. The writings of Bahá'u'lláh and 'Abdu'l-Bahá revealed in Bahá'íyyih Khánum's honour and the tributes of Shoghi Effendi contain valuable insights into different stages of her life. Bahá'íyyih Khánum spoke to Lady Blomfield about her childhood memories:

> I remember dimly very happy days with my beloved father and mother, and my brother 'Abbás, who was two years my senior . . .
>
> We used to go to our house in the country sometimes; my brother 'Abbás and I loved to play in the beautiful gardens, where grew many kinds of wonderful fruits and flowers and flowering trees; but this part of my early life is a very dim memory.[2]

She remembers her beloved Father being arrested after an attempt on the life of the Sháh 'by a half-crazy young Bábí'.[3] When the assassination attempt took place, Bahá'u'lláh was 'temporarily in the country'; Bahá'íyyih Khánum, then five years old, her older brother, eight, her baby brother and their mother were in Ṭihrán. Her mother learned of the horrifying news from a servant who was with Bahá'u'lláh when He was arrested.[4] Bahá'u'lláh was subsequently imprisoned in the Síyáh Chál (Black Pit) of Ṭihrán. On hearing the news of His arrest, Bahá'íyyih Khánum witnessed her mother's face grow whiter and whiter. Speaking of her own reaction, she says, 'We children were terribly frightened and could only weep bitterly.'[5] She also witnessed the effect of that event on their relatives, friends and servants who, she says, all fled in terror, 'only one man-servant, Isfandíyár, remained, and one woman'.[6] She explains that their 'palace, and the smaller houses belonging to it were very soon stripped of everything; furniture, treasures, all were stolen by the people'.[7] Referring to that incident, 'Abdu'l-Bahá says: 'In Ṭihrán, we possessed everything at a nightfall, and on the morrow we were shorn of it all, to the extent that we had no food to eat.'[8] Of that episode in Bahá'íyyih Khánum's life, Shoghi Effendi says:

> How well I remember her recall, at a time when her faculties were still unimpaired, the gnawing suspense that ate into the hearts of those who watched by her side, at the threshold of her pillaged house, expectant to hear at any moment the news of Bahá'u'lláh's imminent execution! In those sinister hours, she often recounted, her parents had so suddenly lost their possessions that within the space of a single day from being the privileged member of one of the wealthiest families of Ṭihrán she had sunk to the state of a sufferer from unconcealed poverty. Deprived of the means of subsistence her illustrious mother, the famed Navváb, was constrained to place in the palm of her daughter's hand a handful of flour and to induce her to accept it as a substitute for her daily bread.[9]

Bahá'íyyih Khánum spoke to Lady Blomfield about the destitution of her precious mother and how Mírzá Músá, Bahá'u'lláh's brother, who was always very kind to them, helped her mother and her three children to escape into hiding.[10] She related how her mother cared for her children and how with the sale of 'some few of the marriage treasures, which were all of our vast possessions left to us', she 'was able to pay the gaolers to take food to my father in the prison, and to meet other expenses incurred later on'.[11]

Even in her old age Bahá'íyyih Khánum could still recall the horrible sounds she heard at five when, every day, some of those imprisoned with Bahá'u'lláh were removed from the prison to be tortured to the shouts of the crowd and the beating of drums.[12] Her mother could not find out what had happened to her husband and so, despite the danger to herself, she ventured out late at night or very early in the morning to seek news.[13] Bahá'íyyih Khánum describes her own feelings during those dark hours of uncertainty:

> How well I remember cowering in the dark, with my little brother, Mírzá Mihdí, the Purest Branch, at that time two years old, in my arms, which were not very strong, as I was only six. I was shivering with terror, for I knew of some of the horrible things that were happening, and was aware that they might have seized even my mother.
>
> So I waited and waited until she should come back. Then Mírzá Músá, my uncle, who was in hiding, would venture in to hear what tidings my mother had been able to gather.

My brother 'Abbás usually went with her on these sorrowful errands.[14]

Timely action taken by Mírzá Yúsuf, a Russian subject married to Bahá'íyyih Khánum's great aunt and a friend of the Russian Consul in Ṭihrán, who addressed the court fearlessly threatening to avenge any wrong inflicted upon Bahá'u'lláh as a consequence of its decision, averted the passing of a death sentence on Him and forced the governor to give orders that He 'should be permitted to come forth from that prison with his life. It was also decreed that he and his family were banished.'[15] Bahá'u'lláh confirms the intervention of the Russian Consul in a Tablet revealed in honour of Tsar Alexander II, which says: 'Whilst I lay, chained and fettered, in the prison of Ṭihrán, one of thy ministers extended Me his aid.'[16]

Recalling the feelings of joy evoked by the receipt of the wonderful news of Bahá'u'lláh's imminent release from prison, Bahá'íyyih Khánum says:

> An account of this scene was given to my mother by Mírzá Yúsif that night, and told by her to my uncle, Mírzá Músá, when he came for tidings.
>
> Needless to say how eagerly my brother and I listened, and how we all wept for joy.[17]

Upon His release from prison, Bahá'u'lláh went to live in the two little rooms that Ásíyih Khánum had rented after their own house had been pillaged and its belongings plundered. The joy of His presence was beyond description, yet so was the sadness they felt for the sufferings He had endured. Although Bahá'u'lláh 'spoke very little of the terrible sufferings of that time', the children 'saw the marks . . . where the chains had cut into the delicate skin, especially that of his neck, his wounded feet so long untended, evidence of the torture of the bastinado' and they wept with their mother.[18]

Ásíyih Khánum and the children heard of 'the steadfast faith of the friends, who had gone forth to meet their death at the hands of their torturers, with joy and gladness, to attain the crown of martyrdom'.[19] They also heard that 'Jamál-i-Mubárak [Bahá'u'lláh] had a marvellous divine experience whilst in that prison'. They 'saw a new radiance seeming to enfold him like a shining vesture', the significance of which, Bahá'íyyih Khánum says, 'we were to learn years later. At that time we were only aware of the wonder of it, without understanding, or even being told the details of the sacred event.'[20] She speaks of the great difficulty facing her mother who did her best to nurse Bahá'u'lláh 'that he might have some strength to set out upon that journey'.[21] At the same time she had to make preparations for the 'terrible journey' and ensure the safety and well-being of her three children.

Bahá'íyyih Khánum recalls the hour of departure from Ṭihrán: 'No one of all our friends and relations', she says, 'dared to come to our help, or even to say good-bye, but one old lady' whom she identifies as her great grandmother (the grandmother of her mother).[22] She also speaks affectionately of their 'faithful servant, Isfandíyár, and the one negro woman'[23] who stayed with them.

What affected Bahá'íyyih Khánum's tender heart the most was separation from her younger brother, Mírzá Mihdí, who was left behind. She speaks of his being 'very delicate' and says 'my mother allowed herself to be persuaded to leave the little fellow, only two years old, with her grandmother, though the parting with him was very sad'.[24]

Describing the early stage of Bahá'íyyih Khánum's life and the suffering she endured as a child, Shoghi Effendi says:

> From the beginning of her life, from her very childhood, she tasted sorrow's cup; she drank down the afflictions and calamities of the earliest years of the great Cause of God. In the tumult of the Year of Ḥín [1268 AH/1851–2 AD] as a result of the sacking and plundering of her glorious Father's wealth and holdings, she learned the bitterness of destitution and want. Then she shared the imprisonment, the grief, the banishment of the Abhá Beauty.[25]

Also,

> As far back as the concluding stage of the heroic age of the Cause, which witnessed the imprisonment of Bahá'u'lláh in the Síyáh-Chál of Ṭihrán, the Greatest Holy Leaf, then still in her infancy, was privileged to taste of the cup of woe which the first believers of that Apostolic Age had quaffed.[26]

Shoghi Effendi confirms without the slightest trace of hesitation that Bahá'íyyih Khánum shared from childhood the suffering and hardships of Bahá'u'lláh and 'Abdu'l-Bahá:

> From early childhood she had her share of the sufferings of Bahá'u'lláh, subjected even as He was to hardships and calamities, and she was as well the partner in sorrows and tribulations of 'Abdu'l-Bahá.[27]

Bahá'íyyih Khánum was six when she accompanied her beloved parents on the arduous journey from Ṭihrán to Baghdád. Until then the only trips she had taken were from Ṭihrán to Tákur and Yalrúd, where members of her family on both her father's and mother's sides lived. Those were happy travels, for the joy of seeing her relatives and spending the summer months in the cool surroundings of those small towns in the mountains was immense. The journey that they were now embarking on was very different, a 'fearful journey': 'the weather was bitterly cold, snow was upon the ground . . . the cold was intense' and they 'were not well prepared'.[28]

The journey from Ṭihrán to Baghdád was by mule or on horseback. The women travelled on what Bahá'íyyih Khánum calls 'takht-i-raván' (a palanquin) 'borne on a jolting mule'.[29] Recalling that journey, Bahá'íyyih Khánum says,

> It was bitterly cold, and the route lay over mountains . . . My father was very ill. The chains had left his neck galled, raw, and much swollen. My mother, who was pregnant, was unaccustomed to hardships, and was worried and harassed over our recent trials and the uncertainty of our fate . . . We were all insufficiently clothed, and suffered keenly from exposure.[30]

When they came to a city, they visited the public bath where they could also wash their clothes. They 'sometimes stayed in a caravanserai – a sort of rough inn. Only one room was allowed for one family, and for one night – no longer. No light was permitted at night, and there were no beds.'[31] Bahá'íyyih Khánum says: 'Sometimes we were able to have tea, or again a few eggs, a little cheese, and some coarse bread.'[32]

When the exiles, escorted by Iranian soldiers, reached the border of Iraq, then within the Ottoman domain, they were met by Turkish soldiers and escorted to Baghdád.

Life in Baghdád (April 1853 to April 1863)

Bahá'u'lláh, His family and companions arrived in Baghdád on 8 April 1853 'in a state of great misery, and also of almost utter destitution'. The few personal effects that Bahá'íyyih Khánum's mother had collected before departure 'were nearly exhausted by the time we reached our destination, having been bartered on the journey for necessaries'.[33] In Baghdád, Bahá'íyyih Khánum spent the remaining years of her childhood and the early years of adulthood. As difficult as the decade-long stay in Baghdád was for the family, for her it was even harder. Describing the first place where they lived in Baghdád, she says: 'When we first arrived there, we had a very little house, consisting of my father's room, and another one which was my mother's, and in which were also my eldest brother, the baby,[34] and myself.'[35] The same room served also as a reception room for female visitors. Bahá'íyyih Khánum was very conscious of her beloved mother's delicate health, caused by the hardships she had endured, and was concerned that 'she always worked beyond her force'.[36] Therefore, from early childhood Bahá'íyyih Khánum helped with household chores. Regarding the initial stage of their stay in Baghdád, Bahá'íyyih Khánum says:

> . . . we struggled through this period as bravely as we could, until, after a time, occasional remittances came to us from Tehran, the proceeds of personal effects – jewels, cloth of gold, and other valuable articles which were a part of my mother's dowry – which had been left there to be sold. This money ameliorated our condition to a considerable extent.[37]

As soon as the rigours of life in exile eased somewhat, a problem with far-reaching consequences arose, adding tremendously to the weight of woes sustained by the Holy Family, especially Bahá'íyyih Khánum. That problem was the arrival of an uninvited, arrogant and self-centred guest. Mírzá Yaḥyá Azal, 13 years younger than Bahá'u'lláh, was His half brother, 'over whom' He 'watched for successive years, and who, day and night, served in [His] presence, until he was made to err by one of [his] servants, named Siyyid Muḥammad'.[38] After the attempt on the life of Náṣiri'd-Dín Sháh, Mírzá Yaḥyá fled to Mázandarán, where he lived in disguise for some time. When Bahá'u'lláh and His family arrived in Baghdád, Mírzá Yaḥyá left Iran as a fugitive and went to Iraq disguised as a dervish. There he joined Bahá'u'lláh's family and lived in their house as a guest. Recalling the problems caused by Mírzá Yaḥyá, Bahá'íyyih Khánum says:

> When he arrived at Baghdád he much resented the attitude of reverence shown by all the friends to his majestic elder brother. He claimed the leadership of the Bábís, asserting that His Holiness the Báb had named him His successor . . .
>
> When Ṣubḥ-i-Azal[39] arrived in Baghdád he tried to get the friends to acknowledge him as their leader. They paid scant attention to him, and just laughed at his haughty airs.
>
> He asserted that Jamál-i-Mubárak (Bahá'u'lláh) was preventing the acknowledgement of his position by the people.[40]

To provide Mírzá Yaḥyá with the opportunity to prove himself as the leader he longed to be, Bahá'u'lláh withdrew from Baghdád and lived in seclusion in the mountains of Sulaymáníyyih in Kurdistán for two years. Before leaving Baghdád in 1854, 'he commanded the friends to treat Ṣubḥ-i-Azal with consideration. He offered him and his family the shelter and hospitality of our house,' says Bahá'iyyih Khánum.[41]

Bahá'u'lláh's departure, so soon after His arrival in Baghdád, was most difficult to bear for His family and companions. Describing the emotions surging in their hearts, Bahá'íyyih Khánum says:

> Our grief was intense when my father left us. He told none of us either where he was going or when he would return. He took no luggage, only a little rice, and some coarse bread.
>
> So, we, my mother, my brother 'Abbás and I, clung together in our sorrow and anxiety.[42]

Not only did Bahá'íyyih Khánum endure the pain of separation from her beloved father, she was also deeply affected by the restrictions Mírzá Yaḥyá inflicted upon her. The fear of being discovered prompted him to impose intolerable regulations on the members of Bahá'u'lláh's family. One of his cruel acts was to prevent Bahá'íyyih Khánum from stepping out of the house and associating with other children. Describing his attitude during this time, Bahá'íyyih Khánum says:

> He became at this time more than ever terrified lest he should one day be arrested. He hid himself, keeping the door of our house locked, and stormed at anybody who opened it.
>
> As for me, I led a very lonely life, and would have liked sometimes to make friends with other children. But Ṣubḥ-i-Azal would not permit any little friends to come to the house, neither would he let me go out!
>
> Two little girls about my own age lived in the next house. I used to peep at them; but our guest always came and shouted at me for opening the door, which he promptly locked. He was always in fear of being arrested, and cared for nothing but his own safety.
>
> We led a very difficult life at this time as well as a lonely one. He would not even allow us to go to the Hammám to take our baths. Nobody was permitted to come to the house to help us, and the work therefore was very hard.[43]

One of Bahá'íyyih Khánum's daily arduous tasks was to draw water from a deep well for domestic use. Before plumbing was introduced, wells constituted an essential part of every house. To obtain water, someone had to stand at the edge of the well, lower into it a bucket attached to a long rope, hold it down and manoeuvre the bucket until it was full of water, then pull it up. Buckets were usually made of metal or rubber. Apart from being arduous, the task of drawing water was fraught with danger, especially if effective safeguards were not in place to protect the person who drew water, which was usually the case.

Regarding this aspect of her daily chores, Bahá'íyyih Khánum recalls:

> For hours every day I had to stand drawing water from a deep well in the house; the ropes were hard and rough, and the bucket was heavy. My dear mother used to help, but she was not very strong, and my arms were rather weak. Our guest never helped.[44]

The family tolerated the demands made by Mírzá Yaḥyá because Bahá'u'lláh had requested them to do so. He had told His family 'to respect and obey this tyrannical person', and, Bahá'íyyih Khánum says,'we tried to do so, but this respect was not easy, as our lives were made so unhappy by him'.[45] Bahá'u'lláh had instructed His family to respect and obey Mírzá Yaḥyá not so much because of the man himself but out of respect for the Báb, whose nominee he was.

Bahá'u'lláh and Ásíyih Khánum's son, 'Alí-Muḥammad, who was born soon after their arrival in Baghdád, died while Bahá'u'lláh was in Kurdistán. Bahá'íyyih Khánum describes the circumstances of his death and burial:

> During this time the darling baby brother, born after our arrival in Baghdád, became seriously ill. Our guest would not allow a doctor, or even any neighbour to come to our help.
>
> My mother was heart-broken when the little one died; even then we were not allowed to have anybody to prepare him for burial.
>
> The sweet body of our beautiful baby was given to a man, who took it away, and we never knew even where he was laid.
>
> I remember so clearly the sorrow of those days.[46]

Mírzá Yaḥyá's erratic behaviour continued until Bahá'u'lláh's family moved to a larger house. At that point Mírzá Yaḥyá, to avoid being seen, decided to live with his family in a little house situated behind theirs. However, he continued to depend on the hospitality of Bahá'u'lláh's family, which sent him and his family food. When Mírzá Yaḥyá no longer lived amidst Bahá'u'lláh's family, they gave a sigh of relief and focussed on finding out Bahá'u'lláh's whereabouts. Bahá'íyyih Khánum explains the efforts made by her mother, her brother and her uncle, Mírzá Músá, describing how they made 'every possible inquiry', how her brother on one occasion prayed 'the whole night a certain prayer with the one intention, that our father might be restored to us', and how the very next day they obtained a clue about Bahá'u'lláh's whereabouts and sent an emissary to entreat Him to return to Baghdád.[47] She also expresses the immense joy they felt when the tree of their ardent prayers and hope yielded the fruit of reunion with their Best Beloved.

> At last! At last! As my mother, my brother, and I sat in a breathless state of expectancy, we heard a step. It was a dervish. Through the disguise we saw the light of our beloved one's presence!
>
> Our joy cannot be described as we clung to him.
>
> I can see now my beloved mother, calm and gentle, and my brother holding His father's hand fast, as though never again could he let him go out of his sight, the lovely boy almost enfolded in the uncouth garment of the dervish disguise. I could never forget this scene, so touching and so happy.[48]

When, after two years, Bahá'u'lláh returned from Sulaymáníyyih, Bahá'íyyih Khánum was about nine years old. In Islam nine is the age of maturity for girls, and she was living in a Muslim state. Thus, her childhood years were by then behind her. The decade-long stay in Baghdád was a crucial period in her development. It was during this decade that amidst intense suffering she crossed the threshold of childhood and became an adult. As the eldest daughter of the family, she bore ever-increasing responsibilities on her tender shoulders. Being responsible and conscientious made her a perfect candidate for carrying out missions of great importance.

Bahá'íyyih Khánum's time was so fully occupied with carrying out various household tasks and helping her beloved parents during their years in Baghdád that she had no time for other activities, such as receiving tuition in the arts of reading and writing, as a conversation she had with Lady Blomfield, the author of *The Chosen Highway,* explains:

> 'My mother,' she said, 'sometimes gave lessons to my brother 'Abbás; at other times Mírzá Músá would teach Him, and on some occasions he would be taught by His father.'
>
> 'And *your* lessons?' I asked.
>
> 'But I never had any time for studies,' she said, in a tone which spoke volumes of absolute self-effacement, and this is the keynote of her whole life, no thought of her unselfishness entered her mind.[49]

Lady Blomfield comments:

> During the period of the sojourn in Baghdád, Bahíyyih Khánum, the Greatest Holy Leaf, was her mother's loving helper, working always beyond her strength, in the various household tasks. No childish pleasures or companions were hers. Always with eyes on her mother, alert to spare her any fatigue, she rejoiced beyond measure when she could minister in any way to her or her illustrious father.[50]

The deprivations that Bahá'íyyih Khánum suffered and the hardships that she endured played an important role in forming her distinct personality and character. After coming of age, she exercised the freedom to decide and chose to remain unmarried in order to devote her whole life to serving her beloved parents, the Cause of God and humankind. Lady Blomfield relates: 'As she grew up, she implored her father to allow her to remain unmarried, that she might the better devote herself to her three dearly loved ones. And so it was.'[51] She also quotes an old man to whom Bahá'u'lláh had said: 'I know no man worthy to marry such purity as my daughter.' She asked the man: 'Khánum *must* have been very lovely?' The man had answered, 'I have been told so; naturally, I never saw her.'[52]

Shoghi Effendi describes Bahá'íyyih Khánum's life in the Baghdád period:

> . . . she shared the imprisonment, the grief, the banishment of the Abhá Beauty, and in the storm which broke out in 'Íráq – because of the plotting and the treachery of the prime mover of mischief, the focal centre of hate – she bore, with complete resignation and acquiescence, uncounted ordeals. She forgot herself, did without her kin, turned aside from possessions, struck off at one blow the bonds of every worldly concern; and then, like a lovelorn moth, she circled day and night about the flame of the matchless Beauty of her Lord.[53]
>
> And when at a later time this revered and precious member of the Holy Family, then in her teens, came to be entrusted by the guiding hand of her Father with missions that no girl of her age could, or would be willing to, perform, with what spontaneous joy she seized her opportunity and acquitted herself of the task with which she had been entrusted! The delicacy and extreme gravity of such functions as she, from time to time, was called upon to fulfil, when the city of Baghdád was swept by the hurricane which the heedlessness and perversity of Mírzá Yaḥyá had unchained, as well as the tender solicitude which, at so early an age, she evinced during the period of Bahá'u'lláh's enforced retirement to the mountains of Sulaymáníyyih, marked her as one who was both capable of sharing the burden, and willing to make the sacrifice, which her high birth demanded.[54]

Departure from Baghdád, Journey to and Short Stay in Istanbul

Bahá'u'lláh's exile to Baghdád failed to extinguish the light of His fame. On the contrary, it gained in intensity, attracting many Persians in Iran and

Iraq. Many travelled to Baghdád to attain His presence. The inhabitants of the city were also fascinated by His majesty and desired to learn more about Him. Among them were prominent people and those who held positions of authority. This situation could not be tolerated by the mullás and the fanatic elements in the Persian government. They attempted to have Bahá'u'lláh and His followers sent back to Iran. That attempt failed, for by then many of the exiles had applied for and been granted Ottoman citizenship. The next course of action for the Iranian government was to bring pressure to bear on the Turkish central government to exile Bahá'u'lláh to lands farther away from Iran. That request was entertained and, as Shoghi Effendi describes, it fell on the Governor of Baghdád to convey the decree to Bahá'u'lláh:

> . . . the Deputy-Governor . . . delivered to Bahá'u'lláh in a mosque, in the neighbourhood of the governor's house, 'Álí Páshá's letter,[55] addressed to Námiq Páshá,[56] couched in courteous language, inviting Bahá'u'lláh to proceed, as a guest of the Ottoman government, to Constantinople, placing a sum of money at His disposal, and ordering a mounted escort to accompany Him for His protection. To this request Bahá'u'lláh gave His ready assent, but declined to accept the sum offered Him. On the urgent representations of the Deputy that such a refusal would offend the authorities, He reluctantly consented to receive the generous allowance set aside for His use, and distributed it, that same day, among the poor.[57]

During the ten-year stay in Baghdád, Bahá'u'lláh's family had grown and the number of His companions increased. Therefore it was not easy 'to make preparation for a journey, [they] knew not how long, to a place [they] knew not where'.[58] The suddenness of the decree, the shortness of time they were given to prepare and uncertainties involved caused consternation among the friends. 'There was such turmoil that we could not proceed with our preparations,' says Bahá'íyyih Khánum.[59]

> At this juncture Najíb Páshá, who had become a reverent admirer of Bahá'u'lláh, invited him to bring some of the friends, and come to stay in his garden, a short distance outside Baghdád.
>
> This relieved some of the turmoil, and we worked hard to make ready for the departure.[60]

According to Shoghi Effendi, 'on a Wednesday afternoon (April 22, 1863), thirty-one days after Naw-Rúz, on the third of Dhi'l-Qa'dih, 1279 AH' Bahá'u'lláh 'set forth on the first stage of His four months' journey to the capital of the Ottoman Empire'.[61] On that day, He left 'for the last time, amidst weeping and lamentation, His "Most Holy Habitation" . . . reached the banks of the river, and was ferried across, accompanied by His sons and amanuensis, to the Najíbíyyih Garden, situated on the opposite shore'.[62]

Bahá'u'lláh's arrival in the Najíbíyyih Garden 'signalizes the commencement of what has come to be recognized as the holiest and most significant of all Bahá'í festivals, the festival commemorating the Declaration of His Mission to His companions'.[63] Bahá'u'lláh's family could not join Him for nine days because, it is believed, the overflow of the river made crossing by ferry impossible. 'Abdu'l-Bahá, after accompanying Bahá'u'lláh to the Najíbíyyih Garden, seems to have returned to Baghdád to help the family prepare for the journey; He and the family are believed to have arrived there on the ninth day. On the twelfth day Bahá'u'lláh, accompanied by His family and companions, left for Istanbul:

> The departure of Bahá'u'lláh from the Garden of Riḍván, at noon, on the 14th of Dhi'l-Qa'dih 1279 AH (May 3, 1863), witnessed scenes of tumultuous enthusiasm no less spectacular, and even more touching, than those which greeted Him when leaving His Most Great House in Baghdád.[64]

The journey took three and half months to complete:

> On May 3rd 1863, the exiles set out on their long journey to the capital of the Ottoman Empire . . . It took them one hundred and ten days to reach the port of Sámsún on the Black Sea, where they embarked for Constantinople, and arrived at the metropolis of the Ottoman Empire on August 16th 1863.[65]

Baghdád was the city that Bahá'íyyih Khánum had known since she was about seven years old and it held fond memories of her childhood and early youth. Now she was leaving that city and the people she had come to know there, never to return to it again. The family was going to another unfamiliar place, facing an unknown destiny. She had to cope with the rigours of over one hundred days of travel involving long hours sitting with one or two other women in a litter placed on the back of a mule. What impression did the long and arduous journey leave on her? We will never know, as Bahá'íyyih Khánum did not speak of herself unless specifically asked and she does not seem to have been asked about that experience. There are reasons for this lack of knowledge. Bahá'u'lláh was the focus of the life of the exiles and all accounts revolve around Him. Those who put pen to paper giving eyewitness accounts of the journey did not meet with women. If they did, the encounter was short, not lending itself to a discussion of serious matters. So nothing is known of the women's experience of that journey. What we do know is that whatever happened to Bahá'u'lláh affected them deeply.

With Bahá'u'lláh's arrival in Constantinople 'the grimmest and most calamitous and yet the most glorious chapter in the history of the first Bahá'í century may be said to have opened. A period in which untold privations and unprecedented trials were mingled with the noblest spiritual triumphs was now commencing.'[66]

Upon their arrival in Constantinople, which was 'the capital of the Ottoman Empire and the seat of the Caliphate',[67] Bahá'u'lláh, His family and companions, about 70 of them, were taken to an inn where a small space was allotted to them. 'The Master asked the Governor to let Bahá'u'lláh and His family have a house apart', Bahá'íyyih Khánum relates. 'The house was given, but Ṣubḥ-i-Azal and his family were invited by my father to share this house with us.'[68]

The sojourn in Istanbul lasted but four months, so short that the family hardly had time to settle down. Before they had recovered from the effects of one long journey, they had to start on another, shorter this time but more arduous, for it was undertaken in the heart of a severe winter:

> . . . the infamous edict the Sulṭán had promulgated, less than four months after the arrival of the exiles in his capital, banishing them, suddenly and without any justification whatsoever, in the depth of winter, and in the most humiliating circumstances, to Adrianople, situated on the extremities of his empire . . . an edict which evinced a virtual coalition of the Turkish and Persian imperial governments against a common adversary, and which in the end brought such tragic consequences upon the Sultanate, the Caliphate and the Qájár dynasty.[69]

Life in Adrianople (1863–8)

The journey from Constantinople (Istanbul) to Adrianople (Edirne) was not unlike the one from Ṭihrán to Baghdád:

> Bahá'u'lláh's third exile was reminiscent of His first. Once again it was the heart of winter. Once again the road led out of the capital city of an Islamic realm, the seat of a corrupt tyranny. Once again the exiles were ill-equipped for the rigours of a winter journey.[70]

Bahá'u'lláh Himself, addressing the Ottoman Emperor, Sulṭán 'Abdu'l-'Azíz, says:

> They expelled Us from thy city with an abasement with which no abasement on earth can compare.[71]

> Neither My family, nor those who accompanied Me, had the necessary raiment to protect them from the cold in that freezing weather.[72]

> The eyes of Our enemies wept over Us, and beyond them those of every discerning person.[73]

Bahá'u'lláh, His family and companions travelled 'through rain and storm, at times even making night marches'.[74] They arrived in Adrianople on 12 December 1863 and spent the first three days in the Khán-i-'Arab, a two-storey caravanserai. Then Bahá'u'lláh and His family moved to 'a house suitable only for summer habitation', followed by six months in another house. Finally 'they transferred to more commodious quarters, known as the house of Amru'lláh (house of God's command) situated on the northern side of the mosque of Sulṭán Salím.'[75]

During Bahá'u'lláh's stay in Adrianople, described by Shoghi Effendi as 'the most turbulent and critical period of the first Bahá'í century',[76] events of great significance took place. But what more than anything else had a direct bearing on Bahá'u'lláh's family was the open hostility of His half brother Mírzá Yaḥyá. Although aware of Bahá'u'lláh's declaration in the Garden of Riḍván, Mírzá Yaḥyá still entertained the hope of being the recognized leader of the believers in Iran and abroad. Thus far the fear of being recognized and persecuted had prevented him from taking a stand. In Adrianople he felt secure enough to make known what had been brewing in his heart for many years. However, with the sun of Bahá'u'lláh shining so brilliantly, he knew that he could not succeed. Removing Bahá'u'lláh from the scene was the option that appealed to him. But how could he achieve this? His twisted mind devised a scheme. He invited

> . . . Bahá'u'lláh to his home, where, one day, having smeared His tea-cup with a substance he had concocted, he succeeded in poisoning Him sufficiently to produce a serious illness which lasted no less than a month, and which was accompanied by severe pains and high fever, the aftermath of which left Bahá'u'lláh with a shaking hand till the end of His life.[77]

This treacherous act caused Bahá'u'lláh's family grave concern for His safety. Bahá'íyyih Khánum was then about 19 years old. She was well familiar with Mírzá Yaḥyá's insecurities and meanness. She had herself suffered at his hand at an early age. Therefore she knew what was going on in the mind of her father's half brother. She fully understood the gravity of the situation but could not, owing to restrictions on women, do anything to shield her father from real and potential harm outside the home.

The scheme to poison Bahá'u'lláh was not the only attempt by Mírzá Yaḥyá to get rid of Him. He had also 'poisoned the well which provided water for the family and companions of Bahá'u'lláh, in consequence of which the exiles manifested strange symptoms of illness'.[78] When these attempts failed, Mírzá Yaḥyá tried something different: 'He asked the bath attendant (for a bribe) to assassinate Bahá'u'lláh whilst he should be taking His bath, suggesting how easily it could be done without fear of detection.'[79] Referring to this, Shoghi Effendi says:

> He even had gradually and with great circumspection, disclosed to one of the companions, Ustád Muḥammad-'Alíy-i-Salmání, the barber, on whom he had lavished great marks of favour, his wish that he, on some propitious occasion, when attending Bahá'u'lláh in His bath, should assassinate Him.[80]

Mírzá Yaḥyá witnessed with consuming envy Bahá'u'lláh's unrivalled prominence in the community. He craved to be in His position but knew his lack of credibility made it impossible. However, he stopped at nothing to achieve his evil purpose. What finally caused a permanent separation between Bahá'u'lláh and His followers on the one hand and Mírzá Yaḥyá and his supporters on the other, was the Lawḥ-i-Amr (Tablet of Declaration) revealed by Bahá'u'lláh and sent to Mírzá Yaḥyá by His amanuensis. Soon after reading that Tablet, Mírzá Yaḥyá made a counterclaim that he was the one promised by the Báb and that all had to obey him. That declaration rejoiced the hearts of Bahá'u'lláh's enemies and caused bewilderment among His followers. To provide believers with the opportunity to freely decide their allegiance, Bahá'u'lláh withdrew with His family to the house of Riḍá Big and refused to see any friend or stranger for two months. Shoghi Effendi refers to Mírzá Yaḥyá's presumptuous assertion as 'the signal for the open and final rupture between Bahá'u'lláh and Mírzá Yaḥyá – a rupture that marks one of the darkest dates in Bahá'í history'.[81] Thus all contact between Bahá'u'lláh and his half brother, who had brought nothing to Him but despair, was cut off in 1865.

Referring to the suffering of Bahá'íyyih Khánum in Adrianople and the role she played during that 'most great commotion', Shoghi Effendi says:

> Because of the intense and deep-seated sorrows and the manifold oppressive trials that assailed her – never failing spring of grace that she was,

> essence of loving-kindness – in the Land of Mystery her lovely form was worn away to a breath, to a shadow; and during the Most Great Convulsion, which in the year of 'Stress' made every heart to quake, she stood as a soaring pillar, immovable and fixed; and from the blasts of desolation that rose and blew, that Leaf of the eternal Lote-Tree did not wither.
>
> Rather did she redouble her efforts, urging herself on the more, to servitude and sacrifice. In captivating hearts and winning over souls, in destroying doubts and misgivings, she led the field. With the waters of her countless mercies, she brought thorny hearts to a blossoming of love from the All-Glorious, and with the influence of her pure loving-kindness, transformed the implacable, the unyielding, into impassioned lovers of the celestial Beauty's peerless Cause.[82]

> How staunch was her faith, how calm her demeanour, how forgiving her attitude, how severe her trials, at a time when the forces of schism had rent asunder the ties that united the little band of exiles which had settled in Adrianople and whose fortunes seemed then to have sunk to their lowest ebb! It was in this period of extreme anxiety, when the rigours of a winter of exceptional severity, coupled with the privations entailed by unhealthy housing accommodation and dire financial distress, undermined once for all her health and sapped the vitality which she had hitherto so thoroughly enjoyed. The stress and storm of that period made an abiding impression upon her mind, and she retained till the time of her death on her beauteous and angelic face evidences of its intense hardships.[83]

The period of Bahá'u'lláh's seclusion in Adrianople, according to Áqáy-i-Kalím, was 'marked by tumult and confusion'. 'We were', he says, 'sore-perplexed, and greatly feared lest we be permanently deprived of the bounty of His presence.'[84] Mírzá Yaḥyá and his accomplice, Siyyid Muḥammad, took advantage of Bahá'u'lláh's absence and engaged in extensive correspondence with believers in Iran with the purpose of confusing their minds about Bahá'u'lláh. To save the Cause of God from its detractors, after a duration of two months, Bahá'u'lláh ended the voluntary seclusion He had undertaken. His return calmed the agitation that had seized the community of the faithful, cheered the hearts of His devoted followers and rescued them from the intrigues employed by the enemy from within who were by now well recognized and kept at bay. The stage was now set for a separation which eased the concerns of Bahá'u'lláh's family for His safety. When the separation took place, they gave a sigh of relief that at last they were free from having contact with Mírzá Yaḥyá and his supporters who had spared no effort to destroy Bahá'u'lláh and undermine His Cause.

After living in the house of Riḍá Big for about a year, Bahá'u'lláh and His family returned to the house of Amru'lláh and, after three months, moved to the house of 'Izzat Áqá, where they lived until their departure from Adrianople. Shoghi Effendi says:

> It was in this house, in the month of Jamádíyu'l-Avval 1284 AH (Sept. 1867) that an event of the utmost significance occurred, which completely discomfited Mírzá Yaḥyá and his supporters, and proclaimed to friend and foe alike Bahá'u'lláh's triumph over them.[85]

The event in question was Mírzá Yaḥyá's agreement to meet Bahá'u'lláh face to face 'so that a discrimination might be publicly effected between the true and the false'.[86] Mírzá Yaḥyá nominated the mosque of Sulṭán Salím for the encounter. Bahá'u'lláh went to the mosque on the appointed day and at the fixed time but Mírzá Yaḥyá failed to appear, instead asking for a postponement. However, he failed to respond to the conditions of a postponed meeting. Consequently, his cowardice was exposed and his credibility among the friends diminished drastically.

To discredit Bahá'u'lláh, Mírzá Yaḥyá began a widespread campaign against Him. He sent envoys to Constantinople with complaints that He and His family were being unfairly treated. He also made preposterous accusations against Him which startled authorities at the highest level. The intrigues employed by Mírzá Yaḥyá and his accomplice, Siyyid Muḥammad, played into the hands of Mírzá Ḥusayn K͟hán, Mus͟híru'd-Dawlih, who was responsible for banishing Bahá'u'lláh, His family and companions to the Most Great Prison ('Akká).[87] Other factors were the ever-increasing number of pilgrims coming from Iran to Adrianople to see Bahá'u'lláh, the political instability of the country, the friendly attitude of local authorities and dignitaries towards Bahá'u'lláh, the challenging tone of Bahá'u'lláh's newly-revealed Tablets, and internal dissensions which had shaken the Faith. These are listed by Shoghi Effendi among factors that prompted the central government 'to take drastic and immediate action which would extirpate that Faith, isolate its Author and reduce Him to powerlessness'.[88] According to 'a strongly worded Farmán' issued by Sulṭán 'Abdu'l-'Azíz, Bahá'u'lláh was banished to the penal colony of 'Akká and Mírzá Yaḥyá to Famagusta, Cyprus. There were rumours that other exiles 'were to be dispersed and banished to different places or secretly put to death'.[89] 'Akká was chosen as the final place of Bahá'u'lláh's banishment because it was considered inaccessible to the growing multitude of Bahá'u'lláh's followers. Speaking of 'Akká, Bahá'u'lláh says: 'According to what they say, it is the most desolate of the cities of the world, the most unsightly of them in appearance, the most detestable in climate, and the foulest in water'.[90] Bahá'íyyih Khánum explains how they learned of the decision that they were being banished to yet another place.

> We were sitting one day in our house, when we heard discordant music, loud, insistent! We wondered what could be causing this uproar. Looking from the windows we found that we were surrounded by many soldiers.
>
> The Governor was reluctant to tell Bahá'u'lláh that the order had come for still another banishment. He explained this to Sarkár-i-Áqá ('Abdu'l-Bahá), and we were told that we had three days to prepare for the journey to 'Akká. Then we learnt that we were all to be separated. Bahá'u'lláh to one place, the Master to another, and the friends to still another place.
>
> I well remember, as though it were only yesterday, the fresh misery into which we were plunged; to be separated from our Beloved; and He, what new grief was in store for Him?[91]

'At length we all started together on the journey to Gallipoli,' she says, 'and in three days we arrived, having travelled in carts and wagons.'[92]

Departure from Adrianople and Journey to 'Akká

Bahá'u'lláh, His family and other exiles left Adrianople on 12 August 1868. After nearly five years' stay in that town, the inhabitants had got to know the exiles well. When the townspeople learned of the decree banishing Bahá'u'lláh and His followers from their city, they surrounded His house in dismay. Bahá'u'lláh says: 'The loved ones of God and His kindred were left on the first night without food . . . The people surrounded the house, and Muslims and Christians wept over Us . . .'[93] 'The consuls of that city (Adrianople) gathered in the presence of this Youth at the hour of His departure and expressed their desire to aid Him.'[94]

After four days the travellers reached Gallipoli, where they stayed for three nights:

> Here the Governor announced that he had received orders for our separation. He came to see Bahá'u'lláh and the Master, and becoming friendly, he tried to help us in our distress . . .
>
> At last permission was given for us all to embark together in a Turkish boat. In this small boat we, seventy-two persons, were crowded together in unspeakable conditions, for eleven days of horror. Ten soldiers and two officers were our escort.
>
> There was an appalling smell in the boat, and most of us were very ill indeed.[95]

Shoghi Effendi explains that 'Even in Gallipoli, where three nights were spent, no one knew what Bahá'u'lláh's destination would be':

> The government's original order was to banish Bahá'u'lláh, Áqáy-i-Kalím and Mírzá Muḥammad-Qulí, with a servant to 'Akká, while the rest were to proceed to Constantinople. This order, which provoked scenes of indescribable distress, was, however, at the insistence of Bahá'u'lláh, and by the instrumentality of 'Umar Effendi, a major appointed to accompany the exiles, revoked. It was eventually decided that all the exiles, numbering about seventy, should be banished to 'Akká. Instructions were, moreover, issued that a certain number of the adherents of Mírzá Yaḥyá, among whom were Siyyid Muḥammad and Áqá Ján, should accompany these exiles, whilst four of the companions of Bahá'u'lláh were ordered to depart with the Azalís for Cyprus.[96]

On 21 August 1868 the exiles left Gallipoli for Alexandria, Egypt, aboard an Austrian-Lloyd steamer. One of the believers became very ill on the voyage. When the boat reached Smyrna, where it stopped for two days, 'Abdu'l-Bahá and Mírzá Músá took him to a hospital. 'The Master bought a melon and some grapes; returning with the refreshing fruit for him – He found that he had died. Arrangements were made with the director of the hospital for a simple funeral. The Master chanted some prayers, then, heartsore, came back to the boat.'[97]

In Alexandria, the exiles were transferred to another Austrian-Lloyd steamer and continued their voyage to Haifa via Port Said and Jaffa. The boat reached Haifa on 31 August 1868. Bahá'u'lláh, His family and all but four of His followers, as well as a number of Azalís, disembarked. After a few hours' stay at this port, they were put into a sailing boat and sent to 'Akká. Mírzá Yaḥyá, his supporters and four of Bahá'u'lláh's followers were sent to Famagusta, Cyprus.

Regarding the voyage from Haifa to 'Akká, Bahá'íyyih Khánum says: 'There being no wind, and no shelter from the burning rays of the sun, we spent eight hours of positive misery, and at last we had reached 'Akká, the end of our journey.'[98] As in Haifa, here, too, 'the ladies were taken ashore in chairs . . . There was a detachment of soldiers on shore drawn up in two lines. Between these lines the prisoners walked to the barracks.'[99]

Arrival in 'Akká and Incarceration in the Army Barracks

When the exiles landed in 'Akká they faced a hostile population whom they did not know at all, a population that had been fed rumours beforehand about the prisoners being enemies of God and dangerous criminals. Bahá'íyyih Khánum describes the population's reaction to their arrival and the misery they caused:

> All the townspeople had assembled to see the arrival of the prisoners. Having been told that we were infidels, criminals, and sowers of sedition, the attitude of the crowd was threatening. Their yelling of curses and execrations filled us with fresh misery. We were terrified of the unknown! We knew not what the fate of our party, the friends and ourselves would be.[100]

Shoghi Effendi explains the nature and details of the strict instructions issued by the central government on how the prisoners were to be treated:

> Explicit orders had been issued by the Sulṭán and his ministers to subject the exiles, who were accused of having grievously erred and led others far astray, to the strictest confinement. Hopes were confidently expressed that the sentence of life-long imprisonment pronounced against them would lead to their eventual extermination. The farmán of Sulṭán 'Abdu'l-'Azíz, dated the fifth of Rabí'u'th-Thání 1285 AH (July 26, 1868), not only condemned them to perpetual banishment, but stipulated their strict incarceration, and forbade them to associate either with each other or with the local inhabitants. The text of the farmán itself was read publicly, soon after the arrival of the exiles, in the principal mosque of the city as a warning to the population.[101]

Shoghi Effendi quotes from a letter that the Persian ambassador accredited to the Sublime Porte had written to his government sometime after the arrival of the exiles in 'Akká. The contents of the letter expose the collusion of the two governments in banishing Bahá'u'lláh, His family and companions to 'Akká and confining them to a town where they had no hope of survival:

> The Persian Ambassador, accredited to the Sublime Porte, had thus assured his government, in a letter, written a little over a year after their banishment to 'Akká: 'I have issued telegraphic and written instructions, forbidding that He (Bahá'u'lláh) associate with any one except His wives and children, or leave under any circumstance, the house where He is imprisoned. 'Abbás-Qulí Khán, the Consul-General in Damascus . . . I have, three days ago, sent back, instructing him to proceed direct to 'Akká . . . confer with its governor regarding all necessary measures for the strict maintenance of their imprisonment . . . and appoint, before

his return to Damascus, a representative on the spot to insure that the orders issued by the Sublime Porte will, in no wise, be disobeyed. I have, likewise, instructed him that once every three months he should proceed from Damascus to 'Akká, and personally watch over them, and submit his report to the Legation.'[102]

In 'Akká the prisoners were assigned the army barracks, a place where they could live in complete isolation from the inhabitants of the town and where their movements could be closely monitored. The barracks were situated near the only land entrance to the town. The entrance was watched over by soldiers round the clock and the town itself was cut off by a moat, so that no movement was possible by land except through that entrance. Bahá'íyyih Khánum describes their arrival and imprisonment:

> We were taken to the old fortress of 'Akká, where we were crowded together. There was no air; a small quantity of very bad coarse bread was provided; we were unable to get fresh water to drink; our sufferings were not diminished. Then an epidemic of typhoid broke out. Nearly all became ill.[103]

Shoghi Effendi recounts their suffering in more detail:

> Having, after a miserable voyage, disembarked at 'Akká, all the exiles, men, women and children, were, under the eyes of a curious and callous population that had assembled at the port to behold the 'God of the Persians', conducted to the army barracks, where they were locked in, and sentinels detailed to guard them. 'The first night,' Bahá'u'lláh testifies in the Lawḥ-i-Ra'ís, 'all were deprived of either food or drink . . . They even begged for water, and were refused' . . . All fell sick, except two, shortly after their arrival. Malaria, dysentery, combined with the sultry heat, added to their miseries. Three succumbed, among them two brothers, who died the same night, 'locked', as testified by Bahá'u'lláh, 'in each other's arms'.[104]

Bahá'u'lláh Himself speaks of the cruel treatment to which He was subjected:

> None knoweth what befell Us, except God, the Almighty, the All-Knowing . . . From the foundation of the world until the present day a cruelty such as this hath neither been seen or heard of.[105]

> He hath, during the greater part of His life, been sore-tried in the clutches of His enemies. His sufferings have now reached their culmination in this afflictive Prison, into which His oppressors have so unjustly thrown Him.[106]

Life in the barracks was particularly restrictive and harsh for the women. Simple routine activities, such as going to a public bath, proved complicated. Fifty-two years afterwards Bahá'íyyih Khánum spoke to some of the women pilgrims about the first time the women visited the public bath in 'Akká. Mabel Hyde Paine, who was on pilgrimage in 1920, records:

> After about fifteen days the women asked permission to go to the public bath. Permission was given. They did not realize but what they were going alone until a soldier picked up the handkerchief which Khánum had dropped. At the bath they were told to hurry, as the soldiers were in a hurry to go home.
>
> Khánum said that she cried after she had returned from the bath. She feared they would all come to look like the other women they saw in the bath, yellow skinned and with big hard bellies. This appearance was caused by malaria.[107]

Bahá'íyyih Khánum entered the prison-city of 'Akká as a young woman of about 21. Although from early childhood she had tasted of the chalice of tribulation and throughout her youth had sustained torments of various kinds, the worst was yet to come. The period spent in the army barracks was unparalleled in poignancy with what she had thus far experienced. For nearly two years she and her family lived under appalling conditions with no relief in sight. During this time, to attain Bahá'u'lláh's presence, pilgrims came on foot from Iran. Barred from entry into the city, they 'had to content themselves with a fleeting glimpse of the face of the Prisoner, as they stood, beyond the second moat, facing the window of His Prison. The very few who succeeded in penetrating into the city had, to their great distress, to retrace their steps without even beholding His countenance.'[108] Then a devastating tragedy struck. Nearly two years earlier Bahá'u'lláh and His family had entered the citadel of 'Akká and were assigned the three upper rooms in the army barracks. Bahá'íyyih Khánum's loving brother whom she, as a little girl, had held in her tiny arms and protected against harm when Bahá'u'lláh was in the Síyáh Chál, a brother who was now a lovely young man serving His father as His amanuensis and helping the family and exiles in whatever way he could, fell through a unguarded skylight in the roof of the prison. He died 22 hours later.

Mírzá Mihdí, entitled the Purest Branch, was about three years old when Bahá'u'lláh and His family left Ṭihrán for Baghdád. Because he was so young, constitutionally not very strong and the journey ahead so hard and perilous, he was left behind. Several years later he joined the family in Baghdád. Thenceforth he shared Bahá'u'lláh's successive banishments to Constantinople, Adrianople and 'Akká. Referring to his fateful fall, Shoghi Effendi says:

> He was pacing the roof of the barracks in the twilight, one evening, wrapped in his customary devotions, when he fell through the unguarded skylight onto a wooden crate, standing on the floor beneath, which pierced his ribs, and caused, twenty-two hours later, his death, on the 23rd of Rabí'u'l-Avval 1287 AH (June 23, 1870). His dying supplication to a grieving Father was that his life might be accepted as a ransom for those who were prevented from attaining the presence of their Beloved.[109]

Speaking of His son's highly significant sacrifice, Bahá'u'lláh says: 'I have, O my Lord, offered up that which Thou hast given Me, that Thy servants may be quickened, and all that dwell on earth be united.' Also, addressing His son, He says: 'Thou art the Trust of God and His Treasure in this Land. Erelong will God reveal through thee that which He hath desired.'[110]

The scene of the accident was the second floor of the army barracks, the building that housed the prisoners, and only a short distance from the cell that Bahá'íyyih Khánum shared with her mother and brothers. She was a witness to her mother's anguish at hearing the terrifying sound of the fall. She was likewise a witness to her mother's struggle to embrace the blood-stained body of her beloved son. When her mother passed out and Mírzá Mihdí reached out to hold her in his loving arms, painful as the move was, Bahá'íyyih Khánum's concern for the two people who meant the world to her knew no bounds. She was unaware that divine will had decreed the release of Mírzá Mihdí from the cage of his body in the prime of his youth. He had been singled out for the honour of offering his soul for the unification of the world and the quickening of its people. Much depended on him. He was the ransom for bringing relief to Bahá'u'lláh, so that the work He was to achieve could continue without further delay. Mírzá Mihdí was the worthy candidate for the purpose. He was informed and given a choice. With meekness and resignation He accepted to offer up his soul. Twenty-two hours after his fall, he winged his flight to the world beyond. The words of Bahá'u'lláh at the time his body was being prepared for burial describe the depth of the anguish felt by his loved ones:

> At this very moment My son is being washed before My face, after Our having sacrificed him in the Most Great Prison. Thereat have the dwellers of the Abhá Tabernacle wept with a great weeping, and such as have suffered imprisonment with this Youth in the path of God, the Lord of the promised Day, lamented . . . This is the day whereon he that was created by the light of Bahá has suffered martyrdom, at a time when he lay imprisoned at the hands of his enemies.[111]

When the body was being taken away for burial, Bahá'íyyih Khánum and other members of her family could not accompany Mírzá Mihdí to his resting-place. Although some of the restraints imposed on prisoners had been somewhat eased by then, the more stringent restrictions were still in place.

Mírzá Mihdí's death 'in the most tragic circumstances' 'robbed' Bahá'iyyih Khánum 'of the Purest Branch, her only brother besides 'Abdu'l-Bahá, while still in the prime of youth'.[112] What went through Bahá'íyyih Khánum's mind during those woeful times? How did she deal with her grief? How did she react? How did she mourn the death of a brother she so dearly loved? What impressions did that tragic event leave on her mind? When Bahá'íyyih Khánum related the tale of her brother's tragic death to Madam Canavarro 30 years later, she divulged little of the emotions surging within her and her feelings of loss and grief. She rarely spoke of herself; when she did, it was in response to a question and even then she was careful not to evoke sadness in her listeners. Despite all this, through the words she spoke about the burial of her beloved brother, one cannot fail to feel her pain:

> As we could not leave the barracks, we could not bury our dead; nor had we the consolation of feeling that we could provide for him through others the grateful final tribute of a proper and fitting burial, as we had no means wherewith even to purchase a coffin. After some consideration and consultation among ourselves, finding that we had nothing to dispose of, and at a loss how to proceed, we told our Lord of the sad situation. He replied that there was a rug in his room which we could sell. At first we demurred, for in taking his rug we took the only comfort he had; but he insisted and we sold it. A coffin was then procured, and the remains of my deceased brother placed in it. It was carried out by our jailors, and we did not even know whither it was taken.[113]

Four months elapsed from the date of Mírzá Mihdí's tragic death. '. . . the war between Russia and Turkey was in progress. More barrack room was required for the soldiers. Bahá'u'lláh protested against the friends being crowded in with the soldiers.'[114] Consequently, the exiles were allowed to leave the barracks. 'How we rejoiced in our liberty, restricted though it was. Only three times had we been permitted to go out, for even an hour, from the prison barracks during the whole of that first two years. How tired we were of those three little rooms,' says Bahá'íyyih Khánum.[115]

Life inside the Prison-City

Bahá'íyyih Khánum was 23 years old when she left her prison cell in the army barracks. According to Shoghi Effendi's testimony:

> Not until . . . she had been confined in the company of Bahá'u'lláh within the walls of the prison-city of 'Akká did she display, in the plenitude of her power and in the full abundance of her love for Him, those gifts that single her out, next to 'Abdu'l-Bahá, among the members of the Holy Family, as the brightest embodiment of that love which is born of God and of that human sympathy which few mortals are capable of evincing.[116]

To keep all the exiled men, women and children together inside the city, a very large place was needed. In the absence of such a house, they were accommodated in different quarters. Bahá'u'lláh and His family were initially assigned the house of Malik. After three months in this house they moved to the house of Khavvám for a few months, before moving to the house of Rábi'ih for four months. Finally, about the end of 1871, they moved to the house of Údí Khammár, where they stayed for several years.

It was not long after Bahá'u'lláh and His family had moved to the house of 'Údí Khammár that 'an internal crisis, which had been brewing in the midst of the community, was brought to a sudden and catastrophic climax'.[117] The few Azalís who had been sent with the exiles to 'Akká were hard at work to frustrate attempts to ease the restrictions that had been imposed by the government. They acted as spies and 'embarked on a campaign of abuse, calumny and intrigue, even more pernicious than that which had been launched . . . in Constantinople'.[118] Their misdeeds endangered the life of Bahá'u'lláh and brought misery upon all. Some of His companions, tired of the schemes of the stirrers of mischief, plotted to get rid of them.

> Though He Himself had stringently forbidden His followers, on several occasions, both verbally and in writing, any retaliatory acts against their tormentors . . . seven of the companions clandestinely sought out and slew three of their persecutors, among whom were Siyyid Muḥammad and Áqá Ján.[119]

In consequence of the heinous act committed by a few irresponsible individuals, Bahá'u'lláh was detained for 70 hours, 'Abdu'l-Bahá was imprisoned for a few days, even chained for one night. Twenty-five of Bahá'u'lláh's companions were imprisoned and shackled for six days before suffering confinement for six months, while those responsible remained in prison for several years.

When 'the governor, at the head of his troops, with drawn swords, surrounded [Bahá'u'lláh's] house' and when the 'shouts and clamour of the people'[120] filled the air, Bahá'íyyih Khánum's childhood memories of her father's arrest and their house in Ṭihrán being plundered by the mob rushed through her mind. Did she think that the scenes were being repeated? In Ṭihrán her mother was much younger and stronger, and the children, although tender in age, were all together. Now her father was summoned to the Governorate for interrogation, 'Abdu'l-Bahá was also arrested and Mírzá Mihdí was no longer with them in this world. She was left alone with her mother, who needed much consolation herself. Unlike the time in Ṭihrán, in 'Akká Bahá'íyyih Khánum had siblings, albeit from a different mother. Mahd-i 'Ulyá and probably Gawhar Khánum were also there but none of them had gone through what she and her mother had experienced 20 years before. Bahá'íyyih Khánum's chronicles do not cover this woeful episode in her life. Either the questions she was asked did not relate to this period or she deliberately avoided touching upon matters that evoked sadness in her listeners.

She did, however, speak fondly of Shaykh Salmán and the 'significant mission' he performed about the time this episode occurred:

> It was this devoted and resourceful friend who was entrusted with the significant mission of bringing Munírih Khánum from Isfahán to 'Akká, she who was to become the wife of Sarkár-i-Áqá ('Abdu'l-Bahá) the Master, and my much-loved sister.[121]

It was during the stay of Bahá'u'lláh and His family in the house of 'Údí Khammár, which lasted seven years, that 'Abdu'l-Bahá's marriage to Munírih Khánum took place. Munírih Khánum's arrival in the Holy Land, although arranged months in advance, had coincided with the difficulties encompassing the exiles as a result of the murder of the Azalís. Nonetheless, it was the happiest event in the life of Bahá'íyyih Khánum. The joy of that occasion was beyond anything she had experienced in her adult life. She was glad to see her brother marry at the age of 29, a joy that was shared with her beloved parents who had long hoped to see their firstborn happily married. Bahá'íyyih Khánum was happy to have a 'much-loved sister', almost her age, added to the family, a sister whose friendship and companionship she enjoyed for the next 60 years. Above all, she was overjoyed to see her beloved mother happily preparing for the joyous event.

'Abdu'l-Bahá's marriage on 8 March 1873 marked the beginning of improvements in the grim situation that faced Bahá'u'lláh, His family and companions. Referring to the period after the killing of the Azalís and the dawning of the morn of delivery from strict confinement, Shoghi Effendi says:

> The cup of Bahá'u'lláh's tribulations was now filled to overflowing. A situation, greatly humiliating, full of anxieties and even perilous, continued to face the exiles, until the time, set by an inscrutable Will, at which the tide of misery and abasement began to ebb, signalizing a transformation in the fortunes of the Faith even more conspicuous than the revolutionary change effected during the latter years of Bahá'u'lláh's sojourn in Baghdád.[122]

The effect of the change in the fortunes of the Faith was most conspicuous in the relaxation of rules governing the entry of the Bahá'í pilgrims and visitors into the city. Consequently, eager souls longing to attain Bahá'u'lláh's presence achieved their hearts' desire without impediment. The prisoners were no longer closely watched. They enjoyed freedom of movement within the city. They could also associate with the inhabitants more readily. Some prominent people from abroad came to the Holy Land and attained Bahá'u'lláh's presence. Bahá'u'lláh could move beyond the city limits without objection from the authorities. However, He did not do so until, at the insistence of Shaykh 'Alíy-i-Mírí, the Muftí of 'Akká, He visited what became known as the Riḍván Garden. Finally, He left the prison-city for the Mansion of Mazra'ih.

Although 'Abdu'l-Bahá was the moving force behind the arrangements for Bahá'u'lláh to leave the city and transfer His residence to less inhospitable surroundings, He Himself remained in 'Akká to attend to the work at hand. Along with Munírih Khánum, who remained with Him and continued to live in the house of 'Abbúd, were His mother Ásíyih Khánum and His sister Bahá'íyyih Khánum. By the time Bahá'u'lláh left for the Mansion of Mazra'ih, 'Abdu'l-Bahá and Munírih Khánum may have had two children. The joy that the children brought to the family was tremendous, yet so was the grief and heartache caused by the death of some of them in infancy and childhood.

The Mansion of Mazra'ih, although situated a short distance from 'Akká, could not be easily reached by the women who lived in the city. The primitive means of transportation, the need for women to be veiled and not seen, as well as the need for segregation along gender lines during journeys, indeed in all social undertakings, made travelling very difficult for women. How often did Bahá'íyyih Khánum have the opportunity to visit her beloved father at Mazra'ih and how long did she stay each visit? No information is available regarding either question.

After two years at Mazra'ih, Bahá'u'lláh moved to a magnificent and spacious mansion which 'Údí Khammár had built at Bahjí, in close proximity to 'Akká. 'The drastic farmán of Sulṭán 'Abdu'l-'Azíz,' says Shoghi Effendi, 'though officially unrepealed, had by now become a dead letter.'[123] The short distance between the house of 'Abbúd and the Mansion of Bahjí facilitated more frequent visits to Bahá'u'lláh by Bahá'íyyih Khánum and other women members of the family who lived in 'Akká. Likewise, Bahá'u'lláh visited His family in 'Akká, at times staying several days.

After He left the prison-city in about 1878, Bahá'u'lláh made several visits to Haifa at different times in His ministry. Bahá'íyyih Khánum and other women members of His family may have accompanied Him on some visits.

During Bahá'u'lláh's stay at Bahjí 'the doors of majesty and true sovereignty were flung wide open'.[124] High-ranking officials and prominent people, with whom 'Abdu'l-Bahá had established contact and had friendly relations, longed to be admitted to Bahá'u'lláh's presence. As 'Abdu'l-Bahá says: 'Governors and mutiṣarrifs, generals and local officials, would humbly request the honour of attaining His presence – a request to which He seldom acceded.'[125] 'Abdu'l-Bahá would usually receive such individuals at Bahjí and respond to their questions. His vast range of activities on behalf of His father were rejoiced by Bahá'íyyih Khánum who, although a silent partner, took pleasure in witnessing improvements in the affairs of her family, especially the relative ease and pleasure that her father enjoyed after long years of imprisonment and exile.

Yet just as she and the rest of the family seemed to have a respite from years of hardship, another tragedy struck. Her beloved mother whom she adored and spared no effort to help in whatever way she could, whose long years of suffering she had witnessed with sadness and concern, who had shared Bahá'u'lláh's tribulations to the fullest, had a fall and was confined to bed. Details about how long she lived after that fateful fall are obscure. What is certain is that she lived long enough to see all her loved ones by her bedside, for Bahá'u'lláh attests to it in a Tablet He revealed immediately after Ásíyih Khánum passed away.[126]

The person worst affected by the death of Ásíyih Khánum was Bahá'íyyih Khánum who, from early childhood, was intimately associated with every aspect of her mother's saintly and sacrificial life. Ásíyih Khánum's death in 1886 created a void in Bahá'íyyih Khánum's life that nothing filled to the end of her days.

Six years passed. Another tragedy, far more devastating and potent in its far-reaching consequences, shook the family and the whole Bahá'í community. In late May 1892 Bahá'u'lláh was unwell. Members of His family were gathered by His bedside. To be close to her father during the last days of His earthly life, Bahá'íyyih Khánum had gone to the Mansion of Bahjí. The words that Bahá'u'lláh spoke and the statements that He made during those final days of His life sent a clear message that He had left a Will in which He had entrusted them all to the Most Great Branch, 'Abdu'l-Bahá.

Referring to the deep anguish felt by Bahá'íyyih Khánum during the years that she lived in 'Akká before the ascension of Bahá'u'lláh, Shoghi Effendi says:

> Yet another wound was inflicted on her injured heart by the aggressions and violations of the evil-doers within the prison-fortress, yet another blow was struck at her afflicted being. And then her anguish was increased by the passing of the Abhá Beauty, and the cruelty of the disloyal added more fuel to the fires of her mourning.[127]

The Ascension of Bahá'u'lláh and Its Aftermath

Bahá'u'lláh's earthy life drew to a close in the early morning hours of 29 May 1892. He was buried in the afternoon of same day in the northwestern room of a house in close proximity to the Mansion of Bahjí where His youngest daughter Furúghíyyih Khánum and her husband Siyyid 'Alí Afnán lived. Rafí'ih Shahídí, then six years old, has left the following description of how the women believers gathered in the Mansion of Bahjí and mourned the ascension of Bahá'u'lláh:

> We received the news of Bahá'u'lláh's ascension from my cousin Hayatiyyih Khánum. She came from the blessed Mansion and conveyed with tearful eyes the shocking news. Needless to say how we all felt after hearing what had occurred. Devastated and grief-stricken, all set off for the Mansion of Bahjí.
>
> I, too, went along. The Bahá'ís of Haifa and 'Akká gathered in the Mansion. The Bahá'í women occupied the balcony of the Mansion which had been covered with carpets for the occasion. The sound of their wailing and weeping rose sky high. Whatever they did I copied. They hit themselves on the head, I did likewise. I was then about six years old.[128]

Another eyewitness account by Murassa' Rouhani describes how even non-Bahá'í women mourned Bahá'u'lláh's ascension:

> The news of Bahá'u'lláh's ascension reached the surrounding areas on the day that it took place. Among the people who thronged the Mansion of Bahjí were Arab women from 'Akká and places in the vicinity of the Mansion. They all wore black garments and burqas. Orders were given for carpets to be placed in the central hall of the Mansion of Bahjí. The women sat cross-legged in a circle on the carpets. They chanted mourning verses and beat the back of their hands with their palms. I was then a child. I sat next to them and did the same.[129]

Being the eldest son, 'Abdu'l-Bahá was in charge of all arrangements. Following Bahá'u'lláh's entombment, a period of mourning began which extended over several days. Knowing how eager everyone was to learn of the contents of Bahá'u'lláh's Will, on the ninth day after His ascension 'Abdu'l-Bahá brought together a number of believers. In their presence He opened the Will and asked one of them to read it aloud. The disclosure of the contents of the Will stirred up dormant emotions, exposed hidden ambitions and set in motion a chain of reactions with far-reaching consequences for the family, the exiled members of the community and the believers in general.

To forestall problems faced by the followers of previous religions who suffered disunity and division after the death of the founder because He had not specified in writing the name of His successor and the scope of his duties, Bahá'u'lláh in a sealed document written in His hand stated in unambiguous language that unity was the goal of His Revelation. To safeguard that unity and prevent His followers from schism, in the same document He appointed His Most Great Branch, 'Abdu'l-Bahá, as His successor and the authorized Interpreter of His writings. He also specified that the station of His second son, Mírzá Muḥammad-'Alí, titled the Greater Branch, who was to succeed the Most Great Branch, was beneath that of 'Abdu'l-Bahá.

Since the Book of Bahá'u'lláh's Covenant was written in His own hand and its seals were broken only on the day it was read, its authenticity could not be disputed. 'Abdu'l-Bahá's opponents, disappointed that the document had left no room for ambiguity, decided to accept it but tried to minimize its significance. One way to achieve their purpose was to interpret its contents to suit their aims, knowing that 'Abdu'l-Bahá was not only the Centre of Bahá'u'lláh's Covenant but also the authorized Interpreter of His writings. The attempt to attach self-serving interpretations to the contents of the Will and to spread them far and wide set the stage for the launching of insidious attacks on 'Abdu'l-Bahá. Although unsuccessful and finally defeated in their purpose, for a long while they caused widespread confusion, impeded the progress of the Faith and caused heartache to ‘Abdu’l-Bahá and His family, especially Bahá’íyyih Khánum. Seeing ‘Abdu’l-Bahá caught in the claws of His envious and unfaithful half brothers and their supporters both inside and outside the family circle caused her intense grief and concern. They engaged in a vast campaign of intrigue to rob ‘Abdu’l-Bahá of His legacy by trying to discredit Him in the eyes of Bahá’ís in the Holy Land and abroad, and by bringing false charges against Him before the local authorities.

When the Book of Bahá’u’lláh’s Covenant was read on the ninth day after His ascension, first to a small group of Bahá’ís then to all the believers in the Holy Land, including the members of His family, the mood in the Mansion changed. Once it became clear that ‘Abdu’l-Bahá was indeed the Centre of Bahá’u’lláh’s Covenant, the one to whom all were to turn, Mírzá Muḥammad-‘Alí and those occupying the Mansion who sided with him were utterly disappointed. Although as the eldest son ‘Abdu’l-Bahá was in charge of all arrangements and expenses incurred, it was made known to members of His family that they were not welcome to stay in the Mansion where the family received mourners who thronged its doors to convey their condolences. The awkwardness created by this anomaly was conspicuous. Bahá’íyyih Khánum was Bahá’u’lláh’s eldest daughter. Her absence at such a time was most unusual. Nonetheless, with a heavy heart she returned to ‘Akká together with other members of ‘Abdu’l-Bahá’s family. The unkind treatment she received from her unfaithful kindred at such a poignant time in her life caused her to suffer all the more.

Devastating as the death of Ásíyih Khánum had been for Bahá’íyyih Khánum and the immediate members of her family, it had no apparent lasting effect on the Faith for which she had suffered so much and for so long. But Bahá’u’lláh’s ascension was highly poignant both in the pain and sorrow that it caused and in the repercussions that it had for the Bahá’í Cause and Bahá’u’lláh’s family. His ascension set in motion an internal crisis that left its marks on the family and the community for several generations. It was this crisis that had a direct bearing on Bahá’íyyih Khánum’s future work and destiny, for her unique personality and the true worth of her invaluable services were revealed in full during the ministry of ‘Abdu’l-Bahá:

> Great as had been her sufferings ever since her infancy, the anguish of mind and heart which the ascension of Bahá’u’lláh occasioned nerved her, as never before, to a resolve which no upheaval could bend and which her frail constitution belied. Amidst the dust and heat of the commotion which that faithless and rebellious company engendered she found herself constrained to dissolve ties of family relationship, to sever

> long-standing and intimate friendships, to discard lesser loyalties for the sake of her supreme allegiance to a Cause she had loved so dearly and had served so well.
>
> The disruption that ensued found her ranged by the side of Him Whom her departed Father had appointed as the Centre of His Covenant and the authorized Expounder of His Word.[130]

The evil designs of the faithless members of 'Abdu'l-Bahá's family did not escape the keen eye of other believers. For example, Murassa' Rouhani writes: 'For a few days after the ascension, a large crowd of Bahá'í women also gathered inside the Mansion . . . After a malodour of Covenant-breaking was inhaled, they severed all ties and never returned to the Mansion.'[131]

Bahá'íyyih Khánum during 'Abdu'l-Bahá's Ministry

After Bahá'u'lláh's ascension, the person fully aware of Bahá'íyyih Khánum's station and her capacity for rendering unique service to the Cause of God was the one Bahá'u'lláh had appointed as the Centre of His Covenant and the authorized Interpreter of His writings. 'Abdu'l-Bahá, 'the Most Great Branch', 'the One Whom God hath purposed', who had 'branched' from the ancient stock,[132] made His beloved and self-sacrificing sister His confidant, the companion of His heart. Bahá'íyyih Khánum stood by her brother throughout His ministry and suffered with acquiescence all the pain and tribulations that He endured. The contents of 'Abdu'l-Bahá's Tablets revealed after Bahá'u'lláh's ascension in Bahá'íyyih Khánum's honour reveal the depth of the agonizing pain she sustained:

> O My well-beloved, deeply spiritual sister!
>
> Day and night thou livest in my memory. Whenever I remember thee my heart swelleth with sadness and my regret groweth more intense. Grieve not, for I am thy true, thy unfailing comforter. Let neither despondency nor despair becloud the serenity of thy life or restrain thy freedom. These days shall pass away. We will, please God, in the Abhá Kingdom and beneath the sheltering shadow of the Blessed Beauty, forget all these our earthly cares and will find each one of these base calumnies amply compensated by His expressions of praise and favour. From the beginning of time sorrow and anxiety, regret and tribulation, have always been the lot of every loyal servant of God. Ponder this in thine heart and consider how very true it is. Wherefore, set thine heart on the tender mercies of the Ancient Beauty and be thou filled with abiding joy and intense gladness . . .[133]

The supplication offered by 'Abdu'l-Bahá on behalf of Bahá'íyyih Khánum 'at morn and eventide, with the utmost ardour and humility', discloses the extent of her sufferings:

> Grant, O Thou my God, the Compassionate, that that pure and blessed Leaf may be comforted by Thy sweet savours of holiness and sustained by the reviving breeze of Thy loving care and mercy. Reinforce her spirit with the signs of Thy Kingdom, and gladden her soul with the testimonies of Thy everlasting dominion. Comfort, O my God, her sorrowful heart with the remembrance of Thy face, initiate her into Thy hidden mysteries, and inspire her with the revealed splendours of Thy heavenly light. Manifold are her sorrows, and infinitely grievous her distress. Bestow continually upon her the favour of Thy sustaining grace and, with every fleeting breath, grant her the blessing of Thy bounty. Her hopes and expectations are centred in Thee; open Thou to her face the portals of thy tender mercies and lead her into the ways of thy wondrous benevolence. Thou art the Generous, the All-Loving, the Sustainer, the All-Bountiful . . .[134]

Journey to Egypt

The ascension of Bahá'u'lláh so affected Bahá'íyyih Khánum's health that 'Abdu'l-Bahá was greatly concerned:

> My sister, for a considerable period, that is, from the day of Bahá'u'lláh's ascension, had grown so thin and feeble, and was in such a weakened condition from the anguish of her mourning, that she was close to breakdown.[135]

To help her recuperate from that ordeal to some degree 'Abdu'l-Bahá sent her to Egypt 'to provide her with a change of air'.[136] To Ḍíyá Khánum,[137] whom He sent to accompany her on that trip, He said:

> O Ḍíyá! It is incumbent upon thee, throughout the journey, to be a close, a constant and cheerful companion to my honoured and distinguished sister. Unceasingly, with the utmost vigour and devotion, exert thyself, by day and night, to gladden her blessed heart; for all her days she was denied a moment of tranquillity. She was astir and restless every hour of her life. Moth-like she circled in adoration round the undying flame of the Divine Candle, her spirit ablaze and her heart consumed by the fire of His love . . .[138]

Since her arrival in the Holy Land more than two and a half decades earlier, this was the first time that Bahá'íyyih Khánum had taken a trip outside the place where she and other exiles were confined. Her accommodation in Egypt had to be arranged in a dignified and secure place. 'Abdu'l-Bahá chose the home of Jináb-i-Ḥájí Mírzá Ḥasan-i-Khurásání and his wife for this privilege. In a Tablet revealed in honour of Jináb-i-Ḥájí, 'Abdu'l-Bahá explains the state of Bahá'íyyih Khánum's health after Bahá'u'lláh's ascension and apprises him of His intention to send her to Egypt:

> Although, so far as she was concerned, it was her dearest wish to drain her cup and wing her way to the realms where the Divine Essence shineth in glory, still this servant could not bear to behold her in that state. Then it occurred to me that, God be thanked, I have such an unfailing comforter as Jináb-i-Ḥájí, and it would be well to make him my partner in distress. I therefore determined to send her to Egypt, to provide her with a change of air.
>
> Although this will certainly cause thee trouble and inconvenience, still, I trust that out of God's bounty, it will also bring thee much joy and good cheer.[139]

The extent of 'Abdu'l-Bahá's attachment to and concern for Bahá'íyyih Khánum's well-being, and the intimate bond of friendship that existed between Bahá'iyyih Khánum and Munírih Khánum can be discerned from the contents of this Tablet:

> O thou my affectionate sister!
>
> God be praised, according to what we hear the climate in that land hath proved not unfavourable. It is to be hoped that out of the grace of the Blessed Beauty thy illness will be completely cured and thou wilt return in the best of health, so that once again I may gaze upon that wondrous face of thine.
>
> Write thou a full account of thy condition by every post, for I am most anxious for news of thee. Let me know if thou shouldst desire anyone from here to come to thee, that I may send the person along – even Munírih – so that thou wilt not be homesick.
>
> That thou shouldst spend a few days of peace and rest, is my dearest wish.
>
> We here, God be thanked, are all enjoying the best of health. I have been better lately, and sleeping well at night. Rest assured.[140]

During 'Abdu'l-Bahá's Short Stay in Tiberias

Feeling overwhelmed by the tremendous weight of the anguish caused by Bahá'u'lláh's ascension and the mischief stirred by His faithless kindred, 'Abdu'l-Bahá withdrew to Tiberias. Bahá'íyyih Khánum and the rest of His family stayed in 'Akká. The distance between 'Akká and Tiberias is about 50 kilometres and can be traversed nowadays by car in half an hour. But then it took half a day on mule back. This was the first time after Bahá'u'lláh's ascension that 'Abdu'l-Bahá was absent from 'Akká and the first time that His family suffered separation from Him under the difficult conditions created by His opponents. Bahá'íyyih Khánum was not only the most senior member of the family after 'Abdu'l-Bahá, she was also the woman who had been given a position by Bahá'u'lláh which no one among her sex excelled. She was also the trusted, loving and faithful sister of 'Abdu'l-Bahá. Therefore, for the first time in her life she had to step forward and take on responsibilities she had not undertaken before. Fortunately, 'Abdu'l-Bahá was not far away. He was kept informed of all developments and His approval was sought for every important matter.

A Tablet 'Abdu'l-Bahá sent to Bahá'íyyih Khánum from Tiberias seems to have been revealed by Him soon after His arrival in that town in 1895:

> O My spiritual sister!
>
> God be praised, through the Ancient Beauty's grace and bounty, we have set foot safe and sound upon this shore, and arrived in this town [Tiberias] . . .
>
> These coasts were once the place where the breezes of God's loving kindness blew, and here in this sacred Vale the Son of Spirit [Jesus] raised up His call of 'Here am I, O Thou My Lord! Here am I!' That is why we here perceive, from every direction, the sweet breathings of holiness.
>
> My meaning is, rest thou assured, this servant is suffering neither from any trouble, nor hardship, nor fatigue. I am looking after myself, and keeping away from all mental preoccupations; all, that is, except for one thought, which doth indeed disquiet the mind – and that is, God forbid, that thou shouldst sorrow.
>
> I hope that out of the bestowals and bounties of the Ancient Beauty, He will in His grace bring comfort to every heart.[141]

One of the significant events that took place during 'Abdu'l-Bahá's journey was the marriage of Ḍíyá'íyyih Khánum, 'Abdu'l-Bahá and Munírih Khánum's eldest daughter, with Mírzá Hádí, a great nephew of Khadíjih Bagum, the wife of the Báb. According to Ṭúbá Khánum, 'Abdu'l-Bahá's second daughter, Mírzá Hádí had been to the Holy Land previously and his request to be accepted as 'Abdu'l-Bahá's son-in-law had received Bahá'u'lláh's approval.[142] Now that about three years had elapsed from Bahá'u'lláh's ascension, Mírzá Hádí had come back in the hope of finalizing arrangements for the wedding. 'Abdu'l-Bahá's approval was sought and received. However, He was not physically present at the ceremony, which His instructions said should be simple because the anguish of Bahá'u'lláh's ascension was still so fresh and vivid. In His absence, Bahá'íyyih Khánum was clearly in charge. Regardless of the pain and difficulties caused by Mírzá Muḥammad-'Alí and his kindred, she invited them to the wedding ceremony. Ṭúbá Khánum says, 'My aunt invited the family of Muḥammad-'Alí to come in the evening. They came and jeered at the simplicity of the wedding with great ridicule.'[143]

This marriage, as will be seen later, produced 'Abdu'l-Bahá's prized grandson who was appointed the first Guardian of the Bahá'í Faith and led the community of the Most Great Name for 36 years.

Change of Residence in 'Akká

Shortly after His return from Tiberias, 'Abdu'l-Bahá rented the house of 'Abdu'lláh Páshá in the vicinity of the house of 'Abbúd and adjacent to the army barracks where Bahá'u'lláh and His family had been imprisoned for two years. The move took place in late 1896. The first auspicious event taking place in the house was the birth of Shoghi Effendi on 1 March 1897. His arrival was the most joyous event the hard-pressed family of 'Abdu'l-Bahá had experienced in many years. Other joyful events took place while 'Abdu'l-Bahá and His family lived there. Western pilgrims came to visit 'Abdu'l-Bahá and stayed in the same house. The arrival of western pilgrims, especially the women among them, introduced a huge and happy change in the life of Bahá'íyyih Khánum and other members of 'Abdu'l-Bahá's family. The women pilgrims, who lived in the same house, associated closely with Bahá'íyyih Khánum and other members of 'Abdu'l-Bahá's family. The younger daughters of 'Abdu'l-Bahá had grown up and served as translators. The arrival of the first group of western pilgrims in 1898 marked the initial stage in the establishment of East–West relationships. Bahá'ís from the West, particularly women pilgrims, became intimately familiar with 'Abdu'l-Bahá's family. They saw His sister Bahá'íyyih Khánum as the archetype of the people of Bahá and learned from her lessons in self-effacement and self-sacrifice. At the same time, their visits provided Bahá'íyyih Khánum and other members of 'Abdu'l-Bahá's family with glimpses of the western world and how the light of Bahá'u'lláh's Revelation was rapidly penetrating beyond the Asian and African continents. Some women pilgrims, such as Laura Clifford Barney and Lua Getsinger, spent extended periods of time with the Holy Family, met 'Abdu'l-Bahá frequently, drank deep from the wellspring of His divine knowledge, and gained deeper insights into the way that the Centre of Bahá'u'lláh's Covenant and the most 'outstanding heroine of the Bahá'í Dispensation'[144] lived.

Among the seekers who visited the Holy Land at the beginning of the 20th century with the specific aim of meeting 'Abdu'l-Bahá and investigating the truth of Bahá'u'lláh's Cause were Countess M. A. de S. Canavarro and Myron H. Phelps. To obtain firsthand information about Bahá'u'lláh and His family's successive exiles from Ṭihrán to Baghdád, Constantinople, Adrianople and 'Akká, Mr Phelps arranged to have interviews with Bahá'íyyih Khánum. However, Islamic custom strictly observed by the people of the area and which the Bahá'ís respected 'for the sake of peace and harmony'[145] did not allow him to meet with her personally. Therefore, Madam Canavarro met with Bahá'íyyih Khánum and through a translator received responses to the questions she put to her. The information thus obtained was conveyed to Myron Phelps, who recorded them in his book *Life and Teachings of Abbas Effendi*.

Events of monumental significance took place during the period that 'Abdu'l-Bahá and His family lived in the house of 'Abdu'lláh Pashá. The remains of the Báb and His companion reached the shores of the Holy Land at the end of January 1899, were safely delivered to 'Abdu'l-Bahá's hand and kept in the room of His trusted sister, Bahá'íyyih Khánum. It was also during His stay in the house of 'Abdu'lláh Páshá that 'Abdu'l-Bahá wrote at least the first two parts of His Will and Testament.

Meanwhile, the activities of the stirrers of mischief intensified steadily, causing 'Abdu'l-Bahá and His family, particularly Bahá'íyyih Khánum, increased sorrow and deep concern. 'Abdu'l-Bahá did everything in His power to contain the effect of their misdeeds but the scope of their activities reached such proportions that He had to make them known to the community and warn the faithful against their schemes. The grief and sadness caused by the activities of the opponents of Bahá'u'lláh's Covenant affected 'Abdu'l-Bahá's health. He was persuaded to leave 'Akká for a change of air and recuperation. This time He travelled to Haifa, where He stayed at the lower cave of Elijah. A Tablet to Bahá'íyyih Khánum was written during that visit:

> My sister and beloved of my soul!
>
> Here on the slopes of Mount Carmel, by the cave of Elijah, we are thinking of that Most Exalted Leaf, and the beloved and handmaids of the Lord.

We pass our days in writing and our nights now in communion with God, now in bed to overcome failing health. And although, to outward seeming, we are absent from you all, and far away, still our thoughts are with you always.

I can never, never forget thee. However great the distance that separates us, we still feel as though we were seated under the same roof, in one and the same gathering, for are we not all under the shadow of the Tabernacle of God and beneath the canopy of His infinite grace and mercy?[146]

During the first few years of the stay of 'Abdu'l-Bahá and His family in the house of 'Abdu'lláh Páshá, the Cause of God in the Holy Land and abroad gained in stature and made striking progress, enabling 'Abdu'l-Bahá to purchase land on Mount Carmel in Haifa and begin work on constructing a befitting mausoleum for the remains of the Báb on a site designated by Bahá'u'lláh.

The Covenant-breakers' New Intrigues

The prestige enjoyed by 'Abdu'l-Bahá and His faithful followers tempted Mírzá Badí'u'lláh, the younger half brother of 'Abdu'l-Bahá and Bahá'iyyih Khánum and a strong supporter of Mírzá Muḥammad-'Alí, to make appeals to rejoin the community of faithful believers. He expressed regret for his wrongdoings, made fervent pleas to 'Abdu'l-Bahá to forgive his past transgressions and promised to abide by the requirements of Bahá'u'lláh's Book of the Covenant. Soon after his admission, he betrayed his true intention and continued his subversive activities against 'Abdu'l-Bahá and the Cause He represented. When his misdeeds were exposed, he rejoined Mírzá Muḥammad-'Alí, the Arch-breaker of the Covenant, and his supporters. However, hope for financial gain and continued disagreement with Mírzá Muḥammad-'Alí caused him to use repentance once again as a pretext for seeking forgiveness from 'Abdu'l-Bahá. To give credence to his plea, he used a reputable believer as intermediary. Knowing his craftiness and selfish intentions, 'Abdu'l-Bahá asked that he make his confession in writing and explain what he and Mírzá Muḥammad-'Alí had perpetrated in contradiction to the text of Bahá'u'lláh's Covenant. As a result, his well-known letters of confession enumerating the misdeeds committed against 'Abdu'l-Bahá were written. Yet in spite of his written confessions and claims of sincere repentance, after achieving his purpose he began his vast campaign of scheming against 'Abdu'l-Bahá from inside His house, causing 'Abdu'l-Bahá and His family endless pain and suffering. At least thrice Mírzá Badí'u'lláh repented and went back on the promises he had given.

The malicious and baseless reports that Mírzá Badí'u'lláh sent about 'Abdu'l-Bahá's activities alarmed the authorities and prompted the central government to dispatch designated individuals to carry out extensive investigations of the reported claims. Among the pretexts used by the Covenant-breakers to alarm the authorities were the coming of western pilgrims and the construction of the original rooms of the Shrine of the Báb on Mount Carmel. 'Abdu'l-Bahá was accused of building a fortress in preparation for raising the banner of rebellion at a time when the government was weak and suspicious of any activity that could be interpreted as hostile in nature. During the investigation Mírzá Badí'u'lláh joined hands with 'Abdu'l-Bahá's sworn enemies. The trumped-up charges against Him and the false reports culminated in the re-incarceration of 'Abdu'l-Bahá. Referring to the role played by Bahá'íyyih Khánum in connection with that episode, Shoghi Effendi says:

> In the midst of that storm of violation, the countenance of that rare treasure of the Lord shone all the brighter, and throughout the Bahá'í community, her value and high rank became clearly perceived. By the vehement onslaught of the chief of violators against the sacred beliefs of the followers of the Faith, she was neither frightened nor in despair.
>
> In the days of the Commission of Investigation, she was a staunch and trusted supporter of the peerless Branch of Bahá'u'lláh, and a companion to Him beyond compare.[147]

> With the passing of Bahá'u'lláh and the fierce onslaught of the forces of disruption that followed in its wake, the Greatest Holy Leaf, now in the hey-day of her life, rose to the height of her great opportunity and acquitted herself worthily of her task . . . but for her sleepless vigilance, her tact, her courtesy, her extreme patience and heroic fortitude, grave complications might have ensued and the load of 'Abdu'l-Bahá's anxious care would have been considerably increased.[148]

Shoghi Effendi testifies that Bahá'íyyih Khánum was 'the partner in sorrows and tribulations of 'Abdu'l-Bahá'.[149]

The relentless activities of the violators of Bahá'u'lláh's Covenant to remove 'Abdu'l-Bahá from the scene were about to bear the hoped-for result. They had succeeded in influencing the outcome of the official investigation by lavishing valuable gifts on the authorities and extending bribes to people in power. Recommendations had been made to the central government that 'Abdu'l-Bahá be either executed or banished to a remote and obscure place in North Africa. Just about the time that the decree was to be carried out, the Young Turks' revolution took place in 1908, leading to the release of all political prisoners. Since 'Abdu'l-Bahá had been re-incarcerated on the basis of accusations levelled against Him by His kindred and their supporters that He was involved in carrying out subversive activities against the government, He, too, was set free. Thus the Covenant-breakers' designs were utterly frustrated. Instead of being executed or exiled, 'Abdu'l-Bahá was free. His freedom set the stage for remarkable achievements and opened the way for undreamed-of undertakings.

Supporting 'Abdu'l-Bahá's Undertakings

To fully exploit the opportunities that freedom offered, it was absolutely essential for 'Abdu'l-Bahá to have beside Him someone of the calibre of Bahá'íyyih Khánum. She combined the attributes of a sacrificial nature and being her brother's loving confidant, tireless helper, selfless supporter and a trusted deputy when needed. Shoghi Effendi says:

> And when the storm-cloud that had darkened the horizon of the Holy Land had been finally dissipated and the call raised by our beloved 'Abdu'l-Bahá had stirred to a new life certain cities of the American and European continents, the Most Exalted Leaf became the recipient of the unbounded affection and blessings of One Who could best estimate her virtues and appreciate her merits.[150]

He describes the nature of the services that Bahá'íyyih Khánum rendered after 'Abdu'l-Bahá's release from confinement:

> The decline of her precious life had by that time set in, and the burden of advancing age was beginning to becloud the radiance of her countenance. Forgetful of her own self, disdaining rest and comfort, and undeterred by the obstacles that still stood in her path, she, acting as the honoured hostess to a steadily increasing number of pilgrims who thronged 'Abdu'l-Bahá's residence from both the East and the West, continued to display those same attributes that had won her, in the preceding phases of her career, so great a measure of admiration and love.[151]

Move to Haifa

While the construction of the Shrine of the Báb on Mount Carmel was underway, 'Abdu'l-Bahá was contemplating another building project. Preparations for the construction of the new building were made as He was confined to

His house in 'Akká, with all His activities and movements under surveillance. That project was the house He built below the Shrine of the Báb on the slope of Mount Carmel with specifications He Himself determined. The house was ready for occupation about two years before the remains of the Báb were placed in the mausoleum built for the purpose. According to *The Priceless Pearl*,

> When 'Abdu'l-Bahá first moved into the new home in Haifa (which was in use by members of His family in February 1907, if not earlier) the rooms were occupied by all the members of His family . . .[152]

The transfer from 'Akká to Haifa did not take place at once. Some members of 'Abdu'l-Bahá's family moved to that city first. Before settling in Haifa permanently, Bahá'íyyih Khánum made several trips there. Some of 'Abdu'l-Bahá's Tablets addressed to her were revealed during those visits. Shoghi Effendi's name is mentioned at the end of two Tablets, indicating that by then he was either living and going to school in Haifa, or that he had accompanied his great aunt on her visit:

> O My sister in the spirit, and the companion of my heart!
> God willing, the climate of Haifa hath proved favourable. I hope that out of the bounties of the Ancient Beauty thou wilt gain a measure of peace and health.
>
> I bring thee to mind both night and day. Just recently I had hoped to come to Haifa to visit thee, but various problems and the pressure of work have left me no time; for I want to see the travellers off, and every one of them presented a long list of names. God be thanked, I have written to them all.
>
> Kiss the fresh flower of the garden of sweetness, Shoghi Effendi.[153]

> O My spiritual sister!
> Thou didst go away to Haifa, supposedly for only three or four days. Now it becometh apparent that the spiritual power of the Shrine hath brought thee joy and radiance, and even as a magnet is holding thee fast. Thou surely wouldst remember us as well.
>
> Truly the spiritual quality of the holy place, its fresh skies and delicate air, its crystal waters and sweet plains and charming seascape, and the holy breathings from the Kingdom all do mingle in that Sacred Fold. Thou art right to linger there . . .
>
> Kiss the light of the eyes of the company of spiritual souls, Shoghi Effendi . . .[154]

The following Tablet places Bahá'íyyih Khánum in Nazareth and Haifa:

> O My dear sister!
> It is quite a while now, since thou hast left us, and gone away to Nazareth and Haifa. This journey hath lasted too long. The weather in 'Akká is fine and moderate. If thou comest back, it will rejoice our hearts . . .[155]

At the end of this Tablet, too, 'Abdu'l-Bahá conveys loving greetings to Ḍíyá Khánum and Jináb-i-Áqá Mírzá Hádí,[156] and asks His sister to kiss the spiritual Shoghi Effendi.

'Abdu'l-Bahá continued to live in 'Akká until about 1909. H.M. Balyuzi says:

> During the period immediately following the change of the Turkish régime, 'Abdu'l-Bahá continued His residence in 'Akká. But after the entombment of the remains of the Báb, he chose to live in Haifa, where a house was being built for Him.[157]

After 'Abdu'l-Bahá moved to Haifa, there were times when Bahá'íyyih Khánum went to 'Akká for a visit. This is evidenced by a Tablet 'Abdu'l-Bahá revealed in her honour while she was there:

> O My well-beloved sister, O Most Exalted Leaf!
> Thou didst leave for 'Akká to remain but two days or so and then return, but now thou hast been gone from us for quite a while. We have stayed behind in Haifa, all alone, and it is very difficult to get along. We hear that thou art a little indisposed; the Haifa air would have been better for thee. We had everything ready in Haifa to receive thee, but in fact, this caused thee some difficulty. There is no way but to endure the toil and trouble of God's path. If thou dost not bear these hardships, who would ever bear them?
>
> In any case, no matter how things are, come thou here today, because my heart is longing for thee.[158]

What comes through strongly is the deep affection that existed between 'Abdu'l-Bahá and Bahá'íyyih Khánum. Time and again, when 'Abdu'l-Bahá was separated from His beloved sister, whether the duration was short or long, He expressed His eagerness to reunite with her. During a journey He had earlier taken to Haifa for health reasons, He wrote to her:

> O My affectionate sister!
> God be praised, through His grace and favour, my health and well-being

are now restored, but it is very hard for me to bear thine absence.

We think of thee at all times, here on the slopes of this sacred, holy and blessed Mount Carmel, and we are being happy on thy behalf . . .[159]

The Interment of the Remains of the Báb

The first highly significant project 'Abdu'l-Bahá undertook after gaining freedom was placing the remains of the Báb in the Mausoleum He had built on Mount Carmel. Present at the ceremony were pilgrims from the East and West, as well as local Bahá'ís. It is not clear whether Bahá'íyyih Khánum, who had been the trusted custodian of those remains for a considerable time, and other female members of 'Abdu'l-Bahá's family participated in the ceremony. Traditional restrictions on women in the Middle East may have prevented them from being present. The restrictions included absenting themselves from functions attended by men other than close family members, which encompassed everything in public. Bahá'íyyih Khánum was kept informed of all developments regarding the project, watched its construction from beginning to end with great anticipation and visited the place on many occasions, both before and after the tomb's completion. The reports left of that momentous event indicate that on the morning of Naw-Rúz 1909, the day when the remains of the Báb were placed in the Shrine, 'Abdu'l-Bahá and His family travelled from 'Akká to Haifa. Therefore Bahá'íyyih Khánum and other female members of 'Abdu'l-Bahá's family were in Haifa on that day. If they were not present at the public ceremony, they were most certainly in a place nearby. The absence of any published record regarding their participation in the ceremony or a private visit to the Shrine immediately before or after the interment of the remains makes it difficult to say anything with certainty. The following from the unpublished memoirs of Layla Ábádih'i may provide a clue:

> I heard from Ḍíyá, granddaughter of the King of Martyrs, wife of Mírzá Inayatu'lláh-i-Iṣfahán, who was residing in the Holy Land . . . that when the remains reached Beirut, 'Abdu'l-Bahá instructed that they be brought to 'Akká by boat. The person in charge was Jináb-i-Mírzá Asadu'lláh-i-Isfahání, 'Abdu'l-Bahá's brother-in-law . . . The remains were taken to the home of Jináb-i-Mírzá Asadu'lláh. After a few days, they were transferred to 'Abdu'l-Bahá's house [in 'Akká]. When the Shrine was ready, the remains were taken to Carmel. On the appointed day, 'Abdu'l-Bahá advised the Greatest Holy Leaf and other members of His family to go up to the Shrine and be there for the interment of the remains. 'Abdu'l-Bahá accompanied by Mr . . . [a western pilgrim] went up ahead of time . . .[160]

Deputizing for 'Abdu'l-Bahá

As stated before, the revolution of the Young Turks in 1908 resulted in the freedom of all political prisoners. 'Abdu'l-Bahá was not a political figure but His re-incarceration had been politically motivated. Soon after He gained freedom, He and His family moved to Haifa. The move prepared the ground for significant events that followed. Eighteen months after the remains of the Báb and His companion, Mírzá Muḥammad-'Alíy-i Zunúzí, were ceremoniously interred in a permanent resting-place on Mount Carmel, 'Abdu'l-Bahá embarked on His travels to Egypt, Europe and North America. Shoghi Effendi refers to the vital role that Bahá'íyyih Khánum played as 'Abdu'l-Bahá's vicegerent during His long absence from the Holy Land:

> And when . . . the ban on 'Abdu'l-Bahá's confinement was lifted . . . He with unhesitating confidence, invested His trusted and honoured sister with the responsibility of attending to the multitudinous details arising out of His protracted absence from the Holy Land.[161]

Absence from the World Centre of the Faith for a lengthy period at a time when the Covenant-breakers were actively pursuing their malicious objective of establishing an authority in parallel to that of 'Abdu'l-Bahá was a delicate matter and needed to be handled with special tact. Making the plans of His contemplated visit public would have entailed complications and may have thwarted His purpose. The one whom He could take into His confidence was the person capable of overseeing the affairs of the community in the Holy Land in His absence. He disclosed His plan to Bahá'íyyih Khánum in a Tablet revealed in her honour. The contents of the Tablet, which may have been revealed at the time 'Abdu'l-Bahá was on His way to Egypt, indicate that Bahá'íyyih Khánum prior to the receipt of that Tablet was probably unaware of the plan. The Tablet also confirms that her presence in the Holy Land made it possible for 'Abdu'l-Bahá to undertake the trip with peace of mind. The precariousness of the situation did not allow further disclosure of details which remain to date unclear:

> O thou my sister, my dear sister!
> Divine wisdom hath decreed this temporary separation, but I long more and more to be with thee again. Patience is called for, and long-suffering, and trust in God, and the seeking of His favour. Since thou art there, my mind is completely at rest.
>
> In recent days, I have made a plan to visit Egypt, if this be God's will. Do thou, on my behalf, lay thy head on the sacred Threshold, and

perfume brow and hair in the dust of that Door, and ask that I may be confirmed in my work; that I may, in return for His endless bounties, win, if He will, a drop out of the ocean of servitude.[162]

This was a momentous time in Bahá'íyyih Khánum's life. It is not clear how she reacted to this sudden thrust of responsibility, how she carried out the requirements of her work and, more importantly, how she coped with 'Abdu'l-Bahá's long absence from the Holy Land. Since Bahá'u'lláh's ascension, 'Abdu'l-Bahá had been away from His family for short periods of time but never outside the confines of the Holy Land. And never before had it become necessary for Him to entrust His beloved sister with responsibility for supervising the affairs of the family and the community for such a long time. A detailed history of this period would probably deal with these questions, as well as how the believers in the Holy Land and abroad reacted to His long absence.

'Abdu'l-Bahá initially visited Egypt, a country not far from the Holy Land. There He spent a considerable time before and after a short trip to France and Great Britain. One of the wisdoms of His long stay in Egypt may have been to prepare the ground for His longer absence from the Bahá'í World Centre. Had the means of communication been as elaborate and efficient as they are today, a physical distance of several thousand kilometres between 'Abdu'l-Bahá and Bahá'íyyih Khánum would have been a less daunting prospect. For 'Abdu'l-Bahá to be away from the World Centre of the Faith for such a long time and in places so distant, He needed a person completely trustworthy, utterly selfless, fully devoted and completely faithful to the Covenant. These qualities He found in the person of His highly valued sister, Bahá'íyyih Khánum, the Greatest Holy Leaf. As Shoghi Effendi says, 'At the time of His absence in the western world, she was His competent deputy, His representative and vicegerent, with none to equal her.'[163]

After His arrival in France, 'Abdu'l-Bahá sent the following Tablet to Bahá'iyyih Khánum:

Her Highness, the Greatest Holy Leaf, upon her be Bahá'u'lláhu'l-Abhá! He is the Glory of the Most Glorious! O My beloved sister! Through the bounties of the Blessed Beauty, may My spirit be sacrificed for His Blessed Dust, we have traversed the expanse of deep seas, and have, under the loving protection of the Most Great Name, passed through ports and gulf straits. We are now staying at Grant Hotel in Thonen on the shore of Lake Swiss, thinking of thee and remembering thee. The beauty of the scenery, the pleasantness of the place, the purity of the water, the charm of the horizon, the softness of the breeze, and the lushness of the mountain have combined to produce an extraordinary sight better than which cannot be imagined. However, 'Abdu'l-Bahá is so busied with work and writing that He has no time to look [at the scenery]. But the climate is agreeable. It is hoped that through the favours of the Ancient Beauty, this broken winged gnat will be so strengthened in servitude to the Threshold of the Desired One as to extend new wings. He taketh every breath with such hope, and all dependeth on His aid.

Yea! I swear by the Sacred Dust that the sandy earth beyond 'Akká is so filled with spirituality and luminosity that one span of it is preferable to a thousand gardens, parks, lawns and meadows of this country, for the soil of that land is luminous and its billowing sea high as the firmament. His grace causes its breeze to blow. Its fragrance is the smell of strong-scented musk, its desert the valley of trust, its expanse the Blessed Shrine, and a place blooming with flowers and roses. Therefore, notwithstanding separation from that land, for the people of faith, this is like a prison and portico narrow and dark. Hence, I expect of thee, at the time of visiting the Sacred Court, to place thy face on that perfumed dust, kiss the Holy Threshold, and beseech aid and assistance that 'Abdu'l-Bahá may take a breath in serving that Threshold.

Convey My utmost love and eagerness to the blessed leaf, My sister Furúghíyyih Khánum. She is always in my thoughts. Also, convey My Abhá greetings to her mother.[164]

The water pump for the Shrine Garden has no doubt been installed by now.[165]

And upon His arrival in New York 'Abdu'l-Bahá wrote:

O thou Greatest and Most Merciful Holy Leaf!
I arrived in New York in the best of health, and I have been at all times thinking of thee, and supplicating fervently at the threshold of the Blessed Beauty that He may guard thee in the stronghold of His protection. We are in the utmost fellowship and joy. I hope that thou wilt be sheltered under His bountiful care. Write to me at once about Rúḥá Khánum's and Shoghi Effendi's condition, informing me fully and hiding nothing; this is the best way.[166]

Convey my utmost longing to all.[167]

When His labours in the West bore fruit and the trip became an outstanding success, 'Abdu'l-Bahá wrote to His sister, sharing with her the glad-tidings of the progress achieved:

> O My dear sister!
> Praise be to God, within the sheltering grace of the Blessed Beauty, here in the lands of the West a breeze hath blown from over the rose-gardens of His bestowals, and the hearts of many people have been drawn as by a magnet to the Abhá Realm.
>
> Whatever hath come to pass is from the confirmations of the Beloved; for otherwise, what merit had we, or what capacity? We are as a helpless babe, but fed at the breast of heavenly grace. We are no more than weak plants, but we flourish in the spring rain of His bestowals.[168]

Before closing, 'Abdu'l-Bahá made a special request of His beloved sister:

> Wherefore, as a thank-offering for these bounties, on a certain day don thy garb to visit the Shrine, the ka'bih of our heart's desire, turn thyself toward Him on my behalf, lay down thy head on that sacred Threshold, and say:
>
> 'O divine Providence! O Thou forgiving Lord! Sinner though I be, I have no refuge save Thyself . . . [169]

In another Tablet He said:

> O My cherished sister!
> Thou art never absent from my thoughts.
>
> I speak of thee and call thee to mind at all times. It is my hope that out of God's favour and grace thou mayest keep well and safe, and dost visit the two Sacred Thresholds on my behalf.[170]

There was regular correspondence between 'Abdu'l-Bahá and Bahá'íyyih Khánum during His absence from the Holy Land. Bahá'íyyih Khánum kept 'Abdu'l-Bahá informed of all developments, shared with Him her inner thoughts and sought His advice on matters that needed His approval. At a time when she was feeling unwell and in need of a change, He was asked regarding her taking a trip or introducing some change in her routine.[171] In response, 'Abdu'l-Bahá wrote:

> O My sister, the kindred of My spirit!
> I have perused all the communications that were sent. Regarding a trip to Alexandria, Cairo, Port Said and also from there to Beirut, do thou consider what is best for thee. Whatever leads to an improvement in thy health, the same should be carried out. If the weather proves disagreeable, thou mayest go to Beirut and stay in the home of Jináb-i-Muḥammad Muṣṭafá, upon him be Bahá'u'lláhu'l-Abhá. Also, shouldst thou desire to

> go to Jibál from there, that, too, is permissible. Or shouldst thou wish, we could obtain a place specially for thee in Haifa. Do thou write soon about thy decision.
>
> Convey Abhá greetings on My behalf to all the blessed leaves and also to all the friends. There is no time to mention them one by one.
>
> P.S. I have given Áqá Muḥammad-Taqí the sum of 30 Liras to give to thee. Thou mayest get from 'Aqá Siyyid Yaḥyá [Munírih Khánum's brother] what thou need. I will pay him later.[172]

Another Tablet which seems to have been revealed during 'Abdu'l-Bahá's visit to the West provides evidence that Bahá'íyyih Khánum did make a trip to Egypt at that time.

> Dear sister, beloved of my heart and soul!
> The news of thy safe arrival and pleasant stay in the land of Egypt has reached me and filled my heart with exceeding gladness. I am thankful to Bahá'u'lláh for the good health thou dost enjoy and for the happiness He hath imparted to the hearts of the loved ones in that land. Shouldst thou wish to know of the condition of this servant of the Threshold of the Abhá Beauty, praise be to Him for having enabled me to inhale the fragrance of His tender mercy and partake of the delights of His loving-kindness and blessings. I am being continually reinforced by the energizing rays of His grace, and feel upheld by the uninterrupted aid of the victorious hosts of His Kingdom. My physical health is also improving. God be praised that from every quarter I receive the glad-tidings of the growing ascendancy of the Cause of God, and can witness evidences of the increasing influence of its spread . . .[173]

Reunion in Egypt

After extensive travels in the North American and European continents involving numerous appearances in formal gatherings, meetings with religious and political leaders of various countries, interviews with newspaper reporters and attending gatherings of the friends, 'Abdu'l-Bahá returned to Egypt on 16 June 1913. From there He wrote to Bahá'íyyih Khánum:

> O My beloved sister, the Greatest Holy Leaf!
> My eagerness knows no bound. I have not seen thee for such a long time. My coming to Haifa is somewhat delayed. If possible, come soon to Port Said. Perhaps we could return together to the Holy Land . . .[174]

According to the Hand of the Cause Amatu'l-Bahá Rúḥíyyih Khánum, 'His family hastened to His presence there, among them Shoghi Effendi, who joined Him about six weeks after His arrival'.[175] Shoghi Effendi who was then studying in Beirut could not join his grandfather immediately. He waited for the school year to end after the first week of July. Thereafter, he returned to Haifa 'where he joined some of his family and then sailed from Haifa to Egypt, arriving in the company of the Greatest Holy Leaf and others on 1 August in Ramleh, where 'Abdu'l-Bahá had once again rented a villa'.[176] Writing of the emotions that surged in the heart of the Greatest Holy Leaf when after three years she was reunited with her beloved brother in Egypt, Shoghi Effendi says:

> The enthusiasm and joy which swelled in her breast as she greeted 'Abdu'l-Bahá on His triumphant return from the West, I will not venture to describe. She was astounded at the vitality of which He had, despite His unimaginable sufferings, proved Himself capable. She was lost in admiration at the magnitude of the forces which His utterances had released. She was filled with thankfulness to Bahá'u'lláh for having enabled her to witness the evidences of such brilliant victory for His Cause no less than for His Son.[177]

'Abdu'l-Bahá's extensive travels from 1910 to 1913, apart from spreading the fragrances of the Revelation of Bahá'u'lláh abroad and promulgating the tenets of His Cause, facilitated the achievement of the following two very important purposes:

1) It afforded Bahá'íyyih Khánum the opportunity to act as 'Abdu'l-Bahá's deputy during His ministry. Her deputization made it clear to Bahá'ís everywhere that, after 'Abdu'l-Bahá Himself, the station of no one rivalled that of the Greatest Holy Leaf.

2) It laid the ground for the Greatest Holy Leaf to use her leadership abilities on a scale much wider than hitherto tried. It also prepared her to render vital service immediately after 'Abdu'l-Bahá's ascension and during Shoghi Effendi's absence from the Holy Land.

These points will be discussed in more detail below.

Return to the Holy Land

Bahá'íyyih Khánum returned to the Holy Land with feelings of joy and relief that the Master had safely returned from His extensive and arduous travels in the West. She was also grateful that the project had been highly successful. Upon her return, she resumed her previous work and continued to be the staunchest supporter of the Centre of the Covenant until His ascension on 28 November 1921. One of her laborious responsibilities was overseeing arrangements for feeding the pilgrims and visitors from East and West who, in an increasing number, thronged 'Abdu'l-Bahá's house, a task which she performed with happiness and radiance. To ensure that everything was done in a timely manner, she would get up early in the morning, open the room where provisions were stored and release the amount necessary for that day's meals. She would then personally supervise every stage of the preparation of the food and send pots of cooked food to places where oriental and occidental pilgrims stayed. She was alert that no one should go without food. If one from among the members of 'Abdu'l-Bahá's family were absent, she would send food to his or her home.

The pilgrims were eager to see their Khánum. One would request a name for her child, another would seek blessings from her hand. There were also those who, according to their Islamic background, would bring material for shrouds and ask Khánum to cut it for them, that it might help them rest in their graves with more comfort.[178] Nonetheless, she would find time to attend to the needs of non-Bahá'ís as well. Dr Ḥabíb Mu'ayyad writes in his memoirs:

> Poor and shelterless orphans were the recipients of her special care and affection. She sheltered them in the house of the Master and loved them dearly . . . regardless of whether they were Arab or non-Arab, black or white, Bahá'í or non-Bahá'í. She taught them good manners, the art of relating to others, dawn prayers, reading and writing, home management, embroidery, sewing, cooking, studying the verses of God, fear of God and human perfections. She adorned them with the ornament of knowledge, good character, perfection and fear of God. She turned them into fruitful trees, led them to the highway of guidance, prepared them for living the life, made them prosperous and delivered them to society . . .[179]

World War I

About a year after 'Abdu'l-Bahá's return to the Holy Land, World War I broke out and engulfed areas under the rule of the Ottoman Empire. The threat of bombardment made the inhabitants of the Haifa–'Akká areas very fearful. To spare His family and members of the Bahá'í community unnecessary distress and concern, 'Abdu'l-Bahá responded affirmatively to an invitation from <u>Sh</u>ay<u>kh</u> Ṣáliḥ and sent everyone to Abú-Sinán, a Druze village situated to the east of 'Akká in the Galilee. During the six months that they lived there, 'Abdu'l-Bahá remained with one or two attendants in the Haifa–'Akká area. According to Dr Ḥabíb Mu'ayyad,[180] during that time, 'He visited Abú-Sinán every week, to supervise the affairs of the community there, but returned after a night or two.'[181] In His absence, Bahá'íyyih <u>Kh</u>ánum was in charge and ensured the well-being of those in her care. Dr Mu'ayyad says that although there was a famine, Bahá'íyyih <u>Kh</u>ánum personally prepared food and sent it to the place where he and several others stayed, so they did not go hungry.[182]

The dire consequences of the war affected all, especially the poor and those with a low income. Regarding the services rendered by Bahá'íyyih <u>Kh</u>ánum during the war, Shoghi Effendi says:

> The outbreak of the Great War gave her yet another opportunity to reveal the true worth of her character and to release the latent energies of her heart. The residence of 'Abdu'l-Bahá in Haifa was besieged, all throughout that dreary conflict, by a concourse of famished men, women and children whom the maladministration, the cruelty and neglect of the officials of the Ottoman Government had driven to seek an alleviation to their woes. From the hand of the Greatest Holy Leaf, and out of the abundance of her heart, these hapless victims of a contemptible tyranny, received day after day unforgettable evidences of a love they had learned to envy and admire. Her words of cheer and comfort, the food, the money, the clothing she freely dispensed, the remedies which, by a process of her own, she herself prepared and diligently applied – all these had their share in comforting the disconsolate, in restoring sight to the blind, in sheltering the orphan, in healing the sick, and in succouring the homeless and the wanderer.
>
> She had reached, amidst the darkness of the war days the high watermark of her spiritual attainments. Few, if any, among the unnumbered benefactors of society whose privilege has been to allay, in various measures, the hardships and sufferings entailed by that Fierce Conflict, gave as freely and as disinterestedly as she did; few exercised that undefinable influence upon the beneficiaries of their gifts.[183]

Life After the War

When the war ended it took some time before life returned to normal. One of the activities suspended during the war was pilgrimage. Over the years pilgrims from the East and West had come even during difficult times. Their visits served as a vital link between 'Abdu'l-Bahá and His faithful followers. They also served as a welcome link between the members of His family and the outside world. When the war broke out, life for people living in areas affected by the war was completely disrupted, normal communication stopped, travelling became hazardous and insecurity was a major concern. These combined factors made it necessary to suspend pilgrimage to the Bahá'í World Centre. Those who had permission to come on pilgrimage were advised to postpone their visit. As soon as roads were safe to travel and life assumed some normality, pilgrims were allowed to come again.

Among the western friends who came on pilgrimage in 1919 were Mr and Mrs Randall and their daughter Margaret, whom 'Abdu'l-Bahá named Bahíyyih. She was then 12 years old. In *My Pilgrimage to Haifa, November 1919*, she describes the meetings that she and her mother had with the sister, wife and daughters of 'Abdu'l-Bahá. Some of her observations provide insightful clues to their lives. For example, describing the afternoon of the first day, she says:

> That afternoon we also went to a gathering at the Shrine of the Báb, the Herald of the Bahá'í Faith. Mother and I were sad because the ladies of the Master's household could not be with us. They had to stay at home while we visited the holy places because it was a Muslim rule that men who were not part of their family – and there were many – could not be permitted to enter their company.[184]

The restriction applied also to meals that 'Abdu'l-Bahá had with the pilgrims. Although the women supervised the preparation of meals for the pilgrims, they did not eat with them if men were present. Mrs Mabel Hyde Paine describes a meeting in the Master's house with the Greatest Holy Leaf, the Holy Mother, two of 'Abdu'l-Bahá's daughters and some of His grandchildren:

> After a while dinner was announced. Then these beautiful ladies left us, kissing us as they had at first. We felt sad that custom demanded that they should not eat, as we did, at the same table with men.[185]

On the fourth day of Bahíyyih Randall's pilgrimage there was unusual activity at tea time:

> Many Bahá'í women came and went. The Master's wife was going away, but she had four daughters who would help take care of things. But I had noticed that it was the Greatest Holy Leaf to whom everyone turned for help and advice. She was gentle and loving, but strong, too.[186]

On day five Bahíyyih Randall helped the ladies of 'Abdu'l-Bahá's family and household clean wheat. 'There were great bags of it, and we pulled it towards us little by little, looking for the small stones that cause trouble.'[187] That afternoon she had a private visit with the Greatest Holy Leaf in her room. She was shown 'some interesting pictures and things that she had'. The Greatest Holy Leaf 'spoke little English but her eyes talked. Her face looked dreadfully tired but her eyes were like the Master's, so alive and expressive. She was not like the other ladies . . .' 'The Greatest Holy Leaf was apart, like the Master. It was a joy to be with her. I loved her,' wrote Bahiyyih Randall.[188]

The resident women believers had their share of meetings with the Greatest Holy Leaf as well. Once a week on Wednesday afternoon they congregated in the house of the Master. 'The purpose', says Rafí'ih Shahídí, 'was to attain the presence of the Greatest Holy Leaf, the wife of the Master and members of the Holy Family. After prayers were recited, the Greatest Holy Leaf spoke and expressed loving words which made everyone joyous and happy . . . When we left that rarefied atmosphere, we looked forward to spending a similar day the following week in that blessed house which was everyone's shelter and refuge . . .'[189] The Wednesday afternoon meetings were at times attended by the western women pilgrims. Mabel Hyde Paine says in her memoirs: 'In the afternoon we went to the women's meeting which is held every Wednesday in the Master's House. There were probably about twenty-five there. All were dressed very simply in plain print dresses. Their veils were thrown back on their shoulders . . .'[190]

'Abdu'l-Bahá's Ascension: Bahá'íyyih Khánum's Role During Shoghi Effendi's Absence, 28 November to 29 December 1921

Shoghi Effendi was in England when 'Abdu'l-Bahá passed away. The period between 'Abdu'l-Bahá's ascension and Shoghi Effendi's return to the Holy Land, although very short in duration, is most crucial in the annals of the Bahá'í Faith. 'Abdu'l-Bahá, the Centre of Bahá'u'lláh's Covenant, passed away on 28 November 1921. The one appointed by Him as the Guardian of the Cause of God and the interpreter of the writings was not in Haifa at the time. Moreover, he was unaware of the appointment and the Bahá'í world was uninformed of the provisions of 'Abdu'l-Bahá's Will and Testament. Mírzá Muḥammad-'Alí, who, according to Bahá'u'lláh's Book of the Covenant, would have succeeded 'Abdu'l-Bahá had he not opposed Him and tried to divide the community, was actively pursuing all possible avenues to establish himself as 'Abdu'l-Bahá's rightful successor. Bahá'iyyih Khánum was the only living member of Bahá'u'lláh's immediate family who had remained faithful to His Covenant and stood firmly by 'Abdu'l-Bahá through the 29 years of His ministry. She was the one the Bahá'í world knew as the Greatest Holy Leaf, the one who had served as 'Abdu'l-Bahá's deputy and vicegerent during His long absence from the Holy Land. The eyes of the faithful were turned to her to guide their steps and tell them what was to be done next. Muḥammad-Shafí' Rouhani[191] explains in his memoirs how the friends in Nayríz thought the Greatest Holy Leaf was the leader of the Bahá'í community after 'Abdu'l-Bahá:

> The news of the calamitous event, the ascension of 'Abdu'l-Bahá . . . was conveyed by Áqá Ḥakím, a member of the Local Spiritual Assembly of Shíráz, to Manṣúru's-Salṭanih, the governor of Nayríz. Manṣúru's-Salṭanih sent Shaykh Áqá Fáḍil, an Arabic teacher in the Manṣúrí School, to inform the Local Spiritual Assembly of Nayríz . . . Every night memorial meetings were held in the Ḥaẓíratu'l-Quds. The Assembly provided consolation to the friends by saying that 'Abdu'l-Bahá had not left the community without direction. Another message from the Greatest Holy Leaf was received assuring the friends that 'Abdu'l-Bahá had left a Will and Testament . . . She advised the Bahá'ís in the interim period, until the name of the successor was made public, to read the Tablet of the Holy Mariner. Therefore, every night that Tablet was recited and Jináb-i Fáḍil-i Shírází[192] translated it.[193] From its contents the friends inferred that after 'Abdu'l-Bahá, the Greatest Holy Leaf was in charge of affairs. One night Jináb-i-Fáḍil-i Qaṣru'd-Dashtí said, 'The contents of the Tablet seem to indicate that the Greatest Holy Leaf would be in charge of affairs . . . After 40 days the Will and Testament was read publicly. Its glad-tidings reached Nayríz after a few days. We all heard and obeyed the directives.[194]

Regarding the effect of 'Abdu'l-Bahá's ascension on Bahá'íyyih Khánum and the invaluable services she rendered immediately after His passing, Shoghi Effendi says:

> The ascension of 'Abdu'l-Bahá, so tragic in its suddenness, was to her a terrible blow from the effects of which she never completely recovered. To her He, Whom she called 'Áqá', had been a refuge in times of adversity. On Him she had been led to place her sole reliance. In Him she had found ample compensation for the bereavements she had suffered, the desertions she had witnessed, the ingratitude she had been shown by friends and kindred. No one could ever dream that a woman of her age, so frail in body, so sensitive of heart, so loaded with the cares of almost

eighty years of incessant tribulation, could so long survive so shattering a blow. And yet, history, no less than the annals of our immortal Faith, shall record for her a share in the advancement and consolidation of the world-wide Community which the hand of 'Abdu'l-Bahá had helped to fashion, which no one among the remnants of His Family can rival.[195]

As stated earlier, when 'Abdu'l-Bahá passed away, Shoghi Effendi was studying in England. Passport difficulties delayed his departure. 'Shoghi Effendi cabled Haifa he could not arrive until the end of the month. He sailed from England on 16 December, accompanied by Lady Blomfield and Rouhangeze, and arrived in Haifa by train at 5.20 p.m. on 29 December from Egypt where his boat from England had docked.'[196] Bahá'íyyih Khánum knew of the existence of 'Abdu'l-Bahá's Will and of Shoghi Effendi's appointment as the one to succeed Him. According to *The Priceless Pearl*,

> When 'Abdu'l-Bahá so unexpectedly and quietly passed away, after no serious illness, the distracted members of His family searched His papers to see if by chance He had left any instructions as to where He should be buried. Finding none, they entombed Him in the centre of the three rooms adjacent to the inner Shrine of the Báb.[197]

In the absence of Shoghi Effendi, Bahá'íyyih Khánum stepped forward with absolute resolve and took in her capable hands the leadership of the community until Shoghi Effendi's return on 29 December 1921. During those decisive days she warded off attempts by her unfaithful half brothers who used 'Abdu'l-Bahá's ascension as the pretext to find favour with family and friends. Their intent was to appear as caring siblings participating in the mourning process and using the opportunity to regain their long-lost prestige. Bahá'íyyih Khánum was well familiar with their schemes. She knew too well what they had done during 'Abdu'l-Bahá's ministry to discredit Him and retard the progress of the Cause whose undisputed leader He was. She knew the dark secrets of their hearts. Therefore she sent a message that they were not welcome in the house of the Master where the family lived, where mourners gathered and where all activities in connection with the work of the Faith took place. Her timely action thwarted the plan of the Covenant-breakers, who had resumed their activities with renewed hope to achieve their end of establishing Mírzá Muḥammad-'Alí as 'Abdu'l-Bahá's rightful successor.

The Bahá'ís of the world who had earlier become familiar with Bahá'íyyih Khánum's leadership abilities turned to her wholeheartedly and followed her directives. During this time, under her supervision, arrangements were made for a befitting funeral procession attended by the faithful members of 'Abdu'l-Bahá's family,[198] the resident Bahá'ís and pilgrims, as well as dignitaries, religious and secular leaders alike, and His admirers from all walks of life. Layla Ábádih'i was residing in the Holy Land and served in 'Abdu'l-Bahá's house when He passed away. In her unpublished memoirs written in Persian, quoting from 'Abbás-Quli Khádim about the choice of the burial place, she writes:

> When the ascension of 'Abdu'l-Bahá took place, the Greatest Holy Leaf and other members of the family were wondering where would be an appropriate burial place for Him . . . Jináb-i-Khádim went to the Greatest Holy Leaf and said: 'On the day you came up to the Shrine for the interment of the remains of the Báb, 'Abdu'l-Bahá indicated a place for Himself. After He interred the holy remains in their eternal place, He stepped from the vault into a passageway and ordered the opening to be closed and, pointing to the passageway, said, 'And this should be a place for Us.' The Greatest Holy Leaf said, 'Very well.' She blessed him for what he said and stated: 'That is where it will be.'

After 'Abdu'l-Bahá's ascension, the Covenant-breakers intensified their activities in the Holy Land and abroad, using the media to propagate their claims. About two weeks after His ascension, i.e. on 14 December 1921, Bahá'íyyih Khánum warned the Bahá'ís of the United States against the intrigues of the Covenant-breakers who were very active in that country:

> Now is period of great tests. The friends should be firm and united in defending the Cause. Nakeseens [Covenant–breakers] starting activities through press other channels all over world. Select committee of wise cool heads to handle press propaganda in America.[199]

On 21 December 1921, she assured the Persian and American believers that 'Abdu'l-Bahá had left 'full instructions in His Will and Testament'.[200]

On the afternoon of 29 December 1921, with a broken heart and frail arms, Bahá'íyyih Khánum received Shoghi Effendi in the embrace of her boundless love, bowing before his authority and urging all to do likewise. At that time Shoghi Effendi was 24 years old and Bahá'íyyih Khánum 75.

On 3 January 1922 'the Master's Will and Testament was read aloud to nine men, most of them members of the family of 'Abdu'l-Bahá, and its seals, signatures and His writing throughout, in His own hand, shown to them,' and at Shoghi Effendi's instruction 'a true copy' was made 'by one of those present – a believer from Persia'.[201]

On 7 January 1922 'Abdu'l-Bahá's Will was read 'at his house in the presence of Bahá'ís from Persia, India, Egypt, England, Italy, Germany, America and Japan'.[202]

About the same time, provisions of 'Abdu'l-Bahá's Will were announced at a memorial gathering attended by 'some Bahá'ís and many notables, including the governor of Haifa'[203] following a luncheon held in the central hall of His house. This was the time the governor and other notables learned officially of the provisions of 'Abdu'l-Bahá's Will and Testament and of Shoghi Effendi's appointment as the Guardian of the Bahá'í Faith and expounder of its teachings.

After the contents of 'Abdu'l-Bahá's Will and Testament were made public in Haifa on 7 January 1922, Bahá'íyyih Khánum announced 'to the Bahá'í world the provisions of the Master's Will'.[204] She sent two cables to Iran, informing the friends there of the dispatch of 'Abdu'l-Bahá's Will and Testament and of Shoghi Effendi's appointment as Centre of the Cause. The two cables, dated 7 January 1922, read:

> Memorial meetings all over the world have been held. The Lord of all the worlds in His Will and Testament has revealed His instructions. Copy will be sent. Inform believers.[205]

> Will and Testament forwarded Shoghi Effendi Centre Cause.[206]

On the 16th of January she informed the friends in the United States: 'In Will Shoghi Effendi appointed Guardian of Cause and Head of House of Justice. Inform American friends.'[207]

The crucial role that Bahá'íyyih Khánum played during the few weeks after 'Abdu'l-Bahá's ascension protected the Bahá'í community from the Covenant-breakers' fresh intrigues. She also provided support and assistance to the young Guardian of the Cause of God, who felt overwhelmed under the weight of the grievous loss he had suffered and the colossal responsibilities placed on his shoulders. Shoghi Effendi recounts his debt of gratitude to his great aunt for the glorious work she performed during his own ministry. His moving tributes eloquently testify to the unique personality of the Greatest Holy Leaf:

> After the ascension of 'Abdu'l-Bahá to the realm of the All-Glorious, that Light of the Concourse on High enfolded me, helpless as I was, in the embrace of her love, and with incomparable pity and tenderness, persuaded, guided, and urged me on to the requirements of servitude. The very elements of this frail being were leavened with her love, refreshed by her companionship, sustained by her eternal spirit.[208]

During the Ministry of Shoghi Effendi

Shoghi Effendi was well familiar with Bahá'íyyih Khánum's exceptional capabilities and the invaluable services that she had rendered during different phases of her rich and eventful life. His tributes constitute a mine of precious information about her, yet he felt unable to illustrate adequately what she had done for him and for the Faith of which he was the head:

> That my tongue, my pen could thank thee were a hopeless task, nor can any praise of mine befit thine excellence. Not even a droplet of all thine endless love can I aspire to fathom, nor can I adequately praise and tell of even the most trifling out of all the events of thy precious life.[209]

And again:

> How can my lonely pen . . . repay the great debt of gratitude and love that I owe her whom I regarded as my chief sustainer, my most affectionate comforter, the joy and inspiration of my life? . . . Only future generations and pens abler than mine can, and will, pay a worthy tribute to the towering grandeur of her spiritual life, to the unique part she played throughout the tumultuous stages of Bahá'í history, to the expressions of unqualified praise that have streamed from the pen of both Bahá'u'lláh and 'Abdu'l-Bahá . . . though unrecorded, and in the main unsuspected by the mass of her passionate admirers in East and West, the share she has had in influencing the course of some of the chief events in the annals of the Faith, the sufferings she bore, the sacrifices she made, the rare gifts of unfailing sympathy she so strikingly displayed – these, and many others stand so inextricably interwoven with the fabric of the Cause itself that no future historian of the Faith of Bahá'u'lláh can afford to ignore or minimize.[210]

The last sentence of this momentous passage recalls the warning Bahá'u'lláh voiced in one of His Tablets revealed in honour of Ásíyih Khánum regarding those who would try to deny her station or minimize the value of the services she had rendered. Shoghi Effendi was keenly aware of historians' tendency to ignore or marginalize women's share in shaping major historical events, a trend so apparent in the history of past religions, and even in the early history of our Faith, at least in the Middle East. In *The Dawn-Breakers*, for example, not a single reference to the Greatest Holy Leaf exists. Shoghi Effendi added a footnote to the last pages of the part he translated into English to indicate that at the age of six she accompanied Bahá'u'lláh on His exile from Iran. He then dedicated the exquisite translation of the book to 'The Greatest Holy

Leaf, the Last Survivor of a Glorious and Heroic Age . . . in Token of a Great Debt of Gratitude and Love'.[211]

Bahá'iyyih Khánum saw in Shoghi Effendi the fulfilment of 'Abdu'l-Bahá's highest aspirations: the assurance that the Faith of Bahá'u'lláh was in capable hands and had a worthy and able leader to move it successfully towards its destiny. Thus, after His ascension, she devoted her life completely to the support of Shoghi Effendi and service to the Cause of Bahá'u'lláh. Her heavenly qualities which made her so distinct and valuable a person prompted Shoghi Effendi to say in praise of her:

> If I cry at every moment out of a hundred mouths, and from each of these mouths I speak with a hundred thousand tongues, yet I could never describe nor celebrate thy heavenly qualities, which are known to none save only the Lord God; nor could I befittingly tell of even the transient foam from out the ocean of thine endless favour and grace.[212]

Legal Challenge to Shoghi Effendi's Authority: The Question of the Custodianship of the Most Holy Tomb

The most grievous challenge to Shoghi Effendi's authority as the Guardian of the Faith of Bahá'u'lláh was launched almost immediately on his return to Haifa from England after 'Abdu'l-Bahá's ascension. Acting on the claim that Mírzá Muḥammad-'Alí, 'Abdu'l-Bahá's half brother, was the rightful successor of 'Abdu'l-Bahá, his supporters, most specifically his youngest brother, Mírzá Badí'u'lláh, forcibly seized the keys of Bahá'u'lláh's Shrine from its Bahá'í caretaker on 30 January 1922. Amatu'l-Bahá Rúḥíyyih Khánum describes the circumstances leading to the seizure of the keys:

> . . . [Mírzá Muḥammad-'Alí] applied to the civil authorities to turn over the custodianship of Bahá'u'lláh's Shrine to him on the grounds that he was 'Abdu'l-Bahá's lawful successor. The British authorities refused on the grounds that it appeared to be a religious issue; he then appealed to the Muslim religious head and asked the Mufti of Akka to take formal charge of Bahá'u'lláh's Shrine; this dignitary, however, said he did not see how he could do this as the Bahá'í teachings were not in conformity with Shariah law. All other avenues having failed he sent his younger brother, Badiullah, with some of their supporters, to visit the Shrine of Bahá'u'lláh where, on Tuesday, 30 January, they forcibly seized the keys of the Holy Tomb from the Bahá'í caretaker, thus asserting Muḥammad 'Alí's right to be the lawful custodian of his Father's resting-place. This unprincipled act created such a commotion in the Bahá'í Community that

> the Governor of Akka ordered the keys to be handed over to the authorities, posted guards at the Shrine, but went no further, refusing to return the keys to either party.[213]

Rustam Mihragání was in Haifa on the day the Covenant-breakers seized the key of the Most Holy Shrine from its caretaker. Shoghi Effendi sent him and another resident believer to Bahjí to ensure that nothing inside the Shrine had been disturbed. Mr Mihragání wrote about the incident in his memoirs:

> On the fortieth day after 'Abdu'l-Bahá's ascension, the contents of the blessed Will and Testament were announced. Shortly after that, one evening Shoghi Effendi called me in and instructed me to go up to the Shrine of the Báb, fetch Áqá Raḥmatu'lláh, the Shrine guard, and together go to Bahjí where the Covenant-breakers had forcibly seized the key of the Most Holy Tomb from its caretaker. Once there we were to ensure that the Covenant-breakers had not done anything discourteous. He emphasized that we were not to get entangled with the Covenant-breakers. Áqá Raḥmatu'lláh and I left Haifa at 9:00 p.m. We rode on horseback and had to go slower than usual because it was raining. It took three hours. When we arrived at 12:00 midnight, we saw two friends from 'Akká at the entrance. They gave us the glad-tiding that police had intervened and taken the key from the Covenant-breakers. Whoever wanted to visit the Shrine had to ask the police to open the door. We saw a policeman on horseback present. As soon as we arrived, someone was sent by the Covenant-breakers to spy on us. One of the friends from 'Akká told him to get lost. He complained to the police and was told that there was nothing for him there, therefore should leave the place. He left disappointed. Áqá Raḥmátu'lláh and I went inside the Shrine and saw that nothing had been disturbed. After leaving the Shrine, we stayed for a while. At dawn Áqá Raḥmátu'lláh took the horses and returned to Haifa to inform Shoghi Effendi. I was instructed to remain at Bahjí. After three days His Highness the Guardian, may my spirit be sacrificed for his directives, came to Bahjí, stayed a night and returned to Haifa the following day. I accompanied him back to Haifa.[214]

The illegal seizure of the key and the intervention of the authorities set in motion a lengthy legal battle which continued during the time Bahá'íyyih Khánum was left in charge of the affairs of the Faith. The adjudication of the question of succession after 'Abdu'l-Bahá required the examination of His Will and Testament by the governor's office. One of the provisions of 'Abdu'l-Bahá's Will was the formation of the Universal House of Justice, whose permanent Head was the Guardian of the Faith. This provision of 'Abdu'l-Bahá's Will, as essential as the formation of the Universal House of Justice was, could not be implemented before steps were taken to strengthen the institution of Local Spiritual Assemblies leading to the establishment of National Spiritual Assemblies, pillars of the Universal House of Justice. Soon after the seizure of the key of the Shrine of Bahá'u'lláh, i.e. in March 1922, Shoghi Effendi 'gathered in Haifa a group of representative and well-known Bahá'ís'.[215] Rúḥíyyih Khánum records in *The Priceless Pearl* the gist of a conversation that the Governor of Haifa had 'with one of the Bahá'ís Shoghi Effendi had sent for' on the subject of the formation of the Universal House of Justice. He had felt 'that when the House of Justice was established, and the Bahá'í Holy Places registered in its name, the whole issue would be removed from the status of a family quarrel and placed on the firm legal basis of a permanent religious organization'.[216] Rúḥíyyih Khánum adds:

> This opinion held by not only a British official but some believers and members of 'Abdu'l-Bahá's family as well, reflects clearly the attitude of some of them towards the Guardian. His youth, his own condition at the beginning of his ministry, inclined them to the belief that he needed the other members of the Body of which he was permanent Head to help and advise him, as well as to secure a firmer legal foundation on which to fight the claims being made by the enemies in Palestine and in Iraq according to Muslim Shariah law, to the Bahá'í Holy Places in these countries.[217]

Although the formation of the Universal House of Justice without first strengthening the institutions of the Local as well as National Spiritual Assembly was out of the question, the presence of a number of veteran Bahá'ís from different countries and continents with whom Shoghi Effendi consulted about 'the foundation of the Universal House of Justice',[218] made it clear that serious steps were being taken towards the establishment of that institution which, together with the institution of guardianship, constitute 'Abdu'l-Bahá's twin successors. As Rúḥíyyih Khánum remarks, what it really amounted to was 'that Shoghi Effendi, a little over two months after he became Guardian, began to lay his foundations for the erection of the Administrative Order of the Faith as set forth in the Will of 'Abdu'l-Bahá'.[219]

Bahá'íyyih Khánum's Role During Shoghi Effendi's Absence

The question of the legal custodianship of the Shrine of Bahá'u'lláh was unresolved when Shoghi Effendi left for Europe on 5 April 1922. Before leaving Haifa, he 'appointed a body of nine people to act tentatively as an Assembly'.[220] He also appointed Bahá'íyyih Khánum 'to administer, in consultation with the family of 'Abdu'l-Bahá, and a chosen Assembly, all Bahá'í affairs during his absence'.[221] He confirmed the decision in a letter he wrote in his own hand in Persian. A facsimile of Shoghi Effendi's original letter and its English translation, made by himself, as well as a facsimile of the original letter from Bahá'íyyih Khánum in Persian and its English translation by Dr Zia M. Baghdádi, were published in *Star of the West*:

> This servant, after that grievous event and great calamity, the ascension of His Holiness 'Abdu'l-Bahá to the Abhá Kingdom, has been so stricken with grief and pain and so entangled in the troubles created by the enemies of the Cause of God, that I consider that my presence here, at such a time and in such an atmosphere, is not in accordance with the fulfilment of my important and sacred duties.
>
> For this reason, unable to do otherwise, I have left for a time the affairs of the Cause both at home and abroad, under the supervision of the Holy Family and the headship of the Greatest Holy Leaf until, by the Grace of God, having gained health, strength, self-confidence and spiritual energy, and having taken into my hands, in accordance with my aim and desire, entirely and regularly the work of service I shall attain to my utmost spiritual hope and aspiration.[222]

The English translation of Bahá'íyyih Khánum's letter dated Sha'bán 1340 (April 1922) reads in part:

> His Holiness, the Guardian of the Cause of God, the Primal Branch, the joy of the people of Bahá – Shoghi Effendi – because of this great calamity, most painful event, infinite sorrow and the severity of the effect upon himself – has desired to travel for several days, that he may regain his health and have rest. Then he will return to the Threshold, arise in service to the Cause of God and perform his duties. According to a letter written by his own hand, which is enclosed, he has appointed this prisoner to supervise and manage the affairs of the Cause, through consultation with the Holy Family, during his absence. Therefore, this perishable one, temporarily, has organized an assembly to act according to the advice of the souls who were appointed and nominated by him – His Holiness Shoghi Effendi.[223]

The authorized translation of Bahá'íyyih Khánum's letter is published in *Bahíyyih Khánum, the Greatest Holy Leaf*:

> Shoghi Effendi, the Guardian of the Cause of God, the Chosen Branch and leader of the people of Bahá, as a result of intense and unceasing grief over this great bereavement, this supreme affliction, has determined to absent himself for a short period, in an effort to rest, and to regain his health, after which he will return to the Holy Land and resume his services and obligations to the Cause of God. During his absence, in accordance with his letter herewith enclosed, this prisoner is appointed to administer the affairs of the Faith, in consultation with the members of the Holy Household.
>
> For this reason I have temporarily made arrangements so that the persons named by Shoghi Effendi may meet and the affairs be conducted in consultation with them.[224]

Although it was not specified for how long Shoghi Effendi would be away, it was assumed by almost all concerned that it would be for a brief period. When Bahá'íyyih Khánum met with the friends, especially those coming from abroad who had not had sufficient opportunity to be in the presence of Shoghi Effendi, she consoled them by saying that he would return shortly, urging them on to serve the Faith like never before that they may become the cause of the joy and gladness of his heart.

The prolonged absence of Shoghi Effendi, the person appointed by 'Abdu'l-Bahá in His Will and Testament as the Guardian of the Cause of God, at a time when Covenant-breakers had intensified their activities to establish Mírzá Muḥammad-'Alí as 'Abdu'l-Bahá's successor, was a most delicate matter that needed to be handled with supreme care. Protecting the Bahá'í community from the Covenant-breakers' vicious propaganda and attacks had long been pursued with vigilance. Bahá'íyyih Khánum continued, with full force, the policy of protecting the believers from the Covenant-breakers' intrigues which had now been expanded to include legal challenges to Shoghi Effendi's authority as the rightful leader of the Bahá'í community and custodian of the Most Holy Tomb.

As mentioned earlier, when Shoghi Effendi left the Holy Land in April 1922, the matter of the legal custodianship of the Most Holy Tomb had not yet been settled. To enable Bahá'íyyih Khánum to take whatever action was necessary in that regard or any other matter arising in his absence, without the least hesitation or reservation – unusual as it was in the early 1920s to have a woman in charge of the affairs of a worldwide religious community, especially in this part of the world – Shoghi Effendi wrote to the governor introducing Bahá'íyyih Khánum as his representative. His letter of 5 April 1922 is addressed to the Governor of Phoenicia, Colonel Symes:

> As I am compelled to leave Haifa for reasons of health, I have named as my representative during my absence, the sister of 'Abdu'l-Bahá, Bahíyyih Khánum. To assist her to conduct the affairs of the Bahá'í Movement in this country and elsewhere, I have also appointed a committee of the following Bahá'ís [eight men of the local community, three of them the sons-in-law of 'Abdu'l-Bahá] . . . The Chairman of this Committee, to be soon elected by its members, with the signature of Bahíyyih Khánum has my authority to transact any affairs that may need to be considered and decided during my absence. I regret exceedingly to be unable to see you before my departure, that I may express more adequately the satisfaction that I feel to know that your sense of justice will safeguard the interests of the Cause of Bahá'u'lláh whenever called upon to act.[225]

In her letter of May 1922, Bahá'íyyih Khánum informed the believers throughout the world of the Covenant-breakers' unceasing assaults on the Cause of God since the ascension of Bahá'u'lláh and, she said, their intensification after 'Abdu'l-Bahá's ascension. The opening paragraph of her letter reads:

> It is not unknown to those who stand firm in the Covenant and Testament of God that the centre of violation and his associates, from the day of the ascension of the Ancient Beauty, may His Great Name be ever exalted, have been working night and day and continually putting forth all their efforts, to spread disorder and disrupt the Faith. At this time, because of our terrible affliction, the ascension of 'Abdu'l-Bahá – may the quintessence of our souls be sacrificed to His sacred resting-place – they are busying themselves more than ever with the circulation of false rumours and idle imaginings, their purpose being, one way or another, to instil doubts into the minds, and thus to achieve their vain futile ends . . .[226]

She then apprised them of circumstances leading to the seizure of the key of Bahá'u'lláh's Shrine and set out details of the actions taken to ensure its restoration:

> Briefly, for some time they had been applying to the various government agencies, in the hope that with the government's assistance they would be able to obtain legal support for their empty claims. However, God be praised, they were disappointed. Then came a day, Tuesday. January 30 – that is, four months ago – when the disaffected gathered together at the Mansion of Bahjí, invited in some of the rabble of 'Akká, and after their joint consultation, determined to go to the Holy Tomb, forcibly wrest its

> key from the caretakers, and hand it over to the arch Covenant-breaker, pivot of the violation. Such was the plan, the disgraceful action, devised by the prime mover of mischief and his lieutenant.
>
> They then committed the brazen act. From the caretaker of the Holy Tomb, 'Aqá Siyyid Abu'l-Qásim, they took away the key by force, and he, unable to withstand their attack, at once dispatched his assistant, 'Aqá Khalíl, to Haifa, to report to Shoghi Effendi what had taken place. The news reached Haifa about two hours after sunset, and the matter was instantly referred to the Governor. On his stringent orders, the key was surrendered that very night and placed in Government custody until the matter could be fully investigated to determine the question of rightful ownership.[227]

In the same letter she described the course of action suggested by the government for the resolution of the problem, asked that requests be sent to the British authorities in Jerusalem confirming that Shoghi Effendi was the legitimate leader appointed by 'Abdu'l-Bahá in His Will and Testament, and explained the procedures to be followed:

> Now, after the passage of four months, the Government has rendered its verdict, to the effect that the question should be put to the Bahá'í community, and that whatever decision the Bahá'ís arrive at will be conclusive. If the Bahá'í community considers Mírzá Muḥammad-'Alí to be excommunicated, then he has no rights whatever to the takeover. Therefore, wherever Bahá'ís reside, they must, through the given city's Spiritual Assembly, and bearing the signature of named individuals who are members of the elected body, inform the British authorities in Jerusalem, either by cable or letter sent through His Majesty's ambassadors or consuls, that the Bahá'í community, in conformity with the explicit writings and the Will and Testament of His Eminence 'Abdu'l-Bahá, Sir 'Abbás Effendi, texts well known and available in His own hand – recognize His Eminence Shoghi Effendi as the one to whom all Bahá'ís must turn, and as the Guardian of the Cause of God, and that they have no connection whatever, either material or spiritual, with Mírzá Muḥammad-'Alí, whom they consider to be excommunicated from the Bahá'í Faith, according to the explicit writings of 'Abdu'l-Bahá.
>
> It should be the request, therefore, of Bahá'ís of all countries, both men and women, in every important centre, wherever they may reside throughout the world, that the officials of His Britannic Majesty's Government in Palestine, its Headquarters being Jerusalem, issue a categorical order that the key of the Holy Tomb – which is the Point of Adoration and the sanc-

> tuary of all Bahá'ís in the world – be restored to His Eminence Shoghi Effendi, the Chosen Branch . . .[228]

The Assemblies acted as they had been instructed. Their communications made clear to authorities in Jerusalem that Shoghi Effendi was considered the appointed Guardian of Bahá'u'lláh's Cause and the leader of the Bahá'í community throughout the world in accordance with 'Abdu'l-Bahá's Will and Testament. Helpful as these letters were in conveying the Bahá'ís' unified stand regarding the position of Shoghi Effendi, they did not resolve the question of the Shrine's custodianship. In response to a letter of enquiry from Bahá'íyyih Khánum dated 15 October 1922, the governor wrote to her on 30 October, saying:

> Dear Madam,
> In reply to your letter of the 15th instant I regret that I cannot throw any very new light on the subject. As has been stated publicly the Government feel that the custody of the Shrine at Acre as well as other important questions affecting the Bahá-ist organization should if possible be settled by a Congress of representatives of Bahá'í opinion throughout the World. To judge from messages received from a number of Bahá-ist Centres it would appear that they endorse and uphold the provisions of the Will of the late Sir Abdul Baha Abbas, and as soon as the Congress aforementioned has actually met and given its decision the Government will be prepared to entertain its final recommendations. In the meantime if it is possible to find an individual whose provisional custody of the Key of the Shrine will be offensive to no section of Bahais I shall be only too glad to hand over the key to him until such time as the Congress has met and made its final recommendations in the matter.[229]

Further actions were taken before and after Shoghi Effendi's return to the Holy Land in mid-December 1922, culminating in the government's decision to return the key of Bahá'u'lláh's Shrine to its original Bahá'í caretaker. On 14 March 1923, the District Governor, G. S. Symes, 'instructed the Sub-Governor at Acre to return the key of the Tomb of Baha'Ullah to Es Saiyid Abu'l-Kassim' from whom the Covenant-breakers had forcibly seized it nearly 14 months earlier.

Dealing with the Incessant Activities of Covenant-breakers

After 'Abdu'l-Bahá's ascension, the majority of the Bahá'ís everywhere remained faithful to the Covenant. They were delighted to learn that 'Abdu'l-

Bahá had appointed Shoghi Effendi as the Guardian of the Bahá'í Faith. However, the fainthearted among the believers were severely tested by Shoghi Effendi's appointment as the leader of the Bahá'í community. The ambitious, unwilling to accept the authority of the young Guardian, stood in opposition to him, broke the Covenant and tried their best to instil doubt in the hearts of the inconstant and halfhearted believers. Following the ways of like-minded people of the past, the newly-declared Covenant-breakers joined forces with the old. In the hope of gaining strength and achieving their selfish ends, they unitedly began a widespread campaign against Shoghi Effendi.

Bahá'íyyih Khánum's most urgent task was to protect the believers from the negative propaganda of the disaffected. Following the example of 'Abdu'l-Bahá, through her letters she warned the believers against the Covenant-breakers' intrigues and encouraged them to protect the body of the Cause of God from the darts of people of malice, from those who were intent on destroying what had been achieved painstakingly and with tremendous sacrifice over many years. The letter she wrote in May 1922 explains her concerns:

> At this hour while yet the heart burns with the anguish of sorrow, and the gloom of bereavement still hangs low, my thoughts turn in loving remembrance to my sincere beloved sisters and brothers in the Cause.
>
> The news of your firmness in the Covenant, of your endeavour to work in unity and harmony, and of your untiring zeal and devotion in the Path of Service, has been a source of untold joy to me. For now my sole comfort lies in the loyalty and faithfulness of the friends, and my one joy in the progress of the Cause.
>
> Dear friends! At this critical time through which the Cause is passing the responsibility that has fallen on every individual Bahá'í is great, and his duties are pressing and manifold. Now that the Sun of the Covenant has set on the horizon of the world, the eyes of all the people are turned expectant upon us. Now the time has come for the faithful friends of 'Abdu'l-Bahá, who have been the recipients of the Glorious Light, to shine forth even as brilliant stars. The radiance of our Faith must be such as to dispel the clouds of doubt and guide the world to the Day-spring of Truth.
>
> Our firmness must be such as to cause him who wavers and errs to turn back penitent unto the fold; our unity and love must be such as to cause the peoples of the world to join hands in amity and brotherhood; and our activity in service must be such as to have all parts of the world resound with the echoes of 'YÁ-BAHÁ'U'L-ABHÁ!'[230]

To inspire the hearts of the friends and to provide them with divine guidance, she quoted from Bahá'u'lláh and 'Abdu'l-Bahá's writings about the importance of showing forth fidelity, manifesting steadfastness, seeking divine assistance, remaining united and teaching the Cause of God. She then conveyed the following advice:

> Dear Friends! A great obligation of every Bahá'í is vigilance to protect and shield the stronghold of the Faith from the onslaught of the enemies. In these days their activity has waxed strong. They are constantly on the alert, and exert the utmost endeavour to cause such harm as would impede the onward march of the Cause.
>
> Association with such people will cause discord and unrest among the friends and will be detrimental to the progress of the Cause. Therefore it is urgent that the friends exercise great wisdom and vigilance lest through the evil schemes of the enemies a breach be made in the Faith. The few people whom 'Abdu'l-Bahá pronounced as injurious to the Cause must be shunned by all the friends, as Shoghi Effendi himself tells us to do in his second letter to the American believers.[231]

The Eruption of Hostilities in Iran

Another urgent task faced by Bahá'íyyih Khánum was protecting Iranian Bahá'ís from fanatical elements. The ascension of 'Abdu'l-Bahá, the activities of internal enemies and political instability in the country breathed fresh hope in the hearts of them that were ever ready to stir up trouble and benefit from chaos and disorder. The Bahá'í community in Iran had never enjoyed any measure of freedom. In fact, from the dawn of the Revelation, its members had from time to time suffered severe persecution and many had been killed for their belief. Now that their oppressors found the ground favourable for inflicting fresh tribulations, they began a campaign of incitement against the Bahá'ís in several towns and cities. When reports of renewed persecutions reached the Holy Land, Bahá'íyyih Khánum apprised the Bahá'ís in America and elsewhere of the situation. In her letter of 20 July 1922 to the Bahá'ís of America, she wrote:

> O steadfast ones, gathered beneath the Abhá Beauty's standard of oneness, O faithful lovers of 'Abdu'l-Bahá! Sad news has come to us out of Iran in recent days, and it has intensely grieved the entire Bahá'í world: they have, in most parts of that land, set bonfires of envy and malevolence, and hoisted the banner of aggression against this much wronged community; they have left no means untried, no plot or strategy neglected, and

> have arisen with extreme hostility and spite to pull out by their very roots the trees of this garden of God.[232]

She then explained the seriousness of the situation of the defenceless Bahá'ís and requested that assemblies act urgently, contact the Iranian embassy in their country and seek justice on behalf of their persecuted Bahá'í brothers and sisters in Iran:

> During occurrences of this kind, it is incumbent upon the believers in other countries to immediately adopt prudent and reasonable measures, that through wise methods such fires may be put out . . .
>
> . . . At this time it is urgently needful, and it is the request of this grieving servant, that the assembly of the believers in that area act at once, and take the case to the ambassador of the Iranian government.[233]

She also explained what the petition was to include:

> Let them tell him, 'The holy Cause of Bahá'u'lláh has so unified us who are His world-wide followers, and has brought us so close together, that we have become like a single body. If the foot of a Bahá'í, in the farthest Eastern land, is so much as scratched by a thorn, it is even as if we Bahá'ís here in the West had suffered the same. We have now received word from Iran that in Shíráz, in Sulṭánábád, in Hamadán, in Káshán, even in Ṭihrán, and in other places as well, the fanaticism of the ignorant and heedless has been fanned into flame, and that agitators are stirring up the populace – with the result that our brothers and sisters, who are but well-wishers of all humankind and are indeed the world's only hope for peace, and are obedient and helpful citizens of Iran and her government, find themselves under attack and pushed into the heart of the fire.
>
> 'We therefore request the representative of Iran to ask his government to safeguard our brothers in Iran from the aggressions of their enemies, and to deliver that flock of God's lovers from the claws of the wolf, and provide for their security and well-being.'[234]

She went further in her request, asking,

> And further, if it be possible, you should make this same representation through your own ambassador in Ṭihrán, so that he may direct the attention of the Iranian authorities to these persecutions, and awaken that government to the possibility of divine retribution and to the shameful stigma occasioned by such actions directed against this innocent commu-

nity by the heedless and ignorant amongst the mass of the people.

Let him make them aware that there are thousands of adherents of this Faith of the love of God around the world, who are gazing in astonishment and disbelief at the savage acts now being perpetrated against their brothers, and are eagerly waiting to hear that the government has come to the rescue of this unique, this law-abiding people, who are the well-wishers of mankind, from the attacks of the ravening wolves.[235]

Concern for Shoghi Effendi's Well-being

When Shoghi Effendi left for Europe on 5 April 1922 the hope was that he would return after a short stay abroad. However, his first absence from the Holy Land, which Amatu'l-Bahá Rúḥíyyih Khánum calls 'his withdrawal',[236] extended over several months. The prolongation of his absence caused Bahá'íyyih Khánum anxiety and deep concern. In the letter of lament penned by Munírih Khánum on the first anniversary of 'Abdu'l-Bahá's ascension, she says: 'The absence of the Most Excellent Branch [Shoghi Effendi], and the lack of any news from Him [sic] have completely sapped the strength of the Greatest Holy Leaf [Bahíyyih Khánum] . . .'[237]

After several months elapsed and Shoghi Effendi did not return, Bahá'íyyih Khánum despatched some members of his family to Europe with the mission to find and plead with him to return. According to Amatu'l-Bahá Rúḥíyyih Khánum:

> In the autumn of 1922 the Greatest Holy Leaf, deeply distressed by Shoghi Effendi's long absence, sent members of his family to find him and plead with him to come back to the Holy Land. In the street of a small village in the mountains, as he returned in the evening from one of his all-day walks, Shoghi Effendi, to his great surprise, found his mother looking for him; she had come all the way from Palestine for this purpose, accompanied by another member of the Master's family; with tears she informed him of the distress of Bahíyyih Khánum, the family and friends and persuaded him to return and assume his rightful place.[238]

Finally, after eight and a half months' absence, Shoghi Effendi returned to the Holy Land on 15 December 1922. Unfortunately, in early summer 1923 'for the second time his health failed'.[239] Bahá'íyyih Khánum refers to Shoghi Effendi's second absence in a letter she wrote 'to the members of the Spiritual Assemblies and all the Friends of God in the East' on 28 March 1924: 'at the importunity of this evanescent soul and the urgent entreaties of the Holy Household and the repeated appeals of those in close association with him

– he went away last summer'.[240] From that trip, which lasted several months, he returned in November 1923. In early 1924, he left again. Bahá'íyyih Khánum, in the same letter of 28 March 1924, refers to Shoghi Effendi's departure from the Holy Land and explains the reason:

> . . . once again in some communities, he noted from certain letters an absence of spirituality and good-fellowship among some of the friends, and a lack of respect among some for their Assemblies. Once more, as a result of this, his heart was filled with sorrow and once again he decided on departure. This lowly maidservant and the other members of the Household and all the Holy Leaves did all we could to blot away this grief from his radiant spirit . . . but to no avail.
>
> He told us: 'My heart is sensitive. Just as I feel the ill-feeling that exists between individuals, and am injured by it, so too do I treasure the excellent qualities of the believers; indeed, I hold these dearer than words can tell.'[241]

In her letter of 27 May 1924 to the Spiritual Assembly of Hamadán, Bahá'íyyih Khánum explains:

> We continually receive joyous news of the health and well-being of the Guardian of the Cause of God and eagerly hope that the night of separation may come to an end, that the period of bereavement may soon expire and his blessed person may return to this hallowed Spot with utmost joy and radiance.[242]

Then in a letter written on 19 July 1924, she says:

> I am glad to tell you that the Guardian of the Cause of God is in good health. The splendid attitude of the beloved friends in the East and the West and their wonderfully sacrificial efforts in the service of the Cause have greatly lightened the burden of grief upon his loving heart and so, he may return to the Holy Land towards the end of summer when his entire grief, we hope, will be replaced with joy and fragrances which are being wafted to his dear heart.[243]

Her letter of 18 August conveys a similar sentiment:

> Your numerous letters written to the beloved Guardian and myself have all arrived and brought with them the sweet perfume of your devotion, sincerity, strong faith and active and beautiful services you are inex-

haustibly rendering to the Cause of God . . .

The beloved Guardian of the Cause is nowadays in good health . . . his grief has been lightened and so we have great hope that he will return to the Holy Land before long. Here he will resume his personal touch with the friends the world over and will inspire them with his guidance to still greater activity.[244]

Shoghi Effendi's third absence from the Holy Land also lasted several months. During his absences in 1922, 1923 and 1924, he entrusted the affairs of the Faith to the competent care of Bahá'íyyih Khánum who in 1924 was 78 years old.

What worked to Shoghi Effendi's disadvantage more than anything else was his age. As stated before, at the time of 'Abdu'l-Bahá's ascension, he was only 24 years old. His appointment by 'Abdu'l-Bahá as the Guardian of the Cause of God had disappointed some older Bahá'ís who considered themselves more experienced and qualified and stirred feelings of envy dormant in the hearts of those seeking for themselves positions of authority. Such people for selfish reasons did not want to submit to the authority of a young Guardian. The person who truly understood his delicate situation and whose selfless love and advice he trusted and relied on unhesitatingly was Bahá'íyyih Khánum, the Greatest Holy Leaf. As Rúḥíyyih Khánum says, 'to him she had been an incarnation of 'Abdu'l-Bahá's all-encompassing tenderness and love . . . for him she had always been, next to his grandfather, the most beloved person in the world.'[245] Referring to the close bond that existed between Shoghi Effendi and his great-aunt, she writes:

So close was the communion between Shoghi Effendi and his great-aunt that over and over, in cables and other communications, particularly during the early years of his Guardianship, he included her with himself in such phrases as 'assure us', 'the Greatest Holy Leaf and I', 'we', and so on. In a cable sent in 1931 he even signs it 'Bahíyyih Shoghi'.[246]

Dealing with Matters at Home

During Shoghi Effendi's absence from the Holy Land, Bahá'íyyih Khánum was concerned not only with the worldwide affairs of the Bahá'í Faith, such as matters related to the protection of the Cause of God at home and abroad and with the propagation of Bahá'u'lláh's teachings throughout the world. There were other things requiring her attention and making demands on her time. In addition to members of 'Abdu'l-Bahá's immediate and extended family, there was a sizeable community in the Holy Land that looked to her for guidance, shared with her the difficulties they experienced and sought her advice in solving problems of various kinds. Many worked in the Haifa–'Akká area as custodians of holy places, gardeners, domestic help. They had families. The children needed to be schooled and receive Bahá'í training, the youth were in need of guidance, the parents had to be provided with the means to meet their work and family obligations. Bahá'íyyih Khánum performed the role of a loving mother, just as 'Abdu'l-Bahá had played the role of a benevolent father. She had to ensure that those who had come on pilgrimage and were eager to meet the newly-appointed Guardian of the Faith did not return disheartened and disappointed. Those who had come to serve at the Bahá'í World Centre had to be guided and advised how to perform their duties as they had been envisaged by the newly-appointed Guardian. The members of the local Bahá'í community and those living in surrounding areas needed encouragement and spiritual sustenance. Glimpses into this aspect of Bahá'íyyih Khánum's work is obtained from entries in the diaries and memoirs of the people who were in Haifa at that time.

Ya'qúb Gulkár and two Bahá'í friends from Saysán, Iran, had requested and received permission to come on pilgrimage. They had also expressed interest in remaining, after their pilgrimage, to serve at the Bahá'í World Centre. In his memoirs Mr Gulkár describes the sombre mood that prevailed after the news of Shoghi Effendi's departure was shared with the friends:

> The day after we attained the presence of the beloved Guardian was a Sunday. It was customary for all resident Bahá'ís and pilgrims on such a day to gather at the Haifa Pilgrim House and wait for the arrival of Shoghi Effendi. After the Afnáns and the members of the Holy Family arrived, they stated that His Highness the Distinguished Branch, the Guardian of the Cause of God, may my soul be sacrificed for his loving-kindness, had gone away. This news devastated the pilgrims and caused them immense sorrow and sadness. We could not withhold our tears. This day could not be compared with the previous day. We had attained his presence and enjoyed the sweetness of his utterance only once. The eagerness of our hearts to attain the bounty of reunion had not yet been satisfied. But what could be done with that which had been ordained?
>
> After receiving the news of Shoghi Effendi's sudden trip, everyone reverently visited the Shrines of the Báb and 'Abdu'l-Bahá, and humbly implored God to give us the bounty of seeing him once again. During the first several days the sadness caused by separation from Shoghi Effendi was palpable. As a result of the Greatest Holy Leaf's loving-kindness and consideration, our sorrow gradually dissipated and we learned more clearly our duties and the jobs we were to perform . . . I was assigned the

> duty of serving in the gardens of the Shrine of the Báb and helping Áqá Raḥmátu'lláh of Najafábád, who was the custodian of the Shrine.
>
> The Greatest Holy Leaf, the Remnant of Bahá, arranged for the pilgrims to remain and render service in the holy precincts until the beloved Guardian returned, so that they could attain his presence again. What the Greatest Holy Leaf said was our inner desire . . . Each of us had the privilege of being in the presence of the Greatest Holy Leaf, of receiving her loving-kindness and of engaging in the work we were asked to perform. One day she summoned me to the Blessed House. After showering upon me kindnesses that were characteristic of her, she uttered reassuring words that the Distinguished Branch would soon return and encouraged me to render service in the vicinity of the Shrine of the Báb. I said that we were not worthy of seeing the beloved Guardian more than once. She said: 'You have the merit and the capacity. Be assured.' That meeting and the heavenly smiles of the only Remnant of the Blessed Tree I will never forget. It is imprinted upon my heart forever.[247]

Another pilgrim, Yadu'lláh Tabrízí,[248] writes:

> When the beloved Guardian was away on a trip, the Greatest Holy Leaf carried out all the work of the Faith in the Holy Land, be it big or small. Three days after the beloved Guardian left [April 1922], the Greatest Holy Leaf assigned me the job of guarding the Shrine of Bahá'u'lláh and of looking after the garden of the Shrine.[249]

Mr Tabrízí's memoirs also provide glimpses into the close and loving relationship that existed between Bahá'íyyih Khánum and Shoghi Effendi, explain the way they related to one another, and goes into some detail about how they communicated on a regular basis:

> The Greatest Holy Leaf was the only confidant and true supporter that the beloved Guardian had. For his sake she for many years tolerated the people who were related to him. Her love for the beloved Guardian of the Cause of God was deep and genuine. She lived on the second floor of the house of the Master and the beloved Guardian on the third.[250] Whenever she heard his footsteps, she would involuntarily come out of her room, hold his hand and take him to her room. She would offer him whatever edible she had available and ask him to eat and rest a little. The Greatest Holy Leaf took special pleasure in seeing the beloved Guardian eat. Whenever he stood up to go and visit the Shrine of the Báb, Ḥaḍrat-i-Khánum would stand and walk with him to the door. She rejoiced in watching him

walk. Her captivating eyes followed his gate and her tongue uttered these words: 'O 'Abdu'l-Bahá! What a Guardian you have left behind! He has illumined the world and will continue to shed lustre upon it . . .'

Ḥaḍrat-i-Varaqiy-i-'Ulyá (Her Highness the Greatest Holy Leaf) would pace the hall and the verandah on top of the stairs (leading to the Master's house) until the beloved Guardian returned. As soon as her eyes spotted his blessed person, it was like a lover seeing her beloved. She said, 'He is coming. He is coming.' She would invite him to her room, lock the door from inside, so that they could talk, share what needed to be said and hear what needed to be treasured. She would again bring something for him to eat, unwind and take a little rest. I believe that only the Greatest Holy Leaf truly knew the rank and station of the beloved Guardian and he truly knew her true rank and station. These two holy beings most certainly loved one another dearly.[251]

An Exhilarating Experience

After Bahá'u'lláh's ascension, Fáṭimih Khánum, titled Mahd-i-'Ulyá, and her children continued to live in the Mansion of Bahjí. When the odour of their rebelliousness against the Centre of Bahá'u'lláh's Covenant spread far and wide, the ties of relationship between them and 'Abdu'l-Bahá and His family were severed. Bahá'íyyih Khánum lived with 'Abdu'l-Bahá and His family in 'Akká and later in Haifa. While the Covenant-breakers occupied the Mansion, Bahá'íyyih Khánum could not visit her Father's final earthly abode. After Mahd-i-'Ulyá passed away, the Covenant-breakers continued to live in the Mansion but did nothing to maintain it. Its condition deteriorated until it became absolutely necessary to do something about it. The Covenant-breakers made it known that the building was in need of major repair which they were unable and unwilling to undertake. Shoghi Effendi offered to have the necessary repairs carried out only after they had vacated the place. They had no choice but to leave. The repairs took some time. When completed, Shoghi Effendi had it recognized as a historical site, furnished it befittingly and had a most pleasant surprise ready for Bahá'íyyih Khánum. He wanted her to visit that exalted holy place and spend some time there before anyone else. An eyewitness account gives details of that historic visit. Yadu'lláh Tabrízí has written the memoirs of his years of service in the Holy Land:

> After the ascension of Bahá'u'lláh, the blessed Mansion of Bahjí was for nearly 40 years in the hand of the Covenant-breakers. During that period the Mansion had not been repaired and its trees had not been watered. Every winter rainwater would make them turn green and save the roots

> but the stock of orange and tangerine trees had become weak. The beloved Guardian several times promised to take the Mansion out of the hands of the Covenant-breakers and deliver it into our hands.
>
> The beloved Guardian sent a message to Mírzá Muḥammad-'Alí, the arch-breaker of the Covenant, through 'Abdu'r-Raḥmán Jarráḥ saying, 'I am going to repair the Mansion and am waiting for you to vacate it. If you do not vacate it voluntarily, I will appeal to the authorities to evict you.' The negotiations prolonged. In the meantime, his blessed person took a trip. The Covenant-breakers had to turn over the keys of the Mansion to 'Abdu'r-Raḥmán Jarráḥ, the intermediary appointed by the beloved Guardian. 'Abdu'r-Raḥmán Effendi came to the Most Holy Tomb and delivered to me the keys to the Mansion. I immediately went to Haifa with the keys and sought guidance from the Greatest Holy Leaf. Ḥaḍrat-i-Khánum was overjoyed that the keys had been obtained. She said, do water the trees well so that they will become verdant by the time his blessed person returns . . . When the beloved Guardian returned the trees were green and verdant.[252]

Mr Tabrízí says that the restoration work took one and a half years to complete. He explains some details about the way the work was carried out.

> When the restoration of the blessed Mansion was complete, the beloved Guardian arranged for the Greatest Holy Leaf to come and see how it had been furnished and decorated. She was accompanied by three people. As soon as the car in which she travelled arrived, the big entrance door which faces the cities of Haifa and 'Akká (south entrance) was opened and she stepped into the courtyard of the Mansion. As she was unable to climb the set of stairs leading to the upper floor, a large chair was brought in. Khánum sat in it and Isfandyár-i-Síyávash and I carried it up and placed it in the central hall of the Mansion. As soon as the Greatest Holy Leaf entered the hall, she exclaimed in a loud voice, 'O Bahá'u'lláh! The Guardian of your Cause has repaired, furnished and decorated your blessed Mansion.' She then continued, 'O 'Abdu'l-Bahá! What a wonderful Guardian you have chosen for the Cause of God! He has restored the glory of the blessed Mansion.' As she was uttering the words, she was weeping and laughing simultaneously. She then asked that the door to Bahá'u'lláh's chamber be opened. After visiting the room, she came out and said, 'O Bahá'u'lláh! The Guardian of your Cause inflicts harm on himself and causes me anguish.' During the six days that she spent in the vicinity of the Most Holy Tomb, she constantly repeated the above sentence.
>
> She then asked for the box of baklava which she had brought for the

friends serving at Bahjí. A plate with several pieces of baklava on it was brought. She said, '*Nah mádar*,[253] I brought a box of baklava for them.' They brought a box which was half full. She said, '*Nah mádar*, you must bring a whole box.' They finally brought a full box. Her holiness, Khánum, said, 'I brought this box of baklava for you.' I said, 'Tomorrow visitors, Bahá'í and non-Bahá'í alike, will come from 'Akká to visit you. We can leave the box for them.' She responded, 'I have brought for the visitors as well. This belongs to you.'

The Greatest Holy Leaf spent one night in the Mansion and said that she would come down to spend the remaining days in the pilgrim house. I said, 'The beloved Guardian has arranged for you to come to Bahjí and rest in the Mansion.' She said, 'If I stay in the Mansion, tomorrow Bahá'í and non-Bahá'í visitors will come from 'Akká and will dirty the *tirmih* [special brocade material] in the Mansion.' She spent the remaining five days in the pilgrim house. Ḥaḍrat-i-Khánum was very happy during the days she spent at Bahjí and full of humour with whomever she spoke.

As soon as Ḥaḍrat-i-Khánum returned to Haifa, His Highness the beloved Guardian came to visit the Shrine of Bahá'u'lláh. After greetings, he asked if Ḥaḍrat-i-Khánum had a good time. I said, 'Yes, she was ecstatic but during the six days that she was here she constantly said, "O Bahá'u'lláh! The Guardian of your Cause inflicts harm on himself and causes me anguish."' The beloved Guardian while walking on the grass said, 'Yes, Ḥaḍrat-i-Khánum wants me to have a good time at all times and to be comfortable. The Cause has crucial works which I am compelled to do. I have been entrusted with a mission from my three masters.' I took advantage of the opportunity and said, 'In His Will and Testament 'Abdu'l-Bahá has provided for nine persons to help the Guardian of the Cause of God with his work.' His blessed person took a few more steps on the grass, then looked at me and said, 'Those nine must possess certain qualities. They must be trustworthy, truthful, honest, hardworking and serious. They are yet to be found. They will be later.' Then he said, 'As you know, I delegated the work of the Mansion to an appointed body. They talked and talked. In the end they were in disagreement. I supervised the work personally and it was all done very well, don't you think?' I said, '*Balí qurbán* (Yes, may I be your sacrifice).'[254]

The Expected Visit of Queen Marie of Romania

Bahá'íyyih Khánum was nearly 80 years old when in October 1927 Shoghi Effendi extended through Martha Root a 'warm and cordial invitation' to Queen Marie of Romania and her daughter Ileana 'to visit the Holy Land and be received in the Beloved's home'.[255] The prospect of the Queen's visit to Haifa cheered the heart of Bahá'íyyih Khánum. Her joyous anticipation was strengthened in April 1928 when the Queen and her daughter visited Cyprus. They had come so close. The opportunity for a visit to Haifa seemed so real. Had the visit materialized, it would have meant so much to her during the last years of her life. However, it was not to be and the disappointment was great indeed. The reason was evidently 'premature disclosures'. At that time 'the papers . . . published the news that the Queen intended to visit Haifa', which may have 'deterred them from accomplishing their intended pilgrimage . . .'[256]

On 3 December 1929 Shoghi Effendi responded to the Queen's message, which he had received through Martha Root. He closed his letter thus: 'The Family also join me in extending to Your Majesty, as well as to Her Royal Highness Princess Ileana, a most cordial welcome should Your Majesty ever purpose to visit the Holy Land to 'Abdu'l-Bahá's home in Haifa as well as to those scenes rendered so hallowed and memorable by the heroic lives and deeds of Bahá'u'lláh and 'Abdu'l-Bahá.'[257]

The Queen's visit to Egypt in 1930 renewed hopes that she would come to the Holy Land. Amatu'l-Bahá Rúḥíyyih Khánum says:

> Hearing no news of the Queen's plans once she had reached Egypt [Shoghi Effendi] wired to her direct on 8 March:
>
> Her Majesty, the Dowager Queen Marie of Rumania, aboard Mayflower, Aswan.
> Family of 'Abdu'l-Bahá join me in renewing the expression of our loving and heartfelt invitation to your gracious Majesty and Her Royal Highness Princess Ileana to visit His home in Haifa. Your Majesty's acceptance to visit Bahá'u'lláh's Shrine and prison-city of 'Akká will apart from its historic significance be a source of immeasurable strength joy and hope to the silent sufferers of the Faith throughout the East. Our fondest love, prayers and best wishes for Your Majesty's happiness and welfare.[258]

That wire remained unanswered. On 26 March Shoghi Effendi sent another wire in care of the hotel where the Queen and her daughter were staying in Cairo. Two days later he received a wire from the Romanian minister in Cairo. It said: 'Her Majesty regrets that not passing through Palestine she will not be able to visit you.'[259] More than a year later, in her letter of 28 June 1931 to Martha Root, the Queen wrote: 'Both Ileana and I were cruelly disappointed at having been prevented going to the holy shrines and of meeting Shoghi Effendi, but at that time were going through a cruel crisis and every movement I made was being turned against me and being politically exploited in an unkind way.'[260] We read in *The Priceless Pearl* that

> . . . the Greatest Holy Leaf had waited, hour after hour, in the Master's home to receive the Queen and her daughter – for Her Majesty had actually sailed for Haifa, and this news encouraged Shoghi Effendi to believe she was going to carry out the pilgrimage she had planned; time passed and no news came, even after the boat had docked. Later the Guardian learned that the Queen and her party had been met at the boat, informed her visit was impolitic and not permissible, been put in a car and whisked out of Palestine to another Middle Eastern country.[261]

The Mashriqu'l-Adhkár Fund

The construction of the Mother Temple of the West was approved by 'Abdu'l-Bahá in 1903. A religious corporation known as the 'Bahá'í Temple Unity' established in 1907 'for the purpose of choosing the site of the Temple'[262] was incorporated in 1909. The site was dedicated by 'Abdu'l-Bahá during a ground-breaking ceremony held in 1912. The excavation work began in 1920, about a year before 'Abdu'l-Bahá's ascension. Owing to harsh economic conditions, the construction work took many years to complete. About a year before the passing of Bahá'íyyih Khánum, work on the superstructure was complete and 'the first devotional service in the new structure was celebrated'[263] on 1 May 1931. According to Shoghi Effendi, the project was 'associated, in its initial phase, with 'Abdu'l-Bahá, and in the concluding stages of its construction with the memory of the Greatest Holy Leaf, the Purest Branch and their mother'.[264]

In March 1932, about four months before Bahá'íyyih Khánum passed away, Shoghi Effendi wrote to the believers 'urging them to press on with the completion of the dome of "our beloved Temple"' and saying that 'my voice is once more reinforced by the passionate, and perhaps, the last, entreaty, of the Greatest Holy Leaf, whose spirit, now hovering on the edge of the Great Beyond, longs to carry on its flight to the Abhá Kingdom . . . an assurance of the joyous consummation of an enterprise, the progress of which has so greatly brightened the closing days of her earthly life'.[265] Amatu'l-Bahá Rúḥíyyih Khánum says, 'In every act of his life [Shoghi Effendi] associated the Greatest Holy Leaf with his services to the Faith.'[266] In 1939, when he transferred the remains of Ásíyih Khánum and the Purest Branch, the mother and brother of Bahá'íyyih Khánum, from 'Akká to Mount Carmel, he sent a cable, saying: 'Rejoice privilege pledge thousand pounds my contribution Bahíyyih Khánum Fund designed inauguration final drive insure placing contract next April last remaining stage construction Mashriqu'l-Adhkár.'[267]

The Passing of Bahá'íyyih Khánum

Bahá'íyyih Khánum lived for nearly eleven years after the ascension of 'Abdu'l-Bahá. A good part of the first two years of this period Shoghi Effendi was absent from the Holy Land and she was in charge of the affairs of the Cause of God. The remaining years she spent firmly behind Shoghi Effendi in his work and assisted him in whatever way she could. Correspondence signed by her as late as 1926 indicates that she was an active player in the affairs of the Faith until a few years before the end of her earthly life. One of the imperishable services she rendered to the Faith after 'Abdu'l-Bahá's ascension was helping the friends to grasp the importance of the Covenant. She did this through correspondence and through her meetings with the pilgrims.

Of the last years of Bahá'íyyih Khánum's life we know little. One point that comes across in reading *The Priceless Pearl* is that she was frail and in delicate health. We also learn that 'Until the time of her death it was Shoghi Effendi's custom to have his one meal a day alone with her, served on a small table in her bedroom'.[268]

The recollections of Bahá'íyyih Khánum's attendant, Laqá'íyyih Khánum, provide further information about this and other aspects of the final years of the Greatest Holy Leaf's life. With Shoghi Effendi's approval, Laqá'íyyih Khánum had moved in 1926 from 'Ishqábád, where her family lived, to Haifa. The purpose of the move was to marry Jináb-i-Muḥammad-Ḥusayn Kahrubá'í.[269] After marriage, she was assigned the duty of serving the Greatest Holy Leaf. She says:

> During the time I was serving the Greatest Holy Leaf, she was old and frail. Seldom did she go out. Occasionally, one of the ladies of the house would take her out for shopping. Some renowned persons would attain her presence in the house. During the initial years of my stay, once a week there was a women's gathering in 'Abdu'l-Bahá's house. Bahá'í women, pilgrim and resident alike, would come and attain her presence.
>
> It was my duty to set the dinner table, which was placed before Khánum, to bring food from the kitchen and make salad. Every night, after setting the table, I would knock on the door of Shoghi Effendi's room and say, 'The food is ready.' He would come, sit on a chair opposite Khánum. He would first place food on Khánum's plate then on his own, then they would eat.

Ḥaḍrat-i Khánum received the pilgrims at 4:00 p.m. during afternoon tea. One day in the week was fixed for going to the Shrine of the Báb. The Greatest Holy Leaf and ladies of the house would sit in a carriage and go to the Shrine. They also took me and my children. The women gathered in the home of the custodian of the pilgrim house, the men had their meeting in the pilgrim house in the presence of the beloved Guardian. When the meetings ended, all proceeded to the Shrine for a visit. The men occupied one side of the Shrine, the women the other. The two sides were separated by curtains. All would listen to the Tablet of Visitation recited either by the Guardian or another person.

Ḥaḍrat-i Khánum was most loving towards children. She always gave them gifts and food . . .

I recall once I was wearing an ordinary dress when attaining her presence on Naw-Rúz. She said, 'What is this dress you are wearing on a feast day? Go and change into a nice coloured dress.' I went back, wore a pink dress and returned to her. She said, 'Now this is a feast. Since you have such a lovely dress, why did you not wear it earlier?' She also attached much importance to the level of light in the room.

Ḥaḍrat-i Khánum was extremely weak during the last days of her life. She contracted a bad case of bronchitis. Ḍíyá'íyyih Khánum appointed six people to look after her and provide nursing care. Each had a four-hour shift in 24 hours. They were Ḍíyá'íyyih Khánum, Rúḥá Khánum, Munavvar Khánum, the blessed Leaves; and Ṭayyibih Khánum, Fáṭimih Khánum, the mother of Messrs Nakhjavání, and myself. It was arranged for Kahrubá'í to look after the children when I was on duty at night. On the night of her passing, the daughters [of 'Abdu'l-Bahá], the grandchildren and members of the household were gathered around her bed. I went to my room to see how the children were doing. When I returned early the next morning, she had passed away [15 July 1932]. At the time of her passing, only the blessed Leaves and their children were present.

Ḥaḍrat-i-Khánum had herself prepared her shroud and materials necessary for burial. She had them wrapped in a wrapper. Ḍíyá'íyyih Khánum opened it. The items were: a pair of white socks, a white scarf, a white handkerchief and a white dress made of inexpensive material.[270]

Shoghi Effendi was not in the Holy Land when Bahá'íyyih Khánum passed away. This is clear from the message that he sent to the Bahá'ís of the East on 15 July 1932:

> Alas, that I was prevented from being with her at the close of her earthly days, at that moment when she ascended to her Lord, her Master, and

> when her delicate body was placed in the tomb. Not mine that honour, that high privilege, for I was far away, deprived, bereft, excluded.[271]

Upon receiving the news of Bahá'íyyih Khánum's death, Shoghi Effendi sent the following message to the National Spiritual Assembly of the United States and Canada:

> GREATEST HOLY LEAF'S IMMORTAL SPIRIT WINGED ITS FLIGHT GREAT BEYOND. COUNTLESS LOVERS HER SAINTLY LIFE IN EAST AND WEST SEIZED WITH PANGS OF ANGUISH, PLUNGED IN UNUTTERABLE SORROW. HUMANITY SHALL ERELONG RECOGNIZE ITS IRREPARABLE LOSS. OUR BELOVED FAITH, WELL-NIGH CRUSHED BY DEVASTATING BLOW OF 'ABDU'L-BAHÁ'S UNEXPECTED ASCENSION, NOW LAMENTS PASSING LAST REMNANT OF BAHA'U'LLÁH, ITS MOST EXALTED MEMBER. HOLY FAMILY CRUELLY DIVESTED ITS MOST PRECIOUS, MOST GREAT ADORNING. I, FOR MY PART, BEWAIL SUDDEN REMOVAL MY SOLE EARTHLY SUSTAINER, THE JOY AND SOLACE OF MY LIFE. HER SACRED REMAINS WILL REPOSE VICINITY HOLY SHRINES. SO GRIEVOUS A BEREAVEMENT NECESSITATES SUSPENSION FOR NINE MONTHS THROUGHOUT BAHÁ'Í WORLD EVERY MANNER RELIGIOUS FESTIVITY. INFORM LOCAL ASSEMBLIES AND GROUPS HOLD BEFITTING MANNER MEMORIAL GATHERINGS, EXTOL A LIFE SO LADEN SACRED EXPERIENCES, SO RICH IMPERISHABLE MEMOIRS . . . ADVISE HOLDING ADDITIONAL COMMEMORATION SERVICE OF STRICTLY DEVOTIONAL CHARACTER AUDITORIUM MASHRIQU'L-ADHKÁR.[272]

To Iran he sent a similar but shorter cable. The translation reads:

> The Greatest Holy Leaf, the Remnant of Bahá and His Trust, has disappeared from the horizon of the luminous Shrine, ascended to the Sidratu'l-Muntahá and is in the highest chambers of paradise leaning against the immortal throne of glory. The eyes of the people of Bahá are weeping and the hearts of the faithful are on fire. Patience and fortitude are the attributes of the steadfast friends, radiant submission is the characteristic of those near to God. For nine months Bahá'í feasts and celebrations will be completely suspended throughout the east and the west of the Bahá'í world in honour of her station. Her precious body is resting on an elevation in the vicinity of the glorious Shrine.
>
> Signed: Shoghi[273]

Bahá'íyyih Khánum died in the early morning hours of 15 July 1932. She was buried later that day. Shoghi Effendi had designated a spot on Mount Carmel as her permanent resting-place: 'a portion of the school property situated in the precincts of the Shrine of the Báb'.[274] The selection of this spot for Bahá'íyyih Khánum's resting-place was highly significant, for it was 'a further testimony to the majestic unfoldment and progressive consolidation of the stupendous undertaking launched by Bahá'u'lláh on that holy mountain'.[275] By choosing to bury her body on the slopes of Mount Carmel under the shadow of the Báb's Shrine, Shoghi Effendi took the first step in establishing 'that consecrated Spot' which was 'destined to evolve into the focal centre of those world-shaking, world-embracing, world-directing administrative institutions, ordained by Bahá'u'lláh'.[276] The next step was to build the beautiful monument over her resting-place which symbolizes the institutions of the Administrative Order: the steps symbolize Local Spiritual Assemblies, the pillars the National Spiritual Assemblies and the dome the Universal House of Justice.

In December 1939 Shoghi Effendi transferred the remains of Ásíyih Khánum (Navváb) and Mírzá Mihdí (the Purest Branch) – 'who', he cabled 'next twin founders Faith and Perfect Exemplar tower together with Greatest Holy Leaf above entire concourse faithful'[277] – from 'Akká, where they were originally buried, to Mount Carmel in Haifa, and buried them in the immediate vicinity of Bahá'íyyih Khánum's resting-place, thus fulfilling her wish to be buried close to them. He then built two beautiful monuments on their resting-places. In a message sent regarding this remarkable achievement, he wrote:

> O loved ones of God, These two precious and most exalted treasures, these two keepsakes of the sacred Beauty of Abhá, have now been joined to the third trust from Him, that is, to the daughter of Bahá and His remnant, the token of the Master's Remembrance.
>
> Their resting-places are in one area, on an elevation close by the Spot round which do circle the Concourse on High, and facing the Qiblih of the people of Bahá – Akká, the resplendent city, and the sanctified, the luminous, the Most Holy Shrine . . . For joy, the Hill of God is stirred at so high an honour, and for this most great bestowal the mountain of the Lord is in rapture and ecstasy.[278]

After Bahá'íyyih Khánum's passing, Shoghi Effendi sent the following plea to the Bahá'ís:

> O faithful friends! It is right and fitting that out of honour to her most high station, in the gatherings of the followers of Bahá'u'lláh, whether of the East or the West, all Bahá'í festivals and celebrations should be completely suspended for a period of nine months, and that in every city and village, memorial meetings should be held, with all solemnity, spirituality, lowliness and consecration – where, in the choicest of language,

may be described at length the shining attributes of that most resplendent Leaf, that archetype of the people of Bahá. If it be possible for the individual believers to postpone their personal celebrations for a period of one year, let them unhesitatingly do so thus to express their sorrow at this agonizing misfortune. Let them read this letter, this supplication, in their memorial gatherings, that perchance the Almighty will lighten my burden, and dispel the clouds of my bereavement; that He will answer my prayers, and fulfil my hopes, out of His bounty, His power, His grace.[279]

Bahá'íyyih Khánum, the Most Outstanding Heroine of the Bahá'í Dispensation

Many outstanding women have rendered imperishable services to Bahá'u'lláh's glorious Cause in the early years of the Bábí–Bahá'í Faith. The identities of these women remain generally unknown. Some of them have been referenced in relation to their male relatives. Of those few who have been mentioned by name, their particulars are obscure. The rare exceptions are Ṭáhirih and Bahá'íyyih Khánum. Each occupies a unique rank and enjoys a special station in the history of the Bábí and Bahá'í Faiths: Ṭáhirih is the most outstanding heroine of the Bábí dispensation, Bahá'íyyih Khánum, the most outstanding heroine of the Bahá'í dispensation.

Bahá'íyyih Khánum's title was 'the Greatest Holy Leaf'. Bahá'u'lláh originally bestowed this title on Ásíyih Khánum, 'His consort in every one of His worlds'.[280] When Ásíyih Khánum passed away, He bestowed the title on Bahá'íyyih Khánum. To avoid confusion, Shoghi Effendi has translated Ásíyih Khánum's title as 'the Most Exalted Leaf' and Bahá'íyyih Khánum's as 'the Greatest Holy Leaf'. *Varaqih* (leaf) is an Arabic feminine word. Since Arabic was the language of religious discourse and scholarship in the Middle East in the 19th century, its nuances have entered Bahá'í literature. As stated in the introduction, Bahá'u'lláh Himself has been referred to as *Sidrih* (Tree). His male descendants have been referred to as Aghṣan (Branches) and female descendants and relatives as Leaves.[281]

The 'most outstanding heroine of the Bahá'í dispensation' is a designation that Bahá'u'lláh Himself has conferred upon Bahá'íyyih Khánum. In a Tablet revealed in her honour, He says:

> Verily, We have elevated thee to the rank of one of the most distinguished among thy sex, and granted thee, in My court, a station such as none other woman hath surpassed. Thus have We preferred thee and raised thee above the rest, as a sign of grace from Him Who is the Lord of the throne on high and earth below.[282]

Speaking of the rank bestowed on Bahá'íyyih Khánum, Shoghi Effendi says that it is 'comparable in rank to those immortal heroines such as Sarah, Ásíyih, the Virgin Mary, Fáṭimih and Ṭáhirih, each of whom has outshone every member of her sex in previous Dispensations'.[283]

The most outstanding heroines of the Bábí and Bahá'í dispensations, although identical in their intense love for the cause of truth and utter devotion to the person of the Manifestation of God whose Cause they embraced, differ sharply in other respects, especially in the nature of the sacrificial services they rendered. They came from different backgrounds, the circumstances of their lives were different, they undertook different activities and the contribution each made to the progress of the Faiths they espoused could not be more dissimilar. The stark difference in the way they lived and in the manner in which they responded to the needs for change was in accordance with the circumstances of their lives. Circumstances made Ṭáhirih world renowned almost immediately after her death. Bahá'íyyih Khánum, although extraordinary in the feats she accomplished and remarkable in the range of contributions she made to the progress of the Bahá'í Faith, has remained an obscure figure on the world stage. This disparity in the acclaim received by these two most outstanding heroines has intriguing causes.

When Bahá'íyyih Khánum was two years old, a conference was held at Badasht in the province of Khurásán in Iran. At that conference Ṭáhirih was the key player in proclaiming the independence of the Báb's Revelation. In childhood and youth, she enjoyed the blessing of an education reserved for men of the elite class. In spite of her literary accomplishments, she was expected to behave like a traditional Muslim woman. When she came of age, she married her cousin, the son of the Imám-Jum'ih of Qazvín. They lived as husband and wife for several years and she bore three children but she never submitted her will to him. Contrary to the wishes of her family, she corresponded with Siyyid Káẓim and received the title of 'Qurratu'l-'Ayn' (Solace of the Eye). She later espoused the Cause of the Báb by sending Him a letter confessing allegiance to Him. She became the seventeenth Letter of the Living. Her activities as a Bábí woman sealed her fate. When it became clear that her differences with her husband were irreconcilable, she left him and focused her full attention and energy on serving the nascent Faith she had embraced. When she appeared unveiled among the assembled Bábís at Badasht, she registered her defiance of the time-honoured traditions which had kept women backward and subjugated to men for endless centuries. Her action caused consternation among her fellow religionists and created uproar among the Shí'ís, whose spiritual leaders demanded her execution and achieved it. She was strangled, her body thrown in a well. To this day her burial place remains obscure. Ṭahirih attained the full measure of her contribution to humanity through her martyrdom, which caught the attention of the world, and she was widely eulogized for what she stood for.

In contrast, Bahá'íyyih Khánum made her mark on life through long years of laborious service, undetected for decades even by the members of the community she served. Bahá'íyyih Khánum was raised in the cradle of justice and equity and was appreciated for who she was, something Ṭáhirih was deprived of. When Bahá'íyyih Khánum came of age she was left free to marry or remain single. She decided to remain unmarried in order to devote her whole life to the service of Bahá'u'lláh's Cause, and her decision was respected. Ṭáhirih married young and tried in vain to make it work for several years. To free herself from the shackles of a marriage that expected submission to the unreasonable demands of her husband, she gave it up and moved on with matters of conscience and spirituality which she considered far more important and fulfilling than living with the tyrant that her husband was.

Bahá'íyyih Khánum enjoyed for a while all the blessings that life could offer a child. However, at the age of six she tasted the bitterness of destitution and shared the sufferings inflicted on her beloved parents. She then had to leave her homeland at the age of seven and live the rest of her life in exile.

Unlike Ṭáhirih, who was well-versed in all branches of religious knowledge current during her life time, the circumstances of Bahá'íyyih Khánum's life deprived her of a formal education, both religious and secular. The blessing of education enabled Ṭáhirih to engage in religious discourse with prominent scholars and to express her views without fear. It empowered her to stand firm against her opponents and prove herself formidable both among her co-religionists and those who opposed her views on theological matters. She became a well-known public figure not only for her rare intellectual endowments but also for breaking with tradition, for removing her veil, for confronting the *status quo* and fighting injustices perpetrated against womankind.

Ṭáhirih's life, unlike Bahá'íyyih Khánum's, was short. She did not see eye to eye with the clerics in power in her time. This was a serious matter and she knew that she was risking her life for standing against the potentates of the land. Thus she had to achieve the most she could while she had the opportunity. Threatened by the magic of her utterance, the influence of her sharp mind and the charm of her demeanour, the ecclesiastics saw their survival in silencing her. What better and easier way to achieve their purpose than pronouncing the death sentence against her? Ironically, the execution of that sentence and the premature death of a prodigy in the mid-19th century made Ṭáhirih world renowned.

In contrast, Bahá'iyyih Khánum never participated in a public religious discourse, never engaged in arguments over theological issues with the followers of other Faiths. Most of her life she was working quietly behind the scenes and advancing the Cause of God in ways unsuspected by others. The contribution she has made to the Bahá'í community and to society at large, although tremendous, has nevertheless been overshadowed by the immensity of Bahá'u'lláh's Revelation and His grandeur and after Him by 'Abdu'l-Bahá's unique personality and station. These factors naturally determined the part that she played in the history of the Bahá'í Faith and the nature of the contribution that she made to it. Although the duration of the toils she suffered and the exemplary services she rendered extended over a period of 80 years, the true worth of what she achieved was generally unknown until she passed away more than three decades into the 20th century. It was Shoghi Effendi who made her known to the Bahá'í community. His tributes review succinctly the events of her life and let her personality shine through the many decades of selfless service that she rendered. Shoghi Effendi's advice to future historians conveys subtleties that illumine the path of fairness in treating her part in history. He refers to 'the share she has had in influencing the course of some of the chief events in the annals of the Faith, the sufferings she bore, the sacrifices she made, the rare gifts of unfailing sympathy she so strikingly displayed' and says 'these, and many others stand so inextricably interwoven with the fabric of the Cause itself that no future historian of the Faith of Bahá'u'lláh can afford to ignore or minimize'.[284]

The world will undoubtedly recognize the uniqueness of Bahá'íyyih Khánum's place in history and the worth of her contribution to a Faith that has as its pivotal goal the unity of humankind but that recognition will come when the standards of recognizing greatness have changed. At that time, humanity shall 'recognize its irreparable loss'.[285]

The many challenges faced by Bahá'íyyih Khánum and her manner of dealing with them are models for study, especially for those who are wronged, weighed down with numerous injustices and frustrated by the cruel circumstances of their lives. Her childhood, her youth, her adult years and old age inspire fortitude and optimism in those who are passing through these stages.[286] Her sufferings during the darkest days of her life impart hope to the despondent, give energy to the depressed and teach lessons of compassion and tolerance to those bent under the weight of ordeals they have endured. Shoghi Effendi says:

> In the school of adversity she, already endowed by Providence with the virtues of meekness and fortitude, learned through the example and exhortations of the Great Sufferer, Who was her Father, the lesson she

was destined to teach the great mass of His followers for so long after Him.[287]

Bahá'íyyih Khánum's Station and Place in History

Bahá'íyyih Khánum lived from 1846 to 1932. This period is most critical in the world's contemporary history in that it witnessed the advent of Bahá'u'lláh, the Promise of all ages, and the beginning of the spiritual revival of the planet. Two years before her birth the Báb had declared His Mission and heralded the advent of a far greater Revelation than His own, a Revelation that was destined to usher in a process culminating in the unification of the peoples of the world and the establishment of God's Kingdom on earth. The author of that Revelation was Bahá'u'lláh, Bahá'íyyih Khánum's father. He received the intimation of His revelation when Bahá'íyyih Khánum was six and declared His mission when she was about 16 years old. His claim made Him the target of severe persecution, banishment and imprisonment, impacting every stage of Bahá'íyyih Khánum's life from early childhood to old age. She was a co-sharer in her father's sufferings, endured tribulations and restrictions all her life, served Him and His Cause like no other woman believer did, stood firmly by the Centre of His Covenant, served as 'Abdu'l-Bahá's deputy during His travels in the West, was a loving supporter of the person appointed the Guardian of the Faith and for a time served as the head of the worldwide Bahá'í community both in the Holy Land and abroad. Bahá'íyyih Khánum so completely consecrated herself to the promotion of the tenets of her father's Cause that He named her Bahá'íyyih and bestowed upon her a station unsurpassed by any other woman. She lived a holy and immaculate life, served with an ardour, high resolve and selflessness that only 'Abdu'l-Bahá excelled.

The laborious nature of the work Bahá'íyyih Khánum performed during the long years of her life, the extent of the contributions she made to the development of the Bahá'í Faith during the first century of its existence, and her remarkable achievements have won her a unique place in religious history. Bahá'iyyih Khánum stands out among the members of her gender in this dispensation and among the outstanding heroines of other religious dispensations as the most distinguished.

What is known of the lives and contributions of the women who, like Bahá'íyyih Khánum, enjoy the appellation of being the most outstanding heroines of their dispensations, does not compare in magnitude to the richness of the life that Bahá'íyyih Khánum lived and the remarkable contributions that she made. Indeed, to none was given a mandate to take charge of the affairs of the communities established by the founders of those dispensations.

Bahá'íyyih Khánum also stands out, after 'Abdu'l-Bahá, as the foremost among the members of the Holy Family. Shoghi Effendi refers to her 'next to 'Abdu'l-Bahá, among the members of the Holy Family, as the brightest embodiment of that love which is born of God and of that human sympathy which few mortals are capable of evincing'.[288] He laments the meagreness of his 'lonely pen, so utterly inadequate to glorify so exalted a station, so impotent to portray the experiences of so sublime a life . . .'[289]

Confirming the uniqueness of her spiritual station, he says:

> The people of the Concourse on High seek the fragrance of thy presence, and the dwellers in the retreats of eternity circle about thee. To this bear witness the souls of the cherubim within the tabernacles of majesty and might, and beyond them the tongue of God the One True Lord, the Pure, the Most Wondrous.[290]

Bahá'íyyih Khánum's entire life was devoted to serving the Cause of God and the world of humanity at a time when societal restrictions on women, especially in areas where she lived, were most strict. Neither her station nor the mighty contribution she has made to the Bahá'í community, to the cause of womankind and to humanity in general are fully known. When full details of major events in her life and the nature of her undertakings during the ministries of Bahá'u'lláh, 'Abdu'l-Bahá and Shoghi Effendi become known and are studied in depth, the recognition of her station and the unique place she occupies in recorded history will be possible. In the meantime, we can obtain a glimpse of her towering personality by studying the writings revealed in her honour.

Bahá'u'lláh has testified that she appeared in His name, a reference to the fact that of all the members of His family, His eldest daughter was named 'Bahá'íyyih' the feminine form of Bahá'. He also refers to her as the 'Leaf that hath sprung' from the 'Pre-existent Root', and the 'fragrance' of His 'shining robe'.[291]

'Abdu'l-Bahá has addressed Bahá'íyyih Khánum as 'My well-beloved, deeply spiritual sister', 'dear sister, beloved of my heart and soul', 'my honoured and distinguished sister', 'my affectionate sister', 'my sister and beloved of my soul', 'my cherished sister', 'my sister in the spirit, and the companion of my heart', 'Greatest and Most Merciful Holy Leaf'.

Although all His life 'Abdu'l-Bahá faced tribulations of every kind and endured sufferings like no other believer experienced, yet He wrote to Bahá'íyyih Khánum:

> My sorrow and regret concern not myself; they centre around thee.

> Whenever I recall thine afflictions, tears that I cannot repress rain down from mine eyes . . .[292]

'Abdu'l-Bahá was well aware of the nature and extent of Bahá'íyyih Khánum's suffering. He knew too well what cruelties she had endured at the hand of her unfaithful kindred. He knew also the unjust restrictions she had to observe by virtue of her gender and the weight of the responsibilities she had to shoulder. How He wished, when He was witnessing the outpouring of Bahá'u'lláh's bountiful confirmations and favours in the West, that she could see with her outward eye. Alas, the circumstances of life and travel, as well the responsibilities that she had to undertake during 'Abdu'l-Bahá's absence, did not make it possible. Indeed, Bahá'íyyih Khánum never left the Holy Land and its surrounding lands. The farthest place to which she travelled was Cairo.

Those heavenly attributes that endeared Bahá'íyyih Khánum to Bahá'u'lláh and 'Abdu'l-Bahá were also responsible for the deep love that Shoghi Effendi cherished in his heart for her. In one of his tributes he speaks movingly of a celestial love that bonded him to her, a love that manifested itself in a most cordial and intimate relationship that will endure forever. In the same passage he praises those who love Bahá'iyyih Khánum, walk in her footsteps, remember her sufferings and pay homage to her resting-place. At the same time he sternly warns those who may try to dispute her rank and station and deny the excellence of her ways:

> O thou Maid of Bahá! The best and choicest of praises, and the most excellent and most glorious of salutations, rest upon thee, O thou solace of mine eyes, and beloved of my soul! Thy grace to me was plenteous, it can never be concealed; thy love for me was great, it can never be forgotten. Blessed, a thousand times blessed, is he who loves thee, and partakes of thy splendours, and sings the praises of thy qualities, and extols thy worth, and follows in thy footsteps; who testifies to the wrongs thou didst suffer, and visits thy resting-place, and circles around thine exalted tomb, by day and by night. Woe unto him, retribution be his, who disputes thy rank and station, and denies thine excellence, and turns himself aside from thy clear, thy luminous and straight path.[293]

In other of his writings Shoghi Effendi refers to Bahá'íyyih Khánum as 'the Most Exalted, the pure, the holy, the immaculate, the brightly shining Leaf'; 'the Remnant of Bahá'; 'His trust'; the 'eternal fruit' and 'the one last remembrance of the Holy Tree', 'that rich mine of faithfulness', that Orb of the heaven of eternal glory', 'torch of tender love', 'source of grace and mercy'; 'symbol of bounty and generosity', 'day-spring of detachment in this world of being', 'trust left by Bahá among His people', 'remnant left by Him among His servants', 'sweet scent of His garment', 'that quintessence of love and purity within the towering pavilions of eternity', 'this heavenly being', 'never failing spring of grace', 'essence of loving-kindness', 'that Leaf of the eternal Lote-Tree', 'that rare treasure of the Lord', a 'trusted supporter of the peerless Branch of Bahá'u'lláh, and a companion to Him beyond compare', 'His competent deputy', 'His representative and vicegerent, with none to equal her', 'Liege Lady of the people of Bahá', 'that most resplendent Leaf', 'that archetype of the people of Bahá'.[294]

Addressing Bahá'íyyih Khánum, he says:

> Except for a very few, whose habitation is in the highest retreats of holiness, and who circle, in the furthermost Sanctuary, by day and by night about the throne of God, and are fed at the hand of the Abhá Beauty on purest milk – except for these, no soul of this nether world has known or recognized thine immaculate, thy most sacred essence, nor has any befittingly perceived that ambergris fragrance of thy noble qualities, which richly anoints thy brow, and which issues from the divine wellspring of mystic musk; nor has any caught its sweetness.[295]

Shoghi Effendi's praises of Bahá'íyyih Khánum, the Greatest Holy Leaf, are prolific and profound. When it was customary for men of high stature to ignore or minimize women's contributions and conceal their true worth, Shoghi Effendi proclaimed the station of his great-aunt and showered high praise on the glorious services she had rendered to the Cause in general and to him in particular. Excerpts from some of the passages quoted from his statements indicating her unique personality and the value of her work are set out below.

In a letter written on behalf of Shoghi Effendi, we read

> That sacred treasure, that jewel of Heaven, was the very sign and token of spiritual attributes and qualities and perfections, the very model of high honour and nobility and heavenly ways. The sufferings she bore in the pathway of God were the cruellest ones, the afflictions that assailed her were the severest of all. Fortitude was the rich dress she wore, serenity and tranquil strength were her splendid robe, virtue and detachment, purity and chastity, were all her jewels, and tenderness, care and love for humankind, her beauty's bright adornings.[296]

He explains that except for Bahá'u'lláh, the Báb and 'Abdu'l-Bahá, no one had endured in the path of God as much as she did:

> . . . she who did endure with patience in God's way from [her] earliest childhood and throughout all [her] life, and did bear in His pathway what none other hath borne, save only God in His own Self . . . and before Him, His noble Herald, and after Him, His holy Branch . . .[297]

Shoghi Effendi's description of Bahá'íyyih Khánum's demeanour is matchless in clarity and beauty:

> In the heaven of severance, she shone like the Morning Star, fair and bright, and through her character and all her ways, she shed upon kin and stranger, upon the learned, and the lowly, the radiance of Bahá'u'lláh's surpassing perfection . . . With the waters of her countless mercies, she brought thorny hearts to a blossoming of love from the All-Glorious, and with the influence of her pure loving-kindness, transformed the implacable, the unyielding, into impassioned lovers of the celestial Beauty's peerless Cause.[298]

He further states that she personified the attributes of Bahá'u'lláh:

> To this bear witness the Company on High, and beyond them God Himself . . . that during all thy days . . . thou didst personify the attributes of thy Father, the Matchless, the Mighty. Thou wert the fruit of His Tree, thou wert the lamp of His love, thou wert the symbol of His serenity, and of His meekness, the pathway of His guidance, the channel of His blessings, the sweet scent of His robe, the refuge of His loved ones and His handmaidens, the mantle of His generosity and grace.[299]

The Guardian's statements about the spiritual potency of the resting-places of the Greatest Holy Leaf, her exalted mother and martyred brother are as illuminating as his messages about their personalities and stations.

And finally, he refers to the Greatest Holy Leaf as the 'noble and well-favoured scion of a heavenly Father'[300] and asks her to intercede on his behalf and on behalf of all the sincere and devoted believers. Interceding effectively on behalf of others is a function reserved for well-favoured souls, souls that have left the world fully detached from worldly shackles, souls totally concerned with the betterment and well-being of the loved ones they have left behind. It is in that capacity that Shoghi Effendi, addressing Bahá'íyyih Khánum, says:

> Intercede, O noble and well-favoured scion of a heavenly Father, for me no less than for the toiling masses of thy ardent lovers, who have sworn

undying allegiance to thy memory, whose souls have been nourished by the energies of thy love, whose conduct has been moulded by the inspiring example of thy life, and whose imaginations are fired by the imperishable evidences of thy lively faith, thy unshakable constancy, thy invincible heroism, thy great renunciation.[301]

Bahá'íyyih Khánum's Distinguishing Characteristics

Distinction characterized Bahá'íyyih Khánum's life from beginning to end. Every stage of her life was marked by evidences of uniqueness. The Tablets revealed in her honour and Shoghi Effendi's writings extolling her virtues testify to the distinctive qualities she possessed. Yet some of her characteristics stood out more prominently than others. To learn what were her most distinguishing characteristics, we turn to those who knew her well. Foremost among those who knew her intimately is Shoghi Effendi. These are his testimonies:

> A purity of life that reflected itself in even the minutest details of her daily occupations and activities; a tenderness of heart that obliterated every distinction of creed, class and colour; a resignation and serenity that evoked to the mind the calm and heroic fortitude of the Báb; a natural fondness of flowers and children that was so characteristic of Bahá'u'lláh; and unaffected simplicity of manners; an extreme sociability which made her accessible to all; a generosity, a love, at once disinterested and undiscriminating, that reflected so clearly the attributes of 'Abdu'l-Bahá's character; a sweetness of temper; a cheerfulness that no amount of sorrow could becloud; a quiet and unassuming disposition that served to enhance a thousandfold the prestige of her exalted rank; a forgiving nature that instantly disarmed the most unyielding enemy – these rank among the outstanding attributes of a saintly life which history will acknowledge as having been endowed with a celestial potency that few of the heroes of the past possessed.[302]

> . . . in the management of the affairs of His Household in which she excelled, or in the social relationships which she so assiduously cultivated in order to shield both Bahá'u'lláh and 'Abdu'l-Bahá . . . in the unfailing attention she paid to the everyday needs of her Father, or in the traits of generosity, of affability and kindness, which she manifested, the Greatest Holy Leaf . . . abundantly demonstrated her worthiness to rank as one of the noblest figures intimately associated with the life-long work of Bahá'u'lláh.[303]

In his messages Shoghi Effendi confirms the similarity of Bahá'íyyih Khánum's attributes with those he had seen in 'Abdu'l-Bahá:

> . . . she was the living symbol of many an attribute I had learned to admire in 'Abdu'l-Bahá. She was to me a continual reminder of His inspiring personality, of His calm resignation, of His munificence and magnanimity. To me she was an incarnation of His winsome graciousness, of His all-encompassing tenderness and love.[304]

Those who knew Bahá'íyyih Khánum well had nothing but praise for her heavenly attributes. Among her admirers were some from the western world, such as Lady Blomfield:

> After those terrible days in Ṭihrán, and the not less terrible journey to Baghdád, during the sojourn in this city, she grew into a beautiful girl, very much like her lovely mother in grace of body and character, a gentle, slender maiden with large, grey-blue eyes, golden-brown hair, and warm, ivory-coloured skin. Her sense of humour was keen and her intelligence remarkable.[305]

Mabel Hyde Paine, whose recollections of the Greatest Holy Leaf have been quoted earlier in this account, describes Bahá'íyyih Khánum's manner when she spoke: 'She spoke in a most unassuming way and would not have spoken at all had we not begged her to.' She adds, 'No face I saw at Haifa is clearer in my mind than hers. It is the face of a person of exquisite susceptibilities who has suffered, who has shrunk from the suffering and who has also accepted it with infinite sweetness and resignation. And upon this sweet resignation has broken the light of great day . . .'[306]

Keith Ransom-Kehler, posthumously designated by Shoghi Effendi as a Hand of the Cause of God, was in the Holy Land in June 1932 before going to Iran on a special mission given to her by Shoghi Effendi. Writing in her diary about Bahá'íyyih Khánum she says:

> From the Greatest Holy Leaf streamed an effulgence of beauty and heavenly love that I have never witnessed from any human being. To come into her presence was to hush and exalt the soul. She was like a bird at dawn, the coming of spring, a city on a far horizon; everything that wakes our wonder and reveals the depths and not the tumults of the heart . . .
>
> On the eve of my departure I went to tea with the ladies of the Household. Khánum was very feeble . . .
>
> Her thoghtfulness, her loving kindness, her self-mastery, her complete

dedication to the things of the spirit never ceased to the last hour that I saw her, just a month and a day before her ascension.

As I was making my farewells Ḍíyá assisted her to her feet in spite of my protests. She folded me oh, so tenderly in her precious arms and said: 'When you are come to Persia, I want you to give my love to every Bahá'í in all that land, to the men the same as to the women. And when you reach the holy city of Ṭihrán enter it in my name, and teach there in my name.'[307]

Another western pilgrim, Marjory Morten, describes some of the attributes that distinguished Bahá'íyyih Khánum from others:

You were sure that if one tried to hurt her she would wish to console him for his own cruelty. For her love was unconditioned, could penetrate disguise and see hunger behind the mask of fury, and she knew that the most brutal self is secretly hoping to find gentleness in another. She had that rarest heart-courage, – to uncover the very quick of tenderness to any need. And so deep was her understanding that she plumbed all the miseries of the human heart and read their significance, blessing both the victim and the valid pain itself.

So alive was she to the source of all bounty that she had no consciousness of her own bounty. When she made a gift she seemed to be thanking you for it. The prompting included gratitude. When she gave joy she blessed you for it. It was almost as if she did not distinguish giving from receiving . . . she took nothing for granted in the way of devoted service and even in her last hours she whispered or smiled her thanks for every littlest ministration . . . She delighted in making presents, – sweetmeats and goodies and coins for the children, and for others flowers, keepsakes, – a vial of attar of roses, a rosary, or some delicate thing that she had used and cared for. Anything that was given her she one day gave to someone else, someone in whom she felt a special need of a special favour. She was channel rather than cup; open treasury, not locked casket.

And as she would not lock away her small treasures, neither would she store up her wisdom and her riches of experience. In her, experience left no bitter ash. Her flame transmuted all of life, even its crude and base particles, into gold. And this gold she spent. Her wisdom was of the heart. She never reduced it to formula or precept: we have no wise sayings of hers that we can hang motto-like on our walls, just by being what she was she gave us all that she knew.

. . . Something greater than forgiveness she had shown in meeting the cruelties and strictures in her own life. To be hurt and to forgive is saintly

> but far beyond this is the power to comprehend and not be hurt. This power she had . . . She was never known to complain or lament. It was not that she made the best of things, but that she found in everything, even in calamity itself, the germs of enduring wisdom. She did not resist the shocks and upheavals of life and she did not run counter to obstacles. She was never impatient. She was as incapable of impatience as she was of revolt. But this was not so much long-suffering as it was quiet awareness of the forces that operate in the hours of waiting and inactivity.
>
> Always she moved with the larger rhythm, the wider sweep, toward the ultimate goal. Surely, confidently, she followed the circle of her orbit around the Sun of her existence, in that complete acquiescence, that perfect accord, which underlies faith itself.[308]

Bahá'íyyih Khánum lived 80 years of her life as an exile in several unfamiliar places but never lost her love for Iran and did not feel the Persian tongue to be alien. She preserved the good traditional values of her birthplace and passed them on to the generation of exiles who accompanied Bahá'u'lláh on His banishment from land to land.

Marjory Morten reflects on Bahá'íyyih Khánum's demeanour:

> Her graciousness and courtesy reflected the courtly Persia of another day. Even with her family she observed some of the punctilio of that day, gestures that for her were a part of a living ritual rather than a dead form; delicate values of human relationships that outlast all form and fashion and that expressed her innate respect and consideration for every fellow-being.[309]

Elaborating the point she says:

> It is a charming Persian habit to wrap a gift in an embroidered silk or linen cloth, as fine in its way as the thing enclosed. So, always, she gave a gift within the gift. You took the happy warmth of contentment you felt when you were with her and only later came to realize that this was the fine wrapping of a deeper joy, a richer core.[310]

To show her appreciation for what people could do well and to make them feel good about their accomplishments, Bahá'íyyih Khánum provided them with opportunities to reveal their talents. She then used the occasion to reward them unobtrusively with acts of loving-kindness. When Miss Qudsíyyih Ashraf[311] was on pilgrimage in 1920, Bahá'íyyih Khánum learned that she was talented in making women's clothes. One day she asked Miss Ashraf to make her a warm coat since winter was approaching, and provided her with a piece of woollen fabric. Miss Ashraf has written in her memoirs:

> I got busy taking measurements and started cutting the fabric. Only once she tried it on and the fitting was done. The garment was ready close to sunset. Ḥaḍrat-i-Khánum wore it and said, 'You worked very hard. You are a good tailor. You have made me a lovely dress.' While she was uttering these words, she put her arm under mine and said, 'You have become tired. Let's go into the garden and walk a little.' We walked towards the private entrance of the house, exited the hall and started walking. Ḥaḍrat-i-Khánum was talking softly and I was all ears. I was so intoxicated with the sweetness of her voice and the words she uttered that I lived in a different world. Suddenly I felt a ring being slipped onto my little finger. She had taken a ring off of her delicate and angelic finger and put it on mine. The reader may be able to create in her or his mind how ecstatic I felt at that particular time but describing the experience is an impossible task not only for me but also for the most able writer, the most eloquent speaker or celebrated poet . . . I do not recall having uttered a word of thanks for the priceless gift. I was so puzzled I could not speak. I was in a world unlike this one with its customs and traditions. I was melted into a world that was absolute servitude. I do not know what happened and how I left her presence.[312]

In her book *Prophet's Daughter* Janet Khan has focused attention on resilience as one of the outstanding characteristics of Bahá'íyyih Khánum. She has devoted a section in the last chapter[313] to a discussion of this significant attribute and its manifestations in Bahá'íyyih Khánum. She concludes: 'The Greatest Holy Leaf is a model of resilience in the face of a lifetime of suffering and tribulation.' She adds: 'Shoghi Effendi attests that, while these sufferings "left their traces upon her feeble form", they did not in the least affect "her spirit of joy and hopefulness", nor did they undermine her faith in the future.'[314]

Bahá'íyyih Khánum's Writings

The Greatest Holy Leaf's writings consist of letters that she wrote to Bahá'í Assemblies and individuals. A collection of her letters available in Iran was for the first time published by the Bahá'í Publishing Committee of the National Spiritual Assembly of the Bahá'ís of that country in 129 BE (1972 AD) under the title of *Dastkhatháy-i-Haḍrat-i-Varaqiy-i 'Ulyá* (Letters of Her Highness the Greatest Holy Leaf). On the fiftieth anniversary of her passing in 1982, the English translation of a large number of her letters, together with the translation of the writings of Bahá'u'lláh, 'Abdu'l-Bahá and Shoghi Effendi to and about her, were published by World Centre Publications under the title of *Bahíyyih Khánum, the Greatest Holy Leaf.* The facsimile of her handwriting is published on page 156 of that book. The same book has also been published in Persian.

Bahá'íyyih Khánum's Monument Symbolic of Her Station and Personality

In a luxuriant garden on the slopes of Mount Carmel and under the shadow of the Shrine of the Báb stand four monuments. Of the three built at a higher elevation two are identical; they belong to Bahá'íyyih Khánum's mother, Ásíyih Khánum, titled Navváb and the Most Exalted Leaf, and her martyred brother, Mírzá Mihdí, titled the Purest Branch. The third and most prominent is the one built over Bahá'íyyih Khánum's resting-place. At a lower level stands a smaller and less ornate monument, the resting-place of Munírih Khánum, the wife of 'Abdu'l-Bahá. Shoghi Effendi built these monuments in that particular spot for a specific purpose. The subject of a befitting burial place for Bahá'íyyih Khánum was on his mind during the closing years of her life. He wished to have her buried in a spot befitting her station and rank, a spot where he could also have the remains of her mother and brother interred, thus fulfilling her wish of being buried close to them. In 1932, before he left on a trip to Switzerland, he left instructions regarding the spot on Mount Carmel where Bahá'íyyih Khánum was to be buried if she died while he was away. Shoghi Effendi then planned 'for her grave a suitable memorial which he hastened to Italy to order'.[315] Hand of the Cause of God Amatu'l-Bahá Rúḥíyyih Khánum says, 'No one could possibly call this exquisitely proportioned monument, built of shining white Carrara marble, anything but what it appears – a love temple, the embodiment of Shoghi Effendi's love.'[316]

The path leading from the street to the monument of the Greatest Holy Leaf is lined on both sides with cypress trees. The monument, surrounded by green grass, fruit-bearing trees and flowers is built of three distinct parts. Three steps lead to the circular platform forming the base of the monument. In the centre of the platform, on a prominent piece of black marble, is engraved her full name, i.e. Bahá'íyyih Khánum, and the dates of her birth and death (1846–1932).

Nine columns with ornate pedestals surround the circular platform of the base. These pillars uphold the crowning part of the monument, the dome. Around the base of the circular dome is inscribed in gold Bahá'u'lláh's testimony in Arabic for His illustrious daughter. The English translation of the Tablet reads:

> This is My testimony for her who hath heard My voice and drawn nigh unto Me. Verily, she is a leaf that hath sprung from this preexistent Root. She hath revealed herself in My name and tasted of the sweet savours of My holy, My wondrous pleasure. At one time We gave her to drink from My honeyed Mouth, at another caused her to partake of My mighty, My luminous Kawthar. Upon her rest the glory of My name and the fragrance of My shining robe.[317]

A Persian pilgrim who was in the presence of Shoghi Effendi in 1952 has recorded in his memoirs the following about the significance of the Monument Gardens:

> Regarding the Monument Gardens Shoghi Effendi said: 'Tomorrow you will visit the Monuments of the Greatest Holy Leaf, the Purest Branch and their esteemed mother. This is a very important centre. It looks like a garden but its significance will become evident in the future. This new creation is one of the evidences of the establishment of the Shrine of the Báb which 60 years ago the Ancient Beauty created on Mount Carmel. I had told the pilgrims repeatedly that this will be a very important international administrative centre. The friends must read the Tablet of Carmel and ponder upon it, both its allegories and its prophecies. The spiritual centre is the Shrine of the Báb. It is a place of pilgrimage, a holy place. The administrative centre will be later established around these monuments. [In the Tablet of Carmel] there is mention of Madinatu'lláh (the city of God) and of Safinatu'lláh (the Ark of God). These refer to a great prophecy that is yet to happen . . .'[318]

The accessibility of the resting-place of the Greatest Holy Leaf, its open space, the vibrant colours of grass, trees and flowers that surround it, all combine to give it a striking appeal. It can be visited by the friends at any time of the day and one can spend in its vicinity any amount of time, to pray and meditate.

At times when the weight of tribulations and ordeals are overwhelming and hold one back from approaching the Sacred Shrines, when the spirit longs to commune with God but the heart feels heavy and down, one feels beaconed by the Greatest Holy Leaf to lay down in the open surroundings of her monument one's burden of sorrows, to refresh the spirit, cleanse the heart and make preparations for communing again with the One who is the desire of the world. I have often stood before that monument feeling embraced by the motherly love of the Greatest Holy Leaf, assured of her intercession on behalf of humanity and overcome with feelings of utter calm and tranquillity. When Shoghi Effendi sought her intercession on his behalf, he also confirmed her power of intercession on behalf of all humanity:

> Then intercede thou for me before the throne of the Almighty, O thou who, within the Company on High, dost intercede for all of humankind.[319]

It is her power to intercede on behalf of humanity that is most reassuring, for no matter how severe our shortcomings, we know that they will not be allowed to stand in the way of attaining our heart's desire if it is to serve the Cause of God. As we pray through her gentle and saintly spirit, we feel unperturbed by the vicissitudes of this world and know that the outpourings of divine assistance will embrace us and ensure our success in promoting the Cause to which she consecrated her life.

The Greatest Holy Leaf's monument is a vivid reminder of her loving and caring personality, of her serenity, supreme compassion and, above all, her accessibility: she was always ready to embrace those desiring to approach her. It summons us to draw nigh to its peaceful surroundings, it gives ear silently to our inmost feelings, stretches a loving hand to embrace us lovingly and provides the atmosphere conducive to feelings of tranquillity. It invites visitors to express their desires uninhibited and offer supplications through her to the object of their adoration. It affords happiness to the despondent and solace to the grief-stricken. It reinforces the resolve of those who seek confirmation to continue their service and opens up the hearts of those who dare not share their inner feelings with other human beings. It stands in a perfect spot on Mount Carmel which unites the spiritual and administrative centres of the Faith. It serves as a reminder that these two centres are inseparable. Anyone who traverses the beautiful gardens interposed between the sacred Shrines in Haifa and the Seat of the Universal House of Justice cannot fail to fathom the symbolic significance of the monument of the Greatest Holy Leaf, whose resting-place, along with those of her saintly mother and martyred brother, constitute the focal point of the world administrative institutions of the Faith.

In December 1939, about seven and a half years after the passing of Bahá'íyyih Khánum, Shoghi Effendi transferred the remains of Ásíyih Khánum and Mírzá Mihdí from 'Akká where they were originally buried, to the spot on Mount Carmel where Bahá'íyyih Khánum is buried. The transfer of their remains and the building of their monuments in that 'consecrated spot' on Mount Carmel completed the plan he had devised many years earlier. Regarding these precious resting-places he says:

> The conjunction of these three resting-places, under the shadow of the Báb's own Tomb, embosomed in the heart of Carmel, facing the snow-white city across the bay of 'Akká, the Qiblih of the Bahá'í world, set in a garden of exquisite beauty, reinforces, if we would correctly estimate its significance, the spiritual potencies of a spot, designated by Bahá'u'lláh Himself the seat of God's throne. It marks, too, a further milestone in the road leading eventually to the establishment of that permanent world Administrative Centre of the future Bahá'í Commonwealth, destined never to be separated from, and to function in the proximity of, the Spiritual Centre of that Faith, in a land already revered and held sacred alike by the adherents of three of the world's outstanding religious systems.[320]

Other statements by the Guardian about the spiritual potency of the resting-places of the Greatest Holy Leaf, her exalted mother and martyred brother are quoted in chapter 6 of the present book.

Sacred Writings Revealed in Bahá'íyyih Khánum's Honour

Authentic statements by the founders of previous religious dispensations and their successors revealed in honour of the female members of their families are scarce, if not non-existent. In contrast, a wealth of material is available in the hand of the Central Figures of the Bahá'í Faith, as well as by Shoghi Effendi, in honour of the women of the twin Holy Families.

Scriptural references to Bahá'íyyih Khánum are numerous. Some of the writings of Bahá'u'lláh and 'Abdu'l-Bahá revealed in her honour have been quoted throughout this account. There is yet more. Speaking of the feelings of joy and delight that her presence evoked, Bahá'u'lláh says:

> How sweet thy presence before Me; how sweet to gaze upon thy face, to bestow upon thee My loving-kindness, to favour thee with My tender care, to make mention of thee in this, My Tablet – a Tablet which I have ordained as a token of My hidden and manifest grace unto thee.[321]

8

Fáṭimih Khánum, Titled Mahd-i-'Ulyá, the Second Wife of Bahá'u'lláh

Family Background

Fáṭimih Khánum was born to Malik Nisá' Khánum, Bahá'u'lláh's paternal aunt, and Mírzá Karím-i Namadsáb,[1] both from the Núr district of Mázandarán. She had one sister called Maryam, titled Varaqatu'l-Ḥamrá (the Crimson Leaf). Maryam married Mírzá Riḍá Qulí, Bahá'u'lláh's half brother. Unlike her husband, she was a devoted and active believer. Fáṭimih Khánum and Maryam had a brother, named Mírzá Muḥammad-i Vazír. He married Ḥavvá Khánum, the daughter of Bahá'u'lláh's half sister, Sakínih (Ṭallán) Khánum, and Mírzá Muḥammad, a younger half brother of Mírzá Buzurg. Mírzá Muḥammad-i Vazír and Ḥavvá Khánum were both devoted believers.

Birth and Early Life

Fáṭimih Khánum was born in Núr *circa* 1828. Nothing is known of her childhood and early life. Indications are that she was raised in Núr. Considering that some close members of her family, including her sister, lived in Ṭihrán, it would not be unreasonable to assume that she visited the capital from time to time.

Marriage

When she was about 14 years old Fáṭimih Khánum married a renowned mujtahid of Núr named Mullá Muḥammad-Taqí. He was several decades older than she. The marriage took place in 1842 and lasted about a year. For those who may wonder why a young girl of 14 would marry an old mullá in the sunset of his life, they need to know that in those days, and even today, some Muslim families in Iran and other Islamic countries consider it an honour to give their young daughters in marriage to a well-known religious figure. Mullá Muḥammad-Taqí was renowned in the district of Núr. His pre-eminence as a spiritual leader must have been a major factor in the decision of Fáṭimih Khánum's parents to give her to him in marriage. He may have been distantly related to the family. He was an honest and trustworthy man and served as the executor of the will of Mírzá Buzurg, Bahá'u'lláh's father. Mullá Muḥammad-Taqí died in 1843, before the Báb declared His mission. Fáṭimih Khánum had no children from this first marriage.

In 1849, nearly six years after the death of Mullá Muḥammad-Taqí and 14 years after Bahá'u'lláh's marriage to Ásíyih Khánum, Bahá'u'lláh married Fáṭimih Khánum. The circumstances leading to the marriage are unclear. The popular belief is that since Fáṭimih Khánum had been widowed at the age of 15 or 16 and tradition required that a male member of the family, well placed and able, provide her with security and protection, her mother had set her hopes on Bahá'u'lláh and made entreaties to Him in this regard.

After the declaration of the Báb in 1844, Bahá'u'lláh was preoccupied with promoting the Bábí Faith. He visited Núr several times for the purpose of teaching the Bábí Faith to the inhabitants of Tákur and its surrounding areas, particularly to the members of His own family. It seems that Fáṭimih Khánum accepted the Bábí Faith then. After the conference at Badasht, which took place in the summer of 1848, Bahá'u'lláh made two trips to the district of Núr. The first trip was immediately after the Badasht conference. It was in conjunction with His visit to the fort of Ṭabarsí for the purpose of inspecting the fortifications there. The second trip was in 1849 when the battle between the defenders of the fort and government forces was in full swing. During that trip Bahá'u'lláh spent several days in Tákur to make preparations for joining the fort of Ṭabarsí defenders. His marriage to Fáṭimih Khánum, whose mother lived in Núr, may have taken place then. Adib Taherzadeh states that the marriage took place in Ṭihrán.[2] Fáṭimih Khánum's mother had set her hopes on Bahá'u'lláh marrying her young widowed daughter; it is believed that at any opportune moment she would raise the subject. It seems that it was in response to His aunt's repeated pleadings that Bahá'u'lláh entered into a marriage contract with Fáṭimih Khánum. Until this and similar assumptions are backed by evidence, they should be treated as conjecture.

The marriage ceremony must have been small and low-key, for unlike His marriage to Ásíyih Khánum, for which there is an elaborate marriage certificate and detailed accounts, we know almost nothing of Bahá'u'lláh's marriage to Fáṭimih Khánum.

If the marriage indeed took place in Núr during Bahá'u'lláh's stay there in connection with His effort to join the defenders of the fort at Ṭabarsí, it is unlikely that Fáṭimih Khánum moved to Ṭihrán immediately afterwards. In fact, she could not have done so because of the events that transpired thereafter. The period between the closing months of 1849 and Bahá'u'lláh's departure for Baghdád was the most difficult in His life before leaving Iran. When He attempted to join the defenders of Fort Ṭabarsí late in 1849, He was captured and imprisoned in Ámul. Shortly after His return to Ṭihrán, at the suggestion of the prime minister of Iran, He left for Karbilá, where He spent nine months. When He returned to Iran the attempt on the life of Náṣiri'd-Dín Sháh occurred, culminating in His arrest and imprisonment in the Síyáh Chál for four months. And about one month after His release, He went into exile.

Exactly when Fáṭimih Khánum joined Bahá'u'lláh in Ṭihrán is uncertain. A logical time seems to be after His release from the Síyáh Chál and before His departure from Iran. She may have in fact joined Him during His brief stay in the home of her sister, Jináb-i-Maryam, and her husband, Mírzá Riḍá Qulí, Bahá'u'lláh's half brother.

The accounts of Bahá'u'lláh's four months' imprisonment in the Síyáh Chál are clear about where Ásíyih Khánum and her children lived during that time. They are similarly clear about where Bahá'u'lláh stayed in Ṭihrán for recuperation during the interim between His release from prison and His departure for Baghdád. The accounts reveal that during Bahá'u'lláh's stay in the house of Mírzá Riḍá Qulí and Jináb-i-Maryam, it was Maryam who nursed Bahá'u'lláh until He regained sufficient strength to undertake the trip to Baghdád. The account also indicates that Ásíyih Khánum and the children did not live with Bahá'u'lláh during His stay in the house of Mírzá Riḍá Qulí and Jináb-i-Maryam. Although the accounts are silent about the whereabouts of Fáṭimih Khánum, it may be reasonably assumed that in order for her to accompany Bahá'u'lláh on His journey to Baghdád, she would have moved to Ṭihrán at least during the last days of that period.

Layla Ábádih'í's memoirs suggest that the marriage actually took place in Ṭihrán before Bahá'u'lláh and His family left for Baghdád:

> One day when I was attending to the Greatest Holy Leaf in the bath, she said, 'When the Blessed Beauty was released from the Síyáh Chál of Ṭihrán, He stayed in the home of my uncle Áqá Mírzá Ḥasan,[3] for Bahá'u'lláh was unwell and that house was close to the Síyáh Chál. Bahá'u'lláh was in that house for two weeks. During that time, my uncles suggested that He marry with the mother of Mírzá Muḥammad-'Alí [i.e. Fáṭimih Khánum]. They said that it would be better if He married her and secured for Himself a clan of supporters. Bahá'u'lláh did not consent to the marriage in the beginning. My uncles insisted until He agreed and the marriage took place.'[4]

Life in Exile

Fáṭimih Khánum accompanied Bahá'u'lláh and His family on the journey from Ṭihrán to Baghdád. No accounts are available about how she fared during that arduous trip. She being young and not yet with child must have made it easier for her to cope. Her life in Baghdád is likewise shrouded in obscurity. A few things are certain:

1) Her first child, Mírzá Muḥammad-'Alí, was born in 1854, probably before Bahá'u'lláh left for Kurdistán.

2) She seems to be the only member of Bahá'u'lláh's immediate family who returned to Iran shortly after arrival in Iraq. This may indicate that she was not officially among the exiles and was free to travel back to Iran. The details of the trip, including exactly when it took place and how long she stayed in Iran, are unclear.

3) When she returned to Baghdád in 1858 she brought with her Mírzá Mihdí, the Purest Branch. Mírzá Mihdí was about three years old when Bahá'u'lláh and His family left for Baghdád. He was too young and delicate to withstand the rigours of travel during the severe winter months.

Fáṭimih Khánum accompanied Bahá'u'lláh and His family on subsequent exiles to Istanbul, Adrianople and 'Akká. Bahá'u'lláh and Fáṭimih Khánum had five children, all of whom were born in exile.[5] They were Mírzá Muḥammad-'Alí, Mírzá Ḍíyá'u'lláh, Ṣamadíyyih Khánum, Mírzá Badí'u'lláh and Sádhijíyyih Khánum, who died in infancy.

Information about Fáṭimih Khánum's life in Istanbul and Adrianople is scanty. However, through the activities of her children, especially her eldest son, Mírzá Muḥammad-'Alí, entitled the Greater Branch, we gain insights into her life.

Mírzá Muḥammad-'Alí was about ten years younger than 'Abdu'l-Bahá and very different from Him in many respects. As he grew older, so did his desire to assume a leading role among Bahá'u'lláh's followers grow. Many believe his mother played a role in instilling that desire in him. Exactly when the process began and how his egotistic tendencies and covetous nature were nurtured is not certain. The seed was undoubtedly planted long before Mírzá Muḥammad-'Alí's malicious schemes caused himself, his mother and his siblings a severe test of faith.

When 'Abdu'l-Bahá, the Most Great Branch, was growing up in Baghdád, at His father's behest He accompanied His uncle, Mírzá Músá, who represented Bahá'u'lláh in official circles. Later He carried out this function on His own. When Bahá'u'lláh and His companions left Baghdád for Istanbul and Adrianople, 'Abdu'l-Bahá was 19 years old and visibly in charge of the caravan that took the exiles farther away from Iran. Upon arrival in 'Akká, He attended to all matters pertaining to the life of the exiles. He also dealt with the authorities and shielded Bahá'u'lláh from outside harm. In the meantime, Mírzá Muḥammad-'Alí was growing older, completely overshadowed by the distinctive personality of the Most Great Branch.

The first time Mírzá Muḥammad-'Alí acted upon his impulse to prove that he could rival not only the Most Great Branch but Bahá'u'lláh Himself was in Adrianople. To prove his worth, he claimed that he was the recipient of verses from God. According to Adib Taherzadeh,

> When he [Mírzá Muḥammad-'Alí] was in his early teens in Adrianople, he composed a series of passages in Arabic and without Bahá'u'lláh's permission disseminated them among some of the Persian Bahá'ís, introducing them as verses of God which, he claimed, were revealed to him. He intimated to the believers that he was a partner with Bahá'u'lláh in divine Revelation . . .
>
> This controversy prompted Ḥájí Muḥammad-Ibráhím, entitled Khalíl, to write a letter to Bahá'u'lláh begging Him to clarify His own station and the station of His sons. Ḥájí Khalíl was already confused about the claims of Mírzá Yaḥyá and wished to be enlightened and find the truth.[6]

Mírzá Muḥammad-'Alí's claim exposed his unconstrained ambition and earned him the wrath of Bahá'u'lláh, whose rebuke included chastising him 'with His own hands'.[7] In His Tablet to Ḥájí Khalíl, which became known as the Lawḥ-i-Khalíl (Tablet of Khalíl), Bahá'u'lláh declared His own station. Regarding His children He stated that so long as they

> observe the commandments of God, persevere in edifying their souls, testify to what has been revealed by God, believe in Him Whom God shall make manifest, do not create divisions in His Cause and do not deviate from His revealed laws, they can be considered as the leaves and branches of His Tree of holiness and members of His family. Through them will the light of God be diffused and the signs of His bounty be made manifest.[8]

In another Tablet, referring to Mírzá Muḥammad-'Alí, Bahá'u'lláh says: 'He, verily, is but one of My servants . . . Should he for a moment pass out from under the shadow of the Cause, he surely shall be brought to naught.'[9]

In yet another Tablet He says: 'By God, the True One! Were We, for a single instant, to withhold from him the outpourings of Our Cause, he would wither, and would fall upon the dust.'[10]

Bahá'u'lláh's stern and emphatic warning made Mírzá Muḥammad-'Alí and those who cherished high hopes for him realize that he would be doomed if he tried to do anything foolish. However, neither did he nor those who promoted him abandon the hope of seeing him in a position of authority after Bahá'u'lláh passed away. They knew that Bahá'u'lláh would some day appoint the one who was to succeed Him, so they set their hopes on that, despite knowing that Mírzá Muḥammad-'Alí did not stand a chance. What stood between him and the realization of his hope to succeed Bahá'u'lláh was the person of 'Abdu'l-Bahá, the Most Great Branch, very much loved and trusted by Bahá'u'lláh:

> In the *Tablet of Khalíl* Bahá'u'lláh alludes to 'Abdu'l-Bahá in terms which immensely exalt Him above the others. He refers to Him as One among His sons 'from Whose tongue God will cause the signs of His power to stream forth', and as the One Whom 'God hath specially chosen for His Cause'.[11]

When 'Abdu'l-Bahá got married in 'Akká at the age of 29, Mírzá Muḥammad-'Alí was 19 but nowhere close to 'Abdu'l-Bahá in personality and stature when He was that age. Fáṭimih Khánum was not blind to the glory of the destiny awaiting the Most Great Branch and wanted the same for her firstborn son. As a mother, judging on a purely human level, the feeling of wanting the best for her son may be understandable. However, acting on that feeling and going against the explicit wishes of Bahá'u'lláh whose station she claimed to have recognized and bowed before is inexcusable. What makes her behaviour towards the Most Great Branch reprehensible is the extensive actions she took to realize her fanciful desires. Her actions were initially clandestine but gradually became apparent and eventually flagrant.

In *The Covenant of Bahá'u'lláh*, Adib Taherzadeh has written in some detail about Mírzá Muḥammad-'Alí's ambitious behaviour during Bahá'u'lláh's lifetime. He has also written about his attempts to appear on a par with, or even superior to, the Most Great Branch and that his conduct had to be monitored and kept in check.[12] However, there is almost nothing regarding the role played by Fáṭimih Khánum in the process, especially after Bahá'u'lláh's ascension. The absence of detailed information in this regard does not mean that she was unaware or did not participate in what transpired. In fact, there are indications that she and several other members of the family were involved in unwittingly causing Mírzá Muḥammad-'Alí's downfall and, in the process, causing 'Abdu'l-Bahá and His family intense sorrow and suffering.

When Bahá'u'lláh moved to the Mansion of Mazra'ih, 'Abdu'l-Bahá stayed in the House of 'Abbúd together with His family, which included also His mother, Ásíyih Khánum, and His sister, Bahá'íyyih Khánum. Bahá'u'lláh's change of residence from the House of 'Abbúd to the Mansion of Mazra'ih, which 'Abdu'l-Bahá had worked so hard to make possible, afforded Fáṭimih Khánum and her children the opportunity to be with Bahá'u'lláh and enjoy constant close physical access to Him. Nothing has come to hand regarding how the physical separation affected the way that Fáṭimih Khánum related to Ásíyih Khánum. However, we have 'Abdu'l-Bahá's commentary on the 54th chapter of the book of Isaiah revealing to our eyes invaluable insights. He first confirms that the chapter 'refers to the Most Exalted Leaf, the mother of 'Abdu'l-Bahá'.[13] Then, regarding verse 11, which begins: 'O thou afflicted, tossed with tempest, and not comforted,'[14] He says:

> And truly the humiliation and reproach which she suffered in the path of God is a fact which no one can refute. For the calamities and afflictions mentioned in the whole chapter are such afflictions which she suffered in the path of God, all of which she endured with patience and thanked God therefor and praised Him, because He had enabled her to endure afflictions for the sake of Bahá. During all this time, the men and women (Covenant-breakers) persecuted her in an incomparable manner, while she was patient, God-fearing, calm, humble and contented through the favour of her Lord and by the bounty of her Creator.[15]

After Bahá'u'lláh left the prison-city of 'Akká, contacts between Him, 'Abdu'l-Bahá and His family were through visits and written communications. Since travel was by primitive means, roads were bad and the weather not agreeable, it is unlikely that the women were able to visit Bahá'u'lláh frequently. However, Bahá'u'lláh visited 'Akká for the purpose of being with 'Abdu'l-Bahá and His family and when He visited, He stayed for some time. Some of the Tablets addressed to the members of the family in 'Akká were revealed when Bahá'u'lláh sent them written messages during their physical separation.

The available information on how the women of Bahá'u'lláh's family lived and the activities in which they engaged during the years Bahá'u'lláh resided at Mazra'ih and Bahji is scanty indeed. Women who had the opportunity to visit Bahá'u'lláh's family were not many and very few of them had the ability to write their observations. One such woman was Rafí'ih Shahidi. She was a little girl when she accompanied her grandmother on a visit to the Mansion of Bahji. She later wrote:

> One day I went in the company of my grandmother to the Mansion of Bahji. We entered a room which had a window opening to Bahá'u'lláh's chamber. It was the living room of the mother of Mírzá Muḥammad-'Alí [Fáṭimih Khánum] . . . When the women believers went to the Mansion of Bahji intending to attain Bahá'u'lláh's presence, they gathered in that room and waited until they were summoned by Bahá'u'lláh. On that day all the women pilgrims were gathered in that room. Suddenly the curtain on the window was drawn to one side. Bahá'u'lláh walked to the window. We all rose up to our feet. The eye of Bahá'u'lláh's loving-kindness was turned towards me. Then addressing my grandmother, He enquired whether I attended school . . .[16]

It is not unprecedented in religious history for women among the kindred of the Manifestation of God to play crucial roles in helping the Cause of God to go forward or adversely affect its progress. The Old Testament cites a number of instances. In Christianity, since Christ did not marry and was crucified young, there are fewer examples but none as prominent as the Virgin Mary, the mother of Jesus Christ. Islamic history has recorded active roles played by Muḥammad's wives, especially Khadíjih and Ayishíh, and His daughters, particularly Fáṭimih.

Human nature has changed little since the beginning of recorded history. Envy still remains an incurable malady. Uncontrolled ambition and love for supremacy and leadership still cause untold suffering and threaten prospects for unity and coexisting amicably. Some women members of Bahá'u'lláh's family undoubtedly suffered from the spiritual diseases afflicting humanity in general. What is different in Bahá'u'lláh's Cause, however, is that a firm Covenant has been established, making it impossible for those with malicious intentions to succeed in their attempts to undermine God's purpose or gain ascendancy over the appointed centre of authority.

To avoid the pitfall of blaming women for whatever goes wrong in religion, it must be admitted that Fáṭimih Khánum was not solely responsible for fanning to flame the fire of Mírzá Muḥammad-'Alí's ambitious tendencies. He had other supporters within the immediate family circle. Mírzá Muḥammad-'Alí's brother-in-law and cousin, Mírzá Majdu'd-Dín, who was married to Ṣamadíyyih Khánum, Fáṭimih Khánum's daughter, was his accomplice and partner in mischief. Mírzá Majdu'd-Dín was notorious for his hostility towards 'Abdu'l-Bahá and, unlike his father, Áqáy-i-Kalím, who served Bahá'u'lláh to the end of his life with devotion and distinction, Mírzá Majdu'd-Dín threw in his lot with Mírzá Muḥammad-'Alí and worked assiduously to undermine 'Abdu'l-Bahá's authority. Other members of Mírzá Muḥammad-'Alí's family lent him their support. The result was the loss of their sacred heritage. Fáṭimih Khánum lost the inestimable honour she had gained when Bahá'u'lláh married her. In the end she reaped what she had sown. The crushing fall she suffered was because she turned her back on 'Abdu'l-Bahá and broke the Covenant of Bahá'u'lláh. Her children followed her example and were reduced to naught, as Bahá'u'lláh had said in His Tablet, quoted above.

That Mírzá Muḥammad-'Alí himself was an ambitious person there is no doubt, for without that essential element in his personality no amount of allegiance, support and encouragement could have made him do what he did to the Centre of Bahá'u'lláh's Covenant. The element of rebellion was there early on. As stated earlier, during Bahá'u'lláh's lifetime, he made claims that displeased Him intensely. How much responsibility Fáṭimih Khánum bears for planting the seed of opposition to 'Abdu'l-Bahá in Mírzá Muḥammad-'Alí is unknown. What is certain is that her own ambitions caused her to feed the ambitious tendencies of a son who was willing to do whatever it took to discredit 'Abdu'l-Bahá, with the purpose of pushing Him aside and occupying the seat of authority after Bahá'u'lláh's ascension.

After the Ascension of Bahá'u'lláh

The real test of Fáṭimih Khánum's faith came when Bahá'u'lláh's earthly life came to an end. Almost immediately after Bahá'u'lláh's ascension, Fáṭimih Khánum felt free to put into action what she considered necessary for the realization of the hope she had for so long cherished in her heart, the hope of undermining the Most Great Branch and installing her eldest son, Mírzá Muḥammad-'Alí, in His place.

Shoghi Effendi in *God Passes By* describes how during the last days of His earthly life Bahá'u'lláh advised His kindred and those of His followers, who were in His presence, of the Will He had left with the Most Great Branch:

> Six days before He passed away He summoned to His presence, as He lay in bed leaning against one of His sons, the entire company of believers, including several pilgrims, who had assembled in the Mansion, for what proved to be their last audience with Him. 'I am well pleased with you all,' He gently and affectionately addressed the weeping crowd that gathered about Him. 'Ye have rendered many services, and been very assiduous in your labours. Ye have come here every morning and every evening. May God assist you to remain united. May He aid you to exalt the Cause of the Lord of being.' To the women, including members of His own family, gathered at His bedside, He addressed similar words of encouragement,

> definitely assuring them that in a document entrusted by Him to the Most Great Branch He had commended them all to His care.[17]

The very fact that Bahá'u'lláh had entrusted the Most Great Branch with the Will He had entitled *The Book of My Covenant* conveys His complete trust and confidence in His eldest Son. During His ministry Bahá'u'lláh had made His intention clear regarding the one who was to follow Him by treating the Most Great Branch with special consideration and requiring the members of His family and followers to do likewise. To leave no ground for disputation regarding the subject of succession, He also left a document in His own hand elaborating on passages in the Kitáb-i-Aqdas which deal with the matters of succession and interpretation of the holy writ, emphasizing that all had to turn to the Most Great Branch, the Centre of His Covenant and the authorized Interpreter of His words. However, neither Bahá'u'lláh's utterances, nor His written injunctions, or the way He educated the believers to refer to the Most Great Branch as the Master and treat Him as such stopped Fáṭimih Khánum from lending Mírzá Muḥammad-'Alí her full support in executing his malicious designs.

At first Mírzá Muḥammad-'Alí and his supporters tried to lay their hands on Bahá'u'lláh's Will by going through the contents of the two cases containing His papers. These two cases had been entrusted to the Most Great Branch during the last days of Bahá'u'lláh's earthly life. The family members who were hard at work to thwart Bahá'u'lláh's will and usurp the right of primacy from 'Abdu'l-Bahá for Mírzá Muḥammad-'Alí, vainly imagined that the will had been placed in one of those two cases and set their hearts on gaining access to them at an opportune time. The opportunity presented itself when Bahá'u'lláh's body was being washed and prepared for burial:

> When the ascension took place, 'Abdu'l-Bahá's grief knew no bounds. The shock He sustained as a result of this calamitous event was so intense that He found it difficult to describe it. He says that in the morning, along with His brother, He began the task of preparing the remains for burial. When they were about to wash Bahá'u'lláh's blessed body, Mírzá Muḥammad-'Alí suggested to 'Abdu'l-Bahá that since the floor would become wet, it would be better to take the two cases out of the room into Badí'u'lláh's room. 'Abdu'l-Bahá was at that point in such a state of shock and grief that He was almost unconscious of His surroundings. He never thought that behind this suggestion could be a treacherous plot designed to rob Him of that precious trust.
>
> He agreed, and the two cases were taken out and that was the last He saw of them.

The sacred remains were laid to rest that same day. 'Abdu'l-Bahá was disconsolate and heartbroken. He says that for three consecutive days and nights He could not rest a single moment. He wept for hours and was in a state of unbearable grief. The Light of the World had disappeared from His sight and all around Him had been plunged into darkness. On the fourth night after the ascension, He arose from His bed around midnight and walked a few steps hoping that it might help to bring a measure of tranquillity to His agonized heart. As He began to pace the room, He saw through the window a scene His eyes could scarcely believe. His unfaithful brothers had opened the cases and were looking through Bahá'u'lláh's papers, those papers which had been entrusted to Him!

'Abdu'l-Bahá was deeply disturbed by the treachery of His brothers so soon after the ascension of their Father. This act of unfaithfulness committed so dishonourably against the most sacred trust of God, inflicted further pain and suffering upon His sorrow-laden heart. He returned to His bed immediately after this incident, for He did not wish His brothers to know He had seen them interfering with the contents of the cases. At this point 'Abdu'l-Bahá thought to Himself that since His brothers had not seen the *Will and Testament* of Bahá'u'lláh, which was in 'Abdu'l-Bahá's possession, they were trying to find some document among His Writings with which to justify their intended action of undermining the foundations of the Cause of God and creating a division within the ranks of its avowed supporters. However, 'Abdu'l-Bahá hoped, when they saw the *Will and Testament*, their efforts would be frustrated and they would then return His trust to Him.

But alas, this did not happen![18]

That Fáṭimih Khánum had a hand in schemes designed to install Mírzá Muḥammad-'Alí as the Branch intended to succeed Bahá'u'lláh is evident from the role she played after His ascension. An early believer residing in 'Akká has left an account of the events that transpired immediately after Bahá'u'lláh's ascension. In a letter to Áqá Khalíl, Ḥájí Muḥammad-Ḥusayn-i Tabrízí writes:

The heaven of the sanctified temple had not yet been hidden from mortal eyes when idle talk from the people of malice circulated among the non-Bahá'ís and reached the believers' ears. The believers with utter astonishment heard the non-believers say: 'We wonder what has caused Mírzá Muḥammad-'Alí to become Bahá'u'lláh's successor despite the Master being present!' The friends were bewildered as to whence the rumour originated and from whom. After investigation it became evi-

> dent that non-Bahá'í women who had gone to the Mansion to convey their condolences had asked who Bahá'u'lláh's successor was. Certain persons, who had malicious intentions from the beginning, had made the statement. The friends were heartbroken and grieved that the blessed temple was not yet buried when such talk found currency causing indignation and sowing in the hearts the seeds of discord, in utter contradiction to the will of God. Moreover, they were saying that which was obviously untrue . . .[19]

To make Bahá'u'lláh's wishes regarding His successor and other matters known to the members of the family and believers alike, on the ninth day after His ascension, 'Abdu'l-Bahá chose a number of believers to witness the unsealing of Bahá'u'lláh's Book of the Covenant. In their presence Bahá'u'lláh's Will was opened and the contents read aloud by one of the witnesses. The document was in Bahá'u'lláh's hand. It left no doubt regarding Bahá'u'lláh's rightful successor. It enjoined upon all to turn their faces toward the Most Great Branch. The position of the Greater Branch, the document specified, was beneath that of the Most Great Branch. In the afternoon of the same day, Bahá'u'lláh's Book of the Covenant was read to all the believers assembled in the Most Holy Shrine. To ensure that the women of the Holy Family and other female believers were aware of Bahá'u'lláh's Will, the document was also read to them in the Mansion.

The announcement of the contents of Bahá'u'lláh's Will should have put an end to speculations and rumours originated from those living in the Mansion. The document should have rallied members of the community in general and Bahá'u'lláh's kindred in particular around the Most Great Branch. But this was not the case. According to Ḥájí Muḥammad Ḥusayn-i Tabrízí:

> After a short while the 'Akhtar'[20] newspaper announced the news of Bahá'u'lláh's ascension. In the same issue it announced that there were differences between the Branches. We all wondered what the reason for such a statement could be. Was there again a discussion of this nature going on? Suddenly we realized that some were secretly spreading rumours that although outwardly the Most Great Branch was the centre of authority, the true successor was Mírzá Muḥammad-'Alí. And when they [rumour-mongers] discussed the subject, they made the enquirers promise that they would not divulge the name of the person who had made the statement. Ironically, the Branches heard what was discussed and did not object. On the contrary, they were intimate friends with and at one with the people who spread the rumours.[21]

In spite of the fact that Fáṭimih Khánum had openly sided with her son, Mírzá Muḥammad-'Alí, and actively engaged in attempts to undermine 'Abdu'l-Bahá, He treated her most respectfully and evinced the reverence and consideration due to a surviving wife of Bahá'u'lláh. Ḥájí Muḥammad Ḥusayn-i Tabrízí says:

> Whenever Bahá'u'lláh's wife visited 'Akká, she was received with a degree of reverence beyond which cannot be imagined. When she wanted to visit Tiberias, 'Abdu'l-Bahá had a litter made for her and Himself supervised its construction. He sent them to Tiberias with such honour, glory and grandeur that astonished and surprised friend and foe alike . . . 'Abdu'l-Bahá wanted nothing but the preservation of their station, the glorification of the Cause of God, and the spreading abroad of the breezes of holiness . . .[22]

Then came a time when the malevolent designs of Mírzá Muḥammad-'Alí, his mother and other members of his family became blatantly clear, causing a breach between the steadfast supporters of Bahá'u'lláh's Covenant and those who violated its provisions. The separation cleansed the Bahá'í community from the effects of discord eating into its fabric and afforded 'Abdu'l-Bahá the opportunity to focus full attention on deepening the believers in their understanding of the tenets of Bahá'u'lláh's Cause and spreading its sweet savours abroad.

Just as 'Abdu'l-Bahá and His family seemed to enjoy a brief respite from the effects of the storm of Covenant-breaking, another plot by the violators of the Covenant was in the making. The self-seeking and treacherous Mírzá Badí'u'lláh,[23] Mírzá Muḥammad-'Alí's younger brother, suffering from heavy financial debt and seeking a way out, decided to break ties with Mírzá Muḥammad-'Alí, confess their malevolent deeds, expose their schemes, beseech 'Abdu'l-Bahá's forgiveness and join the community of the faithful believers.[24] During the short period of time he pretended to have severed ties with the violators of the Covenant, he stirred much mischief and caused 'Abdu'l-Bahá untold grief. While enjoying 'Abdu'l-Bahá's generosity and hospitality, he was clandestinely in touch with Mírzá Muḥammad-'Alí. Fáṭimih Khánum acted as the intermediary to effect reconciliation between the two brothers. This fact is confirmed by 'Abdu'l-Bahá in a Tablet He revealed in response to an enquiry from a western believer, most probably Laura Clifford Barney, regarding Mírzá Badí'u'lláh. It explains his clandestine activities after he had repented and rejoined the community. It also explains the role that his mother, Fáṭimih Khánum, played in bringing about a reconciliation between him and Mírzá Muḥammad-'Alí.

. . . By God, I am not offended by Mírzá Badí‘u’lláh, or by the harm he inflicted on Me which caused My renewed incarceration and stirred up mischief against Me, causing members of the local government in ‘Akká to be displeased with Me. However, I am offended that he acted against the Cause of God, broke the Covenant and caused sedition in the Faith of God. After the ascension of the Blessed Beauty, he arose with intense envy, inflicted whatever harm he could, united with his brother Mírzá Muḥammad-‘Alí, noised abroad false accusations against Me, and stirred up great mischief. I endured everything patiently. After some time he was overcome with remorse and realized that he was in manifest loss. He repented and confessed his transgression. He announced that he was duped and misled by Mírzá Muḥammad-‘Alí, that Mírzá Muḥammad-‘Alí interpolated the Book of God, that he broke the Covenant of God with all his power, and that he [Mírzá Badí‘u’lláh] was coerced to join him in opposition to Me. That epistle [Mírzá Badí‘u’lláh’s confession] has been translated in the United States. A copy is being sent . . . For every disease there is a cure and for every wound a balm, but for the sickness of envy there is no remedy, and love and fidelity yield no result.

Yea! I paid off all his debts with the utmost difficulty and hardship. Indeed, I postponed the payment of My own debts and paid off his. I provided for him every means of comfort and happiness, all to no avail. His sense of envy boiled over again. Three months elapsed from the time of his return when secretly he reconciled with Muḥammad-‘Alí and made a friendship pact with him. They used their mother as the intermediary for the truce. He conveyed to Mírzá Muḥammad-‘Alí in the dead of the night all the private affairs of the Cause of God, My every movement, My conversations with the friends, and the news coming in from all over the world. Nonetheless, I endured patiently and uttered not a word.[25]

‘Abdu’l-Bahá explains how Mírzá Badí‘u’lláh continued his mischievous deeds within and outside the community, instigated the populace, including a certain foreign national, against Him. Mrs Rosamond Templeton, an American with a self-imposed mission of reforming the ‘backward’ people of the Orient, was by her own admission duped by Mírzá Badí‘u’lláh. Mrs Rosamond Templeton is the same as Rosamond Dale Owen, author of *My Perilous Years in Palestine*, published in 1928. In a chapter entitled ‘The Behai’s (or Babists)’,[26] she describes among other things how Mírzá Badí‘u’lláh took advantage of her generosity:

During my stay in Haifa I have been led to interest myself especially in three persons. Frau F., the elderly daughter of the founder of the German

Colony . . . The second was Carlos . . . The third was Bedi-Allah, the youngest surviving son of Baha'o'llah. He was a political prisoner in St Jean d'Acre for a number of years, and I found that he and his family of seven persons were about to starve. So I helped them to the best of my ability. When he was released later, at the time the Young Turks came into power, my task grew more trying, for I found that both he and an able-bodied brother-in-law, living in his home, still failed to exert themselves seriously in order to make a living. As they had very little property, they were always in difficulty, and often the Voice bade me help them, until I had spent on them a very considerable sum of money. It had been difficult under these circumstances to keep my vow, to give, to forgive, to believe, especially when the following circumstances arose:

I had been going through a long period of money stress, made the more difficult by the drain on my purse through Bedi-Allah. Finally, I received an unexpected sum of money, and began to breathe freely after a prolonged anxiety about ways and means. But my relief did not last long, for Bedi-Allah came a week or two after, and asked to let him have four hundred pounds. I was obliged to pray all night before my soul was sufficiently free from bias to hear the Voice of Christ and to obey His touch. When I attained this balance the Voice said, 'Give.' Later Bedi-Allah confessed to me that he had asked for this money, four hundred pounds, in order to save from exposure a Turk, whom we will call Halim Effendi, and who had been robbing a Government strong-box put temporarily under his charge. When Bedi-Allah saw that through his foolish act I was reduced again to poverty, he was very sorry and tried to get back the money, but in vain.

It had been very difficult under these circumstances to keep my threefold vow to give, to forgive, to believe. For I urgently needed the money the thief had received; I was tempted to be much irritated with Bedi-Allah; and my faith was strained, when I realized the Voice had told me to give for so unworthy a purpose. Still, a sweet peace flowed through me, when I was able to overcome, and it seemed to me that I had done what Christ meant me to do; although I could not see what good purpose it had served, and hence it was an act of blind obedience.

It was about this time the three brothers, Abbas, Mohammed Ali, and Bedi-Allah, desired me to act as arbitrator in order to settle the disputes between them, Abbas Effendi adding: 'I want you to look well into the affair of Halim Effendi.' Bedi-Allah had already confessed how foolish he had been in yielding to the entreaties of Halim Effendi, and with a good deal of effort I had forgiven him; hence it was not necessary for me to investigate this detail. I had obtained from Halim Effendi a legal

> acknowledgment of the loan, but it was useless, as he had no money and no property upon which I could levy.[27]

The story makes one wonder whether Mrs Templeton bestowed money on Mírzá Badí'u'lláh out of the generosity of her heart, as a result of which she was turned poor, or was spending money on a scheme aimed at obliterating 'Abdu'l-Bahá from the scene. Did she refuse 'to look into the affair' of the man with the fictitious name 'Halim Effendi' because she was so forgiving, or was she avoiding self-implication in a failed plot against the Centre of Bahá'u'lláh's Covenant?

Mrs Templeton says in her book that she had known Mírzá Badí'u'lláh for 25 years. Since the book was first published in 1928, they probably met in 1902 or 1903. This date coincides with Mírzá Badí'u'lláh breaking with Mírzá Muḥammad-'Alí and turning to 'Abdu'l-Bahá for forgiveness. The account he wrote confessing his wrongdoings and exposing the odious activities of Mírzá Muḥammad-'Alí and his accomplices against 'Abdu'l-Bahá is dated February 1903. Fáṭimih K͟hánum was still alive. When Mrs Templeton visited the two brothers in their homes, i.e. the Mansion of Bahji, did she also meet with their mother and other women members of the family? It is curious that Mrs Templeton does not mention having met them, neither does she mention the fact that it was 'Abdu'l-Bahá who paid Mírzá Badí'u'lláh's debts. Two letters from her to 'Abdu'l-Bahá on the subject are extant. They speak of the arrangements made for the repayment of Mírzá Badí'u'lláh's debts. They also indicate that she cancelled a pre-arranged meeting with 'Abdu'l-Bahá. Her description of mundane details and omission of important facts make one wonder why a woman of Mrs Templeton's claimed honesty and piety who was able to forgive Mírzá Badí'u'lláh's glaring shortcomings, had such palpable contempt for 'Abdu'l-Bahá. The extent of her contempt for Him is evidenced by the contents of the chapter under discussion. Not only did she make no mention of the considerable sum of money she received from 'Abdu'l-Bahá, she actually blamed Him for the seeming poverty of His half brothers and their families. How much of her contempt for 'Abdu'l-Bahá was based on false information she was fed when she visited the home of the half brothers of 'Abdu'l-Bahá and their families and how much on sheer prejudice and bias against the one who by her own admission had the admiration of millions of Christians, is something worth pondering. Mrs Templeton's statements betray her true intentions. Her true colours come across loud and clear in the several pages she has devoted to the 'Behais (or Babists)' in her book.

Assisted by people like Mrs Templeton who financed the illegal activities of the like of 'Halim Effendi', Mírzá Badí'u'lláh managed to turn the pillars of the central government into 'Abdu'l-Bahá's avowed enemies. While he was busy spying on 'Abdu'l-Bahá, Mírzá Muḥammad-'Alí and Mírzá Majdu'd-Dín were hard at work sending alarming reports to the governor of the province of Syria, Náẓim Pásḥá, aimed at inducing him to have 'Abdu'l-Bahá deported from the Holy Land. Mírzá Muḥammad-'Alí's envoy to Damascus was Mírzá Majdu'd-Dín, the son-in-law of Fáṭimih Khánum. Adib Taherzadeh says:

> Majdu'd-Dín arrived back from his mission in a jubilant mood, having secured the Governor's promise of aid. But events now took a different turn. Upon receiving the Governor's report, Sulṭán 'Abdu'l-Ḥamíd became alarmed and ordered that incarceration be reimposed upon 'Abdu'l-Bahá, His brothers and his followers. Consequently, to the surprise of Majdu'd-Dín, his plans misfired and he himself, as well as his chief, Mírzá Muḥammad-'Alí, together with Mírzá Badí'u'lláh, were incarcerated in the city of 'Akká by the order of the Sultan.[28]

After the unexpected reincarceration, Mírzá Muḥammad-'Alí tried in vain to secure his release. Finally, 'Abdu'l-Bahá met with the civil and military authorities, interceded on behalf of his half brothers, as well as other detainees, secured their release, and offered to endure the restrictions Himself, which continued until the revolution of the Young Turks in 1908. Regarding what caused the Sultan to order the renewed incarceration of the exiles, Taherzadeh says:

> As to the cause of the restrictions, Mírzá Muḥammad-'Alí: he first flatly denied having had any communication with the Governor of Damascus and Majdu'd-Dín did likewise. They both alleged that the edict of the Sultan for re-incarceration had been issued as a result of the publication of a book by Mírzá Abu'l-Faḍl, the great Bahá'í scholar, but the truth soon surfaced. Ḥájí 'Alíy-i-Yazdí has described in his memoirs the circumstances which exposed the treachery of Majdu'd-Dín and Mírzá Muḥammad-'Alí. According to Ḥájí 'Alí, Majdu'd-Dín had delivered two petitions personally, one to Náẓim Pásḥá and the other to Faríq Pasḥá. The latter was a high-ranking military officer friendly towards 'Abdu'l-Bahá. It appears that the second petition was presented in response to a question raised by Faríq Pásḥá, who wanted to know the nature of disagreements between 'Abdu'l-Bahá and His brothers.
>
> In order to confuse the issue for Faríq Pásḥá, who was a Sunní Muslim, Mírzá Muḥammad-'Alí and Majdu'd-Dín forged a document which they attributed to Bahá'u'lláh; they sent this document along with their peti-

> tion. In this document they composed, in the name of Bahá'u'lláh, certain complimentary passages in praise of 'Umar, the second Caliph of Sunní Islám. In so doing, they made it seem that Bahá'u'lláh was a follower of Sunní Islám. The other document which they sent to the Pá<u>sh</u>á contained parts of the *Lawḥ-i Hizár Baytí (Tablet of One Thousand Verses)* in which 'Abdu'l-Bahá condemned 'Umar in strong terms. In their petition they then alleged that 'Abdu'l-Bahá was inciting His followers to arise in enmity against the Sunnís, whereas the rest of Bahá'u'lláh's family were admirers of 'Umar and the Sunní community.
>
> Mírzá Muḥammad-'Alí and Majdu'd-Dín continued to deny having sent any petition to Damascus until Faríq Pá<u>sh</u>á at last sent it to 'Abdu'l-Bahá, who upon receiving it sent it to the mother of Mírzá Muḥammad-'Alí so that she could see the treachery of her offspring and son-in-law Majdu'd-Dín.[29]

To a mother fully convinced of her son being beyond reproach and deserving to be on a par with the Centre of Bahá'u'lláh's Covenant, if not higher in stature, the evidence of his treachery must have come as a shock. Fáṭimih <u>Kh</u>ánum believed and acted as though Mírzá Muḥammad-'Alí was the embodiment of his father's virtues, a true defender of His Cause, someone who could do no wrong. The evidence showed that in his efforts to discredit 'Abdu'l-Bahá, he was willing to turn his back not only on what the Bahá'ís believe to be true but on the basic tenet of <u>Sh</u>í'í Islam, to which Fáṭimih <u>Kh</u>ánum's parents and ancestry belonged. What did Fáṭimih <u>Kh</u>ánum do in the face of that irrefutable evidence? Her continued and unqualified support for her sons and son-in-law, who were determined to destroy 'Abdu'l-Bahá by every means at their disposal, indicates that, alas, she did nothing to redeem herself, thus missing the last opportunity to make amends for her failures and becoming worthy of the honour Bahá'u'lláh bestowed in His Book of the Covenant on His kindred and the members of His household.

The Passing of Fáṭimih <u>Kh</u>ánum and a Brief Review of Her Life

Fáṭimih <u>Kh</u>ánum outlived Bahá'u'lláh by 12 years. She passed away in 'Akká in 1904 and was buried in a plot of land close to Bahjí which became an exclusive cemetery for the members of Bahá'u'lláh's family who violated His Covenant and their families.

The intervening years between Bahá'u'lláh's ascension and Fáṭimih <u>Kh</u>ánum's passing were the most turbulent in the history of the Covenant established by Bahá'u'lláh, the purpose of which was to safeguard the unity of His followers. 'Abdu'l-Bahá, the Centre of that Covenant, was assailed by formidable assailants. They included Bahá'u'lláh's two surviving wives, their children and in-laws, as well as Bahá'u'lláh's amanuensis, Mírzá Áqá Ján. They teamed up with 'Abdu'l-Bahá's external enemies and created conditions that put His life in danger. The most senior of 'Abdu'l-Bahá's opponents among the family of Bahá'u'lláh was Fáṭimih Khánum. While she enjoyed the honour and respect accorded her by virtue of her position, not only did she do nothing to put out the fire of enmity ignited by her sons against the Most Great Branch, she actually fuelled it behind the scenes.

Some oriental believers implicate Fáṭimih Khánum in the rebellion of Mírzá Muḥammad-'Alí. They cite in support of their argument her consuming envy for 'Abdu'l-Bahá and her burning desire to see her eldest son established on the throne of authority. Historians, on the other hand, list her as a breaker of Bahá'u'lláh's Covenant for siding with Mírzá Muḥammad-'Alí, who became known as the Centre of Sedition after violating the provisions of Bahá'u'lláh's Book of the Covenant. They do not present her as a main player on the Covenant-breaking scene. There are reasons for this.

1) Bahá'u'lláh's injunction that believers should show respect to His wives and kindred has caused them to withhold the pen from portraying in detail the hostile attitude of Fáṭimih Khánum towards the Most Great Branch.

2) The general tendency to underestimate the influence, good or bad, of the women on the course of religious history, the belief being that women's influence, if any, was negligible. Hence Fáṭimih Khánum has not been taken to task for what she has done or failed to do in the fulfilment of the requirements of the high esteem in which she was held by virtue of her position in the community. This was the case even after she defied the provisions of the document which required the believers to show her respect. The same applies to her daughter, Ṣamadíyyih Khánum, to her stepdaughter and her mother, Furúghíyyih Khánum and Gawhar Khánum, respectively, about whose activities against 'Abdu'l-Bahá we know very little. The historians have generally focused their attention on the male line. The women were considered adjuncts to the men, therefore not deserving historical treatment.

3) The activities of the female members of the family, unlike those of the male, were clandestine and conducted out of view. The reason for this is the traditions of the time and place in which they lived. Not allowing the women to be directly and openly involved in activities that were considered beyond their domain encouraged them to conduct their work behind the scenes. As a result, women could at times achieve clandestinely and

with impunity what men could not openly. Here lies the core of the secret of men often using the women to attain their ends.

In His Book of the Covenant, Bahá'u'lláh had provided for Mírzá Muḥammad-'Alí to succeed 'Abdu'l-Bahá. Fearful that he may not outlive 'Abdu'l-Bahá, he did what he could to usurp from Him the right of primacy. Fáṭimih Khánum was happy and willing to help him succeed. In the process, she went down in history as the mother of the arch-breaker of Bahá'u'lláh's Covenant, taking with her down the path of perdition all of her children and their families. Her hostility towards 'Abdu'l-Bahá intensified as she grew older and reached its height after Bahá'u'lláh's ascension.

Had Fáṭimih Khánum remained faithful to the Covenant of Bahá'u'lláh, things would have been very different. As Bahá'u'lláh's wife and the mother of the Greater Branch, who would have succeeded 'Abdu'l-Bahá had he remained faithful to the Covenant, Fáṭimih Khánum would have occupied an exalted position in the history of the Bahá'í Faith. But she chose to violate the provisions of the document which safeguarded her interests and made it incumbent upon the believers to show her respect. Consequently, she went down in history as the mother and supporter of the Centre of Sedition. She could have had an enviable position in the Bahá'í community had she remained faithful to Bahá'u'lláh's Covenant. Her impatience and ambition, however, caused the faithful to look upon her as the supporter of a son whose 'soul-festering' jealousy drove him to the brink of extinction.

Fáṭimih Khánum from the Eye of a Westerner

A woman missionary, Miss S. Louie Barker, wrote in her Annual Letter dated December 1891 of her visit to the Mansion of Bahji in the month of October of that year. During that visit she met Fáṭimih Khánum and Gawhar Khánum. Speaking of them she says: 'The ladies were most warm in their reception. Judging from their delight and their naive remarks, I should say we were the first European ladies they had seen!'[30] Moojan Momen has quoted in *The Bábí and Bahá'í Religions, 1844–1944: Some Contemporary Western Accounts* 'a much more condescending account' written by Miss Barker for *The Children's World*, the children's magazine of the CMS. Although her comments provide nothing of substance, nonetheless they convey a glimpse of the kind of life that the women led. Miss Barker says the two ladies did 'most of the talking in very imperfect Arabic'. She also says: 'They asked heaps of questions, and were greatly surprised at my not being married. One of the wives [Fáṭimih Khánum] said how she would like me for her son . . .' Miss Barker further explains, 'Some ladies who came in, hearing the English ladies were there, kissed the hem of the dresses of the two wives, and also the sons' wives [the wives of Mírzá Muḥammad-'Alí and Mírzá Ḍíyá'u'lláh], and afterwards saluted us.' She then speaks of tea being served two or three times and quotes the comment of one of the ladies that 'they drank tea nearly the whole day long!' She also says: 'They showed us the house, etc. and even took us on the verandah. They so seldom go out – they are shut up more than the Moslems – that one told me it was years since she has been even on this verandah.'[31]

The Fate of Fáṭimih Khánum's Children

As we have seen, Fáṭimih Khánum had three sons – Mírzá Muḥammad-'Alí, Mírzá Ḍíyá'u'lláh and Mírzá Badí'u'lláh – and two daughters, Ṣamadíyyih Khánum and Sádhijíyyih, who died in infancy. Mírzá Ḍíyá'u'lláh passed away shortly after Bahá'u'lláh's ascension. He was married to Sorayya (Thurayyá), daughter of Shaykh Káẓim Samandar. They had no children. After the death of her husband, Sorayya Khánum did not return to Iran, something her family wished her to do. She lived in the Mansion of Bahjí with the members of the family who broke the Covenant and herself became a Covenant-breaker.

Mírzá Muḥammad-'Alí had two wives. One of them was Laqá'íyyih Khánum, the daughter of Áqáy-i-Kalím. Mírzá Muḥammad-'Alí had four children, one daughter and three sons. Mírzá Shu'á'u'lláh was the most notorious. He went to the United States, teamed up with Dr Khayru'lláh and was a great mischief-maker. Mírzá Badí'u'lláh may have got married after Bahá'u'lláh's ascension. He had several children, none of whom remained within the orb of the Faith. In brief, Fáṭimih Khánum became a fallen Leaf causing the downfall of her children and grandchildren who followed in her footsteps in opposing the Centre of Bahá'u'lláh's Covenant and severing ties with the Tree of Life.[32]

Writings Revealed in Honour of Fáṭimih Khánum

The writings of Bahá'u'lláh revealed in Fáṭimih Khánum's honour or about her which have come to hand are few in number. The two Tablets addressed to her personally are brief and seem to have been revealed in the latter part of Bahá'u'lláh's earthly life. These were probably revealed when He spent time away from the Mansion, visiting 'Abdu'l-Bahá and His family or Áqáy-i Kalím and his family in 'Akká.

> He is the Helper!
>
> Mahd-i 'Ulyá! As divine favour is these days all-embracing and the Afnáns, upon them be God's Glory, are under the Sidrih, a robe of honour

> was bestowed, a robe whose warp is the bounty of God and whose woof is His grace. From the beginning of the world until now no one had outwardly attained such a robe. Verily, God hath made this bounty a treasure and honour for thee.[33]

The second paragraph speaks of two kinds of fabric that were sent. Each fabric was enough to make two garments. The names of the recipients are mentioned in the Tablet. Bahá'u'lláh instructs that the garments be made and given to the people named, that on 'Special Days they may adorn their temples [with those garments] and engage in remembering God and those Days'. At the end, He sends His greetings to all.

The second Tablet is revealed in honour, collectively, of Mahd-i 'Ulyá and other members of the family:

> He is the Extoller, the All-Knowing!
>
> O Mahd, O members of the Household!
>
> Tonight, after supper, the portal of bounty was opened and the Wronged One engaged in mentioning you. This day is different from other days and this time is likewise different. Please God, ye may attain that Light which is preserved from extinction and that Bounty which mortality overtaketh not. Glory be upon you from God, the Most Mighty, the Most Praised.
>
> As God loves unity and togetherness, We mentioned all on one page.[34]

Fáṭimih Khánum is also mentioned as 'Mahd' in a Tablet revealed in honour of her eldest son, Mírzá Muḥammad-'Alí, titled Ghuṣn-i Akbar (the Greater Branch):

> He is the Most Wise!
>
> O Greater Branch! Upon thee be My Glory and My favour. Praised be God Who hath enabled Mahd and members of the Household to do that which hath been revealed in the Qur'án . . .
>
> . . . We send greetings to members of the Household, Mahd and others. Their deeds are accepted and their efforts appreciated.[35]

9

Gawhar Khánum, the Third Wife of Bahá'u'lláh

Family Background

Little is known about Gawhar Khánum's background. She was born to a couple in Káshán. Her father's name was Mírzá Aḥmad-i-Rawḍihkhán (preacher). He was an erudite man. The name of her mother is not known: she is referred to in Tablets Bahá'u'lláh revealed in her honour as 'Umm-i-Ḥaram, K' (mother of the honoured wife, Káshán). She seems to have visited Gawhar Khánum in 'Akká and remained there to the end of her life.

Mírzá Aḥmad and his wife had four children: two daughters and two sons. They were all Bahá'ís. Two of them, Gawhar Khánum and Mírzá Mihdí,[1] were renowned. Gawhar Khánum's other brother and sister were also honoured with Tablets from Bahá'u'lláh.

Another outstanding member of Gawhar Khánum's family – probably the first to become a believer – was her paternal aunt. She was referred to as Ḥáj 'Ammih Khánum. She became a well-known Bahá'í through her early recognition of Bahá'u'lláh and belief in His Cause. She stood firm in the Faith despite severe opposition from her husband, Mullá 'Alí Akbar, and his family. She raised her children as Bahá'ís, attained Bahá'u'lláh's presence in 'Akká and rendered outstanding services to His Cause and the friends of God. Some of her family adopted Muhtadi as a family name and remained steadfast in the Faith after Gawhar Khánum and her offspring became Covenant-breakers.

Birth and Early Life

Information about Gawhar Khánum's life, especially the early years, is scant. The date of her birth is not known. If she was 15 when she went to Baghdád with her brother in about 1862, she would have been born in about 1847. She was born and raised in Káshán, where her parents lived.

Journey to Baghdád and Marriage

Gawhar Khánum was a young woman when her brother, Mírzá Mihdí, took her to Baghdád. The exact date of that trip is unknown. Indications are that it was towards the end of Bahá'u'lláh's stay in that city. Regarding what prompted Mírzá Mihdí to take his sister to Baghdád, some have conjectured that, influenced by old tradition and belief, his intention was to ask Bahá'u'lláh to allow her to serve in the *andarún*, hoping that He would eventually marry her. In Shí'í Islam, a man who takes in a maid enjoys all rights and prerogatives over her.[2] Since the Kitáb-i-Aqdas had not yet been revealed, the believers lived according to the practices of their old belief.

There has also been the suggestion that since, according to the Bayán, a believer had 'the duty of offering' before the throne of Him whom God would make manifest 'priceless gifts from among his possessions', a requirement annulled in the Kitáb-i-Aqdas,[3] and since in those days men regarded women as objects they possessed, a notion still widespread in some countries, her brother took her to Baghdád to fulfil what he considered a 'religious' duty.

Gawhar Khánum and her brother seem to have reached Baghdád shortly before Bahá'u'lláh left for Istanbul. All sources indicate that Gawhar Khánum did not accompany Bahá'u'lláh and His family on their exiles to Constantinople and Adrianople. At Bahá'u'lláh's behest, she and her brother remained in Baghdád and lived in His house.

After Bahá'u'lláh's departure from Baghdád, disturbances broke out in that city against the believers, culminating in the authorities rounding up the Persian Bahá'ís and sending them as exiles to Mosul. Gawhar Khánum and her brother were among these. They were later released and went to 'Akká to join Bahá'u'lláh. 'Abdu'l-Bahá describes in *Memorials of the Faithful* the story of Mírzá Mihdí:

> . . . he left his homeland and journeyed to 'Iráq, the focal centre of the new Light, where he gained the presence of all mankind's Beloved.
>
> He spent some time here, in the friends' company, composing verses that sang the praises of Bahá'u'lláh. Later he was given leave to return home, and went back to live for a while in Káshán. But again, he was plagued by yearning love, and could bear the separation no more. He returned, therefore, to Baghdád, bringing with him his respected sister, the third consort.
>
> Here he remained, under the bountiful protection of Bahá'u'lláh, until the convoy left 'Iráq for Constantinople, at which time Mírzá Mihdí was directed to remain behind and guard the Holy House. Restless, consumed with longing, he stayed on. When the friends were banished from

Bag͟hdád to Mosul, he was among the prisoners, a victim along with the others. With the greatest hardship he got to Mosul, and here fresh calamities awaited him; he was ill almost all the time, he was an outcast, and destitute. Still he endured it for a considerable period, was patient, retained his dignity, and continually offered thanks. Finally he could bear the absence of Bahá'u'lláh no longer. He sought permission, was granted leave to come, and set out for the Most Great Prison.[4]

Ustád Muḥammad-'Alíy-i-Salmání, Bahá'u'lláh's barber, mentions the sister of Mírzá Mihdí of Ká͟shán in *My Memories of Bahá'u'lláh*:

Mírzá Mihdí of Ká͟shán had a sister whom he wished to marry to Bahá'u'lláh, saying that she could live in the andarún and serve. The sister was in Bag͟hdád when Bahá'u'lláh left that city, and He placed the girl in the household of her brother, and did not take her as His wife. Mírzá Mihdí then wrote that he wished to come to 'Akká. He begged and begged to come, and finally he and his sister arrived in the area . . .[5]

Life in the Holy Land

After a 'long and hard' journey, Mírzá Mihdí and Gawhar K͟hánum 'reached the 'Akká prison . . . during the time when the Blessed Beauty was imprisoned within the citadel, at the centre of the barracks'.[6] Referring to Mírzá Mihdí's journey and arrival in 'Akká, 'Abdu'l-Bahá says:

Despite the terrible hardships, Mírzá Mihdí spent some days here, in great joy . . . His illness worsened; from day to day he failed; then at the last, under sheltering grace, he took his flight to the inexhaustible mercy of the Lord.[7]

Since Gawhar K͟hánum and her brother arrived in 'Akká at a time when Bahá'u'lláh, His family and companions were still incarcerated in the army barracks, they may have taken up residence inside the city and lived together until Mírzá Mihdí passed away. Bahá'u'lláh and His family left the barracks in the latter part of 1870. Gawhar K͟hánum seems to have joined Him after that date. She spent the rest of her life in the Holy Land. She was with Bahá'u'lláh at Mazra'ih and Bahjí. She gave birth to one daughter, Furúg͟híyyih. The exact date of her birth is unknown. Although 1873 has been suggested as a possible date, it may have been earlier than that.

Furúghíyyih Khánum's Marriage and Subsequent Developments

Furúghíyyih Khánum married Siyyid 'Alí, a nephew of Khadíjih Bagum, the wife of the Báb. This was the first marriage between the families of the Báb and Bahá'u'lláh. As a result, Gawhar Khánum, the bride's mother, moved into the limelight. However, the brilliance of that light was immediately dimmed by the betrayal of Siyyid 'Alí of the solemn promise he had made to his aunt, Khadíjih Bagum, to accompany her to the Holy Land where she could attain Bahá'u'lláh's presence, if and when his wish to marry Bahá'u'lláh's daughter was granted. Later developments caused that light to fade further and completely lose its lustre.

When Khadíjih Bagum submitted a request to Bahá'u'lláh through Munírih Khánum that the two Holy Families be linked through marriage, she had in mind a marriage between her nephew Siyyid 'Alí, the son of her eldest brother, Siyyid Ḥasan, and one of Bahá'u'lláh's daughters. The petition received Bahá'u'lláh's blessing, as this extract from a letter written by Munírih Khánum to Khadíjih Bagum describes:

> . . . Yea! You have written about the requested matter. Your petition was presented in the Holy Court and received acceptance. Praise and glory be to God! You are the recipient of such bounty and favour that something sublime you wished has been accepted and granted.[8]

Several years intervened between the time Khadíjih Bagum submitted the original request and the time when the marriage of Siyyid 'Alí and Furúghíyyih Khánum took place. At the time the request was presented to Bahá'u'lláh (1873), none of Bahá'u'lláh's daughters were married. The eldest, Bahá'íyyih Khánum, by then 26 years old, was determined to remain unmarried and devote her life to the service of her parents and the promotion of the Cause of her beloved father. The youngest, Furúghíyyih Khánum, was either unborn or a mere infant. Ṣamadíyyih Khánum, whose mother was Fáṭimih Khánum (Mahd-i-'Ulyá), had just come of age.[9] She married her cousin Mírzá Majdu'd-Dín, the son of Áqáy-i-Kalím.

Several years elapsed. Khadíjíh Bagum renewed her request, this time through 'Abdu'l-Bahá, whom she asked to intercede on behalf of her nephew, Siyyid 'Alí, and to beseech Bahá'u'lláh to accept him as His son-in-law. 'Abdu'l-Bahá attained the presence of Bahá'u'lláh and implored Him to gladden the heart of Khadíjih Bagum, who had suffered so much in the path of God, by granting her request.[10] Bahá'u'lláh did so. Siyyid 'Alí began making preparations for the journey which included his parents and sister but not Khadíjih Bagum, whom he had promised to take with him. He wrote to

Khadíjih Bagum informing her of the arrangements and presenting excuses for not being able to fulfil his promise at that time. When Khadíjih Bagum heard the news, she was deeply saddened by the betrayal of her nephew. She realized that her only opportunity to attain Bahá'u'lláh's presence was lost. The deprivation was beyond what she could bear, and the one who had caused it was her own nephew for whom she had done so much to achieve his heart's desire. She bemoaned her plight day and night. When her grief became too much to bear, deep depression set in and claimed her life.[11]

Before she passed away in August 1882 Khadíjih Bagum wrote to her unfaithful nephew complaining about his failure to honour the promise he had made to her. Siyyid 'Alí's response, published in *Khándán-i-Afnán*[12] reveals something of his disposition. He writes at length and tries in vain to exonerate himself of responsibility for breaking her heart. Instead of taking steps to redress the unfortunate consequences of his action and using all means at his disposal to find a satisfactory solution, he becomes defensive, calls her communication unkind, her complaint unjustified. When he received her letter, he and his family had not yet left Iran. He still could have gone to Shíráz and fetched her. Instead, he informed her that it was not possible for him to return to Shíráz and expected her to believe his feeble excuses. In his letter, while Siyyid 'Alí appears to be contrite by saying he is disappointed in himself, he remarks that it was Khadíjih Bagum's 'unkind' remarks that caused him to feel this way, rather than his own misbehaviour. He does not accept that by breaking his promise to her he has in fact failed to be of service, and takes no responsibility for his actions, rather blaming his father for the situation. He refuses to make good his promise by returning for her but suggests a unsatisfactory way to remedy the problem by making some unrealistic promises about arranging her travel through others and meeting her along the route. One wonders how Siyyid 'Alí viewed his life, after Khadíjih Bagum passed away brokenhearted as a direct result of his failure to fulfil a solemn promise? That is if he ever realized the gravity of what he had done.

When Siyyid 'Alí and his family reached 'Akká, they had to wait for a considerable time for the marriage to take place. One reason for the delay may have been that Furúghíyyih Khánum had not yet come of age. Exactly how long they waited is unknown. In the meantime, Khadíjih Bagum passed away.

In a Tablet revealed in honour of one of the Afnáns, Bahá'u'lláh refers to the request that Khadíjih Bagum had made several years earlier, a request which, He says, had been adorned with the ornament of acceptance. He then refers to the arrival sometime earlier of the members of the party for the purpose of attaining His presence and for the matter they had been promised.[13]

The marriage is believed to have taken place in 1885–6. The marriage ceremony was elaborate and 'Abdu'l-Bahá supervised the arrangements. The invited guests fondly remembered the ceremony many years after the occasion.

After Bahá'u'lláh's Ascension

After the passing of Bahá'u'lláh, Gawhar Khánum continued to live at Bahjí where her daughter Furúghíyyih Khánum and son-in-law Siyyid 'Alí as well as the rest of Bahá'u'lláh's immediate family – other than 'Abdu'l-Bahá and Bahá'íyyih Khánum – lived. Siyyid 'Alí, who had betrayed Khadíjih Bagum, his own aunt, did not remain faithful to 'Abdu'l-Bahá either.

Siyyid 'Alí and his family lived in close proximity to the hotbed of Covenant-breaking activity. Association with the Centre of Sedition, Mírzá Muḥammad-'Alí, and his supporters who lived in and around the Mansion of Bahjí was, for a person of Siyyid Alí's calibre, disastrous and proved fatal. He became a willing instrument of those who worked day and night to frustrate 'Abdu'l-Bahá's efforts to unite the community and promote the Cause of Bahá'u'lláh. The intense animosity towards 'Abdu'l-Bahá brewing constantly in his heart affected the spiritual health of every member of his family. He joined hands with the Covenant-breakers, fell from grace and caused the downfall of his entire family, Gawhar Khánum included.

On the day Mírzá Badí'u'lláh, the younger brother of Mírzá Muḥammad-'Alí and his staunch supporter, confessed his wrongdoings in writing and requested 'Abdu'l-Bahá to forgive his transgressions and accept him back into the fold, Siyyid 'Alí did likewise. Indeed, he wrote a letter dated 4 February 1903 verifying Mírzá Badí'u'lláh's statement, repenting his own misdeeds and seeking forgiveness. However, like Mírzá Badí'u'lláh, Siyyid 'Alí repented more than once, was forgiven by 'Abdu'l-Bahá, but slipped back into his usual pattern of behaviour. Eventually his schemes, which were carried out clandestinely while he claimed loyalty to the Covenant, were exposed. He was confronted with evidence showing that he was working secretly with 'Abdu'l-Bahá's enemies who wanted Him dead.

When he rejoined the Bahá'í community, the members of his family, including Gawhar Khánum and Furúghíyyih Khánum, followed his example. In those days, men were regarded as the head of the family. Whatever decisions they made, be they routine or crucial matters of faith and spirituality, impacted on the entire family. Women of a family generally stood with their men. They did not have an identity of their own; their identify was very much contingent on the men they followed.

In a Tablet revealed in honour of Bahá'íyyih Khánum at the beginning of His trip to the West, 'Abdu'l-Bahá conveys His loving greetings to His dear sister, Furúghíyyih Khánum, and to her mother, Gawhar Khánum. This Tablet seems to have been revealed during the period when Siyyid 'Alí had repented for a second time and, together with his family, had rejoined the community of the faithful.

During 'Abdu'l-Bahá's travels in the West, He was informed that the weather at Bahjí did not suit Gawhar Khánum's health and that she wished to move into a rented house in Haifa. 'Abdu'l-Bahá did not consider a rented house suitable for her. He had a house built for her on a plot of land that the family owned in Haifa. It is not clear exactly when she moved to Haifa and for how long. She may have also visited Tiberias.

A cable sent by Shoghi Effendi in 1952, after the death of Nayyir Afnán, the second son of Furúghíyyih Khánum and Siyyid 'Alí, makes it clear that Gawhar Khánum broke the Covenant and joined 'Abdu'l-Bahá's opponents soon after Bahá'u'lláh's ascension:

> History will brand him [Nayyir] one whose grandmother, wife of Bahá'u'lláh, joined breakers of His Covenant on morrow of His passing, whose parents [Furúghíyyih Khánum and Siyyid 'Alí] lent her undivided support, whose father [Siyyid 'Alí] openly accused 'Abdu'l-Bahá as one deserving capital punishment, who broke his promise to the Báb's wife to escort her to Holy Land, precipitating thereby her death, who was repeatedly denounced by Centre of the Covenant as His chief enemy . . .[14]

In the same cable Shoghi Effendi refers to Gawhar Khánum's eldest grandson, Siyyid Ḥusayn, as the one who 'through deliberate misrepresentation of facts inflicted humiliation upon defenders of the House of Bahá'u'lláh in Baghdád'.[15] He also speaks of all of Gawhar Khánum's grandchildren as the ones who attributed to 'Abdu'l-Bahá 'responsibility for fatal disease which afflicted their mother'.[16]

To understand the background to Siyyid 'Alí's hostility towards 'Abdu'l-Bahá, which had no apparent justifiable cause or basis, it is helpful to know his personality. 'Abdu'l-Bahá ascribes his enmity towards Him and the difficulties that he caused within the Faith to Siyyid 'Alí's complete lack of will power. He says anyone could work on him and overpower his will. In the same unpublished Tablet 'Abdu'l-Bahá enumerates a number of instances when He extended to him vital assistance and each time received from him not only ingratitude but incredible hostility. He says if Siyyid 'Alí had any will power, he would not have allowed himself to be so influenced by those surrounding him who appeared in the garb of friends, that is, members of Bahá'u'lláh's family whose consuming jealousy had turned them against 'Abdu'l-Bahá.

The Passing of Gawhar Khánum and a Brief Review of Her Life

Gawhar Khánum passed away as a Covenant-breaker. Almost every stage of her life is wrapped in obscurity. The only aspect of her life that is well known is her siding with 'Abdu'l-Bahá's opponents and her support for the breakers of Bahá'u'lláh's Covenant. Not only did she, her daughter and son-in-law, break Bahá'u'lláh's Covenant but her grandchildren, through marriages with 'Abdu'l-Bahá's grandchildren, introduced Covenant-breaking into His family as well.[17] These are the people referred to by Shoghi Effendi as the ones 'who over twenty years schemed to undermine the position of the Centre of the Faith through association with representatives of traditional enemies of Faith in Persia, Muslim Arab communities, notables and civil authorities in Holy Land'.[18] One last shameful act Nayyir, Gawhar Khánum's grandson, was unable to undertake owing to his death was his scheduled appearance 'as star witness on behalf of daughter of Badí'u'lláh [Sádhijih] in recent lawsuit challenging the authority conferred upon Guardian of Faith in 'Abdu'l-Bahá's Testament'.[19]

Had Gawhar Khánum remained faithful to Bahá'u'lláh's Covenant, she might have had a salutary influence on her daughter and son-in-law and saved herself from the stigma of being a fallen leaf from the Divine Tree.

10

The Sisters of Bahá'u'lláh

Family Background

Mírzá 'Abbás-i-Núrí, titled Mírzá Buzurg, had several wives and many children.

Muslim men in the 19th century, regardless of where they lived and what the circumstances of their lives by and large were polygamous. They enjoyed the right of having simultaneously up to four legally wedded wives. One of the byproducts of polygamy was the intricateness of the families they established. The desirability of marriage between first cousins added to the complexity of such households. As stature and wealth provided better opportunities for Shí'ís of Iran to have, in addition to four wives, as many concubines as a man could afford, including female slaves and orphans in their employ,[1] men of means and influence were excellent candidates for establishing highly complex and intricate families. Mírzá Buzurg-i-Núrí combined wealth, artistic talents, stature, good looks and influence. These were alluring attributes for attracting the kind of women one wanted to marry. As many marriages in those days were based on considerations of political and public relations, the wives usually came from diverse backgrounds and widened the man's circle of influence.

Mírzá Buzurg had four wives, the maximum allowed in the Qur'án at any given time, and three concubines. There is no limit to the number of concubines Shí'í Muslims can have. Mírzá Buzurg's wives and concubines bore him 14 children: nine sons and five daughters. With his first wife, Khán Nanih, Mírzá Buzurg had no daughters, only two sons. With his second wife, Khadíjih Khánum, he had five children: three sons and two daughters. The daughters were Sárih Khánum and Nisá' Khánum. With his third wife, Kulthúm Khánum, he had five children: two daughters and three sons. The daughters were Sháh Sulṭán Khánum ('Izzíyyih) and Fáṭimih Sulṭán Khánum. Of the three concubines only one had a daughter, named Ḥusníyyih Khánum. Her mother's name was Nabát Khánum.

The complexity of Mírzá Buzurg's family was enhanced when he married Khadíjih Khánum, Bahá'u'lláh's mother, who already had three children, one son and two daughters, from her first marriage. She married Mírzá Buzurg after the death of her first husband. Her daughters were Sakínih Khánum and Ṣughrá Khánum. Sakínih Khánum married Mírzá Buzurg's younger brother. Thus Bahá'u'lláh had two sisters with whom He shared both parents and five half sisters with whom He shared only one parent. Two of the half sisters were from His mother's side and three from His father's side.

One of Bahá'u'lláh's full sisters, Nisá' Khánum, died before Bahá'u'lláh's declaration in 1863. The other, Sárih Khánum, was utterly devoted to Him, as we shall see. Of the sisters from His mother's side, more is known about Sakínih Khánum, known as Ṭallán Khánum, who married Bahá'u'lláh's paternal uncle at the time her mother married Mírzá Buzurg. Although devoted to Bahá'u'lláh, as evidenced by a visitation prayer revealed in her honour by 'Abdu'l-Bahá, she does not seem to have been an active believer, probably owing to the circumstances of her life. About Ṣughrá Khánum we know almost nothing.

Of the three half sisters from Mírzá Buzurg's side, nothing is known about Ḥusníyyih Khánum, whose mother was originally from Gurjistán (Georgia). One may safely assume that she was neither a believer nor an opponent of Bahá'u'lláh, for otherwise we would have heard something of her activities. Of the other two, Sháh Sulṭán Khánum was the most notorious. She sided with Mírzá Yaḥyá Azal and actively opposed Bahá'u'lláh. Fáṭimih Sulṭán Khánum's standing is not very clear. Initially, she seemed close to Bahá'u'lláh, probably because she was married to His nephew, Mírzá Maḥmúd, son of Mírzá Muḥammad-'Alí, Khadíjih Khánum's son from her first marriage. Fáṭimih Sulṭán Khánum and Mírzá Maḥmúd later turned to Mírzá Yaḥyá Azal, probably because two of their children, a daughter and a son, were married to two of Mírzá Yaḥyá's children. Consequently, these two sisters lost their legacy.

The members of Bahá'u'lláh's family, who remained in Ṭihrán and Núr after His departure from Iran, can be divided into three distinct categories: 1) those who remained faithful to Bahá'u'lláh and suffered persecution as a result of their allegiance to Him, 2) those who concealed their belief and outwardly appeared indifferent and 3) those who actively opposed Him. The gulf between the sisters who were devoted to Bahá'u'lláh and the ones who turned against Him widened with Mírzá Yaḥyá's active and open opposition to Bahá'u'lláh towards the end of His stay in Adrianople. In the complex web of family relationships were entangled some who remained outwardly unaffected by His Revelation. To survive the onslaught of their persecutors, they appeared indifferent. Bahá'u'lláh's mother, one of His half sisters, as well as some of His nieces, aunts and cousins, maternal and paternal alike, fall into this category.

To compensate for his intrinsic shortcomings and the inability to rival Bahá'u'lláh's conspicuous glory and popularity, Mírzá Yaḥyá had long before his defection carried out a scheme which had helped him to broaden the scope of his influence within and without the family. The scheme involved marrying a number of women from a wide range of backgrounds. Several of them were close family members, including the daughters of Bahá'u'lláh's sister from His mother's side. Mírzá Yaḥyá's children did likewise. When it became clear in Adrianople that Mírzá Yaḥyá was determined to follow the promptings of his ego and claim a station on a par with Bahá'u'lláh, those who had close family ties with him generally remained in his camp; others were severely tested by the agitations of Sháh Sulṭán Khánum, who exerted great influence on them. Sháh Sulṭán Khánum was the eldest daughter of Mírzá Buzurg and Kulthum Khánum. She had great sympathy for Mírzá Yaḥyá, the half brother she had raised and loved like a son. Consequently, those female relatives who recognized Bahá'u'lláh's station and were completely faithful and devoted to Him suffered intense hostility from their kindred who supported Mírzá Yaḥyá. A study of the life of Bahá'u'lláh's sisters unfolds the way that each responded to the challenge.

The Full Sisters of Bahá'u'lláh

Sárih Khánum, Titled Ukht

Birth and Early Life

Sárih Khánum[2] was born to Mírzá Buzurg and Khadíjih Khánum. The exact date of her birth is unknown. Being the sibling born before Bahá'u'lláh, whose birth occurred on 12 November 1817, one may surmise that her birth date was around 1814–15. As Mírzá Buzurg's settling in Ṭihrán seems to have coincided with his marriage to Khadíjih Khánum, all their children were most probably born and raised in that city. It is clear from accounts of Bahá'u'lláh's childhood that the family of Mírzá Buzurg and Khadíjih Khánum visited the district of Núr in Mázandarán frequently. They spent the hot summer months in Tákur, where they owned a beautiful palace, and visited its surrounding areas where they had relatives and friends. Other than that we know nothing of Sárih Khánum's early life.

Marriage

One of the families with whom Mírzá Buzurg and Khadíjih Khánum had close ties was that of Mírzá Ismá'íl Vazier-i Núrí. They lived in Yálrúd, a village near Tákur. The bond between the two families was strengthened when Sárih Khánum married Mírzá Maḥmúd-i Khálú, son of Mírzá Ismá'íl Vazier-i Núrí.

The details of Sárih Khánum's life before and after her marriage to Mírzá Maḥmúd are murky. It is not known when she got married, how old she was at the time of her marriage, where she and her husband lived, in Núr or Ṭihrán, and whether her husband had other wives. What is certain is that she played an important role in the marriage of Bahá'u'lláh and Ásíyih Khánum, her husband's sister.[3]

Sárih Khánum and Mírzá Maḥmúd had one son whom they named Mírzá Ismá'íl. He married his cousin Zahrá Khánum, titled Thamarih, the daughter of Jináb-i-Maryam (Crimson Leaf) and Mírzá Riḍá Qulí, Sárih Khánum's half brother. Zahrá Khánum and Mírzá Ismá'íl had three children. (More information about them can be found in the chapter on Jináb-i-Maryam.) Mírzá Ismá'íl died in 1322 AH (about 1895) and was buried next to his mother, Sárih Khánum, in Bíbí Zubaydih.

Conversion

It is not clear exactly when Sárih Khánum accepted the Bábí Faith. It may have been during the time Bahá'u'lláh was engaged in intensive teaching activities in the district of Núr. According to M. A. Malik-Khusrawví, most of His relatives paid allegiance to the Bábí Faith during that time. Sárih Khánum was an ardent lover of Bahá'u'lláh and believed in Him wholeheartedly. Exactly when she heard and embraced His Cause is unclear.

When Bahá'u'lláh was arrested in Níyávarán and imprisoned in the Síyáh Chál in the latter part of 1852, Sárih Khánum may not have been in Ṭihrán. This assumption is based on the absence of any reference to her in connection with this episode in the early history of the Bábí–Bahá'í Faith. Had she been in Ṭihrán and informed of the plight of her beloved brother and His family, she would have undoubtedly arisen to render whatever assistance she could, as did her younger sister Nisá' Khánum and her younger brother Mírzá Músá. That there is a reference[4] to Sárih Khánum having a Qur'án purportedly in the handwriting of Imám 'Alí[5] which she presented to Áqá Khán-i-Núrí, the then Prime Minister of Iran, to spare Bahá'u'lláh's life, does not necessarily mean that she was living in Ṭihrán at the time.

During the month intervening between Bahá'u'lláh's release from the Síyáh Chál and His departure for Baghdád together with His family and companions, there is likewise no evidence indicating that Sárih Khánum was in Ṭihrán or that she was fully aware of what was going on. On the whole, nothing has come to hand to shed light on when Sárih Khánum heard about Bahá'u'lláh's plight and how she reacted to events leading to His imprisonment and subsequent departure from Iran. Considering that He left Iran so soon after His release from prison and that His life was so circumscribed before His departure, it seems most unlikely that she would have heard anything about the intimation He had received in the Síyáh Chál regarding His glorious mission.

After Bahá'u'lláh's Departure from Iran

The cloud of obscurity casting its shadow over Sárih Khánum's childhood and youth overshadows every stage of her life. Not only do we know nothing about how she dealt with the imprisonment of her brother, we are similarly uninformed of her subsequent separation from Him, a separation that was not followed by a reunion in this world. If it were not for Bahá'u'lláh's writings revealed in her honour, we would know almost nothing about her life and what she went through by virtue of her being His loving and faithful sister who was caught in the claws of His enemies in her homeland. It is through Bahá'u'lláh's writings that we learn of her love for and allegiance to Him, an allegiance that made her a target for persecution. Her tormentors included close members of her family. There are indications that her own husband was unsympathetic towards Bahá'u'lláh's claim. His attitude added to the weight of Sárih Khánum's ordeals and increased the burden of the tribulations she sustained in His path. Bahá'u'lláh testifies that 'She was indeed oppressed and quietly endured that which none but God is able to recount. Blessed is she. My glory be upon her for having endured patiently for the sake of God and for having sustained hardships in His straight path.'[6]

In a Tablet revealed in her honour Bahá'u'lláh describes her plight, praises her devotion and beseeches God to console her heart and solace her eyes.

> Ṭá
> Ukht, upon her be the Glory of God
> He is the Most Holy, the Most Great!
>
> Thou seest, O My Lord, one of the Leaves grown out of the Tree of Thy Oneness and the mighty stock of Thy Singleness, surrounded by unbelievers, men and women alike. Thou knowest that she hath verily turned to Thee, hath clung to the cord of Thy bounty and held fast to the hem of Thy favours. Consequently there befell her that which hath come to pass.
>
> I beseech Thee, O Thou the Possessor of Names and the Fashioner of Heaven, to ordain for her that which will gladden her heart, illumine her eye and delight her bosom. O God! Protect Thy leaves from the transgressors amidst Thy handmaids who have turned away from Thy Beauty,

giving allegiance to those who have refuted Thee and Thy Signs. Thou art verily He Whose power hath encompassed all who are in the heavens and on earth. The dwellers of the Kingdoms of Creation and Command are unable to frustrate Thy purpose. No God is there but Thee, the Most Powerful, the All-Knowing, the Most Wise.

O God, look upon her with Thy eye of favour and cast upon her a glance of Thy mercy. Protect her then from the stones of the suspicions of other women and from the darts of the vain imaginations of the sinful. Give her to drink at all times from the wine of Thy bounty, from the river of Thy favour and the wellspring of Thy mercy. Verily Thou art the Ruler of the world and Thou art powerful over nations. Thou ordainest for whosoever Thou desirest what Thou wishest. No God is there but Thee, the Giver, the Forgiver and the Merciful.

[Bless Thou, O Lord my God, the Divine Lote-Tree and its leaves, and its boughs, and its branches, and its stems, and its off-shoots, as long as Thy most excellent titles will endure and Thy most august attributes will last. Protect it, then, from the mischief of the aggressor and the hosts of tyranny. Thou art, in truth, the Almighty, the Most Powerful.][7]

It is clear from the contents of other Tablets revealed in her honour or about her that the relationship between Bahá'u'lláh and Sárih Khánum was very close. One particular Tablet revealed in Arabic verse shows the depth of Bahá'u'lláh's feelings for his sister. In several places He refers to her as 'Qurratí' (the Solace of My Eye).[8] The loving bond that existed between Bahá'u'lláh and Sárih Khánum remained strong to the end.

All the Tablets addressed to 'Ukht' (Sister), unless followed by a name identifying another of Bahá'u'lláh's sisters, are believed to have been revealed in honour of Sárih Khánum, who was explicitly referred to as 'Ukht'. These Tablets contain salient points about Bahá'u'lláh's life in exile and disclose the fact that information about His sufferings and whereabouts may not have been readily available to her.

He is God, Exalted is He!

O My sister! It hath been a long time since thy news hath reached this Prisoner. As Jináb-i-Shaykh Muḥammad was in recent days travelling to that region, thou wert remembered with these few words. Shouldst thou desire to find out about this Stranger's affairs, by God neither am I able to recount nor art thou able to hear. Such hath been ordained for My Self from the celestial Kingdom of the Lord, the Powerful, the Mighty, the Self-Subsisting. By now thou hast most certainly heard certain news. If thou hast not heard by now, soon thou shalt. Yea! My situation is beyond what the pen can recount, My affliction is beyond mention and My tribulations innumerable. No one is aware of My plight except God, the All-Knowing, the All-Informed.

Do thou always write about thy affairs. May Jináb-i-Áqá[9] be ever in the safe-keeping of God! And upon thee be Glory.[10]

Once, when Bahá'u'lláh had not heard from His sister for a long time, He wrote and enquired about her affairs. The reference in this Tablet to seclusion and solitude, which she may have chosen for herself, is significant. She may not have written to Bahá'u'lláh because credible information about Him was kept from her or she may have chosen silence as a means to avoid persecution:

He is God, the Most High!

It hath been a long time since news of thee hath been received. It seemeth that thou hast secluded thyself from the world and its people, choosing solitude.

I swear by the Peerless and Eternal Beloved that this Servant hath ever sought and will continue to seek that state for Himself, for in seclusion one's soul findeth peace whilst through association with others the spirit is consumed.

The former is the attribute of the near ones who believe in God's oneness, the latter is the characteristic of the heedless. However, there are times when solitude is rejected and association desired. Thus hath it been ordained by the One Who is Mighty and Powerful. Nonetheless, I have all My life sought but not attained it.

Upon My arrival in Iraq, detached from all else save God, I withdrew for two years. Singly and alone I departed for the wilderness and severed Myself from the world and its peoples. But during that period of withdrawal solitude was not granted to me. Those joyous days soon passed and came to an end, and it hath not been My portion ever since. Thus hath it been recorded by the Pen of Decree by the Finger of Splendour and Sanctity.

Shouldst thou desire to know My situation, 20 years have passed since I have seen the light of day.[11] I swear by the Sun of the Celestial Beauty that during this time I have not partaken even a glass of water in comfort and have been denied even a moment's rest owing to the venom of the ungodly. Like unto one constantly tormented in the mouth of a dragon, I have ever been confined in the prison of envy and afflicted by the claws of enmity. The tale of this Youth increaseth sorrow, His remembrance a book does not suffice and its end the pen of creation is unable to describe.

O My Sister! By God, I have so blotted out from memory the remembrance of everything that I know not what hath been written down. Sorrow hath so surrounded Me that I have forgotten Mine own Self, how much more the writing of letters. O that My Mother had never given birth to Me!

May thou be always under the protection of God and abide in the shade of His mercy. Convey My sincere wishes to honourable mother.[12]

In His writings Bahá'u'lláh confides in Sárih Khánum the intensity of His sufferings. The tone of His writings is intimate and similar to the Tablets He revealed in honour of Jináb-i-Maryam (the Crimson Leaf). These women knew from personal experience what longsuffering and tribulations entailed and could well understand what Bahá'u'lláh was going through. The Tablets disclose movingly what He endured at the hand of His internal and external enemies and how His breast was the target of the dart of the envious.

In the Name of God, the Eternal!

We have verily sent forth a fragrant breath from the holy fragrances of this exalted Paradise that the world may be perfumed in these days when the Temple of Immortality hath been established upon the throne of names and attributes with a new Revelation, and that My sister may obtain from it the sweet savour of My garment, may soar in the atmosphere of nearness, and hearken to the melodies through which the hearts of the near ones have been stirred.

Give ear, O My Leaf, to My call raised from the direction of oneness that the Divine Summons may draw thee to the Heavenly Throne and help thee to hear the melodies of birds singing sweetly upon the twigs in praise of My Mighty and All-Knowing Self. Know thou that thy Brother hath verily quaffed from the cup of calamity at all times. Thus hath it been ordained for Him from the One Who is Mighty and Powerful. By God, the Sidratu'l-Muntahá hath verily been bowed, the Countenance of the One Who hath shone brightly amongst the people of the world hath clouded, and His black hair hath turned white by virtue of that which the host of unbelievers hath inflicted upon Him.

Verily, the intensity of her sorrows maketh Me weep and causeth My heart to address her, saying: Understand thou well the heat which is consuming Me that thou mayest praise God for thy plight, and thy soul may find abundant joy. And My liver addresseth My heart saying: Wert thou to be informed of how I burn and blaze, thou wouldst find the fire thou art in to be light and cold. Thy Lord is a witness to what I say and He is the All-Knowing. And My inner being addresseth them collectively, saying:

Be thankful for that of which thou art unaware. Verily, I am consumed silently in a fire one ember of which, should it appear between the heavens and the earth, will consume the inhabitants of the world. Such is the tale of this Youth and such are the circumstances surrounding Him on all sides as a result of that which hath been perpetrated by the hands of them for whose protection We have made Our bosom a shield, that the darts of the envious may not touch them. Verily, thou shouldst remember thy Lord for that which hath been expounded by the Tongue of Revelation in this wondrous Tablet.

Praise be to Thee, O my God and my Desire! I know not whether to make My plaint about Thy forbearance in spite of Thy knowledge of all things, or about Thy patience in spite of Thy power over all things. How long wilt Thou abandon the Manifestation of Thy Self to the hands of the tyrants? I beseech Thee, O my God, by Thy name which hath encompassed all created things, to show forth the signs of Thy power over Thy creatures, and through it to raise up the weak among Thy loved ones during Thy days and to encompass the downfall of the arrogant among Thine enemies. I beseech Thee further, O my God, that Thou prevent me not from recognizing Thee and suffer me not to be deprived of meeting Thee. Ordain for me the good of this world and of the next. Verily, Thou art the Possessor of all existence. No God is there but Thee, the Mighty, the Most Powerful. Praised be God, the Lord of all worlds.[13]

In one of His Tablets Bahá'u'lláh describes how suffering had ignited the flame of His longing for more tribulations. He speaks of the transient nature of this world and all that pertains to it. He encourages His sister to cling tenaciously to the truth and reminds her of the blessings that God has bestowed on her.

My sister, upon her be God's Glory.
In the name of the Friend!
O thou Fragrant and Blessed Leaf!

Shouldst thou enquire about the body, it is severely afflicted, and shouldst thou ask about the physical frame, it is surrounded by countless calamities. But shouldst thou ask after the spirit, it is in the utmost joy and happiness. I have not complained about My calamities in the path of God. Rather am I accustomed to adversity and tribulation in the path of His love, just as the infant is accustomed to its mother's breast. But, alas, life is still continuing and I am yet to quaff the chalice of martyrdom in the path of God, although every moment requireth a fresh sacrifice. Praise be to the Best Beloved of the world that, in spite of all our troubles and difficulties, We are occupied with the remembrance of the Friend and are detached from all else but Him.

This world is not something eternal that man should attach his heart to it or grieve because of the events which transpire upon it. Erelong all things will perish and be as naught. That which doth remain and will ever remain is God, glorified be His might and exalted be His station. Regard the troubles endured in His path as a mercy and the calamities borne for His sake as a blessing. Concealed in all that We have endured is a wisdom inscrutable to all but God.

Thou hast ever been and will continue to be before Mine eyes. Hold fast to the Truth and turn away from all else. Render thanks to the Lord that the bond of kinship hath not been severed, and that thou art reposing in the shade of the heavenly Tree. This is a great blessing from God. The reward of every deed is concealed in His inviolable Treasury. When the time arriveth, it will appear in the most excellent adornment. Verily, thy Lord is the Conferrer of rewards to His servants, women and men alike. Convey My salutations and greetings to those who are in thy presence. Glory be upon thee and upon those who are with thee.[14]

In a prayer specially revealed for Sárih Khánum to recite, Bahá'u'lláh calls to mind divine favours vouchsafed to her:

Ṭá
Ukht, upon her be Bahá'u'lláh

In His Name, the Most Holy, the Most Glorious!

O My sister and the leaf of My Tree! Give ear to the call of this Wronged One raised from the direction of His renowned and infamous Prison: 'There is no God save Him, the Help-in-Peril, the Self-Subsisting', and say: All grace, O Thou Beloved of the world, and all bounty and generosity, O Possessor of nations, are Thine for having called me to the heaven of Thy recognition and the ocean of Thy reunion. Thou hast aided me to recognize the Dawning-place of Thy Revelation and the Dayspring of the splendours of Thy Oneness. I beseech Thee by Thy name through which Thou hast conquered all the dwellers of earth and heaven, to ordain for me and for Thy handmaids that which will draw them close to Thee in every world of Thy worlds. Write down, then, for me and for them, from Thy Supreme Pen, that which will be of benefit to me and to them in this world and the next. Verily, Thou rulest over whatever Thou desirest. Thou art verily the Most Powerful.[15]

The Passing of Sárih Khánum

According to her tombstone, Sárih Khánum died in 1296 AH (1880). Assuming that she was born about 1815, at the time of death she would have been about 65 years old. She was buried in the vicinity of the shrine of Bíbí Zubaydih, situated between Ṭihrán and the shrine of 'Abdu'l-'Aẓím. The following Tablet of Bahá'u'lláh has been identified by the author of *Akhtarán-i-Tábán* as a visitation prayer revealed in honour of Sárih Khánum:

> The first remembrance uttered by the Tongue of Majesty and Grandeur rest upon thee, O thou exalted leaf shining from the horizon of Command in the days of God, the Possessor of Names! I bear witness that thou didst turn toward the all-highest Paradise and didst attain unto that which most of the people have not attained. I testify moreover that thou didst verily bear hardships and tribulations in the path of God, the Fashioner of the heavens. So unwavering was thy conviction that neither the blame of blamers nor the denial of the ungodly among the women held thee back in the Cause of God.
>
> Blessed art thou and them that visit thy shrine and seek thee through that which hath appeared from the Pen of God, the Most Exalted, the Most Glorious, the One Whom the oppressors have imprisoned in the citadel of 'Akká. I testify that thou verily surrendered thy spirit while separated [from Him] after being ablaze with the fire of longing during the days of God, the Lord of the Judgement Day.
>
> Wretched be those who have recognized not thy station and who drank not from the chalice of thy remembrance, and happy are those that remember thee through that wherewith God hath remembered thee in His Books and Tablets.[16]

Regarding her resting-place, in one of His Tablets, Bahá'u'lláh says: 'He who visiteth Ukht[17] and Masíḥ[18] in Rayy,[19] it is as though he hath visited Me.'[20]

Sárih Khanum's Station and Her Place in History

In several of His Tablets Bahá'u'lláh testifies to the staunchness of Sárih Khánum's faith, her meekness and the sufferings she endured by reason of her allegiance to Him. His testimony uncovers to the eyes of the believers her glorious station. In a Tablet addressed to the believers in Ṭihrán in which He extols the virtues of that land, He says:

O Land of Ṭá! Call to remembrance when thou wert the Seat of the Throne and thy surroundings reflected its splendours. Numerous are the sanctified and assured souls who have offered up their lives and sacrificed their spirits in the path of thy love. Blessed art thou and those who reside in thee. Those endowed with a perceiving sense will inhale from thee the fragrance of the Desired One. In thee appeared that which was hidden, and from thee emerged that which was concealed. Which of the true lovers who have given up their souls and been buried in thy soil should We mention? The fragrances of the heavenly robe have never been and shall never be withheld from thee. We make mention of thee and all the wronged ones, men and women alike, who repose beneath thee.

Verily, We mention My sister as a sign of My favour and as an expression of My faithfulness. She returned to God in the utmost meekness. Only My all-encompassing knowledge is informed of it.

O Land of Ṭá! Through God's bounty thou art even now the gathering place and centre of the friends. Blessed art thou and those who have migrated to thee in the path of God, the Possessor of this wondrous Day . . .[21]

In a Tablet addressed to one of the believers, after greeting the friends, Bahá'u'lláh pays a moving tribute to Sárih Khánum:

We verily mention Our friends collectively, greet them from the direction of My Prison, send them salutations and remember them every morn and eve . . . We verily exhort thee to be joyful, even as We remember Our sorrow in this day wherein the news of the tribulations suffered by Our sister at the hands of the people of tyranny have reached Our ears. We testify that verily she believed, attained and soared in the atmosphere of My good pleasure, and that she moved by My leave and will. Thus testifieth the Pen of the Most High, but most people are in conspicuous doubt.

Blessed is the one who visiteth her, who turneth towards her purely for the sake of His Lord, the Bountiful, the Giver and the Beneficent.

O Jamál! The Point of the Bayán sayeth that all have been created for the purpose of being mentioned in that sanctified, luminous and exalted presence. Behold now and appreciate this bounty, that the Pen of the Most High hath mentioned His Friends at a time when sorrow hath surrounded Him from every side.

. . . This year several calamitous events have taken place and recently the news of the Ukht [Sister] hath outwardly reached the Holy Presence. She was indeed oppressed and quietly endured that which none but God is able to recount. Blessed is she. My glory be upon her for having endured

patiently for the sake of God and for having sustained hardships in His straight path.
27 Jamadiyu'l-Ula 1297 (1880)[22]

And addressing the mother of a man named Muḥammad-Ḥasan who served Bahá'u'lláh in the Holy Land, He says:

> . . . The Land of Ṭá hath been the seat of the Throne and the dawning place of the Desired Morn. It is the place of the Ukht [Sister] and where the friends of God repose.
>
> Happy is the one who hath attained the love of the Ukht and of the friends of the Lord. Verily, from this Spot We greet the countenance of My Sister and My loved ones who have uttered My praise and have been neither moved by the tempestuous winds of idle fancies, nor kept back by the tumult raised by those who have disbelieved in God, the Lord of all worlds.
>
> Render praise to God that He hath given thee a son who, since his arrival until now, hath been engaged in serving God. Blessed is he, blessed is he! Beseech God to enable thee to drink from the oceans of favour that are concealed in these words, and behold the splendours of the Sun of Mercy . . .[23]

In a Tablet revealed in honour of the handmaid of God (Amatu'lláh) Hudhud, Bahá'u'lláh makes mention of His sister:

> . . . O Hudhud! We make mention of thee through remembering Our sister [Ukhtí], and her days, and how her heart was ablaze with the fire of her Lord's love . . .[24]

In another Tablet, after recounting His sufferings in the path of God, Bahá'u'lláh reaffirms His absolute love for Him and submission to His decree, then offers a prayer in which He mentions His faithful sister:

> . . . Praise be to Thee, O My God, for all that hath transpired, for verily this hath been the rule prescribed for Thy Chosen Ones and Thy conduct with those who love Thee. I swear by Thy Might, O My God and My Master, shouldst Thou slay me with the swords of Thy Decree, torment Me with every torment, or burn Me with the fire of Thy justice and vengeance, My soul will not be emptied of its love for Thee, nor My tongue stilled from mentioning Thee, nor My heart busied with anyone save Thyself. My inner being will not cling to anyone but Thee, My feet will not move

except towards Thee and My hands will not be raised save unto Thee.

Praised be Thou, praised be Thou! I beseech Thee by Thy Primal Light through which the ocean of Thy Oneness hath surged and the arks of Thy Will and the paths of Thy Guidance have been fashioned, to suffer Me to be pleased with Thy Decree, to seek Thy calamity, and to long for Thy presence, as promised in Thy Book. Cause then My sister to become one of Thy handmaids who believe in Thee and are steadfast in Thy love. Shelter her moreover in the precincts of Thy mercy and grant her to dwell under the shadow of the Tree of Thy bounty, that her heart may be assured, her spirit calmed and her soul at peace. Thou art, verily, the Most Powerful, the Mighty, the Self-Subsisting.[25]

‘Abdu’l-Bahá and Sárih Khánum

Bahá’u’lláh and His family left Iran for Iraq in late 1852 or early 1853 when ‘Abdu’l-Bahá was about nine years old. While growing up in Ṭihrán, ‘Abdu’l-Bahá often visited His ancestral home in the district of Núr and enjoyed a close and loving relationship with those members of the family who lived there, particularly Sárih Khánum, His paternal aunt, who was married to His maternal uncle, Mírzá Maḥmúd-i-Khálú. After Bahá’u’lláh’s banishment from Iran, the loving aunt and nephew never saw each other again in this world but kept in touch through correspondence. The following two Tablets written during the ministry of Bahá’u’lláh, which have come to hand, testify to the loving bond that existed between Sárih Khánum and her illustrious nephew:

The Blessed Leaf, the Honourable Aunt, upon her be the Glory of God.

He is the Most Illustrious, the Most Glorious!

Praised be Thou O Lord my God! This is one of the leaves of the Tree of Thy Oneness and a fruit of the Tree of Thy Singleness whose root is firmly established in the land of eternity and whose branch reacheth the highest heaven.

O God, verily calamities have so encompassed her in Thy path that her flesh hath melted away and her bones crumbled to dust. She wasteth away as a burning candle in her separation from Thee and weepeth as a bereaved mother in her remoteness from Thee. O God, send down upon her that which will comfort her. Verily, Thou art powerful over all things.

Convey My Abhá greetings to Jináb-i Áqá Mírzá Ismá‘íl.[26]

He is God, the Almighty, the Self-Subsisting!

O kind Aunt! Thy letter adorned with God’s remembrance hath been perused. On the one hand it caused exceeding happiness, on the other much sorrow. Happiness, because it sang the praise of the Desire of the world; sadness because like unto a fire blazing in separation from the Beauty of the Omnipotent Lord it burned and consumed the heart and soul. However, it is clear and evident that true reunion is spiritual nearness attainable only by walking in the path of His good pleasure. Therefore, if a person is physically one hundred thousand miles away but blessed with God's good pleasure that one is in truth among those who enjoy nearness to Him. Otherwise, that which looks outwardly near is in fact distant. Therefore, it is proven that that blessed Leaf is at all times present in the Court of Holiness and nourished with the blessing of His proximity and reunion.

Why art thou sad? Thou dwellest in God's realm of happiness. And why art thou dejected since thou hast been addressed with the call of the supreme glad-tidings? The world of happiness circleth round thee and the sun of felicity and gladness is shining from the horizon. Erelong shall the heedless awaken and their remorse shall be made manifest.

We send loving greetings to thy son and to other loved ones and friends of God, men and women alike.[27]

Nisá' Khánum

Birth and Early Life

Nisá' Khánum is the youngest of Mírzá Buzurg and Khadíjih Khánum's children. She was probably born in Ṭihrán. No information is available about the date of her birth and nothing is known about her early life.

Marriage

Nisá' Khánum married Mírzá Majíd-i Áhí. The marriage must have taken place in Ṭihrán where Mírzá Majíd had a job at the Russian legation. The date of the marriage is unknown. Since she died in childbirth about 1853, assuming that it was her first pregnancy, it may not be unreasonable to presume that the marriage had taken place around 1850–1. Mírzá Majíd and Nisá' Khánum had no surviving children. After Nisá' Khánum died, Mírzá Majíd remarried and had children from his second marriage.

During Bahá'u'lláh's Arrest, Imprisonment and Exile

Nisá' Khánum's name is mentioned in the early history of the Bábí–Bahá'í Faith in connection with Bahá'u'lláh's arrest subsequent to the attempt on the life of Náṣiru'd-Dín Sháh by two Bábí youths in 1852. On the day of His arrest, Bahá'u'lláh was returning from Afchih to Níyávarán in the district of Shimírán, which was then the Iranian army headquarters. Nisá' Khánum and her husband lived in the village of Zarkandih, also in the district of Shimírán, where Mírzá Majíd 'acted as secretary to the Russian minister [Prince Dolgorouki] and was invited by him to stay at his home, which adjoined that of his superior'.[28] It was in Zarkandih and while Bahá'u'lláh was a guest in His sister and brother-in-law's home that He was arrested. Referring to the episode, Nabíl says:

> The attendants of Ḥájí 'Alí Khán, the Ḥájibu'd-Dawlih, recognized Him and went straightway to inform their master, who in turn brought the matter to the attention of the Sháh.
>
> ... Náṣiri'd-Dín Sháh ... was amazed at the bold and unexpected step which a man who was accused of being the chief instigator of the attempt upon his life had taken. He immediately sent one of his trusted officers to the legation, demanding that the Accused be delivered into his hands. The Russian minister refused, and requested Bahá'u'lláh to proceed to the home of Mírzá Áqá Khán, the Grand Vazír, a place he thought to be the most appropriate under the circumstances. His request was granted ...
>
> As Bahá'u'lláh was leaving the village of Zarkandih, the minister's daughter, who felt greatly distressed at the dangers which beset His life, was so overcome with emotion that she was unable to restrain her tears. 'Of what use,' she was heard expostulating with her father, 'is the authority with which you have been invested, if you are powerless to extend your protection to a guest whom you have received in your house?' The minister, who had a great affection for his daughter, was moved by the sight of her tears, and sought to comfort her by his assurances that he would do all in his power to avert the danger that threatened the life of Bahá'u'lláh.[29]

Nabíl explains how Mírzá Áqá Khán failed to honour the promise he had made to the Russian minister and how Bahá'u'lláh was mistreated on the way from Shimírán to the Síyáh Chál, the place where He was imprisoned. The news undoubtedly devastated Nisá' Khánum, the first member of Bahá'u'lláh's family to witness the event. Regrettably, her reaction to the arrest and what she may have done to mitigate its effects have not been passed down either orally or in writing. To penetrate the darkness of not knowing the actual facts, seeking enlightenment from the power of imagination remains our only solace and hope. That she was distraught to see her beloved brother being arrested and mistreated while an honoured guest in her home there can be no doubt. Under those circumstances, would it be unreasonable for her to alert the daughter of Prince Dolgorouki to intercede with her father and ensure the safety of Bahá'u'lláh? Someone must have involved the Russian minister's daughter. Who other than Nisá' Khánum could have done it? If she did not do it, then who did? In the absence of accurately recorded information, the suggestion that Nisá' Khánum may have alerted the minister's daughter to the dangers facing Bahá'u'lláh and sought her assistance remains only a conjecture.

Whether after that episode Nisá' Khánum saw Bahá'u'lláh again we are not informed. After four months' imprisonment in the Síyáh Chál, Bahá'u'lláh spent one month in the home of His brother and sister-in-law, Mírzá Riḍá Qulí and Jináb-i-Maryam, before going into exile. About what happened during that month, who visited or had the right to visit Him, whether Nisá' Khánum was forced to stay away for fear of persecution or spent time with Him no information is available.

The Passing of Nisá' Khánum

It is unclear exactly how long after Bahá'u'lláh's departure from Iran Nisá' Khánum passed away. Indications are that she died soon after His departure for Baghdád. Therefore she was not alive when His declaration took place in 1863. Nisá' Khánum was pregnant with her first child at the time of Bahá'u'lláh's departure from Iran and she died in childbirth. Her child did not survive either.

Nisá' Khánum's corpse was sent to Iraq for burial. It reached Baghdád after Bahá'u'lláh's arrival there. According to Mr Malik-Khusrawví, Bahá'u'lláh buried Nisá' Khánum in Baghdád.[30] The reason that Iranian Shí'ís sent the bodies of their loved ones to Iraq for burial was so that they could be buried in Najaf or Karbilá, the twin holy cities where Imám 'Alí and Imám Ḥusayn are buried. The reason for Nisá' Khánum's burial in Baghdád is not clear.

Nisá' Khánum died very young. At the time of death she was probably in her teens. Her untimely and tragic death occurred about the time Bahá'u'lláh and His family arrived in a foreign land and were surrounded by woes and tribulations of every kind. She was the only one of Bahá'u'lláh's siblings to be buried by Him. No Tablet revealed in her honour has come to light.

The Half Sisters of Bahá'u'lláh

Sakínih Khánum

Birth and Early Life

Sakínih Khánum, known as Ṭallán Khánum, was born to Khadíjih Khánum and her first husband. The date of her birth, her age when her father died, where and how she was raised are unknown. She moved into the limelight when her mother married Mírzá Buzurg-i-Núrí. At that time Sakínih Khánum married Mírzá Buzurg's younger brother, Mírzá Muḥammad. As a result, her children became at once Bahá'u'lláh's nieces and nephews as well as His cousins.

Marriage

No information is available about the exact date of Sakínih Khánum's marriage to Mírzá Muḥammad. They may have lived in Núr and visited Ṭihrán frequently. At the time of her marriage she was at least nine years old, the minimum age of marriage for girls in Islam.

Sakínih Khánum and Mírzá Muḥammad had three daughters and one son. The daughters were Ḥavvá Khánum, Fáṭimih Khánum and Ruqyih Khánum. Her son's name was Mírzá Abu'l-Qásim.[31] Sakínih Khánum's second and third daughters, i.e. Fáṭimih Khánum, also known as Ḥájíyih, and Ruqyih Khánum, both married Mírzá Yaḥyá Azal. Fáṭimih Khánum was Mírzá Yaḥyá's first wife. That marriage produced only one child, Mírzá Muḥammad Hádí, whom the Azalís call Áqá; they call his mother 'the mother of Áqá'. During the onslaught on the Bábís of Tákur in 1268 (1852) carried out by a representative of the central government, Fáṭimih Khánum and 34 other believers were captured and sent to Ṭihrán in chains.[32] After her release she returned to Tákur where she lived with her son.

Mírzá Yaḥyá also married Ruqyih Khánum, Fáṭimih Khánum's younger sister. Ruqyih Khánum had five children: Mírzá Vaḥíd, Mírzá Taqí'd-Dín, Fu'ád, Muḥtaram Khánum and Maryam Khánum. Ruqyih Khánum accompanied Mírzá Yaḥyá to Cyprus and died there.[33]

Having two of her daughters married to Mírzá Yaḥyá, who was relentless in his enmity towards Bahá'u'lláh, and one (Ḥavvá Khánum) married to Bahá'u'lláh's faithful cousin and brother-in-law Mírzá Muḥammad-i Vazír, undoubtedly placed Sakínih Khánum in an awkward situation. According to 'Abdu'l-Bahá's visitation prayer, she was a faithful aunt. However, she may not have openly shown support for Bahá'u'lláh during His ministry and that must be the reason why there is no Tablet from Bahá'u'lláh revealed in her honour. In addition to having children with split loyalties, she was surrounded by other members of her family hostile to Bahá'u'lláh, such as 'Izzíyyih Khánum and Fáṭimih Sulṭán Khánum. They were her daughters' sisters-in-law and her husband's nieces. In addition, Fáṭimih Sulṭán Khánum was married to Sakínih Khánum's nephew, Mírzá Maḥmúd-i Namadsáb, son of Mírzá Muḥammad-'Alí, whose children (one son and one daughter) were married to Mírzá Yaḥyá's children. How Sakínih Khánum dealt with the complex circumstances of her life is unclear. A visitation prayer 'Abdu'l-Bahá revealed in her honour after her death confirms that she died as a devoted believer.

Among the children of Sakínih Khánum, Ḥavvá Khánum was the closest to Bahá'u'lláh and most devoted to Him. She was married to Mírzá Muḥammad-i Vazír, the brother of Jináb-i-Maryam and Fáṭimih Khánum, Bahá'u'lláh's second wife. When Mírzá Muḥammad-i Vazír passed away, Bahá'u'lláh revealed 'Kalimát-i 'Álíyát' (Most Exalted Words), also known as 'Ḥurúfát-i 'Álín' (Sublime Letters), in her and Maryam's honour. In a Tablet revealed in honour of Ḥavvá Khánum, He addresses her as the daughter of His uncle and sister, which makes her at once His cousin and niece:

> Varaqih Ḥavvá, the daughter of [My] uncle and sister, upon her be the Glory of God!
>
> In the name of the All-Knowing Announcer!
>
> Render thanks to the Lord that through the confirmations of God, glorified be His grandeur, thou hast entered the lofty tabernacle raised in His Name and drunk deep of the river of utterance. Whoever recognizeth the Days of God, that soul is accounted among the inmates of Paradise in the Crimson Book. Beseech God to confirm thee in protecting this precious gem. By My life, were the assessors of the world to gather together, they would find themselves powerless to estimate its worth. Betrayers are many and trustees few. Some mistaken souls have forsaken the River of Mercy for a foul pond. Woe to them and to those who have denied God and His sovereignty and turned away from the Countenance shining brilliantly from the celestial horizon, after the annihilation of all things.
>
> O thou the daughter of My uncle and of My sister! Give ear to My Call, then remember Thy Lord with such steadfastness that the promptings of the evil ones will not shake thee. May God enable thee to cling to the cord of the favour of the Desire of the world at all times, for no deed is more praiseworthy than this.
>
> We mention thy son named Mihdí and give him the joyful news of the favour of his Munificent and Compassionate Lord. The poem he

had previously composed in His tribute was received, and the servant in attendance recited what he had composed. We verily heard him and answered him with a perspicuous Tablet.

We send greetings to all the brothers and sisters. We hope from God that they have been and will continue to be protected by Him, glorified be His grandeur. This is a lofty station. May its effects become clear and evident!

Should the intended affair happen joyfully and with radiance, it is very praiseworthy.[34] However, should it entail any harm for that handmaid or her relatives, it would not be praiseworthy before this Wronged One, for one must act according to the requirements of the time and the dictates of wisdom.

Jináb-i Ismulláhu'l-Mihdí is travelling in that direction. Do thou that which is discreet. He verily enricheth and assisteth thee, and He is the Most Bountiful, the Most Generous.

Glory be upon thee and upon all the kindred who have clung to the sure handle and held fast to the hem of the garment of the Sovereign of the world.[35]

Reaction to Bahá'u'lláh's Revelation

Sakínih Khánum died a devoted believer. A Tablet from 'Abdu'l-Bahá revealed in her honour after her death leaves no room for doubt in this regard. However, she seems to have kept a low profile during Bahá'u'lláh's ministry. Her attitude was probably dictated by the requirements of wisdom because two of her daughters were married to Mírzá Yaḥyá Azal. Had she been active in the Faith and carried out worthwhile activities, we would have seen indications of it in the writings that would have been revealed in her honour or about her.

Sakínih Khánum's Passing and a Brief Review of Her Life

Sakínih Khánum passed away during the ministry of 'Abdu'l-Bahá. This is deduced from the visitation prayer He revealed in her honour. She died in Tákur and was buried in the northwestern chamber of Takíyyih where her husband, Mírzá Muḥammad, and their daughter, Ḥavvá Khánum, were also buried.[36] In the visitation prayer revealed in her honour, 'Abdu'l-Bahá testifies to her love for Bahá'u'lláh and discloses her true station in the Faith.

Visitation prayer for her highness 'Abdu'l-Bahá's Aunt, Ṭallán Khánum, wife of the late Mírzá Muḥammad, upon her be Bahá'u'lláhu'l-Abhá

He is God!

Upon thee be salutations and praise, O pride of the female kindred of that Blessed Tree whose Root is firmly established and whose Branch reacheth to the heavens! I testify that all the days of thy life thou wert denied even a drink of water with ease and comfort, that thou wert surrounded by tribulations and woes and wert trapped beneath the talons of ferocious beasts and the claws of the enemy. Thou wert denied rest, even for the blink of an eye, because of the persecution of the adversary and the ascendancy of the ignoble, and wert prevented from reposing in comfort upon thy couch all the days and nights of thy separation and remoteness from the divine Countenance. At every moment the enemy aimed at thy bosom the darts of reproach and the arrows of hatred and vilification. And all these ordeals and calamities thou didst patiently and without plaint endure for the love of the exalted Lord. Thou didst remain thankful, patient and dignified in that luminous village until thou didst hear the call 'O thou assured soul, return to thy Lord pleasing and well-pleased.' Then thou didst answer the call and thy spirit soared to the Kingdom of Abhá. God's blessings be thine and glad-tidings from thy Master. Well done, well done, O thou pure and blessed handmaid of the Lord of the Highest Heaven!

How often do I recall the days when I was a child and came to thee with love and devotion! Thou didst take me up in thy warm and affectionate embrace, and I delighted in the goodly fruits of the garden of thine abundance. I beseech God to make thee the symbol of forgiveness, surround thee with mercy and bounty, make thy countenance bright, thy station exalted, and thy face illumined like the clear morn.

Blessed is the one who delighteth his senses with the fragrance of the dust of thy luminous tomb. May the faithful visitors be perfumed therewith. Upon thee be salutation and praise. 'Abdu'l-Bahá 'Abbás.[37]

Fáṭimih Sulṭán Khánum

Birth and Early Life

Fáṭimih Sulṭán Khánum was born to Mírzá Buzurg and his wife Kulthúm Khánum. The date of her birth is unknown. She was probably born in Ṭihrán where her parents lived. She was the youngest of Mírzá Buzurg's children and may have been about 15 years younger than Bahá'u'lláh. Nothing is known about her childhood and early life.

Marriage

Fáṭimih Sulṭán Khánum married one of Khadíjih Khánum's grandsons. He was Mírzá Maḥmúd-i Namadsáb, son of Mírzá Muḥammad-'Alí, Khadíjih Khánum's son from her first marriage. The date of Fáṭimih Sulṭán Khánum's marriage is not known.

Fáṭimih Sulṭán Khánum and Mírzá Maḥmúd had five children: three daughters and two sons. One of their daughters, Fakhríyyih Khánum, married Mírzá Muḥammad Hádí, the eldest son of Mírzá Yaḥyá Azal, and one of their sons, Mírzá Muḥammad Khán, married Maryam, one of Azal's daughters. Fáṭimih Sulṭán Khánum's other children were Zamzam Khánum, wife of Mírzá 'Abdu'l-Báqí Sharíf; Ibráhím Khán; and Ḥamídih Khánum, who married Mírzá Faḍlu'lláh Niẓámu'l-Mamálik, son of Bahá'u'lláh's eldest brother, Mírzá Muḥammad-Ḥasan, firm believers in Bahá'u'lláh.

Fáṭimih Sulṭán Khánum's Standing in the Cause of Bahá'u'lláh

Among the early adherents of the Cause of the Báb in Núr were Fáṭimih Sulṭán Khánum and her husband, Mírzá Maḥmúd. They were attracted to the Bábí Cause through Bahá'u'lláh's teaching activities in that district. Mírzá Maḥmúd suffered imprisonment after the attempt on the life of Náṣiri'd-Dín Sháh and was with Bahá'u'lláh in the Síyáh Chál.[38] After Bahá'u'lláh's departure from Iran, under pressure from hostile elements that were at work to arouse His kindred against Him, the couple joined His opponents.

Fáṭimih Sulṭán Khánum had an older sister, named Sháh Sulṭán Khánum, who fiercely opposed Bahá'u'lláh and sided with Mírzá Yaḥyá Azal. Fáṭimih Sulṭán Khánum and her family fell under this sister's spell and succumbed to pressure to renounce Bahá'u'lláh. Whether she decided to oppose Bahá'u'lláh and outwardly support her sister, as did her brother Mírzá Riḍá Qulí, is hard to know. The marriage tie between two of Fáṭimih Sulṭán Khánum's children with two of Yaḥyá Azal's children may have been another reason for changing her allegiance from Bahá'u'lláh to Mírzá Yaḥyá Azal later in her life.

The Passing of Fáṭimih Sulṭán Khánum and a Brief Review of Her Life

The date of Fáṭimih Sulṭán Khánum's death is not known. She died in Ṭihrán and was buried in Imámzádih Ma'ṣúm, where some other members of her family are buried.

Although initially an ardent lover of Bahá'u'lláh, Fáṭimih Sulṭán Khánum later changed the course of her spiritual journey. Had she continued on the path that she was on, she would have attained the pinnacle of glory destined for firm believers, especially for a leaf so closely connected to the Divine Tree. Unfortunately the circumstances of her life and the temptations of the people of tyranny caused her to slip away and abandon the journey that would have won her immortality in the annals of the Faith. There are no indications that she ever actively opposed Bahá'u'lláh; nonetheless, as a result of her inaction she lost the legacy that she came so close to claiming.

Writings Revealed in Honour of Fáṭimih Sulṭán Khánum

Bahá'u'lláh has revealed a number of Tablets in honour of Fáṭimih Sulṭán Khánum. They bear no date but seem to belong to the earlier period of Bahá'u'lláh's exile. The contents reveal how close she was initially to Bahá'u'lláh:

> The younger sister, the blessed leaf, Fáṭimih Khánum
>
> He is the Mighty, the Most Exalted!
>
> O My sister! We beseech God to protect thee from the harms of the world. There hath been no news from thee for some time. God willing, thou art established in the abode of God's love with the utmost happiness and joy. Shouldst thou wish to know how this mortal Prisoner is, by God, the tongue is speechless and pens are broken into pieces when attempting to mention it. However, We are at all times thankful and patient. Other than total submission and perfect acquiescence nothing is desired.
>
> May thou be always engaged in mentioning the true Beloved and be illumined with the rays of the eternal and sanctified Sun. And upon thee be Glory.[39]

> My sister Fáṭimih
>
> He is God!
>
> Take up the exalted Pen, O Servant, move it on the snow-white tablet and call to remembrance Thy sister, Fáṭimih, that the bounty upon her and upon all who dwell on earth may be complete.
>
> O My Fáṭimih! We have verily sent thee this garment from this Announcer of good news that thou mayest inhale therefrom the fragrances of holiness and be recorded in the Mother Book by the Manifestation of Attributes. Rejoice thou for seeing Paradise in the days of God, soar towards the magnificent abode mentioned in the Tablet, then recognize the blessings that God hath vouchsafed to thee. He hath singled thee out from amongst most handmaids for His favour, and He hath caused thy name to be mentioned with sanctity in the mighty Tablets. Verily, He is the True One. No God is there but Him. He bestoweth dominion on whosoever He

desireth, and the decree hath been firmly established in the foundation of destiny from the Dawning-place of Command. May the light of God shine upon thy face and upon those who are in thy company.[40]

One of the Tablets of Bahá'u'lláh revealed in honour of Fáṭimih Khánum is very different in tone and content from His other writings. It starts with a dialogue between Him and Mahd-i-'Ulyá about whether the Tablet was to be revealed in Arabic or Persian. He then invites the recipient to ponder upon deep spiritual matters underlying the message conveyed:

Fáṭimih Khánum

In the name of the Friend!

Mahd-i 'Ulyá says, 'Letters written to the Iraqi friends would be better in the Persian tongue.' I say that they are also informed of the melodies of Ḥijáz. She says that the accents of Iraq are more appealing. I say that the melody of Ḥijáz is more beloved, for members of the Household have drunk deep from the Kawthar of enchantment and quaffed from the ocean of oneness. They have issued forth from the innate Nature and have sprung from the heavenly Branch. To those endowed with innate ability all tongues are one and all accents proceed from the Beloved. They may find the melody of the Nightingale of Ḥijáz to be enchanting but the warbling of the Songbird of Persia to be intoxicating. All lamentations emanate from the heart. Should those invested with the power of hearing hearken, they would most certainty offer up their souls. However, this bird of the spirit hath other utterances in another tongue.

O sister! Shouldst thou hearken with the ear of the spirit, thou wouldst abandon thy veil and direct thy steps in thy Brother's path until, in thy quest for reunion, thou dost lay down thy life. A thousand Ḥijází eagles obey this Iraqi Bird and a thousand celestial birds serve this Mystic Dove. Upon thee be greetings, O My sister.[41]

Sháh Sulṭán Khánum ('Izzíyyih)

Birth and Early Life

Sháh Sulṭán Khánum was born to Mírzá Buzurg and his third wife, Kulthúm Khánum. She was born about 1810–11 and raised in Ṭihrán where her parents lived. She was the eldest of Mírzá Buzurg's daughters. Nothing is known of her childhood years and early life. She had two siblings from the same set of parents. They were Mírzá Riḍá-Qulí and Fáṭimih Sulṭán Khánum. She was semi-literate. This was much more than what the generality of women of her era in Iran enjoyed and gave her an advantage over them.

Adulthood and Later Years

Sháh Sulṭán Khánum is the most notorious of Mírzá Buzurg's daughters. She gained her notoriety through opposing Bahá'u'lláh and siding with Mírzá Yaḥyá Azal. Ambition, rapaciousness and love for temporal authority set her apart from her sisters and other female contemporaries. Opting to remain single and independent, Sháh Sulṭán Khánum wielded power over many of her siblings and influenced the course of events associated with them and their children, especially those who lived in Ṭihrán and Núr. She was addressed by the members of the family as Khánum Buzurg and Ḥáj 'Ammih Khánum. She had earned the title 'Ḥáj' by going on pilgrimage to Mecca, not a common phenomenon for a single Iranian woman of that era. The titles indicate her status among the members of her family.

Sháh Sulṭán Khánum was particularly close to her half brother Mírzá Yaḥyá, who was about 18 years her junior. She had helped raise Mírzá Yaḥyá and was very attached to him. The relationship was more like a mother and son. She was his staunch supporter and an effective instrument in steering things in his favour. To please him, she did what she could to inflict harm on Bahá'u'lláh and His family. The Azalís refer to her as 'Izzíyyih, meaning mighty, honourable. The title indicates her position and stature within the Azalí community. The Azalís went as far as writing a book in repudiation of Bahá'u'lláh's Cause and attributing its authorship to 'Izzíyyih. According to Mr Malik-Khusrawví, the book *Tanbíhu'n-Ná'imín* (Awakening the Slumbering) was authored by Mírzá Aḥmad Amínu'l-Aṭibbáy-i Rashtí.[42]

That Sháh Sulṭán Khánum fiercely opposed Bahá'u'lláh and acted vindictively towards Him are historical facts. In a Tablet revealed in honour of Amatu'lláh Sakínih, Bahá'u'lláh refers to His sufferings caused by His sister's denial and the activities in which she and other opponents engaged.

> . . . O My handmaid! Ponder upon that which hath befallen My Beauty from My kindred and from the adherents of former Faiths, causing the heaven to be cleft asunder and the earth split. Despite all this, My own sister hath risen up against Me with a manifest sword. We beseech God to open her eyes and to purge her from worldly things that she may recognize her Lord, for verily thy God's bounty is abundant.
>
> Recite unto thy Lord: Praised be Thou, O My God! I beseech Thee by Thy Beauty through which the Sun of Thy Oneness hath risen upon all

creation, to protect the Manifestation of Thine Essence from the handmaids who have denied Thee. Thou art verily the Possessor of names and attributes. O my God! Thou beholdest Thy Best Beloved imprisoned amidst Thy enemies and saddened by what hath befallen Him at the hands of Thy servants. Notwithstanding that He is surrounded by deniers from every direction, He hath also been wronged by His sister whom Thou hast fashioned and created through Thy power and inspiration. I beseech Thee at this time, O My God, by Thyself to protect Him from her and from the harm of Thy creatures. Thou art verily the Powerful, the Mighty and the Beneficent.[43]

In another Tablet revealed in honour of one of the handmaids of God, Bahá'u'lláh says:

. . . O My handmaid! Verily, the nations of the earth have arisen to harm me, and supporting them are those who wield power as well as the community of the Bayán. By God, because of them there hath befallen Me that which hath made the eye of the Merciful to weep in the Riḍván of His Name, the Most Subsisting, causing tears to flow from the eyes of the Concourse on High and those who are sincere.

This is a Bird imprisoned in the cage of the world. Both His enemies as well as His kindred among Our heedless servants are intent upon His harm. O My handmaid! Meditate upon My plight and upon that which hath befallen Me in the path of My Best-Beloved. At a time when every nation had turned against Me, My own sister joined in opposition and committed that which caused the letter Ṭá[44] to weep in the Abhá Paradise and the inmates of heaven to lament, and beyond them the celestial maids who dwell in the inviolable chambers of the Lord, the Almighty, the All-Praised. Her fascination with the world made her cling to the love of the most abject and turn away from the Best Beloved of the universe. By God, she committed that which caused the Most Great Spirit and the Spirit of Trust to lament. When entering the abode of the infidels, she would say, 'Verily I have disbelieved in God, the Lord of all who dwell on earth.' And when entering the seat of the believers in God's unity, she would say, 'Verily I am the first handmaid to believe in God, the Best Beloved of the universe.'

O My sister! Hast thou desired, through what thou hast committed, the sadness of My heart? By God, naught will affect it, for God hath established Himself therein with conspicuous sovereignty. Verily, shouldst thou, with thine own hands, marry to Mine enemies all the women residing in the households related to My Name, My luminous heart would

> not be saddened,[45] for God hath verily made it the repository of His Revelation, the wellspring of His knowledge, the Dawning-place of His Cause and the Seat of His mighty throne. Yet it is difficult for Me to bear that thou takest pride in serving the ungodly and associating with them. This is what saddens My heart and the hearts of the righteous.
>
> O My sister! What wrongdoing hath caused thee to abandon Me and embrace those who have denounced God? I have desired what is best for thee and thou hast desired for Me grief. I leave My affairs to God, the Most Glorious, the Most Informed.[46]

Bahá'u'lláh explains that the real reason for Sháh Sulṭán Khánum's opposition to Him and her contempt for the Cause of God stemmed from something concealed in her heart by reason of what she had perpetrated in times past. He then confirms: 'Thus, doth God expose them that deceive with the eyes and all that is concealed in the hearts of the malevolent.' Bahá'u'lláh further explains the reason for severing the tie of relationship with His sister, saying: 'Should one of My sons transgress the divinely revealed laws, by God, the glance of Mine eye will never be turned toward him, and to this beareth witness every fair-minded and informed person.' He further admonishes His followers to turn away from any of His brothers and sisters who turn against God, and fix their gaze on the Best Beloved. The Tablet ends with a prayer for His siblings, especially for Sháh Sulṭán Khánum, that they may not be deprived of the effect of His Revelation.[47]

Despite the harm that Sháh Sulṭán Khánum inflicted on Bahá'u'lláh and the wrongs that she committed, He revealed a Tablet in her honour responding, it seems, to a missive someone had sent to Him regarding her. In it, Bahá'u'lláh refers to Sháh Sulṭán Khánum's failure to recognize Him and expresses the hope that she may be divinely aided to do so.

> 'Izzíyyih
>
> He is God!
>
> Praised be Thou O Lord My God. This is My sister who hath believed in the Manifestations of Thy unity appearing in the garments of Thy eternity and recognized the Dawning-places of Thy constancy in the holy temples of Thy sovereignty. She hath ascended to the station that is detached from all save Thee and hath returned from Thee toward Thee. I ask of Thee, O My God, to free her from the insinuations which have hindered her from entering Thy Crimson Sea and from dwelling in the chambers of eternity on the exalted shore that she may haply recognize Thee in the Manifestation of Thy Beauty, the most hidden Dawning-place. In truth, Thou doest what Thou pleasest. Verily Thou art the Self-Subsisting Who

rulest supreme over all things.

To continue: Thy sweet letter hath been presented in the court of the presence of this ephemeral One. We beseech God to gather us together in the gardens of immortality near unto the twin glorious bows, that haply thou mayest witness the secrets of God's decree within this crimson and effulgent countenance, that the blessing of God upon thee and upon all who are on earth may be made complete.

The Spirit be upon thee and upon the new believers.[48]

One of Sháh Sulṭán Khánum's flagrant transgressions against Bahá'u'lláh and His family was the intrigue she employed to prevent the marriage of 'Abdu'l-Bahá to Shahrbánú Khánum, His cousin, the daughter of Mírzá Muḥammad-Ḥasan, the eldest son of Mírzá Buzurg. When Sháh Sulṭán Khánum heard of the arrangements that had been made for Shahrbánú Khánum to travel to Adrianople where she was to marry 'Abdu'l-Bahá, she (Sháh Sulṭán Khánum) devised a scheme to frustrate that plan. Shahrbánú Khánum was brought from Tákur to Ṭihrán by an envoy sent by Bahá'u'lláh to make preparations for her journey to Adrianople. Upon arrival in the capital, Sháh Sulṭán Khánum took Shahrbánú Khánum to her house and began laying the ground for her to marry 'Alí Khán, the son of Mírzá Áqá Khán-i Núrí, the prime minister of Iran whose hostility towards Bahá'u'lláh was well known. Her treacherous act caused Bahá'u'lláh and 'Abdu'l-Bahá immense sorrow. They have referred to it in some of their writings. In the Epistle to the Son of the Wolf Bahá'u'lláh recounts that episode:

> . . . Our late brother Mírzá Muḥammad-Ḥasan's daughter – upon him be the glory of God and His peace and His mercy – who had been betrothed to the Most Great Branch ('Abdu'l-Bahá) was taken by the sister of this Wronged One from Núr to her own house, and from there sent unto another place. Some of Our companions and friends in various places complained against this, as it was a very grievous act, and was disapproved by all the loved ones of God. How strange that Our sister should have taken her to her own house, and then arranged for her to be sent elsewhere! In spite of this, this Wronged One remained, and still remaineth, calm and silent. A word, however, was said in order to tranquillize Our loved ones. God testifieth and beareth Me witness that whatever hath been said was the truth, and was spoken with sincerity. None of Our loved ones, whether in these regions or in that country, could believe Our sister capable of an act so contrary to decency, affection and friendship. After such a thing had occurred, they, recognizing that the way had been barred, conducted themselves in a manner well-known unto thyself and

> others. It must be evident, therefore, how intense was the grief which this act inflicted upon this Wronged One. Later on, she threw in her lot with Mírzá Yaḥyá. Conflicting reports concerning her are now reaching Us, nor is it clear what she is saying or doing. We beseech God – blessed and glorified be He – to cause her to turn unto Him, and aid her to repent before the door of His grace. He, verily, is the Mighty, the Forgiving; and He is, in truth, the All-Powerful, the Pardoner.[49]

In the same book Bahá'u'lláh describes another treacherous act committed by Sh_áh Sulṭán Kh_ánum and explains the background to her hostilities towards Him:

> Ḥasan-i-Mázindarání was the bearer of seventy Tablets. Upon his death, these were not delivered unto those for whom they were intended, but were entrusted to one of the sisters of this Wronged One, who, for no reason whatever, had turned aside from Me. God knoweth what befell His Tablets. This sister had never lived with Us. I swear by the Sun of Truth that after these things had happened she never saw Mírzá Yaḥyá, and remained unaware of Our Cause, for in those days she had been estranged from Us. She lived in one quarter, and this Wronged One in another. As a token, however, of Our loving-kindness, our affection and mercy, We, a few days prior to Our departure, visited her and her mother, that haply she might quaff from the living waters of faith, and attain unto that which would draw her nigh unto God, in this day. God well knoweth and beareth Me witness, and she herself testifieth, that I had no thought whatsoever except this. Finally, she – God be praised – attained unto this through His grace, and was adorned with the adornment of love. After We were exiled and had departed from 'Iráq to Constantinople, however, news of her ceased to reach Us. Subsequent to Our separation in the Land of Ṭá (Ṭihrán), We ceased to meet Mírzá Riḍá-Qulí, Our brother, and no special news reached Us concerning her. In the early days we all lived in one house, which later on was sold at auction, for a negligible sum, and the two brothers, Farmán-Farmá and Ḥisámu's-Salṭanih, purchased it and divided it between themselves. After this occurred, We separated from Our brother. He established his residence close to the entrance of Masjid-i-Sh_áh, whilst We lived near the Gate of Sh_imírán. Thereafter, however, that sister displayed toward Us, for no reason whatever, a hostile attitude. This Wronged One held His peace under all conditions.[50]

In another Tablet, He says:

> . . . One of the relatives, named Muḥammad-Ḥasan, came to this land, and on his return he bore seventy Tablets for the servants of God. Upon arriving in Ṭihrán he was imprisoned and then sent to a certain village [Tákur], where he ascended. A woman stole those Tablets and sent them to My sister in Ṭihrán. God alone knoweth what she hath done with them, giving them to people in her own name or in that of Mírzá Yaḥyá. By God, she hath not been with Us and knows nothing of this Cause.
>
> A grievous transgression she committed: She sent one of the leaves enlisted as a friend,[51] who was related to her, to the house of an enemy for the sake of worldly glory. She then turned on her heels and did cling to another than Me. Her conduct is well known to many. She is incapable of reading a Tablet, but so capable of increasing the baseless imaginations of the doubters that none but God knoweth the extent. Verily He heareth and seeth, and He is the All-Hearing, the All-Seeing. She hath not been with Us and is uninformed, having been in a different land.
>
> Yea, her deed caused her own despair and she turned to others.[52] Gracious God! She is sixty years old and to this day she hath attained nothing worthwhile. Her love for the things of this world and for status hath prompted her to commit that which hath caused the sighs of the near ones to ascend and the tears of the sincere to flow.
>
> Apparently, she hath also been trying to obtain the Kitáb-i-Íqán. It is not known what her intentions are. We beseech God to aid her to return, to repent, and to humble herself [before God]. Verily, He is the Forgiver of sins, the Pardoner, the Merciful, and He is the Bestower, the Bountiful, the Mighty, and the Generous.[53]

When Jináb-i Varqá reported that a woman had embraced the Bahá'í Faith, Bahá'u'lláh revealed a Tablet in his honour and referred to God's way of making those who are high on earth to lose their status and cause the lowly to ascend to the heights of honour. Then He said:

> Ponder and reflect upon that which hath come to pass: The sister of this Wronged One hath been miles distant from the truth while the aforementioned handmaid hath attained nearness and union. Yea, the banner of 'no relationship existeth amongst you'[54] hath been hoisted, and the standard of 'the day on which men take flight'[55] hath been planted upon the highest peak. This sister hath not been with Us and hath not seen Yaḥyá in this Cause. For the love of the world and because of her relationship with people of power and wealth, she hath abandoned this Wronged One and joined hands with the oppressor. As a consequence of her most treacherous act, she became one with the enemy and is now burning with the fire

of hatred. She hath shown such duplicity that the world of being hath been astonished.

She is completely uninformed of this Cause. However, she hath learned countless schemes from those who are the manifestations of the Evil One. She hath arisen with intense malice and is bent upon inflicting harm on this Wronged One.

Convey greetings to the new leaf, and gladden her heart with the splendours of the rays of the Sun of Truth. Blessed is she and the one who hath helped her to recognize the truth, the one who taught her and guided her to the path of the Lord of the heavens and the earth, the Possessor of this world and the next.[56]

After Bahá'u'lláh's ascension, 'Abdu'l-Bahá revealed a long Tablet in honour of His unfaithful aunt, laying bare before her the greatness of Bahá'u'lláh and His Cause, reminding her of the sufferings inflicted upon the Prophet Muḥammad by His kindred and those who came from His birthplace, pleading with her to open her eyes and recognize the truth. He then says:

O kind aunt! The world hath been stirred into motion by the life-giving breezes of the disposition of thy august Brother. The mirror of the cosmos is illumined and distinguished by the splendours of His Countenance. The fame of His greatness is resounding in the universe, and the praises of His beauty are ringing in the highest heaven. Is it fair that a leaf from that blessed Stock be forsaken and a fruit from that pure Tree be deprived? Nay, by God! That esteemed aunt should be foremost among the holy leaves and a lighted candle in the assemblage of the attracted handmaids. She should be a manifest verse in the illustrious book and an exalted title in the annals of the leaves that have attained certitude. By Him Who is the Most Great Name, I write these words and utter these phrases with immense sorrow.

O kind aunt! This wanderer in the wilderness of God's love, because of His special love for thee since early childhood, hath written these words and hath committed to paper these sentences. I am the bearer of the message that must be conveyed. Dost thou recall how attached I was to thee in My childhood? And even now, I swear by His blessed dust, the focal centre of the adoration of the Concourse on high, that I still hold tremendous love for thee, and thus the sorrow and regret that I feel.

O affectionate aunt! Know the value of this chance while there is yet time, and barter not the Joseph of the heavenly city for a paltry sum. 'The tale of Joseph is better than a few coins.' And by 'a few coins' here is meant those who become the veil that covereth that luminous Face. If thou ponderest awhile, thou shalt clearly see the station and rank of every person from his bearing and conduct . . .

O honoured aunt! . . . Of a necessity the sun hath its rays and the rose garden its sweet perfume. The ocean must have its surging waves and the eagle the lofty peak. The advent of the Manifestations of Oneness hath, as its sole object, raising up the spirits of men to a new life and clothing them in the garment of a new creation. The splendours of the Sun of Truth are purely for the education and advancement of the people in every degree in this glorious age. Notwithstanding this, how could an obscure person who is intrinsically in need of an educator, protector, and helper become the educator of the world and the conferrer of bounty upon those who are steadfast in the Covenant? Nay, by God! 'How can the one who hath not received life from the Source of existence become himself the giver of life?'

. . . O beloved aunt! The sons of a certain claimant who calls himself the educator of all and the midmost heart of the highest firmament took refuge in this blessed Spot. In accordance with their capacity they composed treatises professing their own devotion and certitude, setting forth arguments in support of the blessed Cause and the invalidation of all else. These treatises in their own handwriting are extant with Amatu'lláh Khadíjih Sulṭán. However – I swear by His blessed Dust – their actions, their bearing, and their upbringing caused Me such shame and embarrassment before stranger and friend alike that I compelled them to return. Now consider, when water is tainted with mud at the source, how can it be refreshing and bestow life? 'Take heed, O people of understanding!' Is it fair to be content with a polluted drop and deprived of the life-giving sea and the sweet waters, or to be content with a spark and veiled from the world-illuminating sun? Nay, by God! Nay, by God! Nay, by God!

O clear-sighted aunt! I swear by that Spot round which circumambulate the Concourse on high that thou excellest in wisdom, understanding, intellect, and judgement those who claim to be the pivot of God's universe. The child thou didst raise in the bosom of thy loving kindness was in all respects unlike his brothers and was entirely lacking in capacity.

O honourable aunt! Granting that one unfamiliar with Arabic may not recognize clarity and eloquence, nor understand what is correct and incorrect in that tongue, and therefore misunderstand matters, the Persian odes and poems which are extant should suffice. By God, what is this obstinacy and harmful zeal which have blinded the eyes and deafened the ears? Gracious God! What is this mystery? After the ascension of His Holiness the Exalted One,[57] may My spirit be His sacrifice, until the present time, what signs of might and greatness have been manifested

> from any other than the True One[58] that have veiled the eyes from beholding the Sun of Truth, notwithstanding what His Holiness the Exalted One, may the spirit of the world be His sacrifice, hath said explicitly? 'Beware, beware, lest the first váḥid of the Bayán become a veil, for that verily is His creation.' And the first váḥid of the Bayán compriseth the eighteen Letters of the Living, the nineteenth being His Holiness Himself. Behold! He saith, let not Myself and My Letters become the cause of thy denial, and condition not thy belief upon our confession and acceptance of Him. And one of the Letters is Jináb-i-Quddús under whom, according to the Bayán, are thirteen váḥids of Mir'át (Mirror).[59]
>
> O loving aunt! Tarry awhile in the rose garden of the utterances of His Holiness the Exalted One, may the spirit of existence be a sacrifice for the wrongs He suffered, and peruse some of the chapters of the Bayán. Ponder upon what He saith in numerous places about the station, rank, and reality of the Mirrors. The truth will then become clear and manifest as the sun.
>
> O My aunt! How long wilt thou remain fast asleep and recumbent upon thy couch? Arise from thy slumber with humility and self-effacement. By the One True God, the sun hath verily risen, the clouds have poured down, the winds have blown, and 'the earth hath stirred, swelled, and put forth in pairs every kind of luxuriant herb.'[60]
>
> Shouldst thou listen with an attentive ear, by God, thou wouldst hear the call of the trumpet from the Concourse on high in praise of thy Lord, the Most Glorious.[61]

At the end of the Tablet 'Abdu'l-Bahá speaks of the effects of His aunt's wilful blindness and prejudices which cause her to be happy and satisfied with the least when through the recognition of Bahá'u'lláh's Revelation she could have enjoyed the full measure of God's all-encompassing blessings.

'Abdu'l-Bahá's loving and candid Tablet reached its intended recipient. Sháh Sulṭán Khánum and her Azalí friends deemed it necessary to come up with an answer. One of them composed a response and circulated it in her name. H.M. Balyuzi refers to it in *Edward Granville Browne and the Bahá'í Faith:*

> . . . we have the curious testimony of a tract attributed to a sister of Ṣubh-i-Azal. In an effort to make her see how untenable the position of Mírzá Yaḥyá was, 'Abdu'l-Bahá wrote her a long Letter, in which He addressed her as 'O my affectionate Aunt'. The aforementioned tract is her supposed answer to 'Abdu'l-Bahá's Tablet. *Risáliy-i-'Ammih* – The Aunt's Treatise – as it has come to be known, is an apologia for Ṣubḥ-i-Azal.[62]

The Passing of Sháh Sulṭán Khánum and a Brief Review of Her Life

Shah Sulṭán Khánum outlived most, if not all, of her siblings. She died in Ṭihrán in 1322 AH (1905–6) at the age of 95 and was buried in Imámzádih Ma'ṣúm.

Through her obstinate and wilful opposition to Bahá'u'lláh and her engagement in dishonourable activities against Him and against those devoted to Him, Sháh Sulṭán Khánum has earned for herself an unrivalled abominable place among the female members of His family. She will go down in the annals of the Bahá'í Faith as a sister of the Supreme Manifestation of God who was consumed with the fire of envy for Him and as a person of influence who used her full power to discredit Him. She lived long enough to witness the rising Sun of Bahá'u'lláh's Revelation from the horizon of His exiled land and the glory of His Covenant. She saw the futility of the activities in which she engaged before she died, disillusioned and despondent.

11

Jináb-i-Maryam, Titled the Crimson Leaf,[1] Bahá'u'lláh's Cousin and Sister-in-law

Family Background

Jináb-i-Maryam was born to Malik Nisá' Khánum, Mírzá Buzurg-i-Núrí's sister, and Mírzá Karím-i Namadsáb. Mírzá Karím was probably related to Khadíjih Khánum, Bahá'u'lláh's mother, who was also from the Namadsáb tribe. Jináb-i-Maryam had two siblings: Fáṭimih Khánum and Mírzá Muḥammad. For an account of the life of Fáṭimih Khánum, see chapter 8 on Fáṭimih Khanum, titled Mahd-i-'Ulyá.

Mirzá Muḥammad was a devoted believer. He married Ḥavvá Khánum, Bahá'u'lláh's niece, also a devoted believer. Mírzá Muḥammad died young. Bahá'u'lláh revealed, after his death, Ḥurúfát-i 'Állín (the Exalted Letters) in honour of his sister, Maryam, and his wife Ḥavvá.[2]

Birth and Early Life

Maryam was born about 1826. Since her parents had a house in the village of Fuyúl situated to the southeast of Tákur in the district of Núr, it is assumed that is where she was born and spent her childhood and early years. Judging from what is left of the poetry she composed, she may have been instructed in the art of reading and writing in her childhood. Unfortunately, no information is available about her early life. The fame that she enjoys in the annals of the Bahá'í Faith is due to the Tablets Bahá'u'lláh revealed in her honour. These Tablets are known as Alváḥ-i Maryam and occupy a unique place in the body of Bahá'u'lláh's writings. Maryam's legendary fame, however, does not match the historical treatment accorded her. On the whole, very little information is available about her life, especially the period between her birth and marriage. Influenced by the Shí'í bias against women, early Bahá'í historians rarely delved into the lives of prominent believing women in the early stages of the development of the Faith. As a result, information about the early women believers and their contribution to the Faith is scanty and obscure. The scantiness and vagueness apply more particularly to the lives of the female members of Bahá'u'lláh's family. One such woman is Maryam, Bahá'u'lláh's cousin. She rendered Him remarkable service at a very crucial juncture in His life. Also, despite the precarious circumstances of her life, she remained in touch with Him through correspondence and devoted her whole life to the promotion of His Cause.

Marriage

In his unpublished memoirs known as *Áfáq va Anfus* (*Places and Peoples*), A. Ishráq-i-Khávarí says that according to their marriage certificate, which was in the possession of Mr Malik-Khusrawví, a member of the Núrí family and the author of *Iqlím-i-Núr*, Maryam and Mírzá Riḍá Qulí[3] got married in 1260 (1844). Furúgh Arbáb says Maryam married Mírzá Riḍá Qulí two years before the Báb's declaration, i.e. in 1842.[4] Maryam and Mírzá Riḍá Qulí had a house in Ṭihrán, where they lived.

The fruit of Maryam's marriage with Mírzá Riḍá Qulí was a daughter named Zahrá, titled Thamarih (Fruit). A Tablet revealed by Bahá'u'lláh in honour of Maryam speaks of her sorrows caused by her separation from Him and the death of her sons. This indicates that she bore more children than the one who survived. Ishráq-i-Khávarí states that Mírzá Taqíy-i Ḥakamí was born to Mírzá Riḍá Qulí and Maryam. Other sources say that Mírzá Taqí and Kulthúm were from Mírzá Riḍá Qulí's second wife, Qamar Khánum who, according to Ishráq-i-Khavarí, was nine years old when, after Maryam's death, she married Mírzá Riḍá Qulí. According to the same source, Mírzá Riḍá Qulí died at the age of 92.[5]

Zahrá Khánum, also known as Fakhru'l-Ḥájíyih, married Mírzá Ismá'íl, son of Sárih Khánum (Bahá'u'lláh's sister) and Mírzá Maḥmúd (Ásíyih Khánum's brother). They had two children: Zíbandih Khánum Thamarí and Náṣir Khán Thamarí. More information about Zahrá Khánum and her family is given at the end of this chapter.

Conversion

It is not clear exactly when Maryam joined the Bábí Faith. Bahá'u'lláh states in an as yet unpublished Tablet that as soon as she heard the call, she believed. He also testifies that she was inflamed with the fire of the love of God before that fire touched her, that the promptings of the deniers did not influence her and the whisperings of the Covenant-breakers did not keep her away from the path of Truth, that she was steadfast in her love for the Cause of God and that her high spiritual station was concealed ere her passing.

Maryam's allegiance to Bahá'u'lláh and His mission was categorical and complete. She openly supported Him when her husband remained ostensibly indifferent. Some close members of her family, such as her sister-in-law, Sháh Sulṭán Khánum, known as 'Izzíyyih, publicly opposed Bahá'u'lláh and supported His enemies. Maryam's allegiance to Bahá'u'lláh and her support for Him caused her intense suffering. After Bahá'u'lláh left Ṭihrán for Baghdád, she became a target for criticism and condemnation and her activities were tightly controlled. But she never wavered in her belief in the truth of the Cause she had embraced.

Offering Hospitality to Bahá'u'lláh after His Release from the Síyáh Chál

Maryam's name will be forever associated with Bahá'u'lláh's release from the Síyáh Chál (Black Pit). By 1852, when Bahá'u'lláh and Ásíyih Khánum had been divested of their belongings and He had been arrested and imprisoned in the Síyáh Chál, Maryam and her husband were well established in Ṭihrán. It was in her house that He stayed for about a month to recuperate from the harsh conditions of that dreadful prison before embarking on His long journey to Baghdád. When Bahá'u'lláh was released from prison, He had no house to retire to. His house had been pillaged. Most of His relatives were panic-stricken. To avoid persecution, some were living in hiding while others did not openly associate with Him and Ásíyih Khánum. His half brother Mírzá Riḍá Qulí had chosen to remain outwardly indifferent to Bahá'u'lláh's plight. It was under those circumstances that Maryam stepped forward and offered hospitality to Bahá'u'lláh. During His stay in her house, she served Him with exemplary devotion and consideration until He regained sufficient strength to undertake the journey to Baghdád.

Although extending assistance to Bahá'u'lláh was a risky affair under the circumstances prevailing in Ṭihrán in those perilous days, after His release from prison Maryam offered her home as a safe abode where He could recuperate from the rigours of the four months' imprisonment. Adib Taherzadeh says:

> Bahá'u'lláh spent the month preceding His exile in the house of His half brother Mírzá Riḍá-Qulí, a physician. The latter was not a believer though his wife Maryam, a cousin of Bahá'u'lláh, had been converted by Him in the early days of the Faith and was one of His most sincere and faithful followers within the family. With great care and affection Maryam, together with Ásíyih Khánum, the wife of Bahá'u'lláh, nursed Him until His condition improved and, though not fully recovered, He had gathered sufficient strength to enable Him to leave Ṭihrán for 'Íráq.[6]

When Bahá'u'lláh was released from the Síyáh Chál, Ásíyih Khánum and her three children were living in two rented rooms in an obscure corner of Ṭihrán. That kind of accommodation was inadequate for Bahá'u'lláh's quick recovery prior to His departure for Baghdád. Therefore the invitation to stay at Maryam and Mírzá Riḍá-Qulí's place was favourably considered. It is generally believed that Bahá'u'lláh stayed at the home of His half brother for about a month. According to Bahá'íyyih Khánum's recollections recorded by Lady Blomfield, Bahá'u'lláh, upon release from prison, joined Ásíyih Khánum and the children in the rented rooms.[7] His transfer to the house of His half brother and Maryam may have been arranged some time after His release from the Síyáh Chál when it became clear how utterly inadequate those rooms were for His recovery. Alternatively, He may have spent some time in either place before His departure from Ṭihrán.

After Bahá'u'lláh's Departure from Iran

Maryam served the Cause of Bahá'u'lláh with the same intense devotion and love with which she served Him. Many obstacles were placed in her path by those who claimed to love her but worked assiduously against her interests and succeeded in drastically circumscribing her activities. Bahá'u'lláh's sworn enemy and half sister, whom the Azalís called 'Izzíyyih, a staunch supporter of Mírzá Yaḥyá Azal, did everything in her power to turn Maryam away from the object of her adoration, causing her tremendous grief.[8] Bahá'u'lláh describes her plight as being 'a stranger in her country and a captive in her home.'

Maryam was deeply affected by Bahá'u'lláh's sufferings and tribulations. After Bahá'u'lláh's departure from Iran, she kept in touch with Him through correspondence. Unfortunately, her letters have not survived but Tablets revealed in response to her letters provide a treasury of information. They reveal the tender tone with which Bahá'u'lláh has addressed her. It is evident from these writings that in her communications Maryam conveyed her devotion to Him, expressed the anguish of her heart in her separation from Him and recounted the ordeals she suffered by virtue of her allegiance to Him. At times she expressed her feelings in verse. Some of her poems have survived. They depict generally the anguish of her soul in separation from Bahá'u'lláh.

In an unpublished Tablet revealed jointly in honour of His sister, Sárih Khánum, Khánum[9] and Maryam Khánum, Bahá'u'lláh speaks of calamities and afflictions descending upon them from the clouds of destiny in rapid succession. He talks about the bleeding hearts and fragmented breasts of the lovers of God and describes the woes they suffered and recounts their ordeals.

He then speaks of His captivity and imprisonment in Ṭihrán, His banishment to Iraq and the 'fresh calamity' which had saddened the hearts, agitated the souls, broken their backbones and severely oppressed their inmost being.[10] He beseeches for them patience under His trials and tranquillity under His ordeals. He says that the lovers' complaints stemmed from the wounds they sustained for the sake of their Best Beloved. He also says that they wished not to complain about what they had experienced in the pathway of love and separation or from burning in the fire of longing but rather to express their devotion before the Beloved and their steadfastness in the path of His love.

The Planned Trip to Baghdád

To quench the fire of her longing, Maryam decided to visit Bahá'u'lláh. She began making preparations for the journey. When her plans were disclosed, 'some members of the family who were ill disposed towards the Faith prevented her from leaving home and she died sad and disappointed'.[11]

The belief that Maryam tried to attain Bahá'u'lláh's presence after He was exiled to Iraq and into Turkey but was prevented from undertaking the journey is based on Bahá'u'lláh's visitation Tablet revealed in her honour, which indicates that she was prevented from attaining reunion with Him. It is not known when she intended to make the trip, what arrangements she made and how her plans were frustrated. Her last attempt was probably made during the period Bahá'u'lláh lived in Adrianople. Her efforts seem to have been aborted by her husband, his sister Sháh Sulṭán Khánum ('Izzíyyih) and other close members of her family 'who were ill disposed towards the Faith'.[12]

The Passing of Maryam

Maryam is believed to have died during the last year of Bahá'u'lláh's sojourn in Adrianople. In his unpublished memoirs A. Ishráq-i-Khávarí notes 6 Rabí'uth-Thání 1284 (circa 1867) as the date of her passing. Both he and Furúgh Arbáb, author of *Akhtarán-i-Tábán*, agree that Maryam was 42 years old when she passed away. Maryam died in Ṭihrán and is buried, according to Mr Malik-Khusrawví, inside the shrine of 'Abdu'l-'Aẓím.

After her passing, Bahá'u'lláh revealed a Tablet of visitation in Maryam's honour.[13] The Tablet lifts the veil of concealment from her station. One of the passages confirms this: 'We concealed her station during her lifetime. When she ascended to the Highest Horizon, God removed the veil and made her known to His servants.' The contents of the Tablet also recount the circumstances under which she lived and the sufferings that she endured.

In the passages that precede the prayer Bahá'u'lláh speaks of the great sorrow occasioned by Maryam's death, which He describes as a grievous calamity, and bids His Pen to recount the afflictions she had suffered. Bahá'u'lláh then reveals the visitation prayer, the opening passage of which reads:

> The first mercy which hath descended from the clouds of the Will of thy Creator, the Most Exalted, the Most Glorious; the first light which hath shone forth from the Horizon of Eternity, and the first salutation uttered by the Tongue of Grandeur in the realm of His indomitable Purpose, rest upon thee, O thou who art the most mighty sign, the most exalted word, the most brilliant pearl, and the countenance of unity in the heaven of his irrevocable Decree. [14]

Bahá'u'lláh speaks further of the lamentation that encompassed the unseen realm upon her death. He affirms that when Maryam heard the divine call she did not hesitate for a moment in recognizing it. Describing her sufferings on earth, Bahá'u'lláh says that she was a stranger in her own land and a captive in her own home, and that she was kept back from the Court of Sanctity in spite of her yearning. He blesses her for forfeiting her desire for that of her Lord and affirms that she remained faithful to the Covenant.

Addressing Maryam as Varaqatu'l-Baqá'íyyih (Leaf of Eternity), Bahá'u'lláh continues:

> By thy righteousness, O nightingale of eternity! How sorely trying it is for Me to see the world but to behold thee not therein, to hear the warbling of nightingales and yet to hear not thy melodious voice lifted up in praise of thy Lord, the Most Exalted, the All-Glorious. I swear by God! On account of thy sorrow all creation hath been overwhelmed with sadness and the embodiments of the names of God have donned garments of black. How can I recount, O beloved of Bahá, the days when thou wouldst sing upon the branches, magnifying the praise of thy merciful Lord in a voice of incomparable sweetness? By virtue of the melodies thou didst pour forth in the praise of thy mighty and beneficent Lord, the rustling of the celestial Tree of utterance hath become audible, and the Dove of divine knowledge hath cooed, and the River that is life eternal hath murmured, and the gentle breeze of Paradise hath whispered, and the Bird of the Throne hath warbled, all of them celebrating the praise of thy Lord, the Most Glorious, the Help in Peril.
>
> Thou art she by virtue of whose praise every created thing hath been prompted to magnify the glory of its Lord, the Mighty, the Loving. In

> mourning thy loss the Nightingale hath fallen silent, and the winds have been stilled, and the lights of felicity have been extinguished, and the waters of salvation have frozen. Blinded be the eye that hath failed to behold in thy countenance the beauty of the All-Merciful and that did not weep over the manifold sorrow that touched thee; and silent be the tongue that recounteth not thy virtues amidst the inhabitants of the world of being.[15]

The Tablet continues with Bahá'u'lláh, referring to Maryam as Al-Musta<u>sh</u>had fí sabíli'l Bahá (the one who died as a martyr in the path of Bahá), recalling with immense sorrow the many nights that she had, while lying on her couch, shed tears in her longing to attain His presence and the days when she had burned in the fire of yearning to reunite with Bahá. He testifies that from His face she sought only the face of her Creator. He calls her the pride of men and testifies that Maryam was a leaf which was moved everlastingly by the breezes of the will of God and that the promptings of the people of dissension who had broken the Covenant and denied God did not affect her. He blesses those handmaids who associated with her, heard her praise, clung to the cord of her love, and through her drew nigh to God. He says that her body was a trust which the Creator had deposited in the bosom of the earth while her spirit had soared towards the Most Glorious Horizon.

At the end of the Tablet Bahá'u'lláh revealed a prayer, to be recited by those who visit Maryam's resting-place.

Writings Revealed in Honour of Maryam

The number of years intervening between Bahá'u'lláh's departure from Ṭihrán (late 1852/early 1853) and Maryam's death (1867) is about 14. Bahá'u'lláh spent ten of those 14 years in Iraq. It was in that country where the fire of Covenant-breaking was first ignited and severely tested the faith of some members of His family who lived in Iran. It was also in that country where Bahá'u'lláh revealed, in Maryam's honour, a number of Tablets describing His plight. As Adib Taherzadeh says:

> To her, from 'Iráq, He addressed some of His Tablets known as the *Alwáḥ-i-Maryam* which are unique in their tone and sentiment. In language at once moving and tender He poured out His heart to her and recounted the afflictions heaped on Him by some of His unfaithful kinsmen and friends within the community.[16]

The most well-known Tablet Bahá'u'lláh revealed in honour of Maryam is the one He wrote after His return to Ba<u>gh</u>dád from Kurdistán. Its tone is moving, the style most appealing and the contents very revealing of His plight during the years of exile in Iraq, His sojourn in the mountains of Kurdistán and His return to Baghdád.[17]

> The wrongs which I suffer have blotted out the wrongs suffered by My First Name (the Báb) from the Tablet of creation.[18]

Bahá'u'lláh speaks of His ordeals and reasons for the sufferings inflicted upon Him. Regarding His banishment from His homeland, He says that it was occasioned by no other reason but His love for the Best Beloved, and His exile from His country had no justification but His seeking the good pleasure of the Desired One. When heavenly ordeals descended, He says, He was enkindled like a bright candle and when calamities struck, He was steadfast like a mountain. He showed forth bounties like a downpour and like a burning flame dealt with the enemies of the Peerless Sovereign. He says the manifestations of His might made the enemy envious and the evidences of His wisdom made the people of malice resentful. He did not rest a single night in a secure place, nor did He raise His head a single morn with ease. After explaining the intensity of His ordeals in the land of His birth, He says:

> O Maryam! From the land of Ṭá (Ṭihrán), after countless afflictions, We reached 'Íráq, at the bidding of the Tyrant of Persia, where, after the fetters of Our foes, We were afflicted with the perfidy of Our friends. God knoweth what befell Me thereafter![19]

Bahá'u'lláh then describes how, singly and alone, He left home and family, risked His life and all that pertains to it, and entered the wilderness of resignation.[20] He speaks of His loneliness and says that His companions during that period were the birds of the field and beasts of the wilderness. He explains how like unto a spiritual lightning He passed through the mortal world, eschewed fellowship with all save God and fixed His gaze on Him alone that perchance the fire of animosity might subside and the heat of envy lose its intensity.[21]

Addressing Maryam again, He says that it was not befitting to divulge mysteries or disclose the wonders of the Almighty. He defines 'mysteries' as the treasures hidden in His inner Being and laments,

> I have borne what no man, be he of the past or of the future, hath borne or will bear.[22]

Bahá'u'lláh confirms that during His absence none of His brothers enquired about His affairs, nor did they have the desire to know.[23] Bahá'u'lláh emphasizes the significance of His absence and says that the good enshrined in His migration exceeded by far the merit of a worship in both worlds, and refers to it as 'the mightiest testimony and the most perfect and conclusive evidence'[24] of the truth of His Revelation.

After explaining the circumstances attending His return, He says that when He got back to Iraq He saw some souls spiritless and withered, even lost and dead. No mention of the Cause of God was left and no understanding heart could be seen.[25] Therefore, Bahá'u'lláh arose to protect the Cause of God and elevated it in such a way that it seemed Resurrection had recurred. As a result of His efforts, He says, the exaltation of the Faith became so evident that sovereigns were compelled to behave with propriety and consideration.[26]

Bahá'u'lláh tells Maryam that the stand He took against the enemies from every denomination and background so increased the adversary's envy that it could neither be described nor perceived. The most important of all things, He emphasizes, is the purification of the heart from all save God and He admonishes Maryam to sanctify her heart from all but the Friend, that she may be worthy to enter the court of His company. He tells her to leave the shackles of imitation and to enter the joyful atmosphere of freedom, to detach her heart from the world and its contents, that she may attain the Sovereign of faith and deprive not herself of the sanctuary of God. He admonishes her to rend asunder the veil of vain imagining with the might of detachment and enter the holy abode of certainty. He advises her to seek communion with God, take refuge under His infallible protection and turn from fleeting shadows to the Sun of everlasting might. He says that all shadows owe their existence and movement to the sun to such a degree that if the bounty is withheld for one moment, they all return to the canopy of non-existence. He expresses pity and regret for those who busy themselves with vanishing phenomena and are prevented from the dawning-place of holiness.

Bahá'u'lláh further counsels Maryam to appreciate the value of the time in which He is living among humanity for, He says, the time is approaching when the Spiritual Youth will no longer be in this world. Then she will see signs of sorrow in all things and reunion with Him will be impossible.

At the end of the Tablet, Bahá'u'lláh refers again to the deterioration in the situation and to His decision to remove Himself from among the 'Gogs'. He explains at such a time His only succourers were the tears He shed, His only attendant the moaning of His heart, His companion His Pen, His comrade His Beauty, His army His trust, and His party His Self-reliance. He thus informs Maryam of the mysteries of this affair that she may be of those who were informed.

Bahá'u'lláh closes the Tablet by saying that all the water in the world and all the rivers therein were from His eyes which had appeared in the form of clouds and poured down as a result of the wrongs He endured. He offered up His head and His soul in the path of the Friend at the beginning that has no beginning and was happy and content with whatever occurred. He cites examples from religious history, saying that at one time His head was on the spear, at another it was in the hand of Shimr. Once He was thrown into the fire, another time He was suspended in the air, and this, He says, was how the infidels dealt with Him.

Bahá'u'lláh called the Tablet Náliy-i Badí'ih (the Latter-day Lamentation) and Garyiy-i Rabí'ih (the Spring Downpour) and sent it to Maryam that she might moan with ease and share in the sorrows of the Ancient Beauty.[27]

At the end of the Tablet Bahá'u'lláh refers to the visit of Jináb-i Bábá, saying that when he attained Bahá'u'lláh's presence, he became aware of some matters. Bahá'u'lláh asks that the Holy Spirit inspire him to speak with certitude and truthfulness and will enable Maryam to catch a glimpse of the story of the Youth.[28]

In a postscript Bahá'u'lláh remembers Ḥusní Khánum and Ṣughrá Khánum.[29] In a more detailed postscript He speaks of Khadíjih Khánum,[30] to whom He had intended to write for some time. He talks about delays caused by problems involved with despatching the writings. He remembers Áqá, the daughters and sons of Ḥavvá Khánum[31] and those intoxicated by the wine of divine love. He ends the postscript by praising those who had drunk deep from the chalice of recognition and advising the partakers to conceal it from the ungodly.

The addressee of a Tablet, referred to as 'the pure leaf', appears to be Maryam. The contents and the tone resemble Bahá'u'lláh's other Tablets addressed to her. Another indication that it is addressed to her is Bahá'u'lláh's reference to 'the pure and brilliant Zahrá'. Maryam had a daughter named Zahrá.

He is God!

O thou pure Leaf! Thy lamentation hath ascended to the heaven of Oneness and the sighing of thy heart hath saddened the inhabitants of the Celestial Paradise. O thou who, after separation, seekest reunion with the Luminary of the universe! Cease thy lamentation and be patient, although teaching patience to the nightingale is like preventing the fire from burning. But in one's nearness to and remoteness from the True One there hath ever been, and will continue to be, a wisdom. The Almighty hath at all times ignited the fire of yearning in the hearts and hath concealed Himself; He hath caused the souls to long for reunion, then separated from them.

Bahá'u'lláh cheers the recipient's heart with humour. He says:

> O that He Who is visible yet concealed would come in truth and the right of that Leaf and other lovers would be extracted from Him! But what can be done? Neither He, nor His sword can be seen.[32]

He then continues:

> O Leaf! Be assured of the bounty of the Sovereign of Oneness and leave thy affairs to the Beloved. He hath never forgotten thee and in the presence of the Great One thou shalt never be absent. The eye of My favour hath ever been and will continue to be turned to thee. Render praise, for divine confirmations have embraced thee in such wise that all created beings testify to thy love. Be not sad. If God wills it He will enable thee to become like unto a moth circumambulating the everlasting Lamp and circling round the divine Light. Convey My greetings to all the believing handmaidens. Convey my remembrances to the pure and brilliant handmaid Zahrá, the one who hath desired to behold My Face and hath attained My glory. Convey greetings on behalf of the Self of God to Khátún Ján and say to her: 'Thou art residing in thy home and the Ancient Beauty is captive in the hand of tyrants.'[33]

Another Tablet addressed to Maryam speaks of the arrival of a certain Mihdí who had returned to Baghdád and, among other things, had talked about Maryam's sorrows caused by pangs of separation and the death of her sons. Bahá'u'lláh says that this was very strange, for she had been given to drink from the Tavern of Núr and was fed from the choice wine of Revelation. All relationships, He says, were linked to her and all spirits referred to her. He then enquires: 'What is causing thy sadness and why art thou sorrowful? Hast thou ever heard of the ocean shedding tears in separation from a river or the sun fearing the pursuit of a star?' He admonishes Maryam to sever the head of heedlessness that she may fathom the mystery of 'verily, to Him we all return'. He says the new creation is wholesome; it is free from every defect, otherwise the verse 'Blessed is God, the Most Perfect of all Creators' will be in vain and meaningless. He ends the Tablet by saying: 'More than this I am not allowed to disclose, and salutation be upon all.'[34]

In a moving Tablet addressed to Maryam, Bahá'u'lláh first describes the devastating effect of the crucifixion of Jesus Christ. He then says that the illumined breast of the lovers is a worthy target for the shafts of the divine decree and their neck an eager recipient for the lasso of infinite ordeals. Where there is an arrow, He says, its recipient is the friends' bosom and where there is a sorrow, it descends on their heart. He says that it behoves the lovers to have moist eyes and the loved ones to be demure and distant. The lamentation of the lover intensifies the loved one's reluctance. He advises Maryam to be ready to sacrifice her life if she desires the chalice of reunion and to enter the valley of privation if she seeks the wine of His Countenance. He then says:

> O Maryam! Exchange thy sorrow for happiness and drink thy sadness from the cup of joy. Shouldst thou desire to enter the path of search, thou must needs be patient; lacerate not thy face, cease thy weeping and be not of those who are impatient. Put on the garb of submissiveness, drink the wine of contentment and barter for a penny the world of being. Accept the decree of fate and be at one with what hath been preordained. Open the eye of true learning and close it to all that is not of the Friend, for erelong we shall gather in the presence of the Sanctified One and turn our faces towards the Exalted Companion. From the Iraqi Songster we shall hear the Ḥijází melody. We shall be united with the Friend, speak that which cannot be spoken, see that which cannot be seen and hear that which cannot be heard. We shall cause the temple of the spirit to dance to the melody of light. In the sanctified arena of the Beloved convene a delightful feast, seize from the cupbearer of glory the chalice of His beauty and quaff the peerless wine in memory of the countenance of the Beauteous One.

At the end of the Tablet Bahá'u'lláh exhorts Maryam to wipe her eyes dry, to drive despondency away from her heart, to free her bosom from sorrow, and sing with the sweetest of melodies:

> If swords rain down in the Beloved's abode
> We lay low our necks for God's decree to hold.[35]

In yet another Tablet addressing Maryam as Al-Varaqatu'l-Ḥamrá' (the Crimson Leaf), Bahá'u'lláh bids her to rejoice for having been remembered by the Beloved, the Most Glorious, who had been wronged and sustained tribulations in the path of God's love, the Possessor of Names and Fashioner of the Heaven. She is then bidden to say:

> Praised be to Thee, O Thou Who hast revealed to me Thy lofty Horizon, aided me to recognize Thy most exalted Word, and drawn me nigh unto the station wherein the Ocean of Thy Oneness hath surged, shedding forth from its horizon the light of Thy unity. O my God! How can I render

thanks to Thee for having blessed me with Thy generosity, assisted me to find the fragrance of Thy garment, and helped me to attain the cup which hath been proffered by the hand of Thy bestowal? I beseech Thee to make me steadfast in Thy Cause and help me to remember Thy verses in such wise that worldly affairs will not prevent me from turning my gaze towards Thee. Thou art verily the Forgiver of sins and the Most Merciful.[36]

Maryam's Daughter

As stated earlier, Maryam and Mírzá Riḍá Qulí had one daughter, named Zahrá, titled Thamarih (Fruit). Zahrá Khánum followed in the footsteps of her illustrious mother and became an ardent lover of Bahá'u'lláh. In a Tablet revealed in her honour, He says:

> Thamarih, upon her be Bahá'u'lláhu'l-Abhá
>
> He is the Most Compassionate, the Most Generous.
>
> O thou My leaf, upon thee be My glory and My favours! O thou the fruit of My Tree, upon thee be My mercy and My bounty! Thou art oft remembered in the Holy and Exalted Court. Praised be God that thou hast perceived the fragrant breezes of divine Revelation and inhaled the sweet savours of the garment of Utterance. Thou hast been and art remembered among the Concourse on High. Render thanks to thy Lord. Verily, He hath remembered thee with that for which all mentions are sacrificed. We beseech God to protect thee and those who are with thee from the one who hath falsely accused Us and stolen Our Tablets and that which We have revealed.[37] We beseech God to assist her to return and adorn her with the ornament of justice and fairness.
>
> O Thamarih! Thou knowest that she is unable to read even one of the Tablets, that she was not with Us in the Land of Ṭá, and that she hath not seen Yaḥyá after the Primal Point declared His Mission. Nonetheless, she hath uttered calumnies the like of which hath not been heard. We beseech God to enable all to do what is loved and praiseworthy.
>
> Glory from Us be upon thee, upon those who are with thee, and upon every firm and steadfast believer.[38]

After Bahá'u'lláh's ascension, Thamarih remained faithful to His Covenant. She received many Tablets from 'Abdu'l-Bahá. In one Tablet, He says:

> The Ancient Beauty, may My spirit be sacrificed for His loved ones, from the beginning had the utmost consideration for that family. He even

> stayed in that house for some time. He Himself guided the members of that family and evinced towards them many loving kindnesses. Through the outpourings of the clouds of bounty that house became a rose-garden and a nest for the birds of the bower of understanding. After the emigration of the Greatest Name, may My spirit be sacrificed for His loved ones, scorching winds from the whisperings of certain souls began to blow, withering and shrivelling the flowers of that garden and causing sadness and regret. Now it is hoped that that Thamariy-i Ṭayyibih (Choice Fruit) may again, with aid from the Ancient Beauty and outpourings from His Kingdom, give that withered garden infinite freshness and refinement, causing the feeble young trees to flourish through the sprinklings of the clouds of divine love, that they may give forth foliage, and the fragrant breeze of the love of God may spread abroad, perfuming every corner of that house . . .[39]

Zahrá Khánum (Thamarih) and her daughter Zíbandih sought permission from 'Abdu'l-Bahá to come on pilgrimage. Their request arrived when He had returned to Egypt from His first trip to Europe and was about to embark on His trip to North America. He responded:

> . . . Thy letter hath arrived. Praised be God, under the sheltering protection of the Blessed Beauty, I have safely returned from the West but will again proceed to America in the near future. After I return, the means may be in place for thee to attain thy highest desire and with Zíbandih Khánum visit the Holy Threshold . . .[40]

Thamarih does not appear to have lived long enough to achieve her heart's desire. She seems to have passed away soon after 'Abdu'l-Bahá's return to the Holy Land. Zíbandih Khánum, however, received permission to come on pilgrimage, 'if it was possible for her to travel with ease'.[41]

In many Tablets 'Abdu'l-Bahá praises Thamarih for her firmness in the Covenant and testifies that in the storms of Covenant-breaking which rocked the foundation of the people of the world, she was well protected from its devastating effects. When she passed away, 'Abdu'l-Bahá revealed special visitation prayers in her honour. She had three children: two daughters, Zíbandih and Malakih, and one son, Náṣir. Malakih appears to have died young. All of them had an ample share of the spiritual attributes of their mother and grandmother and were honoured with Tablets from 'Abdu'l-Bahá.

Maryam's Writings

Nothing has remained of Maryam's missives to Bahá'u'lláh and His family but some of her poetry descriptive of the anguish of her heart in separation from Bahá'u'lláh has survived. Ishráq-i Khávarí has published a selection in *Raḥíq-i-Makhtúm*, volume 2. The English translation of her published poems in Persian is provided below.

Salutary is the effect of the tune that lovers play
Sparks of love's flame animate the world of clay

***

A lover's anguish none knows but lovers
For lovers live in a world unlike others

Behold the glorious banquet spread by the Lord!
And beggars at His door, forgetting body and soul

How splendid the melody played by the flute player of love
It causes my soul to forget this world and the one above

Would that the burning fire of love, O God!
Increase its consuming power in our heart!

***

O Thou whose dwelling is beyond the most great sea!
Behold my broken heart and the sorrow caused by Thee!

Separation from Thee has so filled my heart with grief
That all celestial beings are saddened by my ordeal

***

One or two cups from the chalice of Bahá if I imbibe
After stagnation and death I would rumble and rise

Among the learned I appear slight, thoughtless and blind
But when it comes to loving, well taught, wise and erudite.[42]

Maryam's Station and Place in History

Maryam is a unique figure in the annals of the Bahá'í Faith. The contents of the Tablets revealed in her honour testify to her lofty station. Although surrounded by Bahá'u'lláh's enemies and tormented by her close relatives, she refused to submit to their dictates and continued to express her love and devotion for the object of her being. She suffered in silence but through her poetry let the world know why she was despised and why she had to sustain unbearable ordeals. Despite strong resistance from within the family, she raised her daughter as a devoted Bahá'í. Maryam is the symbol of resistance to traditional and cultural norms which demanded that women be silent and every aspect of their lives tightly controlled. She was a captive in her home, a stranger in her land, her movements closely monitored and her planned trip abroad cruelly cancelled. But all those efforts proved futile. She continued to express her allegiance to Bahá'u'lláh and conveyed her devotion and love despite the consequences she suffered. Bahá'u'lláh's Tablets revealed in Maryam's honour have immortalized her memory. She will be ever remembered for being a loving and trustworthy person in whom Bahá'u'lláh could confide the details of His sufferings and ordeals, especially those caused by His half brother, Mírzá Yaḥyá Azal. Maryam in turn opened up her heart to Bahá'u'lláh and described the agony of her heart and the lamentation of her soul, which will remain legendary throughout this dispensation and beyond.

12

Munírih <u>Kh</u>ánum (Fáṭimih <u>Kh</u>ánum), the Wife of ‘Abdu’l-Bahá

Family Background

Munírih <u>Kh</u>ánum, named Fáṭimih <u>Kh</u>ánum at birth, was born to Mírzá Muḥammad-‘Alíy-i-Nahrí and his wife Zahrá <u>Kh</u>ánum, both believers in the Báb and Bahá’u’lláh.[1] In her autobiography Munírih <u>Kh</u>ánum writes extensively about her father and his ancestors but says very little about her mother, who remains nameless throughout.

Traditionally, when people spoke or wrote about their lineage, they specified who their fathers and paternal ancestors were. This practice is still current in many parts of the world. Women, on the whole, have suffered from historical invisibility and lack of independent identity. In the early history of the Bahá’í Faith, women generally appear nameless. If identification became necessary or desirable, a woman was introduced as an adjunct to a male member of her family. Munírih <u>Kh</u>ánum’s genealogy follows the usual pattern. We know who her father and paternal ancestors were. Her father was the son of Ḥájí Siyyid Mihdíy-i-Nahrí, son of Siyyid Muḥammad-i-Hindí. Siyyid Muḥammad was not from India but his wife, who has, alas, remained nameless, was. Siyyid Muḥammad was born and raised in Zavárih, a suburb of Iṣfahán. When he reached the age of maturity,[2] he went to India. Since he was a Siyyid, i.e. a descendant of Prophet Muḥammad, a woman of the royal family of India married him. Thus he became known as Hindí. Siyyid Muḥammad remained in India and by virtue of that marriage acquired considerable wealth. The marriage produced two sons. Ḥájí Siyyid Mihdí, the grandfather of Munírih <u>Kh</u>ánum, inherited all of his parents’ wealth. The name and fate of his brother is unknown. Ḥájí Siyyid Mihdí did not stay in India. He migrated to Iraq and built a river bank in the twin holy cities of Karbilá and Najaf and became known as Nahrí. Siyyid Mihdíy-i-Nahrí had several children. One of his sons was Mírzá Muḥammad-‘Alíy-i-Nahrí, Munírih <u>Kh</u>ánum’s father.

Birth and Early Life

Mírzá Muḥammad-'Alí had no children from his first marriage contracted in Karbilá. The name of his first wife is unknown. After she died, Mírzá Muḥammad-'Alí returned to Iran and resided in Iṣfahán, his ancestral home, where he married Zahrá Khánum, identified in *Munírih Khánum* as the sister of Ḥájí Áqá Muḥammad.[3] This marriage likewise produced no children for some time. During the Báb's sojourn in Iṣfahán in 1846, Mírzá Ibráhím-i-Nahrí, the brother of Mírzá Muḥammad-'Alí, hosted a banquet in His honour. During dinner, Mírzá Ibráhím informed the Báb that his brother, Mírzá Muḥammad-'Alí, was childless, and begged Him to 'intercede in his behalf and to grant his heart's desire'.[4] According to Nabíl:

> The Báb took a portion of the food with which He had been served, placed it with His own hands on a platter, and handed it to His host, asking him to take it to Mírzá Muḥammad-'Alí and his wife. 'Let them both partake of this,' He said; 'their wish will be fulfilled.' By virtue of that portion which the Báb had chosen to bestow upon her, the wife of Mírzá Muḥammad-'Alí conceived and in due time gave birth to a girl . . .'[5]

Dr John Esslemont, author of *Bahá'u'lláh and the New Era*, also describes this, based on an account that was supplied to him by 'a Persian historian of the Bahá'í Faith'.[6] The account is about 'Abdu'l-Bahá's marriage but includes the following passage about Munírih Khánum's birth:

> When the Báb was in Iṣfáhán, Mírzá Muḥammad-'Alí had no children, but his wife was longing for a child. On hearing of this, the Báb gave him a portion of his food and told him to share it with his wife. After they had eaten of that food, it soon became apparent that their long-cherished hopes of parenthood were about to be fulfilled, and in due course a daughter was born to them . . .[7]

The child that was born to Mírzá Muḥammad-'Alí and Zahrá Khánum in 1847 was named Fáṭimih. She was known by this name until Bahá'u'lláh bestowed upon her the name Munírih (Luminous) after she arrived in 'Akká in late 1872. From this point on she was called Munírih Khánum, the name by which she is known in the Bahá'í world. In the present account she is referred to as Fáṭimih Khánum until shortly before her marriage to 'Abdu'l-Bahá, when Bahá'u'lláh named her Munírih; thereafter she is referred to as Munírih Khánum.

Fáṭimih Khánum was born at a time when the generality of women everywhere, especially in the Middle East, including Iran, suffered strict restrictions, were deprived of the bounty of education, had no identity of their own, had no voice and played no public role. Being born into an affluent family gave Fáṭimih Khánum more opportunities than those enjoyed by many of her contemporaries. One remarkable advantage she had over others was that she was literate. How she was schooled and at what stage in her life is not known. Judging from her developed writing style and oratory skills, whatever elementary education she had as a child must have been augmented by lessons she learned in real life, lessons that improved her Persian and increased her knowledge of Arabic. She may have known Turkish as well, for she spent 65 years of her long life in what was then known as Palestine, which constituted a part of the Ottoman Empire.

She even wrote her own autobiography which, with the approval of Shoghi Effendi, was published in both Persian and English during her lifetime. As a detailed account of her early life is available from her own pen, attention is focused here on some outstanding episodes from that period.

Fáṭimih Khánum had just come of age when she was engaged to her paternal cousin Káẓim. He was the younger brother of Siyyid Ḥusayn and Siyyid Ḥasan, twin luminaries martyred for their belief in Bahá'u'lláh and titled by Him Sulṭánu'sh-Shuhadá and Maḥbúbu'sh-Shuhadá, the King of Martyrs and Beloved of Martyrs, respectively. Fáṭimih Khánum describes the groom as 'a most dignified, loving, pleasant, and attractive person'.[8]

The engagement period ended and the time for their wedding arrived. The marriage ceremony took place, the reception was elaborate, joy and happiness seemed complete but as soon as the bride and groom entered the bridal chamber, a state of bewilderment seized the groom, causing much anguish and concern. According to Fáṭimih Khánum's autobiography:

> Preparations for the wedding were made with the greatest care. The young man would send me letters full of love and happiness every day. A house was specially built for us, and all manner of means for our well-being and comfort were provided. The wedding night arrived and, according to Persian custom, all our friends and acquaintances accompanied us to the house of the bridegroom's uncle. With much kindness and amiability they sang and played and made merry until four in the morning. After four, my cousin welcomed me formally, and we were taken to the house built for us. The crowd then dispersed, except for a few close relatives who soon left the room also.
>
> I saw that the young man was not speaking at all. He did not try to remove the veil from my face. He did not say: Are you a guest or my cousin or an acquaintance? Where were you?

I tolerated this for some hours and did not utter a single word. Then, I detected several people standing behind the lattice, waiting. I had no option but to say to him: 'What is wrong with you that you say nothing?'

He replied: 'I have such a headache that I cannot speak.' And again he fell silent.

What can I say? No one had ever heard of such a situation. Nobody would believe it, except for the people of Iṣfahán who saw with their own eyes and heard with their own ears. His brothers and all the relatives became sad and depressed. They would not speak to him. And that poor soul was bewildered and dejected also. He swore that: 'I am not responsible for this. I cannot approach her. I will submit to anything except intimacy with my cousin. There is surely a wisdom in this that will become apparent.'

Life continued like this, with him remaining silent and confused. He spoke to no one and befriended none. Then one night, we were alone in the house except for a maidservant. She saw his head bowed down onto his lap, and after a while she approached him and saw that he had yielded up his life. Upon him be the mercy of God, and His favour!

This story is related so that, if in the world of being difficulties and trials encompass a person, then he should know that behind the mystic veil there is a wisdom concealed. In reality, that youth was an escort who delivered me to my true goal and ultimate destination. He it was who joined this drop to the Most Mighty Ocean.

After this incident, I forsook the world and its people. I cut myself off from all earthly attachments. With a heart full of the love of God alone, I occupied myself in reading verses and scripture and associating with the believers.[9]

Journey to the Holy Land

A decade intervened between a marriage that was not meant to be and another that seemed predestined. During these long years of uncertainty and puzzlement, nothing of special significance took place in the life of Fáṭimih Khánum. In the meantime, Bahá'u'lláh and His family had been exiled from Baghdád to Constantinople (Istanbul), from there to Adrianople (Edirne) in present-day Turkey and from there finally to 'Akká in present-day Israel, arriving there in the summer of 1868. After two years' incarceration in the army barracks and several months living in different dwellings, they had moved to the House of Údí Khammár when a directive from Bahá'u'lláh changed the course of Fáṭimih Khánum's life completely. He had sent instructions that she and her brother, Siyyid Yaḥyá, should proceed to the Holy Land. The mere thought of having the bounty of living in the land of her Best Beloved caused her tremendous joy. She could devote the rest of her life to the service of a Cause she loved so dearly and yearned to serve, she thought.

When Fáṭimih Khánum was 11 years old, her father went to Baghdád to visit Bahá’u’lláh. Upon returning to Iṣfahán, he told his wife, ‘It is my intention to take Fáṭimih to the Blessed Household.’[10] However, he did not live long enough to fulfil his intention. Now, after the lapse of 15 years, that intention was being mysteriously fulfilled.

At Bahá’u’lláh’s behest Shaykh Salmán made arrangements for the journey and accompanied Fáṭimih Khánum and her brother to the Holy Land. Although the reason for the directive was not divulged,[11] there are reasons to believe that it did not come as a complete surprise. As far back as the time that Fáṭimih Khánum’s intended marriage to her cousin had abruptly ended with the bridegroom’s death, Khurshíd Bagum, known as Shamsu’ḍ-Ḍuḥá,[12] had predicted that a fate far more glorious awaited Fáṭimih Khánum. Shamsu’ḍ-Ḍuḥá had shared her intuitive feelings with Fáṭimih Khánum after a conversation she had had with a returning pilgrim, named Siyyid Mihdí Dahijí. The following is the record of the circumstances leading to that encounter and the gist of that conversation:

> At about that time, Sayyid Mihdí Dahijí came to Isfahan at the instruction of the Ancient Beauty to proclaim the Faith. All the believers came to meet him, to inquire about news from the Holy Land, and to question him about the Beloved. Among them was Shamsu’ḍ-Ḍuḥá, a relative of the King of the Martyrs and my aunt. She asked: While you were in the holy Presence [of Bahá’u’lláh] did you ever hear Him speak of any girl He may have selected to marry the Master?’
>
> Sayyid Mihdí Dahijí replied: ‘I heard nothing about that. However, one day when the Blessed Beauty was in the outer rooms of the house, as He paced about He said, “Áqá Sayyid Mihdí, last night I had a strange dream. I dreamt that the face of the beautiful girl in Tehran, whose hand in marriage we have asked from our brother Mírzá Ḥasan for the Most Great Branch, gradually became darkened and indistinct. At the same time, another girl appeared with a luminous face and a luminous heart. I have chosen her for the Most Great Branch.” That is all I have heard.’
>
> When my aunt returned home and saw me she said, ‘I swear by the one true God, at the very moment when Áqá Sayyid Mihdí told this story, I felt that – without a shadow of a doubt – you are that girl! You will see!’[13]

Fáṭimih Khánum dismissed the idea vehemently, saying with tears in her eyes, 'May God forgive me! How can I be worthy? I beg you not to say this again and not to mention it to anyone.'[14]

A further indication that the directive did not come as a complete surprise is a Tablet revealed in honour of the King of Martyrs in which Bahá'u'lláh wrote, 'We have accounted you as one of our near ones and kindred.'[15] The King of Martyrs decided not to share this Tablet with the believers until its meaning had become evident. Several months elapsed between the receipt of the Tablet and when Shaykh Salmán arrived in Iṣfahán and informed the King of Martyrs:

> I carry glad tidings and untold bounties. Your cousin, the daughter of the late Mírzá Muḥammad-'Alí, is to accompany me to Mecca with the Muslim pilgrims going there, as though we too are making a pilgrimage to the Kaaba. You must make preparations for this journey until the usual time of Ḥajj, when we can set out and travel by way of Shiraz and Bushihr. However, do not give out this news until two or three days before our departure.[16]

Fáṭimih Khánum and her brother travelled to Shíráz to join the caravan of pilgrims going to Mecca. In Shíráz, Fáṭimih Khánum had the privilege of meeting Khadíjih Bagum, the wife of the Báb, and other female members of the Afnán family. After a sojourn of several days in that city, Fáṭimih Khánum, her brother and Shaykh Salmán started off for Búshihr. After a short stay there, they sailed to Jeddah. That voyage lasted 18 days. In Jeddah they met several Bahá'í pilgrims returning from 'Akká and heard with dismay the news of recent developments culminating in the imprisonment of some of the believers and the imposition of fresh restrictions on the community. From Jeddah they proceeded to Mecca, performed the rites of pilgrimage and returned to Jeddah where a message from Mírzá Áqá Ján, Bahá'u'lláh's amanuensis, awaited them. The message read:

> You are instructed to remain in Jeddah until all the pilgrims return to their homelands. From there, you can then proceed to Alexandria where you should wait until you receive our telegram.[17]

They carried out the instruction to the letter. When all the Muslim pilgrims had returned to their home countries, it became clear that 17 other Bahá'ís were also on their way to attain Bahá'u'lláh's presence. They left together for Alexandria and remained there until a telegram arrived instructing them all to disperse except Fáṭimih Khánum and her company of three (her brother,

Shaykh Salmán and a male servant), who were to proceed directly to ‘Akká aboard an Austrian steamer. They were also instructed not to disembark when they reached the shores of ‘Akká until a man, named ‘Abdu’l-‘Aḥad, met them on board and accompanied them ashore. The steamer reached the waters of ‘Akká half an hour before sunset. ‘Abdu’l-Aḥad did not appear until all the passengers had left and cargo was unloaded. By the time he arrived with his private boat to take the passengers ashore, it was dark and the gangplank had been raised. His late arrival caused great concern and anxiety among the Bahá’í travellers, who thought they may have to go back. However, this is probably how the encounter was planned, to avoid recognition of the group as Bahá’ís by the local population, which would have stirred up trouble under the prevailing unfavourable circumstances. ‘Abdu’l-Aḥad’s arrival relieved the passengers of their anxiety. After his arrival, the gangplank was lowered and the passengers disembarked. On reaching the landing, they were greeted warmly by Áqáy-i-Kalím and Khájih ‘Abbúd and taken to the Khán-i ‘Umdán, also known as the Khán-i ‘Avámíd and Khán-i Jurayní.

The morning after their arrival, the women members of Bahá’u’lláh’s family visited Fáṭimih Khánum in the house of Áqáy-i-Kalím and his wife, and together they attained the presence of Bahá’u’lláh. This was the visit Fáṭimih Khánum had awaited for so long and for which she had undertaken an arduous journey to attain. Bahá’u’lláh’s first words to her were: ‘We have received you into this prison at a time when the prison door is closed to all the believers, so that the power of God may become clear and evident to all.’[18]

Fáṭimih Khánum remained in the house of Áqáy-i-Kalím and his wife for five months while preparations were being made for her marriage to ‘Abdu’l-Bahá. During this time she had the honour of attaining Bahá’u’lláh’s presence several times. She also received through Áqáy-i-Kalím messages showing His infinite bounties and, sometimes, a gift. One day ‘Aqáy-i-Kalím returned from His visit to Bahá’u’lláh and, addressing Fáṭimih Khánum, said, ‘I have brought you a wonderful gift. You have been renamed Munírih (Luminous) by Him.’[19] Upon hearing this, she immediately remembered Bahá’u’lláh’s dream that Siyyid Mihdí Dahijí had related to Shamsu’ḍ-Ḍuḥá in Iṣfahán sometime earlier.

Marriage

Before describing the circumstances leading to ‘Abdu’l-Bahá’s marriage to Munírih Khánum, it is important to mention an episode in His life that was not unlike that experienced by Fáṭimih Khánum. As extraordinary as it may appear, ‘Abdu’l-Bahá, too, was to marry his paternal cousin. Her name was <u>Sh</u>ahrbánú <u>Kh</u>ánum and her father was Mírzá Muḥammad-Ḥasan, Bahá'u'lláh's half brother. That marriage did not materialize, despite the efforts that were made. Below are the details.

While in Adrianople, Bahá'u'lláh instructed His brother Áqáy-i-Kalím to write to Mullá Zaynu'l-'Ábidín, their paternal uncle, to make arrangements for the relocation of <u>Sh</u>ahrbánú <u>Kh</u>ánum from Tákur to Adrianople via Ṭihrán and Ba<u>gh</u>dád. He emphasized that the move was to be made without delay. Bahá'u'lláh's instructions were conveyed to Mullá Zaynu'l-'Ábidín, who complied and arranged for <u>Sh</u>ahrbánú <u>Kh</u>ánum's travel to Ṭihrán. Since <u>Sh</u>ahrbanú <u>Kh</u>ánum's father had passed away sometime earlier, the door was wide open for senior members of the family to interfere with her affairs. When she arrived in Ṭihrán, one of Bahá'u'lláh's half sisters, under the guise of providing loving advice and guidance, worked to frustrate the plan of transferring <u>Sh</u>ahrbánú <u>Kh</u>ánum to Adrianople. To achieve her malicious purpose, she started whispering in <u>Sh</u>ahrbánú <u>Kh</u>ánum's ears the advantages, as she perceived them, of marrying a person of means and prominence in Ṭihrán. What <u>Sh</u>ahrbánu <u>Kh</u>ánum did not know was that her aunt was a supporter of Mírzá Yaḥyá Azal and had an ulterior motive. The aunt secured the assistance of her brother Mírzá Riḍá Qulí, who had just returned from exile, to dissuade <u>Sh</u>ahrbánú <u>Kh</u>ánum from leaving Iran. Instead, arrangements were made for her to marry 'Alí <u>Kh</u>án, son of the prime minister of Iran, who was related to <u>Sh</u>ahrbánú <u>Kh</u>ánum through his mother. Referring to this treacherous act, 'Abdu'l-Bahá says:

> We were in Adrianople when the great Aunt,[20] who favoured Yaḥyá, did her utmost to please him. She sent that poor soul [<u>Sh</u>ahrbánú <u>Kh</u>ánum] to the home of the son of the prime minister, Mírzá 'Alí <u>Kh</u>án. It has been reported that she went with tearful eyes and trembling. Within a short span of time she contracted tuberculosis and died of consumption. God's mercy be upon her.[21]

Bahá'u'lláh refers to this episode in *Epistle to the Son of the Wolf*:

> ... Our late brother Mírzá Muḥammad-Ḥasan's daughter – upon him be the glory of God and His peace and His mercy – who had been betrothed to the Most Great Branch ('Abdu'l-Bahá) was taken by the sister of this Wronged One from Núr to her own house, and from there sent unto another place ... How strange that Our sister should have taken her to her own house, and then arranged for her to be sent elsewhere! ... None of Our loved ones, whether in these regions or in that country, could believe Our sister capable of an act so contrary to decency, affection and friend-

ship . . . It must be evident, therefore, how intense was the grief which this act inflicted upon this Wronged One. Later on, she threw in her lot with Mírzá Yaḥyá.[22]

Immediately after the marriage took place, Shahrbánú Khánum realized the gravity of the mistake she had made in marrying 'Alí Khán. She found herself trapped with no glimmer of hope for deliverance. She felt ashamed and remorseful. She had bartered the paradise of being in the land of her Beloved with the hell of living with a man she did not love. She prayed God to hasten her end, relieve her from suffering and the guilt she felt in her heart. She died of tuberculosis a few months later. H.M. Balyuzi records:

> Bahá'u'lláh intended to give His niece, Shahr-Bánú Khánum, the daughter of Mírzá Muḥammad-Ḥasan, in marriage to His eldest son. That was also the great hope of Mírzá Muḥammad-Ḥasan, who hurried to Baghdád and pleaded with Bahá'u'lláh to bring about this union. But he passed away before the Most Great Branch came of age. And when Bahá'u'lláh sent Áqá Muḥammad-Javád-i-Kashání (the father of Áqá Ḥusayn-i-Ashchí) with a ring and a cashmere shawl (as was the custom of the day) to Ṭihrán, to ask the hand of Shahr-Bánú Khánum for 'Abbás, the Most Great Branch, both Sháh-Sulṭán Khánum (known as Khánum Buzurg – the Great Lady), His half-sister who eventually sided with Mírzá Yaḥyá, and His half brother, Ḥájí Mírzá Riḍá-Qulí, who after the death of Mírzá Muḥammad-Ḥasan stood as father to Shahr-Bánú, refused to allow her to go to Íráq to be wedded to the Most Great Branch. She was eventually married to Mírzá 'Alí Khán, a son of the Grand Vizier, Mírzá Áqá Khán. As her brother, Mírzá Faḍlu'lláh, the Niẓámu'l-Mamálik, a devout follower of Bahá'u'lláh, has recorded, Shahr-Bánú Khánum was never reconciled to this marriage forced upon her by her aunt and uncle and pined all the rest of her young life, until consumption took her away.[23]

Shahrbánú Khánum's half brother, Mírzá Faḍlu'lláh, the Niẓámu'l-Mamálik, has recorded in his memoirs the tale of her tragic end:

> In the year 83 or 84 [*circa* 1866–7], my half sister, Shahrbánú Khánum, a devoted and virtuous woman known for her uprightness, who was betrothed to 'Abdu'l-Bahá, may my life be a sacrifice for His immaculate remains, was called to the Holy Land . . . My sister immediately obeyed the instructions and despite the severe winter left in the company of our paternal uncles via Láríján. Upon arrival in Ṭihrán, Ḥájíyih Khánum, the great Aunt, and Ḥájí Mírzá Yaḥyá Khán, my sister's maternal uncle,

became aware of the situation, forced her to change her plan, arranged for her to marry Mírzá 'Alí Khán, and prevented her from attaining her heart's desire. Mírzá Riḍá Qulí, our uncle, had during that year been imprisoned for a month and then exiled to Qum for the name [Bahá'í] and although he had just returned to Ṭihrán, he had no choice but to agree . . .

One day I was sitting with my sister in the veranda [of her house]. She was caressing me when Mírzá 'Alí Khán entered the courtyard in the company of his uncle, Mírzá Faḍlu'lláh, the minister of war. As they were walking, my sister looked at him with sad eyes, then addressed me with these heartbreaking words: 'O *dadash*! Since you are an innocent child, your prayers are answered. I will pray and you say *amin*.' She then raised her hands and said: 'O God, I beseech Thee by those who are nigh unto Thy Court to hasten the end of Shahrbánú's life that she may be freed from this dishonour . . . Two months later she winged her flight to the eternal realm.[24]

The mystery of Shahrbánú Khánum's sufferings and death as well as the death of Káẓim, who died immediately after his marriage to Fáṭimih Khánum, remains in the treasury of God's knowledge. What is certain is that neither 'Abdu'l-Bahá's intended marriage to His cousin, nor Fáṭimih Khánum's marriage to her cousin, despite the efforts that were made towards their realization, actually materialized. Would it be fair then to deny that those tragic events were in a mysterious way linked to the realization of 'Abdu'l-Bahá's marriage to Fáṭimih Khánum?

Regarding the choice of Fáṭimih Khánum to become 'Abdu'l-Bahá's wife, Dr Esslemont writes:

> During the youth of 'Abdu'l-Bahá the question of a suitable marriage for Him was naturally one of great interest to the believers, and many people came forward, wishing to have this crown of honour for their own family. For a long time, however, 'Abdu'l-Bahá showed no inclination for marriage, and no one understood the wisdom of this. Afterwards it became known that there was a girl who was destined to become the wife of 'Abdu'l-Bahá, one whose birth came about through the Blessing which the Báb gave to her parents in Iṣfáhán.[25]

As mentioned earlier, the marriage of 'Abdu'l-Bahá and Munírih Khánum took place five months after her arrival in the Holy Land. She arrived in 'Akká during the final months of 1872 and the marriage took place on 8 March 1873. The exact date has been given by her in a poem she composed in honour of the occasion:

> The seventh night of the fasting month became the date of this delight.[26]
> Rise up to your feet, O Friends, for the most great dawn has arrived.[27]

Munírih Khánum has left us with her own description of her wedding. She says that on that night she wore a white dress which had been given to her by the Most Exalted Leaf, ʻAbdu'l-Bahá's mother. At about three hours after sunset Bahá'u'lláh summoned her. She attained His presence in the company of Ḥaḍrat-i-Khánum, probably a reference to Bahá'íyyih Khánum, ʻAbdu'l-Bahá's sister. Seated under a mosquito net, Bahá'u'lláh addressed Munírih Khánum:

> You have come! You are welcome! O My Leaf and My handmaiden! Verily, we chose thee and accept thee to serve my Most Great Branch, and this is by my grace, which is not equalled by all the treasures of earth and heaven . . .
>
> How many were the girls in Baghdád and Adrianople, and in this Most Great Prison who hoped to attain to this bounty, and whose hopes were not fulfilled. You must be thankful for this most great bestowal and great favour.[28]

After Munírih Khánum left Bahá'u'lláh's presence, she went to the room where she saw the Most Great Branch 'in utmost grace, bounty, and majesty'. Speaking of the feelings of joy and rapture surging within her heart, she says: 'How blessed and exalted was that time! How joyous that hour in that room!'[29]

After about an hour, ʻAbdu'l-Bahá's mother, the wife of Áqáy-i-Kalím, the wife of Khájih ʻAbbúd and her daughters, as well as other female members of Bahá'u'lláh's family joined the couple in their room. Munírih Khánum says:

> The mother of Mírzá Muḥammad ʻAlí had brought Tablets used especially for celebrating holy days and festive occasions. She handed me the Tablet that begins: 'The gates of paradise are opened and the celestial youth hath appeared' and told me to recite it. Without further ceremony, I took it and intoned it in a loud and melodious voice. From then on, whenever the wife of Khájih ʻAbbúd saw me she would say: 'I shall never forget that night and that meeting; the sweetness of your voice still rings in my ears. No bride had ever chanted so at her own wedding![30]

Years later, when speaking to Lady Blomfield, the author of *The Chosen Highway*, about her marriage to ʻAbdu'l-Bahá, Munírih Khánum said:

> Oh the spiritual happiness which enfolded us! It cannot be described in earthly words.
>
> The chanting ended, the guests left us. I was the wife of my Beloved. How wonderful and noble He was in His beauty. I adored Him. I recognized His greatness, and thanked God for bringing me to Him.
>
> It is impossible to put into words the delight of being with the Master; I seemed to be in a glorious realm of sacred happiness whilst in His company.
>
> You have known Him in His later years, but then, in the youth of His beauty and manly vigour, with His unfailing love, His kindness, His cheerfulness, His sense of humour, His untiring consideration for everybody, He was marvellous, without equal, surely in all the earth!
>
> At the wedding there was no cake, only cups of tea; there were no decorations, and no choir, but the blessing of Jamál-i-Mubárak; the glory and beauty of love and happiness were beyond and above all luxury and ceremony and circumstance.[31]

The bridal chamber was the room connecting the eastern part of the house of 'Abbúd, known as the house of Údí Khammár, to the western part of that house.

The faithful followers of Bahá'u'lláh residing in the Holy Land were ecstatic and jubilant. In a poem composed for the occasion, Nabíl expresses the feelings of joy and happiness that permeated the atmosphere and the inner beings of the believers on that joyous night. Here is the English translation of the first several lines:

> Rejoice, O lovers, for the world is a garden of roses tonight
> Adorned with trees and flowers is lovers' gathering tonight
>
> All created things sing love songs, all atoms of the world dance
> You, too, O heart, be joyous, for it is joy upon joy tonight
>
> The time is joyous and happy, the earth is the Heaven's envy
> For there are heaps and heaps of flowers in the feast tonight
>
> Behold, it's the time of wedding, and it's time for kissing
> The eyes of the people of Bahá shine brightly this night
>
> Happiness belongs to us, and happy is the Most Great Branch
> All men and women dance and stamp their feet this night.[32]

From Marriage to ‘Abdu’l-Bahá to Bahá’u’lláh’s Ascension (1873–92)

Munírih Khánum has not written anything about the long years she was married to ‘Abdu’l-Bahá and that for very good reason. Anything she would have written would have encroached not only on the life of ‘Abdu’l-Bahá but also on the private life of other members of the Holy Family whose deeds and words had a bearing on the progress of the fast-developing Faith whose Centre of the Covenant was the Most Great Branch. What follows is based on glimpses obtained from the writings revealed in her honour and on deductions made from available historical information.

Munírih Khánum was married to ‘Abdu’l-Bahá for almost half a century. She was fully aware of the honour bestowed upon her and appreciated beyond measure the blessings and responsibilities the marriage entailed. Highly significant events occurred during the long years of her marriage to ‘Abdu’l-Bahá, 29 of which He was the Centre of His father’s Covenant, the authorized Interpreter of His writings, and the appointed head of the worldwide Bahá’í community.

Munírih Khánum’s marriage to ‘Abdu’l-Bahá took place about four and a half years after Bahá’u’lláh and His family had arrived in ‘Akká, and about two and a half years after they had left the army barracks, the original dwelling assigned to them, and had taken up residence inside the fortress city. ‘Abdu’l-Bahá and Munírih Khánum had been married for over four years when Bahá’u’lláh left the walled city and took up residence in the Mansion of Mazra‘ih situated to the north of ‘Akká. That move entailed additional responsibilities for ‘Abdu’l-Bahá who, together with His family, remained in ‘Akká and continued to live in the house of ‘Abbúd in close proximity to the dwellings of other exiles and to the pilgrims who travelled to the Holy Land to attain the presence of Bahá’u’lláh. With ‘Abdu’l-Bahá were, in addition to Munírih Khánum, His mother, Ásíyih Khánum, and sister, Bahá’íyyih Khánum. By the time Bahá’u’lláh left the house of ‘Abbúd, ‘Abdu’l-Bahá and Munírih Khánum may have had their first two children. Gradually, other believers, such as members of Munírih Khánum’s family, were allowed to come to the Holy Land. They seem to have initially lived in or around the house of ‘Abbúd. Although details are not available, it stands to reason by virtue of ‘Abdu’l-Bahá’s position and responsibilities that His residence in ‘Akká was the centre of activity for the local Bahá’í community, especially during Bahá’u’lláh’s visit to ‘Abdu’l-Bahá and His family, which at times lasted several days.

In addition to the responsibilities she had as ‘Abdu’l-Bahá’s wife, Munírih Khánum was also preoccupied with the arduous task of bearing and raising children in an inhospitable place with an unfavourable climate. Altogether she bore eight children, four of which died in infancy or childhood: Mírzá

Mihdí, Rúḥangíz, Fu'ádíyyih and Ḥusayn Effendi, who lived for several years. All accounts indicate that Ḥusayn Effendi was a very sweet child and very much loved by all. Information about his life is scanty. Bahá'u'lláh's Tablets revealed in his honour and after his death provide valuable insights. Bahá'u'lláh's love for His grandson and attachment to him are evident from the contents of His Tablets. for example:

> Ḥusayn Effendi, upon him be God's peace and favours!
>
> He is God! Exalted is the station of His wisdom and utterance. Praised be God alone, and salutation be upon the One after whom there is no prophet.
>
> O Ḥusayn Effendi! Upon thee be God's peace and His favour. Yesterday We were in Junaynih.[33] Some pomegranate was found and sent. We instructed Muṣṭafá, should he find something else in the city, to procure it and send it with the pomegranate. A small sum of money was also sent.
>
> We greet the chaste one, thy mother,[34] Ḍíyá Khánum,[35] Khánum Effendi, Jamálíyyih, Ḥabíbih, Jání Bagum, and those residing in the House. We commit them to God's care, glorified is His grandeur.
>
> Remembrance, praise and salutation be upon all of you and also His mercy and blessings.[36]

In another Tablet, signed by Khádimu'lláh ('Servant in attendance') and revealed at a time when Munírih Khánum was in Haifa together with Ḥusayn Effendi and Ḍíyá'íyyih Khánum, we read:

> Write to Ḥusayn Effendi to pray for *maṭar* [rain], that God may send rain. Apparently, lack of rain hath become a barrier and kept thee from the Source. God willing, rain will come, roads will be adorned and closeness attained.[37] *Tabáshá* in 'Akká may not be less than *tabásha* in Haifa.[38] We beseech God to protect thee, aid thee, confirm thee, render thee successful and bring thee close to Him. He is the Mighty and Powerful. He is the Answerer of prayers . . .
>
> Day and night We beseech God, glorified be His grandeur, to send to this servant [Khádimu'lláh] that bough of the Blessed Tree, His honour the solace of the world Áqáy-i Ḥusayn Effendi, upon him be peace from the All-Merciful, that the eyes of the longing souls may be brightened and the hearts of the yearning ones may be gladdened and assured. One cannot wish better than this from an offspring. May the world be ever green and verdant through his name, and may humanity rejoice and be enamoured of his love.
>
> The beauty of the world is evident and manifest. However, its adorn-

ments are trees, and trees are adorned with leaves. Therefore, the exalted leaf, the fruit of the Tree, her honour Ḍíyá'íyyih Khánum, upon her be God's Glory, serving the light of eternity, His Highness Ḥusayn Effendi, upon him be a thousand glories and a thousand praises, is engaged in looking after essential affairs. Most certainly, he needs such a companion, and that is the Leaf of the Beauteous Tree, exalted above praise . . .

The contents of the above Tablets make it clear that Ḍíyá'íyyih Khánum was older than Ḥusayn Effendi and that for some time they were the only surviving children of 'Abdu'l-Bahá and Munírih Khánum. The other three children who died in infancy had probably been born and passed away by then.

The dates of the births and deaths of the children who died in infancy and childhood are not available. Therefore, it is not possible to know in exactly what order they were born and at what ages they died. However, from certain indications in the writings inference may be made that Mírzá Mihdí was 'Abdu'l-Bahá and Munírih Khánum's firstborn and the first to die in childhood. In a Tablet addressed to 'Abdu'l-Bahá, Bahá'u'lláh mentions Mírzá Mihdí, for whom He had sent a piece of Syrian silk. Since this Tablet bears the name of none of Mírzá Mihdí's siblings, and since no mention of him appears in the Tablets that were revealed in honour of his siblings later, it is assumed that Mírzá Mihdí was the eldest and for a while the only child. Ḍíyá'íyyih Khánum may have been born after Mírzá Mihdí, followed by Fu'ádíyyih, whose name also appears in a Tablet revealed by Bahá'u'lláh conferring upon her that name. By the time Fu'ádíyyih was born, it seems that Mírzá Mihdí had passed away. Fu'ádíyyih died before Ḥusayn Effendi was born. Rúhangíz may have died in early infancy, for almost no information is available about her. Unlike Ḥusayn Effendi who lived to be several years old, Mírzá Mihdí and Fu'ádíyyih died in early childhood.

The death of the children caused Munírih Khánum immense grief. The following Tablet was revealed after the death of one of the daughters:

> O Munírih! He verily fulfilleth what hath been promised in the Book. Let nothing sadden thee. She verily ascended to God and returned to Him just as she had appeared from Him. She hath returned, rested, rejoiced and is overjoyed. Verily, thy Lord is the All-Knowing, the All-Informed.[39]

Judging from the contents of one of Bahá'u'lláh's Tablets revealed in honour of Munírih Khánum, she was most affected by the death of Ḥusayn Effendi. When he passed away, Munírih Khánum was beside herself with grief. The Tablet reveals what a special child Ḥusayn Effendi had been and how deeply his death affected all, especially his mother:

He is the Most Exalted, the Most Great!

No refuge is there for the servants from God's absolute decree and His precise command. 'Wherever ye are, death will find you out, even if ye are in towers built up strong and high!'[40] When, at the bidding of the Eternal One, the irresistible decree strikes, it is incumbent upon all to submit to it and to be content. Although outwardly separation consumeth the heart, yet it is the cause of reunion and return and, for some children, it is a means of protection. To none are known the exigencies of divine wisdom. The effect of this ascension is in the grasp of God's knowledge, and to divulge it is not permissible. Should We remove the veil from this station, the immense sorrow will be transmuted to great joy, and innumerable souls would take their flight. 'Wealth and sons are allurements of the life of this world: But things that endure, good deeds, are best in the sight of thy Lord, as rewards, and best as (the foundation for) hopes.'[41]

But this son was and continues to be the adornment of the highest Heaven. At this very moment, through God's bounty and divine mercy, We behold Our '*tabáshá*' engaged in '*tamáshá*' in the highest paradise.[42]

O ye members of My Household! Praised be God that ye all believe in and confess this blessed word which is like unto a mighty fortress: 'He is praised for what He doth and obeyed in His command.' Although separation and remoteness after union, togetherness and attachment cause joy and happiness to depart, it hath been and will continue to be powerless to erase that word from the tablet of the heart. He is the Most Patient. He hath commanded them that are nigh unto Him to observe true patience. We beseech God to protect you and to draw you near to Him at all times. He, verily, is the All-Possessing, the Most Exalted.[43]

In a Tablet revealed at a time when Munírih Khánum's mother, brother and sister were in the Holy Land, Bahá'u'lláh mentions all of them, as well as her surviving children:

He is the Most Generous!

God beareth witness that verily there is no God but Him. He guideth to His straight path whomsoever He willeth.

O Munírih! The Lord of humankind maketh mention of thee and giveth thee the glad-tidings of God's mercy and His bounty. Well is it with thee and blessed art thou and [thy son], thy daughters, thy mother, sister and brother who have attained that which hath been willed by God, the Lord of all worlds . . .[44]

The four surviving children of 'Abdu'l-Bahá and Munírih Khánum were, in order of their age: Ḍíyá'íyyih Khánum, Ṭúbá Khánum, Rúḥá Khánum and Munavvar Khánum.

Life in 'Akká during the last decades of the 19th century was arduous. The place was desolate, its climate unfavourable, living conditions primitive and provisions scarce. Under the best circumstances life was hazardous. For the exiles it was much worse. The lives of their children were threatened and the health of the adults adversely affected. 'Abdu'l-Bahá Himself had health problems which forced Him to go to Beirut for the change of climate that was deemed necessary for His recovery. It was on the occasion of that trip that Bahá'u'lláh revealed the well-known Tablet of the Land of Bá in honour of 'Abdu'l-Bahá.[45] While in Beirut, 'Abdu'l-Bahá and Munírih Khánum were in correspondence. In response to one of her letters, 'Abdu'l-Bahá wrote:

> The letter adorned with the True One's mention hath been received.
>
> Praised be God that under divine favours ye are the recipients of the greatest of all bounties.
>
> From the day of arrival in Beirut until now the condition of my health hath improved day by day until at present no trace of illness remaineth. God willing, soon we shall attain that which ye have attained.
>
> I have explained the situation in detail in the letter I sent to His Highness the Greater Branch. Therefore, no need is there to repeat the same in this letter. Thou shalt certainly be informed. Al-Bahá be upon thee and peace.[46]

Another Tablet addressed to Munírih Khánum, written probably during the same journey, reveals the depth of 'Abdu'l-Bahá's loving care and consideration for His mother and sister Bahá'íyyih Khánum:

> Since I intend to return home, therefore, I do not write in detail. Praised be God that we are all safe and secure in the shelter of divine care and protection. There is no sorrow or sadness save in remoteness from His Holy Court. God be praised, I have recovered from My cold. Since My intention is to hasten home, the response to Her Highness, the Mother, as well as to Khánum [Bahá'íyyih Khánum, the Greatest Holy Leaf] will either be written in detail or reported at length in person when I see them. My heart is not happy and content with such a brief response and I have not had the opportunity to write in detail. I hope from divine bounty that under His infinite loving care and favour all will be happy and protected.[47]

During Bahá'u'lláh's lifetime there were times when 'Abdu'l-Bahá had to journey to places in the Holy Land, such as Haifa and Tiberias. The trips sometimes lasted several days and 'Abdu'l-Bahá and Munírih Khánum often communicated with each other while 'Abdu'l-Bahá was away. The following Tablet was revealed in response to a letter He received while in Haifa. It must have been before 1886, for He mentions His mother in the Tablet:

> He is God! O Handmaid of God! . . . All that was written hath become known and been understood. Praised be God, through the bounty and grace of the Beloved of the world, physical wellness is attained in every respect. The weather in Haifa is not bad and there is no trouble except that the Muftí is bothersome. However, he is leaving today or tomorrow.
>
> On behalf of this Servant, make the dust beneath the Blessed Feet the kohl of the true sight.
>
> Convey My utmost eagerness to Her Highness, the Mother, and Her Highness, the Sister, and write in detail about the children.[48]

During His father's lifetime 'Abdu'l-Bahá made another trip either to Beirut or to another place that caused Him to be away from home. In a Tablet to Munírih Khánum in response to her letter, He speaks of Bahá'u'lláh's visit to the 'House in the Most Great Prison', the house of 'Abbúd. The Tablet must have been revealed after the passing of Ásíyih Khánum, i.e. after 1886, for there is no mention of her in it. However, it was written before the passing of Ḥusayn Effendi, who is mentioned in the Tablet. 'Abdu'l-Bahá voices concern that during the heat of the summer Bahá'u'lláh, who was by then living in the Mansion of Bahjí, would be uncomfortable and inconvenienced in the house in 'Akká.

> He is God! Thy perspicuous letter hath arrived. Whatsoever thou didst write hath become known and all that was concealed in the innermost parts of the sentences became manifest. The return of the Blessed Countenance caused utmost anxiety and concern. What will happen to His Blessed Body during the intense heat in that narrow house? Undoubtedly, He would be very much affected by it. Were it during the winter, it would have been easier. But in the summer, in an inadequate place and in the Most Great Prison! I swear by the Ancient Beauty that if tears of blood were shed and hearts were consumed, it would not suffice. And this is all from the greatness of His ancient endurance. Regarding my noble sister, I long for her presence with all My soul, My heart, My spirit and Mine inner being. Day and night she is remembered in Mine inmost thoughts

and feelings. I can say nothing concerning My separation from her, for whatever I write my tears will certainly wash it away.

Ḍíyá Khánum, Rúḥá, and Ṭúbá and all members of the Household, and the family of Sulṭánu'sh-Shuhadá and the members of that household as well as other handmaids of God are all in My thoughts and I am engaged in remembering them. Be certain and never doubt it . . .

Since I have written in detail to Khádim[49] regarding My return, I did not repeat the same in this letter.

Take Ḥusayn Effendi to the Holy Court and let him, on My behalf, prostrate himself at the Blessed Threshold . . .

My physical health, praised be God, is good.[50]

At times 'Abdu'l-Bahá's family visited Haifa, where some members of Munírih Khánum's family had settled, and stayed there for a length of time. The following Tablet was revealed during one such visit:

He is the One desired!

. . . Several days ago we were going to come to Haifa but legal and religious impediments presented themselves . . . God willing, we will come but know not when.

Rúḥá hath arrived. She is somewhat thinner. The observation is that if others are like her, the change of place hath yielded no result. Ḥusayn Effendi is, God willing, radiantly well. Do write in detail about him and others at all times.

It hath been heard that the condition of the esteemed and honourable mother is the same as before.[51] This is the cause of sorrow. We hope that by the bounty and favour of the One True God her condition will improve . . .[52]

Another place visited by 'Abdu'l-Bahá's family was Yarkih, a summer resort not far from 'Akká. In a Tablet addressed to Munírih Khánum, 'Abdu'l-Bahá says:

. . . when I came to 'Akká, it was prescribed for me to go to the sea every day and this was not possible in Yarkih. Moreover, I had a lot of work. Now that I have stopped going to the sea and there is less work, I will go to Mazra'ih tonight and, God willing, I will come there in the next few days. My condition, God be praised and through the grace of the Ancient Beauty, is good. Be assured . . .[53]

Bahá'u'lláh's Ascension and Its Aftermath

During her long years of marriage to 'Abdu'l-Bahá, Munírih Khánum witnessed many developments that shaped the destiny of the newly born Bahá'í world community. The most significant event with far-reaching consequences was Bahá'u'lláh's ascension. Ṭúbá Khánum, one of 'Abdu'l-Bahá and Munírih Khánum's daughters, was 12 years old at the time. Many years later she gave to Lady Blomfield an account, as she remembered, of the happenings immediately before and after that catastrophic event:

> And now a very sad day dawned for us all.
>
> My mother, my Aunt Khánum, my three sisters, and I lived in the bigger house at 'Akká with our beloved Father; Bahá'u'lláh lived at Bahjí . . .
>
> On this day of sadness a servant rode in from Bahjí with a Tablet for the Master from Bahá'u'lláh: 'I am not well, come to Me and bring Khánum.'
>
> The servant, having brought horses for them, my Father and my aunt set off immediately for Bahjí; we children stayed at home with my mother, full of anxiety. Each day the news came that our adored Bahá'u'lláh's fever had not abated. He had a kind of malaria.
>
> After five days we all went to Bahjí; we were very distressed that the illness had become serious . . .
>
> Bahá'u'lláh asked for us, the ladies and children to go to Him. He told us that He had left in His Will directions for our future guidance; that the Greatest Branch, 'Abbás Effendi, would arrange everything for the family, the friends, and the Cause . . .
>
> On the nineteenth day of His illness He left us at dawn.
>
> Immediately a horseman galloped into 'Akká to carry the news to the Muftí . . .
>
> Muslim friends, the Muftí, mullás, Governor and officials, Christian priests, Latin and Greek, Druses from Abú-Sinán, and surrounding villages, and many other friends gathered together in great numbers in honour of the Beloved One . . .
>
> Many of the guests encamped under the trees round the Palace of Bahjí, where more than five hundred were entertained for nine days.
>
> This hospitality entailed much trouble on the Master, Who made all the arrangements and superintended every detail; money also was given by Him on each of the nine days to the poor . . .[54]

Regarding the unsealing of Bahá'u'lláh's Book of the Covenant and the reaction that close members of Bahá'u'lláh's family and the assembled friends showed to it, she says:

> The Master sent to ‘Akká for the box in which the Will of Bahá’u’lláh had been locked up for two years. On the ninth day after the passing of Bahá’u’lláh the Will was read by Mírzá Majdi’d-Dín to all the men friends, in the presence of the Master.
>
> The friends showed great joy that their beloved Master had been appointed by Jamál-i-Mubárak to be their Protector, their Leader, their Guide.
>
> The Master then came to see us, the ladies of the household. We called together the servitors, and, when we were all assembled, the Will was read to us by Majdi’d-Dín, at the request of the Master.
>
> The mother of Muḥammad-‘Alí expressed herself, at that time, as being pleased at the appointment of the eldest son.[55]

However, there were signs of disappointment and displeasure that Mírzá Muḥammad-‘Alí had no immediate role to play in leading the Bahá’í community and guiding the affairs of the friends. ‘Abdu’l-Bahá’s appointment as the immediate successor of Bahá’u’lláh was contrary to Mírzá Muḥammad-‘Alí’s expectation and that of his siblings, their mother and other members of the family who sided with him. Their frustration was so intense that it could not be contained. They first showed their anger by turning on ‘Abdu’l-Bahá’s family, making it clear that they were not welcome at Bahjí. This was at a time when there was an outbreak of cholera in ‘Akká and everyone had fled the town. Ṭúbá Khánum says:

> Whilst we were all at Bahjí there was a serious outbreak of cholera in the town of ‘Akká. Now it was the custom that members of the family should remain in the house of the departed one for a period of forty days. But the mother of Muḥammad-‘Alí, and her other sons, showed us by many discourtesies that they did not wish us to remain.
>
> Accordingly, in spite of the raging cholera, we all, Sarkár-i-Áqá, Khánum, my mother, my sisters, and I, left Bahjí and returned to our house at ‘Akká, trusting in the protection of God . . .
>
> After bringing us back to ‘Akká, the Master went back to the shrine at Bahjí, returning to us next day very sad; the two younger half brothers were with Him. My mother asked them to stay and help Sarkár-i-Áqá with the numberless matters needing to be done. They refused, saying that they were too busy. There was no man of the family to assist our beloved Father in all the work of that difficult time.[56]

Bahá’u’lláh’s ascension caused the malicious intentions of the half brothers of ‘Abdu’l-Bahá and their supporters to become blatantly clear. The storm of Covenant-breaking gathered momentum rapidly and uprooted the shaky foundation of the faith of those who opposed Bahá'u'lláh's appointed successor and authorized Interpreter of His writings. After Bahá'íyyih Khánum, Munírih Khánum was the staunchest supporter of 'Abdu'l-Bahá among the members of His family. She stood firmly by 'Abdu'l-Bahá and saw Him emerge resplendent against the combined formidable internal and external forces leagued together to undermine and discredit Him. She was in her mid-forties when 'Abdu'l-Bahá succeeded Bahá'u'lláh as the Centre of His Covenant. As busy as 'Abdu'l-Bahá was during Bahá'u'lláh's ministry dealing with the authorities, looking after the day-to-day work of the exiled community and looking after the needs of His family, to that was now added responsibility for the affairs of the worldwide Bahá'í community involving the taking of all necessary steps to deal with internal crisis and preserving the unity of Bahá'u'lláh's followers.

Bent under the heavy weight of grief occasioned by Bahá'u'lláh's ascension and dismayed by the misdeeds of the faithless members of His family, 'Abdu'l-Bahá withdrew to Tiberias. The distance between 'Akká and Tiberias is about fifty kilometres and is covered today by car in less than an hour. But in those days by mule, which was the general means of transportation, it probably took more than half a day. 'Abdu'l-Bahá's absence from 'Akká made life for the members of His family, already hard pressed by the actions of His half brothers and their supporters, even harder. The Tablets of 'Abdu'l-Bahá revealed during that time in honour of members of His family, especially Munírih Khánum, provide a glimpse of what they endured. In a Tablet addressed to her, 'Abdu'l-Bahá speaks of His condition, the spiritual atmosphere of the area, the nature of the intrigues employed by people of malice, and the fact that His opponents were using Munírih Khánum as a pretext to cause Him harm. He also discloses the reason for His withdrawal from 'Akká:

> O thou sorrowful Leaf! Be not sad and grieve not. That is the way the world hath been since its beginning. This is God's way. No change and variation wilt thou ever find in God's way.[57] It is exactly the same.
>
> Although this Servant is outwardly alone, the breezes of the Kingdom of Abhá are wafting and the bounties of the Blessed Beauty descending. The remembrance of His Countenance is My companion and from all else I have severed My hope.
>
> In this desert, for many years, His Holiness Christ uttered: 'Here am I, O My God, here am I', and in this wilderness for several centuries the Prophets and the chosen ones associated together. The fragrance of their remembrance hath perfumed the mountains and the field, and their quickening breezes have imbued the desert and the sea with new life. Should

the sense of hearing be refined, it would at this very moment hear those lamentations and supplications, and would perceive those melodies with the inner ear.

Convey my loving greetings to Her Highness the Greatest Holy Leaf, the Abhá holy fruit; also to the blessed Leaf Ḍíyá Khánum, Ṭúbá Khánum, and Munavvar Khánum;[58] the mother of Áqá Mírzá Jalál,[59] Gawhar Bagum,[60] Raḍíyyih Bagum,[61] and other leaves and handmaids of God, upon them be Bahá'u'lláhu'l-Abhá.[62]

Praised be God, I am feeling better, for I am busy with prayers and supplications and weary of all else.

Let not the whisperings of people cause thee grief, and be not saddened by some events. I am the target of these sayings and rumours. It hath been and will become manifest. During Bahá'u'lláh's time, whoever wanted to revolt would first say: 'Dear aunty is the cause of all the Blessed Beauty's anger.' While with his peers, he would say secretly, 'What am I to do? Bibí[63] hath no feelings for me. She is the cause of all the troubles in the Holy Court.' Now they are using you as the scapegoat. I am the target, not you. It hath been in the past and will in the future become very evident. My meaning is this: Engage day and night in remembering the Blessed Beauty and forget all else. I have come here and left the field empty that those who are weak in their faith may do as they please, that they may do it openly, not in secret. 'And soon will the unjust assailants know what vicissitudes their affairs will take!'[64]

During 'Abdu'l-Bahá's absence, the opponents of the Centre of Bahá'u'lláh's Covenant associated freely with the believers and tried hard by all means possible to create confusion and benefit thereby. To spread rumours and mobilize public opinion in their favour, they used unsuspecting men and women as effective instruments. Unaware of the true intention, such men and women would repeat to the willing people they met the information they had been fed and believed to be true. To protect the members of His family and the community from the ill effects of idle talk and gossip, 'Abdu'l-Bahá advised the friends to stay clear of those detestable habits. In a Tablet addressed to Munírih Khánum, 'Abdu'l-Bahá advises that if in the *andarún*[65] women related something about some person, the hearer should observe complete silence, engage in communion with the True One and say that the remembrance of God is best.[66]

Marriage of Ḍíyá'íyyih Khánum and Áqá Mírzá Hádí

Life was most difficult for 'Abdu'l-Bahá's family during His absence in

Tiberias. Saddened and heartbroken by the turn of events, they suffered patiently. This was the first time after Bahá'u'lláh's ascension that 'Abdu'l-Bahá had been away for a considerable time. After Him, the Greatest Holy Leaf was the most senior member of the family and clearly in charge. Not having a close male relative to attend to affairs outside the home posed severe problems. No matter how capable, women were not at liberty to do things they were not expected and allowed to do in public. Going against what was considered the norm – remaining under the veil and attending to domestic chores – would have caused consternation and brought about undesirable consequences for them and members of the nascent community. In that situation serious consideration was given to the proposal of a member of the Afnán family to marry Ḍíyá'íyyih Khánum, 'Abdu'l-Bahá and Munírih Khánum's eldest daughter. Ṭúbá Khánum in her spoken chronicle, published in *The Chosen Highway*, says:

> The time passed on until about three years after the passing of Bahá'u'lláh, when the conditions of our lives, owing to the ceaseless action of the enemy (cunningly devised false representations and accusations), became much more difficult.
>
> Suddenly the Master went to Tiberias to spend some time in retreat. He was accompanied by one servant only.
>
> We, the ladies of the family, were much in despair; we had no man to do anything for us; none that we could trust; our veiling kept us, of necessity, almost prisoners.
>
> There was a certain young man, of the family of the Báb (the members of which were given the name of 'Afnán'), who had for some time been wishing to be accepted by the family of Bahá'u'lláh as husband of the eldest granddaughter . . .
>
> After the Ascension of Bahá'u'lláh, Áqá Mírzá Hádí and his mother went back to their own country, Shíráz in Persia. They constantly wrote letters to the Master, my mother, and my aunt, in which frequent reference was made to their desire for the marriage.
>
> The mother would speak of her great liking for Ḍíyáíyyih Khánum and add praises of her son.
>
> Now, whilst the Master was in retreat at Tiberias, we, the ladies of the household, were in much distress because of being without any man in the family to make whatever necessary arrangements were required from time to time, to which we, because of being veiled, were unable to attend. Our difficulties grew and increased.
>
> We therefore determined to write to the Master, asking Him to permit the marriage of Ḍíyáíyyih Khánum to that spiritually-minded young man,

Áqá Mírzá Hádí Afnán, who was so anxious to be accepted as son-in-law by the Master, and who had been approved by Bahá'u'lláh.

At this time Áqá Mírzá Hádí was actually in 'Akká, as about two years after the ascension of Bahá'u'lláh he had received permission to come back.[67]

'Abdu'l-Bahá consented to the marriage but emphasized that the ceremony had to be very simple. He was not present at the wedding, which took place under the Greatest Holy Leaf's supervision. A small number of people, mainly close family members, were present. 'Abdu'l-Bahá revealed a special Tablet for the occasion. It is in Arabic and not yet translated into English. The translation of another Tablet revealed at that time has been published in *The Chosen Highway*. Referring to the sufferings of His family, He says:

The calamities of my family are beyond endurance, and the troubles of those sorrowful leaves (sister, wife, daughters) are without end.

From all directions the arrows of hardship are being showered upon them, like rain-drops in spring, and the spears of the unfaithful are being hurled upon them without ceasing.

The breezes of peace are being cut off in every direction, so that to breathe is impossible.

Eyes are weeping bitter tears.

Hearts are sore wounded. With hidden wounds are they smitten. Lamentations rend the soul, and the shaft of grief, piercing through all our hearts, joins them together.

This must needs be, for the Sun of the world has gone down below the horizon!

On the table of His departure is set out every kind of harmful viand, and every kind of death-dealing poison!

Verily the table of disaster is spread with every imaginable food!

Oh, family of this sorrowful one, all is sacrifice.

No pleasure is desired by you.

I know your sorrows.

The Mufti may be asked to chant the Marriage Chant at the Holy Shrine on Sunday.[68]

Speaking of the marriage ceremony, Ṭúbá Khánum says:

My aunt invited the family of Muḥammad-'Alí to come in the evening. They came and jeered at the simplicity of the wedding with great ridicule.

None of our friends knew that it was a day of marriage.

My mother, my aunt, and we four girls were together.

Áqá Mírzá Hádí Afnán arrived.

We said 'Bismi'l-láh!'

He kissed the hands of my aunt, my mother, and Ḍíyá'íyyih Khánum.

The Muftí chanted the Marriage Chants, and the marriage ceremony was accomplished.[69]

The marriage of Ḍíyá'íyyih Khánum and Mírzá Hádí took place in late 1895 or early 1896. The expansion of the family required a bigger and more spacious dwelling. 'Abdu'l-Bahá rented the house of 'Abdu'lláh Páshá, situated in close proximity to the house of 'Abbúd. The family moved there in 1896. Shortly afterwards, on 1 March 1897, Shoghi Effendi was born.

His birth presaged the dawn of a new era in the fortunes of the nascent Faith, the Centre of whose Covenant was 'Abdu'l-Bahá. 'Abdu'l-Bahá needed a male offspring to ensure the successful transfer of authority after Him. Thus He appointed Shoghi Effendi as the Guardian of the Cause of Bahá'u'lláh in His Will and Testament while he was still very young. Shoghi Effendi's birth was the spark that illumined the dark tunnel of woes and tribulations suffered by 'Abdu'l-Bahá and His family at a time when the Covenant-breakers were doing everything humanly possible to rob Him of His glorious heritage.

During the long years of marriage to 'Abdu'l-Bahá and thereafter to the end of her life, Munírih Khánum had in the person of Bahá'íyyih Khánum, the Greatest Holy Leaf, an incomparable example to emulate. After Bahá'u'lláh's ascension in 1892, almost all of His kindred leagued against the person He had appointed as the Centre of His Covenant. The Greatest Holy Leaf and Munírih Khánum stood firmly behind 'Abdu'l-Bahá and supported Him with uncompromising loyalty and devotion.

The activities of 'Abdu'l-Bahá's half brothers and their supporters against Him continued unabated until they engulfed every member of Bahá'u'lláh's household except the Greatest Holy Leaf, Munírih Khánum and the family of Bahá'u'lláh's faithful half brother, Mírzá Muḥammad-Qulí. 'Abdu'l-Bahá did all in His power to keep the ill effect of His family's opposition and attacks from spreading far and wide. However, when their misdeeds and misconduct betrayed their true intention and exposed their evil designs, the foul odour of Covenant-breaking permeated the atmosphere, making separation of the faithful followers of 'Abdu'l-Bahá from the opponents of the Covenant inevitable. The separation, when effected, afforded 'Abdu'l-Bahá and His family, especially Bahá'íyyih Khánum and Munírih Khánum, a welcome respite.

‘Abdu’l-Bahá’s Trip to Beirut

‘Abdu’l-Bahá visited Beirut again for health reasons after Bahá’u’lláh’s ascension had taken place. In a Tablet revealed during that trip, He speaks of Bahá’íyyih Khánum most tenderly and expresses the wish that He could arrange for her to visit Beirut:

> He is God!
>
> I have been writing so many letters. The time is now running out and Jináb-i-Ḥusayn Áqá is leaving. Therefore, I write briefly. I was going to leave with this steamer but circumstances made a delay inevitable. Praised be God, the weather in Beirut has been for some time agreeable. However, if the means for return were available, I would not have remained. Right now I feel very well, be assured.
>
> Convey My greetings to everyone. My sister, I know not how to express My eagerness. Whatever I write, My pen would be inadequate. Convey thou the expressions of My eagerness in whatever language thou consider suitable. If means were in place, I would have definitely moved her to Beirut for a change of climate, but the means are not available.[70]

The Arrival of the First Group of Western Pilgrims

Not long after the birth of Shoghi Effendi the first group of western pilgrims arrived in ‘Akká and were accommodated in the house of ‘Abdu’lláh Páshá. Their arrival in 1898 was a long anticipated and happy event in ‘Abdu’l-Bahá’s ministry. It also stirred feelings of deep joy in the hearts of the members of His family. Contact with the western pilgrims opened to the members of ‘Abdu’l-Bahá’s family a window onto the unknown world, a world so different from their own. The pilgrims came in small groups. While in ‘Akká they were guests of ‘Abdu’l-Bahá. They stayed in the house of ‘Abdu’lláh Páshá for a few days and left with feelings of joy and spiritual rejuvenation. Among them were Lua Getsinger and Laura Clifford Barney, who spent a considerable time with ‘Abdu’l-Bahá and His family. Their long stay afforded them the opportunity to get to know the members of the Holy Family more intimately. The close association and intimacy generated spontaneous response from the pilgrims, who addressed Munírih Khánum as the Holy Mother.

Mírzá Badí‘u’lláh’s Intrigues

The period of tranquillity which separation from the Covenant-breakers afforded ‘Abdu’l-Bahá, His family and the Bahá’í community, was short-lived. Mírzá Badí'u'lláh, 'Abdu'l-Bahá's younger half brother, expressed regret for his past behaviour. To ensure that his plea for forgiveness would be granted, he sought and received the intercession of one of 'Abdu'l-Bahá's devoted and trusted followers. As Mírzá Badí'u'lláh's oral statements of regret and repentance were insufficient and to convince everyone of his sincerity, he wrote and published a long letter in which he enumerated the actions that his brother, Mírzá Muḥammad-'Alí, the Centre of Sedition, and his accomplices had perpetrated against 'Abdu'l-Bahá. The publication of this letter exposed the Covenant-breakers' misdeeds and the extent to which they had gone to achieve their evil ends. That letter, better than any other means, made the Bahá'í community aware of the degree of the animosity of 'Abdu'l-Bahá's opponents.

Once he rejoined the community he began a widespread scheme to achieve from inside the community what he could not from outside. He had a twofold objective: 1) he had accumulated a large debt which he wanted 'Abdu'l-Bahá to help him repay and 2) he wanted to familiarize himself with what was going on in 'Abdu'l-Bahá's house and within the Bahá'í community in order to report details to his brother, the Arch-breaker of Bahá'u'lláh's Covenant, Mírzá Muḥammad-'Alí. However, Mírzá Badí'u'lláh could not control his passionate love for mischief-making. He soon proved himself beyond redemption and showed his true face. Consequently, the relatively short span of time that he, under the guise of repentance, spent with the community brought upon 'Abdu'l-Bahá fresh tribulations and ordeals. The false reports that he sent to the authorities caused the central government to dispatch a commission of inquiry to investigate the trumped-up charges against Him. That commission worked closely with 'Abdu'l-Bahá's enemies and imposed fresh restrictions upon His movements and activities. 'Abdu'l-Bahá's re-incarceration in turn affected the people closest to Him, especially the Greatest Holy Leaf and Munírih Khánum.[71]

Munírih Khánum in Egypt

When the situation was somewhat tranquil, Munírih Khánum took a trip abroad. She had come to the Holy Land in the latter part of 1872 and lived under its harsh conditions for over 25 years before it became possible for her to leave. She was not officially an exile and could, like the rest of her family, travel to Iran and back. However, during the first 25 years of her married life she does not seem ever to have left the confines of the Holy Land. Her first trip abroad was to Egypt in the closing years of the 19th century. The approximate date of that trip is confirmed by the contents of a Tablet 'Abdu'l-Bahá revealed in her honour while she was away. Mention is made in the Tablet of a book, most probably *Kitábu'l-Fará'id*, that Mírzá Abu'l-Faḍl was writing in 1897–8, and of the coming of Americans, most probably the first group visiting the Holy Land in 1898. There is also mention of the Centre of Sedition (Mírzá Muḥammad-'Alí), whose nefarious activities against 'Abdu'l-Bahá had by 1898 become public knowledge:

> O Amata'l-Bahá! . . .
> Treat Jináb-i-Áqá Mírzá Abu'l-Faḍl with utmost kindness. Enquire about his health. Sometime visit him thyself and ask him how much of the book he hath written and how much of it is left to be done, and let Me know.
> His health is a very important matter. In this regard, try as much as possible to convince him that someone serve him at all times . . .
> Should the Americans come, show them the utmost kindness . . .
> When thou speakest with anyone regarding the Centre of Sedition, speak not with immense sorrow and regret, for people are weak.[72]

Munírih Khánum made other trips to Egypt. One was during the opening years of the 20th century. At that time Mírzá Badí'u'lláh's clandestine and subversive activities from within the community had reached their height. In a Tablet, 'Abdu'l-Bahá advises Munírih Khánum of Mírzá Badí'u'lláh's activities and the troubles he was causing. He then asks her to gently apprise one of the believers, whose intercession was instrumental in 'Abdu'l-Bahá's pardon of Mírzá Badí'u'lláh:

> O Amata'l-Bahá! The subject of Mírzá Badí'u'lláh hath become extraordinarily strange. My purpose is this: Explain to Jináb-i Ḥájí[73] in detail that the recent troubles stirred by the Committee of Investigation and so forth until the present time are all caused by Mírzá Badí'u'lláh who was constantly reporting to Mírzá Muḥammad-'Alí, and he is presently at the height of his animosity and vindictiveness. Yea, use all possible means to make him understand with utmost gentleness, radiance and kindness what the situation is. There is no time to write more than this. The condition of My health, praised be God, is entirely satisfactory.[74]

Munírih Khánum's trips to Egypt were sometimes for reasons of her health. There are several references in 'Abdu'l-Bahá's Tablets to her health. In one He refers to reports indicating that her condition was the same as before and says that the Exalted Leaves, the daughters of 'Abdu'l-Bahá and Munírih Khánum, were of the opinion that she should go to Egypt. 'Abdu'l-Bahá left the decision to her and expressed the hope 'that through the Blessed

Beauty's bounty and favours thou wilt be completely healed . . .'[75] Another Tablet confirms that she decided to go to Egypt:

> O Amata'l-Bahá! Apparently, thou hast decided to go to Egypt. For the time being, thou wilt explore a new place and wilt be the cause of joy and happiness to the handmaids in that land. I hope from the bounty and favour of the Blessed Beauty that thou wilt return feeling completely well and happy.[76]

In another Tablet, which may have been revealed during one of Munírih Khánum's trips to Egypt, 'Abdu'l-Bahá says:

> O Amata'l-Bahá! Day and night all the Leaves are engaged in remembering thee and await the receipt of news of thy recovery and well-being, that through the bounty and assistance of the Abhá Beauty, may My spirit be sacrificed for His friends, thou mayest return with utmost radiance and joy.[77]

In the same Tablet, 'Abdu'l-Bahá asks Munírih Khánum to write in detail about her condition that all may be reassured. The only other name mentioned in the Tablet is Amatu'lláh Riḍváníyyih Khánum, who may have accompanied Munírih Khánum on that trip.

The Construction of the Shrine of the Báb and the Interment of His Remains

A major undertaking of 'Abdu'l-Bahá's ministry was the construction of the Shrine on Mount Carmel and the interment of the Báb's remains in the mausoleum He had built for the purpose. The construction of the six original rooms of the Shrine took place at a time when the Covenant-breakers were accusing 'Abdu'l-Bahá of preparing to hoist the banner of rebellion against the central government. They used the construction of the Shrine as evidence that He was building a fortress. In spite of His opponents' allegations, misrepresentations, intrigues, and contrary to their false hopes that the imposition of fresh restrictions would hamper 'Abdu'l-Bahá from fulfilling His plans, construction work proceeded and was successfully completed about the time He was released from confinement. Shortly after the completion of the project, 'Abdu'l-Bahá placed with His own hands on Naw-Rúz, 21 March 1909 the wooden casket containing the Báb's remains and those of His companion in the marble sarcophagus, which had been made for the purpose in Rangoon, Burma, sent to the Holy Land and placed in the vault of the Shrine ahead of time. By then 60 years had elapsed from the Báb's martyrdom and ten years since His remains had reached the shores of the Holy Land. After decades of movement from place to place, they finally found rest in the bosom of God's mountain, in a spot designated by Bahá'u'lláh Himself, a spot destined to become the world spiritual and administrative centre of the Bahá'í Faith.

Those present at the ceremony were Bahá'í pilgrims and residents. There is reason to believe that adult female Bahá'ís did not participate. The requirements of the time and place did not allow the women believers, not even the Greatest Holy Leaf and Munírih Khánum, to attend an event together with adult male Bahá'ís. Although physically deprived, they were spiritually very much a part of the long-awaited enterprise. They had for years witnessed its progress with delight and heard with anxiety accounts of how the Covenant-breakers were trying to block its completion. They had rejoiced when its construction advanced unimpeded and shed tears of anguish when they heard there were problems in the way of its accomplishment. They had prayed God to hasten the day when it was successfully finished, when the remains of the Báb had been interred therein. They were now able to see the successful outcome of what Bahá'u'lláh had envisioned and 'Abdu'l-Bahá had achieved. The achievement of this major undertaking at a time when all forces were seemingly leagued against 'Abdu'l-Bahá brought tremendous joy to Him and His faithful followers, especially to the members of His family who watched Him toil day and night to bring to successful completion the Shrine His father had instructed Him to build some two decades earlier.

Change of Residence from 'Akká to Haifa and the Easing of Restrictions

While the construction of the original rooms of the Shrine of the Báb was underway, 'Abdu'l-Bahá was also building a residence on the slopes of Mount Carmel. The site was in close proximity to the Shrine and almost directly below it. By the time the construction of the house began, some members of 'Abdu'l-Bahá's family were living in Haifa, a city gaining in stature and importance. When the house was complete, the family members moved to Haifa in stages. The move, in addition to its logistical advantages, created a welcome distance between the Covenant-breakers and the fast-growing Bahá'í community. The Covenant-breakers occupied the Mansion of Bahjí and its surrounding buildings.[78] The Shrine of Bahá'u'lláh, the pilgrim house, as well as the tea house of 'Abdu'l-Bahá remained in the hands of Bahá'ís.

With the transfer of residence from 'Akká to Haifa came the easing of restrictions on the life and activities of the women members of 'Abdu'l-

Bahá's family. 'Abdu'l-Bahá's house in Haifa was built at a time when, by decree of the government, He was confined to His home in 'Akká and His movements were under surveillance. There are accounts by western female pilgrims indicating that He sent His wife, Munírih Khánum, and other members of the family to Haifa, to welcome them on His behalf. The gradual easing of restrictions made it possible for the female members of 'Abdu'l-Bahá's family to be photographed, something inadmissible for their forebears. It also facilitated their active and public involvement with the work of the Faith.

In her tribute entitled 'In Memory of Munírih Khánum', Corinne True describes meeting 'Abdu'l-Bahá's wife during True's first visit in 1907 and provides valuable insights into Munírih Khánum's life and the nature of the services that she rendered. 'How thoughtful', she says, 'of our beloved Master to send His wife, the revered Munírih Khánum and the little grandson, Shoghi Effendi, together with some other members of His Household, from 'Akká to Haifa to welcome us!'[79] She continues:

> We were permitted to have six days of indescribable joy associating with the members of 'Abdu'l-Bahá's Household, with His wife and with His family . . . His wife had driven all the way from 'Akká to Haifa to greet us and to extend to us her most cordial welcome. It was the beloved Holy Mother, Munírih Khánum, who gave us our first welcome.[80]

Corinne True and two other women pilgrims visited 'the Shrine of the Báb on the slope of Mount Carmel' the next day 'accompanied by the holy women' and dined with them in the house of the Master before receiving permission from 'Abdu'l-Bahá to go to 'Akká the following day. While in 'Akká, they were 'Abdu'l-Bahá's guests and stayed in His House.

> For six days we were guests in this home and daily saw the Holy Mother and the Master's Sister, the Greatest Holy Leaf, and with them the Master's daughters. Very early in the mornings we were permitted to meet in the large reception room where the beloved 'Abdu'l-Bahá and His Family would gather together for an hour of communion. The Master would ask different members of the family to chant the Holy Utterances of Bahá'u'lláh and always the motherly presence of Munírih Khánum filled the atmosphere of that room with the benediction of her great mother heart. She seemed the personification of Universal Motherhood – indeed the 'Holy Mother'. When I was standing beside her one morning the dear Master came and placed my hand in hers, and looking into my face said in English: 'She is your Mother.'[81]

The move to Haifa was followed by the construction of the eastern pilgrim house in the vicinity of the Shrine of the Báb, where pilgrims from the East were accommodated. To provide accommodation for the western pilgrims, a big house close to the house of 'Abdu'l-Bahá was acquired for the purpose. Gradually more property was acquired in that vicinity where members of 'Abdu'l-Bahá's immediate and extended family lived. The move to Haifa, the improvement in living conditions and the amicable relationship between 'Abdu'l-Bahá and the people of Haifa effected a welcome change in the situation of the women of the family. They enjoyed more freedom of movement. They saw more women pilgrims coming from the East. They communicated more effectively with the western women pilgrims. There were a number of grandchildren keeping everyone busy. On the whole, life in Haifa afforded a much happier experience. Munírih Khánum, in the company of the Greatest Holy Leaf, met the women pilgrims. She also accompanied the western women pilgrims to 'Akká.

Munírih Khánum in Samaríyá and Nuqayb

The contents of one of 'Abdu'l-Bahá Tablets addressed to Munírih Khánum indicates that on several occasions she visited Samaríyá and Nuqayb, where the family of Bahá'u'lláh's faithful half brother Mírzá Muḥammad-Qulí lived. As the Tablets are undated, it is not possible to know exactly when those trips took place.

> O Amata'l-Bahá! Think not that because thou art away from the Blessed Shrine, thou art distant and in a forlorn state. Thou art present and visible. The Blessed Leaves, particularly Her Highness, the Greatest Holy Leaf, constantly make mention of thee and remember thee fondly.
>
> It seems that the weather in those parts is agreeable. This time make thou no haste to return, like other times, even when thou hast completely recovered. Spend the months of July and August in Samaríyá and Nuqayb. We will send thee whoever thou may desire.
>
> 'Abdu'l-Bahá's condition through the bounty and favour of the Abhá Beauty is absolutely good. Be assured.
>
> Apparently, the health of the favoured handmaid, the mother of Áqá Mírzá 'Abdu'r-Ra'úf,[82] is suffering from slight disequilibrium. Do ask after her on My behalf and extend to her My loving kindness. She is most certainly better by now . . .
>
> Postscript: Convey My loving greetings to Áqá Mírzá Dhikru'lláh.[83]

It is evident from the contents of most of 'Abdu'l-Bahá's Tablets that Munírih Khánum was very concerned and worried about His health. Whenever she was away, she needed to be reassured about His condition, and when He was away, she needed the same reassurance:

> O Amata'l-Bahá, O Spiritual Leaf! There is nothing wrong with Me. Through the bounty and grace of the Ancient Beauty I am well. The women pilgrims have not arrived and it is not certain when they will. Be at ease and take care of the patient. Do ask after her on My behalf, and also after the others.[84]

During 'Abdu'l-Bahá's Extensive Travels

Munírih Khánum was about 63 years old when 'Abdu'l-Bahá embarked on His long trip to Egypt and the West in the summer of 1910, a journey described by Shoghi Effendi as 'a turning point of the utmost significance in the history of the century'.[85] The account of 'Abdu'l-Bahá's visits to Egypt and countries in Europe and North America is published in several sources, such as Shoghi Effendi, *God Passes By*, *'Abdu'l-Bahá* by H.M. Balyuzi, *Maḥmúd's Diary*, *'Abdu'l-Bahá in Egypt*, and so forth. The aim here is not to repeat what has been published but to provide a glimpse of Munírih Khánum's life during those years.

During 'Abdu'l-Bahá's travels in the West, correspondence between Him and Munírih Khánum was regular. Some of this correspondence contains valuable historical information, which is referred to in this account. 'Abdu'l-Bahá's hectic schedule in the latter part of His travels affected the frequency of communication with His family. In addition to His numerous public appearances, meetings with the friends, visits to the poor and sick, interviews with reporters, meetings with persons of stature and influence, and dealing with the effects of Covenant-breaking in the West, 'Abdu'l-Bahá had to cope with an ambitious, arrogant and self-seeking person in His entourage. Dr Amín Fareed, Munírih Khánum's nephew, accompanied 'Abdu'l-Bahá on His trip to the West and served as His translator. His misconduct and misdemeanours caused 'Abdu'l-Bahá great concern and grief. Being a close member of the family added to the complications of the situation. The consequences of his rebellious behaviour and unbridled ambition eventually engulfed his parents, Munírih Khánum's sister and brother-in-law, and their daughter, Farangees. The situation with Dr Fareed was undoubtedly of great concern to Munírih Khánum. How she reacted to the news of his disingenuous behaviour which brought far-reaching consequences upon himself, his parents and sister, we are unaware.[86] A passage in *The Priceless Pearl* sheds light on how 'Abdu'l-Bahá felt:

> . . . when the Master returned at length to His home in Haifa on 5 December 1913, He proceeded at once to the room of His wife, sat down and said with a feeble voice, accompanied by a grinding gesture of His hand, 'Doctor Fareed has ground me down!'[87]

It is evident from 'Abdu'l-Bahá's Tablets that He kept Munírih Khánum well informed of the details of His travels and plans. In one Tablet He conveys the news of His departure from Port Said for Marseille. He also asks her to convey a message on His behalf to Dr Fallscheer,[88] the family's doctor. It is clear from the message that a person of stature, whose identity is not disclosed, was to meet Him in Marseille. Munírih Khánum was to inform Dr Fallscheer to write to a Miss Astion or Easton immediately, informing her that the person who wanted to see 'Abdu'l-Bahá in Marseille should go there at once. 'Abdu'l-Bahá says that from Marseille He may proceed to America or South Africa, so He emphasizes that the person in question should hasten to Marseille where He would be waiting for him. Who was this person? Was he from the East or the West? Did he succeed in meeting 'Abdu'l-Bahá in Marseille? These questions remain unanswered. What is clear is that 'Abdu'l-Bahá emphasized that details of His plan to visit the western hemisphere not be divulged. The main reason for this was the Covenant-breakers' aspiration to frustrate His plans to advance the Cause of God at home and abroad. Had they known in advance that 'Abdu'l-Bahá was making a trip to the West they would have done everything they could to prevent Him from fulfilling His goal. As it was, as soon as they heard about His departure, they took action which, however, failed to achieve the desired results. According to H.M. Balyuzi:

> . . . Mírzá Muḥammad-'Alí was busy spreading strange rumours. He told the Metropolitan of 'Akká, a cleric in league with him, that 'Abdu'l-Bahá had fled the Holy Land. The Metropolitan telegraphed one of his own men in Jaffa and instructed him to find out whether or not 'Abdu'l-Bahá was on His way to Egypt. That man boarded the Khedivial steamer and came face to face with 'Abdu'l-Bahá. He had the temerity to ask Him to affirm His identity. Ashore, the Metropolitan's man sent this telegram: 'The said person is aboard.' The same thing happened in Port Said. A man came on behalf of the Metropolitan of 'Akká to make certain that 'Abdu'l-Bahá was there.[89]

Therefore, in the Tablet to Munírih Khánum, 'Abdu'l-Bahá advised her how to respond to people's enquiries concerning His whereabouts:

> Should people enquire about My whereabouts, tell them that certain prominent Americans and Europeans have repeatedly sought and received promises that I would make a trip to those areas . . . be evasive as much as possible . . . The less said the better it would be. Tell Dr Fallscheer also not to divulge the truth, and thou shouldst not divulge either as far as possible.

He closed the Tablet thus: 'I hope that thou wilt be protected under the shelter of the Blessed Beauty's favours. Convey my Abhá greetings to all. I do protect myself from cold.'[90]

'Abdu'l-Bahá's intended departure from Egypt for Marseille was postponed considerably. Whether the postponement had anything to do with the person who wanted to meet Him there we do not know. Instead, He went to Alexandria. Again, according to Mr Balyuzi:

> After a month's stay in Port Said, 'Abdu'l-Bahá once again took ship, without previous intimation. He intended to go to Europe, but it became evident that the state of His health did not permit the strenuous work involved. He landed in Alexandria. It was in that ancient city that a sudden change occurred. Journalists in Egypt, who had hitherto shown open hostility, asked to meet 'Abdu'l-Bahá and perceptibly changed their tone. Even more, they wrote in terms of high praise.[91]

From Alexandria, 'Abdu'l-Bahá went to Cairo where He met Shaykh Muḥammad Bakhit, the Muftí of Egypt, and Shaykh Muḥammad Rishád, the Khedive's Imám. 'The Khedive, 'Abbás Ḥilmí II, also met 'Abdu'l-Bahá' and exhibited particular reverence towards Him.[92] After a sojourn of nearly a year, 'Abdu'l-Bahá left for Marseille. The Tablet He revealed in Marseille in honour of Munírih Khánum, whom He often addressed in correspondence as Amatu'l-Bahá, informs her that He and His companions had arrived in Marseille from Alexandria and from there they had gone to Thonon in France. Speaking of Thonon, He says:

> It is truly a delightful place. The mildness of the weather, the freshness of the grass and fields, the lushness and pleasantness of the hills, as well as the beauty of the scenery are most perfect. From the day I left Iran until now I had not seen such a place. For the time being, together with a group of the friends, we are staying in the Grant Hotel Park in Thonon. The weather is most agreeable. Day and night we are thinking of how we can render, through the aid and favour of the Blessed Beauty, may My spirit be a sacrifice for the Threshold of His Dust, some small service.

After emphasizing that aid and confirmation from the Abhá Kingdom were absolutely necessary for the success of any enterprise, He conveys loving greetings to the Holy Leaves, Ḍíyá, Rúḥá, Ṭúbá, Munavvar and some others.[93]

'Abdu'l-Bahá was very careful about how money was spent and kept a record of all expenditures. His strict control of the way the money of the Faith was spent was the cause of unhappiness to some believers who did not like to be accountable and desired the freedom to do as they pleased. Some even used this as a pretext to oppose the Centre of the Covenant. The truth of the matter is that 'Abdu'l-Bahá was just as strict with the immediate members of His own family. Before He left on His lengthy travels, He had arranged for a certain sum to be delivered to Munírih Khánum 'for the expenditures of the house and other expenses'. In a postscript to the above Tablet, He asks her to inform Him of the amount spent. This statement and one at the end of another Tablet, quoted below, show how stringent He was regarding financial matters:

> O Amata'l-Bahá! The luminous page from which the splendours of the light of the Abhá Beauty, may My spirit be a sacrifice for His friends, shone forth has been perused. I render thanks to the Court of the Greatest Name that praised be God all have been and continue to be protected under the shadow of God's loving care. The news of the well being of the friends of God and handmaids of the Merciful in 'Akká and Haifa has been the cause of utmost joy.
>
> Ask Leticia[94] to come back and offer her a sum that would secure her agreement. Also, the sum needed for Shoghi Effendi and Ruhangiz's school must all be paid by Áqá Mírzá Muḥsin[95] . . .
>
> Postscript: I wrote to Khánum, I am writing to you as well: Should major incidental expenses occur, you may every month obtain up to five Liras from Áqá Mírzá Muḥsin.[96]

When 'Abdu'l-Bahá reached the shores of New York, He sent Munírih Khánum the following Tablet:

> O Amata'l-Bahá! With utmost ease I arrived in New York. However, I was not for a moment free of My thoughts for all of you, especially for Rúḥá Khánum and Shoghi Effendi,[97] particularly when remembering Rúḥá's weeping and lamentation as she lay gravely sick in bed.[98] But what could one do? Service to the Blessed Threshold requireth one to sacrifice everything. In that state, I gave her up and entrusted her to the Blessed Beauty, proceeding with the sea voyage, for I am completely resigned [to

> His Will]. It is My hope that thou, too, wilt be patient and steadfast and become the cause of firmness and steadfastness to other souls.
>
> Convey My Abhá greetings to all, especially to the Blessed Leaf, Munavvar Khánum.[99] How I wish she were with Me![100]

Munírih Khánum had at some point sought 'Abdu'l-Bahá's approval to make a trip to Jerusalem. He lovingly advised her against it, explained the reason, suggested an alternative change and provided the means for achieving it:

> O Amata'l-Bahá! All that thou hadst penned down hath been perused. Thou hast written regarding a trip to Quds (Jerusalem). Thou hast not the endurance needed for such a trip, especially through the desert. Therefore, rent thou the house which thou hast written about and provide the means of comfort for thyself. For the new house's rental, I am sending 10 French Liras with Mírzá Amín.[101]

After extensive travels in Europe and North America, 'Abdu'l-Bahá returned to Egypt on 16 June 1913 and was joined by His family shortly thereafter. According to *The Priceless Pearl*:

> At last the long journey was over and the Master, sixty-nine years old and exhausted from His herculean labours, returned to Egypt on 16 June 1913. His family hastened to His presence there, among them Shoghi Effendi, who joined Him about six weeks after His arrival . . . arriving in the company of the Greatest Holy Leaf and others on 1 August in Ramleh, where 'Abdu'l-Bahá had once again rented a villa.[102]

Although her name is not specifically mentioned, it is assumed that Munírih Khánum was among members of the family who went to Egypt to welcome 'Abdu'l-Bahá and be with Him for some time. If she did go, she most probably returned to Haifa when other members of the family returned, which was before 'Abdu'l-Bahá Himself returned.

As she grew older Munírih Khánum seemed fatigued by the tribulations she had endured and the limitations entailed in living in conservative places like 'Akká and Haifa in the late 19th and early 20th centuries. She was especially affected by separation from 'Abdu'l-Bahá. Moreover, she was keenly conscious of the dangers facing Him, which caused her perpetual concern about His safety and well-being. Her concerns and worries were more acute when 'Abdu'l-Bahá was away. To enable her to deal successfully with feelings of sadness and fear, 'Abdu'l-Bahá advised her thus:

O thou Leaf that moveth with the fragrant breezes of God! The written sheet was perused and from its contents the lamentation and cry of thy sorrowful heart heard. While the Blessed Beauty's loving kindnesses are vouchsafed, no one should be saddened by any calamity or fearful of any sound. When the army of sadness attacks, remember those favours that the darkness of sorrow may be transformed to the brilliance of the moon . . .[103]

Life in the Holy Land during World War I

Eight months after 'Abdu'l-Bahá's return from His long trip to Egypt and the West, World War I broke out. By then the Bahá'ís had become a distinct community under the leadership of 'Abdu'l-Bahá who was known and respected not only by the residents of Haifa and the surrounding areas but throughout the world as a prominent religious figure.

When Turkey entered the war on the side of Germany, it set the stage for its eventual defeat, which led to the disintegration and fragmentation of the Ottoman Empire. When the war broke out, the residents of Haifa, alarmed by potential dangers facing the city, moved inland. 'Abdu'l-Bahá was too busy with the work at hand to leave the Haifa–'Akká area for a safer place. However, He accepted an invitation from Shaykh Ṣáliḥ, the Shaykh of Abú-Sinán,[104] and agreed to send His family as well as members of the local Bahá'í community there. 'Abdu'l-Bahá's family stayed in Shaykh Ṣáliḥ's house. The members of the community lived in rented quarters. Speaking of those perilous times, Lady Blomfield writes:

> Soon after its outbreak, Haifa, which was still under Turkish rule, was panic-stricken. Most of the inhabitants fled inland, fearing bombardment by the Allies.
>
> Those Bahá'í friends who were merchants suffered great losses, for all their stores of tea, sugar, etc., were commandeered by the Government, without payment.
>
> The friends, in spite of the reassurances of the Master that no guns would be turned on Haifa, were living in constant fear, and the children, having heard terrible stories which were being told everywhere, grew quite ill, always looking round and about with frightened eyes.
>
> At this time, the Master decided that it would be well to accept an invitation of the Shaykh of Abú-Sinán to remove the Bahá'ís and their children to that peaceful, healthy village, out of reach of the dreaded bombarding. In this village also, the very limited resources of the friends would, with strictest economy, be sufficient for their daily needs, with the

help of the corn from 'Abdu'l-Bahá's storing.

Shaykh Ṣáliḥ placed his house at the disposal of 'Abdu'l-Bahá and His family, Who received the most cordial welcome from this gracious and courteous chief of the Druze village of Abú-Sinán.

The other Persian friends were gladly taken into various houses of the village, where they found themselves in most happy surroundings.[105]

The Holy Family and the friends stayed in Abú-Sinán from November 1914 to 5 May 1915, six months in all. During this time, ''Abdu'l-Bahá Himself stayed in 'Akká with one attendant, and occasionally spent a night or two in Abú-Sinán.'[106] Munírih Khánum, who had been concerned with 'Abdu'l-Bahá's health and well-being while He was away in Egypt, Europe and North America, now had the added worry for His safety and security in a place where the intrigues of His internal and external enemies played a crucial role in shaping events associated with the war. Writing about those hazardous days, Lady Blomfield says: 'The Turks had been so aroused by the enemies of the Master that they had threatened to crucify Him, and all His family, on Mount Carmel.'[107] Mr Balyuzi provides further information:

> . . . in time the constant insinuations of the violators had their effect. Jamál Páshá [the Turkish officer in charge of affairs in Syria, which included the Holy Land] stated that he would crucify 'Abdu'l-Bahá, when he returned victorious from his campaigns.[108]

'Abdu'l-Bahá remained unaffected by such statements, for He held the firm conviction that He was under Bahá'u'lláh's protection, but they intensified His family's concern for His safety. Fortunately, when Jamál Páshá returned, 'he was in full flight, defeated and humiliated, and could not stop to carry out his threat'.[109]

Not until the war ended did the dangers facing 'Abdu'l-Bahá and His family abate. Lady Blomfield has devoted a chapter in her book *The Chosen Highway* to 'Danger to 'Abdu'l-Bahá, His Family and Friends and How it was Averted'. She describes a telephone message she received from 'an authoritative source' in the spring of 1918 relating, ''Abdu'l-Bahá in serious danger. Take immediate action.'[110] She explains how

> . . . a serious tragedy was averted, by the promptness and understanding of Lord Lamington and the power of Lord Balfour, his colleagues in the Cabinet here in London, and by the devotion, efficiency, and promptitude of Major Tudor-Pole at the Turkish end, for Haifa was still in the hands of the Turks . . .

When General Allenby took Haifa, several days before it was believed possible for him to do so, he sent a cablegram to London which caused everybody to wonder, and especially filled the hearts of the Bahá'ís in all the world with deep gratitude to the Almighty Protector.

The cable of General Allenby was as follows: 'Have to-day taken Palestine. Notify the world that 'Abdu'l-Bahá is safe.'[111]

'Abdu'l-Bahá's Ascension

'Abdu'l-Bahá's tireless efforts during His ministry, which lasted 29 years, strengthened the existing Bahá'í communities and spread the Cause of Bahá'u'lláh to many more countries in the East and the West. A large number of people from diverse backgrounds enlisted under the banner of the Greatest Name and their spiritual growth was nurtured through the correspondence which occupied a good portion of His time. As the scope of the Faith widened and the number of believers increased, violators of the Covenant became more strident in their attacks and opposition, requiring His close attention to matters of protection. 'Abdu'l-Bahá lived for three years and two months after the end of World War I. During this time He received pilgrims coming from both East and West, dealt with the authorities, attended to the needs of the poor, engaged in correspondence with believers throughout the world, personally supervised matters regarding His family, which had by then expanded considerably, and the Bahá'í communities in the Holy Land, in addition to leading the global Bahá'í community as it advanced. When His ascension took place on 28 November 1921, the Faith had spread to 35 countries. However, no one in the Bahá'í world or among the members of 'Abdu'l-Bahá's family, except the Greatest Holy Leaf, seems to have known what provisions He had made for the leadership of the community after Him. Had the appointment of Shoghi Effendi been intimated to Munírih Khánum? Had she intuitively understood it to be the case? We do not know for sure. Speaking of the wisdom of her sons dying in infancy and childhood, she said to Lady Blomfield:

> Five of my children died in the poisonous climate of 'Akká.
>
> The bad air was, in truth, only the outside material reason. The inner spiritual reason was that no son of the Master should grow into manhood.
>
> When my darling little son Ḥusayn passed away, Bahá'u'lláh wrote the following:
>
> 'The knowledge of the reason why your sweet baby has been called back is in the mind of God, and will be manifested in His own good time.

> To the prophets of God the present and the future are as one.'
>
> Therefore I understand how that wisdom has ordained the uniting of the two families, that of Bahá'u'lláh and of the Báb, in the person of Shoghi Effendi, eldest son of our daughter, Ḍíyáíyyih Khánum, by her marriage with Áqá Mírzá Hádí Afnán.[112]

On the night of 'Abdu'l-Bahá's ascension, Munírih Khánum was not in the room where He passed away. However, we learn from a letter written to Ella Cooper by Louise Bosch, one of the western pilgrims who, 'soon after 'Abdu'l-Bahá had passed out of this world . . . were allowed into the room where His body lay,'[113] that Munírih Khánum and the Greatest Holy Leaf were in the House:

> We asked the doctors [by then other physicians had been sent for] if he was dead. They said yes, the heart had ceased to beat; they said it was useless to try to revive him – it could not be done. Then after awhile, the mosquito netting over the bed was let down, and this covered from our eyes the earthly remains of our Lord. We got up and went into the adjacent room, and the door of the room out of which we came was closed.
>
> But before this, the blood of the wounds of this blow had begun to flow, and the hurt and the pain and the moans increased with every minute. We five European pilgrims were in the room together with the holy family, and the holy mother held my husband's hand and the Greatest Holy Leaf held mine. After a time we went back to the Pilgrim House, leaving the holy family alone . . .[114]

Munírih Khánum was married to 'Abdu'l-Bahá for nearly half a century. He was not only her beloved master and lord but also her only mainstay for decades. She depended on Him to guide her through life and tell her what to do. His ascension created a huge void that nothing could fill. It left her disconsolate and grief-stricken. Her letters of lament explain the depth of her sorrow. In a letter she wrote in 1922, a year after 'Abdu'l-Bahá's ascension, she included a poem so very descriptive of the feelings of loss surging within her:

> O Bahá, Knower of our inmost thoughts,
> Thou seest the fire in our souls.
> Yet, Thou inquirest not, Thou Self-Subsisting,
> After the nightingales so lovingly nurtured by Thee.
> My home is in ruins, its foundation destroyed;
> I am caught in the talons of the eagle of sorrow.

Call me to that other land, by Thy leave,
To build my home in another nest, another tree.
This wide world, this limitless space
Without Thee, Beloved One, encages me.
Turn our night into day, O Generous One;
Grant us wings to soar towards Thee.
Bestow upon Haifa a new creation,
Whose eyes will never gaze upon the likes of Thee,
Or behold Thy exalted stature,
Or those life-giving smiles of Thine.[115]

In response to Lady Blomfield, who asked Munírih Khánum to speak about 'Abdu'l-Bahá, she said:

> For fifty years my Beloved and I were together. Never were we separated, save during His visits to Egypt, Europe, and America.
>
> O my Beloved husband and my Lord! How shall I speak of Him?
>
> You, who have known Him, can imagine what my fifty years have been – how they fled by in an atmosphere of love and joy and the perfection of that Peace which passeth all understanding, in the radiant light of which I await the day when I shall be called to join Him, in the celestial garden of transfiguration.[116]

The Passing of the Greatest Holy Leaf

After 'Abdu'l-Bahá's ascension, Munírih Khánum stood firmly behind the Greatest Holy Leaf, extending full support to her in the execution of the plans for 'Abdu'l-Bahá's funeral and interment. She also followed her example in bowing before the authority of Shoghi Effendi, her own grandson, whom 'Abdu'l-Bahá had appointed the Guardian of the Faith and authorized Interpreter of the writings. During Shoghi Effendi's absence from the Holy Land, Munírih Khánum was fully supportive of the Greatest Holy Leaf, whom he had appointed as head of a committee to administer the affairs of the Bahá'í world.

Munírih Khánum and the Greatest Holy Leaf were about the same age and lived as two loving sisters and intimate friends for 60 years. Munírih Khánum was well aware of the towering personality and station of Bahá'íyyih Khánum. She had witnessed with admiration the leading role the Greatest Holy Leaf had played during 'Abdu'l-Bahá's absence in Egypt, Europe and North America. She had also watched and learned from 'Abdu'l-Bahá how tenderly and affectionately He had treated the Greatest Holy Leaf. During the several decades that Bahá'íyyih Khánum and Munírih Khánum lived together in the same house, they had a most cordial relationship. After 'Abdu'l-Bahá's ascension, the Greatest Holy Leaf was Munírih Khánum's best comforter and confidant. The Greatest Holy Leaf was most considerate of Munírih Khánum's standing in the community. She always included her in activities with the pilgrims. In the letters that she wrote to the friends, she invariably mentioned Munírih Khánum and other Holy Leaves.

When Bahá'íyyih Khánum passed away in July 1932, Munírih Khánum lost her closest companion and intimate friend. In a letter of lament composed after the passing of the Greatest Holy Leaf, she says:

> I can endure no more. My patience is ended. My powers have declined. I live on Mount Carmel friendless and alone.
>
> O 'Abdu'l-Bahá, I cry out at my remoteness from Thee;
> O 'Abdu'l-Bahá, I commit myself to Thy care.
>
> I have no desire to return to my home. I do not know what to do. It is befitting that I end with the words of Ṭáhirih, O my Master.
>
> Thy radiant face,
> Thy shimmering hair,
> Compel me to Thee,
> Hastily, eagerly.
> O answerer of the needy![117]

And in a letter of lament, penned a year after the passing of the Greatest Holy Leaf, she again gives vent to her feelings of sorrow and grief:

> I sit to write a fitting letter:
> A letter of swelling sorrow;
> Soiled with my heart's blood,
> Patterned with my tears;
> Black as Layli's tresses,
> Laid waste like Majnun's soul;
> Lacerated like a lover's heart,
> Grieved from first to last.
> O Believers! Immersed in my sorrow and woe
> I raise the cup of my own blood to my lips.
> Should I say more, breasts would pound.
> Should I write all, hearts would break.

Whither my Companion, Friend of my soul,
That gentle Confidant of my secret thoughts?
Would that my tears become the sea,
Where I might cast my sorrows.
O woe, O woe, O woe is me,
That our precious Sun should be veiled by a cloud.[118]

When studying the lives of Munírih Khánum and Bahá’íyyih Khánum one is struck by how different they were. Yet they understood each other very well and had the utmost respect for one another. Bahá’íyyih Khánum enjoyed a recognized leading position both within the family and in the worldwide Bahá’í community. She had given up everything, even the thought of marriage and having her own family, in order to devote her whole life to serving Bahá’u’lláh, ‘Abdu’l-Bahá and Shoghi Effendi. Service to the Cause and complete obedience to the centre of authority was what she lived for. Munírih Khánum, on the other hand, was a mother who had spent a good part of her life bearing and raising children. They were ‘Abdu’l-Bahá’s daughters. They were referred to as Holy Leaves. She was emotionally very attached to them and they were to her. They were all married by the time of ‘Abdu’l-Bahá’s ascension and, except for one, all had children. When Bahá’íyyih Khánum passed away, the grandchildren had come of age and at least one was already married to a man whose family had sided with ‘Abdu’l-Bahá’s opponents. In the succeeding years more of her grandchildren married into families who had a chequered history when it came to upholding the provisions of the Covenant. The situation with the grandchildren gradually worsened, threatening the spiritual health of the immediate members of ‘Abdu’l-Bahá’s family. Although none of them was declared a Covenant-breaker during Munírih Khánum’s life, the signs of defiance were there. Instead of being role models supporting Shoghi Effendi in word and deed, they expected to be treated differently and to be allowed to do as they pleased. The consequences were clear. Unless they drastically changed their attitude and obeyed the Guardian of the Faith, their spiritual well-being was in jeopardy. Munírih Khánum could see this but hoped that such a catastrophic outcome would be averted. The emotional effect that such developments had on a grandmother so attached to her children and grandchildren was tremendous, yet based on the contents of ‘Abdu’l-Bahá’s Will and Testament, there was no escape unless they brought themselves in line with what was expected of them.

Munírih Khánum faced the saddest and most grievous challenge of her life after the Greatest Holy Leaf passed away. By then she was in her mid-eighties. During the remaining years of her life she witnessed the worsening of problems besetting the people she most loved, problems arising from their failure to understand and appreciate the implications of 'Abdu'l-Bahá's Will and Testament regarding Shoghi Effendi's guardianship. How exactly the repercussions of this failure impacted Munírih Khánum in her old age we are not informed. What we do know is that with the Greatest Holy Leaf's passing she had lost a salutary influence in her life when she needed it most. That she struggled and toiled to find the right balance and prevent her family from falling apart there is no doubt. Did she succeed? The evidence reveals otherwise. In the end, she had to make a choice, as hard and painful as it was. She decided that what mattered to her the most was Shoghi Effendi's good pleasure.

The Greatest Holy Leaf was passionately concerned with the spiritual well-being of the members of the family and the Bahá'í community but never hesitated to put the interests of the Faith above all other considerations. Her main focus after 'Abdu'l-Bahá's ascension was doing what made Shoghi Effendi happy. Munírih Khánum's strong emotional attachment to her children and grandchildren made finding the right balance somewhat difficult. Indications are that she was particularly vulnerable after the passing of the Greatest Holy Leaf. However, she withstood temptations and stood firmly by the provisions of 'Abdu'l-Bahá's Testament. By so doing, she emphasized once again what she had written in her own hand as early after 'Abdu'l-Bahá's ascension as December 1924. In that letter she addressed 'Ḥaḍrat-i Shoghi Effendi' (His Highness Shoghi Effendi) as 'Gawhar-i Pák' (Pure Pearl), as her dear soul, the beloved of both worlds and the one chosen by the Master of the inhabitants of this world. She explains that, in accordance with the doctors' recommendation, she would be away for a few days and be deprived of seeing him. She sends Shoghi Effendi the gift of a soft blanket which she had received from a friend. Before closing, she beseeches him to pray that she may 'leave the world with an assured heart, complete faith, absolute detachment and utter sincerity', and says that 'this is her highest aim, dearest wish, ultimate hope and cherished desire'.[119]

The Passing of Munírih Khánum

At the time of her passing on 30 April 1938 Munírih Khánum was 91 years old. On the day she passed away the United States National Convention was in session. Shoghi Effendi sent a cablegram informing the delegates of her passing the same day. In that cablegram he announced that Riḍván festivities were to be suspended. He also advised the delegates to devote a special session to her memory and hold a befitting gathering in the auditorium of the Mashriqu'l-Adhkár.

HOLY MOTHER MUNÍRIH KHÁNUM ASCENDED ABHÁ KINGDOM STOP WITH SORROWFUL HEARTS BAHÁ'ÍS WORLD OVER RECALL DIVERS PHASES HER RICH EVENTFUL LIFE MARKED BY UNIQUE SERVICES WHICH BY VIRTUE HER EXALTED POSITION SHE RENDERED DURING DARKEST DAYS ʻABDU'L-BAHÁ'S LIFE STOP ALL RIDVAN FESTIVITIES SUSPENDED STOP ADVISE CONVENTION DELEGATES DEVOTE SPECIAL SESSION HER MEMORY HOLD BEFITTING GATHERING AUDITORIUM MASHRIQU'L-ADKHAR. (Signed) SHOGHI[120]

No information is available regarding Munírih Khánum's last days, the cause of her death, the funeral arrangements and so forth.

Munírih Khánum's Resting-place

Shoghi Effendi chose a spot in close proximity to, but below, the Greatest Holy Leaf's tomb on Mount Carmel to bury Munírih Khánum's mortal remains. Over her resting-place he built a circular monument made of white marble. The base consists of three tiers. In the centre of the top tier is engraved in two lines:

Munírih
Wife of ʻAbdu'l-Bahá

The monument has six plain columns joined together on top by an almost flat roof. It is situated exactly in the axis of the Arc around which the world administrative institutions of the Faith are housed. The lower elevation, size and simplicity of her monument in comparison with the monuments of the Greatest Holy Leaf, her longsuffering mother and martyred brother indicate that her station is overshadowed by theirs.

Shoghi Effendi makes mention of Munírih Khánum's resting-place in conjunction with the transfer of the remains of the Purest Branch and Ásíyih Khánum from ʻAkká to Mount Carmel in December 1939:

BLESSED REMAINS PUREST BRANCH AND MASTER'S MOTHER SAFELY TRANSFERRED HALLOWED PRECINCTS SHRINES MOUNT CARMEL. LONG INFLICTED HUMILIATION WIPED AWAY. MACHINATIONS COVENANT-BREAKERS FRUSTRATE PLAN DEFEATED. CHERISHED WISH GREATEST HOLY LEAF FULFILLED. SISTER BROTHER MOTHER WIFE ʻABDU'L-BAHÁ REUNITED ONE SPOT DESIGNED CONSTITUTE FOCAL CENTRE BAHÁ'Í ADMINISTRATIVE INSTITUTIONS AT FAITH'S WORLD CENTRE. SHARE JOYFUL NEWS ENTIRE BODY AMERICAN BELIEVERS.[121]

In another message, he says:

O Loved ones of God, These two precious and most exalted treasures, these two keepsakes of the sacred Beauty of Abhá, have now been joined to the third trust from Him, that is, to the daughter of Bahá and His remnant, the token of the Master's Remembrance.

Their resting-places are in one area, on an elevation close by the Spot round which do circle the Concourse on High, and facing the Qiblih of the people of Bahá – 'Akká, the resplendent city, and the sanctified, the luminous, the Most Holy Shrine.

Within the shadow of these honoured tombs has also been laid the remains of the consort of Him round Whom all names revolve.

For joy, the Hill of God is stirred at so high an honour, and for this most great bestowal the mountain of the Lord is in rapture and ecstasy.[122]

Munírih Khánum's Station and Place in History

Munírih Khánum's life span covered the latter part of the Báb's ministry, all of the ministries of Bahá'u'lláh and 'Abdu'l-Bahá and almost half of Shoghi Effendi's ministry.

She had the blessing of being born to a devoted Bábí couple who later embraced the Bahá'í Faith and served its interests wholeheartedly. Munírih Khánum herself lived a life of distinguished service. The extraordinary circumstances of her birth and marriage to 'Abdu'l-Bahá for 48 years, her life in the Holy Land in the last decades of the 19th and early decades of the 20th century with all its challenges, her travels, extensive for a woman of her era, her association with women of diverse cultures and backgrounds, as well as her literary accomplishments, place her high on the list of women prominent in the early history of the Bahá'í Faith.

It is neither possible nor fair to measure Munírih Khánum's life achievements in the same balance used to weigh the life work and services of other Bahá'ís. However, it is useful to highlight a few of the remarkable and out-of-the-ordinary things that she did. Being the consort of the Centre of Bahá'u'lláh's Covenant for nearly half a century and grandmother of the one appointed by 'Abdu'l-Bahá as the Guardian of the Faith afforded her a unique position in the Bahá'í world and at the same time placed extraordinary responsibilities on her shoulders. Content with her enviable position, she could have fulfilled the duties expected of her and done nothing else. But that was not the case. She wanted to improve the lives of less fortunate women. Influenced by Bahá'í teachings about the importance of education, she took the initiative to establish a Bahá'í girls' school on Mount Carmel during 'Abdu'l-Bahá's ministry. Although the land was acquired and plans for the building drawn up during His lifetime, its construction did not begin before Shoghi Effendi's guardianship. The letter that she wrote, with Shoghi Effendi's approval, to 'the loved ones of God and handmaids of the Merciful' explains:

> In this most bountiful age, this most fair and splendid century, the Ancient Beauty – exalted be His Most Great Name – has ranked education among the most important matters, in the forefront of His divine and excellent commandments . . .
>
> During the day of the Covenant of 'Abdu'l-Bahá, may our souls be a sacrifice at His Most Pure Threshold, He emphasized this matter of education. He has declared it to be among the greatest of the divine precepts, and accounted its acquisition as an imperative necessity . . .
>
> Indeed, the writings of the Pen of the Covenant overflow with this theme, placing particular emphasis on the instruction and refinement of girls . . .
>
> From early on in my life, I always hoped and envisaged that the means for the progress and success of Bahá'í girls, and indeed, for the girls of all nations, would come about . . .

She explains the genesis of the project:

> When I was in the presence of the Light of the Covenant, the Luminous Orb of the Universe, I said, 'If it is acceptable to You, we should establish a small school in Haifa for the children of the believers, so that they can be trained from their earliest childhood in Bahá'í behaviour and become informed of the history of the Faith.'
>
> 'Abdu'l-Bahá pointed His finger toward Mount Carmel and said, 'This lofty mountain will eventually be covered with schools, hospitals, and guest houses. The promises made by the Prophets will be realized and fulfilled.'[123]

She then describes how the site for the school was acquired during 'Abdu'l-Bahá's ministry, plans for the building prepared and some financial assistance pledged. She further explains her purpose in writing the letter:

> The purpose in writing all this is to say that the land for the school is available . . . I have already contributed a trifling 1,500 lira. Another 1000 lira, or slightly less, has been donated by others. But it is obvious that this excellent and worthy task, requires the magnanimity of the believers, and needs the action of the friends. God willing, in the time of Most Excellent Branch – may the souls of all be a sacrifice to Him – together with the

> efforts of the Holy Leaves, and the aid and assistance of our devoted brothers and sisters, it will be carried out and completed.[124]

In a postscript, Munírih Khánum explains 'the method given by the Guardian of the Cause' regarding the 'method of payment for the school', which required 'anyone sending a contribution' to 'send it in the names of the Blessed Leaves, the daughters of 'Abdu'l-Bahá'. The receipts were also to be signed by the four daughters of 'Abdu'l-Bahá and sent to the contributors. She added, 'The donations will be deposited in the bank in Haifa, in the account of the Blessed Leaves, until such a time when enough money has been collected.' She ends the postscript thus: 'Without a doubt, every beginning was initially but a modest one. Now we too must be content with starting in a small way.'[125]

The structure still stands on the northeast side of the Greatest Holy Leaf's monument. By the time the project was complete, the situation at the Bahá'í World Centre was very different. The school never became functional. At Shoghi Effendi's behest, many Iranian believers who lived in the area returned to their homeland. The building was used for some time as a repository for the sacred relics belonging to the Central Figures of the Faith and was referred to as the Minor Archives. Since the establishment of the Universal House of Justice it has been used as office space and served useful purposes.

Munírih Khánum enjoyed the power of both the pen and utterance. Through her pen she portrayed the mysterious unfolding of her own destiny, using it as a tool to bring hope to those affected by devastating events. She was very fortunate to be literate. Literacy for women in 19th-century Iran was a novelty. Munírih Khánum had good diction and enjoyed the ability to read, write and compose poetry. In addition to Persian, she knew Arabic and probably Turkish. She was good at expressing her emotions, in both prose and poetry.

Munírih Khánum seems to be the first Persian Bahá'í woman to have written her autobiography. Generally, Persians of her time did not speak of their private life in public, let alone write about it. That is the reason we have few autobiographies by Persian women in the 19th and early 20th centuries. Her autobiography covers her early life up to the time of her marriage to 'Abdu'l-Bahá. Its English translation, entitled *Episodes in the Life of Moneereh Khanom*, was published in the United States in 1924. A new English translation together with the translation of eulogies she composed after the passing of 'Abdu'l-Bahá and the Greatest Holy Leaf, entitled *Munírih Khánum: Memoirs and Letters*, has been published more recently. The original Persian of the booklet was published in Haifa in 1934. Munírih Khánum also composed poetry and some of her poems have been published.

Munírih Khánum was an excellent Bahá'í teacher. For insights into her success in the teaching field, we have 'Abdu'l-Bahá's testimony. In a Tablet revealed in her honour during one of her trips to Egypt, He writes:

> According to the news received, thou didst meet with the mother of Náṣiri'd-Dín Mírzá and spoke well. My hope from the grace of the Blessed Beauty is that thou wilt always unloose thy tongue in setting forth proofs . . .[126]

We also have the testimony of Corinne True:

> In November 1919 . . . I was again permitted to make the pilgrimage to the Holy Land; this time under very different circumstances . . . the Holy Family had all moved to Haifa, where life was fairly comfortable after the terrific rigours of imprisonment for so many years.
>
> During this second Pilgrimage we were permitted more intimate association with the Greatest Holy Leaf and the Holy Mother, Munírih Khánum. Almost daily we were received by them in the Master's garden where questions were asked and instructions given to us, clearing up many things that had puzzled the American friends. Here we saw this beloved wife of 'Abdu'l-Bahá as a most wonderful teacher, and through her we grew in the knowledge of the Cause. In the early days one of the greatest privileges of the visiting women pilgrims was this intimate association with these two divine maid-servants of Bahá'u'lláh, Bahíyyih Khánum, the Greatest Holy Leaf, and Munírih Khánum, the Holy Mother. We seldom saw one without the other . . .
>
> On our second visit we saw Munírih Khánum not only as a Universal Mother loving every child of God, but as a great teacher and expounder of the principles of Bahá'u'lláh. She was a teacher who lived these principles before our eyes. Religious history has never known greater examples than these of devotion and sacrifice to God's Holy Messengers! Should we praise God throughout the coming centuries, we could not render praise sufficient for the priceless spiritual heritage bequeathed to us by these holy women. They are the archetypes for the Bahá'í womanhood of the world.[127]

Lady Blomfield, who had the privilege of speaking with Munírih Khánum at length after 'Abdu'l-Bahá's ascension, describes her as 'a majestic woman, stately yet simple, with an innate dignity and strength of character'.[128]

The Fate of Munírih Khánum's Children

As stated earlier, four daughters of 'Abdu'l-Bahá and Munírih Khánum reached maturity, got married and, except for one, had several children each.

Ḍíyá'íyyih Khánum, the eldest daughter, married a great nephew of the wife of the Báb, Mírzá Hádí. He was a grandson of Ḥájí Mírzá Abu'l-Qásim, Khadíjih Bagum's younger brother to whom she was very close until the very end. Ḍíyá'íyyih Khánum and Mírzá Hádí had three sons, Shoghi Effendi, Ḥusayn Effendi, Ríyáḍ (Ríaz) Effendi, and two daughters, Rúḥangíz and Mihrangíz. They adopted Rabbání as a surname.

Ṭúbá Khánum, the second daughter, married Mírzá Muḥsin Afnán, a son of Ḥájí Mírzá Siyyid Ḥasan (the Great Afnán), another brother of Khadíjih Bagum. Mírzá Muḥsin's brother, Siyyid 'Alí, had previously married Bahá'u'lláh's youngest daughter. Ṭúbá Khánum and Mírzá Muḥsin had three sons: Rúḥí, Suhayl and Fu'ád, and one daughter, Thurayyá. They used Afnán as a family name.

Rúḥá Khánum, the third daughter, married Mírzá Jalál, the son of Sulṭánu'sh-Shuhadá (the King of Martyrs) and grandson of Shamsu'ḍ-Ḍuḥá (Khurshíd Bagum).[129] Mírzá Jalál's father and Munírih Khánum were paternal cousins. After his father was martyred in Iṣfahán, Mírzá Jalál and his sister came, at Bahá'u'lláh's behest, together with their mother and grandmother to live in the Holy Land. Mírzá Jalál and his sister grew up there. His sister married Munírih Khánum's brother, Siyyid Yaḥyá. Rúḥá Khánum and Mírzá Jalál had two sons, Muníb and Ḥasan, and three daughters, Maryam, Ḍuḥá and Zahrá. Their family name was Shahíd.

Munavvar Khánum, the youngest daughter, married Mírzá Aḥmad Yazdí, a son of Ḥájí Mírzá 'Abdu'r-Raḥím-i-Qannád. They had no children.

A new storm of rebelliousness brewing in the hearts of the disaffected manifested its devastating effects when Shoghi Effendi's eldest sister, Rúḥangíz, married the second son of Siyyid 'Alí and Furúghíyyih Khánum, Nayyir. The marriage was a clear indication that there was a close association between some members of 'Abdu'l-Bahá's family and His sworn enemies. The fire of rebellion ignited by this marriage spread mercilessly and consumed Shoghi Effendi's siblings, aunts, uncles and cousins in its wake. Even his parents did not remain completely immune. Chapter 32 of Adib Taherzadeh's *The Covenant of Bahá'u'lláh*, entitled 'The Faithless Relatives of Shoghi Effendi', provides detailed information about their misconduct and rebellious behaviour, culminating in the loss of their spiritual heritage.

Among those instrumental in instilling the spirit of Covenant-breaking

> which had lain dormant within the hearts of most members of 'Abdu'l-Bahá's family during the early years of Shoghi Effendi's ministry, were the family of Siyyid 'Alí Afnán . . . He had been an inveterate adversary of 'Abdu'l-Bahá. Now his sons, the grandchildren of Bahá'u'lláh, all Covenant-breakers, inflicted the greatest injury upon the person of Shoghi Effendi.[130]

Ḥasan, eldest son of Furúghíyyih Khánum and Siyyid 'Alí, married Shoghi Effendi's younger sister Mihrangíz. Their third son, Fayḍí, married Thurayyá, the daughter of Ṭúbá Khánum and Mírzá Muḥsin. According to Adib Taherzadeh:

> These inroads made by the old Covenant-breakers into the family of 'Abdu'l-Bahá were fatal, and soon most of its members became Covenant-breakers. Shoghi Effendi usually delayed announcing to the Bahá'í world the misdeeds committed by his relatives. He patiently endured their despicable behaviour and tried to rescue them from their tragic downfall, but eventually he had no choice but to expel them from the community and cut his relationship from them.[131]

The first among Shoghi Effendi's relatives to be excommunicated were his sister Mihrangíz, his aunt Ṭúbá Khánum and her children, Rúḥí, Suhayl, Fu'ád and Thurayyá. The announcement of Mihrangíz's expulsion was cabled to the National Spiritual Assembly of the British Isles while that of Ṭúbá Khánum and her children was cabled to the National Spiritual Assembly of the United States and Canada in 1941. Ṭúbá Khánum's husband, Mírzá Muḥsin Afnán, had passed away in 1927, more than a decade before his wife and children were declared to be Covenant-breakers.

Rúḥá Khánum's son, Muníb, 'married according to the Moslem rites the daughter of a political exile who is nephew of the Grand Muftí of Jerusalem'. His 'treacherous act of alliance with enemies of the Faith'[132] was made known by Shoghi Effendi in November 1944. Rúḥá Khánum's daughter, Zahrá, married Ṭúbá Khánum's son, Rúḥí, who together with his mother and siblings had joined hands with old Covenant-breakers through the marriage of his sister, Thurayyá, with Fayḍí Afnán, the youngest son of Siyyid 'Alí and Furúghíyyih Khánum.

The announcement of Muníb's defection was followed by a cable in April 1945 regarding Shoghi Effendi's brother, Ḥusayn, who had moved in with his sister Rúḥangíz and her husband, Nayyir, Fayḍí's eldest brother:

> My faithless brother, Ḥusayn, after long period of dishonourable conduct,

> has abandoned the Master's home to consort with his sister and other Covenant-breakers.[133]

And in 1951, Shoghi Effendi disclosed that Rúḥá Khánum's son, Ḥasan Shahíd, was planning to marry the granddaughter of Furúghíyyih Khánum and Siyyid 'Alí. In the same cable he announced that his own brother, Ríaz, had established personal contact with 'Majdid-din, redoubtable enemy Faith, former henchman Muhammad-'Ali, Archbreaker Bahá'u'lláh's Covenant'.[134]

Appendix

Outstanding Heroines in Religious Dispensations

Introduction

> . . . it is well established in history that where woman has not participated in human affairs the outcomes have never attained a state of completion and perfection. On the other hand, every influential undertaking of the human world wherein woman has been a participant has attained importance. This is historically true and beyond disproof even in religion.[1]

In every religious dispensation there have been heroines distinguished from other members of their sex for their attainment of spiritual eminence. Such women have, no doubt, been numerous, although little is recorded in history about them and their work. From among such heroines one has always stood out more prominently for manifesting divine attributes. She has, therefore, been acknowledged as the most outstanding of the members of her sex.

The most outstanding heroine of a religious dispensation is generally the one who has been closely associated with the founder of that religion and has discerned at an early stage the light of truth shining through Him. She has shared the trouble-laden life of that Manifestation of God[2] and has accepted suffering and afflictions in the path of His love. She has revealed the exemplary attributes of purity, fidelity, submission to the centre of authority, absolute certitude and modesty, and has proven by her sacrificial deeds and longsuffering attitude to be indeed the most outstanding heroine of a religious dispensation.

Although the most distinguished heroines in religious history are very different in their individual characteristics and personalities, they all share essential prerequisites for the unique station conferred upon them. Their position in religion is not arbitrarily decided and there are no set rules by which to determine their station. Their elevation to the rank is sanctioned by the founder of the religion they espouse or by a subsequent Manifestation of God. Recorded history reveals intriguing information about the contribution, the sacrifices and the station of the following heroines.

The Dispensation of Adam

No woman has been named as the most distinguished heroine of the Adamic dispensation. On the whole, no recorded history exists for that distant period in the annals of humanity except for what is recorded in the first chapters of the Old Testament in connection with the story of creation, according to which Eve was Adam's helpmate, was created in the image of God and after His likeness, as was Adam. Both were then blessed by the Lord and were given the responsibility of being fruitful, of multiplying, of replenishing the earth and of subduing it.[3] Referring to the creation of man, 'Abdu'l-Bahá says:

> . . . God hath created all humankind in His own image, and after His likeness. That is, men and women alike are the revealers of His names and attributes, and from the spiritual viewpoint there is no difference between them.[4]

Although the status of man and woman was originally meant to be equal, there are strong indications in religious history pointing to the gradual undermining of the rights of women. There are also alarming attempts to justify the maltreatment of women which culminated in degrading their status and positioning them as inferior to men. Such justifications include tales about how Eve was made of the rib of Adam, how Eve preceded Adam in partaking of the fruit of the forbidden tree. As a result, the status of woman underwent derogatory changes and deprived the world of humanity of one half of its capability. Man's ignorance and error, according to 'Abdu'l-Bahá, has been responsible for this cruel and manifest injustice: 'To accept and observe a distinction which God has not intended in creation is ignorance and superstition.'[5]

The Dispensation of Abraham

The first religious dispensation for which we have details recorded about its most outstanding heroine is that of Abraham, and the most distinguished heroine of that era is Sarah. She and Abraham were siblings born to the same father but were of different mothers. She shared every aspect of the eventful life of her husband and was an active partner of his woes and tribulations to the end. When they reached the land of Egypt, at her husband's request, she introduced herself as his sister,[6] to spare his life. Had the Pharaoh found her desirable, her marriage to Abraham would have stood in the way of his marrying her and he would have killed Abraham to remove the obstacle. Sarah's statement, according to Genesis, resulted in the Pharaoh's decision to marry her. That decision created a catastrophic situation leading to the expulsion of Abraham and Sarah from the land of Egypt.[7]

The story of Sarah offering her maid, Hagar, to Abraham and allowing Him to take her as a wife that He might have an offspring testifies to her utter devotion to the person of Abraham and His Cause. By so doing, Sarah risked her own position. However, according to Genesis, despite the fact that Abraham was blessed with a son, Ishmael (Ismá'il), who was born of Hagar, it was destined that a son born of Sarah would become His successor. This indicates the significance of Sarah and her preordained station as 'a mother of nations; kings of people shall be of her'.[8]

The Dispensation of Moses

In the history of the Jewish religion there are references to several women who were responsible for saving the life of a child destined to become a Prophet of God. Ukabid, the mother of Moses, and his sister Miriam were determined to ensure that Moses, a newly-born boy, would not suffer the fate Pharaoh had in mind for Him. A third woman, Ásíyih, the daughter of Pharaoh (or his wife, according to the Qur'án),[9] entered the picture through the work of providence. And before these three women there were two others whose contribution to the execution of the plan of God saved the lives of many male babies born at that time. Shiphrah and Puah were two God-fearing midwives who defied the Pharaoh's order to kill boys born to the children of Israel.

Moses grew up in the household of Pharaoh under the protective wing of his daughter;[10] later He became the saviour of the children of Israel and freed them from captivity in Egypt.[11] Of all the women actively participating in saving the life of Moses, the part played by Ásíyih was the most striking. Not only did she save baby Moses from the tyrannical rule of Pharaoh who was intent on annihilating Him but she also fostered Him with motherly care and love. She later became a believer in His divine mission. For her unique contribution to Moses and His Cause she won the appellation of the most outstanding heroine of that dispensation. Although a captive in the hand of a tyrant, Ásíyih succeeded in rendering assistance to God. Indeed, the outward cause of the rescue of Moses was that woman.

The Dispensation of Christ

The story of Mary, the mother of Jesus Christ, and her long years of suffering from the time she conceived her son to the day His blessed body was crucified on the cross, provides a great example of the capacity of women for endurance and fortitude. Although the tale of her sorrow and pain which culminated in her attaining to the glorious station she occupies in the history of Christianity is well known, it is not often remembered that she was as rejected and despised in her lifetime as she is now loved and revered. Mary is believed to have conceived her son through the breath of the Holy Spirit, something that neither she nor anyone else could explain. Her afflictions were such that she had to hide herself from the eyes of the world, leave her home at a time when any woman in her condition would have needed the utmost care and support, at least from those close to her, and take refuge in a stable or under the shade of a tree, as the Qur'án relates,[12] in order to deliver her precious baby. Jesus, son of Mary, is the only Prophet of God known by the name of his mother. He is also the only Prophet of God who is mentioned in the Qur'án as having spoken as a child in His mother's arms, which He did when she made a sign to Him that He should answer the people.[13]

Mary, who suffered the most deplorable circumstances when she delivered her son Jesus, has received the most affectionate treatment in the Islamic scriptures. A whole súrih in the Qur'án is devoted to the story of Mary in which her suffering is recounted and the world is told what she went through as the instrument which gave the world its Saviour. The Súrih of 'Imrán confirms that Mary was chosen 'above all the women of the world'.[14]

In the Bahá'í Faith, Mary occupies the position of the most outstanding heroine of the Christian era. In the Kitáb-i-Íqán (Book of Certitude) which ranks 'foremost among the priceless treasures cast forth from the billowing ocean of Bahá'u'lláh's Revelation',[15] her plight and sufferings are described in a most moving way:

> . . . reflect upon the state and condition of Mary. So deep was the perplexity of that most beauteous countenance, so grievous her case, that she bitterly regretted she had ever been born. To this beareth witness the text of the sacred verse wherein it is mentioned that after Mary had given birth to Jesus, she bemoaned her plight and cried out: 'O would that I had died ere this, and been a thing forgotten, forgotten quite!' I swear by God! Such lamenting consumeth the heart and shaketh the being. Such consternation of soul, such despondency, could have been caused by no other than the censure of the enemy and the cavillings of the infidel and perverse. Reflect, what answer could Mary have given to the people around her? How could she claim that a Babe Whose father was unknown had been conceived of the Holy Ghost? Therefore did Mary, that veiled and immortal Countenance, take up her Child and return unto her home. No sooner had the eyes of the people fallen upon her than they raised their voice saying: 'O sister of Aaron! Thy father was not a man of wickedness, nor unchaste thy mother.'[16]

The Dispensation of Muḥammad

Khadíjah Bint Khuwaylid, Muḥammad's first wife, born about mid-sixth century AD, lived in Mecca at the time Muḥammad was growing up there. 'Trading was her concern and she was seeking someone to whom she could entrust the management of her flourishing business. Her choice fell on Muḥammad.'[17] He was then 15 years old. His impeccable honesty and trustworthiness won Khadíjah's admiration. After a decade when He was 25 and she about 40, they married.[18]

When Muḥammad received the intimation of prophethood, Khadíjah was the first to discern its light shining through His blessed person. Without hesitation she immediately accepted His divine station and believed that He was God's Messenger for the age. With her keen insight, Khadíjah recognized in Muḥammad, an illiterate Arabian man, what the most erudite and learned of the people of Mecca and Arabia failed to perceive even after He manifested Himself and proclaimed His mission. H. M. Balyuzi describes the circumstances of the first revelation that Muḥammad received on Mount Hirrá' and explains Khadíjah's response to it:

> The vehicle of the Revelation which came to Muḥammad on Mount Hirrá' has been traditionally described as the Angel Gabriel. He held up a Tablet to Muḥammad to read. But Muḥammad was untutored and He could not read. Again He was told to read and again He pleaded ignorance. A third time the Angel told Him to read, and once again Muḥammad said that read He could not. Then the words of revelation reached Him: 'Read in the Name of thy Lord Who created; Who created man of blood congealed. Read, thy Lord is the Most Beneficent; Who taught by the Pen; Who teacheth Man what he knoweth not.'[19] Muḥammad was so overcome that He would have hurled Himself down a precipice. Then, the clear voice rang out again, in the stillness of the lone hillside, to tell Muḥammad that God had chosen Him to be His Messenger to mankind. The weight of revelation was too great to bear, and Muḥammad, now aware of His awesome mission to proclaim the Oneness of the Godhead, fled to His home, not more than three or four miles away, and asked Khadíjah, His wife, to cover Him with His mantle. Muḥammad said, on this occasion, that as He lay covered He felt that His soul had left His body for a while. It is related that it became His wont to seek the cover of His mantle, at the approach of a fresh revelation . . .
>
> Muḥammad's wife, Khadíjah, was the first to believe in Him. She had no doubt at all that her husband's experience on Mount Hirrá' was truly a call from God.[20]

Although after the first intimation of His divine mission Muḥammad did not receive any further revelation for a period of three years, Khadíjah did not waver in her belief in Him. She remained faithful without the least reservation. The story of Khadíjah embracing the Cause of her husband at the very outset of the Islamic dispensation is fortunately acknowledged and recorded by early Muslim historians. This was an amazing phenomenon for primitive Arabia where, before the advent of the Prophet Muḥammad, women are said to have meant very little, if anything at all, when it came to such important matters as faith and belief. The fact that the episode has found its place in history and compelled the historians to record the circumstances surrounding the belief of the first believer in the Cause of the Prophet of Islam, goes to show either that Khadíjah was truly extraordinary and soared above all degrading factors affecting the lives of the generality of women in those days, or that the situation with regard to women was not as bad as it later became, reaching its lowest depth about the time the Báb and Bahá'u'lláh revealed their missions.

Although great is the station of Khadíjah and tremendous the contribution she made to the course of the history of Islam, they do not compare in magnitude with those of her youngest daughter, Fáṭimih, titled Batúl (virgin), Zahrá' (resplendent), Siyyidatu'n-Nisá'ul-'Álamín (the world's foremost woman), Khayru'n-Nisá' (most virtuous handmaiden), Ṣadíqih (righteous) and Ṭáhirih (pure).

Historians differ regarding the date of Fáṭimih's birth and the exact date of her death. All believe that she died young; some say that she was as young as 18. She married 'Alí, a paternal cousin of her father, who later became known by the Shí'í adherents of Islam as Amiru'l-Mu'minin (Commander of the Faithful) or Imám 'Alí, when she was about nine years old. The stories related about her life point to the immensity of her suffering in the poverty-stricken house of her father before she married 'Alí and during the years that she shared the eventful life of her husband. She seems to have given birth to four children. Her two sons, Ḥasan and Ḥusayn, became the second and third Imáms following the martyrdom of their father. It is through Fáṭimih, the Lady of Light, that the lineage of Imáms, after Imám 'Alí, trace their descent directly from the Prophet Muḥammad.[21]

According to Shí'í belief, Fáṭimih is the only female member of the Fourteen Pure Souls, the others being Muḥammad and the twelve Imáms. There is a reference to these fourteen in 'Abdu'l-Bahá's commentary on the reference in the Qur'án to 'double seven' or 'twice seven'.[22]

Fáṭimih appears to be the youngest of the most outstanding heroines in religious history, if she indeed died at the age of 18. In spite of her short life span, she is known for her virtuous and exemplary qualities, her acquiescence while enduring enormous suffering, and for her mature wisdom. There are frequent references to her life in various Shí'í publications, and many powerful pens have moved to portray her high station and to extol her unique and godly attributes.

Fáṭimih's name is very familiar in Bahá'í literature because it is associated with the Hidden Words revealed by Bahá'u'lláh. Regarding this book Shoghi Effendi says:

> Revealed in the year 1274 AH, partly in Persian, partly in Arabic, it was originally designated the 'Hidden Book of Fáṭimih', and was identified by its Author with the Book of that same name, believed by Shí'áh Islám to be in the possession of the promised Qá'im, and to consist of words of consolation addressed by the angel Gabriel, at God's command, to Fáṭimih, and dictated to the Imám 'Alí, for the sole purpose of comforting her in her hour of bitter anguish after the death of her illustrious Father.[23]

The Dispensation of the Báb

With the introduction of Islam to the civilized and developed country that Iran was in the 7th century AD, there ensued consequences with far-reaching effects, some of which contributed tremendously to the further advancement of civilization and the discovery of many as yet unexplored fields of sciences, arts and literature. However, it also produced some devastating effects in certain areas of human affairs. Among the most adversely affected were women. Women, under laws made and imposed by men in the guise of religion, lost their freedom, their integrity, their identity, their self-confidence, respect and whatever could be taken away from them in the guise of religion. 'Abdu'l-Bahá says, 'In some countries man went so far as to believe and teach that woman belonged to a sphere lower than human.'[24] This was certainly the case in Iran at the time the Báb manifested Himself. Iran's religious affairs were then dominated by the attitudes and judgements of the 'ulamá in Karbilá, 'the foremost stronghold of Shí'ah Islám', to whom the Guardian of the Bahá'í Faith refers as those 'who relegated women to a rank little higher than animals and denied them even the possession of a soul'.[25]

What is astonishing is that the generality of the population of Iran accepted such a great and unjustified change in the essential fabric of their personal and social life. One reason for it may have been the fear of annihilation, if they resisted the change. Another reason is that Iran, like the rest of the old world, was dominated and ruled by warriors. Women's peace-loving nature prevented them from seeking supremacy through the use of physical force, bloodshed and war. This factor was largely responsible for women's subordination to the outward power and might of men, who appeared as heroes protecting the safety and security of their nations. Although before the advent of Islam women in Iran did not rise to the level of claiming equality with men, they were much more humanely treated than they were by the end of the Islamic dispensation. Two ruling members of the Sasanid dynasty, which preceded the reign of Islam in Iran, were women but the duration of their rule was short.

This tragic historical phenomenon reveals a mysterious tendency in men to strike at and sacrifice at every opportunity, under any pretext, the basic interests of their female counterparts. So much is this the case that the supreme Manifestation of God had to make gender equality one of the cardinal principles of His Revelation, to ensure that the rights of His female followers would be restored to them and protected under the all-embracing banner of His Cause. The only guarantee for such a stride in the evolution of our society is the injunction coming from the author of the Bahá'í Faith Himself:

> Exalted, immensely exalted is He Who hath removed differences and established harmony. Glorified, infinitely glorified is He Who hath caused discord to cease, and decreed solidarity and unity. Praised be God, the Pen of the Most High hath lifted distinctions from between His servants and handmaidens, and, through His consummate favours and all-encompassing mercy, hath conferred upon all a station and rank on the same plane. He hath broken the back of vain imaginings with the sword of utterance and hath obliterated the perils of idle fancies through the pervasive power of His might.[26]

When the state of the women's affairs had fallen to its most degraded depth, Ṭáhirih appeared and with her dramatic decision to embrace the Cause of the promised Qá'im became one of the most outstanding figures in the history of the Bábí Faith. With her extraordinary courage and audacity Ṭáhirih refused to entertain any of those thoughts about women that had been injected into their innermost being for eons. She fought with the sword of utterance and the shield of argument, with their aid she succeeded in confounding whoever ventured to confront her, including her own religiously renowned kinsmen.

Ṭáhirih was born in 1233 AH (1817 AD). She was named Fáṭimih at birth and was given several designations: Umm-i-Salmih, Zakíyyih and Zarrín-táj. She received tuition from a tutor her father had employed to instruct her. She soon proved herself capable of understanding the most complex theological and intellectual questions which had confused the minds of her many contemporaries among the ‘ulamá and the learned class. Her keen insight and inquiring mind led her to the Shaykhí school of thought established by Shaykh Aḥmad-i-Aḥsá’í. She became an adherent of the Shaykhí doctrine during the lifetime of Siyyid Káẓim, one of the ‘twin luminaries’[27] of their time, and maintained a very close and intimate relationship with him through correspondence. However, she never attended the classes Siyyid Káẓim conducted in Karbilá, nor did she meet him personally. Ṭáhirih’s deep perception of religious matters and her rare spiritual qualities prompted Siyyid Káẓim to call her Qurratu’l-‘Ayn (Solace of the Eye).

At Badasht, where Bábís gathered in 1848 to learn of the independence of the Faith they had espoused, Ṭáhirih was instrumental, under the direction of Bahá’u’lláh, in rending asunder the veils beclouding the vision and manner of thinking of the followers of the Báb. She proclaimed the independent nature of the Cause of the Qá’im, which had introduced new laws and ordinances abrogating those of the previous dispensation. It was at that conference that Bahá’u’lláh conferred upon her the appellation of Ṭáhirih (the Pure One). This title was then confirmed by the Báb.

In 1852 when an attempt was made on the life of Náṣiri’d-Dín Sháh, Ṭáhirih, who was then confined in the house of Maḥmúd Khán-i-Kalántar in Ṭihrán, was taken to the Ílkhání garden outside the gates of that city and strangled with a silk kerchief she had readied for that purpose. At the bidding of his drunken masters, a slave ended the precious and noble life of this ‘chaste and holy’ woman.[28] She was 36 years of age when she died as a martyr for her Faith and for the emancipation of women.

There is more available on the life of Ṭáhirih than on any other individual believer in the Cause of the Báb, including those honoured by Him as the Letters of the Living, one of whom was Ṭáhirih herself. She was acknowledged by all, friend and foe alike, to be the wonder of her age and the miracle of her time. She was born and raised in 19th-century Iran, which was tightly in the grip of the time-honoured traditions of Iran’s dark age when the survival of the king and his government depended heavily on how best they served the interests of the self-seeking clergy, who, according to a Tablet of Bahá’u’lláh, did not compare in esteem with ‘a paring from the nail of one of the believing handmaidens . . . in this day’.[29]

The Qur’án’s apparent advocacy of the use of the veil for Muslim women had been interpreted by Muslim judges to encompass their convenient understanding of the Qur’ánic verse to compel women to live under the veil of concealment not only physically but also intellectually and spiritually.[30]

Seeing Ṭáhirih and her revolutionary ideas about the emancipation of women against the background of men’s absolute authority over women makes her personality and accomplishments to shine so much more brightly.

Her fearless approach to matters of religious belief and her pioneering work in seeking liberation for women from men's tyrannical yoke are indeed astonishing.

Women and their work were looked upon with such haughtiness by men that Ṭáhirih's high ideals and the steps she took in manifest opposition to the general trend of thought about women went unchallenged in the beginning. When the seriousness of her ideology and the outstanding success she achieved were laid bare before the eyes of the contemptuous clergy, then no effort was spared to silence her.

Ṭáhirih's acceptance of the Cause of the Báb was as extraordinary as was her general approach to every other field of human endeavour. She was so confident and self-assured in attaining the object of her quest, that of the recognition of the Promised Qá'im, that when she learned of the intention of her brother-in-law to travel with the aim of finding the desired one, she penned her allegiance to the person whom she knew with certainty was the beloved of all those who were earnestly seeking Him and asked that it be presented to Him on her behalf. According to Nabíl:

> It was she who, having learned of the intended departure of her sister's husband, Mírzá Muḥammad-'Alí, from Qazvín entrusted him with a sealed letter, requesting that he deliver it to that promised One whom she said he was sure to meet in the course of his journey. 'Say to Him, from me,' she added, '"The effulgence of Thy face flashed forth, and the rays of Thy visage arose on high. Then speak the word, 'Am I not your Lord?' and 'Thou art, Thou art!' we will all reply."'[31]

Ṭáhirih had thus declared her belief in the one whose advent had not yet been made public and whose appearance others were still awaiting. Unfortunately, the exact date of her petition is unknown. It may have been written before the Báb declared His mission to Mullá Ḥusayn. Such an audacious act is unprecedented in religious history. Ṭáhirih embraced the Cause of the promised Qá'im spontaneously. She was prompted in this venture by divine guidance and strong spiritual insight. As previously stated, Ṭáhirih had never attended the teaching circles of Shaykh Aḥmad and Siyyid Káẓim, whose pupils formed the bulk of the Letters of the Living. Yet she gave her life for the claim of the person she never met on this plain of existence. She was guided to Him and believed in His divine mission unaided by normal means necessary for such recognition. Ṭáhirih's power of judgement, her knowledge of the tenets and laws of Islam and her full familiarity with the signs and requirements of the time won her praise not only from those who followed her lead but also from those who blamed her for going against time-honoured traditions. She was 'the Word which the Qá'im' was 'to utter, the Word which . . . put to flight the chiefs and nobles of the earth!'[32]

She is the one who, according to Nabíl, 'ventured on a few occasions to repudiate the authority of Quddús', saying, 'I deem him a pupil whom the Báb has sent me to edify and instruct. I regard him in no other light.'[33] She is the one who was the subject of one of the three homilies that Quddús had written and had charged Mullá Ḥusayn 'to read aloud to his assembled companions'[34] in the fort of Ṭabarsí, the other two being for the Báb and Bahá'u'lláh. She is the one 'whom the Tongue of Power and Glory . . . named Ṭáhirih [the Pure One]'.[35] She is the one Bahá'u'lláh has called the Point of Attraction. She is the one who addressed Vaḥíd in the House of Bahá'u'lláh in Ṭihrán in the following fashion:

> O Yaḥyá! Let deeds, not words, testify to thy faith, if thou art a man of true learning. Cease idly repeating the traditions of the past, for the day of service, of steadfast action, is come. Now is the time to show forth the true signs of God, to rend asunder the veils of idle fancy, to promote the Word of God, and to sacrifice ourselves in His path. Let deeds, not words, be our adorning![36]

Ṭáhirih has been the envy of both men and women of her time and thenceforth. She was adored to the point of being worshipped by her followers, who called themselves Qurratíyyih, and held in high esteem by world opinion but, alas, hated for her courage and audacity by the ecclesiastics who succeeded with malicious schemes to put an end to her precious and noble life.

Ṭáhirih is a perfect manifestation of 'Abdu'l-Bahá's attestation in one of His Tablets which says, 'when spiritual perfections and virtues and the splendours of the All-Merciful are manifested in the vesture of women, and shine in the lamp of handmaidens, their reflection is more resplendent'.[37]

Ṭáhirih was one of the few Bábís who knew the station of Bahá'u'lláh long before she had met Him. According to Nabíl's testimony, 'As it was with her acceptance of the Faith proclaimed by the Báb when she, unwarned and unsummoned, had hailed His Message and recognized its truth, so did she perceive through her own intuitive knowledge the future glory of Bahá'u'lláh.'[38] Bahá'u'lláh's own testimony is:

> She was with this Servant for a time. She would not barter one moment's meeting with this Youth for the sovereignty of this world and the next, nor for less than an instant did she wish for separation. However, that which had been pre-ordained came to pass.[39]

As early as 1260 AH (1844 AD) Tahirih made the following confession of faith in one of her odes about Bahá'u'lláh: 'The effulgence of the Abhá Beauty hath pierced the veil of night: behold the souls of His lovers dancing, mote-like, in the light that has flashed from His face!' Bahá'u'lláh says: 'Numerous are the verses and poems that she has composed about this new Revelation.'[40]

Ṭáhirih's station as the most distinguished woman of the Bábí dispensation has been confirmed by 'Abdu'l-Bahá, who has also testified that 'in eloquence she was the calamity of the age, and in ratiocination the trouble of the world', that she was a 'brand afire with the love of God' and 'a lamp aglow with the bounty of God'.[41]

Shoghi Effendi has associated the unveiled appearance of Ṭáhirih at Badasht with 'the Islamic tradition foreshadowing the appearance of Fáṭimih herself unveiled while crossing the Bridge (Ṣiráṭ) on the promised Day of Judgement'.[42]

Shoghi Effendi describes Ṭáhirih as a woman 'invested with the rank of apostleship',[43] a poetess 'of bewitching charm, of captivating eloquence, indomitable in spirit, unorthodox in her views, audacious in her acts'.[44] He calls her 'the first woman suffrage martyr'[45] and attests that 'the wondrous story of her life propagated itself as far and as fast as that of the Báb Himself'.[46] In the Epilogue to *The Dawn-Breakers*, Shoghi Effendi refers to Ṭáhirih in the following moving tone:

> Ṭáhirih, that flaming emblem of His Cause who, alike by her indomitable courage, her impetuous character, her dauntless faith, her fiery ardour and vast knowledge, seemed for a time able to win the whole womanhood of Persia to the Cause of her Beloved, fell, alas, at the very hour when victory seemed near at hand, a victim to the wrath of a calumnious enemy.[47]

The memory of Ṭáhirih also caused the beloved Guardian to mention her in the cables he sent in 1951 and 1952 in connection with the centenary of Bahá'u'lláh's imprisonment in the Síyáh-Chál, which witnessed the first emanations of His Revelation. In that same year, Ṭáhirih's martyrdom took place in Ṭihrán.

> . . . the Centenary of the blood bath constituting the most tragic episode in Bahá'í history associated with the martyrdom of the immortal Ṭáhirih, the subjection of Bahá'u'lláh to the rigours of the Síyáh-Chál in Ṭihrán and the barbarous execution of unnumbered heroes and saints of the Apostolic Age of the Bahá'í Dispensation.[48]

And again:

> . . . centenary of the darkest, bloodiest episode in Bahá'í history, associated with the nation-wide holocaust of Ṭáhirih's martyrdom, Bahá'u'lláh's imprisonment in the Síyáh-Chál in Ṭihrán . . .[49]

The Dispensation of Bahá'u'lláh

Numerous are the outstanding heroines of Bahá'u'lláh's dispensation. Some are close members of His own family, an account of whose lives have been given in this book. But the most outstanding of all is His daughter Bahá'íyyih Khánum, whose life and services are recounted in chapter 7.

Bibliography

Ábádih'í, Layla. Unpublished memoirs.

'Abdu'l-Bahá. *Memorials of the Faithful*. Wilmette, IL: Bahá'í Publishing Trust, 1971.

— *Paris Talks*. London: Bahá'í Publishing Trust, 1967.

— *The Promulgation of Universal Peace*. Wilmette, IL: Bahá'í Publishing Trust, 1982.

— *Selections from the Writings of 'Abdu'l-Bahá*. Haifa: Bahá'í World Centre, 1978.

— *Tablets of Abdul-Baha Abbas*. New York: Bahá'í Publishing Committee; vol. 1, 1930; vol. 2, 1940; vol. 3, 1930.

— *Tablets of the Divine Plan*. Wilmette, IL: Bahá'í Publishing Trust, 1993.

— *A Traveler's Narrative*. Wilmette, IL: Bahá'í Publishing Trust, 1980.

Afnán, Abu'l-Qásim. *'Ahd-i A'lá Zindigániy-i Ḥaḍrat-i Báb*. Oxford: Oneworld Publications, 2000.

— *Black Pearls: Servants in the Households of the Báb and Bahá'u'lláh*. Los Angeles: Kalimát Press, 1988.

Áhang-i-Badí' (Bahá'í Youth Magazine published in Iran). Special issue (nos. 6–11), commemorating the fiftieth anniversary of 'Abdu'l-Bahá's Ascension. Ádhar 1350 (November 1971).

Amanat, Abbas. *Resurrection and Renewal*. London: Cornell University Press, 1989.

Arbáb, Furúgh. *Akhtaran-i Tábán*. Ṭihrán: Bahá'í Publishing Trust, 132 BE.

Ashraf, Qudsiyyih. Unpublished memoirs.

The Báb. *Selections from the Writings of the Báb*. Haifa: Bahá'í World Centre, 1976.

Bahá'í News. National Spiritual Assembly of the Bahá'ís of the United States, nos. 172 and 174.

Bahíyyih Khánum, the Greatest Holy Leaf: A Compilation from Bahá'í Sacred Texts and Writings of the Guardian of the Faith and Bahíyyih Khánum's Own Letters. Haifa: Bahá'í World Centre, 1982.

Bahá'u'lláh. *Epistle to the Son of the Wolf*. Wilmette, IL: Bahá'í Publishing Trust, 1988.

— *Gleanings from the Writings of Bahá'u'lláh*. Wilmette, IL: Bahá'í Publishing Trust, 1983.

— *The Kitáb-i-Aqdas*. Haifa: Bahá'í World Centre, 1992.
— *Kitáb-i-Badí'*. Prague: Zero Palm Press, 1992.
— *Kitáb-i-Íqán*. Wilmette, IL: Bahá'í Publishing Trust, 1989.
— *Prayers and Meditations*. Wilmette, IL: Bahá'í Publishing Trust, 1987.
— *Tablets of Bahá'u'lláh*. Wilmette, IL: Bahá'í Publishing Trust, 1988.

Balyuzi, H. M. *'Abdu'l-Bahá: The Centre of the Covenant of Bahá'u'lláh*. Oxford: George Ronald, 2nd ed. with minor corr. 1987.
— *The Báb: The Herald of the Day of Days*. Oxford: George Ronald, 1973.
— *Bahá'u'lláh: The King of Glory*. Oxford: George Ronald, 1980.
— *Edward Granville Browne and the Bahá'í Faith*. Oxford: George Ronald, 1970.
— *Khadíjih Bagum*. Oxford: George Ronald, 1981.
— *Muḥammad and the Course of Islám*. Oxford: George Ronald, 1976.

Blomfield, Lady [Sitárih Khánum; Sara Louise]. *The Chosen Highway*. Oxford: George Ronald, rpt. 2007.

Browne, Edward G. *Materials for the Study of the Bábí Religion*. Cambridge: Cambridge University Press, 1918.

Díván-i-Qaṣá'id va Mathnavíyyát va Tamthílát va Muqatt'át-i Khánum Parvín-i I'tiṣámí. Ṭihrán: Chápkhánih Majlis, 3rd ed., July 1944.

Episodes in the Life of Moneereh Khanom. English title of Munírih Khánum's autobiography *Mukhtaṣarí az Táríkh-i Ḥayát va Tasharruf bih Arḍ-i-Muqaddas*, trans. by Ahmad Sohrab. United States, 1924.

Esslemont, J. E. *Bahá'u'lláh and the New Era*. London: Bahá'í Publishing Trust, 1974.

'Excerpts from Diary of Mrs. Keith Ransom-Kehler'. *Bahá'í World*, vol. 5. Wilmette, IL: Bahá'í Publishing Trust, 1980.

Faizi, Muḥammad-'Alí. *Ḥaḍrat-i Bahá'u'lláh*. Ṭihrán, Bahá'í Publishing Trust, 125 BE (1968 AD).
— *Khánidán-i-Afnán*. Ṭihrán: Bahá'í Publishing Trust, 127 BE (1970 AD).
— *L'aliy-i-Darakhshan*. Ṭihrán: Baha' Publishing Trust, 123 BE (1966 AD).

Gulkár, Ya'qúb. Unpublished memoirs.

The Holy Bible. Authorised King James Version. London: The Gideons, International, 1957.

Ishráq-i-Khávarí, 'Abdu'l-Ḥamíd (ed.). *Áfáq va Anfus*. Unpublished memoirs.
— *Ḥaḍrat-i-Ghuṣnu'lláhu'l-Áthar*. Published one hundred years after the martyrdom of the Purest Branch in Ṭihrán in 127 BE (1971).
— *Má'idiy-i-Ásmání*. 9 vols. Ṭihrán: Bahá'í Publishing Trust, vols. 1 and 6, 128 BE (1972), other vols. 129 BE (1973).
— *Muḥáḍirát*. Hofheim: Bahá'í Verlag, 1987.
— *Raḥiq-i-Makhtúm*. vol. 1 and 2. Ṭihrán: National Bahá'í Publishing Committee, 103 BE.

— *Risáliy-i-Ayyám-i-Tis'ih*. Mu'assisay-i-Millíy-i-Matbú'át-i-Amrí. Hofheim: Bahá'í-Verlag, 4th ed. 127 BE (1971).

Khan, Janet A. *Prophet's Daughter: The Life and Legacy of Bahíyyih Khánum, Outstanding Heroine of the Bahá'í Faith*. Wilmette, IL: Bahá'í Publishing, 2005.

Khúshihá. vol. 14. Khoosh-i-Há'i az Kharman-i-Adab va Honar, annual publication of the Society for Persian Arts and Letters. Wienacht: Landegg International University, 2003.

The Koran. Trans. J. M. Rodwell. London: Dent (Everyman's Library), 1963.

Maghzí, Rúḥá. *Farvardín-námih*. Iran.

Malik-Khusrawví, Núrí. *Iqlím-i Núr*. Shahru'l-Bahá 115 BE (March–April 1959).

Momen, Moojan. *The Bábí and Bahá'í Religions, 1844–1944: Some Contemporary Western Accounts*. Oxford: George Ronald, 1981.

Morten, Marjory. 'Bahíyyih Khánum'. *Bahá'í World*, vol. 5. Wilmette, IL: Bahá'í Publishing Trust, rpt. 1980.

Mu'ayyad, Ḥabíb. *Kháṭirát-i-Ḥabíb*, vol. 1. Hofheim: Bahá'í Verlag, 1998.
— 'Memoirs of Dr Ḥabíb Mu'ayyad'. *Payám-i-Bahá'í*, no. 33, p. 12.

Munírih Khánum: Memoirs and Letters. trans. Sammireh Anwar Smith. Los Angeles: Kalimát Press, 1987.

Nabíl-i-A'ẓam. *The Dawn-Breakers: Nabíl's Narrative of the Early Days of the Bahá'í Revelation*. Wilmette, IL: Bahá'í Publishing Trust, 1970.

Nuqabá'ín, Ḥusám. *Ṭáhirih, Qurratu'l-'Ayn*. Ṭihran: Mu'assissiy-i Millíy-i Matbú'at-i Amri (National Publishing Institute), 128 BE (1972).

One Common Faith. Haifa: Bahá'í World Centre, 2005.

Owen, Rosamond Dale. *My Perilous Years in Palestine*. London: George Allen and Unwin, 1928.

Paine, Mabel Hyde. Unpublished memoirs.

Payám-i-Bahá'í. no. 33.

Périgord, Emily McBride. *Translation of French Foot-Notes of the Dawn-Breakers*. Wilmette, IL: Bahá'í Publishing Trust, 1970.

Phelps, Myron H. *The Master in 'Akká*. Los Angeles: Kalimát Press, 1985.

Rabbání, Rúḥíyyih. *The Priceless Pearl*. London: Bahá'í Publishing Trust, 1969.

Randall Winckler, Bahíyyih (Margaret). *My Pilgrimage to Haifa, November 1919*. Wilmette, IL: Bahá'í Publishing Trust, 1996.

Rouhani, Murassa. Unpublished memoirs.

Rouhani (Rúḥání), Mírzá Muḥammad Shafí'. *Kháṭirát-i Talkh va Shírín* (*Bittersweet Memories*). Hofheim-Langenhain: Bahá'í-Verlag, 1993.

— *Lama'átu'l-Anvár: Depicting the Soul-stirring Episodes of Nayríz*. Bundoora: Century Press, 2002.

Ruhe, David. S. *Door of Hope: The Bahá'í Faith in the Holy Land*. Oxford: George Ronald, 2001.

Salmání, Ustád Muḥammad-'Alí. *My Memories of Bahá'u'lláh*. Los Angeles: Kalimát Press, 1982.

Save the Children: http://www.savethechildren.ca/new_zealand/newsroom/pregnancy.html.

Shahídí, Rafí'ih. Unpublished memoirs.

Shoghi Effendi. *Dawn of a New Day: Messages to India 1923–1957*. New Delhi: Bahá'í Publishing Trust, 1970.
— *God Passes By*. Wilmette, IL: Bahá'í Publishing Trust, rev. ed. 1995.
— 'Lawḥ-i Qarn'. Letter to the Bahá'ís of the East on the Centenary of the Báb's Declaration, Naw-Rúz 101 BE. Ṭihrán: Bahá'í Publishing Trust, 123 BE (1967).
— *Messages to America*. Wilmette, IL: Bahá'í Publishing Committee, 1947.
— *Messages to the Bahá'í World*. Wilmette, IL: Bahá'í Publishing Trust, 1971.
— *The Promised Day is Come*. Wilmette, IL: Bahá'í Publishing Trust, rev. ed. 1980.
— *Tawqí'át-i Mubárakih 1927–1939*. Ṭihrán: Bahá'í Publishing Trust, 119 BE (1963).

Sohrab, Mirza Ahmad. *Abdul Baha in Egypt*. London: Rider & Co., no date.

Star of the West. rpt. Oxford: George Ronald, 1984.

Tabrízí, Ḥájí Muḥammad-Ḥusayn. Unpublished letter to Jináb-i-Áqá Khalíl.

Tabrízí, Yadu'lláh. Unpublished memoirs.

Taherzadeh, Adib. *The Covenant of Bahá'u'lláh*. Oxford: George Ronald, 1992.
— *The Revelation of Bahá'u'lláh*, vol. 1. Oxford: George Ronald, 1974.
— *The Revelation of Bahá'u'lláh*, vol. 2. Oxford: George Ronald, 1977.

True, Corinne. 'In Memory of Munírih Khánum', *Bahá'í World*, vol. 8. Wilmette, IL: Bahá'í Publishing Trust, rpt. 1980.

The Universal House of Justice. Message on the Passing of Amatu'l-Bahá Rúḥíyyih Khánum, 19 January 2000.

Zarqání, Mírzá Maḥmúd. *Badáyi'u'-Áthár.* 2 vols. Bombay, Paris Publishing House, vol. 1, 1914; vol. 2, 1921 (*Maḥmúd's Diary*. Oxford: George Ronald, 1998).

References and Notes

Introduction

1. From a message of the Universal House of Justice, 19 January 2000.
2. ibid.
3. Women in the early Islamic dispensation enjoyed more rights than women who succeeded them: they had their own identity and their lineage could be traced back several generations. Their achievements did not go unacknowledged by historians. Ample information exists about Muḥammad's mother, who passed away when He was an infant. It is known who His foster mother was. Several of His wives were widows of other men before He married them and we know who they were and what contributions they made to the Cause of Islam. We know that His favourite wife, Á'isha, sided with the opponents of Imám 'Alí and participated in a battle against him. We know who Muḥammad's daughters were, who they married and what became of them. In brief, there is much more historical information about the female members of Muḥammad's immediate family than there is about those related to Bahá'u'lláh and the Báb and that is due to the fact that there were fewer restrictions on early Islamic historians in writing about women than there were on those who wrote the early history of the Bábí–Bahá'í Faith.
4. *Díván-i-Qaṣá'id va Mat͟hnavíyyát va Tamt͟hílát va Muqatt'át-i K͟hánum Parvín-i I'tiṣámí*, p. 187.
5. *One Common Faith*, para. 45 (pp. 34–5).
6. ibid. (p. 35).
7. Bahá'u'lláh, *Prayers and Meditations*, p. 313.
8. Bahá'u'lláh, *Kitáb-i-Aqdas*, para. 174.
9. 'I am the true vine, and my Father is the husbandman. Every branch in me that beareth not fruit he taketh away: and every branch that beareth fruit, he purgeth it, that it may bring forth more fruit. Now ye are clean through the word which I have spoken unto you. Abide in me, and I in you. As the branch cannot bear fruit of itself, except it abide in the vine; no more can ye, except ye abide in me. I am the vine, ye are the branches: He that abideth in me, and I in him, the same bringeth forth much fruit: for without me ye can do nothing. If a man abide not in me, he is cast forth as a branch, and is withered; and men gather them, and cast them into the fire, and they are burned' (John 15:1–6).
10. 'And there shall come forth a rod out of the stem of Jesse, and a Branch shall grow out of his roots. . .' (Isaiah 11:1).
11. '. . . Thus speaketh the LORD of hosts, saying, Behold the man whose

name is The Branch; and he shall grow up out of his place, and he shall build the temple of the Lord: Even he shall build the temple of the Lord; and he shall bear the glory, and shall sit and rule upon his throne; and he shall be a priest upon his throne: and the counsel of peace shall be between them both' (Zechariah 6:12–13).

12. Bahá'u'lláh, quoted in *Bahíyyih Khánum, the Greatest Holy Leaf*, p. v.
13. The Báb had only one child, Aḥmad, who died in infancy. The Afnáns are related to the Báb through the families of His wife and His parents, which include His uncles and cousins.
14. Bahá'u'lláh, *Tablets*, p. 254.
15. Bahá'u'lláh, *Epistle to the Son of the Wolf*, pp. 11–12.
16. Bahá'u'lláh, *Gleanings*, p. 218.
17. The Báb, *Selections*, p. 129.
18. ibid. p. 172.

Chapter 1

1. Faizi, *Khánidán-i-Afnán*, p. 24.
2. Nabíl-i-A'ẓam, *Dawn-Breakers*, p. 14.
3. Arbáb, *Akhtaran-i Tábán*, p. 22.
4. ibid.
5. Balyuzi, *The Báb*, p. 32.
6. ibid. p. 39.
7. Nabíl-i-A'ẓam, *Dawn-Breakers*, p. 75, fn. 1.
8. ibid. pp. 72–5.
9. ibid.
10. The Báb, *Selections*, pp. 52–3.
11. Ishráq-i-Khávarí, *Muḥáḍirát*, p. 1035.
12. Balyuzi, *The Báb*, p. 39.
13. Nabíl-i-A'ẓam, *Dawn-Breakers*, p. 77, fn. 1.
14. Faizi, *Khánidán-i-Afnán*, p. 24.
15. See Balyuzi, *The Báb*, p. 41.
16. ibid.
17. Ḥájí Mírzá Ḥabíbu'lláh Afnán was a grandson of the sister of Khadíjih Bagum, the wife of the Báb.
18. Balyuzi, *The Báb*, pp. 45–6.
19. ibid. p. 46.
20. see ibid.
21. ibid.
22. Faizi, *Khánidán-i-Afnán*, p. 193.
23. Nabíl-i-A'ẓam, *Dawn-Breakers*, pp. 76–7.
24. ibid. p. 129.
25. The Báb's Ethiopian servant.
26. Khadíjih Bagum, the wife of the Báb, whose eldest brother was Áqá Mírzá Siyyid Ḥasan.

27. *Núr-i-chashmán* is a term used for referring to one's own children or the children of the family.
28. Provisional translation of a previously unpublished Tablet approved by the Universal House of Justice for inclusion in this book.
29. Men traditionally referred to their wives as 'the mother of the children'.
30. Ishráq-i-Khávarí, *Muḥáḍirát*, pp. 1030–1. Muḥáḍirát says the letter was sent to the Most Great Uncle (i.e. Ḥájí Mírzá Siyyid 'Alí) who was living in Shíráz at that time. The actual recipient of the letter was Ḥáji Mírzá Siyyid Muḥammad, the Greater Uncle.
31. Balyuzi, *Khadíjih Bagum*, p. 19.
32. Ḥájí Abu'l-Ḥasan-i-Bazzáz had met the Báb on His pilgrimage to Mecca and had been impressed with His demeanour; he later espoused His Cause in Shíráz. His wife was a close relative of the Imám-Jum'ih of Shíráz (ibid. fn.).
33. Balyuzi, *Khadíjih Bagum*, p. 20.
34. Nabíl-i-A'ẓam, *Dawn-Breakers*, p. 151.
35. ibid.
36. ibid.
37. ibid. p. 191.
38. ibid. p. 195.
39. Balyuzi, *Khadíjih Bagum*, pp. 16–17.
40. ibid. p. 17.
41. Balyuzi, *The Báb*, p. 104.
42. Nabíl-i-A'ẓam, *Dawn-Breakers*, p. 197, fn. 1; *Traveler's Narrative*, p. 11; Balyuzi, *The Báb*, p. 105.
43. Nabíl-i-A'ẓam, *Dawn-Breakers*, p. 198.
44. Balyuzi, *Khadíjih Bagum*, pp. 21–2.
45. Balyuzi, *The Báb*, p. 105.
46. Balyuzi, *Khadíjih Bagum*, pp. 24–5.
47. ibid. p. 25.
48. ibid. p. 26.
49. Nabíl-i-A'ẓam, *Dawn-Breakers*, pp. 446–7.
50. Balyuzi, *The Báb*, p. 150.
51. Nabíl-i-A'ẓam, *Dawn-Breakers*, p. 448.
52. Balyuzi, *Khadíjih Bagum*, p. 26.
53. 'In some respects woman is superior to man. She is more tender-hearted, more receptive, her intuition is more intense' ('Abdu'l-Bahá, *Paris Talks*, p. 161).
54. Balyuzi, *Khadíjih Bagum*, p. 26.
55. See ibid. p. 27.
56. ibid. pp. 27–8.
57. 'The thirteenth century AH ended in October, 1882 AD' (Nabíl-i-A'ẓam, *Dawn-Breakers*, p. 191, fn. 1).
58. Nabíl-i-A'ẓam, *Dawn-Breakers*, pp. 191.

59. ibid. pp. 191–2.
60. The Báb's second wife was Fáṭimih Khánum. The marriage took place during the Báb's short sojourn in Iṣfahán. For more information about her, see below, chapter 4 'Fáṭimih Khánum, the Second Wife of the Báb'.
61. A reference to the repugnant behaviour of Mírzá Yaḥyá Azal who, after the Báb's martyrdom, married Fáṭimih Khánum, the Báb's second wife. More information about this episode is provided in the account of the life of Fáṭimih Khánum, below.
62. Provisional translation approved for inclusion in this book.
63. Balyuzi, *King of Glory*, p. 418.
64. These memoirs are quoted by Muḥammad-'Alí Faizi in *Khánidán-i-Afnán*, translated into English and published by Adib Taherzadeh in *Revelation of Bahá'u'lláh*, vol. 1.
65. Taherzadeh, *Revelation of Bahá'u'lláh*, vol. 1, pp. 155–7.
66. The Kitáb-i-Badí' is the name of a very long Tablet revealed by Bahá'u'lláh in response to the protests voiced by Mírzá Mihdí Gílání in a letter written to Áqá Muḥammad-'Alí, who presented it to Bahá'u'lláh in Adrianople. Bahá'u'lláh revealed the Tablet in the name of Khádimu'lláh.
67. Provisional translations approved for inclusion in this book. Bahá'u'lláh, *Kitáb-i-Badí'*, pp. 389–91. The reference to the mother and wife of the Báb has been revealed in both Arabic and Persian, hence some parts appear repetitious.

Chapter 2

1. After Ḥáj Mírzá Abu'l-Qásim built a *saqqákhánih* (public drinking place, drinking fountain) close to his business premises in the bazaar, he became known as Saqqákhánih'í (Khándán-i-Afnán).
2. Balyuzi, *Khadíjih Bagum*, p. 1.
3. Shí'í jurisprudence does not accept the mother's guardianship of an underaged child when his or her father dies, hence the necessity for a male member of the family to act as the child's guardian.
4. Balyuzi, *Khadíjih Bagum*, p. 1.
5. The women of that era sought the assistance of a close literate male member of their family to write their correspondence. Those who had no literate relative would pay a scribe to write what they wanted to convey.
6. Balyuzi, *Khadíjih Bagum*, p. 2.
7. Afnán, *'Ahd-i a'lá*, p. 47.
8. ibid. p. 38.
9. Faizi, *Khándán-i-Afnán*, p. 162.
10. ibid.
11. ibid.
12. Munírih Khánum, *Memoirs and Letters*, p. 33.
13. Perigord, *Translation*, p. 9, translating Nabíl-i-A'ẓam, *Dawn-Breakers*, p. 76, fn. 3.
14. Nabíl-i-A'ẓam, *Dawn-Breakers*, p. 76.

15. Balyuzi, *Khadíjih Bagum*, p. 5.
16. ibid. p. 6.
17. ibid. p. 5.
18. ibid. p. 6.
19. ibid.
20. Nabíl-i-A'ẓam, *Dawn-Breakers*, pp. 76–7.
21. 'The Báb oftentimes refers to Himself in the *Qayyúmu'l-Asmá'* as the Qurratu'l-'Ayn – the Solace of the Eyes' (ibid p. 9).
22. ibid. Shoghi Effendi included A.L.M. Nicolas's translation in *The Dawn-Breakers*. Here is an English translation from the French:

    > Glory be to God Who in truth has given to the 'Delight of the Eyes', in her youth, a son who is named Aḥmad. Verily, we have reared this child toward God! (Perigord, *Translation*, p. 9, translating Preface to A.L.M. Nicolas's translation of 'Le Bayan Persan', vol. 2, p. 11, quoted in Nabíl, *Dawn-Breakers*, p. 76, fn. 4).

23. Súratu'l-Qarába (the Chapter of Kinship). See ibid. p. 7.
24. 'The term 'Dhikr', here translated as 'Remembrance', was frequently used by the Báb to refer to Himself' (Balyuzi, *Khadíjih Bagum*, p. 8 fn.).
25. The daughter of the Prophet Muḥammad.
26. Balyuzi, *Khadíjih Bagum*, pp. 7–9. Shoghi Effendi included A.L.M. Nicolas's translation of this passage in *The Dawn-Breakers* (p. 52, fn. 1). Here is an English translation from the French:

    > Know that the benevolence of the Dhikr Sublime is great, O dearly beloved! Because it is the benevolence which comes from God, the Beloved. Thou art not like other women if thou obeyest God with regard to the Dhikr Sublime. Know the great truth of the Holy Word and glory within thyself that thou art seated with the friend who is the Favourite of the Most High God. Truly the glory comes to thee from God, the Wise. Be patient in the command which comes from God concerning the Báb and his family. Verily, thy son Aḥmad has a refuge in the blessed heaven close to the great Fáṭimih! (Perigord, *Translation*, p. 9, translating Nabíl-i-A'ẓam, *Dawn-Breakers*, p. 76, fn. 3).

27. For information about Bíbí Dukhtarán, see Balyuzi, *Khadíjih Bagum*, p. 7; see also Faizi, *Khánidán-i-Afnán*, p. 193 fn.
28. Faizi, *Khánidán-i-Afnán*, p. 195.
29. ibid. pp. 194–5. Summary translation.
30. ibid. p. 195.
31. Nabíl-i-A'ẓam, *Dawn-Breakers*, p. 191.
32. Arbáb, *Akhtaran-i-Tábán*, vol. 1, pp. 9–11.
33. Balyuzi, *Khadíjih Bagum*, pp. 10–14.
34. Balyuzi, *Khadíjih Bagum*, p. 14.
35. Munírih Khánum, *Munírih Khánum*, p. 34.

36. Nabíl-i-A'ẓam, *Dawn-Breakers*, p. 129.
37. A reference to the Prophet Muḥammad, His daughter Fáṭimih, His cousin and son-in-law Imám 'Alí, and His grandsons, Imám Ḥasan and Imám Ḥusayn.
38. Amanat, *Resurrection and Renewal*, pp. 240–1.
39. Munirih Khánum, *Munirih Khánum*, pp. 34–6.
40. Nabíl-i-A'ẓam, *Dawn-Breakers*, pp. 190–1; see above, ch. 1.
41. ibid. p. 191; see also above, ch. 1.
42. Faizi, *Khánidán-i-Afnán*, p. 133.
43. Nabíl-i-A'ẓam, *Dawn-Breakers*, p. 143.
44. ibid. pp. 191–2.
45. See ibid. p. 27.
46. Munírih Khánum, *Munírih Khánum*, p. 36.
47. Muḥammad-Shafí' Rouhani, *Lama'átu'l-Anvár*, p. 159.
48. Balyuzi, *Khadíjih Bagum*, p. 30.
49. Taherzadeh, *Revelation of Bahá'u'lláh*, vol. 2, pp. 383–4.
50. Munírih Khánum, *Munirih Khánum*, pp. 28–30.
51. ibid. p. 32.
52. Faizi, *Khanidán-i Afnán,* p. 243.
53. Taherzadeh, *Revelation of Bahá'u'lláh*, vol. 2, p. 383.
54. Quoted in ibid. pp. 383–4.
55. Balyuzi, *Khadíjih Bagum*, pp. 30–1.
56. Provisional translation of a previously unpublished Tablet approved for inclusion in this book.
57. ibid.
58. ibid.
59. Munírih Khánum, *Munírih Khánum*, p. 37.
60. Balyuzi, *Khadíjih Bagum*, p. 33.
61. Bahá'u'lláh, *Kitáb-i-Aqdas*, para. 32 and Question 29.
62. When the house of Zahrá Bagum and her husband, Áqá Mírzá Zaynu'l-'Ábidín, was burgled, the title deed of the property, which was kept in their house, was stolen together with their personal effects (Faizi, *Khánidán-i-Afnán*, p. 204). The date of the burglary is unknown.
63. Nabíl-i-A'ẓam, *Dawn-Breakers*, p. 191.
64. Balyuzi, *Khadíjih Bagum*, p. 29.
65. A facsimile of the original Tablet has been published in Balyuzi, *The Báb,* facing p. 193.
66. During the ministry of 'Abdu'l-Bahá, the House of the Báb was restored to its original design and rebuilt from its foundations under the supervision of Áqá Mírzá Áqá, who was familiar with the way it looked during the time the Báb lived in it.
67. See Balyuzi, *Khadíjih Bagum*, pp. 33–4.
68. Provisional translation of a previously unpublished Tablet approved for inclusion in this book.

69. Balyuzi, *Khadíjih Bagum*, p. 35.
70. Munírih Khánum, *Munírih Khánum*, p. 37; see also Taherzadeh, *Revelation of Bahá'u'lláh*, vol. 2, p. 387; and Faizi, *Khánidán-i-Afnán*, pp. 176–7.
71. Balyuzi says 'three hours before sunset' (Balyuzi, *Khadíjih Bagum*, p. 35).
72. English translation of Faizi, *Khánidán-i Afnán*, pp. 179–80.
73. Provisional translation of a previously unpublished Tablet approved for inclusion in this book.
74. Provisional translation of an excerpt from a previously unpublished Tablet approved for inclusion in this book.
75. Provisional translation of an excerpt from a previously unpublished Tablet approved for inclusion in this book.
76. Faizi, *Khánidán-i-Afnán*, pp. 177–8.
77. ibid.
78. Balyuzi, *Khadíjih Bagum*, p. 35.
79. ibid.
80. Zahrá Bagum, the mother of Áqá Mírzá Áqá and the sister of Khadíjih Bagum.
81. Provisional translation of an excerpt from a previously unpublished Tablet approved for inclusion in this book.
82. Provisional translation of an excerpt from a previously unpublished Tablet approved for inclusion in this book.
83. ibid.
84. Bahá'u'lláh, *Kitáb-i-Badí'*, pp. 389–91. Provisional translation approved for inclusion in this book.
85. Paraphrased from a previously unpublished Tablet approved for inclusion in this book.
86. Provisional translation of an excerpt from a previously unpublished Tablet approved for inclusion in this book.
87. Provisional translation of an excerpt from a previously unpublished Tablet approved for inclusion in this book.
88. Faizi, *Khánidán-i-Afnán*, pp. 184–6. Provisional translation approved for inclusion in this book.
89. Provisional translation of a previously unpublished Tablet approved for inclusion in this book.
90. Faizi, *Khánidán-i-Afnán*, p. 181. Provisional translation approved for inclusion in this book.
91. Faizi, *Khánidán-i-Afnán*, pp. 180–1.
92. ibid. p. 191.

Chapter 3

1. For more information about Zahrá Bagum's siblings, see the chapter 2 of the present book: 'Khadíjih Bagum, the Wife of the Báb'.
2. The Báb and Khadíjih Bagum had one son, Aḥmad, who died in infancy.

Jináb-i Siyyid 'Alí and Ḥájíyih Bíbí Ján Ján also had one son, Javád, who died at a young age.

3. The facsimile of the original of Bahá'u'lláh's Tablet in His own hand can be viewed in Balyuzi, *The Bab*, facing p. 193. For more information about the House of the Báb, see chapter 2 of the present book.
4. Faizi, *Khánidán-i-Afnán*, p. 219.
5. This Siyyid 'Alí is the nephew of Zahrá Bagum, who married the youngest daughter of Bahá'u'lláh, Furúghíyyih Khánum, and lived in the Holy Land. For more information about him, see chapters 2 and 9 of this book.
6. Zahrá Bagum's niece and daughter-in-law. Maryam Sulṭán Bagum was the daughter of Jináb-i Ḥáj Mírzá Abu'l-Qásim, the younger brother of Khadíjih Bagum and Zahrá Bagum.
7. Paraphrase of a Tablet of Bahá'u'lláh, in Faizi, *Khánidán-i-Afnán*, pp. 190–200.

Chapter 4

1. Nabíl, *Dawn-Breakers*, p. 208.
2. ibid. p. 214.
3. Browne, *Materials*, p. 220, n. 2.
4. Afnán, *'Ahd-i A'lá*, p. 218.
5. Translated from ibid. pp. 218–19.
6. Bahá'u'lláh's younger half brother who arose against Him and advanced the claim that he was the Báb's successor. He had as many as eight wives and six concubines. They came from various backgrounds and provided him with a broad base of support.
7. Afnán, *'Ahd-i A'lá*, pp. 220–1.
8. See also H. M. Balyuzi's account of this episode in *Edward Granville Browne*, pp. 34–5n.
9. Afnán, *'Ahd-i A'lá*, p. 221.
10. In a footnote to his *Edward Granville Browne and the Bahá'í Faith*, H. M. Balyuzi writes:

    > The Báb, during His six-months' sojourn in Iṣfahán, took as His second wife a sister of . . . Mullá Rajab-'Alí, named Fáṭimih. Perforce, she had to stay in her native town, when the Báb was taken away from Iṣfahán by the orders of Ḥájí Mírzá Áqásí, the Grand Vizier of Muḥammad Sháh (father of Náṣiri'd-Dín Sháh). The Báb had forbidden marriage, after Him, with either of his two wives. In spite of this interdiction, Mírzá Yaḥyá married the sister of Mullá Rajab-'Alí . . . (Balyuzi, *Edward Granville Browne*, p. 34).

11. Bahá'u'lláh, *Kitáb-i-Badí'*, p. 295.
12. Bahá'u'lláh, *Epistle*, pp. 176–7.
13. Translated from an unpublished Tablet of 'Abdu'l-Bahá, authorized for inclusion in this book.

Chapter 5

1. Malik-Khusrawví, *Iqlím-i Núr*, p. 107.
2. In one of His Tablets Bahá'u'lláh addresses a female relative as the daughter of His uncle and His sister, i.e. someone who was at once His niece and cousin. That lady was Ḥavvá. the daughter of Sakínih Khánum and Mírzá Muḥammad.
3. Balyuzi, *King of Glory*, p. 13.
4. Nabíl, *Dawn-Breakers*, p. 12. According to H. M. Balyuzi, 'Mírzá Buzurg was appointed vizier to Imám-Virdí Mírzá, the twelfth son of Fath-'Alí Sháh, who was the *Ílkhání* (chief of the clans) of the Qájár tribe (to which the royal family itself belonged)' (Balyuzi, *King of Glory*, p. 12).
5. Nabíl, *Dawn-Breakers*, p. 12.
6. ibid. pp. 12–13.
7. Ishráq-i-Khávarí, *Risáliy-i-Ayyám-i-Tis'ih*, pp. 62–3.
8. ibid.
9. ibid.
10. ibid.
11. Balyuzi, *King of Glory*, p. 17.
12. ibid. p. 23.
13. Nabíl, *Dawn-Breakers*, p. 107.
14. ibid. p. 116.
15. ibid. p. 119.
16. Some sources introduce the wife of Mírzá Yúsif as Bahá'u'lláh's aunt, others as Ásíyih Khánum's great aunt. Since Bahá'u'lláh and Ásíyih Khánum were distantly related, both accounts may be correct.
17. Ruhe, *Door of Hope*, pp. 142 and 158–9.
18. Ruhe, *Robe of Light*, p. 165.
19. Quoted by Shoghi Effendi in 'Lawḥ-i Qarn', p. 77. Provisional translation approved for inclusion in this book.
20. Provisional translation approved for inclusion in this book.
21. Provisional translation of a previously unpublished Tablet approved for inclusion in this book.
22. See chapter 10 of this book.
23. The vast majority of the people of Iran were illiterate in the 19th century. To enable them to enjoy communicating with their loved ones who lived away from home, there was a system. Scribes offered their service in places frequented by people and charged a fee which varied according to the level of the scribe's competence and the time and effort each task required. Confidentiality, however, could not be guaranteed, especially when the communication was between a mother and her son who claimed to be the Promise of all ages.

Chapter 6

1. 'Vazír' means 'minister' in Persian. It indicates that Mírzá Ismá'íl had an

important government position in Yálrúd, a village in the district of Núr in the province of Mázandarán, Iran.
2. 'Abdu'l-Bahá, *Tablets*, vol. 1, p. 218.
3. ibid. pp. 208–9.
4. It is the draft of a letter that she wrote to her son, the Most Great Branch, on the day He took a trip to Tiberias. The contents indicate that she was not feeling well and 'Abdu'l-Bahá did not awaken her to say goodbye. When she woke up and realized that He had left without saying goodbye, she was sad and poured her heart out in the letter.
5. The purpose of the dowry was to provide married women with some financial support and independence, especially if the marriage ended in divorce. However, in practice, it rarely served the purpose for which it had been instituted. Women who were deprived of the right of ownership and prohibited from seeking divorce were pressed hard by their husbands until they agreed to forgo their dowry before they could be granted divorce.
6. Balyuzi, *King of Glory*, p. 23.
7. Arbáb, *Akhtarán-i-Tábán*, p. 91.
8. Blomfield, *Chosen Highway*, p. 39.
9. Ásíyih Khánum's mother.
10. 'Abdu'l-Bahá
11. The faithful servant of Imám 'Alí, titled Amíru'l-Mu'minín (Commander of the Faithful).
12. Provisional translation approved for inclusion in this book.
13. Blomfield, *Chosen Highway*, p. 39.
14. Mírzá Taqí, known as 'Allámiy-i-Núrí.
15. Balyuzi, *King of Glory*, p. 21.
16. Blomfield, *Chosen Highway*, p. 40.
17. On the effects of child and early teen pregnancy see http://www.savethechildren.ca/new_zealand/newsroom/pregnancy.html.
18. Bahá'u'lláh, *Epistle*, p. 170.
19. This is the house where Mírzá Riḍá Qulí and Maryam lived and where Bahá'u'lláh stayed for about a month after His release from the Síyáh Chál. This house was recently demolished by order of the authorities in Ṭihrán.
20. Balyuzi, *King of Glory*, p. 17.
21. Oriental houses in those days comprised two sections: the *andarún* or the inner section, which remained beyond the reach of men who were not immediate members of the family; and the *bírúní* or outer section, where male guests were received and entertained. The set-up of the two sections of the house was such that women from behind curtains in their quarters could see what was going on in the *bírúní* but those in the *bírúní* could not see into the *andarún*.
22. 'Abdu'l-Bahá, *Memorials of the Faithful*, p. 200.
23. Blomfield, *Chosen Highway*, p. 22.

24. Nabíl, *Dawn-Breakers*, p. 299.
25. ibid. pp. 440–1.
26. For information regarding Bahá'u'lláh's second marriage, see chapter 8 below on Fáṭimih Khánum, Titled Mahd-i-'Ulyá.
27. Nabíl, *Dawn-Breakers*, p. 591.
28. Blomfield, *Chosen Highway*, pp. 40–1.
29. Isfandíyár returned to Ṭihrán after a while to take care of the debts that his purchases for the family had entailed. Thereafter he returned to Mázandarán (Afnán, *Black Pearls*, pp. 29–30).
30. Bahá'íyyih Khánum, in Phelps, *Master in 'Akká*, p. 17.
31. Mírzá Muḥammad-Qulí, Bahá'u'lláh's youngest half brother.
32. *Qiran* is same as *riyal*, which is the monetary unit in Iran.
33. Maḥmúd Zarqání, *Badáyi'u'l-Áthár*, vol. 2, pp. 205–6, translated in Ma'ani, *Ásíyih Khánum*, pp. 27–8.
34. ibid.
35. Blomfield, *Chosen Highway*, pp. 41–2.
36. ibid. p. 42.
37. The weakness of the central government in those days had increased Russia's influence in the internal affairs of Iran. One way of extending influence was offering, with the knowledge of the government of Iran, Russian citizenship to Iranians living in different parts of the country.
38. ibid. pp. 42–3.
39. ibid. pp. 44–5.
40. Shoghi Effendi, *God Passes By*, p. 109.
41. *Takht-i-raván*: a portable couch mounted on a mule, horse or camel. The English equivalent of this term is palanquin or litter.
42. Six months may be more accurate.
43. Blomfield, *Chosen Highway*, pp. 45–6.
44. This must be the house of Ḥájí 'Alí Madad in the old city, a rented house into which Bahá'u'lláh and His family moved in early May 1853.
45. Blomfield, *Chosen Highway*, p. 47.
46. ibid. p. 51.
47. He was the last child born to Bahá'u'lláh and Ásíyih Khánum.
48. Blomfield, *Chosen Highway*, pp. 51–2.
49. Isaiah 54:6–8.
50. Shoghi Effendi, *God Passes By*, p. 241.
51. ibid. pp. 129–30.
52. *Raḥíq-i-Makhtúm*, pp. 200–1.
53. The 12 days that Bahá'u'lláh spent in the Garden of Riḍván are associated with the declaration of His mission and are designated the Riḍván Festival or the King of Festivals. The 21st of April, the date of His arrival in the garden, the 29th when His family joined Him and the 2nd of May, the date of departure, are holy days during which work is suspended.
54. Shoghi Effendi, *God Passes By*, pp. 158–9.

55. Bahá'u'lláh, quoted in ibid. p. 161.
56. Shoghi Effendi, *God Passes By*, p. 167.
57. For details about Mírzá Yaḥyá's treacherous behaviour towards Bahá'u'lláh, see chapter 7 below on Bahá'íyyih Khánum, under the sub-heading 'Life in Adrianople'.
58. Shoghi Effendi, *Tawqí'át-i-Mubárakih*, vol. 2, p. 299.
59. Shoghi Effendi, *God Passes By*, p. 179.
60. ibid. pp. 185–6.
61. Blomfield, *Chosen Highway*, p. 66.
62. Ishráq-i-Khávarí, *Ḥaḍrat-i-Ghuṣnu'lláhu'l-Athar*, pp. 9–14.
63. Shoghi Effendi, *God Passes By*, p. 188.
64. Ishráq-i-Khávarí, *Ḥaḍrat-i-Ghuṣnu'lláhu'l-Athar*, pp. 9–14.
65. ibid.
66. Bahá'u'lláh, *God Passes By*, p. 188.
67. Bahá'íyyih Khánum, in Phelps, *Master in 'Akká*, p. 90.
68. Nearly 70 years later the remains of the Purest Branch were transferred by Shoghi Effendi to the slopes of Mount Carmel, where were also buried the remains of his mother, transferred from another cemetery in 'Akká. Their monuments were built next to each other in close proximity to the monument of Bahá'íyyih Khánum in a garden known as the Monument Gardens.
69. Bahá'íyyih Khánum, in Phelps, *Master in 'Akká*, p. 90.
70. Shamsu'ḍ-Ḍuḥá was a prominent believer in Iran. She was married to Mírzá Hádíy-i-Naharí, Munírih Khánum's uncle. When in Karbilá she was arrested and tortured in place of Ṭáhirih. For further information, see 'Abdu'l-Bahá, *Memorials of the Faithful*, pp. 175–90.
71. Fáṭimih Bagum was the wife of the King of Martyrs. Her mother's teaching activities before and after her husband's martyrdom caused them untold suffering. They were called to the Holy Land because there was no peace and protection for them in their home country.
72. Bahá'u'lláh, *Tablets*, pp. 227–8.
73. Bahá'íyyih Khánum, the Greatest Holy Leaf.
74. Provisional translation, approved for inclusion in this book, of an excerpt from a previously unpublished letter of 'Abdu'l-Bahá to His wife.
75. Provisional translation approved for inclusion in this book.
76. Siyyid Asadu'lláh-i Qumí came from Iran and served in the Holy Land during the ministry of Bahá'u'lláh and later during the ministry of 'Abdu'l-Bahá. He had the honour of meeting Ásíyih Khánum. He says in his memoirs: 'One afternoon Navváb, 'Abdu'l-Bahá's mother, paid me a visit at my home which was also my shop. With her visit she honoured this unworthy one.'
77. Balyuzi, *King of Glory*, p. 369.
78. The title 'Varaqatu'l-'Ulyá' was first bestowed by Bahá'u'lláh upon Ásíyih Khánum. After her passing He conferred the title upon Bahá'íyyih

Khánum. To avoid confusion, Shoghi Effendi translated Ásíyih Khánum's title as 'the Most Exalted Leaf' and Bahá'íyyih Khánum's as 'the Greatest Holy Leaf'.
79. Bahá'u'lláh, quoted in Shoghi Effendi, *Messages to America*, pp. 34–5.
80. Bahá'u'lláh, quoted in ibid. p. 35.
81. Shoghi Effendi, in *Bahiyyih Khánum*, p. 61.
82. Shoghi Effendi, *Tawqí'át-i-Mubárakih*, vol. 2.
83. Isaiah 54:2–15.
84. 'Abdu'l-Bahá, quoted in Shoghi Effendi, *Messages to America*, pp. 35–6.
85. Provisional translation approved for inclusion in this book.
86. Blomfield, *Chosen Highway*, pp. 39–40.
87. ibid. pp. 93–4.
88. To frustrate Shoghi Effendi's efforts, the Covenant-breakers objected to the transfer of her remains and those of the Purest Branch from 'Akká to Haifa stating that they were related to them and thus had the right to oppose the planned transfer.
89. Shoghi Effendi, in *Bahíyyih Khánum*, pp. 60–1.
90. Shoghi Effendi, *Messages to America*, p. 31.
91. The original coffin has been preserved.
92. Rabbaní, *Priceless Pearl*, pp. 259–60.
93. ibid. pp. 262–3.
94. Shoghi Effendi, cable of 26 December 1939, quoted in ibid. p. 262.
95. Shoghi Effendi, *Messages to America*, pp. 31–2.
96. Shoghi Effendi, in *Bahíyyih Khánum*, p. 61.
97. Bahá'u'lláh, in *Ásíyih Khánum*, p. 71. This verse in the Persian letter of Shoghi Effendi in ibid. but not translated in the English version.
98. Shoghi Effendi, *God Passes By*, p. 348.
99. Shoghi Effendi, *Tawqi'át-i-Mubárakih*, p. 242.
100. Shoghi Effendi, *Messages to America*, p. 36.
101. ibid. The Mashriqu'l-Adhkár project was launched on Naw-Rúz 1909 when the remains of the Báb were placed by 'Abdu'l-Bahá in the vault of the Shrine He had built on Mount Carmel.
102. ibid. p. 37.
103. Shoghi Effendi, *God Passes By*, p. 348.
104. Shoghi Effendi, *Messages to America*, pp. 32–3.
105. ibid. p. 33.
106. ibid.

Chapter 7

1. Bahá'u'lláh, in *Bahíyyih Khánum*, p. v.
2. Blomfield, *Chosen Highway*, pp. 39–40.
3. ibid. p. 40.
4. Phelps, *Master in 'Akká*, pp. 14–15.
5. Blomfield, *Chosen Highway*, p. 41.

6. ibid.
7. ibid.
8. Balyuzi, *'Abdu'l-Bahá*, p. 9.
9. *Bahíyyih Khánum*, pp. 32–3.
10. Blomfield, *Chosen Highway*, p. 41.
11. ibid.
12. ibid. p. 42.
13. ibid.
14. ibid. pp. 42–3.
15. ibid. p. 44.
16. Bahá'u'lláh, *Epistle*, p. 57.
17. Blomfield, *Chosen Highway*, p. 44.
18. ibid.
19. ibid. p. 45.
20. ibid.
21. ibid. To provide a better environment for recuperation, Bahá'u'lláh also spent some time in the house of His half brother and sister-in-law, Mírzá Riḍá Qulí and Maryam, entitled Varaqtu'l-Ḥamrá' (the Crimson Leaf).
22. ibid.
23. ibid.
24. ibid.
25. Shoghi Effendi, in *Bahíyyih Khánum*, p. 26.
26. ibid. p. 32.
27. ibid. p. 75.
28. Blomfield, *Chosen Highway*, pp. 45–6.
29. ibid. p. 46.
30. Phelps, *Master in 'Akká*, p. 19.
31. Blomfield, *Chosen Highway*, p. 46.
32. ibid.
33. Phelps, *Master in 'Akká*, p. 20.
34. Ásíyih Khánum was pregnant when the exiles left Iran. The baby was born soon after their arrival in Baghdád. He was named 'Alí-Muḥammad.
35. Blomfield, *Chosen Highway*, p. 47.
36. ibid.
37. Phelps, *Master in 'Akká*, p. 22.
38. Bahá'u'lláh, *Epistle*, p. 70.
39. Morn of Eternity, one of Mírzá Yaḥyá's titles.
40. Blomfield, *Chosen Highway*, pp. 48, 50.
41. ibid. p. 50.
42. ibid. p. 51.
43. ibid.
44. ibid.
45. ibid.
46. ibid. pp. 51–2.

47. ibid. p. 53.
48. ibid. pp. 53–4.
49. ibid. p. 69. It is not clear exactly when and how Bahá'íyyih Khánum was instructed in the art of reading and writing. A specimen of her writing is included in *Bahíyyih Khánum, the Greatest Holy Leaf.* It is also clear that later in her mother's life, she helped in writing letters for her.
50. ibid. p. 68.
51. ibid. p. 69.
52. ibid.
53. Shoghi Effendi, in *Bahíyyih Khánum*, pp. 26–7.
54. ibid. p. 33.
55. 'Álí Pashá was the grand vizier of Sulṭán 'Abdu'l-'Azíz.
56. Námiq Páshá was the governor of Baghdád.
57. Shoghi Effendi, *God Passes By*, p. 148.
58. Blomfield, *Chosen Highway*, p. 57.
59. ibid.
60. ibid. pp. 57–8.
61. Shoghi Effendi, *God Passes By*, p. 148.
62. ibid. p. 149.
63. ibid. p. 151.
64. ibid. p. 155.
65. Balyuzi, *'Abdu'l-Bahá*, p. 17.
66. Shoghi Effendi, *God Passes By*, p. 157.
67. ibid.
68. Bahá'íyyih Khánum, quoted in Blomfield, *Chosen Highway*, p. 59.
69. Shoghi Effendi, *God Passes By*, pp. 158–60.
70. Balyuzi, *'Abdu'l-Bahá*, p. 18.
71. Bahá'u'lláh, quoted in Shoghi Effendi, *God Passes By*, p. 161.
72. ibid.
73. ibid.
74. ibid.
75. ibid. pp. 161–2.
76. ibid. p. 162.
77. ibid. p. 165.
78. ibid. p. 166.
79. Blomfield, *Chosen Highway*, p. 60.
80. Shoghi Effendi, *God Passes By*, p. 166.
81. ibid. p. 167.
82. Shoghi Effendi, in *Bahíyyih Khánum*, pp. 27–8.
83. ibid. pp. 33–4.
84. Shoghi Effendi, *God Passes By*, p. 167.
85. ibid. p. 168.
86. ibid.
87. Referring to Mushíru'd-Dawlih, Bahá'u'lláh says in *Epistle to the Son of*

the Wolf: 'It was he who was responsible for the arrival of these wronged ones in the Most Great Prison ('Akká).' (Bahá'u'lláh, *Epistle,* p. 69).

88. Shoghi Effendi, *God Passes By*, p. 179.
89. ibid.
90. From Lawḥi-i-Sulṭán, quoted in ibid. p. 186.
91. Blomfield, *Chosen Highway*, p. 62.
92. ibid.
93. Bahá'u'lláh quoted in Shoghi Effendi, *God Passes By*, p. 179.
94. ibid. p. 180.
95. Blomfield, *Chosen Highway*, pp. 62–3.
96. Shoghi Effendi, *God Passes By*, p. 181.
97. Blomfield, *Chosen Highway*, p. 65.
98. ibid. p. 66.
99. Memoirs of Mabel Hyde Paine, pp. 37–8. Mabel Hyde Paine and her daughter, Sylvia, were on pilgrimage in 1920. They heard the Greatest Holy Leaf speak about the conditions of life on her arrival in 'Akká and during the early days in the barracks. Mrs Paine included in her recollections the English translation of the Greatest Holy Leaf's words.
100. Blomfield, *Chosen Highway*, p. 66.
101. Shoghi Effendi, *God Passes By*, p. 186.
102. ibid.
103. Blomfield, *Chosen Highway*, p. 66.
104. Shoghi Effendi, *God Passes By*, pp. 186–7.
105. Bahá'u'lláh, quoted in ibid. p. 187.
106. ibid.
107. Memoirs of Mabel Hyde Paine, p. 38.
108. Shoghi Effendi, *God Passes By*, p. 187. The only one who succeeded in seeing Bahá'u'lláh during the time He was in the army barracks was Ḥájí Abu'l-Ḥasan-i-Ardikání. It was arranged for him to see Bahá'u'lláh in a public bath but he was advised against 'approaching Him or giving any sign of recognition' (ibid.).
109. Shoghi Effendi, *God Passes By*, p. 188.
110. Bahá'u'lláh, quoted in ibid.
111. Bahá'u'lláh, quoted in Shoghi Effendi, *Messages to America*, p. 33.
112. Shoghi Effendi, in *Bahíyyih Khánum*, p. 37.
113. Phelps, *Master in 'Akká*, pp. 89–90.
114. Blomfield, *Chosen Highway*, p. 68.
115. ibid.
116. Shoghi Effendi, in *Bahíyyih Khánum*, p. 34.
117. Shoghi Effendi, *God Passes By*, p. 189.
118. ibid.
119. ibid.
120. ibid. p. 190.
121. Blomfield, *Chosen Highway*, p. 68.

122. Shoghi Effendi, *God Passes By*, p. 191.
123. ibid. p. 193.
124. 'Abdu'l-Bahá, quoted in ibid.
125. ibid.
126. For details, see chapter 6 on the life of Ásíyih Khánum.
127. Shoghi Effendi, in *Bahíyyih Khánum*, p. 28.
128. Translated from the unpublished memoirs of Mrs Rafí'ih Shahídí, whose family resided in the Holy Land at the time of Bahá'u'lláh's ascension.
129. Translated from the unpublished memoirs of Mrs Murassa' Rouhani.
130. Shoghi Effendi, in *Bahíyyih Khánum*, pp. 36–7.
131. Translated from the unpublished memoirs of Mrs Murassa' Rouhani.
132. Bahá'u'lláh, quoted in Shoghi Effendi, *God Passes By*, p. 239.
133. 'Abdu'l-Bahá, in *Bahíyyih Khánum*, p. 7.
134. ibid. pp. 8–9.
135. ibid. p. 14.
136. ibid. p. 15.
137. 'Abdu'l-Bahá's eldest daughter.
138. 'Abdu'l-Bahá, in *Bahíyyih Khánum*, p. 10.
139. ibid. pp. 14–15.
140. ibid. pp. 10–11.
141. ibid. pp. 15–16.
142. Blomfield, *Chosen Highway*, p. 113.
143. Ṭúbá Khánum, quoted in ibid. p. 114.
144. Shoghi Effendi, *God Passes By*, p. 9.
145. Phelps, *Master in 'Akká*, p. xxiv.
146. 'Abdu'l-Bahá, in *Bahíyyih Khánum*, pp. 13–14.
147. Shoghi Effendi, in ibid. p. 28.
148. ibid. pp. 37–8.
149. ibid. p. 75.
150. ibid. p. 38.
151. ibid. pp. 38–9.
152. Rabbaní, *Priceless Pearl*, p. 13.
153. 'Abdu'l-Bahá, in *Bahíyyih Khánum*, p. 17.
154. ibid. p. 15.
155. ibid. pp. 16–17.
156. Shoghi Effendi's parents.
157. Balyuzi, *'Abdu'l-Bahá*, p. 132.
158. 'Abdu'l-Bahá, in *Bahíyyih Khánum*, pp. 12–13.
159. ibid. p. 16.
160. Translation of the unpublished memoirs of Layla Ábádih'i.
161. Shoghi Effendi, in *Bahíyyih Khánum*, p. 39.
162. 'Abdu'l-Bahá, in ibid. p. 13.
163. Shoghi Effendi, in ibid. p. 28.
164. Indicating that at that time Furúghíyyih Khánum and her mother Gawhar

<u>Kh</u>ánum were not regarded as Covenant-breakers.
165. Provisional translation approved for inclusion in this book. It is not clear whether the water pump was for the Shrine Garden at Bahjí or Haifa.
166. At the time 'Abdu'l-Bahá left for New York, Rúḥá <u>Kh</u>ánum was lying in bed very sick. This is clear from the Tablet He wrote to Munírih <u>Kh</u>ánum. See above p. 173.
167. 'Abdu'l-Bahá, *Bahíyyih <u>Kh</u>ánum*, pp. 17–18.
168. ibid. p. 11.
169. ibid. p. 12. The full text of the prayer can be found on p. 12 of ibid.
170. ibid. p. 17.
171. Tablets often do not bear dates, which make it most difficult to know exactly when they were revealed. The contents of this Tablet seem to indicate that it was revealed during 'Abdu'l-Bahá's long absence from the Holy Land.
172. Provisional translation approved for inclusion in this book.
173. 'Abdu'l-Bahá, *Bahíyyih <u>Kh</u>ánum*, p. 9.
174. Provisional translation approved for inclusion in this book.
175. Rabbaní, *Priceless Pearl*, p. 21.
176. ibid.
177. Shoghi Effendi, in *Bahíyyih <u>Kh</u>ánum*, pp. 39–40.
178. Memoirs of Dr Ḥabíb Mu'ayyad, in *Payám-i-Bahá'í*, no. 33, p. 12.
179. ibid.
180. Dr Mu'ayyad was a physician who had recently graduated from medical school. At 'Abdu'l-Bahá's behest, he stayed in Abú-Sinán and looked after the medical needs of the population of that village and the surrounding area at a time when men had been conscripted into the army and physicians were in great demand.
181. Mu'ayyad, *<u>Kh</u>áṭirát-i-Ḥabíb*, vol. 1, pp. 192–3.
182. ibid. p. 196.
183. Shoghi Effendi, in *Bahíyyih <u>Kh</u>ánum*, pp. 40–1.
184. Randall, *My Pilgrimage to Haifa*, p. 14.
185. Pilgrimage memoirs of Mrs Mabel Hyde Paine and Sylvia Paine, who were on pilgrimage in 1920.
186. Randall, *My Pilgrimage to Haifa*, p. 37.
187. ibid. p. 43.
188. ibid. p. 49.
189. Translated from the unpublished memoirs of Mrs Rafí'ih <u>Sh</u>ahídí.
190. From the memoirs of Mabel Hyde Paine.
191. The present author's father.
192. It should read Qaṣru'd-Da<u>sh</u>tí.
193. Towards the end of His life 'Abdu'l-Bahá had advised the friends to read that Tablet and ponder upon its contents.
194. Rouhani, *<u>Kh</u>áṭirát-i-Tal<u>kh</u> va <u>Sh</u>írín*, p. 104.
195. Shoghi Effendi, in *Bahíyyih <u>Kh</u>ánum*, pp. 41–2.

196. Rabbaní, *Priceless Pearl*, p. 42.
197. ibid.
198. There is nothing to indicate that Bahá'íyyih Khánum and other female members of 'Abdu'l-Bahá's family accompanied the cortege or were present at the time of the interment of the body.
199. Rabbaní, *Priceless Pearl*, p. 49.
200. ibid. p. 45.
201. ibid. p. 46.
202. ibid.
203. ibid. p. 47.
204. ibid.
205. ibid.
206. ibid.
207. ibid. p. 48.
208. Shoghi Effendi, in *Bahíyyih Khánum*, p. 29.
209. ibid.
210. ibid. pp. 31–2.
211. Shoghi Effendi, dedication to Nabíl, *Dawn-Breakers*, p. v.
212. Shoghi Effendi, in *Bahíyyih Khánum*, p. 55.
213. Rabbaní, *Priceless Pearl*, pp. 53–4.
214. From the unpublished memoirs of Rustam Mihragani.
215. Rabbaní, *Priceless Pearl*, p. 55.
216. ibid.
217. ibid. pp. 55–6.
218. ibid. p. 56.
219. ibid.
220. ibid. pp. 56–7.
221. ibid. p. 57.
222. Shoghi Effendi, in *Bahíyyih Khánum*, p. 21; and *Star of the West,* vol. 13, no. 4, p. 80.
223. *Star of the West*, ibid. pp. 82–3.
224. Bahá'íyyih Khánum, in *Bahíyyih Khánum*, p. 115.
225. Rabbaní, *Priceless Pearl*, p. 276.
226. Bahá'íyyih Khánum, in *Bahíyyih Khánum*, pp. 117.
227. ibid. pp. 118–19.
228. ibid. pp. 119–20.
229. Letter of the governor held in the Bahá'í World Centre Archives.
230. Bahá'íyyih Khánum, in *Bahíyyih Khánum*, pp. 162–3.
231. ibid. pp. 164–5.
232. ibid. p. 165.
233. ibid. pp. 167–8.
234. ibid. pp. 168–9.
235. ibid. p. 169.
236. Rabbaní, *Priceless Pearl*, p. 62.

237. *Munírih Khánum*, p. 59.
238. Rabbaní, *Priceless Pearl*, p. 63.
239. Bahá'íyyih Khánum, in *Bahíyyih Khánum*, p. 205.
240. ibid.
241. ibid. pp. 205–6.
242. ibid. p. 217.
243. ibid. p. 222.
244. ibid. p. 223.
245. Rabbaní, *Priceless Pearl*, p. 145.
246. ibid. p. 146.
247. From the unpublished memoirs of Ya'qúb Gulkár.
248. An Iranian believer who served at Bahjí for many years as a guard and gardener.
249. From the unpublished memoirs of Yadu'lláh Tabrízí.
250. The house of the Master in Haifa has three floors: a basement, a floor built several steps above the ground, and a top floor, which was added later by the Greatest Holy Leaf for the use of Shoghi Effendi.
251. From the unpublished memoirs of Yadu'lláh Tabrízí, pp. 15–17.
252. ibid. pp. 24–5.
253. 'Mádar' means mother in Persian. Literally, 'nah Mádar' means 'no mother' and 'balih mádar' means 'yes mother', usually meaning 'no, dear' or 'yes, dear'. The Greatest Holy Leaf used these expressions often.
254. From the unpublished memoirs of Yadu'lláh Tabrízí, pp. 18–21.
255. Rabbaní, *Priceless Pearl*, p. 111.
256. ibid. p. 112.
257. ibid. p. 113.
258. ibid. pp. 113–14.
259. ibid. p. 114.
260. ibid. p. 115.
261. ibid. p. 115–16.
262. Shoghi Effendi, *God Passes By*, p. 349.
263. ibid.
264. ibid. p. 350.
265. Rabbaní, *Priceless Pearl*, p. 144.
266. ibid. p. 147.
267. ibid. p. 262.
268. ibid. p. 146.
269. Mr Kahrubá'í, originally from Yazd, was a trained electrician. At 'Abdu'l-Bahá's behest, he had gone to Haifa in 1921, to instal electric generators in the holy places. The work continued well into Shoghi Effendi's ministry. 'Abdu'l-Bahá bestowed upon him the name 'Kahrubá'í' (electrician).
270. *Payám-i-Bahá'í*, no. 192, pp. 17–18.
271. Shoghi Effendi, in *Bahíyyih Khánum,* pp. 23–4.
272. ibid. pp. 22–3.

273. *Payám-i-Bahá'í*, no. 33, p. 14.
274. Shoghi Effendi, in *Bahíyyih Khánum*, p. 63.
275. ibid.
276. Shoghi Effendi, *Messages to America*, p. 32.
277. Shoghi Effendi's cable dated 26 December 1939, quoted in *The Priceless Pearl*, p. 262.
278. Shoghi Effendi, in *Bahíyyih Khánum*, p. 61.
279. ibid. p. 30.
280. Bahá'u'lláh, quoted in Shoghi Effendi, *God Passes By*, p. 348.
281. The relatives of the Báb are all known as Afnáns regardless of their gender.
282. Bahá'u'lláh, in *Bahíyyih Khánum*, p. 3.
283. Shoghi Effendi, *God Passes By*, p. 347. For information about the most outstanding heroines of past religious dispensations, see appendix.
284. Shoghi Effendi, in *Bahíyyih Khánum*, p. 32.
285. ibid. p. 22.
286. *Khúshihá*, vol. 14, p. 97.
287. Shoghi Effendi, in *Bahíyyih Khánum*, p. 36.
288. ibid. p. 34.
289. ibid. p. 31.
290. ibid. pp. 25–6.
291. Bahá'u'lláh, quoted in Shoghi Effendi, *God Passes By*, p. 347.
292. 'Abdu'l-Bahá, in *Bahíyyih Khánum*, p. 8.
293. Shoghi Effendi, in ibid. p. 57.
294. *Khúshihá*, vol. 14, p. 115.
295. Shoghi Effendi, in *Bahíyyih Khánum*, pp. 55–6.
296. ibid. p. 83.
297. ibid. p. 25.
298. ibid. pp. 27–8.
299. ibid. p. 56.
300. Shoghi Effendi, in *Bahíyyih Khánum*, p. 44.
301. ibid. pp. 44–5.
302. ibid. pp. 42–3.
303. ibid. pp. 34–5.
304. ibid. p. 42.
305. Blomfield, *Chosen Highway*, p. 69.
306. From Mabel Hyde Paine's pilgrimage recollections.
307. 'Excerpts from Diary of Mrs. Keith Ransom-Kehler', *Bahá'í World*, vol. 5, p. 187.
308. Morten, 'Bahíyyih Khánum', *Bahá'í World*, vol. 5, pp. 182–5.
309. ibid. p. 181.
310. ibid.
311. Qudsíyyih Ashraf was the first Bahá'í woman to go to the United States for higher education. She was in New York when 'Abdu'l-Bahá arrived for His visit to North America. She studied nursing and upon her return to Iran

rendered outstanding services to the Faith and the people of Iran. While she was on pilgrimage 'Abdu'l-Bahá arranged for her to live with the Holy Family.

312. Translated from Persian from the memoirs of Qudsíyyih A<u>sh</u>raf.
313. Khan, *Prophet's Daughter*, pp. 242–53.
314. ibid. p. 251.
315. Rabbaní, *Priceless Pearl*, p. 146.
316. ibid. pp. 146–7.
317. In *Bahíyyih <u>Kh</u>ánum*, p. v.
318. Translated from the unpublished memoirs of Dr Habibu'llah <u>Th</u>abiti.
319. Shoghi Effendi, in *Bahíyyih <u>Kh</u>ánum*, p. 55.
320. Shoghi Effendi, *God Passes By*, p. 348.
321. Bahá'u'lláh, in *Bahíyyih <u>Kh</u>ánum*, p. 4.

Chapter 8

1. Bahá'u'lláh's mother also came from the Namadsáb clan. Her family was from the village of Fuyúl in Núr.
2. Taherzadeh, *Covenant of Bahá'u'lláh*, p. 117.
3. It should be Áqá Mírzá Riḍá Qulí.
4. The unpublished memoirs of Layla Ábádih'í, who served in the House of 'Abdu'l-Bahá in Haifa and was the Greatest Holy Leaf's attendant.
5. Adib Taherzadeh says that she 'gave birth to six children of whom four survived' (Taherzadeh, *Covenant of Bahá'u'lláh*, p. 117).
6. Taherzadeh, *Covenant of Bahá'u'lláh*, pp. 126–7.
7. ibid. p. 127.
8. ibid.
9. Bahá'u'lláh, quoted by Shoghi Effendi, *God Passes By*, p. 251.
10. ibid.
11. Taherzadeh, *Covenant of Bahá'u'lláh*, pp. 127–8.
12. ibid. pp. 129–31.
13. 'Abdu'l-Bahá, quoted in Shoghi Effendi, *Messages to America*, p. 35.
14. Isa. 54:11.
15. 'Abdu'l-Bahá, quoted in Shoghi Effendi, *Messages to America*, pp. 35–6.
16. From the unpublished memoirs of Rafi'ih Shahidi.
17. Shoghi Effendi, *God Passes By*, p. 222.
18. Taherzadeh, *Covenant of Bahá'u'lláh*, pp. 149–50.
19. Translated from Letter of Ḥájí Muḥammad-Ḥusayn-i Tabrízí to Jináb-i Áqá <u>Kh</u>alíl, p. 5.
20. A Persian weekly newspaper established in 1875 by Áqá Muḥammad-Ṭáhir-i Tabrízí.
21. Letter of Ḥájí Muḥammad-Ḥusayn-i Tabrízí to Jináb-i Áqá <u>Kh</u>alíl, p. 7.
22. ibid. pp. 14–15.
23. Mírzá Badí'u'lláh, according to a Tablet of 'Abdu'l-Bahá published in *Raḥíq-i-Ma<u>kh</u>túm*, vol. l, p. 243, repented at least three times. Each time,

after his selfish motive was exposed, he rejoined the Covenant-breakers and openly engaged in malicious activities against 'Abdu'l-Bahá.

24. Mírzá Badí'u'lláh's confession, written and signed by him and dated 4 February 1903, reveals the treacherous acts committed by Mírzá Muḥammad-'Alí and his supporters against 'Abdu'l-Bahá.
25. Provisional translation approved for inclusion in this book.
26. Owen, *My Perilous Years in Palestine*, pp. 230–1.
27. ibid.
28. Taherzadeh, *Covenant of Bahá'u'lláh*, p. 228.
29. ibid. pp. 228–9.
30. Momen, *Bábí and Bahá'í Religions*, p. 232.
31. ibid. pp. 232–3.
32. The degree of Mírzá Ḍíyá'u'lláh's involvement with the activities of his family against 'Abdu'l-Bahá is uncertain. Whatever his stand may have been, after his passing, 'Abdu'l-Bahá forgave what he had done to harm Him.
33. Provisional translation approved for inclusion in this book.
34. Provisional translation approved for inclusion in this book.
35. Provisional translation approved for inclusion in this book.

Chapter 9

1. For a brief account of the life of Mírzá Mihdíy-i-Káshání, see 'Abdu'l-Bahá, *Memorials*, pp. 95–7.
2. Note 90 of Kitáb-i Aqdas explains this provision, which Bahá'u'lláh has annulled. See Bahá'u'lláh, *Kitáb-i-Aqdas*, para. 63 and Note 90.
3. ibid. para. 114. See also Note 141.
4. 'Abdu'l-Bahá, *Memorials*, p. 96.
5. Salmání, *My Memories of Bahá'u'lláh*, p. 90.
6. 'Abdu'l-Bahá, *Memorials*, p. 96.
7. ibid. pp. 96–7.
8. Faizi, *Khánidán-i-Afnán*, p. 175.
9. Ṣamadíyyih Khánum was born in Baghdád in 1857.
10. Some members of Bahá'u'lláh's family trying to undermine 'Abdu'l-Bahá had in the meantime arranged for an engagement ring to be placed on Furúghíyyih Khánum's finger, giving the impression that she was already engaged to another person. By granting 'Abdu'l-Bahá's request, Bahá'u'lláh frustrated that design.
11. For more information about Khadíjih Bagum, see chapter 2 above.
12. Faizi, *Khándán-i-Afnán*, pp. 177–8; for the English translation of the text of the letter, see chapter 2 above.
13. ibid. p. 175.
14. Shoghi Effendi, *Messages to the Bahá'í World*, p. 25.
15. ibid. The reference is to the House of Bahá'u'lláh in Baghdád, which He designated as the 'Most Great House' and ordained as one of the two focal

centres of pilgrimage in the Bahá'í world. For more information, see Shoghi Effendi, *God Passes By*, pp. 110, 129–30; Bahá'u'lláh, *Kitáb-i-Aqdas*, para. 32 and Questions and Answers no. 29.

16. Shoghi Effendi, *Messages to the Bahá'í World*, p. 25.
17. Nayyir Afnán married Shoghi Effendi's eldest sister, Rúhangíz. Nayyir's brother, Ḥasan, married Mihrangíz, Shoghi Effendi's younger sister. Nayyir's youngest brother, Fayḍí, married Thurayyá, daughter of Ṭúbá Khánum, 'Abdu'l-Bahá's second daughter, and Mírzá Muḥsin Afnán.
18. Shoghi Effendi, *Messages to the Bahá'í World*, p. 25.
19. ibid.

Chapter 10

1. A concubine, according to the Oxford Concise Dictionary is 'a woman who lives with a man but has lower status than his wife or wives'. Its Arabic equivalent is *mut'a or sígha*, terms used to denote temporary marriage contracted for a fixed time period varying from an hour to 99 years. This kind of marriage is legal among Twelver Shí'ís.
2. According to M.A. Faizi, her full name was Sará Khátún Khánum (*Haḍrat-i-Bahá'u'lláh*, p. 9).
3. For more information, see the chapter on Ásíyih Khánum.
4. Arbáb, *Akhtarán-i-Tábán*, vol. 1, p. 117.
5. The Qur'án was compiled during the caliphate of 'Uthmán. Shí'ís believe that the original Qur'án contained references to Imám 'Alí which were omitted from the book compiled during the ministry of 'Uthman. A Qur'án in the handwriting of Imám 'Alí would have been an original version and most precious indeed.
6. Provisional translation of an excerpt from a Tablet of Bahá'u'lláh approved for inclusion in this book.
7. Provisional translation approved for inclusion in this book. The last paragraph enclosed in square brackets forms the last but one sentence of the Tablet of Visitation for Bahá'u'lláh and the Báb and has been translated by Shoghi Effendi. The Tablet of Visitation consists of excerpts from several Tablets revealed by Bahá'u'lláh. After Bahá'u'lláh's ascension, 'Abdu'l-Bahá asked Jináb-i Nabíl to select suitable excerpts to be recited by the friends visiting the Most Holy Tomb. The selected excerpts, known as the Tablet of Visitation, are recited in both the Shrine of Bahá'u'lláh and the Shrine of the Báb.
8. The original of this Tablet has been published in Malik-Khusrawví, *Iqlím-i-Núr*, p. 152.
9. Mírzá Ismá'íl, son of Sárih Khánum.
10. Provisional translation approved for inclusion in this book.
11. If a calculation is made from the date of Bahá'u'lláh's departure from Iran, this Tablet would have been revealed in about 1872. By then Bahá'u'lláh was living in 'Akká.

12. Provisional translation approved for inclusion in this book.
13. Provisional translation approved for inclusion in this book.
14. Provisional translation approved for inclusion in this book.
15. Provisional translation approved for inclusion in this book.
16. Arbáb, *Akhtaran-i Tábán*, p. 439. Provisional translation approved for inclusion in this book.
17. Sárih Khánum. Her full name, according to Mr M. A. Faizi, was Sará Khátún Khánum (*Ḥadrat-i-Bahá'u'lláh*, p. 9).
18. Mírzá Masíḥ was a devoted believer from Núr related to Bahá'u'lláh through the wife of His brother Mírzá Muḥammad-Ḥasan. He was a nephew of Mírzá Áqá Khán-i Núrí, the Prime Minister of Iran at the time Bahá'u'lláh was imprisoned in the Síyáh Chál and when He was banished from Iran.
19. The old city replaced by Ṭihrán.
20. Malik-Khusrawví, *Iqlím-i Núr*, p. 151. Provisional translation approved for inclusion in this book.
21. Provisional translation approved for inclusion in this book.
22. Provisional translation approved for inclusion in this book.
23. Provisional translation approved for inclusion in this book.
24. Provisional translation approved for inclusion in this book.
25. Provisional translation approved for inclusion in this book.
26. Sárih Khánum's son. The provisional translation of this previously unpublished Tablet has been approved for inclusion in this book.
27. Provisional translation approved for inclusion in this book.
28. Nabíl, *Dawn-Breakers*, p. 603.
29. ibid. pp. 603–4.
30. Malik-Khusrawví, *Iqlím-i-Núr*, p. 150.
31. ibid. pp. 94 and 107.
32. ibid. p. 142.
33. ibid. pp. 140–3.
34. Ḥavvá Khánum may have written to Bahá'u'lláh regarding her intention to embark on a trip with the aim of visiting Him. If so, there is no evidence that her intention was fulfilled.
35. Provisional translation approved for inclusion in this book.
36. Malik-Khusrawví, *Iqlím-i-Núr*, p. 111.
37. Provisional translation approved for inclusion in this book.
38. Malik-Khusrawví, *Iqlím-i-Núr*, p. 108.
39. Provisional translation approved for inclusion in this book.
40. Provisional translation approved for inclusion in this book.
41. Provisional translation approved for inclusion in this book.
42. Malik-Khusrawví, *Iqlím-i-Núr*, p. 185.
43. Provisional translation approved for inclusion in this book.
44. The numerical value of Ṭá is the same as Bahá'.
45. Sháh Sulṭán Khánum was responsible for preventing Shahrbánú Khánum,

'Abdu'l-Bahá's cousin who was betrothed to Him, from leaving Ṭihrán for Adrianople and arranged for her to marry 'Alí Khán, the son of Áqá Khán-i Núrí, the prime minister of Iran.

46. Provisional translation approved for inclusion in this book.
47. ibid.
48. Provisional translation approved for inclusion in this book.
49. Bahá'u'lláh, *Epistle*, pp. 170–1.
50. ibid. pp. 169–70.
51. Shahrbánú Khánum, Bahá'u'lláh's niece.
52. Reference to Shahrbánú Khánum's death a few months after her marriage with Mírzá 'Alí Khán. According to Bahá'u'lláh's statement, it was after that incident, which took place while Bahá'u'lláh was in Adrianople, that Sháh Sulṭán Khánum turned to Mírzá Yaḥyá Azal. So, by the time Bahá'u'lláh severed ties with Mírzá Yaḥyá, Sháh Sulṭán Khánum was already in Mírzá Yaḥyá's camp.
53. Malik-Khusrawví, *Iqlím-i-Núr*, pp. 186–8. Provisional translation approved for inclusion in this book.
54. Qur'án 23:101.
55. Qur'án 80:30.
56. Malik-Khusrawví, *Iqlím-i-Núr*, pp. 188–9. Provisional translation approved for inclusion in this book.
57. The Báb
58. Bahá'u'lláh
59. Mírzá Yaḥyá Azal, whom Sháh Sulṭan Khánum followed, was known as a Mir'át.
60. Qur'án 22:5.
61. 'Abdu'l-Bahá, *Makátíb-i-'Abdu'l-Bahá*, vol. 2, pp. 179–86. Provisional translation approved for inclusion in this book.
62. Balyuzi, *Edward Granville Browne*, p. 44.

Chapter 11

1. In some of His Tablets Bahá'u'lláh addresses Maryam as Varaqatu'l-Ḥamrá' (the Crimson Leaf). Some believe the reason for the designation was Maryam's red hair. The title does not seem to have been exclusively given to the Maryam with whose life this account is concerned. It has been used in at least one more instance in connection with 'leaf of the leaf of the Sacred Tree', who was also named Maryam and who was born when Bahá'u'lláh was in the Most Great Prison.
2. For information regarding *Ḥurúfát-i-'Állín* see Taherzadeh, *Revelation of Bahá'u'lláh*, vol. 1, pp. 122–5.
3. Bahá'u'lláh's half brother.
4. Arbáb, *Akhtarán-i-Tábán*, p. 91.
5. The unpublished memoirs of 'Abdu'l-Ḥamíd Ishráq-i Khávarí.
6. Taherzadeh, *Revelation of Bahá'u'lláh*, vol. 1, pp. 12–13.

7. See chapter 7 of this book on Bahá'íyyih Khánum; see also Blomfield, *Chosen Highway*, p. 44.
8. Among Bahá'u'lláh's half sisters 'Izzíyyih Khánum is notorious for her animosity towards Him. She exerted great influence upon her siblings and upon those with whom she was in contact. She is the one who prevented the marriage of her niece, Shahrbánú Khánum, to 'Abdu'l-Bahá and arranged for her to marry the son of the prime minister of Iran which caused her much misery and ended in her premature death. Knowing Maryam's great love for and deep devotion to Bahá'u'lláh, 'Izzíyyih Khánum is believed to have used her influence to curtail Maryam's movements and activities.
9. Khánum (Lady) may be in this instance a reference to Bahá'u'lláh's mother.
10. The 'fresh calamity' may refer to His exile from Baghdád to Constantinople and Adrianople.
11. Taherzadeh, *Revelation of Bahá'u'lláh*, vol. 1, p. 13.
12. ibid.
13. The same visitation Tablet is to be recited at the tomb of Ṭáhirih, according to Bahá'u'lláh's instruction, which reads: 'Moreover, whoso desireth to visit the grave site of the letter Ṭá (Ṭáhirih), who offered up her life as a martyr, let him make his visitation by reciting this Tablet.' The exact location of Ṭáhirih's grave is to be determined in future.
14. Provisional translation approved for inclusion in this book.
15. Provisional translation approved for inclusion in this book.
16. Taherzadeh, *Revelation of Bahá'u'lláh*, vol. 1, p. 13.
17. The set-in verses are Shoghi Effendi's translations published in *God Passes By*, p. 118. The rest is a paraphrase.
18. Bahá'u'lláh, in Shoghi Effendi, *God Passes By*, p. 118.
19. ibid.
20. This is a reference to His unexpected departure from Baghdád and His retirement in the mountains of Sulaymáníyyih in Kurdistán, Iraq, where He spent about two years from 1854 to 1856.
21. A reference to Mírzá Yaḥyá Azal whose animosity towards Bahá'u'lláh and his intense envy of Him were notorious and the main cause of Bahá'u'lláh's migration.
22. Bahá'u'lláh, in Shoghi Effendi, *God Passes By*, p. 118.
23. Maryam's husband was one of the brothers implicated in this statement.
24. Bahá'u'lláh, in Shoghi Effendi, *God Passes By*, p. 124.
25. Evidence of Mírzá Yaḥyá's impotence to exert salutary influence on the Bábí community whose leader he claimed to be.
26. Reference to improvements in the way the exiles were treated by the authorities in Baghdád.
27. Bahá'u'lláh, *Má'idiy-i-Ásmání*, vol. 4, pp. 329–34. *Raḥíq-i-Makhtúm*, vol. 2, pp. 991–6.
28. ibid.

29. Bahá'u'lláh's half sisters. Ḥusní is the abbreviated form of Ḥusníyyih.
30. Khadíjih Khánum is the name of Bahá'u'lláh's mother but it is most unlikely that He would have referred to her by her first name. Therefore, another Khadíjih seems to be intended here.
31. Bahá'u'lláh's niece who married Mírzá Muḥammad, Maryam's brother.
32. Like the Sunnís, Shí'ís are divided into many sects. Some believe in twelve Imáms and are known as Shí'í twelvers. They believe that the twelfth Imám disappeared from sight in infancy and has been living for over a thousand years. They say that he will reappear at the appointed time on the day of resurrection and wipe out injustices with his mighty sword. Thereafter, the rights of the oppressed will be restored, peace and tranquillity will reign in the world.
33. Provisional translation approved for inclusion in this book.
34. Provisional translation approved for inclusion in this book.
35. Provisional translation approved for inclusion in this book.
36. Provisional translation approved for inclusion in this book.
37. A reference to Sháh Sulṭán Khánum ('Izzíyyih), Bahá'u'lláh's half sister and Zahrá Khánum's paternal aunt, who turned against Bahá'u'lláh and sided with Mírzá Yaḥyá.
38. Provisional translation approved for inclusion in this book.
39. Provisional translation approved for inclusion in this book.
40. Provisional translation approved for inclusion in this book.
41. Provisional translation approved for inclusion in this book.
42. *Raḥíq-i-Makhtúm*, vol. 2, pp. 990–1.

Chapter 12

1. The name appears in a visitation prayer revealed by 'Abdu'l-Bahá in honour of Munírih Khánum's mother when she passed away.
2. In Islam, the age of maturity for men is 15.
3. *Munírih Khánum*, p. 12.
4. Nabíl, *Dawn-Breakers*, p. 208.
5. ibid. pp. 208–9. This episode is also mentioned in *Bahá'u'lláh, The King of Glory*, p. 341. The author, H.M. Balyuzi, bases his account on Munírih Khánum's own account.
6. Esslemont, *New Era*, p. 52.
7. ibid.
8. *Munírih Khánum*, p. 22.
9. ibid. pp. 22–4.
10. ibid. p. 20.
11. After what happened to Shahrbánú Khánum (see chapter 10), it was probably deemed unwise to divulge the reason for calling Fáṭimih Khánum to the Holy Land.
12. Shamsu'ḍ-Ḍuḥá was married to Jináb-i Mírzá Hádíy-i Nahrí, Fáṭimih Khánum's paternal uncle. She was Ṭáhirih's companion in Iraq and

suffered persecution and confinement in Karbilá. 'Abdu'l-Bahá has given an account of her life in *Memorials of the Faithful,* pp . 175–90.

13. *Munírih Khánum*, pp. 24–5.
14. ibid. p. 25.
15. Bahá'u'lláh, quoted in ibid.
16. ibid. p. 26.
17. ibid. pp. 40–2.
18. Bahá'u'lláh, quoted in ibid. p. 44.
19. ibid. p. 46.
20. Sháh Sulṭán Khánum; she was also known as Ḥájíyih Sulṭán Khánum and Khánum Buzurg.
21. 'Abdu'l-Bahá, in Malik-Khusrawví, *Iqlím-i Núr*, pp. 213–14.
22. Bahá'u'lláh, *Epistle*, pp. 170–1.
23. Balyuzi, *King of Glory,* pp. 342–3.
24. *Áhang-i-Badí*, special issue (nos. 6–11), Adhar 1350, pp. 305–6.
25. Esslemont, *New Era*, p. 52.
26. The Bahá'í month of fasting (2–20 March) seems to be intended. Muslims generally do not get married during Ramaḍán. In consideration of the sensitivities of the populace, especially in those early years of Bahá'u'lláh's stay in 'Akká, it seems most unlikely for 'Abdu'l-Bahá's marriage to have taken place during that month.
27. Maghzí, *Farvardín-námih*, p. 145.
28. *Munírih Khánum*, p. 49.
29. ibid. p. 51.
30. ibid.
31. Blomfield, *Chosen Highway*, p. 89.
32. Maghzí, *Farvardín-námih*, pp. 146–7.
33. A garden situated between 'Akká and Nahariyyih.
34. Munírih Khánum
35. 'Abdu'l-Bahá's eldest daughter and Ḥusayn Effendi's eldest sister. She later became Shoghi Effendi's mother.
36. Provisional translation approved for inclusion in this book.
37. A Tablet from 'Abdu'l-Bahá revealed at about the same time makes it clear that Munírih Khánum, Ḥusayn Effendi and Ḍíyá'íyyih Khánum had gone to Haifa for reasons of Ḥusayn Effendi's health. In the Tablet 'Abdu'l-Bahá advises Munírih Khánum, who wanted to return to 'Akká, that it was better for her to be patient, for until rain came, the weather in Haifa was more favourable.
38. The word for sightseeing in Persian is '*tamáshá*'. Ḥusayn Effendi could not pronounce the word '*tamáshá*' properly. Instead he said '*tabáshá*'. He loved sightseeing and often said that he wanted to go for '*tabáshá*'. Bahá'u'lláh's choice of words in this and another Tablet revealed after Ḥusayn Effendi's death, betokens this.
39. Provisional translation approved for inclusion in this book.

40. Qur'án, 4:78 (Yusuf Ali translation).
41. Qur'án 18:46.
42. An indication that Ḥusayn Effendi pronounced the word '*tamáshá*' (sightseeing) as '*tabásha*'.
43. Provisional translation approved for inclusion in this book.
44. Provisional translation approved for inclusion in this book.
45. The translation of parts of this Tablet is published in Taherzadeh, *Covenant of Bahá'u'lláh*, p. 137. See also Balyuzi, *'Abdu'l-Bahá*, p. 38.
46. Provisional translation approved for inclusion in this book.
47. Provisional translation approved for inclusion in this book.
48. Provisional translation approved for inclusion in this book.
49. Mírzá Áqá Ján, Bahá'u'lláh's amanuensis.
50. Provisional translation approved for inclusion in this book.
51. This seems to be a reference to Munírih Khánum's mother.
52. Provisional translation approved for inclusion in this book.
53. Provisional translation approved for inclusion in this book.
54. Blomfield, *Chosen Highway*, pp. 105–7.
55. ibid. p. 109.
56. ibid. pp. 109–10.
57. Qur'án 35:43.
58. 'Abdu'l-Bahá's youngest daughter. The third daughter, Rúḥá Khánum, whose name does not appear in the passage, may not have been in 'Akká at the time.
59. Munírih Khánum's cousin. She was the daughter of Shamsu'ḍ-Ḍuḥá and the wife of the King of Martyrs.
60. Munírih Khánum's sister.
61. Munírih Khánum's sister.
62. This passage is significant because it indicates the names of the close members of the family who were living in 'Akká at the time.
63. Venerable lady.
64. Qur'án 26:227. Provisional translation approved for inclusion in this book.
65. Oriental houses in the Middle East in the 19th and early 20th centuries had a *bírúní* (outer section) and an *andarún* (inner section). The women used the *andarún* for getting together, the men the *bírúní*. Thus complete gender segregation was observed.
66. From an unpublished Tablet; provisional translation approved for inclusion in this book.
67. Blomfield, *Chosen Highway*, pp. 112–13.
68. ibid. p. 114.
69. ibid.
70. Provisional translation approved for inclusion in this book.
71. For more detailed information on Mírzá Badí'u'lláh's intrigues, see chapter 7 on Bahá'íyyih Khánum and chapter 8 on Faṭímih Khánum, Titled Mahd-i-'Ulyá.

72. Provisional translation approved for inclusion in this book.
73. The person Mírzá Badí'u'lláh had used as an intermediary to express repentance for the transgressions he had committed against 'Abdu'l-Bahá and the Cause of God.
74. Provisional translation approved for inclusion in this book.
75. Provisional translation approved for inclusion in this book.
76. Provisional translation approved for inclusion in this book.
77. Provisional translation approved for inclusion in this book.
78. The subsidiary buildings were later razed and the rubble became part of the gardens surrounding the Mansion.
79. True, 'In Memory of Munírih Khánum', *Bahá'í World*, vol. 8, p. 265.
80. ibid.
81. ibid.
82. Grandson of Mírzá Muḥammad-Qulí.
83. Provisional translation approved for inclusion in this book. Mírzá Dhikru'lláh is the son of Mírzá Muḥammad-Qulí.
84. Provisional translation approved for inclusion in this book. It is not known who the patient was.
85. Shoghi Effendi, *God Passes By*, pp. 279–80.
86. They broke the Covenant and stirred up a temporary turmoil, the effects of which were felt especially in the United States and United Kingdom.
87. Rabbaní, *Priceless Pearl*, p. 19.
88. Josephine Fallscheer, born 1866, graduated from medical school in Germany in 1891. She and her family lived in Haifa from 1905 to 1912. She attended to the medical needs of 'Abdu'l-Bahá's family and members of the local Bahá'í community. She was also a close and trusted friend of 'Abdu'l-Bahá's family. In her 'Abdu'l-Bahá had confided the guarded secret of the appointment of Shoghi Effendi as His successor.
89. Balyuzi, *'Abdu'l-Bahá*, pp. 135–6.
90. Provisional translation approved for inclusion in this book.
91. Balyuzi, *'Abdu'l-Bahá*, p. 136.
92. ibid. pp. 138–9.
93. Provisional translation approved for inclusion in this book.
94. Leticia was a European, probably Italian, woman who had earlier worked for the family.
95. Áqá Mírzá Muḥsin Afnán was the son-in-law of 'Abdu'l-Bahá and Munírih Khánum. He was married to Ṭúbá Khánum.
96. Provisional translation approved for inclusion in this book.
97. Shoghi Effendi accompanied 'Abdu'l-Bahá on His second sea voyage to Europe and was to accompany Him to North America. When they reached Naples he was denied the necessary health clearance and could not proceed to America.
98. Rúḥá Khánum was with 'Abdu'l-Bahá in France. As the Tablet indicates, she was gravely ill when 'Abdu'l-Bahá had to continue His journey westward.

99. 'Abdu'l-Bahá and Munírih <u>Kh</u>ánum's youngest daughter.
100. Provisional translation approved for inclusion in this book.
101. Provisional translation approved for inclusion in this book. Mírzá Amín Fareed, Munírih <u>Kh</u>ánum's nephew.
102. Rabbaní, *Priceless Pearl*, p. 21.
103. Provisional translation approved for inclusion in this book.
104. A village situated to the east of 'Akká in the Galilee. It is near Yarkih, where Bahá'u'lláh had once stayed for three months as the house guest of <u>Sh</u>ay<u>kh</u> Marzúq. The inhabitants of these areas were predominantly Druze.
105. Blomfield, *Chosen Highway*, p. 189.
106. Balyuzi, *'Abdu'l-Bahá*, p. 411.
107. Blomfield, *Chosen Highway*, p. 219.
108. Balyuzi, *'Abdu'l-Bahá*, p. 414.
109. ibid.
110. Blomfield, *Chosen Highway*, p. 219.
111. ibid. pp. 219–20.
112. ibid. p. 90.
113. Balyuzi, *'Abdu'l-Bahá*, p. 463.
114. Louise Bosch, quoted in ibid.
115. *Munírih <u>Kh</u>ánum*, p. 58.
116. Blomfield, *Chosen Highway*, pp. 89–90.
117. *Munírih <u>Kh</u>ánum*, pp. 75–6.
118. ibid. p. 69.
119. From a handwritten letter of Munírih <u>Kh</u>ánum, December 1924.
120. Cable of Shoghi Effendi received 30 April 1938, in *Bahá'í World,* vol. 8, p. 260.
121. *Bahíyyih <u>Kh</u>ánum*, pp. 60–1.
122. ibid. p. 61.
123. *Munírih <u>Kh</u>ánum,* pp. 77–9.
124. ibid. p. 80.
125. ibid. p. 81.
126. Provisional translation approved for inclusion in this book.
127. True, 'In Memory of Munírih <u>Kh</u>ánum', *Bahá'í World*, vol. 8, pp. 265–6.
128. Blomfield, *Chosen Highway*, p. 72.
129. See 'Abdu'l-Bahá, *Memorials of the Faithful*, pp. 175–90 for an account of her life and services.
130. Taherzadeh, *Covenant of Bahá'u'lláh*, p. 359.
131. ibid.
132. Cable of Shoghi Effendi, in *Bahá'í News*, no. 172, quoted in ibid. p. 361.
133. Cable of Shoghi Effendi, in *Bahá'í News*, no. 174, quoted in ibid. p. 362.
134. Shoghi Effendi, *Messages to the Bahá'í World*, p. 16.

Appendix
1. 'Abdu'l-Bahá, *Promulgation*, p. 134.

2. Tahirih is an exception. She never personally met the Báb.
3. Gen. 1:26–8.
4. 'Abdu'l-Bahá, *Selections*, pp. 79–80.
5. 'Abdu'l-Bahá, *Promulgation*, p. 76.
6. In a letter to an individual Shoghi Effendi's secretary writes: 'Concerning the passage in the Old Testament in which Abraham is reported to have addressed his wife as his sister, the interpretation given it by some Christians cannot hold, as it implies that the Messengers of God are all sinners. A much more plausible explanation would be, that in doing so Abraham wished to emphasize the superiority of the spiritual relationship binding him with his wife to the purely physical and material one' (*Dawn of a New Day*, pp. 197–8).
7. Gen. 12.
8. Gen.16; 17:16.
9. Qur'án 28.
10. Ex. 2:1–10.
11. Exodus.
12. Qur'án 19:23.
13. Qur'án 19:31.
14. Qur'án 3:37.
15. Shoghi Effendi, *God Passes By*, p. 138.
16. Bahá'u'lláh, *Kitáb-i-Íqán*, pp. 56–7.
17. Balyuzi, *Muḥammad and the Course of Islam*, p. 18.
18. Khadijah had been married and widowed twice before.
19. Qur'án 96 ('Congealed Blood'): 1–5.
20. Balyuzi, *Muḥammad and the Course of Islam*, pp. 22–3.
21. Shí'ís believe that Prophet Muḥammad revealed a Tablet in honour of His daughter, Fáṭimih, and in it He recounted the names and sufferings of his successors, i.e. Imám 'Alí, Fáṭimih's husband, and the eleven Imáms following him. In this Tablet He foresees the calamities and afflictions confronting the Imáms and envisages their future glory inasmuch as the Promised One would be from their lineage. He also prophesies the tribulations and adversities surrounding the followers of the Qá'im and vividly depicts their sufferings. This Tablet is known as the Tablet of Fáṭimih. Portions of it have been quoted by Bahá'u'lláh in the Kitáb-i-Íqán.
22. 'Abdu'l-Bahá, *Tablets of the Divine Plan*, p. 6.; see also 'Abdu'l-Bahá, in *Má'idiy-i-Ásmáni*, vol. 7, p. 75.
23. Shoghi Effendi, *God Passes By*, p. 140.
24. 'Abdu'l-Bahá, *Promulgation*, p. 133.
25. Shoghi Effendi, *God Passes By*, p. 73.
26. Bahá'u'lláh, in *Compilation*, vol. 2, no. 2093, p. 357.
27. Shaykh Aḥmad and Siyyid Káẓim are referred to in *The Dawn-Breakers* as 'twin great lights' of divine guidance (pp. lxiii, 134); Shoghi Effendi

referred to them as 'twin luminaries that heralded the advent of the Faith of the Báb' (Shoghi Effendi, *God Passes By*, p. 101).

28. 'Abdu'l-Bahá, *Memorials of the Faithful*, p. 190.
29. Bahá'u'lláh, quoted in Shoghi Effendi, *Promised Day is Come*, p. 88.
30. The use of '*ḥijáb*' (veil) is contained in a general exhortation to both men and women to restrain their eyes from immodest deeds. Addressing the believing women the Qur'án says, 'let them throw their veils over their bosoms, and not show their ornaments, unless to their husbands . . .' (Qur'án 24:31 [Súrih of Light]). Concerning Muḥammad's wives, He says: 'And when ye ask of the Prophet's Wives what ye may have occasion for, ask it of them from behind a curtain. This will be more pure for your hearts and their hearts' (Qur'án 33:53 [Súrih of the Confederates]). For Qur'ánic references to the use of 'veil' or 'outer garments' for women, see Qur'án 33:59 and 24:59.
31. Nabíl, *Dawn-Breakers*, pp. 81–2.
32. ibid. p. 296.
33. ibid. p. 297.
34. ibid. p. 353.
35. ibid. p. 84.
36. Ṭáhirih, quoted in 'Abdu'l-Bahá, *Memorials of the Faithful*, p. 200.
37. 'Abdu'l-Bahá, *Makátíb*, vol. 7, pp. 51–2. Provisional translation approved.
38. Nabíl, *Dawn-Breakers*, p. 285.
39. Ḥusám Nuqabá'í, *Ṭáhirih, Qurratu'l-'Ayn*, p. 12.
40. ibid.
41. Shoghi Effendi, *God Passes By*, p. 75.
42. ibid. p. 32.
43. ibid. p. 7.
44. ibid.
45. ibid. p. 75.
46. ibid. p. 76.
47. Nabíl, *Dawn-Breakers*, p. 655.
48. Shoghi Effendi, *Messages to the Bahá'í World*, p. 10.
49. ibid. p. 28.

Index

This index is alphabetized word for word; thus *'Abdu'l-Vahháb* precedes *'Abdu'lláh Páshá*. Hyphens are treated as spaces; connecting letters -i- and y-i- are ignored, as are 'and', 'at', 'for', 'in', 'of', 'on', 'the' and 'to' in entries.